I0754960

Presented to

President Angell

for the Library of

The University of Michigan.

by Eliza Susan Quincy.

5 Park St. Boston. Massachusetts.

February 4. - 1872

Josiah Quincy

Æt. LV.

LIFE

OF

JOSIAH QUINCY

OF MASSACHUSETTS.

BY HIS SON

EDMUND QUINCY.

BOSTON:
FIELDS, OSGOOD, & CO.
SUCCESSORS TO TICKNOR AND FIELDS.
1869.

Entered according to Act of Congress, in the year 1867, by
EDMUND QUINCY,
in the Clerk's Office of the District Court for the District of Massachusetts.

FIFTH EDITION.

UNIVERSITY PRESS: WELCH, BIGELOW, & CO.,
CAMBRIDGE.

PREFACE.

AT the time of my father's death many of his friends expressed a wish that a somewhat extended account of his long life, so much of which had been spent in the public service, should be prepared for the press. I was a little doubtful as to this myself, considering that it was more than fifty years since he left the scene of national affairs, and nearly twenty since he resigned the Presidency of the University, and withdrew finally to private life. Having met with well-educated persons who had never heard of Fisher Ames, and even with gentlemen of the law whose notions of Samuel Dexter were nebulous to the last degree, I doubted whether it were reasonable to hope that my father's name and public services should have escaped the oblivion which is so swift to swallow up American reputations. But I was willing to be persuaded that it was otherwise by his friends, and, still more, by his children. And, indeed, the intense interest and active part he had taken in the political struggles of the last ten years of his life had perhaps made him sufficiently familiar to the minds of this third generation of men with whom he had lived, to make them not unwilling to learn something of his life before they, or perhaps their fathers, were born.

It was the wish of the family that this filial duty should be performed by my eldest sister, Eliza Susan Quincy, who had long been my father's confidential friend and literary adviser, when engaged on any of his published works, and whom he had appointed, by his will, the custodian of his papers. As she declined, after mature consideration and some preparation, to fulfil our hopes and expectations in this particular, I consented to undertake the Life which I now offer to the public. Had it not been, however, for the assistance afforded to me by her careful arrangement of the materials confided to her by my father, it is safe to say that the task would never have been begun or ended. And it is to her watchful supervision and judicious criticism that the accuracy of the details of this work — the only merit that I claim for it — is largely owing.

I thought it indispensable to the proper understanding of my father's Congressional life, to connect its several parts by a thread of historical narrative, which I have endeavored to make as slight as was consistent with the object I had in view. It is a portion of history less familiar to this generation than it deserves to be, in view of its intrinsic interest and its close connection with the events of later years. In telling this portion of my father's life, I have given ample extracts from his speeches, — for his speeches *were* his life, the very breath of his nostrils, at that period of his history.

I am well aware that such excerpts are very apt to be but cursorily glanced at, or even entirely passed over. I have no fear, however, that any one who will take the pains to read those selections will think that they are too many or too long.

I have made free use of my father's diaries, and of some autobiographical sketches he left behind him; and, as far as they go, I have endeavored to make him draw the outline of his own likeness. Where I lacked that assistance, my desire has been to tell, as simply and briefly as I could, the events and occupations of his life, in the hope that the reader might be thus enabled to complete for himself the portraiture of a character not unworthy of admiration and imitation. How well I have succeeded in this endeavor, it is for the public to decide.

DEDHAM, MASSACHUSETTS,
August 20, 1867.

CONTENTS.

CHAPTER I.

1633-1784.

CHAPTER II.

1772-1790.

CHAPTER III.

1790-1798.

CHAPTER IV.

1798-1805.

CHAPTER V.

1805-1807.

CHAPTER VI.

1807-1808.

CHAPTER VII.

1808.

CHAPTER VIII.

1808-1809.

CHAPTER IX.

1809-1811.

CHAPTER X.

1811-1812.

CHAPTER XI.

1812.

CHAPTER XII.

1812-1813.

CHAPTER XIII.

1813.

CHAPTER XIV.

1814-1815.

CHAPTER XV.

1813-1823.

CHAPTER XVI.

1823-1828.

CHAPTER XVII.

1828 - 1833.

CHAPTER XVIII.

1833 - 1845.

CHAPTER XIX.

1845 - 1855.

CHAPTER XX.

1854 - 1863.

CHAPTER XXI.

1864.

LIFE OF JOSIAH QUINCY.

CHAPTER I.

1633 – 1784.

ANCESTRY.

EDMUND QUINCY, the first of the name in New England, landed at Boston on the 4th of September, 1633, in company with the Rev. John Cotton. Not much is known of him or his history previous to his emigration, excepting that he came from Achurch in Northamptonshire, and owned some landed estate thereabouts. That he was a man of substance may be inferred from his bringing six servants with him; and that he was a man of weight among the founders of the new commonwealth appears from his election as a representative of the town of Boston in the first General Court ever held in Massachusetts Bay. He was also the first named on the committee appointed by the town to assess and raise the sum necessary to extinguish the title of Mr. Blackstone to the peninsula on which the city stands. In company with William Coddington, afterwards Governor of Rhode Island, he bought of Chickatabut, Sachem of Mos-wachuset, a tract of land at Mount Wollaston, confirmed to them by the town of Boston in March, 1636,* a portion of which is yet in the family. Mount Wollaston, from which grew the plantation called Braintree, now Quincy, was the scene, a few years earlier, of the revels of the graceless Morton and his rabble rout, — "setting up a May-pole, drinking and dancing about it, and frisking about it, like so many fairies, or furies rather." †

* See "Mr. Coddington's and Mr. Quincy's Grant," Records of the Town of Boston, Lib. I. fol. 4.

† Morton's New England Memorial.

He changed the sober name of the place to Merry Mount, and so scandalized the neighboring colony at Plymouth by these excesses, and yet more reasonably by selling arms and ammunition to the Indians, that the stalwart Captain Miles Standish was despatched to deal with him, who arrested him, dispersed his crew, and put an end to his reign of misrule. The historian, Motley, made this curiously picturesque episode in our infant annals the subject of one of his earlier works, a romance entitled "Merry Mount," which gave brilliant promise of that glowing power of description which illuminates his later pages. The part of the grant which embraces Mount Wollaston itself afterwards came by inheritance and purchase to President John Quincy Adams, and is now the property of his son, Mr. Charles Francis Adams.

Edmund Quincy died the year after making this purchase, in 1637, at the age of thirty-three. He left a son Edmund, and a daughter Judith. The son lived, in the main, a private life on the estate in Braintree. He was a magistrate and a representative of his town in the General Court, and Lieutenant-Colonel of the Suffolk Regiment. When the people of Boston deposed and imprisoned the Royal Governor, Sir Edmund Andros, who had made himself as odious by his tyranny on this side the ocean as his master James II. had done on the other, in the spring of 1689, Edmund Quincy was made one of the Committee of Safety which formed the provisional government of the Colony until the new charter of William and Mary arrived. Though this Colonial revolution may seem but an obscure underplot of the great English revolutionary drama, still it was inspired by the same love of constitutional freedom, and required quite as much readiness to venture life and estate for its establishment on a sure foundation, in the Colony as in the mother country, and all who ran the risks of the attempt deserve equally the gratitude of after generations. Judith Quincy married John Hull, who, when Massachusetts Bay assumed the prerogative of coining money, was her mint-master, and made a large fortune in the office, before Charles II. put a stop to that infringement of his royalties. There is a tradition that, when he married his daughter to Samuel Sewall, afterwards Chief Justice, he gave her for her dowry her weight in pine-tree shillings. From this marriage has sprung the eminent family of the Sewalls, which has given three Chief Justices to Massachusetts and one to Canada, and has been distinguished in every generation by the talents and virtues of its members. There is another association with the name of Judith Hull, which I fear may not commend it to the blessings of my readers, — at least, of such of them as are accustomed to pass between Boston and New York by the way of Long Island Sound. For John Hull owned lands in the Narragansett country, and, in giving Christian names to those savage places, he conferred that of his wife on the ill-reputed headland, the terror of all seasick passengers, ever since known as Point Judith. If the good man could have had a prophetic glimpse into futurity, he would hardly have sought to perpetuate so beloved a name by bestowing it on that pernicious promontory.

Lieutenant-Colonel Edmund Quincy, who was a child when brought to New England, died in 1698, aged seventy years, having had two sons, Daniel and Edmund. Daniel died during his father's lifetime, leaving an only son, John, who graduated at Cambridge in 1708, and was a prominent public man in the Colony for near half a century. He was a Councillor, and for many years Speaker of the Lower House. He died in 1767, at the time of the birth of his great-grandson, John Quincy Adams, who therefore received the name which he has made illustrious. Edmund, the second son, graduated in 1699, and was also in the public service almost all his life, as a magistrate, a Councillor, and one of the Justices of the Supreme Court. He was also Colonel of the Suffolk Regiment, at that time a very important command, since the County of Suffolk then, and long after, included what is now the County of Norfolk, as well as the town of Boston. In 1737, the General Court selected him as their agent to lay the claims of the Colony before the home government, in the matter of the disputed boundary between Massachusetts Bay and New Hampshire. He died, however, very soon after his arrival in London, February 23d, O. S., 1737–8, of the small-pox, which he had taken by inoculation. He was buried in Bunhill Fields, where a monument was erected to him by the General Court, which also made a grant of a thousand acres of land in the town of Lenox to his family, in further recognition of his public services.

Judge Edmund Quincy had two sons, Edmund and Josiah. The first-named, who graduated at Cambridge in 1722, lived a private life at Braintree and in Boston. One of his daughters married John Hancock, the first signer of the Declaration of Independence and afterwards Governor of Massachusetts. Josiah was born in 1709, and took his first degree in 1728. He accompanied his father to London in 1737 – 38, and afterwards visited England and the Continent more than once. For some years he was engaged in commerce and ship-building in Boston, in partnership with his brother and his brother-in-law, Edward Jackson. A rather singular adventure was the prosperous occasion of his withdrawing from business. In 1748 the partners owned a ship named the Bethell,* which had been on a voyage to the Mediterranean. At that time England was engaged in the war with France and Spain which the Colonists distinguished as King George's War, and the Spanish privateers were the especial dread of English commerce. By way of precaution, the Bethell had taken out a letter of marque, and was armed, though six of her twenty guns appear to have been of the Quaker persuasion. Not long after issuing from the Straits into the Atlantic, she fell in, just at nightfall, with a ship of greatly superior force, under Spanish colors. Escape was impossible; so, instead of attempting it, she bore down upon the Spaniard, and peremptorily summoned her to surrender. The captain, by way of putting as good a face upon the matter as possible, made the best display he could of lanterns in the rigging, and had all the spare coats and hats which the sailors' chests contained picturesquely disposed, so as to make the enemy believe that his ship was full of men. The Spanish captain, after some demur and parley, taking the Bethell

* The Bethell was named for Slingsby Bethell, an eminent merchant of London, afterwards Lord Mayor, who was the correspondent and agent of the Boston firm, and, there is some reason to think, a partner in some sort, at least in this adventure. He was the ancestor of the great lawyer, Sir Richard Bethell, successively Solicitor and Attorney General, and afterwards Chancellor, with the title of Lord Westbury.

for an English sloop-of-war, struck his colors, and gave up his ship without firing a gun. His rage and that of his crew, on discovering the stratagem to which they had fallen victims, was infinite, but unavailing. The gallant captain of the Bethell, Isaac Freeman, whose name certainly deserves to be preserved, says, in his letter to his owners: "At Daylight we had the last of the Prisoners secured, who were ready to hang themselves for submitting, when they saw our Strength, having only fourteen Guns, besides six wooden ones; and you may easily imagine we had Care and Trouble enough with them till they were landed at Fyal." The Jesus Maria and Joseph was a "register ship," bound from Havana to Cadiz, with one hundred and ten men and twenty-six guns; while the Bethell had but thirty-seven men and fourteen guns. Her cargo "consisted of one hundred and sixty-one chests of silver and two of gold, registered," besides cochineal and other valuable commodities. The prize was brought safely into Boston, duly condemned, and the proceeds distributed. My great-aunt, Mrs. Hannah Storer, Mr. Quincy's daughter, who died in 1826, at ninety, used to describe the sensation this event caused in Boston; and how the chests of doubloons and dollars were escorted through the streets, by sailors armed with pistols and cutlasses, to her father's house, at the corner of what is now Central Court and Washington Street, where they were deposited in the wine-cellar, and guard mounted over them by day and night while they remained there.

Though Mr. Quincy was but about forty years old at this time, he soon afterwards retired from business and removed to Braintree, where he lived for thirty years the life of a country gentleman, upon his share of the ancestral acres, occupying himself with the duties of a county magistrate, and amusing himself with field sports. Game of all sorts abounded in those days in the woods and along the shore, and marvellous stories have come down, by tradition, of his feats with gun and rod. He was Colonel of the Suffolk Regiment, as his father had been before him; but not otherwise in public life, excepting that he was sent by the government of the Province, in 1755, during the Old French War, to Pennsylvania as Commissioner to ask the help of that

Colony in an attack which Massachusetts Bay had planned upon Crown Point. He succeeded in his mission, by the help of Doctor Franklin, who relates the transaction at large in his Autobiography.* "A most cordial and affectionate friendship," to use Dr. Franklin's own words, subsisted between them for the next thirty years. Whenever he came to Boston, Dr. Franklin always visited Colonel Quincy (as he was usually styled) at Braintree, and an intimate correspondence was kept up between them as long as the latter lived. It was at the end of one of these letters, dated at Passy, September 11, 1783, that Dr. Franklin made use of the expression, which has become almost as much a proverb in men's mouths as any of Poor Richard's, — "May we never see another war! For, in my opinion, *there never was a good war or a bad peace!*" †

Colonel Josiah Quincy, by his first marriage, had three sons, Edmund, Samuel, and Josiah, and one daughter, Hannah. His first wife was Hannah Sturgis, daughter of John Sturgis, one of his Majesty's Council, of Yarmouth. The tradition in the family runs, that Judge Edmund Quincy saw this young lady, when on circuit, at her father's house, and was so much struck with her charms, that he ordered or advised his youngest son to pay his addresses to her, without delay, — he himself and his eldest son being already matrimonially provided for. The young man dutifully obeyed the paternal behest, and wooed and won her for his bride; an act of filial piety for which he was rewarded by an excellent wife, well-accomplished according to the standard of female education at that day. Her daughter Hannah we may infer, from the way in which she is mentioned in John Adams's early diary, to have been not the least of the attractions of her father's house in the eyes of the young Braintree lawyer. He speaks of her sometimes by her own proper name, and sometimes as O., the initial of Olinda, the name which she assumed in correspondence and intimate society, according to the romantic custom of young ladies of that day, of which Mrs. Adams tells us in her Letters published by her grandson. They remained friends through their long lives, and died within a few weeks of each

* Sparks's Life and Works of Franklin, I. 180.

† Ibid., X. 9.

other, in 1826. She married, first, Dr. Bela Lincoln (H. C. 1754), brother of Major-General Benjamin Lincoln, of the Revolution; and secondly, Ebenezer Storer (H. C. 1747), for many years Treasurer of the College.

Her eldest brother, Edmund, graduated in 1752, after which he became a merchant in Boston. He was in England in 1760, for the purpose of establishing mercantile correspondences, and, as appears from the Memoirs of Thomas Hollis, of ascertaining from the Society of Arts and Commerce what encouragement he might expect for the manufacture of potash in the way of a premium on its importation into England. Dr. Franklin, in a letter to Colonel Quincy, April 8, 1761, says of him, touching this matter: "His ingenuous, manly, and generous behavior in a transaction here with the Society of Arts gave me great pleasure, as it was very much to his reputation."* In this operation it appears, from a letter of his own to Thomas Hollis, July 25, 1766, that he was successful. In the same letter, he tells Mr. Hollis of his endeavors to introduce the silk culture into New England. He says: "I doubt not, in the course of four or five years, or as soon as the mulberry-trees can be brought to be of use, we shall make some figure in that article, for we find by experience that the severity of our winters is no detriment to the eggs of the silkworm, wherever deposited." † Whether he would have "made some figure" in the rearing of silkworms and the culture of silk, had he lived, cannot be known; but I believe his successors in the experiment have made but an indifferent one, up to this time. The attempt, however, at that period, is curious, as showing the activity and enterprise of the New England mind, — then, as now, seeking out new fields and forms of industry. Edmund Quincy died at sea in 1768, on his return from a voyage for his health to the West Indies. While on the subject of his industrial schemes, it may not be amiss to mention that his father, Josiah Quincy, engaged in the first manufacture of glass ever set up in America, in company with Joseph Palmer, afterwards known as General Palmer, an Englishman, who came over in 1744. These glass-works were upon a penin-

* Sparks's Franklin, VII. 225.

‡ Memoirs of Thomas Hollis, I. 337.

sula in Quincy harbor, called Germantown, now the site of the Sailors' Snug Harbor. It was called Germantown from the fact that the glass-blowers were mainly emigrants from Germany. More strictly speaking, they were from Holland; of which fact evidence is yet extant in the remains of the dykes which they painfully constructed, on their arrival, to keep out the sea from land which had never been overflowed since the general deluge. The Revolutionary War put an end to this establishment; and nothing remains of it but the name of the place, and the German names of a few families in Quincy, descended from that industrious colony.

The second son of Colonel Quincy, Samuel, graduated in 1754, and studied the law with Benjamin Pratt, made Chief Justice of New York in 1759. He was of about the same standing as John Adams, and they were intimate friends until their friendship was broken up by the Revolution. They were admitted to the bar on the same day, November 6th, 1758, and Mr. Adams gives a lively account of the ceremony in his diary, some part of which reads oddly in the light of his later celebrity. Mr. Quincy was to be presented to the court by Jeremiah Gridley, the Attorney-General, and the first lawyer in the Province. Mr. Adams had also applied to him for the same service, and, though they had no previous acquaintance with one another, the impression he made at the time of this application was so favorable, that Mr. Gridley agreed to oblige him. On the important day Mr. Gridley had not come to town, and young Adams says:—

"I began to grow uneasy, expecting that Quincy would be sworn and I have no patron, when Mr. Gridley made his appearance, and, on sight of me, whispered to Mr. Pratt, Dana, Kent, Thacher, about me. Mr. Pratt said nobody knew me! 'Yes,' says Gridley, 'I have tried him, and he is a very sensible fellow!' At last he rose up and bowed to his right hand and said, 'Mr. Quincy,' when Quincy rose up; then he bowed to me, 'Mr. Adams,' when I walked out."

He then presented the young candidates to the bench with a few complimentary remarks,—

"when," the Diary goes on, "the clerk was ordered to swear us after the oath, Mr. Gridley took me by the hand, wished me much joy and recommended me to the bar. I shook hands with the bar and received their congratulations, and invited them over to Stone's to drink some punch, where most of us resorted, and had a very cheerful chat." *

The intimacy between the two friends lasted until the heady currents of the Revolution swept them asunder. In the Appendix to Mr. Charles Francis Adams's Life of his grandfather is a letter from Mr. Adams to Mr. Quincy, which his grandson prints as one of those early papers "which, considering all the circumstances by which Mr. Adams was surrounded, are much the most remarkable of his life." Samuel Quincy became eminent in his profession, and rose to be Solicitor-General. He sided with the Crown at the time of the Revolution, went to England at the evacuation of Boston, in March, 1776, and received the appointment of Attorney-General of Antigua by way of compensation for his exile and his losses. He held this office until his death in 1789, having never returned to his native land.†

The youngest son of Colonel Josiah Quincy bore his name, and was therefore known to his contemporaries, and takes his place in history, as Josiah Quincy, Junior, he having died before his father. He was born February 23, 1744, and graduated at Harvard College in 1763. Three years later, on taking his Master's degree, he delivered an English oration, the first in our academic annals, on the characteristic subject of "Patriotism," by the rhetorical merits and graceful delivery of which he gained great reputation. Colonel Timothy Pickering, who was his classmate, said, fifty years afterwards, "I was not much acquainted with Mr. Quincy in College, but I never shall forget his oration on 'Patriotism,' and the tone of voice with which he said, 'A Patriot!' and then proceeded to give the character of one." He studied law with Oxenbridge Thacher, one of the principal lawyers of that day, and succeeded to his practice at his death, which took place about the time he himself was called to the bar. He took a high rank at once in his profession, although his atten-

* Life and Works of John Adams, by his Grandson, Charles F. Adams, II. 49.

† There is a biography of Samuel Quincy in the Appendix to Curwen's Journal, edited by George A. Ward, and an excellent letter to him from his sister Hannah, of whom I have just spoken.

tion to its demands was continually interrupted by the stormy agitation in men's minds and passions which preceded and announced the Revolution, and which he actively promoted by his writings and public speeches. On the 5th of March, the day of "the Boston Massacre," he was selected, together with John Adams, by Captain Preston, who gave the word of command to the soldiers that fired on the crowd, to conduct his defence and that of his men, they having been committed for trial for murder. His wife, to whose excellent virtues I shall presently give the testimony of her son, was summoned to the hall door, on the morning of that fateful day, by the formidable apparition of a grim sergeant in King George's livery, asking for Mr. Quincy. Her first and natural apprehension was, knowing how odious he had made himself to the Provincial authorities, that the errand of this redoubtable messenger was to arrest him. She was soon relieved, however, by finding that his mission was to ask the aid of her husband for a prisoner, and not to make him one.

At that moment of fierce excitement, it demanded personal and moral courage to perform this duty. His own father wrote him a letter of stern and strong remonstrance against his undertaking the defence of "those criminals charged with the murder of their fellow-citizens," — exclaiming, with passionate emphasis, "Good God! Is it possible? I will not believe it!" Mr. Quincy, in his reply, reminded his father of the obligation his professional oath laid him under, to give legal counsel and assistance to men accused of a crime, but not proved to be guilty of it; adding: "I dare affirm that you and this whole people will one day rejoice that I became an advocate for the aforesaid criminals, *charged* with the murder of our fellow-citizens. I never harbored the expectation, nor any great desire, that all men should speak well of me. *To inquire my duty and to do it, is my aim.*" * He did his duty, and his prophecy soon came to pass. There is no more honorable passage in the history of New England than the one which records the trial and acquittal of Captain Preston and his men, in the midst of the passionate excitements of that time, by a jury of the town maddened to rage but a few months before by

* Memoir of Josiah Quincy, Junior, by his Son, pp. 34-36.

the blood of her citizens shed in her streets. At the time of taking so prominent a part in this trial, which Mr. Adams well said was "as important a cause as was ever tried in any court or country in the world," Mr. Quincy was but twenty-six years old.

Notwithstanding his youth, he was taken into the counsels of the elder patriots, and his fervid eloquence in the popular meetings, and his ardent appeals through the press, were of potent effect in rousing the general mind to resist the arbitrary acts of the British ministry. He was one of the first that said, in plain terms, that an appeal to arms was inevitable, and a separation from the mother country the only security for the future. In 1774 he went to England, partly for his health, which had suffered much from his intense professional and political activity, but chiefly as a confidential agent of the patriotic party to consult and advise with the friends of America there. His presence in London, coming as he did at that most critical moment, excited the notice of the ministerial party, as well as of the opposition. The Earl of Hillsborough denounced him, together with Doctor Franklin, in the House of Lords, "as men walking the streets of London who ought to be in Newgate or at Tyburn." He had interviews, by their own invitation, with Lord North and Lord Dartmouth, and was received and treated in the kindest and most confidential manner by Doctor Franklin, Lord Shelburne, Colonel Barré, Governor Pownall, and many others of the leading men in opposition at that time. The precise results of his communications with the English Whigs can never be known. They were important enough, however, to make his English friends urgent for his immediate return to America, because he could give information *viva voce* which could not safely be committed to writing. His incessant devotion to his work undid all the good which the change of air and the varieties of travel had seemed to promise at first. Doctor Franklin says of him, in a letter to James Bowdoin, February 25, 1775: "It is a thousand pities his strength of body is not equal to his strength of mind. His zeal for the public, like that of David for God's house, will, I fear, eat him up." His health had failed seriously during the latter months of his residence in England, and his physician, Dr. Fothergill, strongly advised against his undertaking a winter voyage, assuring him that the Bristol waters and the summer season would restore him to perfect health. His sense of public duty, however, overbore all personal considerations, and he set sail on the 16th of March, 1775, and died off Gloucester, Massachusetts, on the 26th of April. In his last hours, he repeated again and again his heart's desire for one hour with Samuel Adams or Joseph Warren, when he should die content. The citizens of Gloucester buried him with all honor in their graveyard. The next year, when the raising of the siege of Boston opened the communication with Braintree, he was removed thither and placed in a vault, built by his direction for himself and his wife, in the burying-ground there, not far from the family tomb. His contemporaries always spoke of his gift of eloquence as something never to be forgotten, and as of a higher strain than that of the other famous orators those times called forth. His voice is described as combining strength, sweetness, and flexibility in an extraordinary manner, and old citizens have told me that they could hear him at the head of State Street when he was speaking in the Old South Church. John Adams speaks of him "as aptly called the Boston Cicero, the great orator of the body meetings." In a letter to his father, dated Philadelphia, 29th July, 1775, Mr. Adams says: —

"We jointly lament the loss of a Quincy and a Warren; two characters as great, in proportion to their age, as any that I have ever known in America. Our country mourns the loss of both, and sincerely sympathizes with the mother of the one and the father of the other. They were both my intimate friends, with whom I lived and conversed with pleasure and advantage. I was animated by them in the painful, dangerous course of opposition to the oppressions brought upon our country, and the loss of them has wounded me too deeply to be easily healed. *Dulce et decorum est pro patria mori.* The ways of Heaven are dark and intricate, but you may remember the words which, many years ago, you and I fondly admired, and which, upon many occasions, I have found advantage in recollecting, —

'Why should I grieve, when grieving I must bear,
And take with guilt what guiltless I might share?'" *

* Life and Works of John Adams, Vol. IX. p. 360.

Josiah Quincy, Junior, was barely thirty-one years of age when he thus died, as truly perhaps in the cause of his country as his friend Warren, who fell, less than two months afterwards, on Bunker Hill. Their names have been commonly and not unjustly associated, together with that of James Otis, who had been already removed from active life by mental disease, as those of men to whom the Revolution was largely owing, though they were not permitted to assist in its progress, or to witness its triumph.

His father, Colonel Quincy, lived on at Braintree during the whole of the war. The estate bounds on the ocean, and was in danger of boat attacks from the British fleet which commanded the harbor during the siege of Boston. He remained throughout stoutly at his post, though the ladies of his family, at times of special danger, would take refuge with Mrs. Adams in the modest farm-house at the foot of Penn's Hill where Mr. Adams was born. The following extracts from some of his letters to his daughter-in-law, Mrs. Josiah Quincy, Junior, then at Norwich, in Connecticut, describe the alarms to which the family was exposed, and recount some of the gossiping rumors by which they were occasionally beguiled.

"It is now upwards of three months since you left us, and scarcely a week has passed without our being alarmed from the land or water. Great part of our valuable effects are removed. For, although we have five companies stationed near us, yet the shells thrown from the floating batteries and the flat-bottomed boats, which row with twenty oars, carry fifty men each, and are defended with cannon and swivels, keep us under perpetual apprehension of being attacked whenever we shall become an object of sufficient magnitude to excite the attention of our enemies. Our circumstances are truly melancholy, and grow rather worse than better. . . . .

"On the other hand, if we may credit the unanimous report of those who have lately been permitted to come out of Boston, the King's troops, and many of their officers, are sickly and greatly discouraged. So much so, that a fortnight since, when orders were given to strike their tents, as soon as they understood they were to march over the Neck, they refused to proceed, and immediately pitched their tents again. . . . .

"Lieutenant-Colonel Pitkin, who is posted for the defence of Squan tum, informed me last evening that the mate of a vessel who was seized and carried to Boston overheard an officer say to his friend, that General Gage had positive orders to attack the rebels at all hazards. But upon acquainting his officers, they unanimously refused to go, because it would be certain death to them, as we were so strongly intrenched. And that they had rather give up their commissions than hazard their lives at so great a disadvantage."

During the siege of Boston, Colonel Quincy conceived a scheme for blockading the port by means of fortifications thrown up at proper points on the islands commanding the ship-channels, so as to compel the surrender of the whole British force. This plan he communicated to Dr. Franklin, who dined with him in company with James Bowdoin, Professor John Winthrop, and the Reverend Doctor Samuel Cooper, in October, 1775, at the time of the visit of the Commission of the Continental Congress to the camp at Cambridge. Doctor Franklin advised him to impart his scheme to General Washington, which he did, offering his personal services and whatever assistance his own perfect knowledge of the harbor, the islands, and the channels could lend to the accomplishment of the design. General Washington, in replying to this letter, November 4, 1775,* admits the importance of the plan, were it possible to carry it out. "We are," he says, "in a manner destitute of cannon, and compelled to keep the little powder we have for the use of the musketry. The knowledge of this fact is an unanswerable argument against every plan, and may serve to account for my not having viewed the several spots which have been so advantageously spoken of. I am not without intentions of making them a visit, and shall certainly do myself the honor of calling upon you."

On the 10th of October, 1775, Colonel Quincy had the satisfaction of seeing, from an upper window, Governor Gage sail for England with a fair wind, — of which fact he made a record with his ring on one of the panes of glass, yet extant. After an anxious winter, he had the yet higher pleasure of seeing the whole British fleet under sail on its final departure, on the 20th of March, 1776. For the three days that the ships remained in the

* Sparks's Life and Writings of Washington, Vol. III. p. 141.

harbor, after the evacuation of Boston on the 17th, he and his family had been under reasonable apprehensions of foraging attacks, from which they were thus happily relieved. The following letter to General Washington, written the day after, gives a lively description of the scene as it passed before his eyes.

COLONEL QUINCY TO GENERAL WASHINGTON.

"BRAINTREE, March 21, 1776.

". . . . Nothing less than an inveterate nervous headache has prevented my paying in person those compliments of congratulation which are due to you from every friend to liberty and the rights of mankind, upon your triumphant, and almost bloodless victory, in forcing the British army and navy to a precipitate flight from the capital of this Colony. A grateful heart now dictates them to a trembling hand, in humble confidence of your favorable reception. . . . . Since the ships and troops fell down below, we have been apprehensive of an attack from their boats, in pursuit of live stock; but yesterday, in the afternoon we were happily relieved, by the appearance of a number of whale-boats, stretching across our bay, under the command (as I have since learned) of the brave Lieutenant-Colonel Tupper, who in the forenoon had been cannonading the ships with one or more field-pieces, from the east head of Thompson's Island, and I suppose last night cannonaded them from the same place, or from Spectacle Island. This judicious manœuvre had its genuine effect; for, this morning, the Admiral and all the rest of the ships, except one of the line, came to sail, and fell down to Nantasket Road, where a countless number is now collected. In revenge for their burning the castle *last night*, were we provided with a sufficient number of fire-ships and fire-rafts, covered by the smoke of the cannon from a few row galleys, *this night* might exhibit the most glorious conflagration that ever was seen upon the watery element, and the probable consequence of it, a period to the present war; otherwise, humanity revolts at the destruction of so great a number even of our enemies. If my wishes must not be gratified, either in a visit to or from your Excellency, the best I can form will constantly attend you, while memory and reflection are continued to your Excellency's

"Faithful and obed't serv't,

"JOSIAH QUINCY."

The British fleet remained a few days longer in Nantasket Roads, still within sight of the house at Braintree. Colonel

Quincy kept up a sharp lookout upon its motions, and reported them to General Washington, by his request, conveyed in an immediate answer to the foregoing letter, forwarded by a special messenger, a son of Major-General Ward. To this Colonel Quincy replied, March 25, in a long letter, giving minute particulars of the signals and motions of the fleet.

". . . . Agreeable to your Excellency's desire, as fast as I can find trustworthy persons I shall give them directions to make diligent search after such characters as you have described, and, upon good ground of suspicion, to apprehend and carry them to head-quarters, or bring them to me for further examination as may be most convenient. . . . . I expected Mr. Ward would return with Colonel Tupper, and have dined with me; from them I hoped to have gained further intelligence, but am disappointed. I hear the Colonel is preparing a formidable fire-raft, which I wish may effectually operate, but fear a single one will avail little. Your Excellency's tender concern for the restoration of my health (which, thanks to the Father of Mercies, is much mended) lays me under fresh obligation to subscribe myself, with cordial gratitude and esteem,

"Your Excellency's obliged and faithful, humble servant. . . . .

"P. S. 7 o'clock. Mr. Ward and Colonel Tupper are just arrived. They are of opinion that the ships which sailed to-day carried off all the Tories, and are bound with them to Lewisburgh."

The postscript then brings the account of the signalling and manœuvres of the fleet in the minutest detail down to the latest possible moment. Letters continued to pass occasionally between Colonel Quincy and General Washington during the war. The last letter preserved bears date, Braintree, November 27, 1780 : —

"I am happy to hear by my worthy friend, Dr. Crosby, that my last letter to your Excellency, with the papers enclosed, was not only favorably received, but revived the remembrance of one whom you are so good as to rank among the number of your friends. Would to God my abilities were equal to my inclinations, for then I would endeavor to render myself worthy of that honor by some eminent public services in defence of my injured country. But, alas! threescore years and ten are past with me!"

He then enlarges on the mischiefs of the paper currency of the time, in a vein of indignant argument, perhaps not entirely inapplicable to a later period of our history. He affirms, —

"that there never was a paper pound, a paper dollar, or a paper promise of any kind, that ever yet obtained a general currency but by force or fraud; *generally*, by both. . . . . Fictitious wealth that represents nothing but Taxes, to be made a medium of trade, or measure of commerce, an adequate reward for public services, and an equivalent for specie borrowed either on public or private contract, before such fictitious wealth had an existence, is certainly going out of the road of Truth and Justice!"

Such were the old-fashioned notions of a retired man of the world of the old school, as he watched the moving scene of things through the loopholes of his retreat, ninety years ago!

It must have been with feelings in which private sorrow struggled with public joy, that the stout-hearted old man saw the British fleet drop down the harbor; for it bore away, never to return, his only surviving son, Solicitor-General Samuel Quincy, who, as I have already related, remained loyal to the crown. Such partings were common griefs then, as ever in times of civil war, — the bitterest, perhaps, that wait upon that cruelest of calamities. The war now rolled away to the southward, and the dangers and annoyances attendant upon its near neighborhood ceased. Colonel Quincy had his full share of the losses and anxieties growing out of the disturbance of public and private affairs caused by the war; but he survived till after the peace of 1783, and thus lived to see his country received into the family of nations. He died on the 3d of March, 1784. His passion for field-sports remained in full force to the end. Indeed, he may be said to have died a martyr to it; for his death was occasioned by exposure to the winter's cold, sitting upon a cake of ice, watching for wild ducks, when he was in his seventy-fifth year. His friend, John Adams, described him as a man of graceful and polished manners, and distinguished for the elegance of his dress and the completeness of his equipage and appointments. He was fond of books, too, as well as of his gun; and his private letters, and some political essays he left behind him, show a cultivated taste, and a familiarity with English literature and also with the classic authors, his acquaintance with whom he seems to have kept up to the last.

CHAPTER II.

1772–1790.

Birth and Childhood. — School Days at Andover. — College Life. — First Man of his Year. — College Friends. — Thomas Boylston Adams and Joseph Dennie.

JOSIAH QUINCY was born in Boston, on the 4th of February, 1772, in a house the walls of which are still standing, but masked by a new brick front, in the part of Washington Street then known as Marlborough Street. At that time it was the sixth house from Milk Street, and stood not far from the Old Province House, the scene of the Provincial state of the royal Governors for more than a century, and of Hawthorne's delightful legends of the same, but on the opposite side of the way. The bulk of the population lived then at the "North End," or that part of the town lying north of Queen Street, now Court Street. In the newer part the houses stood well apart, many with court-yards before them, shaded by ancient elms, and with gardens full of fruit-trees and flowers behind them. The house in which Josiah Quincy, Junior, lived when his son was born unto him was a modest one of this description, suitable to the means and prospects of a young lawyer already well established in business, and with a still rising reputation. But the shadows of public and private calamity were already beginning to steal over that happy home when it was thus made happier by the birth of a son. The town of Boston was occupied by what its inhabitants regarded as an enemy's garrison. The evils of the present and the uncertainties of the future bore heavily upon their prosperity. The fierce passions which were so soon to break out into revolutionary violence had already begun to separate families, to divide friends, and to break up society. There seemed to be no remedy for the oppressions under which they suffered but an appeal to the sword and the chances of battle at fearful odds. It was plain to all sagacious watchers of the signs of the times, that the storm of civil war was gathering fast; and it was sure to burst first of all over Boston. It was a time of stern agitations and profound anxieties. In these emotions Mr. Quincy and his wife shared deeply and passionately. But a private and particular sorrow mingled with their public griefs. His professional labors and political excitements had begun to tell on a constitution that was never robust. He had been obliged in 1773 to seek for health under the warmer skies of Carolina; but with only a temporary relief. And the next year, as I have already related, he left his home, never to see it again, on a visit to England, undertaken partly with this same object, but chiefly in the hope of doing his country some service. Thus the infancy of the long life we are about to enter upon passed away in a home ennobled by devotion to high and unselfish purposes, chastened by the anxieties of domestic love, and consecrated by the tears of a returnless parting.

Josiah Quincy was not quite three years old when his father went away to die. His mother, however, was a woman of good natural parts, sound judgment, and great force of character, which fitted her admirably to make good to him, in childhood and youth, the want of the watchful guardianship of a father. She was so scrupulously careful lest the passionate fondness of a young widow for her only son should overflow in a hurtful indulgence, that she even refrained, as he used to tell, from the caresses and endearments which young mothers delight to lavish upon their children. This self-command was attended by no harshness or severity of manners. Her maternal tenderness was the guiding principle of her life, and wisely directed her whole conduct towards her son, who returned it with more than filial affection. He attributed the excellent health which he had during his long life to his good early training, and the correct physical habits he acquired under his mother's tuition. Some of her hygienic practices might not be now received with universal acceptance, notwithstanding the success which attended them in this particular case, either because, or in spite, of them. Locke was the great authority at that time on all subjects which he touched, and in conformity with some suggestion of his, as my father supposed, Mrs. Quincy caused her son, when not more than three years old, to be taken from his warm bed, in winter as well as summer, and carried down to a cellar-kitchen, and there dipped three times in a tub of water cold from the pump. She also brought him up in utter indifference to wet feet, — usually the terror of anxious mammas, — in which he used to say that he sat more than half the time during his boyhood, and without suffering any ill consequences. This practice, also, he conceived to have been in obedience to some suggestion of the bachelor philosopher.

Soon after the departure of his father for England, it grew more and more manifest that war was close at hand. The British troops, under Governor Gage, were shut up in Boston, while those of the Colonies were rallying to the inevitable conflict. The wealthier inhabitants of the town withdrew themselves, as they had opportunity, from the impending siege to distant places of safety. Among these, William Phillips, the father of Mrs. Quincy, had provided a city of refuge for himself and his family at Norwich in Connecticut. He was a merchant of the first eminence, and had acquired a fortune vast for those days, and large even for these. Notwithstanding the stake he had at risk, he had been a firm and unflinching Whig from the beginning of the disputes, and did not now shrink from the chances of civil war, when most of the wealthier colonists clung to the protection of the mother country. In the month of April, about the time of the battle of Lexington, he removed his family, including Mrs. Quincy and her son, to Norwich. At first Governor Gage permitted the inhabitants to leave without objection ; but afterwards he forbade it, at the instance of the Tories in the town, who hoped that the presence of the families and friends of the besiegers might deter them from bombarding it. The very earliest recollection of my father was connected with this domestic event, which he thus relates : —

" The tradition in my family was, that my grandfather's carriage was the last which, at this moment of his decision, Gage permitted to leave the town. It was my lot to be with my mother and her two sisters in that carriage. The following fact probably impressed my childish fancy, and was the occasion of my remembering it. The small-pox was then in Boston, and was at that day the terror of the country. At the line which separates Boston and Roxbury there were troops stationed, and a sentry-box on the east side of the street erected. At this point the carriage was stopped, all its inmates made to descend and enter the sentry-box successively. On each side of the box was a small platform, round which each of the inmates was compelled to walk, and remain until our clothes were thoroughly fumigated with the fumes of brimstone cast upon a body of coals in the centre of the box. This operation was required to prevent infection."

Very soon after the establishment of the family at Norwich, Mrs. Quincy heard of the arrival of her husband at Gloucester. She set out at once to meet him, and had reached the house of the Reverend Doctor Gordon, the first historian of the Revolution, then minister of Jamaica Plains, before she heard of his death. She proceeded immediately to Braintree to share her grief with the sorrowing household there. On arriving, she found the family scattered. An alarm of a boat attack had caused the ladies to take refuge with Mrs. Adams at the foot of Penn's Hill, whither Mrs. Quincy went without delay, and received all the consolation and support that sympathy, affection, and friendship could afford. She soon returned to her fatherless son at Norwich, where they remained together until after the evacuation of Boston. Then Mr. Phillips removed his family, first to Jamaica Plains, to the house now occupied by Mr. David S. Greenough, and thence back to Boston.

"Of this part of my life," says my father, "I have few and very obscure recollections. All I remember is, that during my childhood I imbibed the patriotism of the period, was active against the British, and with my little whip, and astride my grandfather's cane, I performed prodigies of valor, and more than once came to my mother's knees declaring that I had driven the British out of Boston."

From the time of the flight to Norwich until he was sent away to school, his mother and himself made a part of the family of his grandfather. This was made necessary by the unsettled state of the times. It was not advisable to settle his father's estate at the usual time, because the debts would have been paid in the depreciated paper money of the period. Consequently, until his own property could be advantageously realized, which was not until after the peace of 1783, he was dependent on his grandfather for support. In his extreme old age he wrote as follows concerning this part of his childhood: —

"My mother imbibed, as was usual with the women of the period, the spirit of the times. Patriotism was not then a profession, but an energetic principle beating in the heart and active in the life. The death of my father, under circumstances now the subject of history, had overwhelmed her with grief. She viewed him as a victim in the cause of freedom, and cultivated his memory with veneration, regarding him as a martyr, falling, as did his friend Warren, in the defence of the liberties of his country. These circumstances gave a pathos and vehemence to her grief, which, after the first violence of passion had subsided, sought consolation in earnest and solicitous fulfilment of duty to the representative of his memory and of their mutual affections. Love and reverence for the memory of his father was early impressed on the mind of her son, and worn into his heart by her sadness and tears. She cultivated the memory of my father in my heart and affections, even in my earliest childhood, by reading to me passages from the poets, and obliging me to learn by heart and repeat such as were best adapted to her own circumstances and feelings. Among others, the whole leave-taking of Hector and Andromache, in the sixth book of Pope's Homer, was one of her favorite lessons, which she made me learn and frequently repeat. Her imagination, probably, found consolation in the repetition of lines which brought to mind and seemed to typify her own great bereavement.

'And think'st thou not how wretched we shall be, —
A widow I, a helpless orphan he?'

These lines, and the whole tenor of Andromache's address and circumstances, she identified with her own sufferings, which seemed relieved by the tears my repetition of them drew from her. These extracts, and others from prose-writers, were my frequent exercise, so that during this period of my childhood I was invariably brought forward at the family meetings to amuse the company with my boyish oratory. What other effect these exercises may have had on my character, besides deepening my regard for my father's memory, I know not; but they certainly increased my powers of memory and elocution, so that during my subsequent course at the Academy I was always brought forward among the best speakers."

He had scarcely completed his sixth year when Mrs. Quincy parted with her son for twelve years, having his society only at vacation-times, until after he had taken his degree. The Phillips Academy at Andover had just been founded, mainly by the contributions of his grandfather and other members of the Phillips family; and it was thought expedient that the founders should show their confidence in the school by sending their children and grandchildren to it. "It was a sacrifice," my father says, "of both the feelings and the judgment of my mother to an incumbent necessity, to which she yielded, as I have heard my aunts, her sisters, say, not without an abundance of tears." For there was this further reason for the separation. His grandfather's house was, of necessity, the home for the time of both mother and son. "Mr. Phillips," to use my father's own words, "was advanced in life, of a stern and peremptory temperament. I was noisy, heedless, and troublesome, and it was for his interest as well as for mine that we should be separated." To Andover, then, he went, twenty-two miles away; a great distance in those days before steam, and even before stage-coaches. And at six years old he took his seat on the lowest form by the side of a man nearly thirty years of age, and they began their Cheever's Accidence together.

This mature schoolfellow, Cutts by name, had been a surgeon in the Continental army, who, having scrambled into as much surgical skill as was then thought sufficient for that position without any early advantages of education, was made so sensible of his deficiencies, through associating with the cultivated men he was thrown among in the army, that he resolved to supply them as soon as he had an opportunity. Resigning his commission, he came to Andover Academy, and went regularly to school for two years, to make up in some degree his classical shortcomings. Out of school, of course, he associated on equal terms with the Preceptor and the other gentlemen of the town. He was a man of wit and talent, and the two ill-mated form-fellows were friends in later years. Various romantic stories are told of him, of which this is one. During his military service he had won the heart of the daughter of a rich Virginia planter, who would not consent that her hand should go with it to the penniless young surgeon. His scholastic training as well as his military career being ended, Dr. Cutts, after various adventures, went to Europe, where he lived for many years, nobody knew how. After long years a letter from the lady of his youthful love found him out, which told him that her father, and I think her husband, and whatever other obstacles had hindered the course of their true love from running smooth, were now out of the way, and that, if he retained his old affection for her, and chose to claim her early promise, she was ready to fulfil it. On this hint he hastened home, married his early love, and spent the rest of his life at ease, in the enjoyment, as I suppose, of the paradise for which the Irish patriot, Mitchell, sighed in vain, — "a good plantation, well stocked with fat, healthy negroes." All this I remember my father telling us at breakfast, many years ago, on reading in the newspaper the death of his old schoolfellow, somewhere near Alexandria, at a good old age.

The Phillips Academy was then under the mastership of the Rev. Eliphalet Pearson, LL. D., afterwards Hancock Professor of Oriental Languages at Cambridge, and subsequently Professor of Sacred Literature in the Theological Seminary at Andover, in the establishment of which he had taken an active part. He was a good classical scholar and a lover of learning, but of a stern and severe temper. He had no gift for smoothing the thorny paths of knowledge, and making them paths of pleasantness. The following is his pupil's account of his own entrance upon them: —

"The discipline of the Academy was severe, and to a child, as I was, disheartening. The Preceptor was distant and haughty in his manners. I have no recollection of his ever having shown any consideration for my childhood. Fear was the only impression I received from his treatment of myself and others. I was put at once into the first book of Cheever's Accidence, and obliged, with the rest of my classmates, to get by heart passages of a book which I could not, from my years, possibly understand. My memory was good, and I had been early initiated, by being drilled in the Assembly's Catechism, into the practice of repeating readily words the meaning of which I could not by any possibility conceive. I cannot imagine a more discouraging course of education than that to which I was subjected.

"The truth was, I was an incorrigible lover of sports of every kind. My heart was in ball and marbles. I needed and loved perpetual activity of body, and with these dispositions I was compelled to sit with four other boys on the same hard bench, daily, four hours in the morning and four in the afternoon, and study lessons which I could not understand. Severe as was my fate, the elasticity of my mind cast off all recollection of it as soon as school hours were over, and I do not recollect, nor believe, that I ever made any complaint to my mother or any one else.

"The chief variety in my studies was that afforded by reading lessons in the Bible, and in getting by heart Dr. Watts's Hymns for Children. My memory, though ready, was not tenacious, and the rule being that there should be no advance until the first book was conquered, I was kept in Cheever's Accidence I know not how long. All I know is, I must have gone over it twenty times before mastering it. I had been about four years tormented with studies not suited to my years before my interest in them commenced; but when I began upon Nepos, Cæsar, and Virgil, my repugnance to my classics ceased, and the Preceptor gradually relaxed in the severity of his discipline, and, I have no doubt, congratulated himself on its success as seen in the improvement he was compelled to acknowledge. During the latter part of my life in the Academy he was as indulgent as a temperament naturally intolerant and authoritative would permit."

By means of Cheever's Accidence, or in spite of it, my father laid at Andover the foundation of the excellent knowledge of Latin, and the moderate acquaintance with Greek, which he kept up all his active life, and which formed the chief amusement of his old age. And, notwithstanding the hardships of the school-room, his health was undoubtedly strengthened by the simple habits of the country, and the pure air of the beautiful town where those early years were passed. The Academy, scarcely bigger than the little square red school-houses yet lingering in some remote rural districts, stood on the crest of the hill where its successor and the Theological Seminary — which, springing from the same root, has almost overshadowed it — now stand. The view from the hill is as fine a one as well can be, of no greater extent. I well remember its splendor in the early summer mornings, stretching away blue and beautiful to the Monadnock in the distance, the Merrimack sending up its incense of mist between, as it flowed along its valley. At the foot of the hill was the little village, and in it the old-fashioned house, with its roof sloping to the ground behind and its picturesque well-pole on one side, where the good minister of the parish lived, and where the happiest hours of my father's school-life were spent. As witness his own words: —

"The comfort of my life was the family where I boarded. Jonathan French, the minister of the parish, and his wife, were father and mother to me. They were both kind and affable, consulted my wants, and had consideration for my childhood. Before entering the service of the Church, Mr. French had been a soldier in the service of the Colony. While a sergeant at Castle William, in Boston harbor, he had seen something of mankind, and he was conciliating in his temper and manner. He took an interest in my progress, and occasionally assisted me in my studies. His wife was amiable and affectionate, but she had an increasing family, so that the care of the boys, my schoolfellows, six or eight in number, devolved on her maiden sister, Ruth Richards by name, who took care of our rooms, saw to our clothes, and had the general care of us. Aunt Ruthy was consequently an object of great importance to the boys, whose affections she found means to gain. We slept in one large chamber, in which were three or four beds, two boys occupying each. The family table was sufficient, but simple, the food being of the most common kind. Beef and pork were the standing dishes, with an ample supply of vegetables. As to bread, there being little or no intercourse with the South, rye and Indian bread was our only supply, and that not always thoroughly baked. The minister alone was indulged in white bread, as brown gave him the heart-burn, and he could not preach upon it. Our time out of school was diminished by a lesson to be prepared for the next morning, and also by morning and evening prayers. On Sunday our time was filled up by morning and evening prayers and a commentary on some portion of Scripture, or by an exercise to be got by heart, — either a hymn or a passage from the Bible. At meeting, both morning and afternoon, we carried our ink-bottles, and took down the heads and topics of the sermon, of which, at evening prayers, we were called upon to give such an account as we could. The Sabbath was anything but a day of rest to us. The old Puritan restrictions, though wearing away and greatly reduced, were still wearisome and irksome. . . . .

"One recollection of my boyhood is characteristic of the spirit of the times. The boys had established it as a principle that every hoop and sled should have *thirteen* marks as evidence of the political character of the owner,—if which were wanting, the articles became fair prize, and were condemned and forfeited without judge, jury, or decree of admiralty."

Thus were eight years of my father's life passed, from six to fourteen, at which age he went to college. During this long time he enjoyed the society of his mother only in the three brief vacations by which the weary year was diversified. Of his visits to his Grandfather Quincy, during these joyful episodes in the monotony of school-boy life, he gives this account:—

"As early as 1780, it was a rule with my mother to take me at least once a year, during the summer vacation, to visit my grandfather at his seat in Braintree, now Quincy. It was always to me a delightful and eagerly expected visit, lasting generally three or four days, and it never failed to be a season of perfect and uninterrupted boyish felicity. My grandfather's family at that time consisted, besides himself, of his wife and three daughters, to all of whom my visits were a kind of jubilee. And they were rendered more delightful to the family from my being accompanied by my mother, who was the delight of them all, from my grandfather downward. She was in the prime of life, very handsome, full of life and vivacity, and qualified in every way to be a universal favorite of the old and the young, the grave and the gay. These visits were the most joyous days of my childhood, made so by the kindness and affection of my grandparents and aunts, the memory of which is ever fresh in my mind. The only particular event out of the common way, that I remember, connected with these visits, is the neighborhood of the French fleet, under Count d'Estaing, which lay in Nantasket Roads during the winter of 1780–81. The officers had letters to my grandfather, and frequently came to the shore of his estate in their boats, and paid visits to his family, making themselves very much at home and very agreeable. While the officers were thus visiting my grandfather and the ladies of his family in the parlor, the sailors would throng the kitchen, and make merry with the servants. And if the maids should happen to lay down their knitting-work, the tars would often take it up and finish their task for them.

"My grandfather died in March, 1784, when I was barely twelve years old. I was not present at his funeral, as the weather, the roads, and the distance made it impracticable to send to Andover for me. By his will he left me his estate at Braintree, according to his previously announced intention, and his portrait by Copley. The shares of his other descendants, however, were of greater value than mine."

In the spring of 1786, Dr. Pearson removed to Cambridge, having been appointed Hancock Professor there; and he was succeeded in the preceptorship by Ebenezer Pemberton, a graduate of Princeton College in 1765. Towards him my father entertained sentiments of warm respect and affection as long as he lived. He says of him, "Mild, gentle, conciliatory, and kind, inspiring affection and exciting neither fear nor awe, while he preserved and supported discipline, he made himself beloved and respected by his pupils," — a tribute confirmed by all who enjoyed his instruction, — among whom I believe were James Madison and Aaron Burr, — during a life chiefly devoted to teaching. This gentleman lived till 1836, and was past ninety when he died. I well remember the handsome old man, and the beautiful picture of serene and venerable age which he presented, seeming in old-world courtesy and costume to have stepped out of the last century into this, and the pride with which he spoke of the eminent men who had been his pupils, and especially of his having offered two Presidents — Kirkland and Quincy — to Harvard. Under these milder auspices my father was presented in July, 1786, to his *Alma Mater*, under whose charge he remained for the next four years. He had selected for his chum, or roommate, Peter Holt, a man twenty-four years old, of a staid and grave character. This judicious choice he regarded as having been greatly conducive to his steadiness and diligence while an undergraduate. Though Mr. Holt never assumed the office or the tone of a Mentor, the respect his young friend felt for him exercised a salutary influence over his character and conduct. Mr. Holt entered the ministry, and was settled at Epping in New Hampshire, where he died in 1851, in his ninetieth year. Though their personal intercourse in after life was necessarily infrequent, the two college chums preserved the friendship of their youth unimpaired through life.

The studies imposed by the college authorities of that day upon the youth under their tuition were not severe in their nature, nor inordinate in their amount. A little Latin and less Greek, and not much mathematics, with a sprinkling of rhetoric, logic, metaphysics, and ethics, filled up the course of four years. My father, having been "well fitted" for college, did not find it difficult to master them all sufficiently to become *facile princeps* among his fellows. And in 1790, when he took his Bachelor's degree, he had the English Oration assigned to him, which was the highest honor of his year. His life during those trying four years was exemplary, according to the testimony of his contemporaries, and remarkably free from such follies and vices

> "As are companions noted and most known
> To youth and liberty."

On this point he thus speaks himself: —

"Through my youth and early manhood the main stay and stimulus to virtue were my affection for my mother, and my respect and interest in the memory of my father, which she never ceased to impress on my heart, and to make a motive for my life. He was naturally of an ardent, anxious, and passionate temperament, which gave direction and expression to his affection for his child, which, in its turn, enkindled a corresponding affection in my heart, as soon as my thoughts were sufficiently ripened to comprehend him."

The following clause in the will of Josiah Quincy, Junior, had a strong influence upon the character and feelings of his son: —

"I give to my son, Josiah, when he shall have arrived at the age of fifteen years, Algernon Sydney's Works, in a large quarto; John Locke's Works, in three volumes, folio; Lord Bacon's Works, in four volumes, folio; Gordon's Tacitus, in four volumes; Cato's Letters, by Gordon; and Trenchard's and Mrs. Macaulay's History of England. May the spirit of liberty rest upon him!"

He never received any of the books thus impressively bequeathed to him, his father's library having been burnt in a warehouse where it had been stored for safe-keeping. But, nevertheless, he goes on to say: —

"The principles those writings inculcate have been during my whole life among my chiefest studies, — not more out of respect for the recommendation of my father, than from my perception of their truth and intrinsic excellence, and my conviction that on their prevalence the happiness and prosperity of every society depend."

The class of 1790 was not remarkable for the eminence of its members in after life. Mr. Quincy says of them: —

"My classmates were almost all successful in the professions to which they devoted their lives. Among them I recognize sound divines, good lawyers, skilful physicians, — men who acted their parts well, filling the stations in life which Providence had assigned them with acceptable faithfulness. Many of them were my friends through life, and some were united to my heart by affections given and reciprocated."

His most intimate friend during his college days and his early youth was Thomas Boylston Adams, the third son of President John Adams. He was a handsome man, of fine manners and address, and of an agreeable vein of conversation. After leaving college, he lived at New York and Philadelphia, his father being then Vice-President. In 1794, when Mr. John Quincy Adams was sent Minister to the Hague, he accompanied his brother, and spent several years abroad. On his return to America, he was at the bar for a few years in Philadelphia, but returned to Massachusetts early in the century, and lived in Quincy until his death, in 1832. He practised law there, and was for a time one of the Judges of the Court of Common Pleas. During the first few years after leaving college, a brisk exchange of letters was kept up between the two friends, which does great credit to their intelligent interest in the politics of the time. I regret that the inexorable laws of space compel me to omit the extracts I had made from this youthful correspondence.

The member of the class of 1790 who was the most widely known in after life was Joseph Dennie, of whom my father speaks thus in recalling the images of those early companions: —

"The most talented, taking light literature as the standard, was Joseph Dennie, whose acquaintance with the best English classics was uncommon at that period. His imagination was vivid, and he wrote with great ease and felicity. In after life he attained local eminence as an essayist, — first by a series of essays, under the title of 'The Lay Preacher,' then by others written in connection with Royall Tyler, under the firm of 'Colon & Spondee,' and finally as editor of a literary periodical called 'The Portfolio,' published in Philadelphia, and which obtained uncommon celebrity and circulation. While at college he might unquestionably have taken the highest rank in his class, for he had great happiness both in writing and elocution; but he was negligent in his studies, and not faithful to the genius with which nature had endowed him."

Mr. Dennie was a most charming companion, brilliant in conversation, fertile in allusion and quotation, abounding in wit, quick at repartee, and of only too jovial a disposition. My father used to tell of the gay dinners which celebrated the not infrequent visits Mr. Dennie made him when he was keeping house with his mother. On these white days he would summon the flower of the youth of Boston to enjoy the society of their versatile friend, and the festivity which set in at the sober hour of two would reach far into the night before the party were willing to break up. In those good old three-bottle days, and indeed for the greatest part of his life, my father was visited with a mortal headache, not merely after any excess in wine, but even after the least indulgence in the good creature. This made him, perforce, for many years, practically "a teetotaller," though he never accepted the philosophy of total abstinence; and it may be that this enforced abstemiousness, especially in the hard-drinking days of his youth, was not without its influence on the perfect and unbroken health of his long life.

Mr. Dennie made a profession of studying the law, but he did not waste much of his time upon the practice of it. The story goes that he opened an office in Charlestown, N. H., ready for the entertainment of clients. On a day one strayed in, but the interruption he caused to the leisure and favorite occupations of his counsel learned in the law was so great, that a repetition of the annoyance was carefully guarded against. Mr. Dennie thenceforward kept his office-door locked on the inside, and bade defiance to the busy world without. But as this mode of practising the law, however agreeable in itself, was not greatly remunerative, he soon afterwards wisely abandoned the profession, and betook himself to the more congenial pursuits of literature and editorship. "The Portfolio," which he established in Philadelphia, and conducted from 1800 until his death in 1812, was very far superior in literary ability to any magazine or periodical ever before attempted in this country. Indeed, it was no whit behind the best English magazines of that day, and would bear no unfavorable comparison with those of the present time on either side of the water. Its influence was greatly beneficial in raising the standard of literary taste in this country, and in creating a demand for a higher order of periodical literature, and for more exact and careful editorship. It was strongly Federalist in its politics, and Mr. Dennie had the assistance of some of the best minds of that party in the political portions of his magazine. Among others, Mr. Quincy furnished a series of papers, under the signature of "Climenole," the name of the "flappers" employed by the philosophic inhabitants of the island of Laputa to awake them from their scientific reveries, as is related by that veracious voyager, Captain Lemuel Gulliver. These prolusions excited much attention at the time, and much curiosity to know who wrote them, the authorship having been kept a secret for a season. They were satirical in their vein, pungent and spicy in their style, and showed a turn for a lively way of writing, from which their writer refrained after entering on the serious responsibilities of public life. Mr. Dennie became the centre of a brilliant circle of scholarly and accomplished men in Philadelphia, to whose social and convivial virtues the poet, Thomas Moore, has recorded his authentic testimony in his "Poems relating to America." While in Philadelphia, in 1804, he was made free of this congenial guild, and shared with them the pleasures of their *symposia*. It was to them that he addressed the passage in the Letter to Spencer, beginning,

"Yet, yet forgive me, O you sacred few,
Whom late by Delaware's green banks I knew;
Whom, known and loved through many a social eve,
'T was bliss to live with, and 't was pain to leave!"

We were not fortunate enough in this country to please the young Irish Anacreon, as a general thing; and, as he says in a note to this poem, it was "in the society of Mr. Dennie and his friends" that he passed the few agreeable moments of his tour. Whatever value we may attach to Mr. Moore's opinions as to American institutions, he may be admitted as a competent witness as to the quality of

"... . the nights of mirth and mind,
Of whims that taught and follies that refined,"

which he passed in that gay society; and also as to "the love for sound literature, which he feels so zealously himself, that Mr. Dennie had succeeded in diffusing through this cultivated little circle." Some of Moore's poems appeared first in the Portfolio, among which was the beautiful song beginning,

"Alone by the Schuylkill a wanderer roved."

Whenever Mr. Quincy passed through Philadelphia on his way to and from Washington, his personal intercourse with his old college friend was renewed, and their intimacy was interrupted only by the death of Mr. Dennie, in 1812. The Portfolio languished on for a few years, but did not long survive its founder.

CHAPTER III.

1790 - 1798.

Studies the Law. — Boston Seventy Years since. — Federalists and Democrats. — Despatchful Courtship. — Visits to New York and Philadelphia. — Recollections of Washington. — Marriage. — Death of his Mother.

AFTER taking his Bachelor's degree, Mr. Quincy returned to live permanently with his mother. She had taken possession, in 1786, of a house in Court Street, adjoining the estate now known as Tudor's Buildings, which had been assigned to her by the General Court for a term of years in satisfaction of some claim of her husband upon the State. On the site of Tudor's Buildings lived Mr. William Tudor, or Colonel Tudor as he was called from his rank as Judge Advocate in the Continental Army; and an intimate acquaintanceship ensued between Mrs. Quincy and himself and his wife, a woman of remarkable talents and force of character. He was a lawyer of respectable standing, and several eminent men had studied the law with him, among whom may be mentioned Fisher Ames and Isaac Parker, afterwards Chief Justice of Massachusetts. The neighborhood and intimacy of the two families undoubtedly suggested him as a convenient and proper person to initiate young Quincy in the first mysteries of the law. He had at first proposed studying his profession at Newburyport, under the auspices of Theophilus Parsons, afterwards Chief Justice, then at the head of the bar, and one of the greatest lawyers this country, or any other, ever produced. John Quincy Adams had just issued from under his instruction, and other young men of promise and subsequent eminence sat at his feet, both before and afterwards. Mrs. Quincy, however, naturally enough, objected to any further separation from her son, and he abandoned his first intention in obedience to her wishes. He accordingly entered his name as a student with Mr. Tudor, and remained under his professional tutelage during the three years of probation. Mr. Tudor, in the words of his pupil, "was gentlemanly and intelligent, but loved society better than labor, and literature more than law. His business was small, his clients few." What there was to learn of practice, and what there was to do of business, Mr. Quincy learned and did to the satisfaction of his patron. The time, however, which this easy pupilage left upon his hands he did not waste in idleness. To use his own words: "Of my progress with Mr. Tudor I have nothing to boast of, and little to regret. I read much, and laid such a foundation of a knowledge of the great principles of the Common Law, and of Civil and Public Law, as has enabled me to conduct my private and public life with a moderate degree of honor and success."

In 1793 he was admitted to the bar, and entered upon practice. He had so far gained the confidence of his master that, on leaving Boston for a tour in Europe, Mr. Tudor left him in charge of such business and clients as he had. Mr. Quincy was properly diligent in business, but his practice was never large. He had the reputation, a good deal exaggerated, of being a young man of good estate and large expectations; and clients, then as now, preferred giving their business, other things being equal, to men whose fees were their daily bread. As he used to say of himself, "he hung rather loosely on the profession"; for both the memory of his father and the expectations of his contemporaries directed his thoughts rather to public than professional life. He sometimes regretted this, and would blame himself for not having confined himself more strictly to the practice of law. But it is not likely, from the quality of his mind and the turn of his character, that he would have reached high eminence in the law; or, if he had, that his life would have been as useful or as happy as it was made by his unstained and unselfish public career. During his apprenticeship to the law, and until his mother's death, he lived with her in the happiest of relations. Of this part of his life he thus speaks: —

"In the society of my mother the natural affections of a son were strengthened by the cultivated affection of a friend. We lived together for about seven years, with a mutual confidence and respect of which there are few parallels, and could be none superior. Our interest in each other was complete. I had no thought which I could not confide to her. I had no wish she did not gratify. The bonds which united us, in feelings and opinions, were the purest and the strongest human nature is capable of maintaining. Her temper was amiable, and full of vivacity, — the delight of the social circle, — and I can conceive of nothing stronger than the mutual love and respect which bound us together. Of a long life, the whole of which has been singularly happy, I can recall no happier portion than the period that I thus passed with my mother. I had every source of rational enjoyment for the present. I had no cause of apprehension for the future. I cannot express too strongly my sense of the wisdom, as well as of the kindness, with which she conducted her intercourse with me, and I attribute such success as I have had in life to the principles and spirit which she early infused into me by her advice and example."

In 1792 Mrs. Quincy and her son removed from Court Street to a house in Federal Street, and, in about a year afterwards, to a larger one, which her father had bought for her use, in Pearl Street. It stood on the slope of one of the three hills which gave to Boston its second title of Trimountain. My eldest sister, in a privately printed Memoir of my mother, thus describes it and its surroundings, at the beginning of this century. The house then stood in the midst of open fields.

"These are now covered by brick houses and granite stores, and its site is marked by the Quincy Block. It was a handsome edifice of three stories, the front ornamented with Corinthian pilasters; and pillars of the same order supported a porch, from which three flights of steps of red sandstone, and a broad walk of the same material, descended to Pearl Street. Honeysuckles were twined round the porch, and high damask rose-bushes grew beneath the windows. The estate extended to High Street; and at the corner of Pearl Street stood the stable and coach-house. The grounds ascending toward Oliver Street were formed into glacis, and were adorned by four English elms of full size and beauty, the resort of numerous birds, especially of the oriole, or golden robin."

In this charming home, with so admirable a companion, those fresh years of life glided happily away. Boston, though the second town in importance in the United States, contained but eighteen thousand inhabitants. It was full of "garden-houses," such as lingered in London as late as Milton's time, and in one of which he once lived. Many of its streets — and Pearl Street was one of them — resembled those of a flourishing country-town rather than of the capital of a sovereign State. Cows were pastured, long since this century came in, where the thick houses of a dense population now crowd one another for room. Boys played ball in the streets without disturbance, or danger from the rush of traffic. The Common was then, and for a quarter of a century later, properly and technically "a common," upon which every inhabitant had the right of pasturing his cow. These "milky mothers," indeed, were very prominent members of society at that time, and for long afterwards, and had or took the freedom of the city with a perfect self-complacency, perambulating the streets at their own free will and pleasure. The same privileges and immunities were enjoyed by them in Boston that were extended then, and until within my own observation, in New York, to less pastoral and uncleaner beasts. Those were days of small things and slow communications. The American cities and communities were then individual and distinct in their characteristics, to a degree scarcely conceivable in these days of multiplied population and universal travel. A journey to New York, then a small city of thirty thousand souls, was a much rarer event in life then than a voyage to Europe now. It took nearly as long, and was attended with greater danger and discomfort. Two stage-coaches and twelve horses sufficed for the travel between the two chief commercial places on the continent in 1790, and the journey consumed a week. The visits of strangers were rare events, and always the occasions of general and eager hospitality. The Boston of that day was a pleasant place to live in. It was well recovered from the financial embarrassments which accompanied and followed the Revolutionary war; and the revival of commerce, and the opening of fields to the enterprise of the merchants, closed against them in the days of colonial dependence, were the cause of a great and growing prosperity.

The intercourse of the cultivated society for which Boston was distinguished was conducted on simple and easy terms. The hours were early. Private parties were elegant, according to the style of the time, but infrequent in comparison with friendly gatherings of a more informal and unceremonious kind. Public assemblies collected the principal inhabitants once a fortnight in Concert Hall, where the minuet and country-dance yet held their own against revolutionary innovations. Solemn dinner-parties, after the English fashion, were of common occurrence, often long protracted over the discussion of politics, and of the rare growths of Madeira, then the favorite wine, and, indeed, almost the only one in use. My father's account of one of these entertainments may be worth preserving. He was probably by a good many years the last survivor of the hundreds, not to say thousands, of guests that John Hancock used to entertain with profuse hospitality. The historical house in which the famous Governor lived and died, the last of the Revolutionary period, just ruthlessly swept away, though of fair proportions, had no dining-room sufficient for his hospitable occasions as originally built. So he had a banquetting-room, taken down many years ago, built out on the north side of the house, extending towards what is now the State-House yard. My father had invited Governor Hancock to the entertainment he had given at Cambridge on Commencement Day, on the occasion of his graduation; and in return he was invited, though so young a man, to dine with his Excellency. The party consisted of not less than fifty or sixty persons, and the dinner and its appointments were in keeping with the rank and fortune of the host. He, however, did not sit at meat with his guests, but dined at a small table by himself, in a wheel-chair, his legs swathed in flannel. He was a martyr to the gout, of which circumstance he made an excuse for doing as he pleased in political as well as social life. Thus, when the adoption of the Federal Constitution hung doubtful in the balance in the Massachusetts Convention of 1788, the gout was made the convenient reason for his staying away, until he was made to see that his indecision must cease, and he interpose, to secure the ratification. My father was in the gallery of the Old South Church at the time, and used to describe how Hancock, wrapt in flannels, was borne in men's arms up the broad aisle, when he made the speech which caused the Constitution to be accepted by nineteen majority. On the occasion with which we have now to do, when the Governor had despatched the frugal repast to which his infirmities condemned him, he wheeled himself about the general table to pay personal attention to his guests, and to take part in the conversation. While thus engaged, and when the animation of the company was at its loudest, it was interrupted by a fearful crash. A servant, in removing a cut-glass *épergne*, which was the central ornament of the table, let it fall, and it was dashed into a thousand pieces. An awkward silence fell upon the company, when Hancock, with the presence of mind of true good-breeding, relieved their embarrassment by exclaiming, good-naturedly, "James, break as much as you please, but don't make such a confounded noise about it!" And under the cover of the laugh thus raised the fragments were removed, and the talk went on, as if nothing had happened.

The ancient severity of manners and strictness of opinions had already begun to give way before more genial habits of society and a greater freedom of thought. The intellectual movement of the eighteenth century in Europe, which went before and prepared the way for her great political revolutions, was not unfelt in New England. Though there was no open schism in the Congregationalism which was the prevailing religious denomination in Boston and throughout New England, there had long been an undercurrent of dissent from its sterner doctrines, and of resistance to its austerer practices, which had already made itself manifest on the surface of social life, as it did, not many years later, on that of ecclesiastical affairs. Boston was then, as she has continued to be, her enemies being her witnesses, the headquarters of free inquiry and daring discussion, which have done so much to modify and control religious and political opinions in all parts of the country. The animated discussions, incident to a transition stage of thought, which diversified the conversation of intelligent and educated men, were favorable to the development of growing minds. The practices and habits of society, too, had undergone a great change. For instance, the theatre had fought its way over the prejudices, or the sound objections, of Puritan tradition, and had established itself as one of the recognized institutions of the town. Mr. Quincy, like most lively and intelligent young men, loved a play, and took a warm interest in the conflict which raged for a while, between the old ideas and the new, over this innovation. He used to assist, in the French sense of the word, at the "Moral Lectures," entitled "The School for Scandal," or "The Belle's Stratagem," under which disguise the drama sought at first to avoid the penalties of the old prohibitory laws. He was present when the sheriff, by Governor Hancock's directions, made his first appearance on any stage in the midst of a performance, arrested the actors, and carried them off in custody to answer for their misdeeds. He helped to swell the public opinion which, provoked by this severity of persecution, as the friends of the drama esteemed it, not long afterwards compelled the repeal of the old laws, and procured the charter of the Boston Theatre. And he was one of the crowd that thronged its auditorium on the opening night, to celebrate the triumphant issue of the contest, and to witness what really marked an epoch in the history of the manners of New England.

But this period of Mr. Quincy's youth, while he was fitting himself for active life, and when he first entered upon it, was a time of great collision of opinions and passions, which stirred men's minds much more deeply than disputes about stage-plays, or even about creeds. The Constitution of the United States had just been adopted, and an event so unprecedented in history was accompanied by many fears, as well as by many hopes. The contagion of the French Revolution, then at its fieriest height, made the fermentation of popular thought and feeling yet more active and intense. That stupendous phenomenon, which some minds regarded as another Star in the East, — the harbinger of peace and good-will on earth, — and others, as a baleful comet that "from its horrid hair shook pestilence and war," shed its influences for good or evil upon the New World as well as the Old. It inspired terror or joy, according as the eyes which watched its progress looked for its issues of life or of death in faith or in fear. The differing elements of human character subjected to this fierce effervescence soon crystallized into the parties of the Federalists and the Democrats, or, as they at first styled themselves, the Republicans. These were natural parties, having their origin in the constitution of human nature. It was inevitable that different men, equally honorable and patriotic, should be very differently affected by so novel a spectacle as the establishment of governments recognizing the People as the source and ultimate depositary of the sovereign power. The sanguine and hopeful, in the fulness of their faith in the virtue of the people, had no doubts as to the success of the experiment, and looked with jealousy on the possible interference of the new central power with the freedom of the several States. The more saturnine and cautious, on the other hand, especially among the educated and wealthier classes, had less confidence in popular wisdom and self-control, and feared that attacks upon the rights of property, in particular, might be made by the ignorant and poor, under the leadership of artful demagogues. Such desired a strong central government, which should check and control the supposed tendency of the lower classes to these excesses. The Federalists hoped to find the general government one of checks and balances, resembling, as far as the different circumstances of the two countries would allow, that of England, which should secure the fullest enjoyment of individual liberty consistent with the fullest protection of common rights. The Democrats feared that it might grow into a tyranny seeking to aggrandize the power and glory of the whole nation at the expense of the rights of its constituent States, and of the personal freedom of the individual citizen. The one admired the theory and practice of the mixed government of England, the defects of which, in its operation upon those living under its immediate dominion, they trusted they had guarded against; while the other yet remembered bitterly the injustice and sufferings that government had inflicted on their country as a remote dependency, and feared that the new President and Congress might prove to be the old King and Parliament under other names. These parties sprang naturally into being out of the fermentation of opinions and the ebullition of passions of that transitional period, and it is nothing strange that they should have clashed fiercely and angrily in political discussion and political action.

It is curious to remark how little the lurking mischiefs of slavery were suspected in those first days after the adoption of the Constitution. It was the poor laborer at their own doors, and not the rich slave-master a thousand miles off, that our anxious fathers regarded with suspicion and dread. Mr. Quincy was one of the earliest to see afar off the dangers to which the recognition of an oligarchy, resting on ownership of human beings, as a constituent part of our national polity, exposed the future of the young Republic; and from his first entrance into public life to his death, this pervading and prevailing feeling gave the key-note to his fiercest utterances, and furnishes the explanation of his most misinterpreted actions. As one of the most promising young men of his time, he was approached and courted by the prominent Anti-Federalists of that day; but he deliberately cast in his lot with the party of Washington, and never wavered in his allegiance to it as long as it had a name to live. Indeed, to the day of his death he professed and called himself a Federalist, and nothing else. After the final dispersion of the Federal party, he voted with various parties according to his estimation of their merits; yet he never regarded himself as belonging to any of them, not even to the Republican party of his old age, though he gave his vote and the weight of his influence to its candidates and its policy. In his choice between the parties of his youth, he was solely guided by his sense of what public duty demanded of him; but he was doubtless confirmed in it by the example and advice of many able men, most of them much his seniors, in Massachusetts, who then illustrated the Federal ranks, and who bestowed on him their countenance and friendship. Among these may be named George Cabot, Fisher Ames, Samuel Dexter, Harrison Gray Otis, the John Lowells, father and son, Theophilus Parsons, Stephen Higginson, and the like. By John Adams he was honored with a continuance of the friendship which had subsisted between his father and himself; and with John Quincy Adams, as a contemporary, he was ever on terms of cordial intimacy. At the time of which we now speak the two Adamses were prominently and thoroughly identified with the Federal party. And though their views of public duty led them both to separate themselves from it at a later period, this circumstance never affected the personal relations of Mr. Quincy with either of them. He began at an early age to take part in politics, and to speak in the town-meetings and the caucuses of the Federal party. Boston was then entirely in the possession of the Federalists, who welcomed his assistance, but were in no haste to reward it. He was content to bide his time, and he waited patiently while the seats in the State legislature, the first objects of young American ambition, were filled by more eager or more fortunate aspirants. He says himself on this subject: —

"Both branches of the Legislature were filled with able and aspiring men, who were not willing to give way to a man younger and as yet untried. Nor, on my part, was I very desirous of place. The habits of my mind made me regard political position as a post of labor and service, and that the honor of holding it was counterbalanced, if not outweighed, by the responsibilities and obligations it involved. I contented myself, therefore, without complaint or solicitation, with waiting for several years without any notice from my fellow-citizens of my party labors."

In effect, he never sat in the lower house of the General Court, excepting for a very short time many years later, and it was not until 1804 that he was elected to the State Legislature as one of the Senators of the Boston district. Notwithstanding the good sense and philosophy with which he accepted his fate, there can be little doubt that he did not consider himself as well treated by his party friends.

The year 1794 was a memorable one in the history of my father, as being the date of his first acquaintance with the lady who afterwards became his wife. In September of that year, Miss Eliza Susan Morton accompanied one of her brothers on a journey he made from New York to Boston on business. She was the daughter of John Morton, a native of the North of Ireland, of Scottish descent, who came to America in the commissary department of the British army about the middle of the last century, and afterwards became a thriving merchant in the city of New York. When the Revolutionary troubles began, he was a prosperous and wealthy man, and he might have remained under British protection during the occupation of that city, if his Whig principles would have permitted it. But "the Rebel banker," as he was styled by the Tories, cast in his lot with his adopted country. He removed with his family first to Elizabethtown, and afterwards to Baskingridge, in New Jersey, having first deposited the bulk of his fortune in the Loan Office. The Governor of New Jersey appointed him one of his aides-de-camp, but he died of a fever before seeing any active service. He married, in 1761, Maria Sophia Kemper, who was born at Caub on the Rhine in 1739, but came to America in infancy with her parents, — persons of easy if not affluent circumstances, who, yielding to a species of epidemic of emigration prevailing in Germany at that time, exchanged a comfortable home and refined circle of society in Europe for the hardships and privations of a new country. After the evacuation of New York, Mrs. Morton returned to the city, and brought her children up well, and lived creditably on what could be recovered of her husband's property.* Miss Morton, at the time of her first visit to Boston, was about twenty years old, not handsome, but with an intelligent face and pleasing person, with very winning manners and most agreeable powers of conversation. My father's fate was decided at their first interview. In a week from the day that he first met her and learned the fact of her existence, he was engaged to be married to her! It is proper to say, however, that he did not commend the abstract prudence of his conduct in this particular, fortunate as its results happened to be, or advise his sons, or any ingenuous youth who might seek his counsel, to imitate the precipitate energy of his example. But I have no doubt that my readers would rather have his own account than mine of this interesting passage of his life.

* This excellent lady spent the last years of her life in Mr. Quincy's family, and died at Cambridge during his Presidency, September, 1832, in her ninety-fourth year.

"On a Sunday evening in September, 1794, I went, as was my habit, to the house of Ebenezer Storer, the husband of my paternal aunt (Hannah Quincy). It was a hospitable, pleasant family, entertaining their friends most agreeably, of whom it was the resort on the Sunday evenings. On this evening I was casually introduced to a young lady from New York, a Miss Morton, of whose existence I had never before heard. There was nothing uncommonly prepossessing in her appearance, and she made no impression on my mind or fancy. Another of my aunts, Mrs. Guild, was also present, and soon asked me to retire with her to an adjoining room, as she wished my advice on some business matters. While thus engaged, the stranger lady, at the request of the company in the parlor, began to sing one of the beautiful songs of Burns, with a clearness of voice and an exquisite taste and feeling which, though I was not very impressible by music, at once struck a chord in my heart never touched before, and excited emotions I had never before experienced. I at once threw down Mrs. Guild's papers, saying I could attend to nothing else while that lady was singing, and returned to the company. At the request of the company the young lady sung several other songs of Burns with equal excellence and a like effect on myself. I immediately entered into conversation with her, which strengthened and increased my previous impression in her favor. I found an intelligence of no common order, and a well-educated mind, with no apparent desire to attract admiration, and I felt my heart drawn towards her by an impulse apparently irresistible. On inquiry I found she was to remain in Boston but a single week, and was at a boarding-house with her brother. I knew of no means to pursue a further acquaintance, to seek which I was impelled by a power of which I had previously no conception. My difficulty in this respect, however, was soon removed. She was taken from her boarding-house by Mrs. Craigie, the wife of Andrew Craigie, a gentleman of fortune, who lived in great style at Cambridge in the fine house which had been Washington's head-quarters, and is now the residence of the poet Longfellow. Here I soon found means to cultivate her acquaintance, and had an opportunity of learning the extraordinary personal interest taken in her, and the admiration felt for her character and attainments by those who had had the opportunity of knowing her. Of these I found several among the most excellent and cultivated members of our own society. Mr. Craigie, who had lived in New York, and was intimately acquainted with her and her family, and George Cabot, who had known her intimately when he was Senator of the United States, and Mrs. Cabot, were loud in her praises.

My uncle by marriage, Edward Dowse, had known her mother in New York, and spoke of her as a lady of exemplary life and manners, religious and refined, of a good family, once rich and still able to keep on the level of the best families in New York, though her property had been much diminished by the war. He said the young lady was highly valued by all that knew her, and that she was especially intimate with Mr. and Mrs. Oliver Wolcott, of Connecticut, he then being Secretary of the Treasury of the United States, and also with the Reverend Dr. Samuel Stanhope Smith, the President of Princeton College, in whose family she had been educated,* and by the members of which she was greatly beloved. She was also intimate with the family of Theodore Sedgwick, afterwards Speaker of the House of Representatives, and usually spent some months of every summer with them at Stockbridge."

It was fortunate, perhaps, for his own satisfaction at the time, that my father was able to find such excellent testimony to the worth of the lady with whom he thus linked his fate for life with characteristic despatch, and it was still more fortunate for himself and his children that it was all more than borne out by the experience of fifty-three years; but it is not likely, in the state of mind which he was then in, that the absence of all evidence in her favor, or the presence of any amount of it to her disadvantage, would have deterred him from taking the step he did. He says himself, after giving this account of the transaction: —

"I have been thus particular on points which give a semblance of justification to my conduct in this, the most critical act of my life, and the one which has contributed more than any other to its happiness, because I regard it as having *apparently* no element of wisdom or prudence. But I have always encouraged myself to believe that all men are at times, if not always, subject to invisible influences, suggesting thoughts and communicating impulses which give direction to the whole course of their lives. That there *is*, as the poet expresses it,

'. . . . a divinity that shapes our ends,
Rough-hew them how we will.'

True or false, this belief is consolatory and useful.'

* My mother was not, strictly speaking, "educated" in President Smith's family; but he took great interest in her improvement, directed her reading, and assisted her by his advice in that self-education which is the best of all educations.

However this may have been, whether it were "God's good providence," or "a lucky hit," this sudden choice of a wife was not one of those made in haste to be repented of at leisure. It was justified by the experience of more than half a century, and not only constituted his chief domestic happiness, but was a constant incentive and assistance to his public service. Miss Morton returned to New York at the end of her memorable week's visit. A correspondence was kept up between the betrothed pair, but the engagement was kept a secret even from their nearest relatives and dearest friends. It would seem as if there were no sufficient reason for this concealment, as the parties were of full age, and of an equality of condition which must have prevented any objections to the suitableness of the match. The only excuse given for it was a tour in Europe which Mr. Quincy contemplated, and until the completion of which they preferred to keep their relations to each other to themselves. The next winter my father made his arrangements for this tour, and took New York and Philadelphia in his way, with the ostensible purpose of seeing the world, but with the real one of seeing the lady of his love. His own account of this journey and visit is as follows: —

"I set out from Boston, the end of December, 1794, or the beginning of January, 1795, in the line of stages lately established by an enterprising Yankee, Pease by name, which at that day was considered a method of transportation of wonderful expedition. The journey to New York took up a week. The carriages were old and shackling, and much of the harness made of ropes. One pair of horses carried the stage eighteen miles. We generally reached our resting-place for the night, if no accident intervened, at ten o'clock, and, after a frugal supper, went to bed with a notice that we should be called at three the next morning, — which generally proved to be half past two. Then, whether it snowed or rained, the traveller must rise and make ready by the help of a horn lantern and a farthing candle, and proceed on his way over bad roads, — sometimes with a driver showing no doubtful symptoms of drunkenness, which good-hearted passengers never failed to improve at every stopping-place by urging upon him the comfort of another glass of toddy. Thus we travelled, eighteen miles a stage, sometimes obliged to get out and help the coachman lift the coach out of a quagmire or rut, and arrived at New York after a week's hard travelling, wondering at the ease as well as expedition with which our journey was effected."

Mr. Quincy's companion on this journey was William Sullivan, a young man two or three years his junior, who had just been admitted to the bar, at which he afterwards rose to eminence. A great intimacy had lately sprung up between the two young men, which endured without interruption until the death of Mr. Sullivan in 1839. He was the only confidant of the love-secret which was the real occasion of their expedition. Mr. Sullivan had every engaging quality that should invite friendship, and every solid excellence that should confirm it. Those of us who remember his winning address, the charm of the mingled sense and pleasantry of his conversation, and the absolute perfection of his manners, can readily imagine what an incomparable friend he must have been in his youth and at such a conjuncture. Political sympathy also was a strong tie to unite the two friends. Mr. Sullivan was a Federalist of the Federalists, although his father, James Sullivan, was a leader of the Democracy, and ultimately became Governor of the State through the support of that party. "This difference of opinion with his father," says Mr. Quincy, "occasioned him great pain, and subjected him to many temptations which he had the principle to withstand. He was a true and faithful friend, and in all respects a worthy and useful citizen of the Republic."

Mr. Quincy took letters to the family of Miss Morton, and thus had free access to her society. He also had introductions to many of the principal inhabitants of New York, from whom he received very flattering attentions. One of the distinguished acquaintances he thus made was Alexander Hamilton, who, if Washington was the head, was then the leader of the Federal party. I am not sure whether it was at General Hamilton's table at this time, or at his own when Hamilton afterwards visited Boston, that a conversation occurred which I have often heard my father repeat. It turned on the character and talents of his deadly rival, Aaron Burr. In reply to the question whether Burr was a man of great talents, "Not of great talents," replied Hamilton. "His mind, though brilliant, is shallow, and incapable of broad views or continued effort. He seldom speaks in court more than twenty minutes, and though his speeches are showy and not without effect upon a jury, they contain no proof of uncommon powers of mind. But," he added, suiting the action to the word, and describing a circle about his head with his hand, "he has an ambition that will never be satisfied until he has encircled his brows with a diadem!" The openness with which Hamilton expressed his contempt for the talents and character of Burr, of which this striking statement to a young stranger was but a casual example, was doubtless a main cause of the personal bitterness on the part of his antagonist which pursued him to the death.

After a delightful visit of a fortnight to New York, Mr. Quincy proceeded to Philadelphia. He put up at the hotel where Vice-President Adams had his apartments, who showed his young friend much kindness, and invited him to make use of his private parlor as if it were his own. He received from the most prominent gentlemen of Philadelphia, to whom he brought letters or was introduced by Mr. Adams, in his own words, "a series of attentions which I can never forget." He mentions, particularly, Robert Morris, the financier of the Revolution, William Bingham, Samuel Breck, and John Vaughan, as among those to whom he was especially indebted for hospitable attentions. At the table of Mr. Bingham he met Talleyrand, who was then in this country in temporary exile. It was during this unwilling residence in America, in the intermediate state of humiliation through which he passed from the bishopric of Autun to the principality of Beneventum, that the cynical diplomatist formed the opinion as to the pleasures of society in this country at that time, of which he gave an epigrammatical expression twenty years later. A French lady of rank, who had also been an emigrant to America at the same time with Talleyrand, on presenting an American to him in 1815, added, "You have not forgotten, Prince, the ball you and I were at together in Philadelphia?" — "Ah, no!" replied the Prince, re-enforcing the sneer by an indescribably eloquent shrug of the shoulders; "the Americans are a hospitable people, a magnanimous people, and are destined to be a great nation, — *mais leur luxe est affreux!*"

Of course Mr. Quincy was presented to President Washington, who then held his regular levees every other Tuesday, at which he received such persons as were thought to be entitled to the distinction. The court of Washington was modelled "in little" after that of the England of that time in its forms and rules. The indiscriminate admissions of later days were undreamed of. No one was admitted unless introduced by one of the members of the Cabinet, or by some private gentleman personally known to the President. These receptions were held in the dining-room of the house on the south side of Market Street, between Fifth and Sixth, which Washington occupied during his official residence in Philadelphia. This room, which was in the rear of the house, looking into the garden, was used for this purpose, as being the largest in the house. The President stood fronting the door of entrance, in the full dress of Stuart's full-length portrait, and the strangers were successively presented to him. This done, and the guests, including those previously received, having all arrived, the company took their places in a circle round the room. The circle formed, the President made the circuit of it, addressing a few words to each individual, after which the party broke up. The receptions were held from three to four in the afternoon.

I was curious to know how my father's recollections of the personal appearance of Washington agreed with the popular descriptions and pictorial representations of it with which we are all familiar. He was not an imaginative man, and never dressed his heroes in the colors of fancy. No man had a profounder reverence for Washington than he, but this did not affect his perceptions of physical phenomena, nor his recollections of them. My mother, on the contrary, was "of imagination all compact," and Washington was in her mind's eye, as she recalled him, more than a hero, — a superior being, as far above the common race of mankind in majesty and grace of person and bearing as in moral grandeur. This was one of the few subjects on which my father and mother differed in opinion. He maintained that Stuart's portrait is a highly idealized one, presenting its great subject as the artist thought he ought to live in the minds of posterity, but not a strong resemblance of the actual man in the flesh. He always declared that the portrait by Savage in the College dining-room in Harvard Hall, at Cambridge, was the best likeness he had ever seen of Washington, though its merits as a work of art are but small. With this opinion my mother could not away. Stuart's Washington could hardly come up to the gracious figure that dwelt in her memory. One day, when talking over those times in his old age, I asked my father to tell me what were his recollections of Washington's personal presence and bearing. "I will tell you," said he, "just how he struck me. He reminded me of the gentlemen who used to come to Boston in those days to attend the General Court from Hampden or Franklin County in the western part of the State. A little stiff in his person, not a little formal in his manners, not particularly at ease in the presence of strangers. He had the air of a country gentleman not accustomed to mix much in society, perfectly polite, but not easy in his address and conversation, and not graceful in his gait and movements." From the recollections of Mr. Sullivan, which he published many years afterwards, it would seem that the impression made upon him by Washington, who was the object of his political idolatry, was much the same as that made upon his friend. He says: "In his own house his action was calm, deliberate, and dignified, without pretensions to gracefulness or peculiar manner, but merely natural, as might be expected in such a man. When walking in the street, his movement had not the soldierly air which might have been expected. His habitual motions had been formed long before he took command of the American armies, in the wars of the interior, or in the surveying of wilderness lands, — employments in which elegance and grace were not likely to be acquired." * It certainly was perfectly natural that Washington's manners should have been those of a country gentleman living remote from cities, he having been engaged in rural occupations the chief of his life,

* "Familiar Letters on Public Characters and Public Events from the Peace of 1783 to the Peace of 1815." A book full of interesting matter, long out of print, and well deserving to be reprinted.

moving in a very narrow circle of society, when he was called at the age of forty-three to the leadership of the Revolution.

While thus pleasantly occupied in Philadelphia, Mr. Quincy was making his preparations for his European tour. His plan was to travel overland on horseback — then the only tolerable mode of locomotion in the regions he proposed visiting — through Virginia and North Carolina to Charleston in South Carolina. Having thus seen what were then the principal portions of his own country, he intended to take passage in a merchant-vessel, for as yet packet-ships were not, from Charleston for Europe. In this design he bought two horses, hired a confidential servant, and was on the eve of departure. The very day before he was to begin his journey southward, he received letters from Boston announcing the failure of a mercantile house, which involved a considerable portion of his own property, and a material part of that of some of his female relatives. This news changed his plans at once. He sold his horses, dismissed his servant, and returned forthwith to Boston, making only a flying visit to Miss Morton as he passed through New York. "Thus ended," he says, "a project of an American and European tour which I had never afterwards the opportunity or inclination to revive." My father never seemed to regret the loss of this opportunity of foreign travel. It was a means of mental improvement of which he always undervalued the benefits and exaggerated the disadvantages. I cannot but think, however, considering the interesting state of Europe at that time, and the excellent introductions he had with him, that such an experience would have been of great advantage to him as a part of his preparation for his political career, as well as the fit conclusion of a liberal education.

The next two years he spent in the pursuits of law and of politics, with moderate success in the one, but with increasing interest in the other. Party spirit ran high in Boston, as in all other parts of the country. Jay's treaty, French insolence, English aggressions, agitated and inflamed the general mind. The Federalists were accused by the Democrats of aristocratic and monarchical leanings towards England, while the Democrats were believed by the Federalists to be ready to second the mad schemes of France, and eager to follow in her bloody footsteps. The art of political lying was carried to a perfection which has hardly admitted of improvement in our later times. The calumnies heaped on the head of Abraham Lincoln at the beginning of his Presidency were not more atrocious nor more malignant than those poured out upon that of George Washington during his second administration. He was accused of moral imbecility, of personal cowardice, of want of military capacity, of treachery to the liberties of his country, and even of pecuniary dishonesty. Mr. Quincy had an opportunity of a nearer view of the workings of the Anti-Washington faction than Boston could afford him, on his first visit to Philadelphia, the hot-bed in which its rankest lies were forced, and again at a second visit he paid to that city in the autumn of the next year. He made a journey to Princeton in September, 1796, to attend the Commencement of the College there; but more particularly, it may be believed, to meet Miss Morton, who was then on a visit to Dr. Smith, the President of the College. He was received and treated with great distinction by President Smith, who obtained for him, of his own mere motion, the honorary degree of Master of Arts. Thence he attended Miss Morton to Philadelphia to the house of her mother's sister, Mrs. Susan Jackson, who is yet remembered by many of all ranks in Boston and Philadelphia, — between which cities her later years were divided, — and by the poor even more warmly than by the rich, as a beautiful example of a serene and happy old age, —

> "Whose cheerful day benevolence endears,
> Whose night congratulating conscience cheers, —
> The general favorite as the general friend."

Her husband, Dr. Jackson, was one of the most zealous of the Anti-Washington party, and the intimate associate of Dallas, Duane, Gallatin, McKean, and others, who never spoke of Washington in their political cabals but as Montezuma, and whose labors to destroy his power and influence by blackening his character were industrious and unceasing. All the personal kindness and amiable qualities of Dr. Jackson could not make the factious virulence of his party less abhorrent to young Quincy, and he returned home more fixed and fervent in his Federal zeal than ever.

The following letter from President Adams was occasioned by an entertainment given in Concert Hall to Citizen Adet, the Minister of the Directory to the United States, at which several of the prominent Federalists had been induced to assist. Mr. Adams expresses with characteristic energy his sense of the unwisdom of the friends of the Administration in thus giving their countenance to that troublesome and insolent envoy of French democracy. I cannot say whether my father was one of the party or not; but I think it very improbable, as it was not a kind of trap he would be likely to fall into.

President Adams to Mr. Quincy.

"Philadelphia, February 21, 1797.

Dear Sir:—I received in its time your favor of the 2d inst., and thank you for your clear and satisfactory answers to my questions.

"Pray tell me, *entre nous*, whether you were one of the citizens who fraternized with Citizen Adet at Concert Hall? Whether Citizen Lincoln and Citizen Higginson were not a little in the compunctions for the illegitimate embraces they gave and received on that day? They seemed to me to be stolen amours at the time.

"We may smile a little *sub rosa* at these runnings astray after stolen waters of our good friends, and meritorious characters. But it is a serious thing. It is very dangerous for private persons to exhibit these ostentatious feasts to foreign ambassadors, which lead to political consequences of the first magnitude, and embarrass the best-intentioned government in the world. The enthusiasm of the American people for the French Revolution, a thing beyond their knowledge to judge of, and of no importance to their interests or engagements, has been countenanced in Boston by the best friends of the American government, and even by the best newspaper in that town, to the detriment of our public affairs upon many occasions. This must be in confidence. You must conceal with great care my correspondence with you, otherwise it may tend to the disadvantage of both.

"I enclosed to Mrs. Adams a power of attorney to you. If she should have occasion to prosecute some hardy trespasser, she will employ you,—so that we shall have business to write about.

"I am, sir, your most obed't,

"John Adams."

It was during this visit to Princeton and Philadelphia that the time of their marriage was arranged between my father and mother, and fixed for the next summer. But my readers will prefer his own account of this matter to mine.

"At the end of the year 1796 I thought it was time to make my engagements with Miss Morton public, and bring them to completion. I made my purposes known to my mother early in January, who at once acceded to my views. An only son, with whom she had lived in mutual harmony and confidence for eleven or twelve years, ever since his entry into college, could not wish to be separated from her, and her own wishes entirely coincided with my own. It was only the introduction of a single individual, and she her son's wife, into a house amply sufficient for a large family, that was the subject of consideration. The whole matter was settled in one evening. Although she had never seen Miss Morton, she had heard of her through others, and she had also entire confidence in my judgment, and wished to see me married."

Although my father seems to have considered his mother's ready consent to this arrangement entirely a matter of course, I cannot but think that she deserves more credit for the good sense and good temper she showed on this occasion than he accords to her. It must have been a most painful moment to her maternal feelings, however well she may have concealed it, when her only son disclosed to her that he had been secretly engaged to be married for more than two years, and to a stranger whom she had never seen, and whom he proposed bringing home to her house. Fortunately, the connection proved an eminently happy one for herself as well as for her son, and gave to the brief remainder of her life the new happiness of the love and society of a daughter. My father thus continues his narrative:—

"With her [his mother's] entire approbation I communicated my intentions to Miss Morton, and in the month of May, 1797, I set off for New York on my matrimonial tour. My mother could not be persuaded to accompany me. A journey to New York was not then such an occasion of pleasure as it is now; and without any expectation that any one of my family relations would be present at the ceremony of my marriage, I reached New York, and settled all preliminaries with the lady's friends, fixing the day on which the marriage was to take place, of which I duly informed my friends in Boston. To my surprise, two days before the appointed day my uncle, Edward Dowse, with my aunt, Mrs. Dowse, appeared, having come on solely for my wedding. I had always been a great favorite with them, and their presence gave me great delight.

"On the 6th of June, 1797, I was married to Miss Morton, by Dr. Samuel Stanhope Smith, President of Princeton College, who came from Princeton for that purpose, the lady having been always a favorite with him, and often an inmate in his family. The next day we set forth in a coach and four, for the state of the roads at that day did not permit travelling such a distance, with any expedition, with less equipage. The stage-coaches were intolerable, and the passage through the Sound still worse. After a journey of about five days we reached the house of the Rev. Asa Packard, in Marlborough. He was the minister of the parish, and had married my aunt, the youngest daughter of my grandfather, Josiah Quincy of Braintree. With Mr. and Mrs. Packard resided my grandmother, Mrs. Ann Quincy, and here my mother met us. The happy unison of mind and spirit between my wife and my mother which was soon apparent, and which grew into perfect affection, filled the measure of my happiness. We proceeded at once to Boston, and from that time we formed a happy, happy family. My mother found my wife all she had desired, more than she had hoped, and by my wife these feelings and affections were cordially reciprocated."

This happiness did not remain long unbroken. In March, 1798, just before the birth of my father's first child, his mother was suddenly seized with an inflammation of the lungs, of which she died on the 23d of the month, in the fifty-fourth year of her age. At the time of this calamity my mother was in a very critical condition, and her physician told my father that the knowledge of it would probably prove fatal to her. It may be well imagined how much this circumstance must have aggravated the agony of his grief at the loss of such a parent, who had been to him, in his own words, "father and mother, brother and sister, a combination of all the relations of which human nature is capable, my friend, my adviser, my guide, and my guardian." In accordance with the advice of Doctor Danforth, Mrs. Quincy's death was kept concealed from her daughter-in-law, who supposed her all the time to be in the opposite bedroom. For a whole fortnight, whenever my father went into my mother's room, he was obliged to assume an appearance of cheerfulness, exchange his mourning for his common dress, have his hair powdered, — powder, it seems, being inconsistent with mourning, — answer her anxious questionings, and quiet her apprehensions as best he might. It is right to say, however, that my mother, who detested the cruel kindness of what is called "the breaking" of ill news, considered these precautions to have been as ill-judged in regard to herself as they were distressing to her husband. The uncertainty and anxiety of her mind, and the haunting sense from which she could not escape of some dread mystery brooding over the house which was kept concealed from her, she believed to have been more likely to do her a mischief than the full knowledge of the worst, at the moment it happened.

In this state of things, it was of course impossible that the funeral of my grandmother should proceed from the house in Pearl Street; and she was, accordingly, removed to that of her brother, William Phillips, in Tremont Street, opposite the King's Chapel Churchyard. Here the funeral services were performed on Thursday, the 29th of March. Funerals in those days were conducted with much more pomp and circumstance than now attend them, and the position of Mrs. Quincy in society, and the admiration and affection of her troops of friends, made hers a large and impressive one. In the night after the funeral services, my father, accompanied only by a most intimate friend, John Phillips, followed his mother to her appointed resting-place in the tomb built by her husband's orders, at Quincy, for himself and her, in which none other was to be laid. It was midnight with the moon at full when he reached the spot, and directed the sepulchre to be opened. Descending into it, he laid his mother by the side of the husband of her youth, and then closed its door forever.

CHAPTER IV.

1798–1805.

"JOHN ADAMS'S WAR." — FOURTH OF JULY ORATION. — DEFEATED FOR CONGRESS. — JOHN QUINCY ADAMS SUPERSEDES HIM, AND IS ALSO DEFEATED. — IN THE STATE SENATE. — ATTACKS THE SLAVE RATIO OF REPRESENTATION. — ELECTED TO CONGRESS. — PREPARATION FOR PARLIAMENTARY LIFE. — JOURNEY TO WASHINGTON. — VISIT TO NEW HAVEN. — CONNECTICUT FEDERALISTS. — FEDERALISTS OF NEW YORK. — JACOB AND WASHINGTON MORTON. — LIFE AT WASHINGTON.

AFTER this rapid succession of joys and sorrows, Mr. Quincy resumed the course of professional and political life which the death of his mother had interrupted for a season. The gloom which that sudden calamity had spread over his home was in due time dispersed by the presence and society of the young wife of his choice, and it became again the scene of every domestic happiness. In his profession he was moderately successful, but he refused to give that undivided attention to the law which so jealous a mistress demands. His thoughts were more earnestly given to public affairs, which were then in a most interesting and critical condition. The insults of the French Directory, encouraged by the ferocious bitterness of their partisans in this country, had reached a point where armed resistance or the surrender of national independence seemed to be the only alternative left to the American people. Talleyrand had reported to the Directory, as the result of the observations of his exile, that the United States were of no more consequence, and need be treated with no more ceremony, than Genoa. As soon as the Federal party — or the English party, as the French government chose to regard it — had succeeded in electing Adams to the Presidency over Jefferson, then considered the champion of French ideas, the Directory proceeded to act upon this hint. On the slightest pretexts of breaches of neutrality, American ships were seized and confiscated; it was ordained that American seamen taken on board British ships, even if it could be proved that they had been impressed against their will, should be considered and treated as pirates; and the requisitions for the qualification of a ship as neutral were so adjusted as to make that character almost an impossibility. As commerce was then the main resource of the country, and especially of its Northern section, this state of things not only touched nearly the national honor, but affected the business and livelihood of almost the entire population. Then the affronts offered to the nation in the persons of her envoys, Pinckney, Marshall, and Gerry, whom President Adams, as a last attempt to obtain redress without war, had despatched to France, and the attempt to extort tribute for the French Republic, and bribes for its officials, as the price of their reception, raised the indignation of all who valued the honor of the country to a white heat. The measures which usually precede and announce a declaration of war had been taken. Merchant-vessels were permitted first to arm in their own defence, and afterwards to make prize of ships making depredations on our commerce. Later, public and private vessels were authorized to capture any armed French ships, the army and navy were increased, Washington was appointed Commander-in-Chief, the treaties with France were abrogated, intercourse with her citizens prohibited, and soon Stewart, Hull, the two Decaturs, Rodgers, and Bainbridge, besides the veterans Barry and Truxton, began to make our infant navy respected by its brilliant successes upon the ocean. In the stormy excitement caused by these foreign exasperations, and by domestic conflict with the party which he in common with all the Federalists believed to be in secret alliance, as it was in open sympathy, with these insolent enemies of the nation, Mr. Quincy shared with all the energy of his ardent temperament and uncompromising spirit.

In the very heat of these agitations, he was asked to deliver the oration on the 4th of July, 1798, at the town celebration of the anniversary of Independence. The effect which his oration produced upon the audience in the Old South Church was long remembered by those who heard it, for the fiery enthusiasm it aroused, and the passionate tears it drew forth. The interest it excited was not confined to the public to which it was addressed. It was reprinted in Philadelphia, then the seat of government, and elicited many gratifying expressions of their sense of its timeliness and its merits from eminent men in different parts of the country. Its style was not free from the usual rhetorical excesses of young orators, but it breathed the spirit of liberty, and was informed with the spirit of the times, and is not uninteresting now as an expression of the prevailing passions that inspired it. The following letter from the President of the United States is the only one for which I have room.

PRESIDENT ADAMS TO MR. QUINCY.

"PHILADELPHIA, July 16, 1798.

"DEAR SIR:—I have received and read with great pleasure your brilliant oration. It is as sensible as it is eloquent. It is one of the most precious morsels that our country has produced upon such occasions. I hope it will be the means of bringing you forward out of that domestic repose in which you seem to place too much of your delight. I cannot blame you, however.

"I love you the better for the motto on your title-page.* It is an amiable tribute from such a son to such a father.

"My compliments to Mrs. Quincy.

"I am, dear sir, yours, &c.,

"JOHN ADAMS."

It was a good deal owing to the reputation Mr. Quincy gained by this oration, that the Federalists selected him as their candidate for Congress at the election of November, 1800. He was twenty-eight years old, but this was regarded then as so infantile an age for a member of Congress, that the Democratic papers called aloud for a cradle to rock the Federal candidate in. His antagonist was Dr. William Eustis, who had served on the medical staff of the Revolutionary army, and was an active partisan of the anti-Washington school of politics. He was afterwards Secretary of War, under Jefferson and Madison, and later Governor of Massachusetts, in which office he died in 1825. The election of 1800 was a hotly contested and very close one. Mr. Quincy had a majority of the votes of the town of Boston, but

* An extract from the "Observations on the Boston Port Bill," &c., by Josiah Quincy, Jr.

these were overborne by those of the country towns, now forming the county of Norfolk, which then made a part of the First Congressional District. This success of an Anti-Federal candidate in the very stronghold of Federalism was a part of the political revolution which destroyed forever the national ascendency of the Federal party. For at the national election held at this same time, John Adams was defeated, and the Federal party fell with him, as a national force. This result was due in some degree to divisions in the Federal ranks, arising partly from animosities personal to Mr. Adams, but chiefly from his nomination of a Minister Plenipotentiary to France. He did not take this step, however, until the Directory, through Talleyrand, then Minister for Foreign Affairs, had given him the assurance of a respectful reception for his envoy, which he had exacted as a condition precedent of a renewal of diplomatic intercourse. The great body of the Federalists, under the lead of Hamilton, were eager for a war with France, partly from abhorrence of her revolutionary excesses and from sympathy with the English crusade against them, and partly from the belief that it would rally the country to their side, and secure their continuance in power. Mr. Adams acted as the head of the nation, and not as the head of a party, and took the responsibility of saving his country from a war sure to be disastrous and possibly fatal to her, without consulting his Cabinet, or regarding the hostility of the Senate, or of the party at large. The courage and firmness which he evinced at this most critical point of our history, though he thus forfeited the good opinion and good will of multitudes of old friends and former political associates, and in some degree embittered the long remainder of his life, are now fitly recognized by history, and his conduct in this difficult dilemma is accepted as the crowning act of his administration, and the fit rounding of his life-long career of public service. But it is not likely that any degree of unanimity between the head and the members of the Federal party could have saved it from dissolution. The time had come for the party of the old ideas to yield to the party of the new. It was the next step in the great succession of revolutions, none of which ever go backward. A reprieve for four years was all that victory itself could have won for it. Its extinction was a moral and political necessity. The Federalists failed in a desperate and indefensible attempt to substitute Burr for the detested Jefferson in the choice between the two Democratic candidates who had an equal number of votes in the Electoral College, and they never again recovered the control of the national government. Still, they counted in their ranks a great proportion of the wealthy, intelligent, and educated classes, and the moral influence of their resistance to the opinions and the policy of the opposite party was not without a modifying effect upon the one and the other.

As a necessary consequence of the fall of Mr. Adams, the diplomatic career of his son, John Quincy Adams, came to an end for a season. He returned to America in 1801, established himself in Boston, and resumed the practice of the law. He was immediately placed in the State Senate, and when the election of 1802 approached, the Federal managers conceived the idea, not unreasonably, that his name and reputation would secure his election to Congress over Dr. Eustis. The proposition was accordingly made to him, but he positively refused to stand in Mr. Quincy's way. Mr. Quincy, however, would not stand in the way of the success of his party, if it could be gained by the substitution of a more acceptable candidate in his place. So he absolutely declined being a candidate as against Mr. Adams, whose nomination was finally arranged. But the result did not answer the expectations of any of the parties to the transaction. For Dr. Eustis was chosen and Mr. Adams beaten, and that by rather more votes than Mr. Quincy had been two years before. Some portion of the disfavor with which the father was regarded by many of the Federalists was doubtless visited upon the son, and made them cool in their support of him. He had also himself offended his party by proposing in the State Senate that a certain proportion of the Councillors, then chosen by the Legislature, should be given to the Democrats. This magnanimity did not commend itself, in those high party times, to men yet smarting under a national defeat, but who still retained the control of their own State. Indeed, it was looked upon by many of them as an overture for Democratic grace and favor. Accordingly, when Mr. Adams was a candidate to fill a vacancy in the United States Senate, in February, 1803, against Colonel Timothy Pickering, whom his father had dismissed from the Secretaryship of State, this same feeling of disapprobation and distrust nearly defeated him. He was finally elected, however, which left the candidateship for the House of Representatives open to Mr. Quincy, who prevailed over his old competitor by a good majority, in November, 1804. At the spring election of that year he had been placed in the State Senate, a promotion not undeserved by his long and patient service of his party, and, especially, by his handsome behavior in the matter of the nomination of Mr. Adams two years before. Thus his first public position was in the Upper House of the State Legislature, without having passed through the usual probation in the lower branch.

At the national election of November, 1804, when Mr. Quincy was chosen to Congress, Mr. Jefferson received the unexpected compliment of the vote of Massachusetts. Up to that year the State had chosen Presidential Electors through the Legislature, which had always been in the hands of the Federalists. The Democrats had all along demanded that the choice should be made by popular vote, and this year their importunity had so far prevailed that the General Court consented that the people should pass upon the question, but insisted that it should be done by "general ticket," which, it was thought, would insure the choice of Federal electors. To their great surprise, which was hardly greater than that of their antagonists, the Democratic candidates prevailed. This was a cruel mortification to the Federalists of all shades of opinion, and none the less because it was largely owing to their own divisions and over-confidence. The following letter from Mr. John Quincy Adams, who was then in full fellowship with the Federal party, was written on the occasion of this catastrophe.

MR. J. Q. ADAMS TO MR. QUINCY.

"WASHINGTON CITY, 4th December, 1804.

"DEAR SIR: — I received your favor of the 23d instant the evening before last, and am happy to find you enjoying so good spirits amid the discomfiture of honest principles which has occurred in our good old parent Massachusetts. This event, though altogether unexpected to me, is easily accounted for after it has happened. I do not, however, impute it to the measures adopted by the Legislature at their summer session. All I can believe on that subject is, that those measures were not adequate to produce the good effects intended by them. They were good medicines rendered ineffectual by the patient's habit of body.

"The causes which have produced the revolution in the politics of Massachusetts are many, — more than I have time to detail. But above all, — more than any Federalist I have seen or heard is willing to allow, — the want of union, and consequently of zeal among themselves, is among the most potent of these causes, though of this we hear little or nothing. The Federalists differ among themselves upon many *fundamental points* to such a degree that they cannot act with the vigor which concert always produces. Many of them are too much devoted to personal and selfish views to make any sacrifice to party purposes. Such men never can be of much use, and yet they are always heavy burdens upon the party with which they are associated. In the days of Cato and Cæsar, the men who had no affections but for their gardens and their statues and their palaces were destined to be vanquished, and were so. Our situation has many points of resemblance with that, and, though with much milder symptoms, we shall find the same virtues and vices characterize both the rival parties. Besides all this, the influence of Federalism must sink before the increasing popularity of Mr. Jefferson and his administration, — a popularity founded on the prosperity of the nation, which his blunders have not been able to counteract, and of which he has all the credit. The mischiefs of which his immoderate thirst for that popularity are laying the foundation, are not immediately perceived; their effects are not yet felt, and probably will not be felt during his life. His political persecutions, as they oppress only individuals, are not interesting to the mass of the people, and during the four years of his Presidency Fortune has taken a pleasure in making his greatest weaknesses and follies issue more successfully than if he had been inspired with the profoundest wisdom. How long this state of things will last, it is only in the hands of Providence to decide; but while it does last, the Federalists must count upon being in a minority, and as the majority consists of men of violent temper and malignant passions, this minority will be as much persecuted and oppressed as they will dare, and as the people will countenance them in.

"From this view of things I lament the change in Massachusetts, because it opens prospects of injustice and of corruption, the extent of which cannot be easily foreseen. But I lament it, as I lament the ravages of an earthquake or a hurricane, — as an evil which human wisdom cannot avert, and which Heaven doubtless intends for wise though inscrutable purposes. In saying this I do not intend to express anything like despair of the public weal. There is but one set of principles which appear to me applicable to all times and to all places, — to success or defeat, — to public or private life. In the steady pursuit of those principles, the rise and fall of parties or of nations ought no more to affect us, when we are ourselves involved in the issue, than when they are mere objects of philosophical contemplation. I have no doubt but that, sooner or later, new divisions of parties and new objects of public interest will occur, upon which we may expect to share more of the public favor in continued efforts for the public interest.

"I shall subscribe for you, according to your wish, to the National Intelligencer, which is something more than demi-official, — which contains the most important of the public documents, and the most accurate reports of the debates in the House of Representatives. Its *candor* and its *falsehoods* are moreover so perfectly characteristic of the system it supports, that an indifferent person of tolerable penetration might take the measure of our administration, heart and head, from this paper, as accurately as a profile may be taken by physiognotrace.*

"I have scarcely room to say how much I am yours,

"J. Q. ADAMS."

While a member of the Senate of Massachusetts, 1804-5, Mr. Quincy made his first public manifestation of that sense of the dangers with which slavery threatened the liberties of the nation, which informed so large a part of his public action from that time down to the end of his life. During his Senatorship at this time he principally distinguished himself by actively promoting a movement for eliminating from the national Constitution the clause permitting the Slave States to count three fifths of their slaves as a part of their basis of representation. Though he could not have fully foreseen the tyrannical power with which this clause of the Constitution was destined to invest a compact oligarchy resting on the ownership of human beings, nor all the ills which

* Or "physiognotype." The word is dubious in the origina. writing

were to flow from it, still his moral and political sagacity discerned that a harvest of evils was included in this germ of mischief, of which he showed that the first fruits had been already perceived in the defeat of Adams by Jefferson, and in the ascendency of the Democratic party in the country. "The Northern States must and will," said he, "keep up the struggle; and if gentlemen do not now agree with us, the time will come when all will concur in this common cause. On the adoption of this amendment the prosperity and the continuance of the Union depend." It is a curious fact in the natural history of parties, that the prophetic instinct of the Democrats led nearly, if not quite, all of them to vote against this resolution, which was adopted by an almost strict party vote. So early did they begin to justify the taunt of John Randolph, inspired by the contempt the slaveholders always felt for their Northern tools, and which they did not take the trouble to conceal, — "Northern gentlemen think to govern us by our *black* slaves; but, let me tell them, we intend to govern them by their *white* slaves!" Perhaps there was no man who divined sooner, and indicated more clearly and more persistently, the fatal nature of slavery, and the necessity of instant and constant resistance to its aggressions, than Mr. Quincy. On this point he never wavered. During the calmest of the halcyon days of the "Era of Good Feeling," his prescient soul foreboded the coming storm. I well remember more than once during my boyhood being present at conversations between himself and his friends, in which he spoke of the certainty of great convulsions in the future, to arise from this attempt to make a union out of parts which could not coalesce in the nature of things. "You and I may not live to see the day," he would say to his friends; "but before that boy is off the stage, he will see this country torn in pieces by the fierce passions which are now sleeping!" His friends would generally smile and shake the head, regarding him as a prophet of ill, and of ill that could never come to pass. Indeed, it was the earnestness of his convictions on this point and cognate ones, and the strength of expression with which he uttered them, that made his party friends rather afraid of him, and gave him the reputation of imprudence and violence, — which is at once the proof and the penalty of being in advance of one's time, and which doubtless stood in the way of his higher political advancement. He did, however, live to see the fulfilment of his prophecies, and with singular literalness, as we shall see by and by, and to rejoice to know that the storm which he had prognosticated with such assured certainty only cleared and purified the air, and destroyed nothing the destruction of which was not a blessing.

This same winter he began to make his preparations for the new duties upon which he was about to enter, with characteristic zeal and industry. Of these he gives the following account: —

"In consequence of my election as member of Congress, I began, on the 1st of January, 1805, a course of preparatory studies, having for their object a minute knowledge of American history and politics, especially that part of both comprised between the adoption of the Federal Constitution and that period. As this knowledge was only to be acquired by a recurrence to the debates, newspapers, temporary pamphlets, and official reports of the intervening years, I set myself at work immediately to examine and digest these documents, arranging them, and the principles and questions agitated in them, so that as far as possible I might obtain a command of all the topics which then or before had divided the American people. With this design I opened a folio commonplace-book, on John Locke's plan, embracing abstracts and researches into the history of the United States relative to all the topics I deemed it proper for me to understand, — a work which cost me no small labor. The scantiness of documents, and the difficulty then of obtaining them, made the procuring, analyzing, and abstracting them — from the minuteness required, and the little interest of their nature — irksome as well as laborious. Many things were inserted in that commonplace-book which I afterwards found to be of little use, or to be more fully acquired elsewhere. But the design was good and honorable, and I never regard well-directed labor as lost."

As a part of his preparation for Congressional life, my father diligently applied himself to the study of the French language, of which he had already the smattering then, not to say now, thought sufficient for the occasions of a university education. In this he so far succeeded as to speak French well enough to converse easily with the foreign ministers, and other European visitors whom he met at Washington, who were not at home in English. The facility of speaking it he lost with the disuse of the habit after leaving Congress; but he retained to the last the accurate knowledge of the language which comes of a thorough study of its principles and grammatical structure. In the year 1805 he began keeping a copious diary, in which he recorded his studies, which were various in kind and surprising in amount, especially when we consider that he was an active member of the State Legislature, and much occupied with private affairs and the demands of society. Dinner-parties and visitors are constantly interrupting his studies. Besides records of conversations, which are only too few and brief, it contains remarks on the works of literature he was reading, with long extracts in English, Latin, and French. And this in addition to the dry and laborious researches of which I have already given his own account. And besides these serious studies he appears to have amused himself with the pursuit of botany, from which, however, he was soon driven by the exactions of politics. I will here insert a few extracts from this diary.

"*January* 3.— In conversation with Theophilus Parsons on the strength of the prejudices of religious sectaries, he related this anecdote. The disputes between the Calvinists and Arians ran high in Newburyport. Two of the former, men of excellent morals,— and, religious prejudices out of the question, of ordinary candor,— were conversing together concerning a neighbor who adhered to the latter doctrines. 'It is a strange thing,' said one, 'that a man so perverse in his doctrines should be so exemplary in his life.' 'I have often thought so,' said the other; 'I have narrowly watched that man for ten years past, and it seems as if *the very Devil helped him to be good!*'"

The next name in the diary will recall to the minds of many of my readers the image of the courteous, cheerful, lively gentleman of the old school whose hospitalities they have enjoyed on the banks of the Kennebeck. Born in England about the middle of the last century, the son of Samuel Vaughan (whom Junius has damned, I believe very unjustly, to everlasting fame), a pupil of Dr. Priestley, educated at Cambridge, Edinburgh, and the Inns of Court, the friend and editor of Franklin, the intimate of the

Whig celebrities of the period of Burke and Fox, a member of Parliament, a voluntary exile from England at the time of Pitt's "Reign of Terror" for his sympathy with the French Revolution, Benjamin Vaughan came to this country about 1795, and established himself at Hallowell, in Maine, then on the frontiers of civilization, created there an elegant and hospitable home, and drew around him a cultivated circle of society. The acquaintance the beginning of which is here set down ripened into a friendship which continued until the death of Mr. Vaughan, in 1834.

"*January* 5.—Benjamin Vaughan, Esq., of Hallowell, an Englishman who has emigrated to this country on account of some political complications, passed the evening with me. His extensive reading and acquaintance with many of the present European actors on the political theatre, particularly those of the opposition, joined with a happy communicativeness of temper, render him a pleasing and instructive companion.

"He said that Swinburne, a celebrated traveller, had assured him that in Italy the thermometer had in one year at Rome stood for thirteen days from three to five degrees below cipher of Fahrenheit. This fact he deemed important to show that the Italian climate had not ameliorated, as some had pretended, in modern times."

"*January* 17. — In the evening, Vaughan at my house mentioned a fact relative to the state of Greek learning in France and England which surprised me. Just before the French Revolution, said Vaughan, the Archbishop of Toulouse informed me that the Greek language had gone much out of repute in France with literary men. He did not believe there were four noblemen in the kingdom who understood it. In England, said Vaughan, it was then and is still considered an essential branch of education for the nobility, — many of them are very good Greek scholars."

"*April* 23. — In conversation with Fisher Ames, — were speaking of the dispositions which made men the least manageable partisans. 'It has long been my opinion,' said he, 'that of all passions *vanity* is the greatest corrupter of good dispositions. Others subside occasionally. Avarice sometimes sleeps. But vanity is a perpetual trade-wind, always moved by a single cause, and always setting one way.'"

"*June* 29. — Dined at Mr. (Theodore) Lyman's. Ex-President John Adams went to town with me in my carriage. In course of conversation Mr. Adams said: 'No writer has ever yet displayed all the terrors of democracy in our language. All the learned men in Europe have had an interest in throwing a veil over its enormities, as they have all felt the necessity of preserving a portion of its spirit in their constitutions. In the history of Naples and of the Italian republics the truest picture of its progress and fate is drawn.' Speaking concerning the merits of history, he said that it ever gave a poor representation of the causes of events and of the motives of the actors, and even of the most important agents in the revolutions of the world. History is always occupied about the painted head of the ship. It says nothing about the helmsman, or the common sailor, to whose skill and activity success is really attributable. It is well known that, in the revolution of Holland, a private individual, whose name is scarcely remembered, did more towards exciting, and making it successful, than William the First. But William had fortune and military skill, was connected with one of the most influential families by marriage, and, what was of full as much consequence as all, he was of a noble family, with a title.

"At dinner the conversation turned on Bonaparte and the probability of his successful establishment of a new dynasty. Dr. Dexter thought that he would transmit the French empire to his family; that the French were tired of revolutions, and must have a master; and that the head of the army must be king. I controverted the probability of the continuance of power in the Bonapartian race, because it was little likely that any of Bonaparte's brothers would be able to keep the army, who would always follow, in a military government, the actual and not the titular leader.

"The dispute growing somewhat ardent, Adams interrupted us, saying: 'Dr. Dexter, you have certainly the Roman legions against you. This conversation, however, reminds me of an anecdote. About the time of the National Convention Dr. Priestley breakfasted with me. He was exulting at the prospect which the French had of now finally establishing their freedom. "But do you believe, Doctor, that liberty is now finally established, and that monarchy in some shape or other will not again be reinstated in France?" "Yes," said he. "And why?" "Why," replied the Doctor, "because I believe the French monarchy to be the *tenth horn of the beast*, mentioned in the Revelations, and that it has now fallen forever." Observing, I suppose, from my countenance, that I was not altogether a convert to his opinion on that ground, after a moment's hesitation, he proceeded: "I confess, however, I have had some doubts. No longer ago than yesterday I was reading the travels of a Frenchman in England, in the year 1658,—the year of Cromwell's death, and just before that event. The writer says that he finds considerable diversity of opinion in private circles concerning the merits and character of the Protector; but *in one thing*, says he, *all men of all parties and all characters are agreed,—that in no shape will monarchy be ever again reinstated in this island, and above all, not in the ancient family!*'"'

One would think that the most scrupulous conscientiousness might have been satisfied with the abundant and various industry of which, as I have described it, my father's diary is the record. It was not enough, however, to content his own, and he more than once laments his "neglect of that moral and mental cultivation" which he regards as "the noblest of human pursuits." And with most superfluous penitence, on one occasion he says: "I resolve, therefore, in future to be more circumspect,—to hoard my moments with a more thrifty spirit—to listen less to the suggestions of indolence, and so quicken that spirit of intellectual improvement to which I devote my life." And at a later date he thus laments over his shortcomings, in a spirit of most gratuitous self-reproach, inasmuch as it seems to spring from regret that he could not employ all his time in two different ways at once.

"*September* 18, 1805.—Since the above, my studies have been progressive, although this record has been stationary. I have maintained a regular course of pursuit, with as little deviation as calls of duty or the interruptions of friendship would permit. The difficulty of obtaining public documents in a successive series has made unavoidable a change in my original plan of political inquiry; and the quick step with which the session is hastening upon me has made necessary a particular reference to such investigations as the state of present politics made most imperiously requisite. To these objects the literary projects I had connected in my plan of study have been forced to yield. My botanical spirit has been permitted to rest, although Nature has solicited it with her later flowers. De Retz and the factions of the sixteenth century have been lost amid the nearer tumults of the beginning of the nineteenth. Even Shakespeare and Quinctilian have been forgotten under the pressure of incumbent and irksome researches. Among the filth of party newspapers and pamphlets I have been drawing forth minute but important facts, and extracting the slight thread of a cobweb policy. The necessity to abstract, in order to preserve the result of my inquiries, has imposed much tedious labor, which has given me an apology for neglecting this short record."

At length the time was at hand when he was to enter on his new career of Congressional life, and he made his serious preparations for the journey to Washington. It was no holiday excursion in those days before steam, before tolerable stage-coaches, before passable roads, and before bridges. The taverns along the road were of a very indifferent description, even for that day, when the best city hostelries were the horror of civilized travellers. My mother used to describe the discomforts and the dangers even of the journeys to Washington, as things to remember to the end of a long life. The accidents caused by the horrible condition of the roads, the distance from help in the solitary places through which the route mostly lay, the terrors of the ferry-boats on the rivers that had them, and the yet greater terrors of fording those that had them not, made those expeditions anything but pleasurable to make or to remember. The universal nomadic public of the present day, when, as Thackeray says, "we no longer travel, we only *arrive*," can form but an inadequate notion of the weariness and the actual bodily suffering which their fathers endured in the pursuit of business or pleasure, stretched on the rack of the old-fashioned stage-coaches, and broken upon four wheels at once. If they could, they would be more patient than they are if they arrive in New York too late for dinner, after breakfasting in Boston, or are delayed more than two days in their flight from the Atlantic to the farthest Western frontier of civilization. We who have lived on the debatable ground between the old and the new, when steam had bridged the sounds and the rivers, and shortened by half the time and by more than half the fatigues of travel, yet remember enough of the former days to be able to say with authority that they were not better than these. But this chapter cannot be better ended than by Mr. Quincy's own account of his journey, and his arrangements for his first winter in Washington. He set out early in November, with his wife and eldest daughter, travelling in his own carriage, and was about a month on the road, including short visits in New York,

Philadelphia, and Baltimore. He left a journal of a portion of his journey, and of his visit to New York, which is not without interest. It begins abruptly somewhere in Connecticut.

". . . . Having passed the Sabbath at Ashford, on the succeeding day we arrived at Hartford, and on the next at New Haven. Between these two capitals of Connecticut the distance is shortened by a turnpike, but the beautiful scenery which distinguishes the other road, the pleasant villages and variegated landscapes, are exchanged for a dull monotony of oak-crowned hills and sheep-covered vales, almost without a single village, and for miles without a house to break the tiresome uniformity of this rustic scene. It was our lot, however, to find one object to interest and occupy our attention, in a French Creole lady from the West Indies, who, with her black female slave, unable to speak a word of English, was travelling under the guidance of a little boy to Middletown. We passed her in the neighborhood of Mendon, and her humble equipage overtook us, travelling slowly, at Ashford. She had just arrived from Martinique, travelling for health. She was emaciated and pale as the native hue of her cheeks would permit. She was ignorant of our climate as of our tongue, and in the beginning of November was travelling in our cold latitudes with little more than would have been comfortable in her tropical country. I furbished up the little French I had, and she received my clumsy offering with a degree of rapture. She had been ten days in the country, and during all that time had not met with a single person whom she could make understand and supply her wants. During her journey she had been put to serious inconvenience through the impossibility of communicating her desires, and oftentimes had been denied what she knew she could have commanded, could she only have made herself understood. Her weak frame could no longer support her painful situation. She was seized with convulsions, and dropped down apparently lifeless on the floor. We had, however, the satisfaction of reviving her, and of offering her against the climate some supernumerary travelling-overcoats, and, taking her under our patronage, we saw her safe within ten miles of Middletown, happy and comparatively comfortable. To her name and real rank we are yet strangers. From circumstances, it was apparent that, if it was not elevated, it was not low.

"At New Haven I found their Legislature in session, and had the good fortune to hear a debate which excited considerable local interest, and called into action the talents of some of their principal speakers. Daggett and Webster on one side, Griswold and Goddard on the other. Daggett was close and logical in argument, and occasionally threw out some scintillations of that native wit in which he is known to abound. His manner was nothing polished, and his language rather forcible than precise. Webster discovered general knowledge, but had neither from nature nor cultivation the qualities necessary for an interesting or powerful public speaker. Goddard was copious, correct, rich in the fountain, but neither easy nor graceful in the delivery of the stream of his eloquence. Griswold, however, made good the deficiency of the others in these respects. His person and action are formed to draw audience and attention. He was eloquent, ardent, and pathetic; in his style, rather declamatory than didactic, and well qualified to impress a popular assembly. The United States, I think, cannot boast many, perhaps none, superior to Griswold in the grace and force of public speaking.

"I passed the evening at Webster's, in company with Griswold, Goddard, and Pitkin, who is Speaker of the House of Representatives, and also lately elected a member of Congress. Mr. Backus, who is also one of the members, and first clerk of their House of Representatives (an office which is the first step to the chair of the House), was also one of the company. The conversation principally turned upon the political state of our country. From what passed I had more than ever cause to lament the loss of Mr. Griswold from the national legislature. At all times knowledge, experience, and talents such as he possesses are of the highest importance, but at present they seem to be almost indispensable. He assured me that Jefferson was *his own minister;* that he was acted upon by none of the heads of departments; that a coolness, it was generally supposed, subsisted between Madison and the President, owing to the disapprobation which the former is known to entertain concerning some of Jefferson's measures, particularly the multiplicity and nature of the removals from office. It was probably on account of this state of things between Mr. Madison and Mr. Jefferson, that the friends of the latter had already begun to turn their attention towards another than Mr. Madison as Mr. Jefferson's successor. Mr. Monroe was undoubtedly the person whom the President favored. And to this predilection might be attributed the numerous important appointments with which Jefferson had successively invested him, — as missions to France, Spain, and England, almost contemporaneously; and all calculated to give him an uncommon elevation in the view of his party and of the people of the United States."

These Connecticut gentlemen, whose acquaintance my father made on this visit, were most of them important public men at that time and afterwards. Webster I take to have been Noah Webster, of lexicographic celebrity. David Daggett was a native of Massachusetts, born in 1764, graduating at New Haven in 1783, and a very eminent lawyer in that city. He was not in Congress with my father, but entered it as Senator in 1813, remaining until 1819. He was afterwards a Justice and the Chief Justice of the Supreme Court of Connecticut. He died in 1851, in his eighty-seventh year. Roger Griswold, born in Lyme in Connecticut, 1762, graduated at New Haven in 1780, was an active member of Congress from 1795 to 1805. His transactions with Matthew Lyon I shall relate elsewhere. Later he was a Judge of the Supreme Court and Governor of Connecticut. He held this office at the breaking out of the war of 1812, and refused to comply with a requisition of President Madison for a militia force to replace the garrisons of regulars which had been sent to the frontier. This was on the ground that the Governor of a State had a concurrent jurisdiction, so to speak, with the President of the United States, over the militia, and might decide whether the emergency existed which would justify him in calling it out. He died in the course of the same year. Calvin Goddard was a native of Massachusetts, born in 1768, graduating at Dartmouth College in 1786, and a member of Congress from 1801 to 1805. He died at Norwich in 1842. Timothy Pitkin was born in Farmington, Connecticut, in 1765, graduated at New Haven, 1785, and was a Representative in Congress from 1805 to 1819. He wrote some laborious statistical and historical works, and died in 1847, in his eighty-third year. My father and he were warm friends through life. I well remember a visit he and Judge Daggett paid my father at Cambridge one Commencement time, about 1834 or 1835, and how the three old Federalists fought their battles o'er again, and showed small mercy to Jefferson and Madison, their following and their works.

During the few days my father stayed in New York he received much attention from the principal Federalists there, — such as Dr. Hosack, Dr. Harris, Colonel Fish, Judge Pendleton, William

Johnson, Jacob Lewis, Mr. Stuyvesant, Mr. Gracie, and Mr. Wolcott, besides his brothers-in-law Jacob and Washington Morton. One of the topics of discussion among these gentlemen at their dinner-parties was, whether it were advisable to change the name of the Federal party, because of the ill odor into which it had fallen. Happily the impossible and the absurd was never attempted.

"Dined at Washington Morton's. Lewis in company. Speaking of John Randolph, member of Congress from Virginia, Lewis said that his (Randolph's) policy was unequivocally hostile to the commercial character of the United States, — that he made no hesitation in expressing his contempt of the carrying trade. One of the heads of departments declared to me, said Lewis, that Randolph, in conversation with him upon the carrying trade, expressed his unequivocal sentiment that no discrimination ought to be made in favor of our own commerce and navigation, — that, in order to promote competition, our ports ought to be open to the ships of all nations. 'He who carries away the produce of my plantation,' said Randolph, 'is like him who *blacks my shoes;* so long as he does it in the best manner, and at the cheapest rate, I employ him; but if another will do either upon more advantageous terms, be he foreigner or native, the other must and ought to lose his employment.'"

Dr. Alexander Hosack, F. R. S., I need hardly say, was the eminent physician of the last generation, and father of the eminent surgeon of the same name of this. Colonel Nicholas Fish served in the Revolutionary army, and was one of the most eminent and honored citizens of his time. He was the father of Mr. Hamilton Fish, sometime Governor of New York. Nathaniel Pendleton was the second of Hamilton in his fatal duel with Burr, by which fact he is chiefly remembered now. He was a judge of some one of the inferior courts. William Johnson is well known to the legal profession by his Reports of the decisions of the highest courts of Common Law and of Equity of New York, in the golden days of Kent, Livingston, and Spencer. Commodore Jacob Lewis was a distinguished naval officer of the old school. Mr. Nicholas Stuyvesant and Mr. Archibald Gracie were gentlemen of wealth and high social position, as their names sufficiently indicate. Mr. Wolcott was, of course, the former

Secretary of the Treasury, afterwards Governor of Connecticut, at that time the president of a bank in New York.

My mother's brothers, Jacob and Washington Morton, were very well-known men to the New York of their day. The image of the former must still live in the memory of the elder and middle-aged portion of the inhabitants of that city. He was born in 1761, and graduated at Princeton in 1778. He studied law, but was diverted from following up the profession by other employments. For thirty years or more he was Major-General of the First Division of the State Militia of New York, until his death, in 1836, in his seventy-fourth year, when he was honored with a great military funeral. During the war of 1812 he was mustered into the service of the United States, and was appointed to the military command of the city of New York. He was the immediate predecessor of General Sandford, who has lately ended a term of service of about the same duration. Many citizens of New York will yet freshly remember the powdered head, erect carriage, alert air, and cordial manners of the kind-hearted and hospitable old General, — a gentleman in breeding as well as politics of the school of Washington, — who was as familiar in the eyes of the New York of thirty years since as the City Hall itself. And speaking of the City Hall, General Morton held some place of trust and emolument there, under the city government, for many years; and so strong was his hold upon the popular regard that no change in the political complexion of the municipal government disturbed his tenure of office. Though a Federalist of the deepest dye in the days when the old Democratic party came into power, and a pronounced Adams man during the excited canvass which resulted in the election of General Jackson to the Presidency, neither Democrats nor Jackson-men ventured to remove him. Perhaps they did not wish to do so. While other heads fell with small mercy under the knife of the political guillotine, his remained safe on his official shoulders until his natural death.

His younger brother, Washington, was born in 1775, and graduated at Princeton in 1792. He was one of Nature's favorite sons, and endowed by her with her best gifts of mind and body.

Splendidly handsome, of great bodily strength and athletic skill, he had also extraordinary powers of mind, from which his contemporaries augured great success in life, and eminence in his profession of the law, — auguries which his early death disappointed of their entire fulfilment. But though not much past thirty when he died, and though perhaps more of his time was given to the pleasures of the world than to its affairs, he had won an honorable place at the bar of New York at that most brilliant period of its history when it bore upon its calendar such names as Alexander Hamilton, Aaron Burr, John Wells, Samuel Jones, Thomas Addis Emmett, Rufus King, David B. Ogden, Peter A. Jay, and others of a national, some of them of a European, reputation. Of his physical powers of endurance and his love of athletic exercises he gave a proof, which made a great noise at the time, by walking for a wager from New York to Philadelphia in one day, then an unprecedented feat. His walk finished and his wager won, after a bath and toilet, as he told the story to my mother, he spent the night with his friends who had accompanied him on horseback, and a party of Philadelphia choice spirits, over a supper-table spread in his honor, at which we may well believe that the conviviality was answerable to the greatness of the occasion.

Being such as I have described him, it is perhaps not surprising, when he and the beautiful Cornelia Schuyler, daughter of General Philip Schuyler of the Revolution, and younger sister of Mrs. Alexander Hamilton, were thrown together, that they should have fallen in love with one another. And perhaps, too, it was nothing strange that the cautious General should have hesitated before consenting to intrust his lovely child to the care of a volatile youth of two and twenty, who, however brilliant might be his prospects and his possibilities, had not yet slackened his pace to the sober rate befitting a steady-going married man. At any rate, he refused his consent to the match, and, exercising the paternal authority then his undisputed right, forbade all communication between his daughter and her suitor. But my uncle Washington was not a man to be turned from his purpose by an obstacle like this. Such an impediment might hinder the course of his true love from running smooth, but, far from staying, only made it run the faster. My readers must supply the intermediate stages of this little romance from their own imaginations, but this was its conclusion. Late one night Washington Morton found himself in Albany, and under the window of the fair Cornelia. At a signal, which I fear must have been preconcerted, the window opened, the young lady appeared, and presently leaped bravely from it into her lover's arms. Whatever may be thought of the prudence of this proceeding, the next step certainly showed that the pair were not wholly without discretion; for they proceeded in all haste, through the watches of the night, to Stockbridge, in Massachusetts, thirty or forty miles away, to seek the counsel and countenance of Judge Theodore Sedgwick, who was the common and intimate friend of both their families. There they suddenly presented themselves to the eyes of that excellent magistrate, who was looking for anything rather than such an apparition, and told the story of their flight. Of course, there was but one thing to do. The parson was sent for, and the twain made one flesh with all convenient speed. It was a good while before General Schuyler could bring himself to forgive this escapade. But in time he was prevailed upon "to take up the mangled matter at the best," and to submit with as good a grace as he could muster to what he could not help.

After the death of Cornelia Morton in 1807, her husband, to dissipate the passionate affliction in which he was plunged by it, went to Europe, and there died, at Paris, in 1810. A romantic story as to the object of his European visit and the manner of his death obtained a good deal of currency at the time, and may possibly yet linger among the traditions of winter-firesides. I was first told of it many years ago in a stage-coach in the State of New York, by a citizen of intelligence and respectability who had no suspicion that I was at all connected with its subject, as an unquestionable fact, and I afterwards learned, on inquiry, that it was extensively believed to be such. I am sorry to be obliged to spoil the story in advance by saying that it was certainly false in its most material circumstance, and that I have no doubt it was altogether a pure fabrication. Washington Morton was well known to have been nearly connected with General Hamilton by marriage, as well as his warm personal friend and ardent political admirer. The story ran that he went abroad with the deliberate purpose of seeking Burr out, challenging him, and avenging the death of Hamilton with his own hand. It went on to say that he traced Burr to Paris, called him out, and they met on the field of honor. Unluckily, however, for the interests of poetical justice, instead of his killing Burr, Burr killed him! And unfortunately for the story, it was contradicted by refractory facts, for Mr. Morton died very suddenly of some disease of the throat, of which event and all its details his family had the testimony of General Armstrong, then our Minister at Paris, and of other Americans residing there at the time. And it is not likely that he undertook his visit to Europe with any such truculent design. For if he had thought himself called upon to be the avenger of blood in the case of Hamilton, Washington Morton was not the man to let the suns of six years go down upon his wrath before entering upon the office. But it is time to return to my father's account of his visit to New York.

"*5th.* — Dined with General Jacob Morton. Jacob Lewis of the company. He was the commander of the celebrated St. Domingo fleet, and had great opportunities of forming correct opinions concerning the state of that island. The continuance of the government in the hands of the blacks he considered as chimerical. It was, undoubtedly, the policy of the British government to get and maintain a footing in the island, either with a view of future perfect occupation, or to have it as an offset at the peace. For this reason they had already taken possession of, and were fortifying themselves in, Jeremie and the Mole. 'The black Emperor,' Lewis said, 'had himself told him, that overtures for this purpose had been made to him by the British agent in behalf of his government, with a threat that, if he opposed or disquieted their possession, they would interdict all commerce with that island, which was contraband. His fear of this had operated to keep him still as to this invasion of his territories. The ostensible reason for taking possession of it at present was to quiet the apprehensions of the inhabitants of Jamaica, who deemed their security hazarded by their proximity to this ferocious and lawless banditti.

"I asked Mr. Pendleton * whether, in the opinion of Mr. Hamilton's friends, Mr. King † had conducted with propriety in leaving New York, previous to the duel, after having been particularly consulted by Hamilton on the subject. Mr. Pendleton answered, 'that the facts were that Hamilton did consult King, and that early. He was that "judicious friend" of whom Hamilton speaks in one of his letters. After having thus been consulted some time previously to the time fixed for the duel, King commenced a journey. I know that this conduct of King has been considered as indicating *great coldness of heart* in King. It certainly does nothing else. A man who had felt deeply the public and private stake which was put at risk, would not, it has been said, have left the vicinity until the final decision, particularly after the marks of confidence he had received from Hamilton. On the contrary, Mr. King says he could have done nothing by staying, — that the duel was inevitable. From political considerations, he might wish to be at a distance from the scene.'"

"*8th.* — Returned Harris's, Stuyvesant's, and Colonel Fish's visits. Went with Dr. Hosack to view his botanic garden and greenhouse. It is only the second year since its commencement, consequently the institution is but in an infant state. The greenhouse is twenty feet high and broad, sixty-three feet long. The whole number of acres destined for the establishment, twenty acres. His collections, considering the time, numerous and various in species.

"*9th.* — Dined with Mr. Gracie, at his country-seat, about eight miles from New York. Gracie is a merchant of eminence, a particular friend of Mr. Wolcott, through his attachment to whom I am probably indebted for his politeness to me, — the dinner having been made particularly on my account. Wolcott's character of Gracie is, that he is one of the most excellent of the earth, — actively liberal, intelligent, seeking and rejoicing in occasions to do good. Certainly I have great reason to be grateful for this attention. His seat is upon the East River, opposite the famous pass called Hell Gate. The scene is beautiful beyond description. A deep, broad, rapid stream glances with an arrowy fleetness by the shore, hurrying along every species of

* Pendleton was one of Hamilton's seconds. I was led to this inquiry because a brother-in-law of mine, Washington Morton, who had married Miss Schuyler (sister of Mrs. Hamilton), a young man of strong passions, had spoken very indignantly of the conduct of King, giving the impression that such was the feeling of his wife's family.

† The celebrated Rufus King; graduated at Harvard University in 1777; Senator from New York and Minister to England. Died in 1827.

vessel which the extensive commerce of the country affords. The water, broken by the rocks which lie in the midst of the current, presents a continual scene of turbulent waves, dashing, foaming, and spending their force upon the rocks. The various courses every vessel has to shape, in order to escape from the dangers of the pass, present a constant change and novelty in this enchanting scene. The shores of Long Island, full of cultivated prospects, and interspersed with elegant country-seats, bound the distant view. The mansion-house is elegant, in the modern style, and the grounds laid out with taste in gardens. Judge Pendleton, Dr. Hosack, Mr. Wolcott, and Mr. Hopkins were of the party."

Arrived at Washington, Mr. Quincy and his family took up their quarters in the house of Chief-Justice Cranch of the District Court, according to an arrangement entered into for the following reasons, as given by himself: —

"Having ascertained the exceeding want of accommodation for a private family at Washington, then only in the sixth or seventh year of its existence, and the many difficulties of keeping house, and the utter discomfort and want of security from intrusion in the boarding-houses, I had made an arrangement with Judge Cranch to receive me and Mrs. Quincy, with one child, into his family, with sufficient adjoining accommodation for my coachman, horses, and carriage, — an arrangement which in its result proved most happy and gratifying to me. Cranch was the son of Richard Cranch, of Quincy, in which town he was born and educated. His father was an early friend of my father, and of myself. Judge Cranch himself was one of the most gentlemanly of men, and eminent for his private virtues and judicial knowledge.

"Of the course of my life during this session I have few remembrances. I had with me my wife and eldest child. My intercourse with Judge Cranch and his family was the solace of my domestic hours, so far as their happiness depended on anything external to my own family. My Congressional friends were our frequent evening visitors, to whom the vivacity, intelligence, and cultivated mind and manners of my wife were never-failing attractions. She was soon visited by several ladies of Washington, with some of whom she afterwards formed interesting friendships. As for myself, my whole thoughts were absorbed in my public duties, the fulfilment of which constituted the constant endeavor and chief pleasure of my life."

CHAPTER V.

1805-1807.

THE NINTH CONGRESS. — STATE OF AFFAIRS. — MR. QUINCY'S OPINION OF MR. JEFFERSON. — OF THE PURCHASE OF LOUISIANA. — MR. MERRY'S RECEPTION BY MR. JEFFERSON. — THE FEDERALISTS AND JOHN RANDOLPH. — THE NON-IMPORTATION ACT. — SPEECH ON COAST DEFENCE. — ABOLITION OF THE SLAVE-TRADE. — LIFE AT WASHINGTON.

THE moment when Mr. Quincy took his seat in the House of Representatives was a very critical one in regard both to the foreign and the domestic affairs of the United States. Mr. Jefferson was in the first year of his second term, and had an unquestionable and unquestioning majority in both houses at his beck. The Federalists were in a hopeless minority in Congress and in the nation. They had but seven Senators, counting John Quincy Adams, who soon went out from among them, and barely twenty-five members of the lower house. A majority even of the Massachusetts delegation (ten out of seventeen) were Democrats. Of course, all that the minority could do was to watch the Administration, to expose its shortcomings and excesses, to resist mischievous measures as well as they could, and record a protest against them when resistance was in vain. The adoption of the Federal Constitution was strictly contemporaneous with the beginning of the French Revolution, and from that time forward American politics had been profoundly influenced by those of Europe. In 1805, Bonaparte was in the midst of his portentous career of victory. His name was a word to conjure with on this side of the Atlantic, as well as on the other. His battles, while they shook the continent of Europe, made that of America tremble also. The Democrats, who had hailed the French Revolution as the dawn of the political millennium, saluted Bonaparte as its heir, and as the instrument appointed for the humiliation of crowned heads and the exaltation of the people. England they regarded as the voluntary champion of the ancient abuses, and the Federalists as in full sympathy with her crusade against struggling liberty. The Federalists, on the other hand, who abhorred the excesses attending the French Revolution, and looked upon Bonaparte as a monster of tyranny to whom that convulsion had given birth, considered England as the only hope of the world for checking his career of universal empire, in which he would accord to the United States only the boon of being devoured the last. And many of them believed the Democrats to be ready to give up the independence of their country, and to surrender it to the Corsican usurper as a virtual dependency, if not as an outlying department, of the French empire. For the quarter of a century between the breaking out of the French Revolution and the Peace of 1815, the hopes and the fears, the passions and the politics of America, were indissolubly and inextricably bound up with those of Europe. This fact supplies the key to much that may seem anomalous or enigmatical in the conduct of American parties during that period.

The situation of public affairs at the opening of the Ninth Congress was substantially this. Bonaparte having sold Louisiana to the United States, in 1803, under circumstances the influence of which has affected our whole subsequent history, the United States were in a state of *quasi* hostility with Spain, who did not see a possession so lately hers, and which she had ceded back to France with no such idea, made over to a rapidly growing Republic conterminous with her other North American possessions. She had solemnly protested against the treaty of 1803 at the time. Disputes as to boundaries were a fruitful cause of collision, and had led to the actual occupation by Spain of soil unquestionably within our frontiers. Irujo, the Spanish Minister, had insulted our government in a manner which showed that Spain probably shared the opinion Talleyrand had expressed to the Directory as to the United States. The President, having taken offence at certain proceedings of his, asked his recall, and when the Secretary of State informed him that his continued presence in Washington was "dissatisfactory to the President," he coolly replied that he should stay as long as suited his convenience, and, further, that he received no orders excepting from the king his master. This state of things certainly called for some military and naval preparation. But this was not all. Up to the year 1805, the United States had enjoyed a most lucrative carrying trade, being the only considerable neutral power during the wars carried on by and against Bonaparte. All the productions of the colonies of France and Holland, and of Spain since her accession to the French alliance, were first brought to some American port, and thence reshipped to the respective mother countries, giving double freights to the ship-owners. The British merchants did not look on this favor shown to American shipping with complacency, and the government also discovered that it gave to France the full benefit of the trade of her own colonies and those of her allies, in war almost as fully as in peace. The Courts of Admiralty, accordingly, reconsidered the old doctrines of international law, and confiscated several valuable cargoes, though protected by the American flag, on the ground that it was merely used to cover a fraudulent transaction, the property never having really belonged to the American merchant, having been landed in the neutral port merely to be reshipped to the hostile one. These decisions, which destroyed an immensely profitable business, caused great dissatisfaction in the commercial centres, and were the beginning of the unfriendly relations with England which at last ended in the war of 1812. And France and Spain, notwithstanding the advantages they derived from the neutral character of the United States, could not keep their hands off the rich prizes which came in the way of their cruisers, and which were taken on small pretexts, or simply robbed without any, and thus gave rise to most of those French and Spanish claims of which we have heard so much in later years.

Mr. Jefferson, in his Message on the opening of Congress, in 1805, drew attention to the aggressions of Spain, and to "the new principles interpolated into the law of nations" by Great Britain, and to the necessity of preparation to defend the rights of the nation in both cases. In his extreme fear of spending money, however, he limited his recommendation of defensive measures to the employment of gunboats for the defence of the harbors, and to a classification of the militia, so that the younger portion might be called into the field in case of emergency. The new policy of Great Britain was perplexing to the Federalists, not merely because the strength of the party lay in the commercial region, which was the one most immediately affected by it, but because it would be an occasion to the French party, as they esteemed the Democrats, to give more effectual help to the conqueror of Europe. It was a nice task to maintain the rights of neutral commerce against the new doctrines of England, and at the same time to do nothing to cripple her in her conflict with the common enemy of mankind, as they regarded Bonaparte. And the question grew more and more perplexing as the relations of the three countries became more and more complicated as time went on. The state of Federal feeling on this subject may be gathered from the following extract from a letter of Fisher Ames, than whom there was no man more admired or revered by the Federalists, to Mr. Quincy, written just before the session, but received after it began. After speaking of the anxiety caused by the English confiscations, he goes on :—

"I am very willing the British should turn out exceedingly in the wrong in regard to condemning our vessels when laden with colonial produce. If they are not in the wrong, I see not the policy or fitness of hazarding our commerce, peace, and prosperity on an untenable point. Force of guns is on their side. I would not voluntarily have the force of argument against us also. In case a candid examination should create many doubts of our assumed principles, as I think it will, why should we make the retracting the contrary principles by England a *sine qua non* of our measures? . . . .

"To reduce France within moderate limits will require an age of battles, and England is alone possessed of the means, and forced to display the courage, to fight them with the necessary perseverance. I expect reverses and disasters, and that Great Britain, now on the high horse, will dismount again. The time will come, therefore, when negotiation may effect much. Menace and the base hostility of confiscation (of debts) will surely prevent its being effected. I could fill a dozen sheets with speculations, because I should deal in conjectures. I will spare you. Why should one Yankee help another to guess?" *

* Works of Fisher Ames, edited by his Son, Seth Ames, Vol. I. p. 339.

The following are some passages from Mr. Quincy's answer to Mr. Ames: —

"I will not anticipate your sentiments of the Message. Considering the rickety habits of our President, some think he shows great strength. I leave that to those who have andrometers graduated to his scale to decide; my opinions relate only to particulars. The general character of the man, or his speech, I have no concern with. There are points which demand our most solicitous attention, and on these I shall hereafter take occasion to give you mine, and ask for your thoughts. That which most interests me, because my constituents have the deepest concern in it, relates to those 'new principles interpolated into the laws of nations.' This part of the Message has been referred to the Committee of Ways and Means, of which Randolph is chairman, and of which I have the honor to be a member. I know and feel the importance of the result, and my commercial friends may rely it shall not be a moment out of my thoughts. It is impossible for me to divine the deep mysteries of the President's policy. From an expression he used in conversation with me, I expected a much more direct and vindictive course than his Message contains. 'Great Britain,' said he, with an air indicative of much temper, 'has taken ground which I believe she means to keep, but which the United States never can concede.' Considering my path of politics was known to him, I expected he was preparing me, and those of my political sentiments, for some strong outline of conduct, which, however, it seems he has not had the boldness publicly to draw, but will leave his fancies to be put upon canvas by the Committee of Ways and Means. You know my situation in that committee, — of course in the minority."

It appears from this letter that Mr. Quincy had waited personally upon Mr. Jefferson, — a visit of ceremony, doubtless, considered as due to the head of the nation from all members of Congress. The opinion which he held, in common with all the Federalists, of that celebrated person, was such as to make him decline receiving any personal attentions from him, or holding any social intercourse with him. On this subject he speaks as follows: —

"During my preparatory studies for public life I had imbibed an impression concerning Mr. Jefferson little less than antipathetic. I found that he had no sooner entered Washington's Cabinet, as Secretary of State, than he commenced insidious attacks upon the leaders of the Federal party, — particularly upon Adams and Hamilton. To the former he well knew he had been selected as the rival for the successorship of Washington. The great and overwhelming talents of the latter he both envied and feared. He began at the same period to assail the whole Federal party, calling them 'Tories,' 'enemies of republicanism,' 'British partisans,' and charged them with being actuated by a settled design to change the Federal Constitution into a monarchy. It was well known that, from the first, his language and letters contained unceasing charges of this kind against that whole party; at the same time, as said Hamilton, 'he arraigned to every man that approached him the principal measures of government with undue warmth.' Nor did he fail to insinuate against such men as Adams, Jay, Hamilton, Knox, and many others, the design of introducing changes into the government of this country, and making way for a king, lords, and commons! Calumnies false, injurious, and absurd, for there was no material out of which such a form of government could have been wrought. Yet were they the subject of his open conversation, of his private letters, and, as often as he dared, in the public prints. His assiduity in this course was apparent and undisguised, the end he had in view plain, and the object and result in his own elevation undeniable. I regarded him, in respect of Washington's administration, and indeed of the Federal party, as a snake in the grass, — the more dangerous from the oily, wily language with which he lubricated his victims and applied his venom, — the more seductive and influential from the hollow pretences of respect, and, in regard to Adams, even of affection, with which he accompanied them.

"I came to Washington with an abhorrence of Jefferson's political character. I had no desire to make my course upward in political life, and holding my public station only as a means and opportunity of serving my country, with no wish or intention of continuing in it one moment longer than it was the unsolicited wish of my fellow-citizens, I had not the usual motives of public men to seek the friendship and favor of men in power. I therefore declined several invitations to dine at the White House, which, with some Congressional demonstrations of mine, made Mr. Jefferson understand that I had no wish for their renewal. The developments which subsequent years have made of his course and language at that period amply justify these feelings, if they do not my mode of expressing them. The Federal party have of late years received a full answer to the prayer of Job, 'O that mine enemy had written a book!' This Jefferson has done, and Henry G. Randall has published it. A memoir more suicidal of character was never written, nor one which established by more unquestionable evidence every ill opinion previously entertained of its subject. It will have its effect, all the efforts of the biographer to whitewash the character of Jefferson, and to support his calumnies, to the contrary notwithstanding."

There is no part of Mr. Quincy's public life which has been the occasion of more comment and more censure than his course, in 1811, in relation to the erection of Louisiana into a State. As his motives and conduct have been very extensively misrepresented and misunderstood, it may be well to give in this place his own account, in his own words, of his views as to the manner in which the original purchase was made. At this distance of time, removed from the influence of contemporary passions, I believe that the impartial judgment of the present day will pronounce his opinions and conduct those of a sagacious and far-seeing statesman, and not of a headstrong and violent partisan. If ever prophecies were answered by events, all his predictions of the mischiefs sure to follow from that *coup d'état* have been fulfilled, and more than fulfilled, to the letter.

" Another act of his administration had filled me with inexpressible disgust and apprehension. The purchase of Louisiana was wise and popular in view of the danger that then seemed threatening. An apprehension prevailed that Bonaparte had compelled Spain to transfer Louisiana to him, he intending to plant a French colony there. It was believed that the troops he had sent to St. Domingo were destined for New Orleans when they had done their work in that island. Then the people of the Western States were clamorous for the free opening of the Mississippi. These circumstances gave general interest and importance to the purchase. Had Jefferson confined his policy to that object, it would have received the approbation even of the Northern States. But he coupled it with a design insidious and unprincipled. The clause in the Constitution giving the power to Congress to admit into the Union other States, had unquestionably sole reference to the admission of States within the limits of the original territory of the United States. No original document, argument, or treatise, at the time of the formation of the Constitution, can be adduced to give color to the opinion that it was intended to extend to territories then belonging to foreign powers, beyond the limits of the original thirteen States. Mr. Jefferson himself was so convinced of this fact, that he declared, previous to the purchase of Louisiana, that it could not be done except by receiving the sanction of the several States, without a violation of the Constitution.

"In a letter to Mr. Breckenridge, dated Monticello, August 12, 1802, Mr. Jefferson writes: 'The treaty (for the purchase of Louisiana) must of course be laid before both Houses. They, I presume, will see their duty to the country in ratifying and paying for it. But I suppose they must then appeal to *the nation* for an additional article in the Constitution, approving and confirming an act which the nation had not previously authorized. The Constitution has made no provision for our holding foreign territory, still less for incorporating foreign nations into our Union.'

"After this statement, and declaring that the Executive, for the good of his country, had done an act beyond the Constitution, he seriously advises that the Legislature should cast behind them metaphysical subtilties, violate the Constitution and their oaths, and do a thing wholly unauthorized. He likened the act to the case of a guardian making an investment for a minor, without authority, for the good of the minor, which he might alter when he came of age; concealing the utter inapplicability of the case to the proposed assumption of power. For here the minors were of full age. The people of the United States might have had a voice in the question, and the deed thus perpetrated was final, and they never could have an opportunity to disavow it.

"In a letter to Levi Lincoln, August 30, 1803, after his opinion on the constitutionality of admitting Louisiana had been publicly avowed, he says: '*The less that is said about any Constitutional difficulty, the better. Congress should do what is necessary in silence.* I find but one opinion as to the necessity of *shutting up the Constitution for some time.*' On the same page, in a letter to Wilson Cary Nicholas, he recommends, 'Whatever Congress do, as it respects the Constitutional difficulty, should be done with as little debate as possible.' See Jefferson's Writings, published by T. Jefferson Randolph, Vol. III. p. 512, Vol. IV. p. 2; also the edition published by order of Congress by H. A. Washington, 1854, Vol. IV. pp. 500, 504, 505.

"Notwithstanding the perfect conviction of his own mind on this point, as he unequivocally declared, (a fact well known at that time, and subsequently publicly demonstrated,) he yielded to the solicitations and influence of his partisans, silenced his conscientious scruples, and, holding in his hand the omnipotence of the present party power, consented to give his sanction to the violation of the Constitution by admitting Louisiana into the Union without receiving or asking the consent of the several States.

"By this act, as was then foreseen, and the result has proved, Jefferson unsettled and spread the whole foundations of the Union, as established by the original Constitution of the United States, introduced a population alien to it in every element of character, previous education, and political tendency. Had his policy terminated with this result, it would have been sufficiently unprincipled, though less injurious; but it was far-reaching into the future, and in its effects on the destinies of the Union. It was obvious that an appeal to the Free States might be safely made with regard to the admission of Louisiana, the apprehension concerning the ulterior views of Bonaparte, and the wish to obtain the free navigation of the Mississippi, were so universal.

"The policy of Jefferson was not, therefore, adopted from fear of a rejection of the proposition for the admission of Louisiana by the States, but he and the Slave States foresaw that, by seizing the opportunity which they then had, and assuming at once that the Constitution gave Congress authority to multiply States in foreign territories, they would put an end forever to the necessity of applying to the States for such power in future. They foresaw that the territories thus conjoined would open the opportunity and power of multiplying Slave States, for which their climate was adapted, and thus effecting additional weight and ultimate predominancy to the slave power in the Union. To this end the assumption was made, and the subsequent history of the Union is but one tissue of evidence of its nature and consequences."

This strong disapprobation of Mr. Jefferson as a public man, which Mr. Quincy shared with the whole Federal party, was made yet more intense by the fears and hopes which agitated the public mind as the great European contest went on. Mr. Jefferson had made no secret of his sympathy with France, as against England, from the beginning of the French Revolution. He was a witness of its earlier scenes from his post at Paris as Minister from the United States, and had given it his counsels as well as his good wishes. It is believed, I am not sure on what authority, that it was he that suggested the name of "National Assembly" to the Abbé Sièyes, when the States General transformed itself from a constitutional into a revolutionary body. The sympathies of the entire American people were at first with the Revolution; and those of the younger and more hopeful, and such as had the least to lose, remained unchanged in spite of the Reign of Terror and of the insolences of the Directory to their own country. The elder and graver classes, the wealthy and the educated, looked upon the French Revolution with horror and dread. The same differences of temperament, condition, and character influenced the feelings of these classes respectively towards England. The former yet remembered bitterly against England the exasperations of our Revolutionary war, while they gratefully recalled the aid, so essential to its successful issue, which the French alliance had lent to our arms. And of later years, while the demeanor of the Directory towards the country had been insolent and offensive, the conduct of England had been far from conciliatory or friendly. By means of these passions, skilfully managed and worked upon, Mr. Jefferson had raised himself to the Presidency.

Of one of his ways of manifesting his English antipathies, Mr. Quincy's journal gives a curious account. Among the acquaintances he formed during his first winter in Washington was that of Mr. Merry, the English Minister. This gentleman gave him an account of the way in which he was treated by Mr. Jefferson at the time of his official reception. As my father wrote down Mr. Merry's story at the time, it is probably the most correct account that has been given of that remarkable transaction.

"*January*, 1806. — The British Minister, Merry, in conversation with me in January, 1806, spoke with great asperity of the treatment, amounting to studied incivility, which he had received from President Jefferson from the first moment of his presenting his credentials as Minister, and which he considered as political and designed. As an evidence of the ground of this opinion, he stated the following facts. 'On presenting my credentials,' said he, 'I asked Mr. Madison, the Secretary of State, at what time it would be convenient for him to introduce me officially to President Jefferson. Madison replied that he would consult Mr. Jefferson, and would inform me of his determination. Accordingly, Madison soon after informed me of the day and hour appointed for my formal introduction, and on that day and hour I called on Mr. Madison, who accompanied me officially to introduce me to the President. We went together to the mansion-house, I being in full official costume, as the etiquette of my place required on such a formal introduction of a Minister from Great Britain to the President of the United States. On arriving at the hall of audience, we found it empty, at which Mr. Madison seemed surprised, and proceeded to an entry leading to the President's study. I followed him, supposing the introduction was to take place in the adjoining room. At this moment Mr. Jefferson entered the entry at the other end, and all three of us were packed in this narrow space, from which, to make room, I was obliged to back out. In this awkward position my introduction to the President was made by Mr. Madison. Mr. Jefferson's appearance soon explained to me that the general circumstances of my reception had not been accidental, but studied. I, in my official costume, found myself, at the hour of reception he had himself appointed, introduced to a man as the President of the United States, not merely in an undress, but actually standing in slippers down at the heels, and both pantaloons, coat, and under-clothes indicative of utter slovenliness and indifference to appearances, and in a state of negligence actually studied. I could not doubt that the whole scene was prepared and intended as an insult, not to me personally, but to the sovereign I represented.'

"This occurrence, with others of a similar nature, were topics of common conversation in Washington, and received by the opponents of Mr. Jefferson with contempt and disgust, as evidence of his desire to avail himself of a vulgar popularity, and by his friends with applause, as proofs of the republicanism of his spirit and his independence of British influence. In dress, conversation, and demeanor he studiously sought and displayed the arts of a low demagogue seeking the gratification of the democracy on whose voices and votes he laid the foundation of his power."

The Federal party, as I have already said, was in a hopeless and helpless minority of twenty-five, in a house of a hundred and forty members. Besides this small opposition of principle, there was a small faction of Democrats called "quids" in the slang of the day, who had quarrelled with Jefferson over the spoils of victory. It was small, and derived all the importance it had from its leader, John Randolph of Roanoke, as he styled himself, whose wit, talent as a debater, insolence, and unbridled license of tongue made him a thorn in the side of the party he had left. He was a Virginian and only a Virginian, of the narrowest sectional feelings and prejudices, who often acted with the Federalists when he could thus best thwart or annoy his enemy. It is said that he parted company with Mr. Jefferson because he had been refused a foreign mission on which he had set his heart. If this were true, surely the most determined of Mr. Jefferson's unfriends could not include that action of his within the scope of their censures. The Federalists, by agreement among themselves, abstained from making any party demonstrations of their own, and contented themselves with following the lead of Randolph. This policy did not suit the quality of Mr. Quincy's temper or mind, and he resisted it, at the time it was under consideration, as being virtually political suicide. A party that refused to act as a party was to all intents and purposes dead. And though it might be merely sleeping, its sleep was virtual death, and its strength was more likely to be lessened than increased by such a lethargy. Being the youngest member of the party, he could not presume to refuse obedience to the decision of the majority, when his arguments and protestations were of no avail. He adhered to the policy thus laid down for that session, but did not feel himself bound to conform to it after he felt more at home in the business of the House. As to Randolph he says: —

"I had no predilection for John Randolph, and liked not the idea of taking a man so fickle, wayward, and overbearing as a sort of leader. However, I acceded to the policy of my friends during the first session, and was true to it. The first struggle was to get Macon of North Carolina, one of Randolph's friends, into the Speaker's chair, which was effected with some difficulty, to his great joy and the annoyance of the friends of the Administration. Macon immediately appointed Randolph Chairman of the Committee of Ways and Means, for which place, had Jefferson's friends been successful, they had selected Barnabas Bidwell of Massachusetts. I was placed upon the same committee, which gave me an opportunity of a personal acquaintance with Randolph, which resulted in as much intimacy as was practicable between me and a Southern man, haughty and wedded to Southern supremacy, and who made no concealment of his want of general sympathy for Northern men and Northern interests. Towards me personally his manners were polite in the extreme, and during our whole political life nothing ever occurred between us which was not of the most agreeable and friendly character. Our general views concerning Jefferson and his party were, for the most part, coincident, and in debate we seldom came in collision."

Barnabas Bidwell entered Congress at this session for the first time, and sat for but one term. He graduated at Yale College in 1785, and was a lawyer in the western part of Massachusetts. He had been a very active Democratic politician, and brought a very high reputation with him to Washington, and his advent was hailed by the Jeffersonians as that of a great accession of strength to their party. Randolph was especially curious to know what manner of man this new antagonist might be, of whose prowess such tales were told. Accordingly, on the occasion of Bidwell's maiden speech, as my father used to tell the story, Randolph was in his place, which commanded that of the new member, and gave him a profound attention. But, as has often happened before, the performance of the new actor did not come up to the expectations excited by the flourish of trumpets which had announced his entrance upon the scene. Mr. Bidwell, though undoubtedly a man of ability in some sort, was not an orator, as Randolph was, but dull and heavy, both in matter and manner. Randolph soon made up his mind about him, and took a characteristic way of letting the House know his opinion. He was dressed in his usual morning costume, — his skeleton legs cased in tight-fitting leather breeches and top-boots, with a blue riding-coat, and the thick buckskin gloves from which he was never parted, and a heavily loaded riding-whip in his hand. After listening attentively for about a quarter of an hour, he rose deliberately, settled his hat on his head, and walked slowly out of the House, striking the handle of his whip emphatically upon the palm of his left hand, and regarding poor Bidwell as he passed him with a look of insolent contempt, as much as to say, "I have taken your measure, sir, and shall give myself no further concern about *you!*" It helped to extinguish effectually the new light from which the Administration had hoped so much. Mr. Bidwell acquired no weight in the House, and left Congress at the end of his term, in 1807, and took the office of Attorney-General of Massachusetts, which he held until 1810. At that time some financial catastrophe overtook him which rendered his emigration to Canada convenient, if not necessary. There he lived until his death in 1833. His son, of the same name, attained considerable provincial distinction, and was at one time, if I am not mistaken, Speaker of the lower House of the Parliament of Upper Canada.

The first gun, so to speak, of Jefferson's war of commercial restrictions against England was fired at this session, or at least loaded and aimed ready to fire. It was a law prohibiting the importation from Great Britain or her dependencies of certain articles, comprising those which were the chief objects of English commerce. To give England time, however, to repent and avoid this penalty of her misdeeds, the prohibition was not to take effect until the next November. This measure the Federalists regarded as one looking towards war, and they deemed that no time should be lost in making some effectual preparation for such a contingency, should it occur. The practical question, therefore, which divided Congress at this time, was that of the fortification of the Atlantic cities. In view of the uncertain state of our relations with Spain and England, those cities felt a natural uneasiness at the unprotected condition in which a sudden war would find them. As they supplied, through the revenue afforded by their trade, all the means of the government, they thought it reasonable that a fair proportion of the funds they furnished should be applied to their own protection. This reasonable expectation the Southern and Western members were very ill disposed to meet. They were remote from the coast, their farms and plantations were secure from invasion, they felt the ignorant prejudice common to imperfect stages of civilization against commerce, and their sectional jealousies were made more bitter by the sight of the growing wealth of the commercial cities. While they were perfectly willing that those cities should pay the expenses of government, and furnish the credit which enabled it to raise fifteen millions of dollars wherewith to buy Louisiana, and two millions to be used in secret service for the acquisition of the Floridas, they grudged the smallest appropriation for their defence. During the seventeen years since the establishment of the government, only seven hundred and twenty-four thousand dollars had been appropriated for the fortification of the nine chief Atlantic cities! No apprehensions of expense deterred the frugal Jefferson and his Southern and Southwestern supporters, together with their faithful retinue of Northern Democrats, from incurring debt or appropriating revenue for whatever looked to the safety or prosperity of the interior. At this very session appropriations for the extinguishing of Indian titles for the advantage of the Southwest had been made to the amount of four hundred and fifty thousand dollars; while one hundred and fifty thousand was all that Congress was willing to expend for the defence of New York, "worth," as Mr. Quincy truly said, "forty Louisianas." A motion to increase the amount to five hundred thousand was treated with ridicule, and received only twenty-seven votes. Randolph, whose lead the Federalists had thought it expedient to follow in his general opposition to Jefferson, had no disposition to do anything to aid the North. The man whose prejudices against manufactures were so strong that he averred he would go a mile out of his way at any time "to kick a sheep," had as little love for commerce, and the Federalists had no help from him. A few gunboats to lie in wait for the enemy behind the headlands, and a few cannon to be run down to exposed points on the approach of danger, and worked by militia-men taken from the plough and the work-bench, were all that was thought necessary to guard the coasts and protect the great marts of trade. It was on this matter that Mr. Quincy made his first important speech, April 15th, 1806. A few extracts will give some notion of the force and good temper with which he urged the points at which I have just glanced, and the tone of the conclusion is not without "something of prophetic strain."

"Mr. Chairman: — Gentlemen seem disposed to treat this subject lightly, and to indulge themselves in pleasantries, on a question very serious to the commercial cities and to the interest of those who inhabit them. It may be sport to you, gentlemen, but it is death to us. However well disposed a majority of this House may be to treat this bill ludicrously, it will fill great and influential portions of this nation with very different sentiments. Men who have all that human nature holds dear, friends, fortunes, and families, concentrated in one single spot, on the sea-coast, and that spot exposed every moment to be plundered and desolated, will not highly relish or prize at an extreme value the wit or the levity with which this House seems inclined to treat the dangers which threaten them, and which are sources to them of great and just apprehensions. . . . .

"With respect to the general utility of fortifications, I ask, By whom is it denied? By men interested in that species of defence? By the inhabitants of cities? By those the necessity of whose situation has turned their attention to the nature of fortifications and their efficacy? No, sir; these men solicit them. They are anxious for nothing so much. They tell you the safety of all they hold dear, their wives, their children, their fortunes and lives, are staked upon your decision. They do not so much ask for fortifications as a favor, as claim them as a right. They demand them. Who are they, then, that deny their utility? Why, men from the interior. Men who, in one breath, tell you they know nothing about the subject, and in the next pass judgment against the adoption of any measures of defence. It is true, sir, to men who inhabit the White Hills of New Hampshire, or the Blue Ridge of Virginia, nothing can appear more absolutely useless than appropriations for the defence of the sea-coast. In this, as in all other cases, men reason very coolly and philosophically concerning dangers to which they are not themselves subject. All men, for the most part, bear with wonderful composure the misfortunes of other people. And, if called to contribute to their relief, they are sure to find, in the cold suggestions of economy, apologies enough for failure in their social duties. . . . .

"It is impossible to form a just estimate of our obligations to defend the commercial cities, without having a right idea of the nature and importance of commerce to the Eastern States, and attaining a just apprehension of its influence over every class of citizens in that quarter of the Union. From what has fallen from various gentlemen in the House, it is very apparent that they do not appreciate either its nature, its power, or the duties which result from our relation to those who are engaged in that pursuit. The gentleman from Virginia (Mr. J. Randolph) told us the other day, that 'the United States was a great land animal, — a great mammoth, which ought to cleave to the land, and not wade out into the ocean to fight the shark.' Sir, the figure is very happy so far as relates to that quarter of the Union with which that gentleman is chiefly conversant. Of the Southern States, the mammoth is a correct type. But I ask, sir, suppose *the mammoth* has made a league with *the cod*, and that the cod, enterprising, active, and skilful, spreads himself over every ocean, and brings back the tribute of all climes to the feet of the mammoth; suppose he thereby enables the unwieldy animal to stretch his huge limbs upon cotton, or to rub his fat sides along his tobacco plantations, *without paying the tithe of a hair,* in such case, is it wise, is it honorable, is it politic, for that mammoth, because by mere beef and bone he outweighs the cod in the political scale, to refuse a portion of that revenue which the industry of the cod annually produces to defend him in his natural element, if not against the great leviathan of the deep, at least against the petty pikes which prowl on the ocean, and if not in the whole course of his adventurous progress, at least in his native bays and harbors, where his hopes and wealth are deposited, and where his species congregate?

"Other gentlemen have shown an equal want of a just apprehension of the nature and effects of commerce. Some think any of its great channels can be impeded or cut off without important injury. Others, that it is a matter of so much indifference, that we can very well do without it. The gentleman from Pennsylvania (Mr. Smilie) told us some days since, '*that for his part he wished that at the time of our Revolution there had been no commerce.*' That honorable gentleman, I presume, is enamored with Arcadian scenes, with happy valleys. Like a hero of pastoral romance at the head of some murmuring stream, with his crook by his side, his sheep feeding around, far from the temptations, unseduced by the luxuries of commerce, he would

'. . . . sport with Amaryllis in the shade,
Or with the tangles of Neæra's hair.'

I will not deny that these are pleasant scenes. Doubtless they are well suited to the innocence, the purity, and the amiable, unobtrusive simplicity of that gentleman's mind and manners. But he must not expect that all men can be measured by his elevated standard, or be made to relish these sublime pleasures. Thousands and ten thousands in that part of the country I would represent have no notion of rural felicity, or of the tranquil joys of the country. They love a life of activity, of enterprise and hazard. They would rather see a boat-hook than all the crooks in the world; and as for sheep, they never desire to see anything more of them than just enough upon their deck to give them fresh meat once a week in a voyage. Concerning *the land* of which the gentleman from Virginia (Mr. J. Randolph), and the one from North Carolina (Mr. Macon), think so much, they think very little. It is, in fact, to them only a shelter from the storm, — a perch on which they build their eyry and hide their mate and their young, while they skim the surface or hunt in the deep. . . . .

"Every year we get together on this floor to consult concerning the public good. The state of commerce makes a capital object in all our deliberations. We have our committee of commerce and manufactures, and a great part of every session is exhausted in discussing their provisions, limitations, and restrictions, until at last we slide into the belief that commerce is of our creation; that it has its root in the statute-book; that its sap is drawn from our parchment, and that it spreads and flourishes under the direct heat of the legislative ray. But what is the fact? Look into your laws. What are they? Nine tenths — I should speak nearer the truth should I say ninety-nine hundredths — of them are nothing more than means by which you secure your share of the products of commerce; they constitute the machinery by which you pluck its Hesperian fruit, and have nothing to do with the root that supports it, or with the native vigor which exudes into this rich luxuriance. Sir, the true tap-root of commerce is found in the nature and character of the people who carry it on. They and their ancestors, for nearly two centuries, have been engaged in it. The industry of every class of men in the Eastern States has reference to its condition, and is affected by it. Why then treat it as a small concern, — as an affair only of traders and of merchants? Why intimate that agriculture can flourish without it? When, in fact, the interests of these two branches of industry are so intimately connected, that the slightest affection of the one is instantly communicated to the other.

. . . . .

"The state of agriculture is adapted, and has been for centuries, to the supply of the wants of this internal consumption. The farmer is bound to commerce by a thousand intimate ties, which, while it is in its ordinary state of prosperity, he neither sees nor realizes. But let the current stop, and the course of business stagnate, in consequence of any violent disturbance of commerce, the effect is felt as much, and in some cases more, by those who inhabit the mountains, as by those who dwell on the sea-coast. The country is associated with the city in one common distress, not merely through sympathy, but by an actual perception of a union in misfortune. It is this indissoluble community of interest between agriculture and commerce, which pervades the eastern portion of the United States, that makes our treatment of the commercial interest one of the most delicate as well as important questions that can be brought before this legislature. That interest is not of a nature long to be neglected with impunity. Its powers, when once brought into action by the necessity of self-defence, cannot but be irresistible in this nation. Sir, two fifths of your whole white population are commercial; or, which is the same thing as to its political effect, have their happiness so dependent upon its prosperity, that they cannot fail to act in concert, when the object is to crush those who oppress or those who are willing to destroy it. Of the five millions which now constitute the white population of these States, two millions are north and east of New Jersey. This great mass is naturally and indissolubly connected with commerce. To this is to be added the like interest, and that of no inconsiderable weight, which exists in the Middle and Southern States. Are these powerful influences to be forgotten or despised? Are such portions of the Union to be told that they are not to be defended, neither on the ocean nor yet on the land? Will they, ought they, to submit to a system, which, at the same time that it extracts from their industry the whole national revenue, neither protects it abroad nor at home? *It needs no spirit of prophecy to say they will not. It is no breach of any duty to say they ought not.* No power on earth can prevent a party from growing up, in these States, in support of the rights of commerce to a sea and land protection. The state of things which must necessarily follow is, of all others, to be deprecated. As I have said before, when party passions run parallel to local interests of great power and extent, nothing can prevent national convulsions; all the consequences of which can neither be numbered nor measured.

"Mr. Chairman, I do not introduce this idea to threaten or terrify. I speak, I hope, to wise men, — to men of experience, and of acquaintance with human nature, both in history and by observation. Is it possible to content great, intelligent, and influential portions of your citizens by anything short of a real attention to their interests in some degree proportionate to their magnitude and nature? When this is not the case, can any political union be either happy or lasting? Now is the time to give a pledge to the commercial interests that they may be assured of protection, let whatever influence predominate in the legislature. A great majority of this House are from States not connected intimately with commerce. Show then those which are, that you feel for them as brothers; that you are willing to give them a due share of the national revenue for their protection. Show an enlightened and fair reciprocity. Be superior to any exclusive regard to local interest. On such principles this Union, so desirable and so justly dear to us all, will continue and be cherished by every member of the compact. But let a narrow, selfish, local, sectional policy prevail, and struggles will commence which will terminate, through irritations and animosities, in either a change of the system of government or in its dissolution."

The next question of historical importance in which Mr. Quincy took an active part was that of the abolition of the slave-trade, which came up because the year 1808 was at hand, when Congress was permitted by the Constitution to prohibit that traffic if it so pleased. The question was brought to the notice of Congress by the President in his annual Message, and it was referred to a committee of which Mr. Early * of Georgia was the chairman. There was no difference of opinion as to the prohibition of the traffic, or at least no expression of any; but the practical details of the law, the penalties by which it was to be enforced, and, above all, the disposition to be made of such negroes as might be brought into the country in violation of it, gave rise to violent and excited debates. The committee reported a law prohibiting the slave-trade after the 31st of December, 1807, imposing certain penalties for its breach, and providing that all negroes imported after that date should be forfeited. The object of this provision undoubtedly was to obtain directly what the Constitution only gave indirectly and by implication, — the sanction of the government of the United States to the principle of slave-holding, by making it hold and sell men as property. The astuteness of the slave-holding mind on all points touching slavery was shown in this proposition, and all the tactics of bullying and bluster with which later Congressional campaigns have made us familiar, were employed in the debate to which it gave rise. It having been moved that the words "shall be entitled to his or her freedom" should be inserted after the word "forfeited," a furious fight ensued over this amendment. The Southern members resisted it, on the ground that the emancipation of the imported Africans would increase the number of free negroes, who, as Mr. Early affirmed, "were considered in the States where they are found in considerable numbers as instruments of murder, theft, and conflagration." And so craftily was this proposition of forfeiture to the government qualified, that its drift was not at first discerned by the Northern members. For,

* Peter Early, born in Virginia, 1773; educated at Princeton; emigrated to Georgia in 1795; Representative from 1802 to 1807; afterwards a Judge of the Supreme Court of Georgia, and Governor; died, 1817.

strong as was their disapprobation of slavery in the abstract, they felt no disposition to expose their Southern brethren to all the horrors of insurrection which it was assumed would follow the multiplication of free negroes. Indeed, Mr. Early candidly said, that, if these negroes were left free in the Southern States, not one of them would be alive in a year. And although the Federalists as a party, and Mr. Quincy eminently among them, regarded the political element of slavery as full of dangers to the future of the nation, these opinions had worked no personal and social alienation between Northern and Southern men, such as has since taken place. During the ascendency of the Federal party it had the support of many of the wealthiest and most intelligent Southern planters and lawyers in all the Slave States, especially in the Carolinas, and there was still a remnant left that adhered to the old faith, though daily diminishing. There was, therefore, quite disposition enough to arrange this matter in the way the most satisfactory to the masters, without so rigid a regard to the rights of the negroes as, it is to be hoped, would have been had in later times.

Mr. Quincy at first opposed striking out the forfeiture clause, on the ground that this was the only way in which the United States could get the control of the Africans, so as to dispose of them in the manner most for their own interest. He said: —

"May you not do with them what is best for human beings in that condition, — naked, helpless, ignorant of our laws, character, and manners? You are afraid to trust the national government, and yet, by refusing to forfeit, you will throw them under the control of States, all of which may, and some of which will and must, retain them in slavery. The great objection to forfeiture is that it admits a title. But this does not follow. All the effect of forfeiture is, that whatever title can be acquired in the cargo shall be vested in the United States. If the cargo be such that, from the nature of the thing, no title can be acquired in it, then nothing vests in the United States. The only operation of the forfeiture is to vest the importer's color of title by the appropriate commercial term, perhaps the only term we can effectually use, for this purpose, in the United States, without interfering with the rights of the States. Grant that these persons have all the rights of man, will not those rights be as valid against the United States as against the importer? And, by taking all color of title out of the importer, do we not place the United States in the best possible situation to give efficiency to the rights of man, in the case of the persons imported? . . . . . To my mind, if, when we have the power, we fail to secure to ourselves the means of giving freedom to them, under proper modifications, we have an agency in making them slaves."

These views influenced a majority of the Northern members until the question of the final passage of the bill approached. At last they came to a sense of the disgrace which the forfeiture of the negroes to the government, and the permission to it to sel. them as slaves if it so pleased, would bring upon the nation, and the whole matter was recommitted to a committee of one from each State. Mr. Quincy supported this recommittal in common with other Northern members, on the general grounds that they could not consent to any action which should authorize the sale of imported negroes, as slaves, by the government. They were willing that the persons should be forfeited, since the Southern members were so apprehensive of danger from their being set free in their territories; but it was only on condition that it should be done in such a way as to prevent their conversion into slaves. There were also technical objections which called for the revision of a committee. This committee reported a bill providing that such imported negroes should be sent to such States as had abolished slavery, there to be bound out as apprentices for a term of years, at the expiration of which they should be free. This bill produced a scene of great and violent excitement on the part of the slaveholders. Mr. Early declared that the people of the South would resist this provision with their lives! This resistance to a measure which proposed doing all the slaveholders had demanded for their own safety, to wit, removing the imported negroes from the slaveholding domain and providing for them in the Free States, showed that their purpose was, at least in part, to have the negroes sold as slaves to themselves. This object they did virtually gain at last, as the final settlement was by a bill originating in the Senate, providing that, though neither importer nor purchaser should have a title to such negroes, still the negroes should be subject to any regulation for their disposal that should be made by the States into which they might be brought. The design of the slaveholding party to make the United States recognize the rightfulness of property in man was thus avoided, but it was, at the cost of leaving the imported Africans to the tender mercies of the Slave States. The fact that the slaveholders were greatly incensed at the result, and regarded it as an injury and an affront, does not make this disposition of these unfortunates any the less discreditable to Congress or the nation.

During the second as well as the first session of the Ninth Congress, Mr. Quincy had the society of his wife, and they passed the winter, as they had the season previous, as boarders in the family of Judge Cranch, who had changed his residence in the interval to a house at Greenleaf's Point. Their apartments were the resort of a very agreeable set of men, comprising the Federal members of Congress and such residents of Washington as were of Federal leanings, — for the tide of party spirit flowed too high and strong to admit of much social intercourse with persons on the opposite side. Among these eminent and pleasant companions may be mentioned Timothy Pickering, Benjamin Pickman, and Jabez Upham, of Massachusetts; Colonel Benjamin Tallmadge, whose name is associated indissolubly with the touching Revolutionary episode of the captivity and death of Major André, and John Davenport,* Samuel W. Dana, Timothy Pitkin, Uriah Tracy,† and James Hillhouse, of Connecticut; and James M. Broome,‡ of Delaware. Of two of their visitors my father wrote thus to a friend in Boston, after their first visit to him and my mother: —

"Judge Marshall and Judge Washington passed last evening with us. They have more of the true New England look, character, and spirit than I have yet seen from Virginia. It might be association of ideas, but there was something in the manner of Judge Marshall that

* John Davenport, Yale College, 1770; Representative from Connecticut, 1799 to 1817; died, 1830.

† Uriah Tracy, born, 1755; graduated at Yale College, 1778; Representative from Connecticut, 1793 to 1796; and Senator, 1796 to 1807, in which year he died, and was the first tenant of the Congressional burying-ground.

‡ James M. Broome, Representative from Delaware, 1805 to 1807.

brought Judge Minot of Boston* very strongly to my recollection His eye is black, penetrating, and indicative of stronger passion than Minot possessed, or at least exhibited. There is a rare mixture of the expression of goodness, of correct thought, and of intelligence, in the face and eye of Judge Washington. Esteemed as they both are in New England, and disposed as we always are to overrate those at a distance, you may rely that these men lose nothing by approximation and personal acquaintance."

The following extract from a letter to my father from Mr. John Cotton Smith † of Connecticut, who had retired from Congress at the end of the long session, bears a cordial testimony to the charms of the society of which he had made a part, and to which the animated intelligence of my mother's manners and conversation gave grace and tone, will make a fitting conclusion to this chapter. It is dated Sharon, August 25, 1806:—

"I am both happy and proud to abjure the general opinion that friendship, to be ardent and durable, must be exclusively the production of early life. My acquaintance with you, I trust, has furnished an ample refutation to this erroneous sentiment, and I deem a six winters' exile a cheap purchase of so valuable a discovery. . . . . . I do feel a pang in separating from that noble band of chevaliers, who, small as their number is, have become the only depositaries of their country's honor. Nor will I conceal the tender emotions which agitate my breast at the recollection of the charming hours I have passed not many miles from the eastern branch of the Potomac. Imagination will long delight itself in recalling the hospitable salutation, the undissembled courtesy, the wisdom, and the wit, which enlivened and endeared and rendered ever memorable those evenings. But this is a theme I must not pursue. It shall be resumed when we meet. May I hope ever to welcome you under my own roof? Should such an event take place, *sublimi feriam sidera vertice*."

* George Richards Minot, born, 1758; graduated at Harvard College, 1778; died, 1802. Author of some valuable historical works.

† John Cotton Smith, born, 1769; graduated at Yale College, 1783; was a Representative in Congress from 1800 to 1806. He was afterwards Governor of Connecticut, 1812-1817, and Judge of the Supreme Court of that State. He died in 1845.

CHAPTER VI.

1807-1808.

Summer Occupations. — Berlin and Milan Decrees. — British Orders in Council. — Right of Search. — The Chesapeake Outrage. — Extra Session. — Mr. Quincy takes the Lead of the Federal Party in the House. — His Private Life. — The Embargo. — John Quincy Adams joins the Democrats. — Speech on Empowering the President to suspend the Embargo, etc.

SOON after the expiration of the Ninth Congress, on the 3d of March, 1807, Mr. Quincy returned home, and spent the summer as usual at his country-seat. A brief journal which he kept during that season bears witness to his persistent industry. The state of public affairs directed his attention particularly to the law of nations, and especially to those branches of it relating to war and peace, to the right of expatriation, and to the rights of neutral nations. He reviewed carefully the portions of Grotius and Puffendorf which treat of these subjects, and made a thorough study of Bynkershoek's *Quæstiones Juris Publici*, of which he made an abstract with pages of quotations. One of these shows that this learned jurist could relax into a mild jest, especially when the sacred subject of tobacco was in question.

"*July* 10. — Read Bynkershoek, Lib. I., from chap. 4 to 15. In chap. 10 is a rare sample of Dutch wit on a favorite topic. The Spaniards once declared tobacco an article contraband of war. This was so highly resented by the English that they granted reprisals against Spain. The solemn jurisconsult remarks: *Sed an ea controversia de Tabaco tandem in fumum abierit, nescio; hoc scio, me Hispanis non consentire, quia verum est, tabaci nullum esse usum ad cædendum hostem.*" *

Mr. Quincy also gives an abstract of the treatise of M. Hubner

* "But whether that dispute touching tobacco will finally vanish in smoke, I cannot say. This I know, that I cannot agree with the Spaniards; for the truth is, there is no way of turning tobacco to the destruction of an enemy."

De la Saisie des Bâtiments Neutres, with long extracts, and of Robert Ward's "Inquiry into the Foundations and History of the Law of Nations in Europe." And these more serious studies were enlivened occasionally by the variation of Cicero *de Officiis*. He complains frequently of the interruptions made by the calls of society in the course of his studies, and now and then gives a specimen of what they were. For example: —

"*July* 25. — Dined in company with the Trustees of the Agricultural Society at Ex-President John Adams's. An Englishman named Kendall was introduced to us. He has come into the country, as it is hinted, with the design of writing his travels. He was forward, talkative, — willing, however, to hear others, — and apparently very desirous of giving the conversation a political turn. Whether this was through design or natural bias of mind, I was doubtful, but rather believe the former."

"*July* 31. — Whole day with the Selectmen, on their annual visit to Deer Island. Among the guests Major Thomas Pinckney, of South Carolina. A singular mildness and modesty in his manners, with marks of great moderation and firmness of character. Also Mr. Kendall, whom I saw at Mr. Adams's. Well informed, full of observation and research, opinionated."

"*August* 3 *to* 10. — Business and society occupied and engrossed my time. Every day in Boston. No opportunity for regular, and but little for occasional reading. On Tuesday, 4th, dined at Benjamin Joy's, with Major Pinckney, and on the 7th this gentleman, President Adams, etc. dined with me. I am charmed with T. Pinckney. He is a perfect gentleman. Exhibits the man of the world united with the man of retirement. He has seen much and read with observation, yet is in nothing obtrusive. Plain in manners and dress."

"*August* 11. — The engagements of duty and friendship, which have so frequently of late broke in upon my intellectual pursuits, are, in a great measure, terminated. I hope, therefore, for more zeal in my studies and more fruit from my time."

The Mr. Kendall here mentioned did execute his purpose of writing a book on America, which was published in London, and republished in New York in three volumes. Major Pinckney was one of the South Carolina Federalists who remained true to the last. He was the first Minister to England after the formation of the government, afterwards Minister to Spain, and the candidate voted for by the Federalists at the same time with John Adams, under the original provision for the election of President and Vice-President, subsequently a member of Congress, and a Major-General in the war of 1812. He died in 1828.

The threatening aspect of foreign affairs, and the disturbance of prosperity at home, might well demand the most careful preparation of every man called to take part in the business of the nation. The interruption which the European war had caused to the commerce of the Atlantic States had occasioned wide-spread distress, reaching all classes. The victory of Trafalgar having secured to Great Britain the monopoly of commerce through the sovereignty of the sea, Bonaparte devised his Continental System to hinder her enjoyment of it. From the battle-field of Jena he issued the Berlin Decree, declaring the British Islands in a state of blockade, and forbidding all commercial intercourse with them. Although there was at first some pretence of making an exception of American ships, they were soon included in the general condemnation, and it was officially declared that all merchandise obtained in Great Britain or her colonies was lawful prize, on board what ships soever it might be found, and the point was reserved whether the ships were not good prize as well. Soon afterwards, England issued her Orders in Council prohibiting any neutral trade with France or her allies unless through British ports. To these Orders Bonaparte soon replied by the Milan Decree, which declared every neutral vessel good prize which should comply with their requisitions. Thus the sea was effectually shut against the American merchants by this combination of both belligerents against them, for their ships were virtually the only neutral vessels left. The distress thus occasioned was all but universal in the seaboard States.

Another great cause of complaint against the British government was the right it claimed to search merchant-vessels at sea, and to take out of them such sailors as owed allegiance to the King of England. This right the British ministry steadily refused to give up. During the brief ascendency of the Whigs under Lord Grenville, in 1806, the ministry was disposed to mitigate the severity of its enforcement as far as English opinion would permit. They agreed to exercise it only in cases where there was strong ground for suspecting the presence of actual deserters, to enjoin the greatest caution against molesting American citizens, and to provide prompt redress in case of mistake or injury. This treaty, negotiated by James Monroe and William Pinkney of Maryland, with the ministry the most favorable to America that had held power since the peace of 1783, was summarily and arbitrarily rejected by Mr. Jefferson, without laying it before the Senate, or even consulting with any member of his Cabinet, excepting Mr. Madison, the Secretary of State, on the ground that the right of impressment had not been entirely abandoned. Whatever might be the abstract merits of the question, it was certainly unwise and unstatesmanlike for the weakest maritime power in the world, as we were at that time, to reject so beneficial a treaty with the strongest, on a point which the victors of the Nile and of Trafalgar would yield only to force of arms; especially as the ratification of the treaty involved no sacrifice of principle, since the United States did not thereby recognize the right of search. It is no wonder that the Federalists saw in this audacious usurpation of power a proof of the sympathy of the Administration with France and of its hatred to England, nor that the Tory ministry which soon replaced that of Lord Grenville should take the same view of the matter. The United States lost the benefits of a treaty scarcely less advantageous than Jay's, under which they had made such progress in wealth and strength, while the right of search was exercised by England with all its ancient rigor. Neither the terrors of Mr. Jefferson's gunboats, nor the thunders of the Non-Importation Act, which he held "checked in mid-volley," frightened the sturdy Tories, when they came into power, from claiming and exercising the prescriptive right of the strongest, — the law of the British lion at all times.

In a conversation which my father held with Mr. Merry on this subject, that diplomatist related his endeavors to negotiate a treaty with Mr. Madison, which were rendered abortive by the fixed determination of the President as to this disputed point. He assured Mr. Madison that this right had been exercised by

Great Britain so long, that she would as soon abandon her marine as give it up. And to show how unlikely it was that she would be legislated or menaced into resigning the right, he related to the Secretary the following anecdote: —

"The right of receiving the honors of the flag in the narrow seas had long been claimed by Great Britain, and was unquestionably a less important right than impressment. Yet at the Congress of Amiens, at the negotiation of that treaty, Joseph Bonaparte made a proposition that Great Britain should waive claiming that honor from the French. I was at that time Secretary of Legation, and as such was admitted at the Congress Board to discuss the various questions which might arise; Lord Cornwallis, the minister, a military character, (chosen out of compliment to Bonaparte,) not being sufficiently acquainted with diplomatic principles or the French language to undertake that part.

"No sooner was the proposition made than I at once told Joseph Bonaparte that, if that was made a *sine qua non*, the treaty might as well be broken off at once, for my country would never yield. 'O,' said he, 'it is only a name, and the expressions of the treaty might easily be so arranged as to express it by construction, and so slide into use without exciting any popular sensation.' I replied that, though he called it a name, I called it a *thing*. Let the British seaman once find that his ship had not the same honor paid to it which he was accustomed to receive, and he would feel himself degraded; and what effect this would have upon the spirit of the navy it was not possible to foretell.

"Upon my explaining the proposition to Lord Cornwallis, the old and sensible veteran had no other way to express his shame and sense of disgrace at the very idea of such a concession, than by covering his face with his hands and laying it upon the table. 'There,' said I, 'M. Bonaparte, is your answer.'

"Nevertheless he persisted. And so desirous was the French government to obtain this *name*, as he called it, that it offered to make provision for the King of Sardinia, in case we would accede, — an object they knew we had much at heart. On our persisting to decline even considering it, they insisted on our remitting it home to our government. From which we received for answer, that his Majesty would never yield that right while he possessed his crown.

"From this anecdote, I said to Mr. Madison, you will judge the likelihood of success in the object you propose."

The question of impressment was brought home to the mind of the country in the most exasperating shape possible by the affair of the Chesapeake and Leopard, which occurred in June of this year. The British naval officers on the coast were greatly, and not unreasonably, annoyed by the desertion of their men to the United States, where they were protected by public sentiment, and indeed by public law, as there was no treaty stipulation for surrendering them. The British officers complained that they were openly insulted in the streets of the seaports, when they went on shore, by deserters from their own ships. On the 1st of June, Vice-Admiral Berkeley, the commander on the North American Station, issued a circular letter to the captains of the ships of his squadron, in which, after reciting these facts, and also that many of the deserters had enlisted on board the American frigate Chesapeake, he ordered any of the commanders of his Britannic Majesty's ships which should meet with the Chesapeake beyond the limits of the United States to demand permission to search her for deserters, and in case of refusal to proceed to search her without permission, offering to the captain of the Chesapeake the same privilege on board their ships. This was a new construction of public law, worthy of the old Scandinavian sea-kings, but not in accordance with the stricter rulings of the older or later authorities. The right of search and impressment was never held to apply to national ships, which are regarded as part of the soil of the country to which they belong, but only to merchant-vessels In compliance with these orders, the Leopard, Captain Humphries, followed the Chesapeake as she was proceeding to sea on her way to the Mediterranean Station, and, overhauling her, demanded permission to search her for deserters. This being of course refused, he fired several broadsides into her, killing three men and wounding eight or ten more, among whom was her commander, Captain Barron. The Chesapeake had gone to sea with such a culpable lack of preparation, that the only gun which was fired on her side was touched off with a coal brought from the cook's galley. There was nothing for it but to submit. Her flag was struck, and she was searched by officers from the Leopard, and four men — one white and three black — were carried off as deserters. Of these the first was hanged, and the three last pardoned on condition of entering the British navy, though their claim to be Americans was not contradicted. The excitement throughout the country, of mingled rage and shame, was most intense. The President issued a proclamation, ordering British ships to leave the American waters, or, if they refused, — as he had no means of compelling them to obey, — forbidding any intercourse with them; and orders were despatched to Messrs. Monroe and Pinkney to suspend all negotiations until this outrage was disavowed and atoned for. Both of these demands the British government were ready to comply with. They disavowed Admiral Berkeley's letter, recalled him, offered the restoration of the three black sailors, and a pecuniary satisfaction to the wounded and the families of the killed on board the Chesapeake. This reparation, however, was made dependent on the President's re voking his proclamation shutting the American ports against English ships, on the ground that it was stipulated in Jay's treaty that no such hostile demonstration should be made until satisfaction had been first asked and refused. This Jefferson refused to do, and the matter was not finally settled till 1811. But the ministry utterly refused to entertain the proposition to abandon the right of search and of impressment on board merchant-ships, or to renew negotiations on the basis of the treaty which had been so cavalierly rejected by Mr. Jefferson, after its conclusion by the Ministers he had appointed.

The public mind was justly and profoundly incensed by this high-handed outrage, and the Federalists shared in the general feeling of indignation and humiliation. But they saw that the despicably helpless condition of the nation, with a handful of useless gunboats, with no army and almost no fortifications, had invited and made it possible. And they saw, too, that the ruin of our commerce was quite as much the work of France as of England, and the insolence of her demands not less. But England was standing almost alone between Bonaparte and universal empire, and they regarded with apprehension and disgust the endeavors of Mr. Jefferson, as they looked at the matter, to enlist the sympathy and virtual help of the nation on the side of the

H

military despotism which threatened to overwhelm the world. On this matter Mr. Quincy speaks thus: —

"It was this policy of the Administration which the Federalists deemed it their duty, both as men and patriots, to oppose. For Great Britain there was among them no general predilection, but they regarded her as struggling alone against an attempt at universal empire. The measures she adopted were deemed by them irreconcilable with our rights, violent and autocratic, but by us, in our relative state of naval power, irresistible. True policy, they thought, required the United States not to aid the aggressive and ambitious belligerent, but to vindicate our independence against Great Britain by permitting the merchants to arm in the defence of commercial rights, and to take the risk of war. In this course they were far from unanimous. A majority preferred to take the chance of events, and to submit for a time to the injuries of both belligerents, rather than take part with either. The policy of the Administration, to use the commerce of the country as a weapon against Great Britain, they detested, regarding it as self-destructive, in effect aiding France, and doing more injury to ourselves than to England. Their measures of embargo and non-intercourse were symptoms of that hostility to commerce which Southern politicians took no pains to conceal."

Such was the condition of public affairs, and such the opinions of the Federalists respecting them, when the President summoned an extraordinary session of Congress on the 26th of October, 1807, to consult and determine on such measures as in their wisdom might be deemed meet for the welfare of the United States. Mr. Quincy left Boston on the 12th of October, and reached Washington on the 23d. His own account of his way of life, as contained in a letter to his wife, who did not accompany him to the capital, is as follows: —

"I took lodgings at a Mr. Coyle's, an eligible boarding-house, having my friend Colonel Tallmadge * settled in the same house and the room adjoining mine. At half past six in the morning my servant comes into my room, makes my fire, gets my dressing apparatus, and at half past seven I am out of bed, and dressed for the day. My servant, not content with tying my hair simply with a ribbon, works it up into a

* Benjamin Tallmadge, born in Suffolk County, New York, 1754. A distinguished Revolutionary officer. Represented Connecticut from 1801 to 1817; died, 1835.

most formidable queue, at least three inches long, and as big as a reasonable Dutch quill. He says this is the mode in New York, and as I do not wear powder, and it looks a little more trig, I acquiesce. In other respects he follows your instructions, given before my departure, with great particularity. About nine o'clock we breakfast; from eleven to two at Congress; at three, dinner; at seven, tea; at eleven, in bed; all the time not accounted for, in my chamber answering letters or preparing to fulfil the duties I have undertaken."

During this session, and for the rest of his Congressional life, Mr. Quincy practically took the leadership of the small Federal phalanx in the House. Although Mr. Samuel W. Dana,* of Connecticut, was technically the leader of the party, as befitting his greater age and longer parliamentary experience, still Mr. Quincy, from his superiority as a debater and a speaker, was looked upon by friends and foes as the actual champion of its principles and its policy. He had reluctantly fallen in with the plan of the Federalists during the last Congress, of following the lead of Randolph, who had nothing in common with them, excepting his detestation of Jefferson, and from this time forward he acted and spoke as his views of public duty prompted, without regard to any such fancied expediency. His opinions and conduct as to this matter received the approval of many eminent Federalists, whose views were expressed in the following paragraph of a letter of November 19, 1807, from Mr. Harrison Gray Otis, a consistent and active Federalist as long as Federalism was.

"I confess myself incapable of perceiving the policy of that course which gives to our adversaries the exclusive possession of the public ear, and exhibits the Federal minority as a browbeaten and desponding cabal, who either cannot or dare not vindicate their own principles or arraign those of their opponents. It sinks the pride of party and enfeebles the principle. It is in Congress that the principles of Federalism should appear to be embodied. It is thence that its vigor, virtue, and consistency should be reacted upon its scattered votaries."

* Samuel W. Dana, born, 1747; graduated, Yale College, 1775; Representative from 1799 to 1811; and Senator from 1811 to 1821. Considering the prominence of Mr. Dana in the House during twelve most important years, it is singular that Mr. Charles Lanman should not have mentioned the fact of his membership, only of his Senatorship, in his Dictionary of Congress. He died in 1830.

When Congress came together, the whole opposition, including Randolph and his handful of malcontent Democrats, only amounted to twenty-eight votes. The Democratic party was not unanimous as to the Speakership, many of the Southern Democrats refusing to vote for Joseph B. Varnum * of Massachusetts, the candidate of Mr. Jefferson. He was, however, chosen by a bare majority, and signalized his fidelity to his political chieftain by leaving Messrs. Randolph and Quincy, not only off the Committee of Ways and Means, but off all the standing committees. My father describes Mr. Varnum as "one of the most obsequious tools of the Administration, elected through the influence of Jefferson, who courted with the most extreme assiduity the leaders of the Democracy of Massachusetts. He was just capable of going through the routine of the office, — an automaton ready to move in any direction the magician who pulled the strings jerked him."

It was a time of great public anxiety and alarm, especially on the seaboard and among the commercial classes. Commerce had been nearly destroyed by the European belligerents, and what remained was threatened with destruction by the United States government under pretext of protecting it. A very exaggerated idea of the importance of American commerce to Europe, and especially to England, prevailed in the Democratic party. This belief was fostered by Mr. Jefferson, who indeed carried it almost to fanaticism. In the commerce of the country he saw the means of carrying on a bloodless war with the belligerent he hated, and of giving indirect assistance to the one he favored, without any expense excepting the ruin of the merchants and of the multitudes dependent upon trade for their support. He had in earlier times expressed the abstract opinion that it would be happy if the United States could be shut out from the rest of the world, like China, and her inhabitants be all husbandmen. In common with the members of his party from the South and West, he looked with equanimity upon the distresses his interferences with

* Joseph B. Varnum, born, 1759; Representative from 1795 to 1811; Speaker of the Tenth and Eleventh Congresses; Senator from 1811 to 1817; and President *pro tem.* of the Senate; died, 1821.

commerce might work to the commercial region, vainly imagining that agriculture would not suffer through an inevitable sympathy with the destruction of trade. It was, then, with anxious and gloomy anticipations that Mr. Quincy entered upon his second term of service. His personal feelings in view of the conflict before him he thus expressed to his wife: —

"*November* 1, 1807. — Allow yourself to entertain no apprehensions with regard to me. The times are difficult, and a tempest is up in the sky, but that is the very moment to be fearless and collected. . . . . . Fear nothing about my being stung or inflamed by the hornets of the House. Nothing occurring on the floor has or can cost me a single pang. After fatigue duty all day, I come home, read or write all the evening, am asleep at eleven o'clock, and nothing troubles my repose."

In his first movement in Congress Mr. Quincy was successful, although opposed by the men representing the pleasure of the President. Mr. Jefferson had, as before stated, forbidden British armed vessels from entering our harbors. This fact he had stated in his Message. Mr. Quincy moved that he be requested to lay a copy of the Proclamation before the House. It is not easy to see what objection there could have been to this motion, and yet it was violently opposed by Mr. Jacob Crowninshield * of Massachusetts, and Mr. Alston † of North Carolina; both of them authentic mouthpieces of Mr. Jefferson. The real objection to the Proclamation was that it was issued in contravention of the provision of Jay's treaty, that no act of retaliation should be made by either power without a demand for reparation being first made and denied. But this could hardly have been the motive for the resistance to laying it before the House, after it had been published to all the world. The reason probably was that the

* Jacob Crowninshield, Representative from 1803 to 1808, when he died at Washington during the session. He declined the Secretaryship of the Navy offered to him by Mr. Jefferson, at the beginning of his second Administration. Mr. Lanman's article on him implies erroneously that he became Secretary in March, 1805, and left Congress at that time. See Hildreth's History of the United States, Vol. II. p. 567.

† Willis Alston, junior, Representative from North Carolina from 1803 to 1815, and from 1825 to 1831.

motion proceeded from one of the opposition. Samuel Harrison Smith, the editor of the National Intelligencer, the organ of the Administration, had warned his party, speaking of a previous motion of Mr. Quincy, "always to keep an eye upon the enemy, and to treat all the measures that gentleman should propose as they did that one, — *vote him down!*" Mr. Quincy chose to assume that this was the occasion of the opposition to his motion, and he attributed it, in his reply, "to the determination of the House to vote down, at all events, all propositions proceeding from the minority, according to the advice addressed to it by a printer generally understood as speaking demi-official language."

"This light," he says, "thrown directly into the eyes of the majority, made them falter, and they passed my resolution by seventy ayes to thirty-two nays. This was a sad mortification to Crowninshield and Alston. Smith was the only stenographer in the House, and we were wholly at his mercy. In general, however, he was fair, and often submitted his reports of speeches of members of the minority to them for correction."

All Americans of that day who were not possessed with the delusion that their commerce was of such vital consequence to the prosperity, if not to the existence of England, that she would yield to any demands rather than risk its loss, were of the opinion that some reasonable preparations should be made for hostilities in case the irritation of the public mind, kept alive by the aggressions of England on the one side and the suicidal policy of the Administration on the other, should seek relief in war. Nothing was further from the intentions or wishes of Mr. Jefferson and his adherents than a war with England. But there was certainly danger that they might find themselves obliged, in decent consistency, to resort to more direct hostilities to obtain their end, should their favorite policy of destroying their own commerce in the hope of damaging that of England fail of success. Besides, the popular passions, under the constant provocation of the diatribes against England with which the Democratic press teemed, might be raised to a pitch of fury which would carry the party beyond the control of its leaders, and compel them to war in order to retain their power. Fisher Ames, who was regarded by the Federalists as the wisest counsellor, as well as the chief ornament of the party, expresses this general feeling on their part in a letter to Mr. Quincy, dated Dedham, December 6, 1807.

"Our Cabinet takes counsel of the mob, and it is now a question whether the hatred of Great Britain, and the reproach fixed even upon violent men, if they will not proceed in their violence, will not overcome the fears of the maritime States, and of the planters in Congress. The usual levity of a democracy has not appeared in regard to Great Britain. We have been steady in our hatred of her, and when popular passions are not worn out by time, but augment, they must, I should think, explode in war." *

The party in power, however, scouted these forebodings as idle fears, and refused to make any other preparations for possible hostilities than the trifling appropriations for fortifications already spoken of, and for the gunboats which were their main dependence for repulsing an enemy's fleet. This last pet scheme of Mr. Jefferson for the cheap protection of our coasts and harbors was a bitter jest with the Federalists. They scouted its inefficiency as more likely to invite than to repel an attack, and laughed at the reply to the argument that a gunboat could be no possible match for a ship of war, that its very smallness and lightness gave it eminent facilities for running away. After ridiculing the scheme as one well contrived for the encouragement of cowardice, Mr. Quincy said: —

"It was not, therefore, without some regret that I heard my honorable colleague (Mr. Crowninshield) dwell with such an apparent satisfaction on the great advantage which these boats gave of getting out of harm's way, and annoying the enemy from shallows, and concealed behind points of land, retreating as the enemy advanced. I begin to fear lest it may be thought that this is our way of fighting in the Northern States, and that such are the calculations which our

* Fisher Ames's Works, edited by his son, Seth Ames, Vol. I. p. 405. The letters of that eminent man to my father are, most of them, contained in this edition of his works, by which circumstance I am debarred from giving them entire in their order. The familiar and political correspondence of Mr. Ames entitles him to as high a place among the letter-writers as his speeches do among the orators of the world. They have every solid and sparkling quality that goes to make up good letters.

warriors would make when the enemy should come. But, sir, the soil in which Prebles spring yields not men who will seek safety in flight, or who will hide themselves when danger approaches. No, sir. They will meet the enemy at the harbor's mouth. Their bodies will be their country's bulwarks. They will engage at close quarters, and if you will not give them decks of their own to fight upon, they will find means to fight on those of the enemy."

The Non-Importation Act of the year before had been but a kind of reconnoissance in force, preparatory to the opening of the war against England by commercial restrictions. It had been believed that it would bring the enemy to terms by the terror the mere threat would strike to her shop-keeping heart. To give her time for reflection, the date of its going into operation was fixed at a distant day, and was again postponed in the hope that she would relinquish her right of impressment rather than lose our custom. As England made no sign of surrender, Mr. Jefferson brought out of the armory of his invention the engine which he had devised as sure to bring her to his feet, and he lost no time in putting it into position and bringing it to bear upon the enemy. This was the famous Embargo Act, by which all American ships were forbidden the sea and locked up in the ports. On the 18th of December he sent a Message to both Houses, perhaps the shortest on record of those proverbially long-winded documents, consisting of two sentences, recommending, "in view of the great and increasing dangers with which our vessels, merchandise, and seamen are threatened on the high seas and elsewhere from the belligerent powers of Europe," and of the importance "of keeping in safety these essential resources," "an inhibition of the departure of our vessels from the ports of the United States." The Senate signalized its obedience to the higher powers by perhaps the very swiftest despatch ever known in the case of so important a measure. Four hours sufficed to bring in the bill and to pass it through all its stages, under a suspension of the rules. This action was forthwith communicated to the House, already engaged in considering the subject, and it forthwith took up the Senate Bill, gave it its three readings, and referred it to the Committee of the Whole, on motion of Mr. Crowninshield, of Massachusetts, with the view, probably, of disposing of the matter with the same celerity which had distinguished the action of the Senate. But this could not be fully effected, and the bill was discussed in Committee of the Whole for three days and almost as many nights, since the debate was protracted late into the nights in the hope of compelling the Committee to report the bill. Mr. Quincy moved as an amendment, that fishing-vessels might be permitted to go to sea, upon giving bonds that they should carry on no commerce whatever, and return with their fare to the United States. This was voted down by eighty-two nays to forty yeas. This provision, however, was finally incorporated with the bill before it went into operation, during the many amendatory tinkerings it had to undergo in consequence of the haste in which it was concocted and carried through Congress. Another amendment of his, moving "that nothing in this act should be construed to contravene any rights or privileges arising out of any treaties with foreign nations," met with the same fate, by a vote of seventy-five nays to fifty-two yeas. The Embargo finally became a law by eighty-two yeas to forty-four nays. The dismay which the promulgation of this edict, thus registered by Congress, carried to the whole seaboard, was dire, and the ruin which it too truly foreboded was terrible and universal. The people of Massachusetts, which then included Maine, and especially the Boston district, felt most cruelly this blow aimed, not merely at their prosperity, but at their daily bread. And this sense of injury was embittered by the insulting pretext that they were thus ruined in their own defence and for their own good! And it was clearly seen, notwithstanding the pretended impartiality of including both belligerents in the recital of the injuries which called for the measure, that the Embargo was virtually and designedly a co-operation with the Continental System of Bonaparte, the trade with France being infinitesimally small when compared with that of Great Britain. And in this view, as we shall see by and by, Bonaparte himself cordially agreed.

The following extract from the last letter Mr. Quincy ever received from Mr. Ames, in reply to one written while the Embargo was before the Committee of the Whole, gives eloquent utterance to the passionate grief with which he, in common with the other Federal leaders, regarded the condition of his country. It is dated Dedham, December 31, 1807.

"When I read your letter of the 19th (received fifteen minutes since) my heart suffered unusual pangs, and I could not suppress some tears. Had I been alone, perhaps I should have been everything but calm and fearless, as you say a man should be now. Had I no children, I should not weep, nor, it may be, even sigh, to see a people carry chains that has proved so unworthy liberty as ours. But some allowance must be made for them. There is no base thought or propensity among them that has not been courted and nursed into a habit in order that some base man might rise upon it. If Jefferson had to bear the chains he has forged for us all, I should be calm at the prospect before us. Slavery would not degrade its friends. As to writing for our papers, it should be done, and according to the hints you suggest. For a fortnight past I have been too sick to write. Attempting to see company in my parlor at dinner, I left my chamber and took cold. It threatened once more to settle on my lungs. After blisters and a variety of defensive measures, I have recovered to the state of my usual debility, where I must rest till I can ride, which will not be much before May. I will try and do my feeble part. Your exertions merit praise, and I have no doubt obtain it. The speech on the gunboats was all that it should be. *Accende animum famæ venientis amore.*"

Probably the infirm state of Mr. Ames's health gave a darker tinge to the prospect of public affairs as it lay before his mind's eye, than it might have done to a more healthful vision; but his emotions were only more intense in degree than those of the Federalists generally, not different in character. Mr. Ames sunk rapidly from this time forward, and died on the 4th of July next ensuing.

A circumstance very painful to Mr. Quincy, in his private as well as his public capacity, was the change which Mr. John Quincy Adams made at this time in his political relations. He had, up to the time of the Embargo, acted with the Federalists, by whom he had been elected to the Senate; but when Mr. Jefferson's Embargo Message produced the rapid act of legislation we have seen, Mr. Adams joined himself to the majority which hurried through the measure. "The President," he said, "has recommended this measure on his high responsibility. I would not consider, I would not deliberate, I would act. Doubtless the President possesses such further information as will justify the measure." And from that time forward he acted uniformly with the Administration. This change of sides naturally excited great indignation in the party he had left, and his conduct was attributed to the basest and most sordid motives. The leading Massachusetts Federalists regarded his course with anger mingled with contempt, which many of them continued to entertain as long as they lived. This ill opinion, however, Mr. Adams cordially reciprocated, and there was certainly no love lost between them. But Mr. Quincy never entered into these extreme views as to Mr. Adams's course. To his wife he speaks thus temperately on the subject: —

"I am glad you enter into no asperities such as you hear upon the character of John Quincy Adams. There are many reasons why we should be very cautious on that head. Particularly as I have made a most inveterate stand in secret session in the House against a question on which he was in favor, and as warmly, in the Senate. This matter is not yet before the public. But I am anxious that, however we may differ politically, as far as it depends on me it may never terminate in any personal difference. I beg you, therefore, to be more than ordinarily cautious on that subject. He is, I fully believe, as perfectly my friend as ever he was. He has just as good a right to his sentiments as I have to mine. He differs from his political friends, and is abused. Let us not join in the contumely. It can do us no good, and may do him some hurt. And, possibly, should any indiscretion fall from us, it may be attributed by the world, as it certainly will be by his friends, to rivalry, or worse motives. 'To avoid even the appearance of evil,' is as wise a political as it is a moral maxim."

From this letter it appears that the Boston Federalists had conceived suspicions of Mr. Adams's fidelity to their party even before he openly left them. In letters written after the embargo had been made public, Mr. Quincy says: —

"Dana and Goodrich,* of Connecticut, are the only men who agree

* Chauncey Goodrich, born, 1759; graduated at Yale College, 1776; a lawyer of eminence; Representative from 1795 to 1801; Senator from 1807 to 1813; died, 1815.

with me concerning the course of John Quincy Adams. His deviation from his friends is perfectly reconcilable with the peculiar texture of his mind, without resorting to any suspicion of his political integrity. I neither join in, nor sanction, any asperities about him. . . . . . With respect to Adams, he has a right to his opinions, as we to ours. It will be my lot to differ from him, — possibly to oppose him publicly. I shall not court the occasion, nor shall I shrink from it. I am only anxious to be in such a situation that even he shall recognize nothing personal, or of vulgar ambition, in my difference from him in my political sentiments. I mean to identify myself with no set of men. I shall do my duty openly, virtuously, and as intelligently as Heaven permits me. I shall not seek to please by any sacrifice of my real opinion. I shall not fear to offend any, if a just view of my country's interest obliges me to declare truths which will have that effect. This course of conduct may not secure me place, of which I am less than ever solicitous, but it will secure me that sense of a right to personal honor of which I am daily more and more solicitous. Let us cultivate in our own minds a strict sense of duty. Towards others let us extend a candid construction.

"Concerning Colonel Pickering's letter, I shall state my opinion to you when we meet; I have not time now to examine it in all its relations. The nature of our political institutions makes such divisions inevitable among men. Let us judge not party judgment; be very just to others; be as true to ourselves. My object is, not to keep the peace, nor to acquire honors, but to place myself in such a state of mind and of political relations as may enable me to be of most service to my country."

This letter of Colonel Pickering was addressed to Governor Sullivan of Massachusetts, "exhibiting to his constituents a view of the danger of an unnecessary and ruinous war," and setting forth the extreme Federal opinions with great force and clearness. This letter Governor Sullivan refused to lay before the Legislature, according to the request upon its face, on the ground that it was "a seditious and disorganizing production"; but it soon found its way into the papers, and was printed as a pamphlet. To this Mr. Adams responded in another letter addressed to Mr. Harrison Gray Otis, in which he attacked the positions of Colonel Pickering with all the vigor and with much of the acrimony which generally characterized his polemical writings. He virtually admitted that the embargo was aimed rather at England than at France. "The most enormous infractions of our rights (by France) have been more in menace than accomplishment. The alarm was justly great, the anticipation threatening, but the amount of actual injury small." The Berlin and Milan Decrees he considers to be occasioned by the maritime pretensions of Great Britain; he attributes to this power the design of "recovering their lost dominion in America"; and the inference which the Federalists drew from the tone of the whole pamphlet was, that he meant to imply that they were not disinclined, to say the least, to have the design succeed. It is to this letter that Mr. Quincy alludes in writing to his wife.

"*April 5.* — Before this time you will have read the letter of John Quincy Adams, in which you cannot but perceive the gauntlet to be thrown to a part of our friends, and that the consequences will be an inveterate party hostility. No man in the nation is situated in relation to the combatants as I am. The part I shall be called to act will be delicate and no less difficult. My desire at present is to place myself so that in nothing I may appear to take a personal part in the controversy. . . . . As yet both gentlemen are very well disposed toward me. With J. Q. Adams I have had an *éclaircissement* of four hours, and he has asked another. I understand him perfectly, — better, I believe, than he does himself, in this instance. Mr. Pickering lives in the same house with me, and we are in the habit of very friendly intercourse, if not altogether confidential, yet bordering upon it. I will do my duty to both. Above all, I will not fail in a higher duty, which I owe to myself and my country, when the occasion calls. . . . . My mind has been grievously agitated by the flying to pieces of men whose natural interests and stand in society are in many respects similar. But such incidents are to be expected, and we ought to use them, and the circumstances resulting from them, to the best moral and intellectual account. . . . .

"I deem the letter of John Q. Adams to Otis unfortunate, but it was not unanticipated. I subscribe entirely to your reflections on its style.

"I have always known Adams; Pickering not intimately until this winter; but the more I know of them, and the more I compare them together, the more I am impressed with the idea how unsuited they are ever to co-operate. Never were two substances more completely adapted to make each other explode. Fire and gunpowder are nothing to them, when brought into opposition. In this instance it will occasion some party abruption, scorch many, blow up the temporary influence of one or the other, — of which it is uncertain, and more dependent on events not within the control of either than on anything in the intrinsic merits of their respective opinions. How to allay, how to control, how to direct, those events and effects, is the question which their best friends and those of their country have to study."

My father's personal relations with Mr. Adams were never interrupted nor altered by the wide divergence of their political opinions and party connections during the fierce dissensions of the coming years.

The Opposition had all along considered it a strong proof of Mr. Jefferson's Gallican leanings that, while every document that could expose the British violations of our neutral rights was spread before Congress and blazoned to the world, a suspicious reticence was observed as to the equally insolent infractions of them committed by the French under the Berlin and Milan Decrees. It was particularly desired by them to obtain possession of the letter of M. Champagny, Bonaparte's Minister of Foreign Relations, to General Armstrong, the United States Minister at the French Court, in regard to them, and this wish was as resolutely resisted by the Administration. Mr. Quincy made two motions calling for the despatches which would contain it, — one on the 26th of February, 1808, and the other on the 14th of March, the last enforced with a strong but temperate exposition of the reasonableness of the request, — both of which were voted down by large majorities. This speech, although the motion it supported was negatived, undoubtedly had an effect upon public opinion, and upon the fears of the Administration party as to the consequences of a continued refusal. About a fortnight afterwards, on motion of John Randolph, the request was made, and, after a little delay, complied with on the 2d of April. The next day Mr. Quincy wrote to his wife as follows: —

"We yesterday forced out the great letter of Champagny to Armstrong, in which, by the order of the Emperor, he modestly tells him that his Majesty considers the United States at war with Great Britain, and that he shall confiscate all the ships he has seized, unless we make a declaration of it! The language of both nations is now before the public, and it must declare its will at the coming elections, whence alone salvation must spring.

"By the way, tell Mrs. Guild* that this Champagny, now the successor of Talleyrand, is undoubtedly the same person she knew in 1780 or 1782. He was an officer in one of the fleets which lay off Boston Harbor, and Mrs. Guild will remember him as one of those who were accustomed to visit freely at my grandfather's when she was a young unmarried lady living at home with him.

"Obtaining Champagny's letter confirms our apprehension concerning the designs of Bonaparte. The party of the Administration stood their ground two days, voting down every motion for its publication. On Tuesday they began to waver, and in the evening, it is understood, a deputation waited on Jefferson, who kindly relieved them *by sending in his permission;* and then all this supple herd got rid of their scruples, and voted unanimously to publish. I have never seen mortification and chagrin so strongly depicted in the countenances of any men as in theirs on this occasion."

The last legislative action of importance before the adjournment of Congress was an act originating in the Senate, authorizing the President, in the event of peace between the European belligerents during the recess, or of such a change of measures in regard to neutral commerce as should make that of the United States sufficiently safe, to suspend the Embargo in whole or in part. Mr. Quincy made one of his best speeches on this occasion, in which he predicted exactly what would be the effect of the Embargo upon foreign powers, and especially upon England. His words, as the historian Hildreth says of this speech, "were too prophetic." He did not oppose investing the President with the power to suspend the Embargo; he wished to enlarge that power, so as to enable him to do so without being limited by the provisions of the bill. He feared that the pressure of the Embargo might produce such a danger of domestic insurrection that it might be necessary, for the peace and security of the nation, to suspend the measure, or, at any rate, to leave the hope of a possible suspension; while he looked upon the happening of either of

* Mrs. Guild was the daughter of Colonel Josiah Quincy, by the second of his three marriages. She married Benjamin Guild, of the Class of 1769 in Harvard University; afterwards tutor in that institution. The late Mr Benjamin Guild, of the Suffolk bar, was their son.

the conditions in the bill as chimerical, and morally impossible to occur. After asserting the constitutional power of Congress to give the President this power, he said: —

"A whole people is suffering under a most grievous oppression. All the business of the nation is deranged; all its active hopes frustrated; all its industry stagnant. The scene we are now witnessing is altogether unparalleled in history. The tales of fiction have no parallel for it. A new writ is executed upon a whole people. Not, indeed, the old monarchical writ of *ne exeat regno*, but a new republican writ, *ne exeat republica*. Freemen, in the pride of their liberty, have restraints imposed upon them which despotism never exercised. They are fastened down to the soil by the enchantment of law; and their property vanishes in the very process of preservation. It is impossible for us to separate and leave such a people, at such a moment as this, without administering some opiate to their distress. Some hope, however distant, of alleviation must be proffered, — some prospect of relief opened. Otherwise we may justly fear the result of such an unexampled pressure. Who can say what counsels despair might suggest, or what weapons it might furnish?

. . . . .

"In recommending that a discretion, not limited by events, should be vested in the Executive, I can have no personal wish to augment his power. He is no political friend of mine. I deem it essential, both for the tranquillity of the people and for the success of the measure, that such a power should be committed to him. Neither personal nor party feelings shall prevent me from advocating a measure in my estimation salutary to the most important interests of the country. It is true that I am among the earliest and the most uniform opponents of the embargo. I have seen nothing to vary my original belief that its policy was equally cruel to individuals and mischievous to society. As a weapon to control foreign powers, it seemed to me dubious in its effect, uncertain in its operation, — of all possible machinery, the most difficult to set up and the most expensive to maintain.

. . . . .

"But the system is adopted. May it be successful! It is not to diminish, but to increase, the chance of that success, that I urge that a discretion, unlimited by events, shall be vested in the Executive. I shall rejoice if this great miracle be worked. I shall congratulate my country if the experiment shall prove that the Old World can be controlled by fear of being excluded from the commerce of the New

Happy shall I be if on the other side of this dark valley of the shadow of death through which our commercial hopes are passing, shall be found regions of future safety and felicity.

. . . . .

"I do indeed believe that the commerce of the United States is important enough to France and Great Britain to incline both those nations to grant us for its continuance many and great commercial privileges. But that it is so consequential to either as that for its enjoyment the one could be tempted to forego a policy which has for its object to crush the only obstacle in its way to universal empire, or the other induced to abandon a system adopted as the only means for the preservation of its national existence, now in peril on all sides, I confess I am very far from believing.

"We are but a young nation. The United States are scarcely yet hardened into the bone of manhood. Our whole national existence has been nothing but an uninterrupted course of prosperity. The miseries of the Revolutionary war were but as the pangs of parturition. The experience of that period was of a nature not to be very useful after our nation had acquired an individual form, and a manly, constitutional stamina. It is to be feared we have grown giddy with good fortune,— attributing the greatness of our prosperity to our own wisdom, rather than to a course of events and a guidance over which we had no influence. It is to be feared that we are now entering that school of adversity the first blessing of which is to chastise an overweening conceit of ourselves. A nation mistakes its relative consequence when it thinks its countenance, or its intercourse, or its existence, all-important to the rest of the world. There is scarcely any people, and none of any weight in the society of nations, which does not possess within its own sphere all that is essential to its existence. An individual who should retire from conversation with the world for the purpose of taking vengeance on it for some real or imaginary wrong, would soon find himself grievously mistaken. Notwithstanding the delusions of self-flattery, he would certainly be taught that the world was moving along just as well after his dignified retirement as it did while he intermeddled with its concerns. The fate of a nation which should make a similar trial of its consequence to other nations would be the same. The intercourse of human life has its basis in a natural reciprocity, which always exists, although the vanity of nations, as well as of individuals, will often suggest to inflated fancies, that they give more than they gain in the interchange of friendship, of civilities, or of business."

All attempts of the minority to invest Mr. Jefferson with absolute power over the Embargo failed, and the bill passed as it came from the Senate, after an excited debate of thirteen hours, by sixty yeas to thirty-six nays. The motives of this self-denying policy on the part of the Administration were, probably, partly the excellent one of never doing what your adversaries wish you to do, and partly an unwillingness to admit the possibility of any contingency which should justify the suspension of the Embargo, excepting the reduction of Great Britain to the necessity of repealing her Orders in Council, and abandoning the right of search and of impressment through its pacific compulsion. It is hardly necessary to say that Mr. Jefferson was not called upon to exercise the limited powers which, only, he was willing to accept.

CHAPTER VII.

1808.

SOCIETY OF WASHINGTON. — ACQUAINTANCES THERE. — MR. ERSKINE AND MR. ROSE. — MR. GARDENIER AND HIS DUEL WITH MR. CAMPBELL. — DISCOMFORTS OF CONGRESS. — ADJOURNMENT. — SUMMER AT QUINCY. — THE EMBARGO AT HOME AND ABROAD. — PRESIDENT ADAMS ON THE CAUSES OF THE FRENCH REVOLUTION. — RETURN TO WASHINGTON. — KEEPS HOUSE WITH SENATOR LLOYD. — THEIR WAY OF LIFE. — FIRST AND SECOND SPEECHES ON FOREIGN RELATIONS. — EFFECT ON THE ADMINISTRATION MEMBERS. — LETTERS FROM MR. ADAMS AND MR. OTIS.

DURING this session Mr. Quincy went very little into Washington society. Society was not very attractive there at the best, and was then made even less agreeable than usual by the agitation of the question of removing the seat of government to Philadelphia. Of course this proposition was very distasteful to the inhabitants, most of whom had entered into speculations in real estate in Washington, in the faith that it was to be the permanent capital. "I take no part in these intrigues," he wrote to his wife; "but if called upon to vote, I fear it will be my lot to wound our good friends Tayloe and Peter." Jefferson and Madison threw all their influence in favor of Washington, and the main Southern vote went in the same direction, and yet the proposition for removal was defeated by only two votes. So violent was the local feeling on the subject, that Mr. Sloan of New Jersey, who made the original motion, stated in his place that he had been threatened with assassination if he persevered in it. Of Washington as a place to live in, Mr. Quincy thus writes to his wife: —

"I have many visitors from Boston. They have but one sentiment of disappointment and disgust. The place is more indifferent than ever, and my system of receiving none of the attentions of the inhabitants has proved no loss, but a great relief to me. Its society has exceeded its ordinary measure of dulness, and since the question of removal has been agitated, it has been distracted with every species of personality and violence. All which I have, to my great satisfaction, escaped."

"It was my habit," he says in another place, "to refuse all invitations except those I thought my official duty required me to accept. I dined during this session with Mr. Erskine, the British Minister, with Mr. Tayloe, and Mr. Peter (of Georgetown), where I was introduced to Mr. Rose, a special messenger sent by the British government to ours. His appearance and manners were pleasing, exhibiting a degree of modesty mingled with evident knowledge of the world. He was extremely fluent, and showed a general knowledge of European politics. I was very favorably impressed by his language and demeanor. Judge Washington urged upon me a visit to Mount Vernon, and offered to send his carriage for me to Alexandria; but my engagements did not allow of it."

Mr. Tayloe resided on a fine estate in the neighborhood of Washington, where his son, Mr. Benjamin Ogle Tayloe, a graduate of Harvard University in 1815, now lives. Mr. Peter was married to one of the granddaughters of Mrs. Washington, between whom and my father and mother there existed a life-long friendship. Mr. Erskine was the Honorable David Montague Erskine, the eldest son of the great Lord Erskine. Being in this country at the beginning of the century, I believe as an *attaché* to the British Legation, he married in 1800 Miss Frances Cadwallader of Philadelphia, daughter of General John Cadwallader. On the accession of the Grenville ministry and the elevation of Lord Erskine to the peerage, he was returned to Parliament instead of his father for Portsmouth, but soon resigned his seat on his appointment to the post of Minister at Washington. Of his adventures with Mr. Madison and Mr. Gallatin, and of the disgrace into which he fell with his government because of them, I shall give some account in their proper place. After his recall in 1809, he was not employed for many years. In 1825, after his father's death, he was appointed Minister to Stuttgart, and afterwards to Munich, which place he held till 1843. His American marriage was a happy and fruitful one, — fifteen children being born of it, of whom ten or twelve yet survive. Lady Erskine died in 1843, and Lord Erskine was married again twice. He died in 1855, in his eightieth year. Mr. Rose, afterwards the Rt. Hon. Sir George Henry Rose, G. C. H., was the son of the Rt. Hon. George Rose, who was Treasurer of the Navy and Vice-President of the Board of Trade under Mr. Pitt, of whom he was the personal friend and devoted partisan. Sir George H. Rose entered diplomatic life very early, and was member for Southampton in 1807, at the time of his appointment to his special mission to the United States. He was afterwards Minister to Munich and Berlin, and on his father's death, in 1818, succeeded him in the lucrative office of Clerk of the Parliaments, which he held till 1844. He died in 1855 at a good old age. The celebrated General Sir Hugh Rose, distinguished for military successes in Syria, the Crimea, and India, who received the thanks of Parliament in 1859 for his services in suppressing the Sepoy mutiny, and was raised to the peerage last year, 1866, by the title of Lord Strathnairn, is the son of Sir George.

Mr. Quincy's time outside the Capitol was the more fully occupied from the extraordinary conscientiousness which prevented him from writing his letters in the House, which was then as now the general habit of the members. He gave strictly all his time during the sessions to the day's work, and did all his writing at his lodgings. He was almost, if not quite, the only member who was so scrupulous as to the time of the public. It seems, according to one of his stories about John Randolph, that even Mr. Speaker would sometimes while away the weary time with his correspondents when he could snatch a prudent hour. Randolph was speaking one day, and Mr. Speaker thought he was safe for an hour or two, and began privily to indite a letter. It was not long before the hawk's eye of Randolph spied out the inattention, and he stopped short in the middle of a sentence. Mr. Speaker was presently aroused by the stillness, and, supposing that Randolph had done speaking, he returned to his duty, and, seeing the eccentric Virginian still on his legs, inquired whether the honorable gentleman had finished his speech. "Mr. Speaker," returned Randolph, in his high falsetto voice, and pointing his long forefinger at his victim, — "Mr. Speaker, I was waiting until you had finished that letter!" It is safe to say that the Speaker never again relaxed in his attention to that particular orator.

Among the new friends Mr. Quincy made at this session was Barent Gardenier, of New York, a self-made, self-educated man, of fiery temperament, reckless courage, and fluent speech. My father had a warmly affectionate regard for him, and loved to tell of his sayings and doings. He says of him in a letter to my mother: "He is a man of wit and desultory reading, accustomed to the skirmishing and electioneering violence of New York. He brings it all into debate in an honest, unguarded, inconsiderate manner, very well calculated to inflame the party passions opposed to him, but not to make converts; but, withal, he is an excellent fellow." On the 20th of February, 1808, Mr. Gardenier made a fierce onslaught on the Administration in a speech on the Embargo. He charged them with base subserviency to Bonaparte, and taunted them in the most galling terms with not daring to let the people know their real designs, or the true condition of the nation. This attack occasioned a violent commotion among the friends of Mr. Jefferson, and a scene ensued not unlike some that later Congresses have witnessed, as when John Quincy Adams asked what he should do with a petition purporting to come from slaves, or when the Haverhill petition was presented praying for a peaceful dissolution of the Union. He was frequently interrupted, called to order, and even threatened with expulsion. And by way of answer, he was assailed with such a storm of personal abuse, that he considered it necessary to call out Mr. George W. Campbell, a native of Scotland, but long a resident of Tennessee.* Of this duel and its consequences, my father gave the following account at the time in his letters to my mother: —

"*February* 26. — Gardenier and Campbell went out yesterday for the purpose of refreshing, or finishing, their honor at the ends of their

* Mr. Campbell was brought to America in infancy, having been born in Scotland in 1768. He was Representative from 1803 to 1809, and was afterwards Senator, Secretary of the Treasury, and Minister to Russia. He died in 1848.

pistols; Eppes (of Virginia) being second to Campbell, White (of Delaware), of the Senate, to Gardenier. But the populace of Georgetown got knowledge of the affair, and were so anxious *to see the sport*, that, to the utter astonishment of the parties, they found, it is said, a hundred and fifty persons, men, women, and children, on the spot marked out for the bloody arena, who had collected with no desire to prevent, but to share in the pleasure of the spectacle. As the parties had no inclination to fight in public, they were obliged to retire. It is supposed to be utterly impossible to prevent this termination of the affair, although we all regret the circumstance deeply."

"*March* 3, 1808. — Poor Gardenier fell yesterday in a duel with Campbell. His wound was at first thought to be mortal, but strong hopes now exist that he will escape a fatal result. They fought at Bladensburg. I visited him with Dana of Connecticut. The scene was heart-rending. The physicians begin to hope that the ball has not passed through the lungs, but it is a most critical wound. He is in the family of Mr. Lowndes, a private gentleman on whose grounds the battle was fought, who happens to be a violent Federalist, as are several families in his neighborhood, and none of them seem to regard the trouble this circumstance is likely to occasion them.

"The friends of Gardenier detailed themselves to watch with him, and with Pitkin of Connecticut I attended him on the night of the 3d of March. His recovery is devoutly to be wished, as he has a wife and three children dependent on him. He would be a sad victim to the Moloch honor. The ball entered his armpit and came out at his back, lodging in the left shoulder-blade. His sympathy with his family during his illness has been very exquisite. Nothing could prevent him from writing to his wife daily, since the wound has been pronounced not mortal.

"'I shudder,' he said to me, 'at the gulf I have passed. For myself I care but little, but I have a wife whom I love, and, what is a higher consideration at such a moment as this, who loves me as much as one being can love another. I realize dreadfully what would have been the distress brought on my family had this wound been mortal. My children would have been doomed to poverty, neglect, and forgetfulness.' Gardenier is a man of excellent natural heart, but abounding in the chivalrous notions which prevail in New York, — good-natured, thoughtless, possessing wit, and not at all scrupulous in exercising it. In the midst of suffering his wit did not for a moment leave him. He made us smile whenever he broke through the laws of his physicians. As he turned himself with great pain in his bed, he said, 'Well, I have this comfort, Congress will certainly grant me a pension for known wounds received in the service of the United States.'"

Mr. Gardenier was a native of Kinderhook, and all his education, excepting what he gave himself, he received in the common schools of that village. He practised law at Kingston, Ulster County, with much reputation and success. "His handsome person, pleasant voice, and easy flow of language remarkable for its simplicity," to use the words of an eminent gentleman of Kingston, who remembers him, "made him indeed a most attractive and successful speaker." * On his return to New York after his spirited though unsuccessful campaign against Mr. Campbell, he was honored by his party with a public reception. He represented his district in the Tenth and Eleventh Congresses, 1807 – 11, and on leaving Congress removed to the city of New York with the purpose of practising his profession there. But the attractions of politics overcame those of the law, and his success was not answerable to the promise of his earlier professional life. At one time he was editor of a Federal newspaper in New York. He died there in 1818. One of his daughters married the well-known writer and diplomatist, Mr. Theodore S. Fay, formerly our Minister to Switzerland.

The end of the long session at length approached. Congress had not yet learned to protract its sittings until midsummer, and the middle of April was thought late in those primeval days. Early in March Mr. Quincy wrote to his wife: —

"*March* 10. — In Congress we have nothing to do, and do nothing. We are tired of one another and Jefferson of us. Intrigues for the Presidency are the order of the day, and the only business on hand. The only difficulty to be surmounted is, that those who voted for the Embargo do not like to go home with it on, and yet they dare not take it off. Weakness and ignorance are full of fears, and we have a plentiful harvest of both. No person here seems to direct. No one pretends to see the course, or to be able to preside over the destinies, of the House or the nation. We meet and adjourn, do ordinary business, wrangle, and then the majority retire to intrigue for the Presidency."

* Mr. A. Bruyn Hasbrouck, formerly President of Rutgers College, New Jersey, to whom I am indebted for these particulars touching my father's old friend, through the kind mediation of Mr. J. V. L. Pruyn, M. C., of Albany.

"*March* 15. — From all parts of the country discontent with the measures of government begins to extend itself, and disgust with Mr. Jefferson more openly to be expressed. Violent passions toward each other fill the adherents of Madison and Clinton. Virginia is torn into factions between the friends of the former and those of Monroe, — who has unquestionably made a coalition with Clinton."

In another letter, of an earlier date, he thus speaks of some of the other discomforts of his assiduous attendance on the sittings of the House. All he can give her, he tells his wife, in return for her excellent letters are —

"these dribbling communications strained through the interstices of a brain kept in constant tension from the wire-drawing machinery of political demagogues and philosophical charlatans. The heat of the Capitol is noxious and insupportable, and it has affected me to fainting. One of the flues of the furnace is behind my chair. I have at length prevailed on the Speaker to forbid our subterranean fires. The effect produced by them is that upon an oyster baked in a Dutch oven. The daily squabbles on our democratic floor disgust me too much to dwell on. Of books I read nothing, and *when I want pleasure I think of you and my children.*"

On the 25th of April, 1808, this eventful and stormy session closed, — the forerunner of others yet more stormy and more eventful. The next day Mr. Quincy took coach for Baltimore, with his friends Messrs. Tallmadge, Pickering, Hillhouse, Goodrich, and Ely,* —

(Six precious souls, and all agog
To dash through thick and thin !)

as he himself parenthesizes, and thence proceeded to Boston with the deliberate speed which marked the travelling of that day.

He spent the next summer, as usual, at his country-seat. His journals of these months are brief; but they show that he did not relax in his habitual industry. His studies seem to have been chiefly directed to the portions of French history relating to the Huguenot persecutions. He began also a critical comparison of Gilbert Wakefield's "Improved Version of the New Tes-

* William Ely graduated at Yale College, 1787; Representative from Massachusetts from 1805 to 1815; died, 1817.

tament" with the original, in which he appears to my laical apprehension to have shown considerable exegetical acumen. But the cares of this world and the deceitfulness of politics did not permit him to push his inquiries very far in this direction. The Embargo was the topic which would persistently thrust itself on his notice above and through all secular or theological studies. It was the nightmare of the New England States, which chilled the life-blood of their industry, and checked its vital current with hopeless torpor. It pressed upon all classes, paralyzing at once the capital of the rich and the day-labor of the poor. Ships rotted at the wharves; handicrafts and industries dependent upon commerce perished with it; agriculture felt the general distress in the diminished demand for its productions; all trades and occupations suffered by sympathy with the destruction of the chief source of wealth and prosperity. The shadow of the Embargo fell upon every household, and darkened every fireside. The irritation of the popular mind was rendered yet more bitter by the intrusions into private affairs through the despotic powers lodged in the hands of the collectors and the temptations held out to the perjury of informers, by the supplementary laws to prevent and punish evasions of the Act under pretence of the coasting-trade. Altogether, the people of the New England States were growing into a dangerous state of discontent with the government, and the lovers of peace and good order feared that their patience might give way, and they refuse to be ruined quietly for the satisfaction of the political theories of Mr. Jefferson. It was a state of things which might well absorb the thoughts of every reflecting man with any stake in the country, and especially of every one called to take an active part in its affairs.

In the mean time, the effect of the Embargo abroad had not been such as its promoters had hoped. The English merchants in the American trade, indeed, remonstrated against the Orders in Council, and petitioned Parliament for their repeal, and their prayer was supported by the Whig opposition; but without effect. The Orders were sustained by large majorities, and heavy transit duties laid on cotton and tobacco and other articles of American production that might pass through England in neutral vessels under these Orders. At the same time Bonaparte's invasion of the Peninsula had destroyed the old Spanish and Portuguese colonial systems, and, as the colonies adhered to the royal families, the commerce of those countries and their dependencies was opened to the British merchants, while the interdict upon our ships gave them a monopoly of it. This, probably, more than compensated for the loss of our trade after the first disturbance of business consequent upon it was over. The English ministry refused to repeal the Orders in return for our repeal of the Embargo, which Mr. Pinkney proposed by Mr. Jefferson's directions, and the refusal was conveyed by Mr. Canning, the Secretary for Foreign Affairs, in a letter barbed with the bitterest sarcasm. If the measure were meant as retaliation for invasions of neutral rights, it should have been aimed at France, the original author of them, and not, virtually, at England alone. If it were a mere municipal regulation, England had no complaint to make of it. She had no hostility to America, and the ministry were "anxious to do all in their power, short of seeming to deprecate the Embargo as a hostile measure, to facilitate the removal of a restriction so very inconvenient to the American people." And he ended with the hope "that the present experiment would teach that Great Britain was not so absolutely dependent on the trade of America as to be obliged to court a commercial intercourse."

On the other hand, the instinct of Bonaparte discerned the friendly *animus* towards himself which was concealed under the pretended impartiality of the terms of the Act. He made no objection to being joined in the preamble with England, and expressed his cordial approbation of the measure; and to show his readiness to co-operate with it, he issued the Bayonne Decree of April 17, 1808, by which he ordered the seizure and confiscation of all American ships in France, or which might arrive there. And when General Armstrong remonstrated against such an activity of friendship, Bonaparte assured him that it was intended merely as a friendly assistance to the American government in enforcing the Embargo, since no American ships could be lawfully at sea after its passage, and any claiming that character must either be British ships in disguise, or, at any rate, they must have "denationalized" themselves by yielding to the Orders in Council, and so be lawful prize by the Milan Decree.

The oppressive effects of the Embargo were not confined to the Northern States, as its Southern supporters had supposed they would be. It recoiled on the grain-raising and planting States so as to make itself severely felt by them. This was particularly the case with the Southern Atlantic States, — the cotton-growing, rice-planting, and tobacco-raising districts, which largely depended for their gains on an unrestricted trade. To this fact Major Thomas Pinckney of South Carolina bears witness, in a letter dated Santee, May 25, 1808.

". . . . . We are here smarting under the effects of the Embargo, and there are some among us who, in spite of the eloquent address of your Professor of Rhetoric,* cannot relish this mode of defending neutral rights, and still less approve of the system of politics which, by the confession of their own party, has left to our Administration no alternative but war (for which they are so evidently unprepared) or this most ruinous proceeding. . . . . . To the philosopher who coolly tries these tremendous experiments on the welfare of a deluded people, neither the failure of his projects nor the evils of unsuccessful warfare (should such be the consequence) would prove so calamitous as to those who, *quicquid delirant reges, plectuntur*. To *him* the road to Carter's Mountain is as practicable as it was in 1781, from whence, on the return of better days, he might again descend to persuade the people, in a communication to another Mazzei, that the man who had been most instrumental in preserving his country was at the head of a league to deprive that country of its liberty."

The following are a few extracts from my father's journal during this summer. The opinion of the venerable ex-President Adams as to the veto power, though very characteristic of him, has hardly been confirmed by subsequent events. They have rather justified the wisdom of the framers of the Constitution in providing the check they did against its abuse.

"*September* 6. — Dr. Morse† dined with me. Visited President

* Mr. John Quincy Adams, then Professor of Rhetoric in Harvard University.

† Doubtless the Rev. Dr. Jedediah Morse (Y. C. 1783) minister at Charlestown. A very prominent man, politically and theologically, fifty years ago;

Adams. A. regretted the want of an absolute negative in the Executive in all the Constitutions. He had urged it in the Legislature of Massachusetts, but Theophilus Parsons, Jackson, Lowell, and other Essex gentlemen would not injure their popularity. If it had succeeded, it would have been, probably, adopted into that of the United States. 'For what,' said he, 'is the Constitution of the United States but that of Massachusetts, New York, and Maryland. There is not a feature in it which cannot be found in one or the other."

"*September* 15. — Ex-President Adams visited me. I remarked on the number of memoirs of French political actors of the seventeenth century which was possessed by the present age. 'The next,' said he, 'will have as many as ours. In less than a hundred years there will be as many memoirs of the French Revolution, not one of which will assign its true cause. This was in fact the same that exists in every country and period of time, — the jealousy and envy of the second families of the first. The great nobles wished to depress the House of Bourbon, but when the mobility had got the reins, the nobles found their expectation to control them was vain. The Marquis de Lafayette is very dear to the people of this country, and they will scarcely bear the truth relative to his family. But it is unquestionable that the pride and ambition of the family of Noailles pulled down the throne of Bourbon. The Viscount de Noailles told me himself that, when he resigned his charters of nobility to the National Convention, he had no other idea than that he was giving away with one hand what would be restored to the other. The family had undoubtedly some obscure hope of ameliorating the condition of the people, and perhaps obtaining some new securities for personal liberty; but the true source of that revolution was the envy and rivalry between that and some other great families and that of the Bourbons.

. . . . .

"The Count de Mercier attended the levee of Louis XVI. in a very plain and apparently mean suit, but, the buttons being diamonds, it was very costly. Adelaide, the king's aunt, said to him, 'M. le Comte, your dress is not sufficiently splendid for the levee.' 'Upon my word, Madam,' replied he, 'my coat cost ninety thousand livres.' 'Then, M. le Comte,' she retorted, 'you ought to have pinned your tailor's receipt on your shoulders.'

. . . . .

"Mr. Adams said that Mr. Lawrence told him that George Gren-

but who will be better known now and hereafter as the father of Professor Samuel F. B. Morse, to whom the world owes the benefaction of the electric telegraph. Dr. Morse died in 1824.

ville said to him (Lawrence) that the object of the Stamp Act was not merely revenue, 'but,' said he, 'you Americans have spread too much canvas upon the ocean.'"

Congress had adjourned to meet on the 7th of November, and towards the end of October Mr. Quincy proceeded to Washington, without his wife and family, as at the last session. The following is his own account of his arrangements for the winter: —

"On the 26th of October, 1808, I took the stage for Washington, James Lloyd,* Senator from Massachusetts, being my companion, — having each of us a servant. We had taken a house together on Capitol Hill, being supplied with all culinary wants from a hotel. It was an independent and pleasant arrangement. We arrived at Washington on the 5th of November, and took possession of our home with the self-congratulation of ownership. It had been well provided with furniture, and all our arrangements proved satisfactory. On the 9th of November we called upon Mr. Jefferson. Of course he was not communicative with us; but to his political friends his language was, 'The only alternative is embargo or war.'

"My personal situation at Washington was never so eligible, except during those sessions when my family was with me. Our house was our own; we were relieved from the noise and intrusion incident to a boarding-house. Lloyd, as a companion, was pleasant and gentlemanly. We had our whole time at our own disposal, and were free from interruption. We breakfasted at eight; usually spent half an hour over the breakfast-table and in conversation, then to our chambers till eleven. Then till three at the Capitol, then to dinner, and after dinner walked till dark. After tea in our chambers until the next morning. Such was the usual routine. We gave occasionally a bachelor's dinner to friends from Boston who visited Washington. To my wife I wrote daily, but to no one else. The subjects of debate were such as required great labor, and I devoted myself exclusively to my Congressional duties."

Mr. Quincy had the satisfaction of hearing, soon after his arrival in Washington, of his re-election, after a very sharp contest, by the largest majority ever received by any Representative of his district. This approbation of his constituents, and yet more the warm approval of his course by his most valued private

* James Lloyd, born in Boston, 1769; graduated at Harvard University, 1787; a successful merchant; Senator from 1808 to 1813, and again from 1822 to 1826. He removed to Philadelphia after leaving Congress, and died there in 1831.

friends, encouraged and strengthened him for the fierce conflicts in which he was about to engage. He began to keep a diary at the beginning of the session, but, like too many virtuous beginnings, it soon came to an untimely end. I will give a few extracts.

"*November* 8.—In the evening Lewis of Virginia called on us. He represented the sufferings of that State under the Embargo as extreme. If continued, it was impossible that the Federalists should not receive a great accession of strength."

"*November* 13. *Sunday.*—Giles of Virginia and General Smith of Maryland called on us. The former wondered that New England would not bear the Embargo. He said that in Virginia they were willing to bear it, out of regard to *their Eastern friends;* that it was of small consequence to them who were the carriers of their produce, and that out of regard for Eastern interests they had submitted to discriminating duties. As to removing the Embargo, he was in favor of adhering to it at all hazards. He was in favor of putting to trial what the strength of the federal arm was, and if it were not sufficient to enforce its own laws, it might as well be known now as hereafter."

"*November* 15.—At Congress. Early adjournment. In the evening Taggart, Lewis of Virginia, Tallmadge, etc. visited us. Lewis said that there were no traditions circulating in Virginia concerning the youthful period of Washington's life of any great interest. He was always remarkable for great firmness and thoughtfulness, for love of athletic sports, and for great muscular strength, particularly great force of arm. He could throw a stone farther than any man in Virginia; and there was a mark on the side of the Natural Bridge, with Washington's name on the rock, it being the place to which he had, in 1750 or 1760, thrown a stone from below, as is the practice with persons visiting that wonder of nature. Washington's mark is twenty feet higher than any other."

"*November* 16.—Conversation with John Randolph. He said the Embargo was ruining Virginia,—particularly in his part of it (Charlotte County), where the justices of the county courts had persisted in continuing the courts open and business progressing in its usual course. In other parts of the State (and he cited Albemarle County and the neighborhood of Mr. Jefferson) the justices had refused to transact business, and that had in some measure checked the immediate pressure of the measure, and indeed had given it a considerable degree of popularity with all those who, being needy or embarrassed, were willing to find an excuse for delinquency. The people had been deluded. Their sufferance of the measure he attributed solely to their patriotism and to their belief that it had its origin in the real good of the country."

By this refusal to hold the county courts, the neighbors of Mr. Jefferson were of course relieved from the unpleasant necessity of paying their debts, — a privilege of which it seems those of Mr. Randolph were, to his regret and indignation, injuriously deprived. Mr. William B. Giles, whose testimony to the willingness of his constituents to suffer in the cause of their Eastern friends is here recorded, was born in 1762; graduated at Princeton in 1781; and was Representative from Virginia from 1790 to 1798, and from 1801 to 1802, Senator from 1804 to 1815, and Governor from 1826 to 1829. He was a bitter political enemy of Washington, distinguishing himself by making a disparaging speech about him on his retirement from office, and by refusing on a previous occasion to vote for an adjournment of the House on the 22d of February, for the purpose of waiting on him, as was then customary. He was one of the ablest supporters of all the extreme measures of Jefferson. He died in 1830. General Samuel Smith had been a Colonel in the Revolutionary army, and was a General of the Maryland militia. He represented that State in the House or Senate from 1793 to 1833, and was also a warm supporter of the administration of Mr. Jefferson. He died in 1839. Joseph Lewis was, according t Jefferson, "the residuary legatee of Virginia Federalism," and cordial regard and occasional correspondence subsisted betwe him and Mr. Quincy while he lived.

From the following letter of Mr. Adams to Mr. Quincy, a yet more from one I shall give a little later, it will be se though he sustained the Administration generally after it ceived the support of Mr. John Quincy Adams, that the I President did not accept the Embargo with the unquestion enthusiasm of his eminent son.

"QUINCY, Nov. 25, 18(

"MY DEAR FRIEND: — I owe you a thousand thanks, to spea the good old English form of civility, for the speech and the docum You are greatly to be pitied, — I mean all of you, of all parties, -

I see you must labor very hard, and with much anxiety, without the smallest hope, that I can discern, of preserving yourselves and us, the people, from very dull times. If you continue the Embargo, the times will be hard. If you institute a total non-intercourse, the times will not be more cheerful. If you repeal the Embargo, circumstances will occur of more animation, but perhaps not more profit or more comfort. If you arm our merchantmen, there will be war. The blood will not stagnate, it is true; but it may run too freely for our health or comfort. If you declare war against France and England at once, this will be sublime, to be sure, and if we had a Dutch navy and a Van Tromp to sail up the Thames, and a De Ruyter to sail up the Seine, we might gain as much by it as the Dutch did when they warred against England, France, and Spain at once, — that is, we might obtain by it much wealth and a good peace.

"I have made up my mind for hard, dull times, in all events. I reconcile myself to our destiny as well as I can, by considering that we are yet in a much better situation than any other nation, and that we cannot probably be in a worse, whatever may happen.

"I have another resource, too, for reconciling myself to our fate, and that is by running over again the history of the world. I have just finished Voltaire's essay on the Manners and Spirit of Nations, which is a miniature of universal history. When I find that this globe has been a vast theatre, on which the same tragedies and comedies have been acted over and over again in all ages and countries, how can I hope that this country should escape the universal calamity? Despair itself hardens, if it does not comfort. One would think that the consideration that all other nations always have been and now are more miserable than we are, should make one more unhappy; but it has not that effect. It alleviates in some degree our distress. When we see that an evil or a danger is inevitable, we resolve and prepare to meet it.

"An acquaintance of yours, Mrs. Price, Mrs. T. Greenleaf's mother, died this afternoon very suddenly. Last evening she was preparing to go abroad upon a tea-party.

"Mrs. Adams presents her compliments and thanks for the documents, which she takes a satisfaction in reading, because they are well printed, and save her eyes from the torment of reading the newspapers.

"With great and sincere esteem, I am, sir, your obliged servant,

"J. ADAMS."

To this letter, Mr. Quincy replied as follows: —

"WASHINGTON, 15th December, 1808.

"SIR: — Your favor of November 25th found me in the midst of a parliamentary contest, which occupied me too intensely to admit of that early acknowledgment which a deep sense of the honor you have conferred on me dictated. The battle has raged with some warmth, and it has been my fate to be in the hottest of it. Whether my exertions were as wise as they were, I am sure, well intended, I confess I am ignorant, — I had almost said, indifferent. That the country cannot remain in the condition in which it is, I was certain. That it was the determination of the Administration to adhere pertinaciously to the Embargo, I was equally certain. That they and their majority were in a good measure ignorant of the real temper and sufferings of our people, I knew. My object has been, as far as possible, to shake their confidence in that system, which, whatever they believed or intended, I was conscious was ruining the hopes of New England. With respect to subsequent measures, in case the Embargo was removed, there are, indeed, considerable difficulties, growing, however, more out of the character and policy of the men who guide our affairs, than from anything unexampled in the embarrassments of the nation. A policy not unlike that of 1798, with some variation in the detail, resulting out of particular differences in our situation, would yet preserve us, not only in peace, but, as I believe, in the enjoyment of a rich harvest of neutrality. But how can such a 'dish of skim-milk' as now stands curdling at the head of our nation be stirred to so mighty an action as that which he who then led the destinies of the country effected? Fear of responsibility and love of popularity are now master-passions, and regulate all the movements. The policy is to keep things as they are, and wait for European events. It is hoped the chapter of accidents may present something favorable within the remaining three months. And if it does not, no great convulsion can happen during that period. The Presidential term will have expired, and then away to Monticello, and let the —— take the hindmost. I do believe that not a whit deeper project than this fills the august mind of your successor.

"Whether the definite project be to put an end to mercantile enterprise, and make us abandon the water, I know not. The intention is denied; yet all the talents of the friends of Administration are in requisition to convince us of the dreadful consequences to our property and rights,

' . . . . si tamen impia
Non tangenda rates transiliunt vada.'

"How all these things will terminate, indeed I know not. But of one thing I am certain, that, happen what will, I shall never cease to feel and express the very great honor and respect with which I am, &c.

"J. QUINCY."

The questions of the Embargo and of the foreign relations of the United States were necessarily the prominent topics of this session. The Federalists moved at sundry times for the repeal, total or partial, of the Embargo, and for various modifications of it to make its operations less oppressive. But all propositions from that side of the House, and of that complexion, were voted down, and the only legislation on the subject was a law providing for its stricter execution, and for the prevention and punishment of evasions of it. Mr. Quincy maintained, during this session, on his own responsibility, the independent course he had adopted at the last, following his own judgment rather than the lead of Randolph in the discharge of his parliamentary duties.

On the 28th of November, he made his first speech on Foreign Relations, which gave him a more marked position in the House and before the country than anything he had yet done. It was on this resolution, offered by the committee to which had been referred so much of the President's Message as treated of foreign relations: "Resolved, That the United States cannot, without a sacrifice of their rights, honor, and independence, submit to the late edicts of Great Britain and France." One of the inferences of the report from this proposition was, that therefore the Embargo should be continued. As to the resolution, in itself, interpreted by the natural meaning of its words, Mr. Quincy affirmed that it was unobjectionable. It was but the announcement of a determination to perform one of the most common and undeniable of public duties. As to the course advocated in the report for the carrying out of the resolution, "it is," he said, "in my opinion, loathsome; the spirit it breathes, disgraceful; the temper it is likely to inspire, neither calculated to regain the rights we have lost, nor to preserve those which remain to us." And presently he proceeds: —

"I agree to this resolution, because, in my apprehension, it offers a solemn pledge to this nation — a pledge not to be mistaken, and not to be evaded — that the present system of public measures shall be totally abandoned. Adopt it, and there is an end of the policy of deserting our rights, under a pretence of maintaining them. Adopt it, and we no longer yield to the beck of haughty belligerents the rights of navigating the ocean, — that choice inheritance bequeathed to us by our fathers. Adopt it, and there is a termination of that base and abject submission by which this country has for these eleven months been disgraced and brought to the brink of ruin.

. . . . .

"It remains for us, therefore, to consider what submission is, and what the pledge not to submit implies.

"One man submits to the order, decree, or edict of another, when he does that thing which such order, decree, or edict commands; or when he omits to do that thing which such order, decree, or edict prohibits. This, then, is submission. It is to do as we are bidden. It is to take the will of another as the measure of our rights. It is to yield to his power, to go where he directs, or to refrain from going where he forbids us.

"If this be submission, then the pledge not to submit implies the reverse of all this. It is a solemn declaration that we will not do that thing which such order, decree, or edict commands, or that we will do what it prohibits. This, then, is freedom. This is honor. This is independence. It consists in taking the nature of things, and not the will of another, as the measure of our rights. What God and Nature offer us we will enjoy in despite of the commands, regardless of the menaces, of iniquitous power.

"Let us apply these correct and undeniable principles to the edicts of Great Britain and France, and the consequent abandonment of the ocean by the American government. The decrees of France prohibit us from trading with Great Britain. The orders of Great Britain prohibit us from trading with France. And what do we? Why, in direct subserviency to the edicts of each, we prohibit our citizens from trading with either. We do more. As if unqualified submission was not humiliating enough, we descend to an act of supererogation in servility; we abandon trade altogether; we not only refrain from that particular trade which their respective edicts proscribe, but, lest the ingenuity of our merchants should enable them to evade their operation, to make submission doubly sure, the American government virtually re-enact the edicts of the belligerents, and abandon all the trade which, notwithstanding the practical effects of their edicts, remains to us. The same conclusion will result if we consider our Embargo in relation to the objects of this belligerent policy. France, by her edicts, would compress Great Britain by destroying her commerce and cutting off her supplies. All the continent of Europe, in the hand of Bonaparte, is made subservient to this policy. The Embargo law of the United States, in its operation, is an union with this Continental coalition against British commerce at the very moment most auspicious to its success. Can anything be more in direct subserviency to the views of the French Emperor? If we consider the orders of Great Britain, the result will be the same. I proceed at present on the supposition of a perfect impartiality in our administration towards both belligerents, so far as relates to the Embargo law. Great Britain had two objects in issuing her orders. First, to excite discontent in the people of the Continent, by depriving them of their accustomed colonial supplies. Second, to secure to herself that commerce of which she deprived neutrals. Our Embargo co-operates with the British views in both respects. By our dereliction of the ocean, the Continent is much more deprived of the advantages of commerce than it would be possible for the British navy to effect, and by removing our competition all the commerce of the Continent which can be forced is wholly left to be reaped by Great Britain. The language of each sovereign is in direct conformity with these ideas. Napoleon tells the American Minister, virtually, that we are very good Americans; that although he will not allow the property he has in his hands to escape him, nor desist from burning and capturing our vessels on every occasion, yet that he is, thus far, satisfied with our co-operation. And what is the language of George III. when our minister presents to his consideration the Embargo laws. Is it *Le Roy s'avisera?* — 'The king will reflect upon them.' No, it is the pure language of royal approbation, *Le Roy le veut*, 'The king wills it.' Were you colonies, he could expect no more. His subjects as inevitably get that commerce which you abandon, as the water will certainly run into the only channel which remains after all the others are obstructed. In whatever point of view you consider these Embargo laws in relation to those edicts and decrees, we shall find them co-operating with each belligerent in its policy. In this way, I grant, our conduct may be impartial; but what has become of our American rights to navigate the ocean? They are abandoned in strict conformity to the decrees of both belligerents. This resolution declares that we will no longer submit to such degrading humiliation. Little as I relish it, I will take it, as the harbinger of a new day, — the pledge of a new system of measures.

"Perhaps here, in strictness, I ought to close my observations. But the report of the committee, contrary to what I deem the principle of the resolution, unquestionably recommends the continuance of the Embargo laws. And such is the state of the nation, and in particular that portion of it which, in part, I represent, under their oppression, that I cannot refrain from submitting some considerations on that subject.

"When I enter on the subject of the Embargo, I am struck with wonder at the very threshold. I know not with what words to express my astonishment. At the time I departed from Massachusetts, if there was an impression which I thought universal, it was that at the commencement of this session an end would be put to this measure. The opinion was not so much that it would be terminated, as that it was then at an end. Sir, the prevailing sentiment, according to my apprehension, was stronger than this, — even that the pressure was so great that it could not possibly be long endured; that it would soon be absolutely insupportable. And this opinion, as I then had reason to believe, was not confined to any one class, or description, or party, — even those who were friends of the existing Administration, and unwilling to abandon it, were yet satisfied that a sufficient trial had been given to this measure. With these impressions, I arrive in this city. I hear the incantations of the great enchanter. I feel his spell. I see the legislative machinery begin to move. The scene opens, and I am commanded to forget all my recollections, to disbelieve the evidence of my senses, to contradict what I have seen, and heard, and felt. I hear that all this discontent was mere party clamor, — electioneering artifice; that the people of New England are able and willing to endure this Embargo for an indefinite, unlimited period; some say for six months, some a year, some two years. The gentleman from North Carolina (Mr. Macon) told us that he preferred three years of Embargo to a war. And the gentleman from Virginia (Mr. Clopton) said expressly, that he hoped we should never allow our vessels to go upon the ocean again, until the orders and decrees of the belligerents were rescinded. In plain English, until France and Great Britain should, in their great condescension, permit. — Good Heavens! Mr. Chairman, are men mad? Is this House touched with that insanity which is the never-failing precursor of the intention of Heaven to destroy? The people of New England, after eleven months' deprivation of the ocean, to be commanded still longer to abandon it, for an undefined period, — to hold their unalienable rights at the tenure of the will of Britain or of Bonaparte! A people commercial in all aspects, in all their relations, in all their hopes, in all their recollections of the past, in all their prospects of the future, — a people, whose first love was the ocean, the choice of their childhood, the approbation of their manly years, the most precious inheritance of their fathers, — in the midst of their success, in the moment of the most exquisite perception of commercial prosperity, to be commanded to abandon it, not for a time limited, but for a time unlimited, — not until they can be prepared to defend themselves there, (for that is not pretended,) but until their rivals recede from it, — not until their necessities require, but until foreign nations permit! I am lost in astonishment, Mr. Chairman. I have not words to express the matchless absurdity of this attempt. I have no tongue to express the swift and headlong destruction which a blind perseverance in such a system must bring upon this nation.

. . . . .

"Mr. Chairman, other gentlemen must take their responsibilities, — I shall take mine. This Embargo must be repealed. You cannot enforce it for any important period of time longer. When I speak of your inability to enforce this law, let not gentlemen misunderstand me. I mean not to intimate insurrections or open defiances of them. Although it is impossible to foresee in what acts that 'oppression' will finally terminate which, we are told, "makes wise men mad." I speak of an inability resulting from very different causes.

"The gentleman from North Carolina (Mr. Macon) exclaimed the other day, in a strain of patriotic ardor, 'What! shall not our laws be executed? Shall their authority be defied? I am for enforcing them at every hazard.' I honor that gentleman's zeal; and I mean no deviation from that true respect I entertain for him, when I tell him, that in this instance 'his zeal is not according to knowledge.'

"I ask this House, is there no control to its authority? is there no limit to the power of this national legislature? I hope I shall offend no man when I intimate that two limits exist, — NATURE AND THE CONSTITUTION. Should this House undertake to declare that this atmosphere should no longer surround us, that water should cease to flow, that gravity should not hereafter operate, that the needle should not vibrate to the pole, I do suppose, Mr. Chairman, — Sir, I mean no disrespect to the authority of this House, I know the high notions some gentlemen entertain on this subject, — I do suppose — Sir, I hope I shall not offend — I think I may venture to affirm, that, such a law to the contrary notwithstanding, the air would continue to circulate, the Mississippi, the Hudson, and the Potomac would hurl their floods to the ocean, heavy bodies continue to descend, and the mysterious magnet hold on its course to its celestial cynosure.

"Just as utterly absurd and contrary to nature is it to attempt to prohibit the people of New England, for any considerable length of time, from the ocean. Commerce is not only associated with all the feelings, the habits, the interests and relations of that people, but the nature of our soil and of our coasts, the state of our population and its mode of distribution over our territory, render it indispensable. We have five hundred miles of sea-coast; all furnished with harbors, bays, creeks, rivers, inlets, basins, — with every variety of invitation to the sea, — with every species of facility to violate such laws as these. Our people are not scattered over an immense surface, at a solemn distance from each other, in lordly retirement, in the midst of extended plantations and intervening wastes. They are collected on the margin of the ocean, by the sides of rivers, at the heads of bays, looking into the water or on the surface of it for the incitement and the reward of their industry. Among a people thus situated, thus educated, thus numerous, laws prohibiting them from the exercise of their natural rights will have a binding effect not one moment longer than the public sentiment supports them.

. . . . .

"I ask in what page of the Constitution you find the power of laying an Embargo? Directly given it is nowhere. You have it, then, by construction, or by precedent. By construction of the power to regulate. I lay out of the question the commonplace argument, that regulation cannot mean annihilation; and that what is annihilated cannot be regulated. I ask this question, — Can a power be ever obtained by construction which had never been exercised at the time of the authority given, — the like of which had not only never been seen, but the idea of which had never entered into human imagination, I will not say in this country, but in the world? Yet such is this power, which by construction you assume to exercise. Never before did society witness a total prohibition of all intercourse like this in a commercial nation. Did the people of the United States invest this House with a power of which at the time of investment that people had not and could not have had any idea? For even in works of fiction it had never existed.

. . . . .

"But it has been asked in debate, 'Will not Massachusetts, the cradle of liberty, submit to such privations?' An Embargo liberty was never cradled in Massachusetts. Our liberty was not so much a mountain as a sea nymph. She was free as air. She could swim, or she could run. The ocean was her cradle. Our fathers met her as she came, like the goddess of beauty, from the waves. They caught her as she was sporting on the beach. They courted her whilst she was spreading her nets upon the rocks. But an Embargo liberty, a handcuffed liberty, a liberty in fetters, a liberty traversing between the four sides of a prison and beating her head against the walls, is none of our offspring. We abjure the monster. Its parentage is all inland.

"The gentleman from North Carolina (Mr. Macon) exclaimed the other day, 'Where is the spirit of '76?' Ay, Sir; where is it? Would to Heaven that at our invocation it would condescend to alight on this floor. But let gentlemen remember, that the spirit of '76 was not a spirit of empty declamation, or of abstract propositions. It did not content itself with non-importation acts, or non-intercourse laws. It was a spirit of active preparation, of dignified energy. It studied both to know our rights and to devise the effectual means of maintaining them. In all the annals of '76, you will find no such degrading doctrine as that maintained in this report. It never presented to the people of the United States the alternative of war or a suspension of our rights, and recommended the latter rather than to incur the risk of the former. What was the language of that period in one of the addresses of Congress to Great Britain? 'You attempt to reduce us by the sword to base and abject submission. On the sword, therefore, we rely for protection.' In that day there were no alternatives presented to dishearten, — no abandonment of our rights under the pretence of maintaining them, — no gaining the battle by running away. In the whole history of that period there are no such terms as '*Embargo, — dignified retirement, — trying who can do each other the most harm.*' At that time we had a navy, — that name so odious to the influences of the present day. Yes, sir, in 1776, though but in our infancy, we had a *navy scouring our coasts, and defending our commerce, which was never for one moment wholly suspended.* In 1776 we had an army also; and a glorious army it was! not composed of men halting from the stews, or swept from the jails, but of the best blood, the real yeomanry of the country, noble cavaliers, *men without fear and without reproach.* WE HAD SUCH AN ARMY IN 1776, AND WASHINGTON AT ITS HEAD. — WE HAVE AN ARMY IN 1808, AND A HEAD TO IT.

"I will not humiliate those who lead the fortunes of the nation at the present day by any comparison with the great men of that period. But I recommend the advocates of the present system of public measures to study well the true spirit of 1776, before they venture to call it in aid of their purposes. It may bring in its train some recollections not suited to give ease or hope to their bosoms. I beg gentlemen who are so frequent in their recurrence to that period to remember, that among the causes which led to a separation from Great Britain the following are enumerated: *unnecessary restrictions upon trade; cutting off commercial intercourse between the Colonies; embarrassing our fisheries; wantonly depriving our citizens of necessaries; invasion of private property by governmental edicts; the authority of the commander-in-chief, and under him of the brigadier-general, being rendered supreme in the civil government; the commander-in-chief of the army made governor of a Colony; citizens transferred from their native country for trial.* Let gentlemen beware how they appeal to the spirit of '76; lest it come with the aspect, not of a friend, but of a tormentor, — lest they find a warning when they look for support, and instead of encouragement they are presented with an awful lesson.

. . . . .

"Let me ask, *Is Embargo Independence?* Deceive not yourselves. It is palpable submission. Gentlemen exclaim, Great Britain 'smites us on one cheek.' And what does Administration? 'It turns the other also.' Gentlemen say, Great Britain is a robber, she '*takes our cloak.*' And what says Administration? '*Let her take our coat also.*' France and Great Britain require you to relinquish a part of your commerce, and you yield it entirely. Sir, this conduct may be the way to dignity and honor in another world, but it will never secure safety and independence in this.

"At every corner of this great city we meet some gentlemen of the majority, wringing their hands and exclaiming, 'What shall we do? Nothing but Embargo will save us. Remove it, and what shall we do?' Sir, it is not for me, an humble and uninfluential individual, at an awful distance from the predominant influences, to suggest plans of government. But to my eye the path of our duty is as distinct as the milky way, — all studded with living sapphires, glowing with cumulating light. It is the path of active preparation, of dignified energy. *It is the path of* 1776. It consists, not in abandoning our rights, but in supporting them, as they exist, and where they exist, — *on the ocean as well as on the land.* It consists in taking the nature of things as the measure of the rights of your citizens, not the orders and decrees of imperious foreigners. Give what protection you can. Take no counsel of fear. Your strength will increase with the trial, and prove greater than you are now aware.

"But I shall be told, 'This may lead to war.' I ask, '*Are we now at peace?*' Certainly not, unless retiring from insult be peace, — unless shrinking under the lash be peace. The surest way to prevent war is not to fear it. The idea that nothing on earth is so dreadful as war is inculcated too studiously among us. Disgrace is worse. Abandonment of essential rights is worse.

"Sir, I could not refrain from seizing the first opportunity of spreading before this House the sufferings and exigencies of New England under this Embargo. Some gentlemen may deem it not strictly before us. In my opinion it is necessarily. For, if the idea of the committee be correct, and *Embargo is resistance*, then this resolution sanctions its continuance. If, on the contrary, as I contend, *Embargo is submission*, then this resolution is a pledge of its repeal."

This speech made its author as well abused a man in Congress, and by the Democratic press, as was then extant. It had evidently drawn blood, and very bad blood. "You must expect," he wrote that day to his wife, "to hear that your husband has been abused and pecked at by the whole poultry-yard; but he keeps up his health and spirits, and means to repay them in time." The speech was immediately printed as a pamphlet in Boston, and the Democratic abuse which it received was answered by quite as warm Federal praise. The time to which he looked forward when he should repay his assailants arrived on the 7th of December, when he made his second speech on Foreign Relations, of which I subjoin a few extracts.

"When I had the honor of addressing this House, a few days ago, I touched this famous report of our Committee on Foreign Relations perhaps a little too carelessly. Perhaps I handled it a little too roughly, considering its tender age and the manifest delicacy of its constitution. But, Sir, I had no idea of affecting very exquisitely the sensibilities of any gentleman. I thought that this was a common report of one of our ordinary committees, which I had a right to canvass, or to slight, to applaud, or to censure, without raising any extraordinary concern, either here or elsewhere. But from the general excitement which my inconsiderate treatment of this subject occasions, I fear that I have been mistaken. This can be no mortal fabric, Mr. Speaker. *This must be that image which fell down from Jupiter,—present or future.* Surely, nothing but a being of *celestial origin* would raise such tumult in minds attempered like those which lead the destinies of this House.

"Sir, I thought that this report had been a common piece of wood,—

inutile lignum. Sir, just such a piece of wood as any day-laborer might have hewed out in an hour, had he health and a hatchet. But it seems that our honorable Chairman of the Committee of Foreign Relations *maluit esse Deum.* Well, Sir, I have no objections. If the workmen will, a God it shall be. I only wish, when gentlemen bring their sacred things upon this floor, that they would 'blow a trumpet before them, as the Heathens do' on such occasions, to the end that all true believers may prepare themselves to adore and tremble, and that all unbelievers may turn aside, and not disturb their devotions.

. . . . .

"The gentleman from Tennessee (Mr. Campbell) called upon us, just now, to tell him what was disgraceful submission, if carrying on commerce under these restrictions was not such submission. I will tell that gentleman. That submission is '*abject and disgraceful*' which yields to the decrees of frail and feeble power as though they were irresistible, — which takes counsel of fear, and weighs not our comparative force, — which abandons the whole, at a summons to deliver up a part, — which makes the will of others the measure of rights which God and Nature not only have constituted eternal and unalienable, but have also endued us with ample means to maintain.

"My argument on this clause of the report of the Committee may be presented in this form. Either the United States have, or they have not, physical ability to carry on commerce, in defiance of the edicts of both or of either of these nations. If we have not physical ability to carry on the trade which they prohibit, then it is no disgrace to exercise that commerce which these irresistible decrees permit. If we have such physical ability, then to the degree in which we abandon that commerce which we have power to carry on is our submission '*abject and disgraceful.*' It is yielding without struggle. It is sacrificing our rights, not because we have not force, but because we have not spirit, to maintain them. It is in this point of view that I am disgusted with this report. It abjures what it recommends. It declaims, in heroics, against submission, and proposes, in creeping prose, a tame and servile subserviency.

. . . . .

"But war is never to be incurred. If this be the national principle, avow it. — Tell your merchants you will not protect them. But for Heaven's sake do not deny them the power of relieving their own and the nation's burdens by the exercise of their own ingenuity. Sir, impassable as the barriers offered by these edicts are, in the estimation of members on this floor, the merchants abroad do not estimate them as insurmountable. Their anxiety to risk their property in defiance of them is full evidence of this. The great danger to mercantile ingenuity is internal envy, the corrosion of weakness, or prejudice. Its external hazard is ever infinitely smaller. That practical intelligence which this class of men possesses, beyond any other in the community, excited by self-interest, the strongest of human passions, is too elastic to be confined by the limits of exterior human powers, however great or uncommon. Build a Chinese wall: the wit of your merchants, if permitted freely to operate, will break through it, or overleap it, or undercreep it.

'Mille adde catenas,
Effugiet tamen hæc sceleratus vincula Proteus.'

The second branch of the alternative under consideration is equally deceptive. '*War with both nations.*' Can this ever be an alternative? Did you ever read in history, can you conceive in fancy, a war with two nations, each of whom is at war with the other, without a union with one against the other immediately resulting? It cannot exist in nature. The very idea is absurd. It never can be an alternative whether we shall fight two nations, each hostile to the other. But it may be, and, if we are to fight at all, it is, a very serious question, which of the two we are to select as an adversary."

. . . . .

"It was under these general impressions that I used the word *loathsome*, which has so often been repeated. Sir, it may not have been a well-chosen word. It was that which happened to come to hand first. I meant to express my disgust at what appeared to me a mass of bold assumptions, and of ill-cemented sophisms.

"I said, also, that '*the spirit which it breathed was disgraceful.*' Sir, I meant no reflection upon the Committee. Honest men and wise men may mistake the character of the spirit which they recommend, or by which they are actuated. When called upon to reason concerning that which, by adoption, is to become identified with the national character, I am bound to speak of it as it appears to my vision. I may be mistaken. Yet I ask the question, Is not the spirit which it breathes disgraceful? Is it not disgraceful to abandon the exercise of all our commercial rights, because our rivals interfere with a part; not only to refrain from exercising that trade which they prohibit, but, for fear of giving offence, to decline that which they permit? Is it not disgraceful, after inflammatory recapitulation of insults, and plunderings, and burnings, and confiscations, and murders, and actual war made upon us, to talk of nothing but alternatives, of general declarations, of still longer suspension of our rights and retreating farther out of 'harm's way'? If this course be adopted by my country, I hope I am in error concerning its real character. But to my sense this whole report is nothing else than a recommendation to us of the abandonment of our essential rights, and apologies for doing it.

. . . . .

'An honorable gentleman (Mr. Troup of Georgia) was also pleased to speak of '*a paltry trade in potash and codfish*,' and to refer to me as the representative of men who raised '*beef and pork, and butter and cheese, and potatoes and cabbages*.' Well, Sir, I confess the fact. I am the representative, in part, of men the products of whose industry are beef and pork, and butter and cheese, and potatoes and cabbages. And let me tell that honorable gentleman, that I would not yield the honor of representing such men to be the representative of all the growers of cotton, and rice, and tobacco, and indigo, in the whole world. Sir, the men whom I represent not only raise these humble articles, *but* they do it *with the labor of their own hands*, — *with the sweat of their own brows*. And by this their habitual mode of hardy industry, they acquire a vigor of nerve, a strength of muscle, and a spirit and intelligence somewhat characteristic. And let me assure that honorable gentleman, that the men of whom I speak will not, at his call, nor at the invitation of any set of men from his quarter of the Union, undertake to '*drive one another into the ocean*.' But, on the contrary, whenever they once realize that their rights are invaded, they will unite, like a band of brothers, and drive their enemies there.

. . . . .

"Can any nation admit that the trade of another is so important to her welfare as that, on its being withdrawn, any obnoxious policy must be abandoned, without at the same time admitting that she is no longer independent? Sir, I could indeed wish that it were in our power to regulate, not only Great Britain, but the whole world, by opening or closing our ports. It would be a glorious thing for our country to possess such a mighty weapon of offence. But, acting in a public capacity, with the high responsibilities resulting from the great interests dependent upon my decision, I cannot yield to the wishes of love-sick patriots, or the visions of teeming enthusiasts. I must see the adequacy of means to their ends. I must see, not merely that it is very desirable that Great Britain should be brought to our feet by this Embargo, but that there is some likelihood of such a consequence to the measure, before I can concur in that universal distress and ruin which, if much longer continued, will inevitably result from it. Since, then, every dictate of sense and reflection convinces me of the utter futility of this system as a means of coercion on Great Britain, I shall not hesitate to urge its abandonment. No, Sir, not even although, like others, I should be assailed by all the terrors of the outcry of British influence.

"Really, Mr. Speaker, I know not how to express the shame and disgust with which I am filled when I hear language of this kind cast out upon this floor, and thrown in the faces of men standing justly at no mean height in the confidence of their countrymen. Sir, I did, indeed, know that such vulgar aspersions were circulating among the lower passions of our nature. I knew that such vile substances were ever tempering between the paws of some printer's devil. I knew that foul exhalations like these daily rose in our cities, and crept along the ground, just as high as the spirits of lampblack and saline oil could elevate; falling soon, by native baseness, into oblivion. I knew, too, that this species of party insinuation was a mighty engine, in this quarter of the country, on an election day, played off from the top of a stump or the top of a hogshead, while the gin circulated, while the barbecue was roasting; in those happy, fraternal associations and consociations when those who speak utter without responsibility, and those who listen hear without scrutiny. But little did I think, that such odious shapes would dare to obtrude themselves on this national floor among honorable men, — the select representatives, the confidential agents, of a wise, a thoughtful, and a virtuous people. I want language to express my contempt and indignation at the sight.

"So far as respects the attempt which has been made to cast such aspersion on that part of the country which I have the honor to represent, I beg this honorable House to understand, that so long as they who circulated such insinuations deal only in generals, and touch not particulars, they may gain, among the ignorant and the stupid, a vacant and a staring audience. But when once these suggestions are brought to bear upon those individuals who, in New England, have naturally the confidence of their countrymen, there is no power in these calumnies. The men who now lead the influences of that country, and in whose counsels the people, on the day when the tempest shall come, will seek refuge, are men whose stake is in the soil, whose interests are identified with those of the mass of their brethren, whose private lives and public sacrifices present a never-failing antidote to the poison of malicious invectives. On such men, sir, party spirit may indeed cast its odious filth, but there is a polish in their virtues to which no such slime can adhere. They are owners of the soil, — real yeomanry, — many of them men who led in the councils of our country in the dark day which preceded national independence; many of them men who, like my honorable friend from Connecticut, on my left, (Colonel Tallmadge,) stood foremost on the perilous edge of battle, making their breasts, in the day of danger, a bulwark for their country."

Mr. Quincy wrote to his wife as follows on the subject of this speech: —

"*December* 17, 1808. — You will before this perceive that I have thrown off certain shackles of other men's opinions, and, instead of lying still all the session, have taken the responsibility of an early display of my standard. The consequence has been that I have been the object of attack to every one who has spoken, and with not a single Federal aid. (This is *entre nous.*) However, this was so much the better. I made to-day my retort courteous. You will see I have been handled a little roughly, and that I handle not gently in return. . . . . I was a little provoked at the scandalous trick of the editor of the National Intelligencer, who published what he reported as my speech so as to make it absolute nonsense, in order to publish a speech of Ezekiel Bacon, my colleague from Massachusetts, in the same paper, written out and corrected from the printer's report, with alterations and amendments by the author. This was a common trick to give temporary elevation to one speaker, and depression to an obnoxious adversary. My provocation caused me to give more than ordinary asperity to my reply. . . . . I see that the Repertory suggests that Campbell will try to pick a quarrel with any man who finds fault with his report; and, as I have scorched it pretty severely, you may be uneasy. But you know my principles and my sense of duty. Those duties I owe to God, to you, and to my children, will never fail to be always the predominant active principles in my mind, not less than those I owe my country. You will find me on trial possessing *real* courage, not that *bastard* kind which is here fashionable.

"Health, peace of mind, and, after my exertions, an humble conviction of not having disgraced myself, were never more entirely mine. The question and the crisis fill my thoughts, and strength and courage come without bidding. Lloyd enters into my feelings, encourages and supports me. He is an excellent fellow. . . . . I do not believe I shall have many such attacks hereafter from Bacon* & Co. My object in

* Ezekiel Bacon graduated at Yale College in 1794. By the Triennial Catalogue of 1865 he appears to have been still living at that time, and the oldest living graduate. He was a member of Congress, 1807 - 1813, and First Comptroller of the United States Treasury, 1813 - 1815.

my second speech was to show them I did not fear a little *cut and thrust, legislatively,* on the national floor. Ten days have passed, and not a member has replied to my speech. Gardenier came out pretty strongly, and the storm beats upon him, and I have only now and then a brush of the whirlwind. However, in its greatest rage it never *lifted a hair.* . . . . I received a very kind letter from Ex-President Adams to-day, in the style of a friend and a father."

The following is the letter from Mr. Adams, to which I have already referred in this chapter, of which my father speaks. This letter of Mr. Adams, and all the others contained in this volume, are now published for the first time, excepting in a few cases where credit is given to the printed collection of his works.

Mr. Adams to Mr. Quincy.

"Quincy, Dec. 23, 1808.

"Dear Sir: — I thank you for all the fine speeches you send me, and especially for that of Mr. Lloyd and the letter of the 14th enclosed with it. The speech is a chaste, neat composition, very sensible, candid, frank, and manly. I conclude with him, 'remove the Embargo, authorize the merchants to arm their vessels, put the nation in a state of defence, and assert your well-established and indisputable rights, or perish in the contest.' I admire his candor in declaring, 'It would be preferable to have war with France rather than with Great Britain'; though I think it unnecessary, and perhaps imprudent, to declare my opinion either way. If we assert our indisputable right, and arm our merchants, it will soon be left to France and England to determine which of them shall declare war against us. We are not as yet obliged to declare war against both or either. Perhaps we never shall be. We may make a maritime war as large as may be necessary without any declaration. I wish your modesty would have permitted you to send me your own speech, which I have read with pleasure. It deserves as handsome a dress as any of them, which our Boston papers have not given it.

"It would be strange if I did not approve the policy of 1798. I hope you will adopt some variations in the details, and, particularly, — 1. I hope you will not tease the President to appoint a commander-in-chief of the army, whose transcendent popularity can blast the most deliberate and judicious decisions of the President, and defeat the authority given him by the Constitution. 2. I hope you will agree to no eight-per-cent loan. 3. I am sorry you have already imitated and exceeded the policy of 1798 in raising so large an army. 4. I see no use of the 100,000 select militia. A million of cavalry could not save one ship at sea from the most contemptible pirate. The resources of the country ought at present to be appropriated to the sea.

"Our Massachusetts Legislature and our Dedham and Topsfield caucuses have adopted and hazarded some assertions that I regret, because I think they cannot be supported. But I am fully convinced that the Embargo must be removed. It will be extremely difficult, if not absolutely impossible, to carry it into execution. Insurrections, rebellions, and divisions of the Union will not be encouraged in New England so easily as they twice were in Pennsylvania; but to carry such laws into effect against the universal bent of a whole people, would require armies and navies sufficient to carry on a foreign war.

"The nation must be brought to a conviction of the necessity of bearing taxes for their defence.

"It is astonishing to consider the tenacious hold with which prejudices and errors grapple whole nations. Our American people have entertained for forty years an opinion of the vast and essential importance of their commerce to the commerce, manufactures, resources, and naval power of other nations, especially Great Britain. It has been the opinion, the public opinion — not indeed the universal opinion, but the general sense — of all the States and all the Colonies. I have never believed that we could coerce or intimidate, or bring to serious consideration, the government of Great Britain by embargoes, or non-importations, or non-intercourses. Yet I have consented to embargoes and non-importations, because the public opinion, the national sense, imperiously demanded them. In 1774 it was the almost unanimous opinion of Congress that we should obtain a complete redress of all grievances by our non-importation agreement. Gentlemen from all the States produced their documents and calculations to demonstrate the vast amount of our commerce with England, and its close connection with every branch of their prosperity. I voted very cheerfully with them, though I expected no redress of grievances from their measures. I said one evening to the 'greatest orator that ever spoke,' as Mr. Randolph calls him: 'I have agreed to all these petitions, addresses, letters, non-importation agreements, etc., but I consider them all to no other purpose but to unite our people. I expect no redress, but, on the contrary, increased resentment and double vengeance. We must fight.' 'By God,' said Patrick, 'I am of your opinion.' I afterwards showed him a letter from Major Hawley* to me, which he called

* A brief characterization by Mr. Adams of Joseph Hawley will be found in Chapter XV.

broken hints of what he thought we ought to do, in which he said, 'We must come to fighting.' 'By God,' said Henry, again, 'I am of that man's mind.' But I never knew another member of that Congress express a doubt of the efficacy of our measures at the next meeting of Parliament.

"In 1793 or 1794, Mr. Madison carried in the House, and sent up to the Senate, resolutions against the importation of various articles. The Senate was equally divided, and I determined against them. I have been always sorry when any such measures have been proposed, because I know they will produce nothing but anger. The nation, however, has been like all other nations. Experience has been lost upon them, and they must and will have such measures still. Fight we must at last, and we shall be ill advised, I think, if we fight until we are compelled to it, and then only by sea, unless we are invaded.

'If the Embargo is lifted, of what consequence will be the non-intercourse? Britain will obtain everything she wants from us in the places with which we trade, say the Spanish dominions in America, or Europe, or Gottenburg, or any other place.

"If the shackles continue on our commerce, they will produce an animosity and a rancor which will give much uneasiness to Mr. Jefferson's successor, and be very prejudicial to the public service, as well as ruinous to the morals, interests, and habits of obedience of the people. The Federal party will increase daily. That, you will say, will be a blessing, but it may be obtained at too dear a rate.

"I am sincerely yours,

"J. ADAMS.

"Mrs. Adams presents her regards to Mr. Quincy."

Looking back to this time late in life, my father says: "The period was critical. Violence appeared at the elections and on the floor of Congress. The language of the Southern leaders was systematically such as to proffer, according to Southern notions, the alternative of disgrace or a duel. I had, however, in addition to an approving conscience, the open and active support of my friends." The following letter from Mr. Harrison Gray Otis is one of the many he received at this time from his personal and political friends. Besides its intrinsic interest, it is curious as containing the first suggestion that I remember to have seen of the Hartford Convention.

MR. H. G. OTIS TO MR. QUINCY.

"BOSTON, Dec. 15, 1808.

"MY DEAR SIR: — Your friends are highly flattered and edified by the honorable and zealous exertion of talent which you have displayed in the defence of the interests of your country. Your several speeches, in connection with those of our Senatorial friends, have left nothing to be said or wished for; and though the Federal phalanx is deplorably small, it combines all the variety of force, eloquence, and argument necessary for the contest, and sufficient to overwhelm all opposition that is not defended by the impenetrable mail of ignorance and impudence. Judging from appearances, there seems but little prospect of your preventing by any means a perseverance in the fatal and unheard-of policy on which the Administration seems fully bent, and it becomes of great importance that the New England Federalists should determine whether any aid can be furnished by the Legislatures of this session, and if beneficial effects are to be expected from this quarter, the objects should be defined and the means concerted. Our General Court will soon meet, and I doubt not the majority will require the bridle rather than the spur. If I am not mistaken, there will be found among them a fulness of zeal and indignation which can be mitigated only by giving them a direction and an object. This temper, you are sensible, must not be extinguished for want of sympathy, nor permitted to burst forth into imprudent excess. We must look to our friends in Congress for advice. You are together, and can best decide on such a course as would probably be agreed to by Connecticut, New Hampshire, etc., and no other ought to be adopted.

"You are sensible how obnoxious Massachusetts, for a thousand reasons, has already become, and perceive more plainly than any of us the efforts which are made to mark and distinguish this State as the hot-bed of opposition, and this town as the citadel of a British faction. Perhaps our Legislature have said as much as is expedient for them to say, unless they are to be supported by a correspondent spirit in the other States. It would be a great misfortune for us to justify the obloquy of wishing to promote a separation of the States, and of being solitary in that pursuit. The delusion would spread among our wavering or timid adherents, and furnish great means of annoyance to our inveterate adversaries. It would change the next election, and secure the triumph of the dominant party. On the other hand, to do nothing will expose us to danger and contempt, our resolutions will seem to be a flash in the pan, and our apostate representatives will be justified in the opinions which they have doubtless inculcated of our want of union and of nerve. What then shall we do? In other words, what can Connecticut do? For we can and will come up to her tone. Is she ready to declare the Embargo and its supplementary chains unconstitutional, — to propose to their State the appointment of delegates to meet those from the other commercial States in convention at Hartford or elsewhere, for the purpose of providing some mode of relief that may not be *inconsistent with the union of these States*, to which we should adhere as long as possible? Shall New York be invited to join? and what shall be the proposed objects of such a convention?

"It is my opinion, if the session of Congress terminates as we have reason to expect, that recourse ought to be had to some such plan as this, and that the only alternative is, in *your* dialect, submission. But some other State ought to make the proposal, for obvious reasons. Will you, my good sir, talk over this subject with our little Spartan band, and favor me in season with the result of your collected wisdom? Let me know whether you think any good effect would be produced *in Congress* by hints of this kind in the public papers. Sometimes I fear that we are so neutralized by our accursed adversaries, that all efforts will be ineffectual, and that we must sit down quietly and count the links of our chains; but then again their system appears so monstrous, so unprecedented, so ruinous, that I think the time will come that must make resistance a duty.

"Remember me with respectful regards to my friend, Mr. Lloyd, and believe me very truly, dear sir, your obedient servant and friend,

"H. G. Otis."

CHAPTER VIII.

1808 - 1809.

Speech on the Bill for Fifty Thousand Volunteers. — Virulent Democratic Attacks. — The Duel at that Time. — Mr. Quincy's Views touching it. — Correspondence with Eppes. — The Four Frigates. — Speech on the Extra Session. — Renewed Virulence. — "Impeachment of Mr. Jefferson." — Repeal of the Embargo and Substitution of Non-Intercourse. — Discomforts of Washington Life. — His Congressional Friends. — South Carolina Correspondence. — The Extra Session. — President and Mrs. Madison. — Visit to Mount Vernon.

IF Mr. Quincy really flattered himself that he had silenced his Democratic antagonists by his speech of December 7th, he was soon undeceived. The quiet of which he spoke in his letter to his wife of the 17th was but the lull between two storms. Towards the close of the year a bill was introduced into the House for raising fifty thousand volunteers. This proposition caused an excited discussion between the contending parties. The argument of the Administration was, that the nation should be preparing itself for the alternative of war, in case the Embargo was not effectual in bringing the belligerent powers to reason. The Opposition maintained that the precise object of the force should be known before it was voted. If it were intended for national defence, — if the Administration proposed to repeal the Embargo, and go to war, — they were ready to vote for it. If it were intended as a means of enforcing that act, they should resist it with all their might. Mr. Quincy, in his speech of December 30th, argued that the Embargo was unconstitutional, — not merely because the power to regulate commerce could not have been intended to give Congress the power to destroy it, but especially because that power could not be construed to authorize interference with the trade, not merely of the different States, but of the different parts of the same State, with one another. It is unnecessary to recapitulate his arguments, but his arraignment of the majority in Congress for having surrendered the commerce of the country into the hands of the Executive was stern and severe. Even a repeal of the Embargo by the unanimous vote of the House would be inoperative against a veto sustained by twelve Senators, — the full Senate then consisting of thirty-two members. He said: —

"Yes, Sir, we once had a commerce. Once this House possessed the power to regulate it. Of all the grants in the Constitution, perhaps this was the most highly prized by the people. It was truly the apple of their eye. To their concern for it the Constitution almost owes its existence. They brought this, the object of their choice affections, and delivered it to the custody of this House, as a tender parent would deliver the hope of his declining years, with a trembling solicitude, to its selected guardians. And how have we conducted in this sacred trust? Why, we have delivered it over to the care of twelve dry-nurses, concerning whose tempers we know nothing, for whose intentions we cannot vouch, and who, for anything we know, may some of them have an interest in destroying it.

"Yes, Sir, the people did intrust us with that great power, — the regulation of commerce. It was their most precious jewel, richer than all the mines of Peru and Golconda. But we have sported with it as though it were common dust. With a thoughtless indifference, in the dead of night, we surrendered this rich deposit. It is gone; and we have nothing else to do than to beg back, at the footstool of the Executive, the people's patrimony. Sir, I know the answer which will, and it is the only one that can, be given, — 'There is no fear of an improper use of this power by the President and Senate, — there is no danger in trusting this most excellent man.' Why, sir, this is the very slave's gibberish! What other reason could the cross-legged Turk or the cringing Parisian give for that implicit confidence they yield their sovereigns, except that it is impossible that they should abuse their power?"

These strictures caused a great stir on the Democratic side of the House. Extreme impatience was manifested, and frequent interruptions were made, chiefly by members from Virginia, — Mr. Eppes, the son-in-law of Mr. Jefferson, Mr. Nicholas, and Mr. Jackson.* Great violence of language and gross personali-

* John W. Eppes was Representative and Senator from Virginia, with two

ties were used towards him, much worse than one would infer from the printed debates. The Speaker, however, was fair, and overruled all attempts to call him to order, and he finished his speech. His friends apprehended that an attempt might be made to dispose of him by the way of a duel, or in some more irregular way. The next day he wrote to his wife: —

"Do not be alarmed at any harshness the papers may convey to you. I shall live down calumnies; and as to *tongue fighting*, if any one has a longer weapon or a sharper, I must be content to contend at a disadvantage.

. . . . .

"*January* 10. — Lloyd showed me a letter from Boston stating that I had fallen in a duel with Campbell. It had not the most remote foundation! I am, as I believe, on good terms with every member of the House. Some hate me a little, but treat me very well. Old Hillhouse has desired me to tell you never to believe such a report until you had it under his hand. On such occasions he was to be my second; and he always fought from behind a tree with a tomahawk."

This piece of pleasantry on the part of Mr. Hillhouse,* then Senator from Connecticut, alludes to a supposed resemblance which he bore in his personal appearance to the Indian race. He used to affirm, jocosely, that he had aboriginal blood in his veins, and that he could strike straight across country to his end, literally, as he certainly did metaphorically, with the instinct of his tribe. The story goes that he was once challenged, and agreed to accept on condition that he was to be allowed his hereditary privilege of *a tree!*

The duel was at that time still regarded as the *ultima ratio* for the settlement of political quarrels and private grievances, on

intervals of two years each, from 1803 to 1819; died, 1823. Wilson C. Nicholas was Senator from 1799 to 1804; Representative from 1807 to 1809; Governor from 1814 to 1817; died, 1820. John G. Jackson was Representative from 1795 to 1797, from 1799 to 1810, and from 1813 to 1817.

* James Hillhouse was born, 1754; graduated at Yale College, 1773; served in the Revolutionary War; Representative from 1791 to 1794; Senator from 1794 to 1810. He resigned to take charge of the School Fund of Connecticut, which he managed with great success. He was Treasurer of Yale College for fifty years, up to his death in 1832.

both sides the Atlantic. It was hardly ten years since Pitt fought with Tierney, and it was but a little later that Canning fought with Castlereagh, and it was twenty years afterwards that the Duke of Wellington's duel with Lord Winchilsea took place, about the same time with that between Mr. Clay and Mr. Randolph.* The duel was recognized, as far north as New York, as the necessary complement of the deficiencies of the law for redress in certain extremities. Duels were not uncommon in the neighborhood of New York, and the parties were seldom if ever molested because of them. The apparent exception in the case of Burr was owing rather to partisan feelings, and to the belief on the part of great numbers that the duel was a preconcerted plot to put Hamilton out of the way, than to any moral objection to the manner of his taking off. And Burr took his place in the chair of the Senate at the next session without pursuit, and ultimately returned to live out the rest of his life in New York. Even in New England, where the practice of duelling was so sternly condemned, there never was an instance, I believe, of one engaged in any of the few duels occurring there being pursued to punishment. The world had not yet outgrown that relic of barbarism, and the custom had not then been put so effectually under the ban of ridicule as in later times. My father took the ground, from the very beginning of his Congressional life, that he would neither be provoked into sending a challenge, nor shamed into accepting one. The moral and religious grounds on which this determination rested have been already stated in

* Two or three curious analogies between these last two almost contemporaneous duels were noted at the time. The Duke of Wellington was Prime Minister of England; Mr. Clay was Secretary of State, the post the most nearly approaching that position under our form of government. Lord Winchilsea was a member of the Upper House of Parliament; Mr. Randolph, of the Senate of the United States. Lord Winchilsea was numbered among the straiter sect, or Evangelical wing of the Church of England, if indeed he were not a Dissenter, and was prominent at the meetings of Bible Societies, Missionary Societies, and the like; Mr. Randolph had also become, a few years before, what is commonly called "a religious man." Neither of them, however, had the moral courage to stand by their religious convictions when these came in collision with the world's code of honor, and neither, it is but just to the religious public to say, ever recovered the *prestige* they thus forfeited.

a letter to my mother in a previous chapter. In his private conversation with the class of persons who would be likely to call him into the field, he did not dwell particularly on these considerations, which would probably be quite thrown away upon them. He would say to them: "We do not stand upon equal grounds in this matter. If we fight, and you kill me, it is a feather in your cap, and your constituents will think all the better of you for it. If I should kill you, it would ruin me with mine, and they never would send me to Congress again." This reasoning they could comprehend, and the consequence was, that he never was challenged, though it was very currently reported that he had been, with imaginary details. And he always said that he owed his strength and independence in the House largely to this well-known resolution of his. Many of the prominent Federalists did not take this ground, but professed their readiness to accept an appeal to "the tribunal of twelve paces," when duly made, and consequently were very cautious as to what they said that might provoke one. Not that they were any more afraid of taking the chance of a pistol-shot than their Democratic opposites, but they did fear the rebuke and condemnation which they would be sure to encounter at home in such case. Hence they lacked somewhat of that perfect freedom of speech which my father exercised. And I must do him the justice to say that, strong as was the language, fierce the invective, and bitter the sarcasm, with which he assailed the Democratic Administration and their measures, his speeches are remarkably free from personal reflections and attacks on individuals, such as should demand bloody satisfaction according to the strictest construction of the canons of the law of honor. His antagonists gave him ample occasion to call them to account for their personal abuse of himself, carefully prepared with that design; but I think, though he sometimes came pretty near the wind, he always avoided such personalities as were held to make a hostile meeting inevitable among fighting men. And this may be one reason why he was never summoned to one.

The following correspondence shows the readiness and the ingenuity with which the partisans of Mr. Jefferson sought to fasten a quarrel upon one who had attacked his policy with freedom and effect. To show the slight grounds of the offence which Mr. Eppes was anxious to find, I will quote the whole passage which contains it. Mr. Quincy had stated that language to the following effect had been used out of the House by the friends of the Embargo. "It is a measure of the Executive. Suppose this House should repeal it, and he negative the repeal, what effect would result but to show distracted counsels? In the present situation of the country nothing is so desirable as unanimity." Mr. Jackson called for names. Mr. Nicholas angrily denounced the statement as an attempt "to palm upon those with whom he acted opinions which all must disclaim." Mr. Quincy went on: —

"I have no intention to palm upon any gentleman sentiments which they disavow. I did not suppose that the gentlemen who entertained such sentiments would disavow them. I certainly shall not mention names. I do not think the argument derives any strength from the fact that such expressions have been used by any gentleman. They are natural and inevitable from the situation in which gentlemen are placed in relation to the Executive. Men willing to take off the Embargo, yet not willing to counteract the system of the President, are forced to adopt such reasoning as this. It is unavoidable when they come to reflect upon the powers which remain to this House in relation to the repeal of this law."

This correspondence is dated on the day the debate appeared in the "National Intelligencer."

Mr. Eppes to Mr. Quincy.

"Washington, January 11th, 1809.

"Sir: — I certainly did not understand from what I heard of your speech the other day, that it was your intention to insinuate that I was one of those disposed to support the Embargo merely because it was an Executive measure.

"The following sentiment is printed in your speech: 'They are natural and inevitable from the situation in which gentlemen are placed in relation to the Executive.'

"If, sir, you believe that in my public conduct I am influenced by my connection with the Executive, it is proper that I should know it. If a plume is to decorate your cap at the expense of my independence, let the sentiment be openly avowed.

"I call upon you, therefore, to say whether I am to consider the words I have quoted as intended by you to be applied to me.

"I am, sir, your most obedient,

"JNO. W. EPPES.

"HON. Mr. QUINCY, House of Representatives."

MR. QUINCY TO MR. EPPES.

"HOUSE OF REPRESENTATIVES, WASHINGTON CITY, 11 January, 1809.

"SIR:—If a construction such as you intimate has been given to the expressions you quote, it is a justice I owe to myself to assure you that in using them I intended no individual application. The idea I meant to convey had nothing personal, but was altogether general. It was this,—that such arguments were 'natural and inevitable from the situation in which gentlemen are placed in relation to the Executive,' in consequence of their having passed such a law; and it was intended to apply to 'men willing to take off the Embargo, yet not willing to counteract the system of the President.' This was the only bearing of my mind. Your particular relation to the Executive, until your letter was received, did not, in connection with this subject, once come within the scope of my thoughts.

"I hope never to be necessitated, *in my public station, to resort to personalities.* But when, if ever, my duty shall require it, you may be assured there will be nothing obscure or doubtful in my use of them.

"I am, sir, your most obedient servant,

"JOSIAH QUINCY.

"HON. JOHN W. EPPES."

The suspicions which the Opposition had conceived that this extraordinary levy of fifty thousand volunteers was designed for the more stringent execution of the Embargo, rather than for defence against foreign enemies, was confirmed by the bill sent down from the Senate for enforcing the act, and empowering the President to employ any portion of the land or naval forces or the militia for that purpose. The bill for the volunteers was suffered to drop in the House, but that for enforcing the Embargo was passed by a strong party vote on the morning of the 6th of January, after a session of nineteen hours. Mr. Quincy and Mr. Gardenier, at six o'clock in the morning, after a night session, urged the delay of one day, declaring their wish to speak on the subject, and their inability to do so at that time through pure bodily exhaustion. But their request was denied, and the bill passed. But although the will of the President was sufficient to carry this point, he was soon made to feel that the sceptre was about to pass from him. At the election of the previous November, Mr. Madison was chosen President, and the days of Mr. Jefferson's public life were numbered. A relaxation of discipline was manifest in the ranks of his party, and his will was not now always law. If his saving soul dreaded one expense more than another, it was that of the equipment of ships of war. He shared, if he did not originate, the antipathy which the slaveholding States always manifested, but especially in the earlier days of our history, to a naval establishment, — arising, doubtless, from their jealousy of the commercial States, for whose benefit they conceived that a navy was particularly designed. The first open breach in the Democratic ranks was on a bill for arming and manning four frigates, to be stationed near such ports, or to cruise off such parts of the coast as the President might direct. It seems odd to us, accustomed to hear of a navy of hundreds of vessels, and of millions of money cheerfully given to sustain it, to read of the violent debate which followed this proposition, and that for appropriating four hundred thousand dollars to carry it out. Mr. Campbell of Tennessee, the Administration leader in the House, Mr. Eppes of Virginia, Mr. Macon, and the Southern members generally, strongly opposed the measure. Mr. Williams of South Carolina said that, if the assertion of its friends was true, that we should never regain our rights without these frigates, he was ready to abandon them. That at the end of the Revolutionary war we had but one frigate, and the best thing we ever did was to give that one away. The State of South Carolina had fitted out a frigate in that war, and she had not yet rid herself of the debt thus incurred. Notwithstanding the opposition of the Administration, the frigates were voted, sixty-four to fifty-nine, to the great annoyance of Mr. Jefferson, on whom this action was regarded as a virtual vote of censure. Mr. Williams declared that he would willingly give up all his earthly goods if that vote could be recalled, for he valued property and life less than the liberties of his country, which he believed would be destroyed in consequence of that vote! However, the House refused to recommit the bill, and it became a law by Mr. Jefferson's signature.

Mr. Quincy wrote to his wife as follows, at the time of this unexpected success: —

"*February* 12, 1809. — We had the tightest voting I ever knew on a bill from the Senate for fitting out all the frigates. The question in favor was carried, 64 to 59. The result was astonishing to Campbell and the leaders of the Palace troops. They moved a recommitment of the bill, for further discussion, which after a day's debate was lost, 58 to 59. So the frigates are to be fitted out. There will be a new attempt to change the decision. The event is terrible to Jefferson, as the law obliges him to do it. There is a palpable division between the friends of the present and future President. Cutts, Jackson, Bacon, &c. in favor of the equipment; Eppes, Taylor, &c. against it. The battle rages between the old allies. Some of my political friends interfered a little. I not at all, — from reasons personal and political."

The next occasion which Mr. Quincy had of attacking the Embargo fell upon the 19th of January, on a bill for an extra session of Congress, to be held in May instead of December. This measure he opposed, as a mere sop to quiet the excitement of the people under their distress by raising the hope that the Embargo would then be taken off. His argument was, that this hope should not be held out unless a definite limit should be first fixed when the Embargo, now indeterminate in its duration, should expire, so as to restore the control of the question to Congress, and to the public sentiment of the nation acting upon Congress. The hope which the extra session held out he affirmed to be a false one, intended to deceive the people. He charged the Administration with duplicity in assuring the British government "that the Embargo was 'a measure of precaution only,' while alleging to the American people that it was a measure of coercion, which, if persisted in vigorously, would reduce Great Britain to our terms." And he taunted them with vaporing about the alternative of war, when they had no intention of resorting to it in any extremity, and when they were ridiculously unprepared for it. The following are some extracts from this speech, which made a great noise and a great impression at the time:—

"It is very painful to me, Mr. Speaker, to be compelled to place my opposition to this bill on ground resulting from the conduct of the Administration of this nation. I say, Sir, this is very painful to me, because I have no personal animosity to any individual of that Administration. Nor, if I know myself, am I induced to this opposition from any party motive. But, Sir, acting in a public capacity, and reasoning concerning events as they occur, with reference to the high duties of my station, I shall not, when I arrive in my conception at a just conclusion, shrink from any proper responsibility in spreading that conclusion before this House and nation. One thing I shall hope and certainly shall deserve from the friends of Administration,—the acknowledgment that I shall aim no insidious blow. It shall be made openly, distinctly, in the daylight. Be it strong, or be it weak, I invite those friends to parry it. If they are successful, I shall rejoice in it not less than they.

. . . . .

"The proposition which I undertake to maintain consists of three particulars. First. That it was, and is, the intention of Administration to coerce Great Britain by the Embargo, and that this, and not precaution, is and was the principal object of the policy. Second. That it was and is intended to persevere in this measure until it effect, if possible, the proposed object. Third. That it was and is the intention of Administration to do nothing else effectual in support of our maritime rights.

. . . . .

"I come now to my third position. Not only that Embargo was resorted to as a means of coercion; but that from the first it was never intended by Administration to do anything else effectual for the support of our maritime rights. Sir, I am sick, sick to loathing, of this eternal clamor of 'War, war, war!' which has been kept up almost incessantly on this floor now for more than two years. Sir, if I can help it, the old women of this country shall not be frightened in this way any longer. I have been a long time a close observer of what has been done and said by the majority of this House, and, for one, I am satisfied that no insult, however gross, offered to us by either France or Great Britain could force this majority into the declaration of war. To use a strong but common expression, it could not be kicked into such a declaration by either nation. Letters are read from the British Minister. Passions are excited by his sarcasms. Men get up and recapitulate insults. They rise and exclaim, 'Perfidy!' 'Robbery!' 'Falsehood!' 'Murder!'

'Unpacking hearts with words, and fall a cursing, like a very drab, a scullion.'

"Sir, is this the way to maintain national honor or dignity? Is it the way to respect abroad or at home? Is the perpetual recapitulation of wrongs the ready path to redress, or even the means to keep alive a just sense of them in our minds? Are those sensibilities likely to remain for a long time very keen which are kept constantly under the lash of the tongue?

. . . . .

"Again, Sir, you talk of going to war against Great Britain, with, I believe, only one frigate and five sloops of war in commission! And yet you have not the resolution to meet the expense of the paltry little navy which is rotting in the Potomac. Already we have heard it rung on this floor, that if we fit out that little navy our treasury will be emptied. If you had ever a serious intention of going to war, would you have frittered down the resources of this nation in the manner we witness? You go to war, with all the revenue to be derived from commerce annihilated, and possessing no other resource than loans, or direct or other internal taxes! You! a party that rose into power by declaiming against direct taxes and loans! Do you hope to make the people of this country, much more foreign nations, believe that such is your intention, when you have reduced your revenue to such a condition?

. . . . .

"But we are about to raise an army of fifty thousand volunteers. For what purpose? I have heard gentlemen say, 'We can invade Canada.' But, Sir, does not all the world, as well as you, know that Great Britain holds, as it were, a pledge for Canada, — and one sufficient to induce you to refrain from such a project, when you begin seriously to weigh all the consequences of such invasion? I mean that pledge which results from the defenceless state of your seaport towns. For what purpose would you attack Canada? For territory? No; you have enough of that. Do you want citizen refugees? No; you would be willing to dispense with them. Do you want plunder? This is the only hope an invasion of Canada can offer you. And is it not very doubtful whether Great Britain could not, in one month, destroy more property on your sea-board than you can acquire by the most successful invasion of that province? Sir, in this state of things,

I cannot hear such perpetual outcries about war without declaring my opinion concerning them.

"When I say, Sir, that this Administration could not be induced into a war, I mean by its own self-motion. War may — I will not assert that it will not — come. But such a state Administration do not contemplate, nor are they prepared for it. On the contrary, I do believe that the very tendency of all imbecile measures is to bring on the very event their advisers deprecate. Well did the gentleman from Georgia (Mr. Troup) warn you, the other day, not to get into war. He told you it was the design of the Federalists to lead you into that state, in order that they might get your places. Now I agree with the gentleman, if, by your measures, you get this country into a war, that you will lose your places. But I do not agree that in such case the Federalists would get them. No, Sir; the course of affairs in popular revolutions proceeds not from bad to better, but from bad to worse. After Condorcet and Brissot came Danton and Robespierre. Well may gentlemen dread, on account of their places, being involved in war. For let the people once begin to look on the state of the country with that anxiety which the actual perception of present danger never fails to awaken, — let them realize the exigencies which that state involves, and compare with them your preparations for it, — let them see an army, in which perhaps a full half of your citizens cannot confide, — a small navy rendered less by natural decay, and even the few ships we have not in a state to give battle, — our treasury exhausted, as it will soon be, and all the ordinary sources of commercial supply dried away, — and they will hurl you from your seats, with as little remorse, with as much indifference, as a mischievous boy would shy so many blind and trembling kittens, six to a litter, into a horse-pond. Yes, Sir, be assured that war is the termination of your political power, unless you have the prescience to prepare an effectual force, worthy of this nation, worthy of either adversary you may elect to engage. But remember you must rely upon something else than the paltry surpluses of your treasury, which, in fact, in one year will not exist, — upon something else than loans or direct taxes.

. . . . .

"Sir, these are the general reasons which I have to urge against the adoption of this bill. In what I have said, my only view has been to exhibit to this House and nation the real motives which, as I apprehend, caused the original imposition of the Embargo, and which still operate in support of this bill. I do not believe that it is the intention of a majority of this House, at present, to continue this system after May. But I do believe that it is the intention of Administration. My design has been to recall the recollection of gentlemen to the difference between the arguments now urged for its continuance and the official reasons at first given for its adoption. And I would warn them, that, if they mean to gain credit with the people for the intention of repealing the Embargo in May, they will not obtain it, if they leave the next Congress at the mercy of the Executive by rising without affixing some limitation to it."

The next day he wrote to his wife this account of the speech, and of its effect on friends and foes: —

"Yesterday, on the bill for an extra session of Congress, I made an attack on Administration which has called out all the virulence of Eppes, Jackson, &c., and to-day I expect most severe animadversion from Campbell; but my spirits were never better. The ground I took was so grateful to my friends that I had a deputation from Frost's boarding-house, consisting of Tallmadge, Upham,* and Davenport, and another from the Washington Mess, consisting of Vandyke, Lewis, and Van Rensselaer,† to thank me, and to wish my speech should, as soon as possible, be put in a pamphlet."

That same day, January 20th, the attack upon him was renewed with redoubled fury and virulence. It was, indeed, as he wrote to his wife —

"the highest and warmest debate that perhaps this House ever witnessed. Campbell and Jackson came with a determination to oblige me to take the same measure to which they had reduced Gardenier. Accordingly, they levelled at me a series of as gross personalities as were ever uttered on a legislative floor. Fortified by a sense of duty to myself and my country, I had no hesitation to take the course of *true* courage, and repaid them with as much severe language as I had at command, and shall live down their calumnies."

In this reply, after showing that none of his positions had been turned, and scarcely attacked, he went on: —

"Whether the arguments I then urged were sufficient to justify my

* Jabez Upham was born, 1764; graduated at Harvard University, 1785; practised law at Brookfield, Massachusetts; Representative from 1807 to 1810; died in 1811. He was one of my father's most valued friends, to which fact I shall presently give his own testimony.

† William Van Rensselaer, Representative from New York from 1801 to 1811 died, 1845.

condemnation of the Administration, is a question referred to the decision of my fellow-citizens. From that tribunal I shall not shrink, and before it I am not afraid to meet any or all of my political opponents. To these arguments, certainly neither personal nor in any respect unparliamentary, what has been the reply? Why, sir, 'false,' 'malicious,' 'defamatory,' 'cowardly,' 'base detraction,' 'dastardly act,' 'old Tory,' 'friend to Great Britain,' 'Nero,' 'Essex Junto,' and such like. Really, Mr. Speaker, I have no means of reply to such arguments as these. Absolutely, through defect of my education, I can make no answer to them. I never studied in the school of the scavenger; I never took degrees at the oyster-bench; I never sat at the feet of the fishwomen. The gentlemen who resort to such weapons have all the advantage of me. . . . . . If gentlemen expect to prevent investigations of public men and public measures by personal invectives, the nature and tendency of which are too obvious to be misunderstood, so far as it respects myself individually, they have mistaken their weapons and their antagonist. It is a choice satisfaction to my mind, that it is not in the power of any individual, however malignant, (should such a character ever appear on this floor,) long to injure the reputation of any one whose private or public life does not co-operate with their malevolent intentions; and I can assure the gentleman from Virginia (Mr. John G. Jackson), and every gentleman who has spoken in his vein, that I shall never be a half-worker with them probably in anything, but certainly not in the attempt to injure my own character. The sting of satire lies in its truth. The keenness of asperity is in the justness of its application. Where these fail, the sped arrow cuts the air harmless."

That this rejoinder did not pacify the leaders of the Administration party may easily be imagined. The rest of the debate consisted of a succession of vituperative attacks upon him as bitter and personal as malice and skill could supply. Towards the close of the discussion, if such it might be called, Mr. Gardenier of New York was provoked into a brief protest against the conduct and language of the Democratic speakers. Of this my father says: —

"Gardenier was deeply irritated at the treatment I received, and took occasion to remark on the scandal of their proceedings. After some handsome compliments to me, and after observing on the obvious intentions of both Jackson and Campbell to reduce me to the necessity of fighting, he remarked that I had the fortune to dwell in a part of the country where the term cowardice was not known, yet where such a resort, far from being an honor, would disgrace me in public opinion."

This gave Mr. Quincy an opportunity of closing the debate by defining his position in this particular in an unmistakable manner. He said that the indignation Mr. Gardenier had expressed on account of the language which had been addressed to himself was very natural in a gentleman in his situation, and entitled him to a grateful acknowledgment. He then went on: —

"But the course of my education has inculcated other sentiments, and instilled different feelings. I have been taught that the just pride of life is only attained by acquiring real honor among honorable men; and that this can only be effected by an undeviating course of public and private conduct, directed by sound principle, and terminating in a fulfilment of duty. Such a course I have attempted to pursue in this debate, though it has been my lot to be mistaken or misrepresented by almost every gentleman who has undertaken to reply to me. Towards neither of those who have seen fit to resort to such opprobrious language can I feel any resentment. They are welcome to all the advantages they can derive from it.

"It is my fortune — perhaps in the opinion of some it is my misfortune — to represent not only a great, a wise, a powerful, an intelligent, but what in that country is valued more than all, a religious people. Gentlemen very well understand, when they use terms in debate to which the customs of this part of the country admit of but one species of reply, that such a resort is altogether prohibited by the public sentiment of that part to which I belong. They know that, so far from being honor, it is disgrace, in my country, to avenge wrongs of words in the way which is here, in a manner, necessary; and that a successful issue, in such a mode of vengeance, would there terminate the hopes as well of political as of private honor of any man who should adopt it. And I shall not, in order to gain the temporary applause of men whom I cannot respect, forfeit the esteem of those whose good opinion is my most precious reward in this life. This is my situation. I am sent here by such constituents to support their interests and maintain their rights. My duty in these respects I shall fulfil, nor shall I be deterred from performing it by the asperities or the violence of any friends of the present or any future Executive.

"My argument, such as it was, will be laid before the people. Whether I have passed the boundary of parliamentary duty or decorum, I cheerfully refer to their judgment. The observations made in reply to me have been one tissue of mistakes. I ought to have interrupted each gentleman at least twenty times; but if gentlemen cannot, or will not, understand the bearing of an argument, it does not become me to be perpetually correcting them. . . . . However, it was not my intention to enter even thus far into additional elucidations of this kind. Knowing the solid ground on which I stand, I have little solicitude concerning the effect of the diatribes of these gentlemen. The force of their weapon, if it have any, will only be felt in its recoil upon themselves; for I have great consolation in the certainty that where *I* am known nothing these gentlemen can say will injure me, and also in the further belief that the effect will not be greater where *they* are known."

In his letters to my mother written at the time of these encounters, my father thus reassures her as to his personal safety: —

"The duties I am performing are arduous, but they are necessary ones. I know my rights, and shall not be bullied out of them. You may fear, perhaps, some personal attacks out of doors. Be assured there is not the remotest danger. Not only personal fears on their own account will prevent that, but public considerations, and the great anxiety which begins to prevail on the state of things in New England. You need not fear that your husband is brow-beaten, much less terrified. I shall perform my duty, and give to any and all men, as occasion calls, what politicians call a Rowland for their Oliver, and what the ladies term tit for tat."

His friends, however, did not altogether share in his disbelief in the danger of a personal assault outside the House. Mr. Lloyd one day brought him a pair of pocket-pistols, carefully loaded, and begged him to carry them in case of attack. He laughed at the offer, and declined it; and the result showed that his own judgment as to the probabilities of danger was correct. No attempt of the kind was ever made.

The next event in his Congressional life was one that made much talk at the time, and is still sometimes spoken of. I refer to what is usually called his motion for the impeachment of Mr. Jefferson, but which was strictly a motion for the preliminary inquiries which might lead to an impeachment. The facts were these. General Benjamin Lincoln, of the army of the Revolution, had been appointed Collector of the Port of Boston by Washington. His infirmities of age and health made him desirous of resigning this post, and in November, 1806, he wrote to Mr. Jefferson, asking leave to do so at the close of the year. Mr. Jefferson, in reply, asked him as a personal favor to retain it until the next March. To this he consented; but not being relieved in March, and after waiting until September, he again wrote, asking that his resignation might be accepted, he being entirely unable to discharge the duties of his office. To this letter he never received any reply at all. The office was thus kept virtually vacant for more than two years as a provision for General Henry Dearborn, the Secretary of War, after his term of office should expire. The immediate provocation of Mr. Quincy's action was an article in the National Intelligencer, charging General Lincoln with "deliberately conspiring with the disaffected, by pressing his resignation, in their infamous violation of the laws of their country, and with ingratitude for the forbearance of the government in retaining him so long in office in opposition to the wishes of a respectable class in the community"! On the 25th of January, Mr. Quincy made a speech reciting these facts, distinctly charged the government with the favoritism towards General Dearborn just mentioned, and concluded by moving for a committee of inquiry. This unexpected attack upon Mr. Jefferson created a great sensation in the House, and certainly showed the mover's opponents that they had not intimidated him by their attacks. An excited debate, or rather a series of personal attacks on the mover of the resolutions, ensued, after which they were rejected by a unanimous vote, save *one*, — the name of JOSIAH QUINCY standing alone in the affirmative. He had not asked, and did not expect, any support from his party. Indeed, Senator Lloyd, who cordially approved his design, was the only person to whom he had communicated it beforehand. But, though thus defeated, he was victorious. He did all he expected to do. He made the conduct of Mr. Jefferson in the premises known to the world, and he procured the instant release of General Lincoln. He made his motion at the opening of the session of the House, and before the Senate adjourned, on the same day, the nomination of General Dearborn was sent in for confirmation! His political friends in Congress, though they did not support, approved of what he had done, and those in Boston were unanimous in their approbation. In his old age, speaking of this action, he says, "No public exertion of mine has been more fully justified by the reflections of a long life."

The discontents caused by the Embargo had risen to such a height, that the Democrats, especially those from the Northern States, had become alarmed, and a general apprehension prevailed of a forcible resistance to the operation of the Enforcing Act. Mr. Jefferson attributed this defection in the ranks of his followers to "an unaccountable revolution of opinion and kind of panic, chiefly among the New England and New York members." This revolution of opinion and panic, for which Mr. Jefferson could not account, arose unquestionably from their more accurate knowledge of the state of feeling in their own part of the country, and the conviction that their own political prospects as public men would be rendered very doubtful if they obstinately adhered to this odious measure. Mr. Jefferson remained firm in his faith in the omnipotence of his political philosophy of compelling England to his terms through the destruction of American commerce. His faith was in fact too strong to be overcome by sight. For, after the first disturbance of trade was over, the English merchants, instead of asking for a repeal of the Orders in Council, so that the American trade might be restored, wished a greater strictness to be given to them, so that they themselves might have the monopoly of the Continental trade, — thus literally fulfilling the prophecy of Mr. Quincy when the Embargo was first proposed. The importation of cotton into England had been already absolutely forbidden, to cripple Continental manufactures, which Bonaparte wished to encourage as a part of his system. The duty which the Orders required to be paid in England, as the condition of permission to reship merchandise to the Continent, having been represented by the Democratic orators as tribute paid to that haughty power, advantage was taken of their denunciations to prohibit the importation of any American productions whatever for the purpose of re-exportation, and Mr. Canning called the particular attention of Mr. Pinkney to this concession to the sensibilities of the American people! But these things moved not the constant soul of Jefferson, and he resisted to the last what he called "the fatal measure of repeal." But his influence was waning, as the days of his power drew towards their close. The fate of the Embargo was fixed, and all he could do was most reluctantly to consent to the substitution of Non-Intercourse with both belligerents for his favorite policy. This measure, though far from satisfying the needs of commerce, was so far an improvement on the one it replaced, that it opened the trade with the rest of the world, and removed the worst of the obstructions to the coastwise traffic.

This bill gave rise to a long and animated debate, in the course of which many amendments were moved, but its original draft could not be altered materially. Mr. Quincy took occasion, on the 15th of February, to recapitulate his arguments against the policy or the feasibility of coercion by means of commercial restrictions. No extended report of this speech appears to have been made, but the substance of his suggestions as to what the state of foreign relations demanded was to this effect, — that the Embargo should be raised, the Non-Importation Act already in existence as to specified articles of British merchandise repealed, and the Non-Intercourse proposition abandoned. He wished "peace if possible; if war, union in that war." For this reason he wished negotiation to be left unshackled with those impediments. As long as they remained, the people in his part of the country would not deem an unsuccessful attempt at negotiation a cause of war. If they were removed, and an earnest and unrestricted attempt made at negotiation, and it should fail, they would join heartily in one. They would not, however, go to war to contest the right of Great Britain to search American vessels for British seamen; for they believed, if American seamen were properly encouraged, there would be no need of employing foreign sailors. When the question was taken, he found himself, with the other extreme opponents of the Embargo, voting against the bill with its most extreme supporters. But though consistency with himself required him to vote against it, he rejoiced with the rest of the Federalists at the substitution of the lesser evil for the greater, heightened, it may be well believed, by the knowledge of the discomfiture of Mr. Jefferson. The following extracts from letters to his wife give an idea of the varying feelings which the progress of the bill excited as it went forward.

"*February* 2.—There is dreadful distraction in the enemy's camp on the subject of removing the Embargo. Jefferson and his friends are obstinate. Bacon and the Northern Democrats are equally determined that it shall be raised in March. After three days' debate, Dawson, a man of the palace, has moved to postpone the subject indefinitely. I believe the President will succeed in keeping this measure in its present state till June, when he will be snug at Monticello. Others think differently, and I hope that I may be disappointed. But my friends ought not to calculate upon it."

"*February* 3.—The question of postponing the raising of the Embargo until June was lost by a vote of 73 against 40 in favor of it. Of course the chance brightens of its being got off by March. But my friends must not be too sanguine. Jefferson is a host, and is opposed to it, and if the wand of that magician is not broken, he will yet defeat the attempt. But I hope his power is drawing to an end in this world."

"*February* 8.—Great caucusing is the order of the day and the night here. Administration is determined to rally its friends and postpone the removal of the Embargo till May. But I think they cannot succeed. Bacon, I am told, stands firm and obstinate against all their solicitations, and even almost denunciations. However, they had another grand caucus last night. The event is unknown. Jefferson has prevailed."

The result of the caucusing was the substitution of Non-Intercourse for the Embargo. Mr. Quincy expresses the general opinion of the time, that this was the doing of Mr. Jefferson. We now know that he was strongly opposed to any modification of his favorite measure. He only consented to it as a compromise, without which the Embargo would have been unconditionally repealed:—

"*February* 29.—. . . . Jefferson has triumphed. His intrigues have prevailed, Non-Intercourse will be substituted for Embargo. The Non-Intercourse bill passed, 81 ayes, 40 nays, all the Federalists voting against the bill, except Taggart and Livermore."

This was the last act of Mr. Jefferson's administration. On the 4th of March, 1809, his official life came to an end, and James Madison reigned in his stead. The Tenth Congress also died a natural death at the same time, leaving no very fragrant memory behind it. None of its predecessors, however it may have been with those that have come after it, had done so much mischief to the country, counterbalanced by so little good. There were few that were not glad that it was no more.

Of his personal feelings and relations to the society of Washington during the two sessions of the Tenth Congress, my father speaks thus: —

"It is impossible to conceive the comfortlessness and desolation of feeling in which those two years were passed. I had, indeed, house, companion, food, and liberty of thought and action; but I was separated from wife and children, in whom all my happiness was concentrated. There were a few families interesting and respectable with whom I might have associated by riding two or three miles in the mud; but with them I had little sympathy. Our acquaintance authorized only formal association, and we had for our conversation nothing but the politics and events of the day, of both which I had enough elsewhere, *usque ad nauseam*. All the settled inhabitants of the place were slaveholders or office-holders. All were interested in building up Washington. Appropriations out of the public treasury for its improvement were the chief objects of their thoughts. And those who were not willing, or even forward, to aid in these objects, soon perceived that they did not possess the qualifications essential to friendship and attentions. So that subserviency to local and personal interests was the obviously implied condition of social intercourse. To such terms the temperament of my mind did not permit me to submit. I therefore kept aloof from the inhabitants of Washington, and never volunteered visits or accepted attentions but such as were formal and specific.

"In Congress my intercourse with those members who coincided in my political views was regulated by party rather than by personal friendship. The latter we had few and limited opportunities to cultivate. The former was cordially manifested by encouragement and support of every public exertion of mine which harmonized with their feelings and interests. Our association on the floor, and at times in our respective lodgings, led to the reciprocation of friendships which remained intimate and cordial during the continuance of our mutual Congress life, but were soon broken by our subsequent separation in different and often far-distant States. Of this class I love to remember Pickman, Stedman, and Upham, of Massachusetts, Potter of Rhode Island, Champion, Pitkin, Dana, and Tallmadge, of Connecticut, Chittenden of Vermont, Emott, Gardenier, and Van Rensselaer, of New York, Milnor of Pennsylvania, and Goldsborough of Maryland,* with many others, once the objects of strong — alas! of temporary — affection, which our subsequent locations in life did not allow us to cultivate, but who have always remained deeply seated in my memory and heart.

"With the friends of Administration, who at that time composed the great majority of Congress, my intercourse for the most part was polite, but cold and general. The leaders of that party both from the South and the West were violent, overbearing, and insolent, both in manner and language. The slaveholders were accustomed to speak in the tone of masters. Bold in assertion, self-confident both from ignorance and vanity, they were ready to construe contradiction into insult; and as they knew that Northern and Eastern men were restrained by their principles and those of their constituents, they would on the slightest provocation tender a duel, which they knew they could do with impunity.

"The men from the West were also bold in assertion and overbearing

* Benjamin Pickman, a descendant of one of the oldest and most distinguished families of Massachusetts, born, 1763; graduated at Harvard University, 1784; an eminent merchant of Salem; Representative from 1809 to 1811; died, 1843. William Stedman, Harvard University, 1784, was a lawyer of large practice at Lancaster, Massachusetts; Representative from 1803 to 1810; died, 1831. Elisha R. Potter, a man of great talent and wit, was Representative from Rhode Island from 1796 to 1797 and from 1809 to 1815; died 1835. Epaphroditus Champion represented Connecticut from 1807 to 1817; died, 1835. Martin Chittenden, born 1769; graduated at Dartmouth College, 1789; Member of Congress from 1803 to 1813, and afterwards Governor of Vermont; died, 1839. James Emott, born 1770, was an eminent lawyer and Judge in New York; Member of Congress from 1809 to 1813; died, 1850. He was father of James Emott, now one of the Judges of the Supreme Court of that State. James Milnor, born, 1773; educated at the University of Pennsylvania; bred to the law; Member of Congress from 1811 to 1813; in 1814 took orders and became Rector of St. George's Church in New York; died, 1845. Charles W. Goldsborough, Member of Congress from 1805 to 1817; also Governor of Maryland; died, 1834.

in manner, not from the habits of masterdom, but from their education and habits of professional life. For the most part they were lawyers accustomed to speak at barbecues and electioneering canvassings, and their assertions usually partook of the license of tongue incident to a wild and uncultivated state of society. With men of such states of mind and temperament, men educated in the strictness and under the laws which regulate New England debates could have little pleasure in intercourse, less in controversy, and of course no sympathy.

"I have thus cursorily accounted for the solitariness and depression of spirits which predominated at this period of my life, and which led me to resolve that I would not return to Washington again unless accompanied by my family. I accordingly made an arrangement for the next session with a Mr. Woodhouse, the keeper of a boarding-house, for all his rooms and his stable, and thus secured to myself the seclusion and independence of a private family."

I will here insert two letters received during this session from Mr. Henry W. Desaussure of Columbia, South Carolina, one of the most eminent men that State has produced. He was one of the small band of South Carolina Federalists who maintained the faith until the dispersion of that political church. In the interval between the two letters he was elected Chancellor by his political opponents, and held that office for many years. It will be seen that he entertained different views as to the value of the Union from those of his son, Mr. William Ford Desaussure, a graduate of Harvard in 1810, and sometime United States Senator from South Carolina, who was one of the main promoters of Secession. Mr. William Crafts, a letter from whom I also subjoin, was a native of Boston, if I mistake not, who graduated in 1805 at Cambridge, and removed to Charleston, where he won for himself a distinguished position as a lawyer and man of letters. He was a very brilliant talker, and always welcome to the best houses of Boston, at his frequent summer visits, and to none more welcome than to my father's. He died in the prime of life, in 1826. The vaticinations of Mr. Crafts as to the dissolution of the Union, coming as they did from Charleston, and his lamentations over the political subordination of South Carolina to Virginia, read oddly in the light of later days.

Mr. Desaussure to Mr. Quincy.

"Columbia, S. C., December 7, 1808.

"Dear Sir: — It is not a pleasant thing to communicate intelligence of events unfavorable to our wishes. It is proper, however, that you should be apprised of the issue of our election of Electors. Our Legislature appoints in this State. That body is composed of a very great majority of Democrats. There are not more than twelve Federalists in the House of Representatives, and six in the Senate. The result you anticipate, for party spirit governs so absolutely that it sweeps away every other consideration. Neither the very high estimation in which General Pinckney universally stands here, nor the deep conviction which prevails that the times are very perilous, and require the greatest virtues and the greatest talents, civil and military, for the government of our country, could produce the smallest alteration. The arrangements of party must be sacredly adhered to. Accordingly it was settled in caucus that no persons should be elected Electors but those who would vote for Mr. Madison and Mr. Clinton. Accordingly, gentlemen thus pledged were elected yesterday, and to-day they have exercised their automaton office by voting unanimously for Mr. Madison and Mr. Clinton (George). The Federalists, finding that there was not the shadow of a chance, resolved not to set up an opposition ticket, and most of them declined voting for Electors altogether.

"We have before us the resolutions of the State of Virginia for altering the Constitution of the United States, by enabling the President, on the address of both Houses of Congress, to remove any of the Judges from office, and for enabling the Legislatures to recall Senators of the United States before the regular expiration of their term of service. No opinion can be formed what will be the issue here. I rather think that neither of them will be agreed to; though the former is more likely to pass than the latter. I will advise you of the result of both. All our elections are Democratic. Mr. John Drayton was elected Governor to-day.

"It is probable that an address of confidence in the Administration will be proposed, and, if so, it will certainly be carried. Indeed, it is a competition among the leading men here, who shall express most confidence in the Administration, and go greatest lengths with it. He who runs ahead in this career is most popular. Such is our situation.

"We learn that you are warm in your debates, and that a division of the States is hinted at. I hope this greatest of evils is not about to fall upon us. I know that the Eastern States have borne much for the sake of union. I hope their patriotism will still bear more, till all hope of a better state of things be lost. I fear nothing but the discord of the States, and their separation.

"I am, my dear sir, with much respect and esteem, yours truly,

"HENRY W. DESAUSSURE."

CHANCELLOR DESAUSSURE TO MR. QUINCY.

"CHARLESTON, S. C., January 21, 1809.

"DEAR SIR: — I returned lately from the country, and had the pleasure of receiving your favor of the 18th December. I perceive, as you observe, 'that the New England Federalists have been true to their Southern friends, notwithstanding all the calumnies circulated concerning their disposition to desert them'; and that 'nothing can be more false than that it is the wish of the leading men in the Northern States to break up the Union.'

"Be assured no apprehensions have ever been entertained by the Federalists here on these points. The knowledge we have of the leading men in your country — of their liberality, candor, good sense, and good faith — made assurance doubly sure. We have no confidence in the visions of Virginia politicians. And we can never fear that those men in whose wisdom and virtue we place such unlimited confidence could ever desire to break up the Union.

"What we fear is, that, in opposing the weak and wild policy of our Virginia masters, such a deep impression will at last be made on the minds of your people, smarting under the effects of that policy, that their enmity will be excited, and their jealousy roused to such a degree as to sweep away all the attachments which bind them to the Southern States. In that moment of resentment all the counsels of moderation, all the considerations of interest drawn from the infinite and indeed inappreciable value of the Union would be forgotten by the people, and the leading men who should attempt to restrain them would speedily lose their influence. The heads of parties seldom govern them. Mr. Pulteney said truly, that the heads of parties in times of trouble were like the heads of serpents, moved on and governed by the tail. I beg, then, that our Eastern friends would pause, and avoid stirring up those passions among their own people which may become too strong to be controlled, and may lead to measures destructive to the Union and ruinous to the country. The headlong madness of the policy you condemn must sooner or later, by its ruinous effects, open the eyes of the people of the United States generally, and produce a change by the regular and constitutional mean of elections. If it does not, we shall furnish another example of the truth of the maxim, *Quem Deus vult perdere prius dementat.*

"All must, however, be left to the wisdom and the virtue and the moderation of the Federalists in your part of the Union. Here we are but a handful, borne down by numbers, and scarcely having a voice in the Legislature. At our late session, finding that it was utterly hopeless to attempt the smallest resistance, the few Federalists who were in the Legislature agreed not to take any part in what was passing relative to national affairs. Accordingly, most of them did not vote for Electors, or upon any of the measures of the general government.

"Many wise and good men view the course pursued by the Administration as you do, and have the same apprehensions; but they have at present no influence, and make no noise. They take a moderate share in the affairs of our own State, and are respected and permitted to have some share in the management; and they will undoubtedly hereafter be ready to render more extensive service when they perceive the signs of the times favorable. You must not, however, count on us: the regeneration must be general and complete elsewhere before it reaches us. I am myself driven in great measure from an active part in the field of politics by an appointment to our Equity bench, which was as unexpected as it was unsolicited, from our Democratic Legislature. Some old friendships with a number of the Democratic leaders, which existed before the formation of parties, and some difficulty in electing competent men (in their estimation) from their party, produced this effect. A few of them, professing friendship, questioned me closely as to the extent of my politics, and, upon a full avowal of Federal principles, they declared themselves satisfied with my frankness, though not with my principles; but assured me that politics should not influence them in judicial elections.

"Your two speeches do honor to your talents, and would produce effect wherever the head of Medusa had not turned men into stone.

"Yours, very truly,

"HENRY W. DESAUSSURE."

MR. CRAFTS TO MR. QUINCY.

"CHARLESTON, January 30, 1809.

"MY DEAR SIR:—I thank you for the communications which you have been so good as to make to me from Washington. These are truly acceptable; for, being of the proscribed party, no member of Congress from this State would venture to hold correspondence with me. All the information we get, therefore, from them, is through their friends here, who give it to us in such manner as they please.

"I do not permit the papers you send me to remain longer in my hands than to admit my perusal of them; they are then circulated among your friends who still dare to call themselves Federalists, of whom there yet are many. This is our invariable practice; so that the information you give to *one* of us is rendered useful, and is highly acceptable to many.

"I could fill a sheet if I were to convey to you one half of the encomium which is hourly passed on you for the manly, spirited, and honorable struggle you are making in Congress to save our country. I fear, alas! it is vain, and will produce you the gratification only of having deserved, and of receiving, the high approbation of those whose good opinion you desire.

"You will have long since seen, by our measures, that this State is as a parish of Virginia. Her politics and her measures govern us entirely, and we are, as I believe, perfectly contented to rise or fall with Virginia. That Virginia politics will dissolve this Union I have long since predicted, and I look for it at no distant day. *You* must be contented to have no commerce, or yield the point that it is to be protected by the Union, and you must, at the same time, protect and defend us, or this Union cannot last long. I do not believe you will consent to these terms, and therefore I look for its speedy dissolution. I do indeed despair of the Republic.

"I beg you to do me the favor to offer my respect and regard to Colonel Pickering and Mr. Lloyd, and to believe me, with sincere regard and respect, your friend and obedient servant,

"W. CRAFTS."

After the adjournment of Congress, my father hastened home and received a most cordial welcome from his personal and political friends. The brighter prospects which the removal of the Embargo opened to commerce were attributed, in a great degree, to the reclamations which he, even more emphatically than the other Federal members, had made against that mischievous measure, and to the force of his representations of the dangerous discontents which it had occasioned. His vacation was but a short one, however, as the extra session began on the 22d of May. Accordingly he left Boston on the 12th of that month, and proceeded, as rapidly as sloops and stage-coaches could carry him, to Wasnington, by the way of Newport, New York, Philadelphia, and Baltimore. As this session was to be but brief, his resolution never to go to Washington again without his family did not attach to it. His journey must have been a very favorable one, as he was only *nine* days on the road, arriving at his own hired house on the 21st. The next day he took his seat at the opening of the session, it being the first Congress of Mr. Madison's Administration. From his letters to his wife I extract the following sketches of his opinions and doings.

"Mr. Madison's Message is modest and precise, but smacks a little of Jeffersonian slang in sentiment and expression. I attended a Presidential levee for the first time. It was crowded by Federalists and Democrats, old opponents and new converts. The sovereign lady was gracious; and it was a subject of congratulation that a married man was at the head of the nation. Parties will take a curious turn, or I am greatly mistaken. They charge Mrs. Madison with being *a Federalist*, and some nominations of Mr. Madison's indicate a disposition very different from that of his predecessor."

"On the 3d of June, by invitation from Judge Washington, I dined at Mount Vernon, with sixteen or twenty Federal members of Congress. The Judge was extremely pleasant and polite. The view at Mount Vernon is much more beautiful than I remember it when we visited it together in the winter of 1806. The house is put in very good repair, the gardens are well cultivated, and the whole in sufficiently good order. At this season of the year the scenery is indescribably interesting; there is a richness of foliage, and a fulness of flower and herbage, equal to anything I ever saw. Although things are not trimmed to the precision of Mr. Lyman's taste, yet nature appears in a wild, bursting luxuriance, and there is an air of unaffected negligence, if I may so speak, in the drapery of the place, that wins and fascinates. You see that it might be improved to the eye, and yet I doubt whether the attempt might not injure rather than help the effect. At least these were my thoughts.

"I had considerable conversation with Washington's old servant Billy, whom I did not see when here before. The old slave could not talk of his master without tears. He said he did not think he was ever out of his mind for two hours together, and that he scarcely ever passed a night without dreaming of him."

This brief session, which lasted but about a month, was marked by no debates of particular interest, and my father took very slight part in them. He and Mr. Lloyd continued to keep house together, and they were joined by Benjamin Pickman of Salem, whom he describes as his "most esteemed and amiable friend, who added a new, instructive, and most welcome associate" to the little household. Congress adjourned on the 28th of June, when he hastened home, as haste was then, and spent the summer at Quincy.

CHAPTER IX.

1809-1811.

THE ERSKINE ARRANGEMENT. — REJECTED BY ENGLAND. — FEDERAL DISAPPOINTMENT AND DEMOCRATIC CHAGRIN. — MR. MADISON'S QUARREL WITH MR. JACKSON, MR. ERSKINE'S SUCCESSOR. — MR. QUINCY TAKES HIS FAMILY TO WASHINGTON. — SPEECH ON THE JACKSON IMBROGLIO. — THE ADMISSION OF LOUISIANA. — SPEECH UPON IT. — DIVERSITIES OF SECESSIONISM. — CORRESPONDENCE WITH JOHN ADAMS.

THE quiet which marked this extra session was chiefly due to the hopes which were entertained of the repeal of the Orders in Council, in consequence of what was known at the time as "the Erskine Arrangement." Mr. Erskine, the British Minister at Washington, of whom I have given some account in a previous chapter, being connected with this country by his marriage with an American lady, felt a natural and just ambition to be the means of reconciling the differences of the two countries, in both of which he had so deep an interest. For this purpose, he made as favorable representations as the facts would bear out of the better dispositions of the incoming, compared with those of the outgoing, Administration towards England, to Mr. Canning, the Secretary for Foreign Affairs, and suggested a new negotiation. Mr. Canning in reply authorized him to offer as reparation for the attack on the Chesapeake the disavowal of Admiral Berkeley's orders, and the restoration of the men proved to be American citizens taken out of that vessel. If this was accepted as satisfactory, his Majesty, "as an act of spontaneous generosity," would make provision for the families of the men killed at the time of the outrage. But no mark of displeasure was to be demanded against Admiral Berkeley, beyond that manifested in his recall from the North American Station, — a mark of displeasure, be it said in passing, somewhat mitigated by his appointment to another and higher command. This preliminary adjusted, the Orders in Council would be revoked as touching the United States, on condition that all acts of Non-Intercourse and of exclusion of public ships from American ports should be repealed as to England, while they were to remain in force as to France and her allies; and that British men-of-war should be authorized to capture any American ships violating the Non-Intercourse with France and the countries adopting her Decrees. Mr. Erskine was authorized to show the original despatch to the American government; which, however, he did not do, probably in the belief that a departure from the letter of his instructions would be overlooked by his superiors, in view of the great advantages which would accrue to both nations from the restoration of commercial intercourse. Accordingly, in the Arrangement, as it was proclaimed on the 17th of April, 1809, the proposition for a provision for the families of the killed on board the Chesapeake did not contain the essential clause that it was "an act of spontaneous generosity" on the part of the King; the continuance of the Non-Intercourse with France was left to be inferred; and nothing was said of the authority to be given to British ships of war to capture American vessels violating that Non-Intercourse. The Federalists believed that Mr. Madison and Mr. Gallatin well knew that Mr. Erskine had exceeded his instructions, and that they had manipulated the young diplomatist with the dexterity of old politicians to obtain terms which should enable them to fall back with some show of grace from their awkward position, — that, to use my father's figure of speech, "the old pikes had been more than a match for the young dace." It was awkwardly enough done, however. At the extra session the act excluding the ships of both belligerents from the American ports was repealed, which was directly in violation of Mr. Erskine's instructions, and another continuing the Non-Intercourse Act, but permitting trade with Great Britain! This strange circumlocution was meant, of course, to continue the Non-Intercourse with France in the form the least offensive to that mighty power.

The general joy which the proclamation of the Erskine Arrangement in April had spread throughout the commercial region was soon damped by the news that the British ministry had rejected it as unauthorized by their instructions to Mr. Erskine, and had censured him severely for making it. Technically, they were justified in this action, undoubtedly; but it may be questioned whether it were a wise or statesmanlike proceeding. England would gain by the Arrangement everything she demanded, without renouncing the rights of search and impressment. Its acceptance would have prevented the war of 1812, and been greatly for the advantage of both countries. Its rejection was largely owing, probably, to an insulting clause which Mr. Madison insisted upon adding to the one waiving any demand on his part for the further punishment of Admiral Berkeley, to the effect that, nevertheless, "the President was not the less sensible of the justice and utility of such an example, nor less persuaded that it would best comport with what was due from his Britannic Majesty to his own honor"! The King was naturally and justly offended by this affront, and it certainly had no tendency to procure the ratification of the Arrangement. Besides this provocation, however, the contempt felt for the United States as a fighting power, caused by the whole course of Mr. Jefferson's Administration as to national defence, and by the notorious want of preparation for war consequent upon it, and the belief of the British merchants that the monopoly of European trade which our Embargo secured to them was more profitable than the trade with America, doubtless helped to bring about the rejection of the Arrangement. Mr. Madison and Mr. Gallatin were deeply chagrined at this failure of their diplomatic strategy, and yet more by the disclosure of their friendly professions towards England, which followed on the publication of Mr. Erskine's despatches.

On the 9th of August, President Madison issued a Proclamation recalling that of the 17th of April, which had announced the Arrangement. The Federalists were cruelly disappointed by this termination of their hopes of better times, while the Democrats were disgusted at what they regarded as the humiliating nature of the advances made by the Administration to England. Having in vain attempted to induce Mr. Erskine to withdraw or qualify his statements, the President seemed determined to show that his former dispositions towards England were unchanged, by the coolness with which he received Mr. Francis J. Jackson, who was sent out to take Mr. Erskine's place, and the obstacles he threw in the way of the new Minister's attempts at a fresh settlement of difficulties. He accordingly, very soon after Mr. Jackson's arrival, took occasion to find fault with his mode of transacting business, and to decline any further intercourse with him excepting by writing. Soon afterwards he took exception to some expressions of Mr. Jackson, which he construed into an intimation that he knew, at the time the Arrangement was negotiating, that Mr. Erskine had no authority to make it. Though Mr. Jackson disclaimed any such intention, Mr. Madison refused to accept any explanation, discontinued all diplomatic intercourse with him, and demanded his recall of his government.

This was the state of affairs when the first regular session of the Eleventh Congress approached. About the beginning of November, 1809, my father, accompanied by my mother and two of their children, set out for Washington in his own carriage, and, after paying visits to their friends in New York, Princeton, and Philadelphia, took his seat at the opening of Congress on the 27th of November. The house which he had taken for the winter was one of the block called "The Six Buildings," then the last towards Georgetown on the Pennsylvania Avenue. This session, the first in regular course of Mr. Madison's Administration, did not open in the hopeful and cheerful spirit which had marked the extraordinary one in May. All parties were out of humor. The Madisonians were mortified at the failure of the Erskine Arrangement. The Federalists were sore from the disappointment of the hopes that plan had excited. And the Jeffersonians were disgusted at the departure of the President from the temper towards England of their great chieftain, and from his principles and policy. It was of the first importance to Mr. Madison to obtain the sanction of Congress for his conduct towards the British Minister, that being the measure by which he hoped to retrieve his damaged popularity. Accordingly, a joint resolution was moved in the Senate by Mr. Giles of Virginia, on the 5th of December, approving of the refusal of the President to hold diplomatic intercourse with Mr. Jackson; characterizing the expressions of the letter on which that refusal rested as "highly indecorous and insolent"; their repetition, after the President's denial of any knowledge of the insufficiency of Mr. Erskine's powers, as "yet more insolent and affronting"; and pronouncing the circular addressed by Mr. Jackson to the British Consuls, informing them of the discontinuance of his functions, "a yet more direct and aggravated insult to the American people and their government," and "an insidious attempt to excite their resentments and distrusts against their own government, through false and fallacious disguises"; and pledging themselves to stand by the President in his refusal, and to call into action the whole force of the nation to sustain him in it, if necessary. On this subject Mr. Quincy speaks as follows: —

"To my mind the conclusions drawn from his (Jackson's) words were artificially forced, and the charges obviously exaggerated. I deemed myself, therefore, called upon to save the honor of Congress and the nation by doing what I could to prevent the passage of a resolution which I deemed dishonorable to both, by giving public sanction to what seemed to me falsehood.

"On the 28th of December I delivered one of the most carefully wrought and studied efforts I ever uttered. It had, of course, no effect at the time, and will probably have no interest in the future, the occasion being personal and temporary, but it was an attempt to remove the opprobrium of uttering for political purposes what to my mind was false. I cannot regret it, it being, in my judgment, one of the most labored, responsible, and powerful of my efforts."

This speech is so compact and so closely argued, that it is impossible to make extracts from it sufficient to give an idea of its logical force, excepting at a length exceeding my limits. Some specimens of the exordium and the peroration are all for which I have room.

"It is proposed, Sir, that this solemn assembly, the representative of the American people, the depositary of their power, and, in a constitutional light, the image of their wisdom, should descend from the dignity of its legislative duties to the task of uttering against an individual the mingled language of indignation and reproach. Not satisfied with seeing that individual prohibited the exercise of his official character, we are invited to pursue him with the joint terrors of legislative wrath; couched in terms selected to convey opprobrium and infix a stigma. '*Indecorum*,' '*insolence*,' '*affront*,' '*more insolence*,' '*more affront*,' '*direct, premeditated insult and affront*,' '*disguises, fallacious and false*'; — these are the stains we are called upon to cast; these the wounds we are about to inflict. It is scarcely possible to comprise within the same compass more of the spirit of whatever is bitter in invective and humiliating in aspersion. This heaped-up measure of legislative contumely is prepared for whom? For a private, unassisted, insulated, unallied individual? No, Sir. For the accredited Minister of a great and powerful sovereign, whose character he in this country represents, whose confidence he shares; of a sovereign who is not bound, and perhaps will not be disposed, to uphold him in misconduct, but who is bound by the highest moral obligations, and by the most impressive political considerations, to vindicate his wrongs, whether they affect his person or reputation, and to take care that whatever treatment he shall receive shall not exceed the measure of justice, and, above all, that it does not amount to national indignity.

"Important as is this view of these resolutions, it is not their most serious aspect. This bull of anathemas, scarcely less than papal, is to be fulminated in the name of the American people from the high tower of their authority, under the pretence of asserting their rights and vindicating their wrongs. What will that people say, if, after the passions and excitements of this day shall have subsided, they shall find, and find I fear they will, that this resolution is false in fact, — that a falsehood is the basis of these aspersions upon the character of a public Minister? What will be their just indignation when they find national embarrassment multiplied, perhaps their peace gone, their character disgraced, for no better reason than that you, their representatives, following headlong a temporary current, insist on making assertions, such as they may then, and I believe will, realize to be not authorized by truth, under circumstances and in terms not warranted by wisdom?

"Let us not be deceived. It is no slight responsibility which this House is about to assume. This is not one of those holiday resolutions which frets and fumes its hour upon the stage and is forgotten forever. Very different is its character and consequences. It attempts to stamp dishonor and falsehood on the forehead of a foreign minister. If the allegation itself be false, it will turn to plague the accuser. In its train will follow severe retribution, perhaps in war, — certainly in additional embarrassments, — and most certainly in, worst of all, the loss of that sentiment of self-esteem which, to nations as well as individuals, is the 'pearl of great price,' which power cannot purchase nor gold measure.

"In this point of view all the other questions which have been agitated in the course of this debate dwindle into utter insignificance. The attack or defence of Administration, the detection of fault, or even the exposure of crime, are of no importance when brought into competition with the duty of rescuing this House and nation from the guilt of asserting what is false, and making that falsehood the basis of outrage and virulence.

. . . . .

"I have thus, Mr. Speaker, submitted to a strict and minute scrutiny all the parts of this correspondence which have been adduced by any one in support of the fact asserted in this resolution. This course, however irksome, I thought it my duty to adopt, to the end that no exertion of mine might be wanting to prevent this House from passing a resolution which, in my apprehension, is pregnant with national disgrace and other innumerable evils.

"But let us suppose, for one moment, that the fact asserted in this resolution is true, — that the insult has been offered, — and that the proof is not obscure and doubtful, but certain and clear. I ask, is it wise, is it politic, is it manly, for a national legislature to utter on any occasion, particularly against an individual, invectives so full of contumely and bitterness? Shall we gain anything by it? Have such expressions a tendency to strengthen our cause, or add weight and respectability to those who advocate it? In private life do men increase respect or multiply their friends by using the language of intemperate abuse? Sudden anger may be an excuse for an individual. Inability to avenge an insult may afford an apology to him for resorting to these woman's weapons. But what can excuse a nation for humiliating itself to the use of such vindictive aspersions? Can we plead sudden rage, — we, on whose wrath thirty suns have gone down? Is this nation prepared to resort for apologies to its weakness, and to confess that, being unable to do anything else, it will strive to envenom its adversary with the tongue? But our honor is assailed. Is this a medicament for its wounds? If not, why engage in such retaliatory insults? Which is best, — to leave the British monarch at liberty to decide upon the conduct of his Minister, without any deduction or sympathy on account of our virulence, or to necessitate him, in measuring out justice, to put your intemperance in the scale against his imprudence? Railing for railing is a fair offset all over the world. And I ask gentlemen to con sider whether it be not an equivalent for a constructive insinuation.

. . . . .

"But if it would be wise and politic to refrain from uttering this opprobrious resolution in case the insult was gross, palpable, and undeniable, how much more wise and politic, if this insult be only dubious, and has, at best, but a glimmering existence! But suppose the assertion contained in this resolution be, as it appears to many minds, and certainly to mine, false, I ask, What worse disgrace, what lower depth of infamy, can there be for a nation, than deliberately to assert a falsehood, and to make that falsehood the ground-work of a graduated scale of atrocious aspersions upon the character of a public minister?

. . . . .

"But this resolution was devised for the purpose of promoting unanimity. Is there a man in this House who believes it? Did you ever hear, Mr. Speaker, that language of reproach and of insult was the signal for conciliation? Did you ever know contending parties made to harmonize in terms of insult, of reproach and contumely? No, Sir. I deprecate this resolution on this very account, — that it is much more like the torch of the Furies than like the token of friendship. Accordingly, it has had the effect of enkindling party passions in the House, which had begun, in some degree, to be allayed. It could not possibly be otherwise. A question is raised concerning a *constructive insult.* Of all topics of dispute, those relative to the meaning of terms are most likely to beget diversity and obstinacy in opinion. But this is not all. On a question merely relative to the construction of particular expressions, all the great and critical relations of the nation have been discussed. Is it possible to conceive that such a question as this, on which the debate has been thus conducted, could be productive of anything else than discord and contention?

"For my own part, I have purposely avoided all reference to any of the great questions which agitate the nation. I should deem myself humiliated to discuss them under a resolution of this kind, which in truth decides nothing but our opinion of the meaning of Mr. Jackson's language, and our sense of its nature; and has, strictly speaking, nothing to do with any of the national questions which have been drawn into debate.

"I declare, therefore, distinctly, that I oppose and vote against this resolution from no one consideration relative to Great Britain or the United States, — from none of friendship or animosity to any one man or set of men, — but simply and solely for this one reason, that in my conception the assertion contained in this resolution is a falsehood.

"But it is said that this resolution must be taken as 'a test of patriotism.' To this I have but one answer. If patriotism ask me to assert a falsehood, I have no hesitation in telling patriotism, 'I am not prepared to make that sacrifice.' The duty we owe to our country is indeed among the most solemn and impressive of all obligations. Yet, high as it may be, it is nevertheless subordinate to that which we owe to that Being with whose name and character *truth* is identified. In this respect I deem myself acting, upon this resolution, under a higher responsibility than either to this House or to this people."

Among my father's papers is a handsomely printed copy of this speech, in pamphlet, of which he gives this account: —

"One fact concerning this speech is somewhat curious. While Jackson was under the anathema of Administration, and previous to his sailing, this speech was privately printed in New York, without the name of place or printer, and never circulated in this country.

"A copy of it was given to me by a Democratic member of Congress, and the intimation given to me was that it was printed at the expense of Jackson, and taken by him to England to be shown to his government and circulated among his friends, as forming his defence on the charges brought against him by our Administration.

"Of Jackson personally I knew nothing, and have no recollection of ever having seen him."

Of the rest of the session he speaks in the following terms: —

"By the rejection of Erskine's arrangement Non-Intercourse was revived, and the party of the Administration were reduced to a state of absolute distraction. They knew not what to do. All parties were dissatisfied with the restrictive system, — all admitted that it injured us more than it did Great Britain. But pride would not permit them to allow that the policy founded on its efficiency had failed. It would be an acknowledgment that the Federalists had triumphed. The violent spirits declared that war was the only refuge from disgrace, and that, although we could not reach Great Britain by sea, we could revenge and save our unsullied honor in Canada; and now for the first time the idea of vindicating commercial rights by the invasion of the Colonies began seriously to be agitated.

"But such projects found no response in the spirit of Madison. To keep as near as possible to the policy of Jefferson, was the rule of his action, — to keep out of war, not offend Bonaparte, who was then apparently in rapid ascent to universal empire, by any coalescence with

Great Britain, and to serve his demands as far as possible without openly aiding his designs. But Madison did not hold the sceptre of popular despotism, like Jefferson. He could not bring his followers into rank by a word; and, without attempting to guide the car of state, he threw the reins upon the necks of both Houses of Congress, and left the leaders to extricate the nation out of the difficulties in which it was involved. Accordingly a succession of schemes, some mad, some foolish, all incompatible one with the other, constituted the labors of both Houses, in which I took no interest, except occasionally to show their absurdity or inadequacy to the end proposed. As to myself, the session was the happiest I ever spent at Washington. My wife and two of my family were with me. I had the whole house to myself, and had the members of Congress frequently to dine with me. My wife was the ornament and attraction of my establishment. She was admired for her manners and mind, was most kindly received by Mrs. Madison at the palace, and enjoyed the society and friendship of a select circle, both in Washington and Georgetown, among whom were the families of Peter, Lee, Teackle, Smith, Tayloe, Cranch, and a few others."

The following letter from Chief Justice Marshall shows how fully that eminent man shared in the anxieties and the forebodings of the Federal party:—

"RICHMOND, April 23, 1810.

"DEAR SIR:—Permit me to request that you will be so good as to charge yourself with the enclosed letter to Rev. Mr. Eliot.

"The Federalists of the South participate with their brethren of the North in the gloomy anticipations which your late elections must inspire.* The proceedings of the House of Representatives already demonstrate the influence of those elections on the affairs of the Union.

"I had supposed that the late letter to Mr. Armstrong, and the late seizure of an American vessel, simply because she was an American, added to previous burnings, ransoms, and confiscations, would have exhausted to the dregs our cup of servility and degradation; but these measures appear to make no impression on those to whom the United States confide their destinies. To what point are we verging?

"With very much respect and esteem, I am, dear sir, your obedient

"J. MARSHALL."

* At the March elections Elbridge Gerry, the Democratic candidate, had been chosen Governor of Massachusetts, and in New Hampshire John Langdon had defeated Governor Jeremiah Smith.

This turbulent session closed about midnight on the 1st of May, and the next day my father left Washington with his family for Boston. The summer was spent as usual at Quincy. It soon passed away, and I find scarcely any record of it left. Notwithstanding his resolution of never going to Washington again unless accompanied by his family, my father was obliged to forego their society during the session of 1810–11. Of his personal arrangements he gives this account: —

"On the 26th of November, 1810, in company with Colonel Timothy Pickering, I took the stage, and, travelling by the way of Hartford and the usual route, reached Washington and took my seat in Congress on the 5th of December. I took a room at Coyle's boarding-house. I had my own servant, and was as happily established as possible when separated from my family. I visited as little as possible, and never except under a sense of obligation, devoting my whole time to the business of the session."

The session of 1810–11 was a memorable one in the history of the United States. Then was established the precedent for the erection of States out of territory foreign to the original domain of the nation, acquired through purchase or conquest, by the mere act of Congress, without recourse to the people in their sovereign capacity, which delivered over the political destiny of the nation for fifty years into the hands of the slaveholders. It was also a memorable epoch in my father's life. The earnest and impassioned resistance he opposed to that fateful measure, the disastrous consequences of which he foresaw and foretold, is perhaps the part of his public life which is the most generally known. It has been particularly recalled to mind since the breaking out of the Rebellion, and his doctrines have been quoted, — sometimes with an approbation I am sure they do not deserve, — on both sides of the Atlantic, as identical with those of the Secession, and as justifying and sustaining it. In order that my readers may judge for themselves whether or not he is justly obnoxious to this satire in disguise, I shall lay before them the most material portions of his famous speech on this subject. It was delivered on the 14th of January, when the Enabling Act was before the House on its final passage.

"Mr. Speaker, — I address you, Sir, with an anxiety and distress of mind with me wholly unprecedented. The friends of this bill seem to consider it as the exercise of a common power, as an ordinary affair, a mere municipal regulation which they expect to see pass without other questions than those concerning details. But, Sir, the principle of this bill materially affects the liberties and rights of the whole people of the United States. To me it appears that it would justify a revolution in this country, and that in no great length of time it may produce it. When I see the zeal and perseverance with which this bill has been urged along its parliamentary path, when I know the local interests and associated projects which combine to promote its success, all opposition to it seems manifestly unavailing. I am almost tempted to leave, without a struggle, my country to its fate. But, Sir, while there is life, there is hope. So long as the fatal shaft has not yet sped, if Heaven so will, the bow may be broken, and the vigor of the mischief-meditating arm withered. If there be a man in this House or nation who cherishes the Constitution under which we are assembled as the chief stay of his hope, as the light which is destined to gladden his own day, and to soften even the gloom of the grave by the prospect it sheds over his children, I fall not behind him in such sentiments. I will yield to no man in attachment to this Constitution, in veneration to the sages who laid its foundations, in devotion to those principles which form its cement and constitute its proportions. What then must be my feelings? What ought to be the feelings of a man cherishing such sentiments, when he sees an act contemplated which lays ruin at the root of all these hopes? — when he sees a principle of action about to be usurped before the operation of which the bands of this Constitution are no more than flax before the fire, or stubble before the whirlwind? When this bill passes, such an act is done, and such a principle usurped.

"Mr. Speaker, There is a great rule of human conduct which he who honestly observes cannot err widely from the path of his sought duty. It is, to be very scrupulous concerning the principles you select as the test of your rights and obligations, to be very faithful in noticing the result of their application, and to be very fearless in tracing and exposing their immediate effects and distant consequences. Under the sanction of this rule of conduct, I am compelled to declare *it as my deliberate opinion, that, if this bill passes, the bonds of this Union are virtually dissolved; that the States which compose it are free from their moral obligations, and that, as it will be the right of all, so it will be the duty of some, to prepare definitely for a separation; amicably if they can, violently if they must.*

"[Mr. Quincy was here called to order by Mr. Poindexter, Delegate from the Mississippi Territory, for the words in Italics. After it was decided, upon an appeal to the House, that Mr. Quincy was in order, he proceeded.]

"I rejoice, Mr. Speaker, at the result of this appeal. Not from any personal considerations, but from the respect paid to the essential rights of the people in one of their representatives. When I spoke of the separation of the States as resulting from the violation of the Constitution contemplated in this bill, I spoke of it as a necessity deeply to be deprecated; but as resulting from causes so certain and obvious as to be absolutely inevitable when the effect of the principle is practically experienced. It is to preserve, to guard, the Constitution of my country, that I denounce this attempt. I would rouse the attention of gentlemen from the apathy with which they seem beset. These observations are not made in a corner; there is no low intrigue; no secret machination. I am on the people's own ground; to them I appeal concerning their own rights, their own liberties, their own intent, in adopting this Constitution. The voice I have uttered, at which gentlemen startle with such agitation, is no unfriendly voice. I intended it as a voice of warning. By this people and by the event, if this bill passes, I am willing to be judged whether it be not a voice of wisdom.

. . . . .

"I know, Mr. Speaker, that the first clause of this paragraph has been read with all the superciliousness of a grammarian's triumph,— '*New States may be admitted by the Congress into this Union*,'— accompanied with this most consequential inquiry, 'Is not this a new State to be admitted? and is not here an express authority?' I have no doubt this is a full and satisfactory argument to every one who is content with the mere colors and superficies of things. And if we were now at the bar of some stall-fed justice, the inquiry would insure victory to the maker of it, to the manifest delight of constables and suitors of his court. But, Sir, we are now before the tribunal of the whole American people, reasoning concerning their liberties, their rights, their Constitution. These are not to be made the victims of the inevitable obscurity of general terms, nor the sport of verbal criticism. The question is concerning *the intent of the American people*, the proprietors of the old United States, when they agreed to this article. Dictionaries and spelling-books are here of no authority. Neither Johnson, nor Walker, nor Webster, nor Dilworth, has any voice in this matter. Sir, the question concerns the proportion of power reserved by this Constitution to every State in this Union. Have the three branches of this government a right, at will, to weaken and outweigh the influence respectively secured to each State in this compact by introducing at pleasure new partners, situate beyond the old limits of the United States? The question has not relation merely to New Orleans. The great objection is to the principle of the bill. If this principle be admitted, the whole space of Louisiana — greater, it is said, than the entire extent of the old United States — will be a mighty theatre in which this government assumes the right of exercising this unparalleled power. And it will be — there is no concealment, it is intended to be — exercised. Nor will it stop until the very name and nature of the old partners be overwhelmed by new-comers into the confederacy. Sir, the question goes to the very root of the power and influence of the present members of this Union.

. . . . .

"But, says the gentleman from Tennessee (Mr Rhea), 'These people have been seven years citizens of the United States.' I deny it, Sir. As citizens of New Orleans, or of Louisiana, they never have been, and by the mode proposed they never will be, citizens of the United States. They may be girt upon us for a moment, but no real cement can grow from such an association. What the real situation of the inhabitants of those foreign countries is, I shall have occasion to show presently. But, says the same gentleman, 'If I have a farm, have not I a right to purchase another farm in my neighborhood and settle my sons upon it, and in time admit them to a share in the management of my household?' Doubtless, Sir. But are these cases parallel? Are the three branches of this government owners of this farm called the United States? I desire to thank Heaven they are not. I hold my life, liberty, and property, and the people of the State from which I have the honor to be a representative hold theirs, by a better tenure than any this national government can give. Sir, I know your virtue. And I thank the Great Giver of every good gift, that neither the gentleman from Tennessee, nor his comrades, nor any nor all the members of this House, nor of the other branch of the Legislature, nor the good gentleman who lives in the palace yonder, nor all combined, can touch these my essential rights, and those of my friends and constituents, except in a limited and prescribed form. No, Sir. We hold these by the laws, customs, and principles of the Commonwealth of Massachusetts. Behind her ample shield we find refuge and feel safety. I beg gentlemen not to act upon the principle that the Commonwealth of Massachusetts is their farm.

. . . . .

"The immortal leader of our Revolution, in his letter to the President of the old Congress, written as President of the Convention which formed this compact, thus speaks on this subject: 'It is at all times difficult to draw with precision the line between those rights which must be surrendered and those which may be reserved; and on the present occasion this difficulty was increased by a *difference among the several States as to their situation, extent, habits, and particular interests.* The debates of that period will show that the effect of the slave votes upon the political influence of this part of the country, and the anticipated variation of the weight of power to the West, were subjects of great and just jealousy to some of the best patriots in the Northern and Eastern States. Suppose, then, that it had been distinctly foreseen, that, in addition to the effect of this weight, the whole population of a world beyond the Mississippi was to be brought into this and the other branch of the Legislature to form our laws, control our rights, and decide our destiny. Sir, can it be pretended that the patriots of that day would for one moment have listened to it? They were not madmen. They had not taken degrees at the hospital of idiocy. They knew the nature of man and the effect of his combinations in political societies. They knew that when the weight of particular sections of a confederacy was greatly unequal, the resulting power would be abused; that it was not in the nature of man to exercise it with moderation. The very extravagance of the intended use is a conclusive evidence against the possibility of the grant of such a power as is here proposed. Why, Sir, I have already heard of six States, and some say there will be at no great distance of time more. I have also heard that the mouth of the Ohio will be far to the East of the centre of the contemplated empire. If the bill is passed, the principle is recognized. All the rest are mere questions of expediency. It is impossible such a power could be granted. It was not for these men that our fathers fought. It was not for them this Constitution was adopted. You have no authority to throw the rights and liberties and property of this people into 'Hotch-pot' with the wild men on the Missouri, nor with the mixed though more respectable race of Anglo-Hispano-Gallo-Americans who bask on the sands in the mouth of the Mississippi.

. . . . .

"I will add only a few words in relation to the moral and political consequences of usurping this power. I have said that it would be a virtual dissolution of the Union; and gentlemen express great sensibility at the expression. But the true source of terror is not the declaration I have made, but the deed you propose. Is there a moral principle of public law better settled, or more conformable to the plainest suggestions of reason, than that the violation of a contract by one of the parties may be considered as exempting the other from its obligations? Suppose in private life thirteen form a partnership, and ten of them undertake to admit a new partner without the concurrence of the other three, would it not be at their option to abandon the partnership after so palpable an infringement of their rights? How much more in the political partnership, where the admission of new associates without previous authority is so pregnant with obvious dangers and evils! Again, it is settled as a principle of morality among writers on public law, that no person can be obliged beyond his intent at the time of the contract. Now who believes, who dares assert, that it was the intention of the people, when they adopted this Constitution, to assign eventually to New Orleans and Louisiana a portion of their political power, and to invest all the people those extensive regions might hereafter contain with an authority over themselves and their descendants? When you throw the weight of Louisiana into the scale, you destroy the political equipoise contemplated at the time of forming the contract. Can any man venture to affirm that the people did intend such a comprehension as you now by construction give it? Or can it be concealed that beyond its fair and acknowledged intent such a compact has no moral force? If gentlemen are so alarmed at the bare mention of the consequences, let them abandon a measure which sooner or later will produce them. How long before the seeds of discontent will ripen, no man can foretell. But it is the part of wisdom not to multiply or scatter them. Do you suppose the people of the Northern and Atlantic States will or ought to look on with patience and see Representatives and Senators from the Red River and Missouri pouring themselves upon this and the other floor, managing the concerns of a sea-board fifteen hundred miles at least from their residence, and having a preponderancy in councils into which constitutionally they could never have been admitted? I have no hesitation upon this point. They neither will see it nor ought to see it with content. It is the part of a wise man to foresee danger and to hide himself. This great usurpation, which creeps into this House under the plausible appearance of giving content to that important point, New Orleans, starts up a gigantic power to control the nation. Upon the actual condition of things there is, there can be, no need of concealment. It is apparent to the blindest vision. By the course of nature, and conformable to the acknowledged principles of the Constitution, the sceptre of power in this country is passing towards the northwest. Sir, there is to this no objection. The right belongs to that quarter of the country: enjoy it. It is yours. Use the powers granted as you please. But take care in your haste after effectual dominion not to overload the scale by heaping it with these new acquisitions. Grasp not too eagerly at your purpose. In your speed after uncontrolled sway, trample not down this Constitution. Already the old States sink in the estimation of members when brought into comparison with these new countries. We have been told that '*New Orleans was the most important point in the Union.*' A place out of the Union the most important place within it! We have been asked, '*What are some of the small States when compared with the Mississippi Territory?*' The gentleman from that Territory (Mr. Poindexter) spoke the other day of the Mississippi as '*of a high-road between*' — good heavens! between what, Mr. Speaker? — why, '*the Eastern and Western States.*' So that all the northwestern territories, all the countries once the extreme western boundary of our Union, are hereafter to be denominated *Eastern States!*

. . . . . .

"New States are intended to be formed beyond the Mississippi. There is no limit to men's imaginations on this subject short of California and Columbia River. When I said that the bill would justify a revolution, and would produce it, I spoke of its principle and its practical consequences. To this principle and those consequences I would call the attention of this House and nation. If it be about to introduce a condition of things absolutely insupportable, it becomes wise and honest men to anticipate the evil, and to warn and prepare the people against the event. I have no hesitation on the subject. The extension of this principle to the States contemplated beyond the Mississippi cannot, will not, and ought not to be borne. And the sooner the people contemplate the unavoidable result, the better, the more likely that convulsions may be prevented, the more hope that the evils may be palliated or removed.

"Mr. Speaker, what is this liberty of which so much is said? Is it to walk about this earth, to breathe this air, and to partake the common blessings of God's providence? The beasts of the field and the birds of the air unite with us in such privileges as these. But man boasts a purer and more ethereal temperature. His mind grasps in its view the past and future as well as the present. We live not for ourselves alone. That which we call liberty is that principle on which the essential security of our political condition depends. It results from the limitations of our political system prescribed in the Constitution. These limitations, so long as they are faithfully observed, maintain order, peace, and safety. When they are violated in essential particulars, all the concurrent spheres of authority rush against each other; and disorder, derangement, and convulsion are sooner or later the necessary consequences.

"With respect to this love of our Union, concerning which so much sensibility is expressed, I have no fear about analyzing its nature. There is in it nothing of mystery. It depends upon the qualities of that Union, and it results from its effects upon our and our country's happiness. It is valued for 'that sober certainty of waking bliss,' which it enables us to realize. It grows out of the affections, and has not, and cannot be made to have, anything universal in its nature. Sir, I confess it, the first public love of my heart is the Commonwealth of Massachusetts. There is my fireside, there are the tombs of my ancestors.

'Low lies that land, yet blest with fruitful stores;
Strong are her sons, though rocky are her shores;
And none, ah! none so lovely to my sight,
Of all the lands which heaven o'erspreads with light.'

"The love of this Union grows out of this attachment to my native soil, and is rooted in it. I cherish it because it affords the best external hope of her peace, her prosperity, her independence. I oppose this bill from no animosity to the people of New Orleans, but from the deep conviction that it contains a principle incompatible with the liberties and safety of my country. I have no concealment of my opinion. The bill, if it passes, is a death-blow to the Constitution. It may afterwards linger, but, lingering, its fate will at no very distant period be consummated."

To his wife he wrote as follows at the time: —

"I answered my purpose fully. The House were so arrested by my boldness that they heard me throughout, and Poindexter has made my position so prominent that I have no fear but that the nation will do the same. This I deem in principle and consequences the most important question that has ever been decided. If the people in our part of the Union are tame on this question, they deserve to be what they will be, *slaves*, and to no very desirable masters. . . . .

"You have no idea how these Southern demagogues tremble at the word 'separation' from a Northern man, and yet they are riding the

Atlantic States like a nightmare. I shall not fail to make their ears tingle with it, whenever they attempt, as in this instance, grossly to violate the Constitution of my country. Some of them were so outrageous that they talked of a halter for your husband; but upon the whole they have concluded to give me a reprieve until my 'constituents' put on the noose.

"My landlord, Mr. Coyle, came home the other day and told me a clerk in one of the public offices had asked him how I behaved in his house; for that one of the Massachusetts Democratic delegation told him that he thought I WAS CRAZY, adding *that it was a complaint to which my family was subject.* I told Mr. Coyle to tell that clerk to read my speech, and he must agree at least that there was great method in my madness.

"Such are the poor tricks of men ignorant of the rights which belong to public debate, and forgetful of what a public man owes not only to himself and his country, but to posterity. I know not how what I have said will be received by my constituents. I know how it ought to be. But the case is my own. I judge not. . . . . The view I took of that question is not denied to be new here; and had it not to resist all the force of Administration, powerful local interests, and temporary projects deeply interesting to the men in power, I have little doubt it would have been successful. With the people, and in future time, I have no question it will be duly appreciated."

The bill passed the next day, January 15th, by a vote of seventy-seven yeas to thirty-six nays.

Mr. Hildreth, in his History of the United States, pronounces the declaration with which this speech began, — "that, if this bill passes, the bonds of this Union are virtually dissolved, that the States which compose it are free from their moral obligations, and that, as it is the right of all, so it will be the duty of some, to prepare definitely for a separation, amicably if they can, violently if they must," — to have been "the first announcement on the floor of Congress of the doctrine of Secession."* However this may be, I think that it will not require a labored argument to prove to any one who has carefully read the speech, that the secessionism it contains is a very different doctrine from that preached in later times. Mr. Quincy did not maintain that the

* Hildreth's History of the United States, Vol. III. p. 226.

Constitution contained within itself an inherent and indefeasible right of any member of the Union to withdraw from it at pleasure. He affirmed only that when the Constitution was flagrantly violated in the interest of a particular section of the country and of a fatal and encroaching institution, incompatible with the rights and liberties of the whole nation, the moral obligation to maintain it ceased, the right of revolution attached, and the constituent States might resume their several sovereignty, if such were their pleasure. The right of resistance to a high-handed violation of the fundamental compact, admitted to be such by the President who initiated it, himself the accepted high-priest of the Democracy, may be clearly distinguished from that claimed to break up the government on a question of revenue or on the election of a President not to the mind of the minority. The secessionism of Josiah Quincy was the vindication of the rights of freedom against the unconstitutional aggressions of slavery; that of Jefferson Davis, the vindication of the rights of slavery against the constitutional restrictions of freedom. Whether Mr. Quincy spoke like a sagacious statesman and a true prophet, let the history of the next half-century answer, in the long supremacy of the slave-power, chiefly through the operation of the principle of this very bill, and in the convulsion which followed the first successful resistance to its absolute sway and unlimited extension. Right or wrong, however, he himself adhered to the opinion thus expressed, that the moral obligation of the old States to remain in the Union was released by that Act, to the day of his death.

He had, however, the most cordial assurances of approval of his speech from the most prominent members of his party. As, for example, Harrison Gray Otis, in a letter dated February 2d, 1811, says: —

"It [the speech] is in my opinion a very honorable monument of your fame, and proves as well the correctness of your prospective views of the destiny of your ill-fated country as of the force and eloquence by which you are capable of unfolding them. The time will come when that speech will be regarded as prophecy, and when those who are infected by the apathy, or dismayed by the calamities, of the times, will blush at the reflection of having withheld from you a more cordial and animating support."

John Lowell of Boston writes, under date of February 13th, 1811: —

"The boldness of your speech, while it has called forth the most virulent abuse from the Democratic party, and cowardly disapprobation from some of your early *feeble* Federal friends, will do you more credit with posterity than any effort of your mind which you have heretofore made."

In the height of the excitement occasioned by his speech, Mr. Quincy received the following cordial letter from John Adams, to which he replied on the 29th of January.

MR. ADAMS TO MR. QUINCY.

"QUINCY, January 15, 1811.

"DEAR SIR: — I thank you for two presents, the Message and the documents. Mr. Madison follows the example of Mr. Jefferson in this instance; but is the difference between a speech and a message of much importance? Does the aversion to speeches and the partiality for messages arise or proceed from the spirit of democracy or aristocracy?

"The glorious uncertainty of the law is a proverbial expression; and why may we not speak of the glorious uncertainty of politics? It gives you great legislators, philosophers, and orators ample scope for all your genius, experience, sagacity, and eloquence. What can be more glorious for the notables of all parties?

"An old man, however, in his sixteenth lustre, would not willingly exchange for all your glories such a morning as this, when, unencumbered with the least responsibility for anything, he sees the sun rising in an atmosphere as clear as crystal, after an imprisonment of a fortnight or three weeks by bad weather.

"We have now the third flight of beautiful snow and fine sleighing. The two former were dissipated in two or three days. This I hope will last till you come home. The blustering and bullying of France and England disturb me much less than the freezing and thawing of this winter. I know, with submission, that all their power and all their policy can do no more finally than compel Hercules to feel his strength and show his wit.

"I am, sir, as ever, your friend and humble servant,

"J. ADAMS."

MR. QUINCY TO MR. ADAMS.

"WASHINGTON, 29th January, 1811.

"DEAR SIR:—I have the very great pleasure to acknowledge your favor of the 15th instant. Be assured, sir, that I appreciate the honor of your correspondence, and that it will be a precious reward to cultivate and deserve your esteem and confidence.

"'The uncertainty of politics' is indeed as obvious as it is lamentable. I cannot, however, unite with you in applying to it the epithet 'glorious.' It is to me a most humiliating as well as depressing fact. Since there are no guides which are infallible, whom shall we follow? Since there are no principles which seem absolutely settled, what foothold has reason, on which it may tread with firmness? All the lights of reflection fail, all those of history are extinguished at the breath and the bidding of the spirit of party. The wisdom which our fathers taught us is despised; and the liberty with which you and they made us free is little else than a cloak for licentiousness. Temporary projects supersede all the prospective duties resulting from permanent relations; and the pride and patronage expected from an extensive territory are taking place of that consolidating and masculine course of policy which distinguished the two first administrations. I know not what fates await us. And in the mysterious course pursuing I can see no other way than to cast anchor upon long-established principles, and trust my own and my country's fortunes, so far as any agency of mine has an influence upon it, to their firmness.

"You will easily perceive, and I shall not conceal, that the course of my reflection has in some degree been shaped by the very responsible stand I have taken against the admission of New Orleans as a State into the Union. My remarks on that subject will probably have reached you through the papers previously to this letter. I should have had the honor of transmitting them to you personally, and shall soon, but I have been waiting for a copy from Baltimore, where, I am told, they are publishing in a better type than that of our ordinary newspapers. Everything of this kind, now-a-days, takes a party lurch, and is attributed to party projects. Yet the truth is, the ground broken by me was as little anticipated by any one of my own party as by any of the opposite. Whether right or whether wrong, I was irresistibly driven to it by a sense of duty to my country. This I have followed instinctively, and shall, let it lead me where it will, and let it run me foul of whom or what it will. If the consequences I have there drawn be not true, if the anticipations be not real and reasonable, I confess that the guides of my mind are deceptive, and that the lights Heaven has set up in it afford no distinct vision of things. I have not expected, nor do I expect, that the ground there defended will speedily be popular. The evils are distant, at least twice the length of the nose, and that is half as far again as the majority of those who call themselves politicians deign to examine. The expressions at which exception was taken were selected, and the event not altogether unanticipated. My determination was to mark the opposition to the bill distinctly in the public mind, and oblige it to be attentive to the subject. I have thus far attained my end. As to the rest I am indifferent.

"The opportunity your letter gave me has drawn me into this explanation. But it is without any design to attract a reply from you on the topic. You may not incline either to censure or approve. This, however, was a case in which my own sense of duty was so clear and so imperious that, let whatever be the event, I can have no regret. I write to you with the more frankness, because, sir, I confess, there has always been towards you and yours something of the filial and fraternal in my feelings, and whatever casual differences may arise, should any ever exist, they can never affect the pride I feel in, and my sense of, your friendship, or the very great respect with which I can never cease to be

"Your obedient and very humble servant,

"JOSIAH QUINCY."

To this letter President Adams replied on the 9th of February, at length, and his answer may be found in his Works, Vol. IX. page 629. I subjoin a few extracts, from which it will be seen that he did not set up his own times as better than those of his correspondent.

"I ought not to object to your reverence for your fathers, as you call them, meaning, I presume, the government and those concerned in the direction of public affairs, much less can I be displeased at your numbering me among them. But to tell you a very great secret, as far as I am capable of comparing the merit of different periods, I have no reason to believe that we were better than you are. We had as many poor creatures and selfish beings in proportion among us, as you have among you; nor were there then more enlightened men, or in greater number, than there are now.

'Heaven from all creatures hides the book of fate.'

'Le grand Rouleau en haut' cannot be read by our telegraphic telescopes. . . . .

"Your eloquence and oratory upon this question are worthy of your father, your grandfather, and your great-grandfather. You spoke your own sentiments, I doubt not, with integrity, and the sense of a majority of your immediate constituents, and will not only increase your popularity with them, but extend your fame as a statesman and an orator, but will not influence at present the great body of the people in the nation.

"Prophecies of division have been familiar in my ears for six-and-thirty years. They have been incessant, but have had no other effect than to increase the attachment of the people to the Union. However lightly we may think of the voice of the people sometimes, they not unfrequently see further than you or I in many great fundamental questions. And you may depend upon it, they see in a partition of the Union more dangers to American liberty than poor Ames's distempered imagination conceived, and a total loss of independence for both fragments, or all the fragments, of the Union."

The events of the last six years have certainly shown that the patriarch was a prophet as well, and that he knew the American people not only better than their partisan leaders knew them, but better than they knew themselves. Though they had consented to compromise after compromise, and yielded concession after concession, rather than put the Union in jeopardy, yet when the madness which these very yieldings had nursed broke out into open rebellion, they held back no cost of blood and treasure that it might be preserved entire; and this from the very instinct for the preservation of their personal freedom and national independence which the aged patriot had divined.

CHAPTER X.

1811 – 1812.

SPEECH ON PLACE AND PATRONAGE. — ON NON-INTERCOURSE. — WASHINGTON IRVING. — TWELFTH CONGRESS. — MR. CLAY AND THE WAR DEMOCRATS. — FEDERAL PERPLEXITIES. — MR. QUINCY VOTES FOR MILITARY PREPARATIONS. — OFFENDS A PORTION OF HIS PARTY. — SPEECH ON MARITIME PROTECTION.

THE next labor which Mr. Quincy undertook was scarcely less Herculean than the one just described. It was nothing less gigantic than to cleanse the Augean stable of political corruption. Early in the session, Mr. Macon * of North Carolina moved the following amendment to the Constitution: —

"No Senator or Representative shall be appointed to any civil office, place, or employment under the authority of the United States, until the expiration of the Presidential term in which such person shall have served as Senator or Representative."

On the 30th of January, this amendment being under consideration in committee of the whole House, Mr. Quincy moved that the following proposition be added to it: —

"And no person standing to any Senator or Representative in the relation of father, brother, or son, by blood or marriage, shall be appointed to any civil office under the United States, or shall receive any place, agency, contract, or emolument from or under any department or officer thereof."

This amendment he then supported in a speech, from which the following extracts are taken: —

"Upon this subject of offices my sentiments may, perhaps, be too refined for the present condition of human nature. And I am aware, in

* Nathaniel Macon, born in North Carolina, 1757; served as a private in the Revolutionary War, having declined a commission. He was in the House and Senate from 1791 to 1828, — the longest term of Congressional service, I believe, on record. He was Speaker from 1801 to 1807; and President *pro tem.* of the Senate from 1825 to 1828; died, 1837.

what I am about to say, that I may run athwart political friends as well as political foes. Such considerations as these shall not, however, deter me from introducing just and high notions of their duties to the consideration of the members of the Legislature. I hold, Sir, the acceptance of an office of mere emolument, or which is principally emolument, by a member of Congress from the Executive, as unworthy his station, and incompatible with that high sense of irreproachable character which it is one of the choicest terrestrial boons of virtue to attain. For while the attainment of office is to members of Congress the consequence solely of coincidence with the Executive, he who has the office carries on his forehead the mark of having fulfilled the condition. And although his self-love may denominate his attainment of the office to be the reward of merit, the world, which usually judges acutely on these matters, will denominate it the reward of service.

. . . . .

"Such is the opinion which, in my judgment, ought to be entertained of the mere acceptance of office by members of Congress. But as to that other class of persons, who are open, notorious solicitors of office, they give occasion to reflections of a very different nature. This class of persons in all times past have appeared, and (for I say nothing of times present) in all times future will appear, on this and the other floor of Congress, creatures who, under pretence of serving the people, are in fact serving themselves, — creatures who, while their distant constituents, good, easy men, industrious, frugal, and unsuspicious, dream in visions that they are laboring for their country's welfare, are in truth spending their time mousing at the doors of the palace or the crannies of the departments, and laying low snares to catch for themselves and their relations every stray office that flits by them. For such men, chosen into this high and responsible trust, to whom have been confided the precious destinies of this people, and who thus openly abandon their duties, and set their places and their consciences to sale in defiance of the multiplied strong and tender ties by which they are bound to their country, I have no language to express my contempt. I never have seen and I never shall see any of these notorious solicitors of office for themselves or their relations standing on this or the other floor, bawling and bullying, or coming down with dead votes in support of executive measures, but I think I see a hackney laboring for hire in a most degrading service; a poor, earth-spirited animal trudging in his traces with much attrition of the sides and induration of the membranes, encouraged by this special certainty, that at the end of his journey he shall have measured out to him his proportion of provender.

"But I have heard that the bare suggestion of such corruption was a libel upon this House and upon this people. I have heard that we were in this country so virtuous, that we were above the influence of these allurements; that beyond the Atlantic in old governments such things might be suspected, but that here we were too pure for such guilt, too innocent for such suspicions. Mr. Chairman, I shall not hesitate, in spite of such popular declamation, to believe and follow the evidence of my senses and the concurrent testimonies of contemporaneous beholders. I shall not in my estimation of character degrade this people below, nor exalt them far above, the ordinary condition of cultivated humanity. And of this be assured, — that every system of conduct or course of policy which has for its basis an excess of virtue in this country beyond what human nature exhibits in its improved state elsewhere, will be found on trial fallacious. Is there on this earth any collection of men in which exists a more intrinsic, hearty, and desperate love of office or place, — particularly of fat places? Is there any country more infested than this with the vermin that breed in the corruptions of power? Is there any in which place and official emolument more certainly follow distinguished servility at elections, or base scurrility in the press? And as to eagerness for the reward, what is the fact? Let now one of your great office-holders, a Collector of the Customs, a Marshal, a Commissioner of Loans, a Postmaster in one of your cities, or any officer, agent, or factor for your territories or public lands, or person holding a place of minor distinction, but of considerable profit, be called upon to pay the last great debt of nature. The poor man shall hardly be dead, he shall not be cold, long before the corpse is in the coffin, the mail shall be crowded to repletion with letters and certificates, and recommendations and representations, and every species of sturdy, sycophantic solicitation by which obtrusive mendicity seeks charity or invites compassion. Why, Sir, we hear the clamor of the craving animals at the treasury-trough here in this capital. Such running, such jostling, such wriggling, such clambering over one another's backs, such squealing because the tub is so narrow and the company so crowded! No, Sir, let us not talk of stoical apathy towards the things of the national treasury, either in this people or in their Representatives or Senators.

"But it will be asked, for it has been asked, Shall the Executive be suspected of corrupting the national Legislature? Is he not virtuous? Without making personal distinctions or references for the sake of argument, it may be admitted that all Executives for the time being are virtuous, — reasonably virtuous, Mr. Chairman, — flesh and blood notwithstanding. And without meaning in this place to cast any particular reflections upon this or upon any other Executive, this I will say, that if no additional guards are provided, and now after the spirit of party has brought into so full activity the spirit of patronage, there never will be a President of these United States elected by means now in use, who, if he deals honestly with himself, will not be able on quitting his Presidential chair to address it as John Falstaff addressed Prince Hal, — 'Before I knew thee I knew nothing, and now I am but little better than one of the wicked.' The possession of that station under the reign of party will make a man so acquainted with the corrupt principles of human conduct, he will behold our nature in so hungry and shivering and craving a state, and be compelled so constantly to observe the solid rewards daily demanded by way of compensation for outrageous patriotism, that, if he escape out of that atmosphere without partaking of its corruption, he must be below or above the ordinary condition of mortal nature. Is it possible, Sir, that he should remain altogether uninfected? What is the fact? The Constitution prohibits the members of this and of the other branch of the Legislature from being Electors of the President of the United States. Yet what is done? The practice of late is so prevalent as to have grown almost into a sanctioned usage of party. Prior to the Presidential term of four years, members of Congress having received the privileged ticket of admission assemble themselves in a sort of electoral college, on the floor of the Senate or of the House of Representatives. They select a candidate for the Presidency. To their voice, to their influence, he is indebted for his elevation. So long as this condition of things continues, what ordinary Executive will refuse to accommodate those who in so distinguished a manner have accommodated him? Is there a better reason in the world why a man should give you, Mr. Chairman, an office worth two or three thousand dollars a year for which you are qualified, and which he could give as well as not, than this, that you had been greatly instrumental in giving him one worth five and twenty thousand for which he was equally qualified? It is in vain to conceal it. So long as the present condition of things continues, it may reasonably be expected that there shall take place regularly between the President of the United States and a portion of both Houses of Congress an interchange, strictly speaking, of good offices."

However deeply the innuendoes of this speech, as well as its direct assaults, might have been secretly resented, it was listened to with apparent good-humor, and its hits greeted with responsive laughter. Indeed, those whom it misliked sought to parry its thrusts only by a *reductio ad absurdum.* Mr. Wright* of Maryland moved to amend by providing that each Senator and Representative, on taking his seat, should furnish a table of his genealogy. Mr. Seybert said that this amendment would not answer the purpose of the mover, "because a man might marry while a member, and thus change his whole connection." Mr. Wright reduced his motion to writing thus: "Each member of the Senate and the House, when he takes his seat, shall file a list of his relatives precluded by said resolution." When the Committee rose, the question came up on printing the amendments. Mr. Smilie † of Pennsylvania, was in favor of printing Mr. Macon's motion; but doubted whether it would comport with the dignity of the House to print the last two (Mr. Quincy's and Mr. Wright's), which could scarcely be seriously meant. Mr. Troup ‡ of Georgia, on the contrary, was in favor of printing. He thought the proposition (of Mr. Quincy) not only important, but essential to carry into effect the original motion; and he had never heard a proposition more ably supported than that of the gentleman from Massachusetts. Almost every sentiment he uttered had met his assent. Finally, Mr. Quincy's amendment was ordered to be printed, and Mr. Wright's refused the compliment of that ceremony. At a later date Mr. Quincy's amendment, as well as that of Mr. Wright, was rejected, and finally this self-denying ordinance itself failed from a lack of the requisite two thirds in its favor, although it received a large majority of votes.

Mr. Adams wrote a letter, February 18th, thanking Mr.

* Robert Wright, Senator from Maryland, 1801-6; Governor, 1806-9; Member of Congress, 1810-17 and 1821-23. When Governor, in 1808, he distinguished himself by pardoning some rioters who had been convicted and imprisoned for tarring and feathering an unlucky English shoemaker, with high compliments upon their patriotism. Hildreth's History, Vol. III. p. 95.

† John Smilie, an Irishman by birth; served in civil and military capacities during the Revolution; Member of Congress, 1793-95 and 1799-1813, in which last year he died.

‡ George M. Troup, born 1780; graduated at Princeton; Member of Congress, 1807-15; Senator, 1816-18 and 1829-34; Governor, 1823-27; died, 1856.

Quincy for this speech, and praising its rhetorical merits in terms which, it must be allowed, are excessive, not to say hyperbolical. He says: —

"I owe you thanks for your speech on Place and Patronage. The moral and patriotic sentiments are noble and exalted, the eloquence masterly, and the satire inimitable. There are not in Juvenal nor in Swift any images to be found more exquisitely ridiculous than the Charlestown hack and the treasury swill-trough and piggery. But are you right in supposing the rage for office more eager and craving now than it has always been, or more grasping and intriguing for executive offices and for legislative stations?" *

The following letters from two eminent men engaged in academic pursuits in States widely separated from one another belong to this place. Learned men in the professions, and having charge of the principal Universities and Colleges, were, with rare exceptions, Federalists of the most pronounced description. With President Smith my readers are already acquainted, as the friend and adviser of my mother in her girlhood. He was born in 1750, and graduated at Princeton in 1769. After serving as tutor there for a few years he went to Virginia, where he was one of the founders of Hampden-Sidney College in Prince Edward County, and was its first President. He was afterwards recalled to Princeton, where he was first Professor of Theology and Moral Philosophy, and afterwards President. He was the author of several theological and ethical works, and died in 1819. Professor Parker Cleaveland of Bowdoin College, Maine, of which institution he was the pride and ornament for more than forty years, stood in the foremost rank of the scientific men of his time as a chemist, and yet more as a mineralogist, and was a European as well as an American celebrity. He graduated at Harvard in 1799, and died at Brunswick, Maine, in 1858.

President Smith to Mr. Quincy.

"Princeton, Feb. 15, 1811.

"Dear Sir: — Accept my thanks for the copies of your speeches which you have been good enough to transmit to me. One of them I

* Life and Works of John Adams, Vol. IX. p. 633.

had seen before, and had read with great pleasure. The other, on Patronage, was new, and uncommonly full of interest, and of amusement, if anything can amuse an American which displays so pointedly the degradation of his country. You must daily see, hear, and feel the dishonors of this boasted Republic, and the blasting of all our flattering hopes, in the most afflicting manner. But in an assembly of beasts who have only horns, and no brains, is it not almost too hazardous to make them feel so deeply your sovereign contempt? For to reform them seems to be beyond human power. Your only consolation must be shortly to get out of the *hearing* of their folly; for under the *feeling* of its effects you and all of us must long and severely suffer.

"With the most sincere esteem and respect, I am, dear sir, y[r]. m[o]. ob[dt]. and m[o]. h[ble]. serv[t].,

"SAMUEL S. SMITH."

PROFESSOR CLEAVELAND TO MR. QUINCY.

"BRUNSWICK, April 2, 1811.

"DEAR SIR: — Yours of the 21st March was received by the last mail. The *notice* to which you allude has never been received by me; the only knowledge I had of my election* was by the private letters of friends. I am sorry that any additional trouble should arise to you on account of the notice having been mislaid. No inconvenience has arisen to me, as I have not visited Boston since the last autumn.

"The election of Governor has this day taken place. In Brunswick we have twenty-five *less* majority for Mr. Gore than we had the last year. This is not to be attributed to a dereliction from Federalism so much as to the absence of *seamen* and other accidental causes.

"I much fear, however, that the reports respecting General Cobb's *Church establishment* (of which you have probably seen something in the newspapers) have had an unfavorable effect upon many of the *Baptist* denomination.

"There is another story which has been circulated among the Republicans of this neighborhood, in which *your* name is employed.

"It is in substance (as related at a Democratic caucus in this town the last week, at which Federalists were permitted to be *present*, but *not to speak*) as follows: — 'That a Mr. Daniel Reed, who, some five or six years since, was a Federal Representative in our State Legislature from *Lewistown*, says he was then on a committee with *yourself* and others; that you then observed it was necessary to have a *Church*

* Probably, as a member of the American Academy of Arts and Sciences.

establishment and an *order of nobility*; that measures were then taking to effect these purposes; and that, if necessary, England would assist in effecting these purposes.'

"The Federalists intend ascertaining whether Mr. Reed has made the above assertions or not; he is *now* a Democrat.

"I presume, sir, you can hardly be aware of the various arts employed and stories fabricated in the District of Maine to affect the result of elections; or if you can easily suppose all this, you cannot well calculate the *extent* of their baleful influence, without a knowledge of the *peculiar character* of those who inhabit our *back settlements*.

"Where *youth* are deprived of education, and *all* of public worship on the Sabbath, the mind is debased, and the influence of truth and sound argument is entirely lost.

"I am, sir, with much respect, your &c.,

"PARKER CLEAVELAND.

The next speech of Mr. Quincy, and the last he made in this Congress, was on the bill to revive Non-Intercourse with Great Britain. The Non-Intercourse which replaced the Embargo at the close of Mr. Jefferson's Administration had expired by its own limitation in May, 1810. It was then enacted, that, in case either France or England should revoke their Decrees or Orders hostile to neutrality, the President should announce the fact by Proclamation, and in case the other belligerent should not do the same within three months, Non-Intercourse should revive as to the contumacious power. Bonaparte, through his Minister for Foreign Affairs, our old acquaintance Champagny, now Duc de Cadore, laid a snare in the very sight of Mr. Madison which yet was not laid in vain. Professing to be satisfied with the act of May, he informed General Armstrong, the American Minister, in August, that the Berlin and Milan Orders were revoked, and would cease to be operative after the 1st of November, provided England revoked her Orders in Council. Although Bonaparte had been soothing his sensibilities, wounded at his being joined with England in the Non-Intercourse of 1809, by seizing and confiscating all the American ships and cargoes he could lay his hands on, Mr. Madison was so rejoiced at this loop-hole of escape from his political embarrassments, that he issued his Proclamation on the 2d of November, annulling the Non-Intercourse Act, without waiting for the performance by England of the condition precedent. As she, not unnaturally, declined to perform it, the act revived as to her on the 2d of February, of which unpleasant fact Mr. Madison had again to inform the country by Proclamation. There being some question as to the legality of this measure, owing to the issuing of the Proclamation of November before the fulfilment of Bonaparte's conditions, it was thought best to re-enact Non-Intercourse as to England. Bonaparte, be it said in passing, continued to seize American ships under his Decrees, even after the arrival of the President's Proclamation in France, while he peremptorily refused satisfaction for his previous confiscations. This, however, he assured us, was only to insure our enforcement of Non-Intercourse with England. I subjoin the most material paragraphs of Mr. Quincy's speech.

"The proposition contained in these amendments has relation to the most momentous and most elevated of our legislative obligations. We are not now about to discuss the policy by which a princely pirate may be persuaded to relinquish his plunder; nor yet the expectation entertained of relaxation in her belligerent system of a haughty and perhaps jealous rival; nor yet the faith which we owe to a treacherous tyrant; nor yet the fond, but frail hopes of favors from a British regency, melting into our arms in the honeymoon of power. The obligations which claim our observance are of a nature much more tender and imperious, — the obligations which as representatives we owe to our constituents, — the allegiance by which we are bound to the American people, — the obedience which is due to that solemn faith by which we are pledged to protect their peace, their prosperity, and their honor. All these high considerations are materially connected with this policy.

"It is not my intention, Mr. Speaker, to dilate on the general nature and effects of this commercial restrictive system. It is no longer a matter of speculation. We have no need to resort for illustration of its nature to the twilight lustre of history, nor yet to the vibrating brightness of the human intellect. We have experience of its effects. They are above, around, and beneath us. They paralyze the enterprise of your cities. They sicken the industry of your fields. They deprive the laborer and the mechanic of his employment. They subtract from the husbandman and planter the just reward for that product which he has moistened with the sweat of his brow. They crush individuals in the ruins of their most flattering hopes, and shake the deep-rooted fabric of general prosperity.

. . . . .

"This, then, is the state of my argument, — that as this non-intercourse system is not fiscal, nor protective of manufactures, nor competent to coerce, and is injurious, it ought to be abandoned, unless we are bound to persist in it by imperious obligations. My object will be to show that no such obligations exist; that the present is a favorable opportunity, not to be suffered to escape, totally to relinquish it; that it is time to manage our own commercial concerns according to our own interests, and no longer put them into the keeping of those who hate or those who envy our prosperity; that we are the constituted shepherds, and ought no more to transfer our custody to the wolves.

"It is agreed on all sides that it is desirable to abandon this commercial restrictive system. But the advocates of the measures now proposed say that we cannot abandon it, because our faith is plighted. Yes, Sir, our faith is plighted; and that, too, to that scrupulous gentleman, Napoleon, — a gentleman so distinguished for his own regard of faith, for his kindness and mercies towards us, for angelic whiteness of moral character, for overweening affection for the American people and their prosperity. Truly, Sir, it is not to be questioned but that our faith should be a perfect work towards this paragon of purity. On account of our faith plighted to him, it is proposed to continue this Non-Intercourse.

. . . . .

"Before, however, I proceed, I would premise that, while I am doubtful whether I shall obtain it, I am sure that the nature of my argument deserves the favor and prepossession for its success of every member in the House. My object is to show that the obligation which we owe to the people of the United States is a free and unrestricted commerce. The object of those who advocate these measures is to show that the obligation we owe to Napoleon Bonaparte is a commerce restricted and enslaved. Now as much as our allegiance is due more to the people of the United States than it is to Napoleon Bonaparte, just so much ought my argument to be received by an American Congress with more favor and prepossession than the argument of those who advocate these measures. It is my intention to make my course of reasoning as precise and distinct as possible, because I invite scrutiny. I contend for my country according to my conscientious conceptions of its best interests. If there be fallacy, detect it. My invitation is given to generous disputants. As to your stump-orators, who utter low invective and mistake it for wit, and gross personality and pass it off for argument, I descend not to their level, nor recognize their power to injure, nor even to offend.

. . . . .

"We all recollect what a state of depression the conduct of Bonaparte in seizing our vessels, subsequent to the 1st of November, produced, as soon as it was known in this House; and what a sudden joy was lighted up in it when the news of the arrival of a French Minister was communicated. Great hopes were entertained and expressed that he would bring some formal revocation of the Decrees, or disavowal of the seizures, which might retroact and support the Proclamation. It was confidently expected that some explanation, at least, of these outrages would be contained in his portmanteau; that under his powder-puff, or in his snuff-box, some dust would be found to throw into the eyes of the American people which might so far blind the sense as to induce them to acquiesce in the enforcement of the Non-Intercourse without any very scrupulous scrutiny into the performance of the conditions by Bonaparte. But, alas! Sir, the Minister is as parsimonious as his master is voracious. He has not condescended to extend one particle, not one pinch, of comfort to the Administration. From anything in the Messages of our President, it would not be so much as known that such a blessed vision as this new envoy had saluted his eyes. His communications preserve an ominous silence on the topic. Administration after all their hopes have been compelled to resort to the old specific, and have caused to be tipped up on our tables a cart-load of sand, grit, and sawdust from our metaphysical mechanic who seesaws at St. James's as they pull the wire here in Washington. Yes, Sir, a letter written on the tenth day of December last, by our Minister in London, is seriously introduced to prove, by abstract reasoning, that the Berlin and Milan Decrees had ceased to exist on the 1st of the preceding November, of whose existence as late as the 25th of last December we have, as far as the nature of things permit, ocular, auricular, and tangible demonstration. And the people of this country are invited to believe the logic of Mr. Pinkney, in the face of the fact of a continued seizure of all the vessels which came within the grasp of the French Custom-House from the 1st of November down to the date of our last accounts; and in defiance of the declaration of our *chargé d'affaires*, made on the 10th of December, that '*it will not be pretended that the decrees have in fact been revoked,'* and in utter discredit of the allegation of the Duke of Massa, made on the 25th of the same month, which in effect declares the Berlin and Milan Decrees exist, by declaring '*that they shall remain suspended.*' After such evidence as this, the question whether a revocation or modification of the edicts of France has so occurred '*as that they cease to violate the neutral commerce of the United States,*' does no longer depend upon the subtilties of syllogistic skill, nor is to be disproved by any power of logical illation. It is an affair of sense and feeling. And our citizens whose property has been since the 1st of November uniformly seized, and of which they are avowedly to be deprived three months, and which is then only to be returned to them on the condition of good behavior, may as soon be made to believe, by the teachings of philosophy, that their rights are not violated, as a wretch writhing under the lash of the executioner might be made by a course of reasoning to believe that the natural state of his flesh was not violated, and that his shoulders, out of which blood was flowing at every stroke, were in the quiet enjoyment of cuticular ease.

. . . . .

"Cadore is directed to say to Mr Armstrong, 'In this new state of things, I am authorized to declare to you, sir, that the Decrees of Berlin and Milan are revoked, and that after the 1st of November they will cease to have effect; *it being understood that, in consequence of this declaration*, the English shall revoke their Orders in Council and renounce the new principles of blockade which they have wished to establish; or that the United States, conformably to the act you have just communicated, shall cause their rights to be respected by the English.' In this curious gallimaufry of time present and time future, of doing and refraining to do, of declaration and understanding, of English duties and American duties, it is easy to trace the design and see its adaptation to the past and present policy of the French Emperor. The time present was used, because the act of the United States required that previously to proclamation the edicts '*shall be*' revoked. And this is the mighty mystery of time present being used in expressing an act intended to be done in time future. For if, as the order of time and the state of intention indicated, time future had been used, and the letter of Cadore had said *the decrees shall be revoked on the 1st of November next*, then the Proclamation could not be issued, because the President would be obliged to wait to have evidence that the act had been effectually done. Now, as the French Emperor never intended that it should be effectuated, and yet meant to have all the advantage of an effectual deed without performing it, this notable scheme was invented. And, by French finesse and American acquiescence, a thing is considered as effectually done, if the declaration that it is done be made in language of time present, notwithstanding the time of performance is in the same breath declared to be in time future. Having thus secured the concurrence of the American Administration, the next part of the scheme was so to arrange the expression that either the British government should not accede, or, if it did accede, that it should secure to France the point of honor, — a previous revocation by the British; and if they did not accede, that there should be a color for seizures and sequestrations, and thus still further to bind the Americans over to their good behavior. All this is attained by this well-devised expression, '*It being understood that*, IN CONSEQUENCE OF THIS DECLARATION, *the English shall revoke*.' Now Great Britain either would accede to the terms, or she would not. If she did, and did it, as the terms required, *in consequence of this declaration*, then it must be done previous to the 1st of November, and then the point of honor was saved to France, — so that thus France, by a revocation verbally present, effectually future, would attain an effectual previous revocation from the English. But if, as France expected, Great Britain would not trust in such paper security, and therefore not revoke previously to the 1st of November, then an apology might be found for France to justify her in refusing to effectuate that present, future, absolute, conditional revocation.

. . . . .

"Mr. Speaker, let us not be deceived concerning the policy of the French Emperor. It is stern, unrelenting, and unrelaxing. So far from any deviation from his original system being indicated in this letter of the Duke of Cadore, a strict adherence to it is formally and carefully expressed. Ever since the commencement of 'his Continental System,' as it is called, the policy of Napoleon has uniformly been to oblige the United States to effectual co-operation in that system. As early as the 7th of October, 1807, his Minister Champagny wrote to General Armstrong, that *the interests of all maritime powers were common, to unite in support of their rights against England*. After this followed the Embargo, which co-operated effectually, at the very critical moment, in his great plan of Continental commercial restriction. On the 24th of the ensuing November he resorts to the same language, — '*In violating the rights of all nations, England has united them all by a common interest, and it is for them to have recourse to force against her*.' He then proceeds to invite the United States to take '*with the whole Continent the part of guaranteeing itself from her injustice*,' and '*in for-*

cing her to a peace.' On the 15th of January, 1808, he is somewhat more pointed and positive as to our efficient concurrence in his plan of policy. For his Minister Champagny then tells us, that '*his Majesty has no doubt of a declaration of war against England by the United States,*' and he then proceeds to take the trouble of declaring war out of our hands, and volunteers his services gratuitously to declare it in our name and behalf. '*War exists then, in fact, between England and the United States; and his Majesty considers it as declared from the day on which England published her decrees.*' And in order to make assurance doubly sure, he sequesters our vessels in his ports, '*until a decision may be had on the dispositions to be expressed by the United States*' on his proposition of considering themselves '*associated in the cause of all the powers*' against England. Now in all this there is no deception, and can be no mistake as to the purpose of the policy. He tells us as plain as language can speak, that, '*by causing our rights to be respected,*' he means war on his side against Great Britain, — that '*our interests are common,*' — that he considers us already '*associates in the war,*' — and that he sequesters our property *by way of security for our dispositions.*

. . . . .

"Bonaparte has not yielded one inch to our Administration. Now, as he has neither performed the act required by the law of May, 1810, nor produced the effect, nor accepted the terms it proposed, whence arise our obligations? How is our faith plighted? In what way are we bound again to launch our country into this dark sea of restrictions, surrounded on all sides with perils and penalties?

"The true nature of this Cadore policy is alone to be discovered in the character of his master. Napoleon is a universal genius. 'He can exchange shapes with Proteus to advantage.' He hesitates at no means, and commands every skill. He toys with the weak; he tampers with the mean; he browbeats the haughty. With the cunning he is a serpent; for the courageous he has teeth and talons; for the cowering he has hoofs. He found our Administration a pen-and-ink gentry, — parchment politicians; and he has laid for these ephemeral essences a paper fly-trap dipped in French honey. Hercules, finding that he could not reach our Administration with his club, and that they were out of their wits at the sight of his lion's skin, has condescended to meet them in petticoats, and conquer them spinning at their own distaff.

"As to those who, after the evidence now in our hands, deny that the Decrees exist, I can no more reason with them than with those who should deny the sun to be in the firmament at noonday. The Decrees revoked? The formal statute act of a despot revoked by the breath of his servile Minister, uttered on conditions not performed by Great Britain, and claiming terms not intended to be performed by us? The fatness of our commerce secure, when every wind of heaven is burdened with the sighs of our suffering seamen, and the coast of the whole continent heaped with the plunder of our merchants? The den of the tiger safe? Yet the tracks of those who enter it are innumerable, and not a trace is to be seen of a returning footstep. The den of the tiger safe, while the cries of the mangled victims are heard through the adamantine walls of his cave, — cries which despair and anguish utter, and which despotism itself cannot stifle? No, Mr. Speaker, let us speak the truth. The act now proposed is required by no obligation. It is wholly gratuitous. Call it then by its proper name, — the first fruit of French allegiance, — a token of Transatlantic submission, — anything except an act of an American Congress, the representatives of freemen.

"The present is the most favorable moment for the abandonment of these restrictions, unless a settled co-operation with the French Continental System be determined. We have tendered the provisions of this act to both belligerents. Both have accepted. Both, as principals, or by their agents, have deceived us. We talk of the edicts of George the Third and of Napoleon. Yet those of the President of the United States, under your law, are far more detestable to your merchants. Their edicts plunder the rich. His make those who are poor still poorer. Their decrees attack the extremities. His Proclamation fixes upon the vitals, and checks the action of the seat of commercial life.

"I know that great hopes are entertained of relief from the proposed law, by the prospect of a British regency. Between a mad monarch and a simpering successor, it is expected that the whole system of that nation will be abandoned. Let gentlemen beware, and not calculate too certainly on the fulfilment by men in power of professions made out of it. The majority need not go out of our own country, nor beyond their own practice, to be convinced how easily in such cases proud promises may eventuate in meagre performance.

"The whole bearing of my argument is to this point. It is time to take our own rights into our own keeping. It is time, if we will not protect, to refrain from hampering by our own acts the commerce of our country. Put your merchants no longer under the guardianship and caprice of foreign powers. Punish not, at the instigation of foreigners, your own citizens for following their righteous callings. We owe nothing to France. We owe nothing to Great Britain. We owe everything to the American people. Let us show ourselves really independent; and look to a grateful, a powerful, and then united people for support against every aggressor."

As Congress would expire in a few days, the Federalists endeavored to defeat the bill by speaking against time, and the debate was carried on through two nights, as the Democratic majority refused to adjourn, excepting for one brief interval. The bill was finally forced through at the point of the Previous Question, then for the first time decided by the House, on appeal from the Speaker, to have the effect of putting an end to debate. With this ignoble legislation the Eleventh Congress gave up the ghost.

It was on one of these nights that John Randolph, as my father used to tell, took his turn at talking against time. After midnight, when most of the members had composed themselves to sleep as best they might, Randolph began to utter a disconnected farrago of long words, apropos to nothing in the universe. Gradually the whole House, from Mr. Speaker downwards, awoke and looked with wondering eyes upon the orator, supposing that much speaking had made him mad. His purpose thus answered, and the ear of the House secured, turning suddenly upon an honest Dutch member from New York, who never ventured on a longer speech than the zealous yeas and nays with which he sustained the Administration, and who was watching open-mouthed to see whereunto this thing would grow, Randolph cried out, in his shrill, deliberate tones, pointing his "slow, unmoving finger" at his prey, "And now, Mr. Speaker, if you will believe it, the honorable gentleman from New York denies the truth of what I have been saying!" "Good God, Mr. Speaker," sputtered forth the mystified Dutchman, "I have done nothing of the kind!" while the House, now thoroughly aroused, shook with unextinguishable laughter.

In a letter to his uncle by marriage, the Reverend Asa Packard of Marlborough, Massachusetts, he thus recapitulates the doings of the session, and their effect on himself: —

"The ruin of the commercial cities seems determined. What with the refusal to renew the United States Bank, the grasping love of our Administration for its beloved Bonaparte, and the effect of the proposed Non-Intercourse, as much distress impends over the seaboard as it has ever witnessed since the Peace of 1783. Where we shall land, Heaven only knows. But the jealousy and hatred of commerce increases in its power daily. And unless met with unanimity in our quarter of the country, it will perish with that of Europe in the Continental System of the French Emperor. To make sure work, they are about bringing into both Houses of Congress Senators and Representatives from New Orleans, and from beyond the Mississippi. If it be borne by New England, there is an end to our weight in the councils of the nation. I sent you my remarks on that subject. It has made me the object of very gross abuse. Nothing less than 'Burr's fate' and 'a halter' have been threatened your poor friend. But as they have consented I should be hung by my constituents, this is some comfort, and will operate as a reprieve, if not as an acquittal. All this is systematic. No man must speak independently without having set upon him a bully or a blackguard, who are kept in kennel, fleshed for the sport, by the friends of the Administration. However, 'Gallio careth for none of these things.' He sleeps, eats, and works, grows fat, and is comfortable."

One part of this statement he corrected in his old age. "The bullies and blackguards," he says, "were not 'kept in kennel,' but stood on the floor of the House constantly in their own proper persons, from the West or the South, unbridled in tongue, and using language learnt in the backwoods or among their slaves, ready to mistake, misrepresent, and to fight." From these scenes and such associates he hastened home, on the adjournment, to his family and his beloved country-seat, where he passed the summer.

During the winter of 1810–11, Mr. Washington Irving was introduced to my father by Mr. Robert Walsh, as appears from the following extract of a letter from that gentleman, dated February 2, 1811. The letter was chiefly one of thanks for a Review of the Life and Works of Fisher Ames, which my father had written for the Boston Anthology, of which Mr. Walsh speaks in terms of the highest commendation. He then goes on:—

"I have devoured your late speech, and most heartily coincide with you in your doctrine that the admission of Louisiana into the confederation is hostile to the spirit of the Constitution. I had the pleasure of transmitting to you the first number of my work. Mr. Irving, a young gentleman of New York, had the goodness to take charge of it, and I presume, therefore, it reached you in good time. We think and talk of nothing but the Bank in this city."

My father seems to have made a very lively and lasting impression on the imagination and memory of the young man of letters. Visiting our family at Cambridge in 1832, he gave an animated description of his Washington experience, and particularly of my father's speeches, during that memorable winter. He said that he well remembered him walking up and down the lobby while the House were debating points of order raised during his speeches, "like a lion," to use Mr. Irving's own words, "lashing his sides with his tail!" Twenty-five years later I had the happiness of a brief visit to Mr. Irving at Sunnyside, — brief, but never to be forgotten, — as the bearer of a letter of introduction from my father. He at once referred to his visit to Washington that winter, and spoke in high terms of admiration of my father's speeches in the House. And referring to the interruptions to which he was subjected, and his way of meeting them, Mr. Irving employed the same figure of speech, and, indeed, the identical words he had used to describe him at Cambridge. I regard the fact of Mr. Irving's retaining so vivid a recollection of my father's parliamentary oratory, after all the varied experience of his life, which had brought him in contact with all the distinguished men of his time in Europe and America, as a very satisfactory proof that it must have been of a high order of excellence.

The Twelfth Congress was summoned by President Madison to meet a month earlier than usual, in consequence of the alarming aspect of foreign affairs. Mr. Quincy accordingly left home for Washington in October, and took his seat on the 4th of November, at the opening of the session. He again established himself at Coyle's boarding-house, where he formed one of a very pleasant mess, consisting of Messrs. Goodrich, Dana, and Pitkin, of Connecticut, and Milnor of Pennsylvania.

Not long after his arrival in Washington, he was saddened by the news of the death of Jabez Upham of Brookfield, Massachusetts, "who," he says, "had been in former sessions one of my most intimate companions, a man of an excellent heart, and a true friend, whom I respected and loved, and whom I still entwine with the chords of my heart." These feelings of friendship were warmly reciprocated by that excellent and eminent man, as may be seen in the following passage of a letter from him to my father, written about a year before his death: —

"Should I attempt to describe the obligations to you, as I feel them impressed upon my heart, I am sure I should fail to express myself with that correctness and delicacy which the purity of your tastes and feelings would require. This, therefore, I must waive. And I do it with great satisfaction, because I well know you must be convinced that you have excited in my bosom a friendship the most sincere and ardent, which must remain unabated so long as that bosom shall continue to be the depository of a single virtuous or grateful sentiment."

Henry Clay of Kentucky was elected Speaker of the House, in the place of Joseph B. Varnum of Massachusetts, who had superseded Colonel Pickering in the Senate. Mr. Clay, on the other hand, had resigned his seat in the Senate, and been returned to the House, for the purpose, as was well understood, of being elected Speaker, it being important that so influential a position, at so critical a time, should be held by a man of more than the mere routine ability of Mr. Varnum. It was the first time that Mr. Clay had ever been a member of the Lower House, — a circumstance which made his elevation to the Speakership the more significant. It was a sign that the extreme Anti-British party, of which he was the leader, which looked to war as not only the rightful remedy for the national injuries, but as one that would be profitable to the Western section of the country at least, was gaining the ascendant over the more moderate Democrats, with Mr. Madison at their head. Notwithstanding the hostility to England which Jefferson and Madison had stimulated for so many years, neither of them wished or expected that it would ever break out into actual war. In the fulness of their faith in the dependence of England on the commerce of the United States, and in the sufficiency of its prohibition to bring her to their own terms, they had relied on the Embargo and Non-Intercourse as the only weapons of their warfare. Their notions of republican economy had resisted every attempt to increase the military and naval strength of the country, which they did not seem to imagine could ever be plunged into war through the operation of their philosophy of peaceable hostilities. Sagacious and experienced statesmen as they were, they appear to have overlooked the truth of which history is full, that wars and fightings come of the passions rather than the interests of men, who are often found willing to encounter deadly odds themselves in the hope of doing an enemy a deadly mischief. Though the Administration policy of compelling justice from England, by the destruction of our own commerce, had commanded working majorities in Congress up to this time, there had been all along a violent war party, consisting partly of honest enthusiasts, — haters of England and lovers of France, — and partly of adventurers who had nothing to lose, and who might gain something by the changes and chances incident to a state of war. The passions and hopes of both these sorts of men were stimulated to the height by the more violent of the Democratic newspapers, most of them conducted by renegade Englishmen or refugee Irishmen. Of course, there had always been, underlying the policy of the redress of our injuries by the ruin of our commerce, an implied threat that, in case this did not succeed, a sharper warfare with other weapons would replace it. The restrictive system had signally and ridiculously failed. The time for open war had logically arrived, and its advocates, in and out of Congress, had the best of the argument, reasoning from the premises of the Administration itself.

The position of the Federalists in Congress was one of some delicacy and difficulty. It was well known that Mr. Madison was utterly opposed to any war with England, excepting one of commercial restrictions; but it was also evident that the section of his party bent upon an open rupture was very strong in numbers, and yet stronger in talent. For, besides Mr. Clay, there was Mr. Calhoun, who then appeared for the first time upon the scene where he was to take for forty years so conspicuous a part, and

Langdon Cheves,* and William Lowndes,† all of them from South Carolina, and all able advocates of the policy of war. They were young, well educated, knowing what they wanted, and determined to carry their point with all the resolute assurance and impatience of control which the habits of slave-mastership naturally inspired. The question which the Federalists had to decide was whether they should assist in preparing for war, in case of hostilities, or resist all propositions for putting the country in a state of defence. There was a division of opinion on this point in the little Federal minority in Congress, which reflected one existing in yet greater force among their constituents at home. Apprehensions that any help given by Federal members of Congress to the Administration, in the direction of preparing for war, might hasten war itself, prevailed very strongly in the commercial cities, and especially in Boston. As my father wrote to my mother on this point at the time: —

"So unnerving has this apprehension of war with England become, that some Federalists seem almost to have forgotten their political character and principles. A navy, once their boast and hope, begins to be feared, or hated, because it is thought Administration intend to use it against Great Britain. For the same reason, the arming of our merchantmen is looked at with suspicion, and at the same time that we clamor against Administration for protecting us, as they call it, by commercial restrictions, we are not willing to accept from them anything else. The consequence has been, that the Administration has had full leisure to fix upon commerce shackles in what form they will; and men of the most generous principles, and true lovers of their country, have become hated for British affinities, and for their willingness, according to the false maledictions of their enemies, to abandon to that nation every right, without struggle or preparation. I need not expose to you the falsehood and fallacy of these allegations."

* Langdon Cheves, born, 1776; Member of Congress, 1811 - 1816; was Speaker for one session; for a time President of the United States Bank; died, 1857.

† William J. Lowndes, born, 1782; Member of Congress, 1811 - 1822. He died at sea on his way to England in 1822. He was a man of great talents and remarkable eloquence and power as a debater. Thus he was cut off at forty in the midst of a career which it was believed might have conducted him to the very highest station in the country.

His own course was guided solely by his views of duty to the nation, and was not at all affected by the strong disapprobation which it excited in the minds of some of the most prominent Federalists at home. He held that "a war with any nation under heaven, Great Britain not excepted, was a less evil than the perpetuation of the Anti-Commercial System"; and that, while the opponents of a war with England should denounce it as unnecessary and wicked, they should not withhold their vote for making the necessary preparations for it, should it be forced upon the country. Accordingly, on the 16th of December, 1811, he voted for the augmentation of the Federal army; to give the President authority to accept the services of volunteers, not to exceed fifty thousand in number, to order out detachments of the militia, and to put into commission all the vessels belonging to the navy worth repairing.

While my father's course in this particular was regarded with displeasure by some of his warmest party friends, he seems to have received a measure of applause from his political enemies which he neither expected nor desired. Writing to my mother, he says:—

"I dined yesterday at Livingston's,* in company with Gouverneur Morris, De Witt Clinton, Fulton, Bayard, &c. De Witt Clinton told me that the *Boston Chronicle* had some paragraphs, I know not what, *complimentary to me.* This I take to be a master stroke of policy, and probably will double the dissatisfaction and discontent of those who have no higher notion of what is right than the principle that what such malignants commend must be bad. For myself, I am as little moved by the praise of my enemies, as by the suspicions, if such exist, of my friends. In a very complicated case I have chosen to judge for myself, and nothing has occurred to shake my confidence in my judgment.

"On the vote for twenty-five thousand men (regular troops), there were but six Federalists with me. Yet these were a host in themselves, —Bleecker, Gold, Emott, Sullivan, Reed,† Livingston,—all of them

* Robert LeRoy Livingston, of New York; Member of Congress from 1809 to 1812. Fulton was the great man to whom the world is indebted for the steamboat.

† Thomas R. Gold graduated at Yale College in 1786; Member of Congress from 1809 to 1813, and 1815 to 1817; died, 1826. George Sullivan was my

men of talents. Others would have been glad to give the same vote, *had they not feared for their popularity in their districts.* All agree in the importance of permitting the party characters to disappear. In the Senate, Lloyd, Horsey,* Bayard, are all with me. . . . . .

"Federalists, in abandoning the doctrines of Washington, of efficient protection, have lost their discriminative character, and, in their fears about the event of the European contests, *their national character.* Instead of a patriotic opposition to an oppressive government, they are in great danger of degenerating into a mere faction, ready to quarrel with anything which may endanger, or adopt anything which will promote, party success."

It will appear from the following passage of a letter from Mr. Harrison Gray Otis, who had strongly supported Mr. Quincy's views and conduct just narrated, that the opinions of those of his political friends which had been the most adverse to him soon began to undergo a wholesome change. It is a peep into the family history of the Boston Federalists, which, like family histories generally, seems not to have been entirely free from family jars. These domestic discrepancies, however, appear to have been in a fair way to be healed. Chief Justice Parsons and Mr. John Lowell were among the warmest opposers of any action on the part of the Federalists in Congress that looked like assistance or encouragement to a war with England.

"Your letters are constantly burnt the hour at *farthest* after they are received, and I do not even hint at any portion of their contents until I find *such* portion the subject of general conversation. I treat them as I should love-letters, except that instead of sighs they elicit groans. There is a general acquiescence, and I may say approbation, of the course pursued by you in Congress. Mr. L., I hear, says there is no difference of opinion *now* among the Federalists. The Chief Justice, in a conversation which I sought for the express purpose of *an argument,* agreed with me in all points, except that *one* short speech show-

father's classmate; he was a son of General John Sullivan of the Revolution, and nephew of Governor James Sullivan of Massachusetts; Member of Congress from 1811 to 1812; he was a distinguished lawyer, and long Attorney-General of New Hampshire; he died, 1838. William Reed, of Marblehead, was a wealthy merchant, who was prominently connected with religious and benevolent movements; Member of Congress from 1811 to 1815; died, 1837.

* Outerbridge Horsey, born, 1777; an eminent lawyer; long Attorney-General of Delaware; Senator from 1810 to 1821; died, 1842.

ing that you did not vote upon the principle of giving sanction to war would have been grateful to him. There is not one of these sworn brothers who is, or ever was, a politician, or who ever had what old John Adams calls the tact of the feelings and passions of mankind; but they are men of probity, of talent, of influence, and the Federal party may say of them, *Non possum vivere sine te nec cum te!*"

On the 25th of January, 1812, Mr. Quincy made his speech on Maritime Protection. Notwithstanding the chronic enmity of the slaveholding States to a navy, the common sense of the abler Southern members of the war party in Congress perceived the absolute necessity of some naval preparation for the conflict with England which they were determined to bring about. It was at the suggestion of some of these members, and especially of Mr. Calhoun, that Mr. Quincy made this speech. He said he was apprehensive that arguments from that side of the House might be received with so natural a jealousy that more would be lost than gained by them; but the debate had been conducted on so liberal a scale, and his own State had so deep an interest in the question, that "he could not permit the opportunity to pass without bringing his small tribute of reflection into the common stock." He then went on to show the necessity of a navy for the protection of commerce, the importance of commerce to the whole country, and the amount of values exposed to destruction from the smallest squadron, or even from a single ship of war, in the present unprotected condition of the coast. I will give a few extracts from the body of the speech, and the chief of its peroration.

"If this commerce were the mushroom growth of a night, if it had its vigor from the temporary excitement and the accumulated nutriment which warring elements in Europe had swept from the places of their natural deposit, then, indeed, there might be some excuse for a temporizing policy touching so transitory an interest. But commerce in the Eastern States is of no foreign growth, and of no adventitious seed. Its root is of a fibre which almost two centuries have nourished; and the perpetuity of its destiny is written in legible characters as well in the nature of the country as in the dispositions of its inhabitants. Indeed, Sir, look along your whole coast, from Passamaquoddy to Capes Henry and Charles, and behold the deep and far-winding creeks and inlets, the noble basins, the projecting headlands, the majestic rivers, and those sounds and bays which are more like inland seas than like anything called by those names in other quarters of the globe. Can any man do this and not realize that the destiny of the people inhabiting such a country is essentially maritime? Can any man do this without being impressed by the conviction that, although the poor projects of politicians may embarrass, for a time, the dispositions growing out of the condition of such a country, yet that Nature will be too strong for cobweb regulations, and will vindicate her rights with certain effect, — perhaps with awful perils? No nation ever did or ever ought to resist such allurements and invitations to a particular mode of industry. The purposes of Providence relative to the destination of men are to be gathered from the circumstances in which His beneficence has placed them. And to refuse to make use of the means of prosperity which His goodness has put into our hands, what is it but spurning at His bounty, and rejecting the blessings which His infinite wisdom has designated for us by the very nature of His allotments? The employments of industry connected with navigation and commercial enterprise are precious to the people of that quarter of the country by ancient prejudice, not less than by recent profit. The occupation is rendered dear and venerable by all the cherished associations of our infancy, and all the sage and prudential maxims of our ancestors. And as to the lessons of encouragement derived from recent experience, what nation ever within a similar period received so many that were sweet and salutary? What nation in so short a time ever before ascended to such a height of commercial greatness?

"It has been said by some philosophers of the other hemisphere, that Nature in this New World had worked by a sublime scale; that our mountains and rivers and lakes were beyond all comparison greater than anything the Old World could boast; that she had here made nothing diminutive — EXCEPT ITS ANIMALS. And ought we not to fear lest the bitterness of this sarcasm should be concentrated on our country by a course of policy wholly unworthy of the magnitude and nature of the interests committed to our guardianship? Have we not reason to fear that some future cynic, with an asperity which truth shall make piercing, will declare, that all things in these United States are great — EXCEPT ITS STATESMEN? and that we are pygmies to whom Providence has intrusted, for some inscrutable purpose, gigantic labors? Can we deny the justice of such severity of remark, if, instead of adopting a scale of thought and a standard of action proportionate to the greatness of our trust and the multiplied necessities of the people, we bring to our task the mere measures of professional industry, and mete out contributions for national safety by our fee-tables, our yard-sticks, and our gill-pots? Can we refrain from subscribing to the truth of such censure, if we do not rise in some degree to the height of our obligations, and teach ourselves to conceive, and with the people to realize, the vastness of those relations which are daily springing among States which are not so much one empire as a congregation of empires?

. . . . .

"While I am on this point, I cannot refrain from noticing a strange solecism which seems to prevail touching the term FLAG. It is talked about as though there was something mystical in its very nature, — as though a rag with certain stripes and stars upon it tied to a stick, and called a flag, was a wizard wand, and entailed security on everything under it or within its sphere. There is nothing like all this in the nature of the thing. A flag is the evidence of power. A land flag is the evidence of land power. A maritime flag is the evidence of maritime power. You may have a piece of bunting upon a staff, and call it a flag, but if you have no maritime power to maintain it, you have a name, and no reality; you have the shadow without the substance; you have the sign of a flag, but in truth YOU HAVE NO FLAG.

. . . . .

"Mr. Speaker, can any one contemplate the exigency which at this day depresses our country, and for one moment deem it exceptional? The degree of such commercial exigencies may vary, but they must always exist. It is absurd to suppose that such a population as is that of the Atlantic States can be either driven or decoyed from the ocean. It is just as absurd to imagine that wealth will not invite cupidity, and that weakness will not insure both insult and plunder. The circumstances of our age make this truth signally impressive. Who does not see in the conduct of Europe a general departure from those common principles which once constituted national morality? What is safe which power can seize or ingenuity can circumvent? or what truths more palpable than these, — that there is no safety for national rights but in the national arm, and that important interests systematically pursued must be systematically protected?

. . . . .

"Touching that branch of interest which is most precious to commercial men, it is impossible that there can be any mistake. For, however dear the interests of property or of life exposed upon the ocean may be to their owners or their friends, yet the safety of our altars and of our firesides, of our cities and of our seaboard, must, from the nature of things, be entwined with the affections by ties incomparably more strong and tender. And it happens that both national pride and honor are peculiarly identified with the support of these primary objects of commercial interest.

"It is in this view I state that the first and most important object of the nation ought to be such a naval force as shall give such a degree of rational security as the nature of the subject admits to our cities and seaboard and coasting trade; that the system of maritime protection ought to rest upon this basis; and that it should not attempt to go farther until these objects are secured. And I have no hesitation to declare that, until such a maritime force be systematically maintained by this nation, it shamefully neglects its most important duties and most critical interests.

. . . . .

"But it is inquired, 'What effect will this policy have upon the present exigency?' I answer, the happiest in every aspect. To exhibit a definitive intent to maintain maritime rights by maritime means, what is it but to develop new stamina of national character? No nation can have or has a right to hope for respect from others which does not first learn to respect itself. And how is this to be attained? By a course of conduct conformable to its duties, and relative to its condition. If it abandons what it ought to defend, if it flies from the field it is bound to maintain, how can it hope for honor? To what other inheritance is it entitled but disgrace? Foreign nations undoubtedly look upon this Union with eyes long read in the history of man, and with thoughts deeply versed in the effects of passion and interest upon independent States, associated by ties so apparently slight and novel. They understand well that the rivalries among the great interests of such States, — the natural envyings which in all countries spring up between agriculture, commerce, and manufactures, — the inevitable jealousies and fears of each other of South and North, interior and seaboard, — the incipient or progressive rancor of party animosity, — are the essential weaknesses of sovereignties thus combined. Whether these causes shall operate, or whether they shall cease, foreign nations will gather from the features of our policy. They cannot believe that such a nation is strong in the affections of its associated parts, when they see the vital interests of whole States abandoned. But reverse this policy; show a definitive and stable intent to yield the natural protection to such essential interests; then they will respect you. And to powerful nations honor comes attended by safety.

"Mr. Speaker, what is national disgrace? Of what stuff is it composed? Is a nation disgraced because its flag is insulted, — because its seamen are impressed, — because its course upon the highway of the ocean is obstructed? No, Sir. Abstractly considered, all this is not disgrace. Because all this may happen to a nation so weak as not to be able to maintain the dignity of its flag, or the freedom of its citizens, or the safety of its course. Natural weakness is never disgrace. But, Sir, this is disgrace, — when we submit to insult and to injury which we have the power to prevent or redress. Its essential constituents are want of sense or want of spirit. When a nation with ample means for its defence is so thick in the brain as not to put them into a suitable state of preparation; or when, with sufficient muscular force, it is so tame in spirit as to seek safety, not in manly effort, but in retirement; — then a nation is disgraced; then it shrinks from its high and sovereign character into that of the tribe of Issachar, crouching down between two burdens, — the French burden on the one side, and the British on the other, — so dull, so lifeless, so stupid, that, were it not for its braying, it could not be distinguished from the clod of the valley.

. . . . .

"The general effect of the policy I advocate is to produce confidence at home, and respect abroad. These are twin shoots from the same stock, and never fail to flourish or fade together. Confidence is a plant of no mushroom growth and of no artificial texture. It springs only from sage counsels and generous endeavors. The protection you extend must be efficient, and suited to the nature of the object you profess to maintain. If it be neither adequate nor appropriate, your wisdom will be doubted, your motives will be distrusted, and in vain you will expect confidence. The inhabitants of the seaboard will inquire of their own senses, and not of your logic, concerning the reality of their protection.

"As to respect abroad, what course can be more certain to insure it? What object more honorable, what more dignified, than to behold a great nation pursuing wise ends by appropriate means, — rising to adopt a series of systematic exertions suited to her power, and adequate to her purposes? What object more consolatory to the friends, what more paralyzing to the enemies, of our Union, than to behold the natural jealousies and rivalries which are the acknowledged dangers of our political condition subsiding or sacrificing? What sight more exhilarating than to see this great nation once more walking forth among the nations of the earth under the protection of no foreign shield? Peaceful, because powerful. Powerful, because united in interests and amalgamated by concentration of those interests in the national affections.

"But let the opposite policy prevail; let the essential interests of the great component parts of this Union find no protection under the national arm; instead of safety let them realize oppression, — and the seeds of discord and dissolution are inevitably sown in a soil the best fitted for their root, and affording the richest nourishment for their expansion. It may be a long time before they ripen. But sooner or later they will assuredly burst forth in all their destructive energies. In the intermediate period, what aspect does a union thus destitute of cement present? Is it that of a nation keen to discern, and strong to resist, violations of its sovereignty? It has rather the appearance of a casual collection of semi-barbarous clans, with the forms of civilization and with the rude and rending passions of the savage state. In truth, powerful, yet, as to any foreign effect, imbecile. Rich in the goods of fortune, yet wanting that inherent spirit without which a nation is poor indeed; their strength exhausted by struggles for local power; their moral sense debased by low intrigues for personal popularity or temporary pre-eminence; all their thoughts turned, not to the safety of the state, but to the elevation of a chieftain. A people presenting such an aspect, — what have they to expect abroad? What but pillage, insult, and scorn?

"The choice is before us. Persist in refusing efficient maritime protection; persist in the system of commercial restrictions; what now is perhaps anticipation will hereafter be history."

This speech had the felicity, rare enough in my father's case, of meeting with the approbation of both sides of the House. The Federalists throughout the country generally applauded it, though not without important exceptions, as we shall presently see. In a letter to my mother he thus speaks of its effect: —

"The result as respects my own gratification has been beyond anything I ever before experienced. Friends and foes, lovers and haters of the navy, have expressed themselves in terms which I do not choose to repeat even to you, because I know they are not entirely deserved."

He also had the gratification of receiving the following letter from Ex-President Adams, written, as he himself says of it, "in a spirit alike friendly, unequivocal, and characteristic."

The speech was entirely in accordance with the well-known opinions of Mr. Adams as to the importance of a naval establishment.

MR. ADAMS TO MR. QUINCY.

"QUINCY, February 21, 1812.

"MR. QUINCY: — I thank you for your speech in relation to maritime protection, and much more for making it. It is the speech of a man, a citizen, and a statesman. It is neither hyperbole nor flattery in me to say, it is the most important speech ever uttered in that House since 1789. I care not a farthing whom I offend by this declaration. But I am puzzled and confounded to see that not one member from New England has been found to second or support you. It is not less surprising that not a member from the two vast States of New York and Pennsylvania has said a word to assist you. I could give a specious account of this, from motives the meanest, and basest, and most disgraceful to human nature; but none at all from any manly, generous, and natural source, and therefore I will not attempt any solution of the theorem. Again I say, I thank you.

"JOHN ADAMS."

A slip of paper is wafered to this letter, on which is written the following words from the Sixth Epistle of Horace: "Piscemur, venemur, ut olim"; — the precise application of which I do not perceive, unless it be aimed as a sarcasm at the men who would prefer their own selfish gratifications to the honor and safety of their country.

My father had also many other most cordial expressions of approval from prominent Federalists. In his own words, "I was supported in the most gratifying language by men whose praise is worthy of being preserved." On the 17th of February Robert Walsh wrote to him: —

"I am in raptures with your speech on the navy bill. It is truly the work of a philosophical and clear-minded politician."

On the 24th of February Harrison Gray Otis wrote: —

"The speech on the navy is worthy of being read in all the churches. I think it is the best and most popular view of that great question that has ever appeared, and am confident it will be regarded in more auspicious times as an elementary treatise upon the sectional relations and interests of our country, as well as a lucid exposition of the fitness and necessity and means of adjusting them by the instrumentalities of a navy. Some of our lounging cavillers (not cavaliers) dispute the accuracy of the calculations, especially those furnished by Reed. But I silence their nonsense by referring them to the *principles and arguments* contained in the speech, and answering them, that all the errors, if proved, do not vary the result. We shall endeavor to give it a very extensive circulation."

Christopher Gore wrote, on the 26th of February: —

"I am very grateful for your speech in favor of a navy. If reason and argument had weight in Congress, such a discourse could not have failed to produce some effect on the votes of that body. If the commercial part of the community were not contemned by our Southern lords more than their black slaves, some attention would be paid by government to the interests of navigation. But as an oppressed and injured people, it seems we must remain a prey to the malignant envy of our associates of the South, and to the baseness and folly of many of those who affect to represent the interests of New England, which they have not wisdom to discern, or are willing to betray for a little temporary superiority over men whose fame they hate, and whose honorable elevation they can never hope to attain."

Of the immediate occasion of this speech, and of the secret disapproval which it caused among a most influential portion of his constituents and personal friends, my father has left this record: —

"The strong desire of these South Carolina politicians to favor a navy made them express to me a wish that I would present the view of the Eastern States on that subject, which induced me to make that exertion which otherwise I should not have done. For the predominating feeling in the mercantile class was at this moment hostile to every form of warlike preparation, which they persuaded themselves would be applied, not to their defence, but to provoke further hostilities with Great Britain, and in support of the views of the French Emperor. Accordingly, although, as I have said, that effort was publicly applauded by men of all parties, it was far from being acceptable to the leading mercantile interests, so deep were prejudices, and so nervous were they through fear."

CHAPTER XI.

1812.

THE JOHN HENRY SCANDAL. — COURSE OF BOSTON FEDERALISTS TOUCHING IT. — THE WAR DEMOCRATS. — CLAY AND CALHOUN. — THE SIXTY DAYS' EMBARGO. — DESPATCH OF THE NEWS TO BOSTON. — ITS EFFECT, MERCANTILE AND POLITICAL. — THE WAR DEMOCRATS PREVAIL OVER MR. MADISON. — WAR WITH ENGLAND IS DECLARED. — MR. QUINCY DECLINES A RE-ELECTION. — HIS REASONS FOR IT. — EFFECT OF THE WAR ON NEW ENGLAND. — APPREHENSIONS AT QUINCY. — THE CONSTITUTION AND GUERRIÈRE. — HULL AND DECATUR. — MEETING OF JOHN ADAMS AND TIMOTHY PICKERING AT QUINCY. — JOHN RANDOLPH AND HIS NEPHEW. — HIS LETTERS TO MR. QUINCY.

EARLY in the spring of 1812 the curious historical episode of the John Henry scandal occurred. Though it is pretty well known to the readers of the history of those times, I will here give my father's account of it, which is the more lively, perhaps, from his having been himself one of the persons whose hospitality had been abused by that adventurer.

"On the 9th of March, 1812, a message from President Madison opened to Congress and the public a mean and base transaction, in which the secret service fund of the United States Treasury was applied solely to circulate, for electioneering purposes, party aspersions and suspicions against the highest and most honorable men in the Eastern States, and as fuel to the most malignant party passions. From the year 1809 to 1812, there had been residing in those States a man, John Henry by name. He had married a lady of good family in Philadelphia, and with her and two children came to Boston, ostensibly for health and amusement, bringing letters of introduction to many families in the place, — among others to mine. He was received with the attention due to the respectability of the letters he brought, and regarded as a man passing idly through the world, seeking and entitled to no special interest or confidence. He flitted about New England, — sometimes at Windsor, and sometimes at Burlington, in Vermont, — but chiefly resided in Boston. His manners being gentlemanly and his letters of introduction good, he was admitted freely into society, and heard the conversation at private tables, but without any reference to him.

"During all this time, as it afterwards appeared, he was a spy, authorized by Sir James Craig, Governor of the British Provinces in North America, to travel in the Eastern States, to gain and communicate such knowledge as he could of the state of affairs and of the opinions of men, with authority also, if he found any parties or persons of leading influence in those States willing to enter into any political connection with the British government, to receive and communicate such disposition to him, for which purpose he received credentials of his authority in this respect, which in such case he was at liberty to produce. For these services he was paid, and was to receive such pecuniary aid as he might require. After having been three years in this agency, having collected nothing but what every newspaper in the country could communicate, having done nothing, and not having, or pretending to have, found a single individual in the United States, of any section or party, disposed to have any political connection with Great Britain, to whom he could exhibit his secret credentials, he laid before the British government exorbitant claims for services, which they instantly rejected. Excessively indignant at this treatment, he resolved to turn traitor to his government, and opened a negotiation with Madison for the sale of his papers. And although they contained not a word implicating any individual, or any party, nor one important fact, except that the British government had employed a *spy* in the United States for the purpose of being informed of the actual position of affairs within them, yet Madison, availing himself of the power intrusted to him as President over the secret service fund, paid this fellow for his papers fifty thousand dollars out of the public treasury!

"In communicating this purchase, Madison had the art and audacity to declare that this secret agent had been employed in the Eastern States in fomenting disaffection, and in intrigues with the disaffected to bring about resistance to the laws and a political connection with Great Britain, when not an individual was ever intimated as being concerned with Henry, or the slightest evidence adduced of any intrigue with him by any person or party. To such arts could a man placed at the head of the nation condescend, to give food to party malice, and to increase the chances of his re-election, then depending, to the Presidency of the United States! The negotiation was made, and the money paid in Washington early in the month of February.

But to conceal the operation, and, if possible, the fact that the papers had been paid for by the President, Henry left Washington, and wrote a letter from Philadelphia, dated the 20th of February (ten or twenty days after the terms of purchase had been settled and the money paid), in which he apparently made a self-moved and disinterested statement of the patriotic motives which had induced him '*herewith to transmit the public documents in his possession*,' and that this had been *done voluntarily* out of regard to the United States. It afterwards appeared that these documents, so far from having been transmitted from Philadelphia on the 20th of February, were in fact then in the hands of Madison, and that, in accordance with proceedings projected at Washington, these falsehoods were written from Philadelphia to conceal the nature of the transaction, that Henry might escape from the country before it should be publicly known in the United States. Accordingly, before its appearance Henry was on his voyage to France on board the sloop-of-war Wasp, sent to carry despatches to Europe. History has few transactions to record more disgraceful to a government than this, considering its nature, its objects, the manner in which it was conducted, and the means taken to conceal it from public view.

"Some of the influential leaders of the Federal party were so infatuated in their belief of the character of British diplomacy, that they at first discredited altogether Craig's letter to Henry, — pronounced it a forgery, and that it was utterly incredible a British Governor should have been engaged in employing a spy in the Eastern States for any such purpose as this letter indicated. By this confidence in British purity, they at first weakened the effect of these disclosures, and confirmed in public opinion their devotedness to the British nation. Their course of proceeding in relation to these disclosures concurring with their condemning my course in voting for preparation for war, maintaining that by such vote I was committed to vote for war, and thereby condemning me for not yielding my sense of public duty to their fears, effectually disgusted me."

It was in this state of feeling that he wrote to his wife as follows, March 20, 1812: —

"My anxiety to get home is intense; yet it seems my duty to stay and watch this sleeping Ætna, although it will probably do nothing but smoulder; and if it burn, I can interpose no resistance to stay its fury. This session has given me a *quietus* with Congress. They may send me on a mission to Kamschatka rather than here. As to the Federalists, I have preached and practised in order to impress on them their political duty. If they justify Great Britain, or *take violently*, or further than by way of suggestion, the ground that Henry's disclosures are forgeries, they are fools, and the party is not worth the saving. Administration may spread fifty traps in broad day, and they will walk deliberately into them. There is but one high, generous, noble ground. Take the documents for granted. Show an indignant sense of injury at the attempt; and turn the indignation of the country against Madison for the base insinuation contained in his Message, — so different from what the tenor of Henry's papers justifies, — and for the notorious intrigue and waste of public moneys."

On the 22d of March he again wrote on the same subject: —

"I find that the doctrine that Henry's papers are forgeries is the favorite one with the Federalists, and it is just the ground Administration wishes them to take. I have, however, little doubt that Sir James Craig's letter was genuine, — whether previously sanctioned in England I cannot say. But it ought to be viewed with peculiar disgust by the Federal party, to whom it was both an insult and an injury. I find this sentiment is little felt, and less expressed. Men are so run away with by the apprehension of a British war, and with the belief that it is the intention of our government to get us into one, that they forget what is due to their own character as a party. I shall be thought a trimmer by all the violents. My fate is odd. By some I am thought such a raving Federalist as to be shrewdly suspected of being one of Henry's confidants; by others that I am so strongly hostile to the British that I am in danger of turning Democrat. The truth is, that there is an intermediate ground for an American politician to stand upon. That I seek, and when I think I have found it I shall not hesitate to defend it, let who will shake or wonder, condemn or applaud."

In another letter, dated March 26th, he says: —

"Your feelings toward Madison and his party are very natural, but their conduct is precisely such as all history leads us to expect, in popular governments, from ambitious leaders. All governments are but a choice among evils, and with all the struggles to which our form subjects us, and all the apparent intrigues to which it exposes us, I am far from being certain that as much happiness is not to be enjoyed under it as under any other which could be induced. As to knaves and fools being our governors, under what form of government are they not powerful? Either one or the other of that species presides at present over every nation in Europe. Why should we repine at a common destiny? As to my views on *the prospect before us*, if they seem discouraging in your view, that is perhaps the result of the instant effect, rather than of the permanent operation of the measures, or rather the no measures, here progressing. The state of things may be wholesome. It may be about to grow rough and tempestuous weather. I confess it appears hazy. But there are landmarks enough to steer by. The shore is bold, and I see no great danger of shipwreck. We shall have enough 'tossing about,' but that keeps the faculties in play. My opinion has always been, that we should get relief, but through suffering. I hope that what the people of Massachusetts have already felt will make them wise enough to produce at the elections a salutary change. If it does not, they must go to school again. This is the way prescribed by Providence for human instruction, and I quarrel not with its institutions, but endeavor to teach myself to understand, and to conform my life to an admiration of, and acquiescence in, its system. As to the British, there is a foolish leaning upon them among some of our friends, which, at the same time that it does little credit to their patriotism, does infinitely less to their judgment. The truth is, the British look upon us as a *foreign nation*, and we must look upon them in the same light. They are willing to make us the tools of their policy, and we ought not to attribute to them higher motives than those which really actuate them."

On the 27th of March he again wrote:—

"I do not feel the despondence you seem to imagine from my last letter. It is, perhaps, because I look upon life differently from most men, who deem the great objects of it to be peace and security. I believe this scene of things to be destined for exertions and duties. Circumstances may make the first rigorous and the latter critical. It is very little within our power to select either the theatre or the time of action. But the great object in which the mind ought to be absorbed, and on which our felicity should be made dependent, is a thorough performance of duty, and a vigorous exertion of our faculties, according to the nature of the stage, and of the period which a higher than human power has provided for us."

All this time the country was drifting rapidly into a war with England. The war of commercial restrictions having failed to bring that haughty power to terms, the alternative of silent submission or an appeal to the last argument of kings and nations was more and more forced upon men's minds. The faith of Mr. Madison in the compulsory power of Embargos and Acts of Non-Intercourse was not yet shaken, and there was no man in the nation that shrunk from a resort to arms more nervously than he. But the spirit of hatred to England which Jefferson had evoked, and he himself had conjured with, was grown too strong for Mr. Madison to exorcise or to control. As a last resort he induced Mr. Pinkney of Maryland, late Minister to England, and one of the ablest men the country ever produced, to use his influence with the merchants in the different commercial cities to write to their correspondents in England, and ask them to endeavor to persuade the British Ministry to modify the Orders in Council sufficiently to make it possible for the United States to withdraw from their unpleasant position with some show of grace. He succeeded in drawing after him some of the Federal merchants even of Boston, by acting skilfully on their hopes and fears. But it was all in vain. The English Ministry were as fast anchored as their isle, and would make neither concessions nor advances. All this strengthened the war party in Congress. Of this party Henry Clay was the guiding spirit. Of his character and qualifications for this leadership my father speaks thus: —

"Bold, aspiring, presumptuous, with a rough, overbearing eloquence, neither exact nor comprehensive, which he had cultivated and formed in the contests with the half-civilized wranglers in the county courts of Kentucky, and quickened into confidence and readiness by successful declamations at barbecues and electioneering struggles, he had not yet that polish of language and refinement of manners which he afterwards acquired by familiarity and attrition with highly cultivated men. . . . . Such was the man whose influence and power more than that of any other produced the war of 1812 between the United States and Great Britain. . . . . Absurd as an invasion of Canada in defence of our commercial rights would appear, yet, if war were once declared, the nation might be brought up to it, as we could do nothing else; and the measure would be highly beneficial to Kentucky and the Western States. Levies of men could easily be raised among their vigorous and active population, and army supplies would be a bounty upon beef, corn, flour, and their other products, — among them the chief expenditures of the war would be made. All this Clay foresaw, and, in the event, realized. The invasion of Canada advanced Kentucky and the Western States fifty years in prosperous progress."

The war party, however, were willing to indulge Mr. Madison with one more trial of the effect of an Embargo for sixty days. This was the occasion of the following transaction, of which I will give my father's own account.

"On the 31st of March, Mr. Calhoun, a member of the Committee on Foreign Relations, came to me voluntarily, and told me that the Administration had determined to lay another Embargo, — that it would certainly be done, — and that it was the intention of the government that it should be made public. I asked him if I was authorized to communicate that intention to my constituents. He replied, certainly, that it was to that end he had mentioned it to me. I immediately sought an interview with Mr. Lloyd. We agreed the important information ought to be instantly transmitted to the merchants of Boston, and united in a letter to H. G. Otis and T. H. Perkins, with the intelligence Mr. Calhoun had given me. We contracted with a stage proprietor to deliver our despatch in Boston in seventy-six hours. This contract was fulfilled, and on Friday, the 4th of April, the intelligence reached Boston. The effect was electric, the excitement produced never exceeded. On Saturday and Sunday the whole town was in motion, every truck and cart was in requisition, the streets and wharves were crowded by the merchants, anxious to send their ships to sea before the harbor was closed by the Embargo. The loading and sailing continued all Sunday. This news, coming on the eve of the April elections, was met first with disbelief, then with calumny. 'The duty assigned to me,' wrote William Sullivan, 'was to *swear*, at caucus, that the letter you and Lloyd sent to Otis was neither a forgery nor an electioneering trick; both which had been asserted concerning it.' The timeliness of this communication from Mr. Lloyd and myself was evident. Its importance to the interests of the merchants was apparent by the rapid and earnest use they made of it, and its favorable effect upon the State election was undeniable. It was one of the most responsible acts of my public life, taken on the information of a deliberate intention of the Administration, communicated to me voluntarily, not confidentially, by Mr. Calhoun, with express authority from him to transmit it to my constituents, and done solely from a sense of public duty and regard for the interests of the merchants. Yet though it was thus used, generally approved, and even lauded by most of my friends, it was far from being so by those who took the lead in the conduct of the Federal party. They at first sneered and disbelieved the statement, said that, as it respected the elections, the Federalists had lost more votes at the polls by sending away sailors who could vote, than were gained by the excitement produced by the news, and treated very slightly the advantage gained by my letter.

"Mrs. Quincy wrote to me on the 6th of April: 'Isaac P. Davis said to me, there were gentlemen in the party who made a practice of disapproving of everything the Federalists in Congress had done, from the beginning to the end; that they were very few in number, but made up in violence what they wanted in strength.' Facts of this kind clinched my determination never again to engage in a service so arduous, so responsible, so thankless, so subject to be abused by one section of the party and only feebly supported by another, — divided by its interests, passions, affections, and principles."

My father was deeply wounded by the manner in which his conscientious performance of his public duty and his faithful service of his party, subordinated only to the higher allegiance due to his country, had been requited by a portion of the leading Federalists. We have already seen how his displeasure at the conduct of these gentlemen in the Henry matter had helped to make up his mind to withdraw from Congress, and this fresh sense of personal injustice only strengthened that resolution. In a letter to his wife written about this time, he thus expresses his feelings and opinions as to the course of the leaders of his party, and repeats his determination not to return to Washington after the expiration of this term.

"You and my other correspondents are my witnesses, that I have foreseen the renewal of the Embargo. Last November I wrote, 'If you mean to get rid of the restrictive system, you must be willing to wish, prefer, and even demand war,' or words to that effect. But I found I could not be supported by my friends. I have been obliged to content myself with a silent acquiescent course, instead of one open, stimulative, vigorous, such as was due to the crisis, to our country, to our character and hopes as a party. From the friendship of Great Britain we have little to hope. Many Federalists by their belief in it have been ruined. Fear of war with her paralyzes others. But you and the nation shall hear my voice. If my friends choose to be offended, I cannot help it. I do not mean to be a member of Congress after this term, being perfectly convinced that whatever weight my character and exertions can effect had better be applied in my native State. I shall speak truth according to my own conception of it; and if I do not convince or change public sentiment, I will not associate myself or my fate with the destinies of the weak, the timid, or the interested.

"But I fear not. The great body of the American people, when they understand the relations of things, will go with me; and if they do not in vote they will in heart, and sooner or later in vote also. If they do not, and are false to themselves, so be it: I will be true to myself and my country. You will perceive that my heart is full, my head also, with a session of eleven hours, during one of which I was on my feet, uttering, I trust, piercing truths, which were felt deeply enough, though they produced no conviction. All this may appear vanity, but I have a right to offer to you the overflowing of a heart which, however engaged, whether light or serious, active or indolent, in strength or weakness, is always yours."

Through this extraordinary despatch, the news of the impending Embargo was in Boston before it was in Baltimore, a circumstance not well pleasing to the merchants there. Mr. Calhoun was inclined to cavil at the rapidity with which his intelligence had been transmitted by Mr. Quincy to his constituents; but as he could not deny that it was communicated for transmission, it was clear that he had no just ground of complaint. Mr. Quincy took an active part in the discussions on the passage of this Embargo in the secret sessions. What he did and said was of no effect within those closed doors, and of none outside of them, as the debates were not published for years afterwards.

Towards the end of April my father obtained leave of absence from the House, and made a flying visit to Boston. On his return his friend, the Rev. William Ellery Channing, accompanied him, by his invitation, to Washington. The health of that celebrated man being infirm then, as it continued to be all his life long, it was hoped that this journey might be of use to him. He remained with my father as his guest for several days, but had no opportunity of gratifying his desire to attend the debates, as the House was in secret session during his whole stay.

The war party in Congress was now in the ascendant, and all the resistance which the Democratic President and the Federal Opposition could offer to the measure was overborne by the reckless energy and determined purpose of Clay and Calhoun. My father gives the following account of the manner in which the reluctance of Mr. Madison was overcome, and he induced to take the responsibility of recommending a declaration of war against England. In those days, as may be seen in the conclud-ing extract of the speech on Place and Patronage, the candi-dates for the Presidency were agreed upon by the members of Congress of the respective parties, instead of being selected, as at present, by general conventions.

"He was heart and soul a convert to Jefferson's policy, and held to the commercial restrictive system with the grasp of death. A war, he thought, would put an end to his hope of re-election to the Presidency, nor did he quit this grasp till waited upon by a commit-tee of which Henry Clay was the Chairman, and was plainly told that his being supported as the party candidate for the next Presi-dency depended upon his screwing his courage to a declaration of war. To this he reluctantly assented, but intimated his desire that it should, in the incipient stage, commence in the House of Representa-tives. But three or four young men, who had recently become mem-bers of Congress, who, from want of experience were without personal weight, and were comparatively unknown to the nation, were unwill-ing to take the lead in such a measure; and Madison was told he must unequivocally assume himself the responsibility of recommend-ing war. To this condition he finally acceded, and, giving full satis-faction to these overbearing leaders, he received the nomination for the Presidency. On this combination of violence with individual in-terest and ambition was laid the foundation of the war of 1812 with Great Britain."

In fulfilment of his part of the contract, Mr. Madison sent a confidential Message, recommending a Declaration of War, on the 1st of June, 1812, and a bill was passed to that effect by the House on the 4th, by a vote of 79 to 49. It took about a fort-night longer to procure the sanction of the Senate, but this was obtained on the 18th, — nineteen Senators voting for the war, and thirteen against it. Mr. Madison made haste to sign the bill, and the work was done. Mr. Quincy was appointed by the Federalists in Congress to prepare an address of the minority to their constituents, which he did in an ample and satisfactory manner. It may be found in the Appendix to Sullivan's Letters on Public Characters, and fills twenty-five pages of small type It was signed by all the Federal members of the House of Representatives, and published about the time Congress adjourned. It is a clear, forcible, and temperate statement of the views of the minority as to the war and the measures which preceded and led to it, and it was accepted by the Federal party at large as a satisfactory exposition of the opinions, and a conclusive defence of the conduct, of its signers.

The experience of this session only confirmed my father in the resolution he had already formed, of declining another election to Congress, which he now formally announced. This determination the remonstrances and even entreaties of his most valued friends could not shake. His private reasons were his unwillingness to be longer separated from his family. "To live longer separate from them," he says, "I would not. To take them with me to Washington my finances would not permit." Of his public reasons he gives the following account: —

"My personal motives for leaving my seat in Congress are explained; my political, I shall also briefly state. Seven years of observation and experience in the national Legislature had brought my mind to the conclusion that the *Southern*, as then called, but now *the Slave-holding States*, were omnipotent in this Union. That their influence was not temporary, but *permanent*, and that this state of relative power in respect of the Free States was destined to continue for a long series of years, and probably for all future time. Another conclusion my experience had established in my mind, that the principles, prejudices, and interests of those Slave-holding States necessarily led to a policy incompatible with the interests and principles of the Free States, most especially of the commercial States. In this prospective view of the relations of the States, I clearly discerned that a continuance in Congress as a Representative from Boston condemned me to a life-long series of contests, laborious in their nature and hopeless as to their result, to which I had no disposition to condemn myself. I then believed, as the course of my writings and speeches at that time sufficiently indicates, that the slave-holders' power bestrode the Union as the Old Man of the Sea did the shoulders of Sinbad the Sailor, — a power which no exertion could throw off, and which time would not unsettle, but rather confirm. This is not the place to state all the facts and circumstances on which this opinion was formed. It is enough that what was but opinion then the experience of fifty years has proved to be truth.*

"Other circumstances growing out of the relations of public affairs at the time, and the want of unison among Federalists themselves as to the political course to be pursued, disgusted me with the service. I found that a Representative in Congress from Boston, to be supported, must follow the opinion of his constituents concerning their real or imagined interests, and that in an independent course he was sure to be suspected or denounced. It was a state of subserviency which suited neither my pride nor my principles; and, though sufficiently urged to continue, no representations could induce me to abandon my purpose of retirement from this part of the public stage.

"I will not conceal that this determination was not made without regret. I had formed myself for a public man on a large and national scale. I had laboriously prepared for the service, as my private manuscripts will evidence. For the sphere of State politics I had neither taste nor adaptation of mind, but I yielded my wishes to a sense of duty, and never regretted my decision."

This stormy session over and the war with England proclaimed, my father hastened home to his family, already established for the summer at Quincy. It was not a cloudless summer of country occupations and country pleasures. Gloom brooded over the land, and the present hour was embittered by anxiety for the future. The ruin of the commercial States seemed now to be a settled thing, and war invoked to devour whatever Embargo, Non-Importation, and Non-Intercourse had spared. The stagnation of business attending this last blow to commerce carried distress or anxiety into every household. It was small consolation to true lovers of their country, — which the Federalists were most emphatically, — to find their predictions so speedily fulfilled in the disasters which attended our arms everywhere along the Canada frontier in the opening campaign of the war, the thick-coming tidings of which helped to darken the

* This was written in the year 1859.

hours of that memorable season. And a general sense of personal insecurity prevailed all along the seaboard. For the government had vouchsafed no protection sufficient to save the cities from being laid under contribution by a British squadron, or to secure the coast from being laid waste by a single ship of war.

In these last-named apprehensions the family at Quincy had good reason to share. For the estate bounds on the ocean, and the fears of boat-attacks and foraging-parties which had haunted that roof thirty years before returned again to disturb its repose. Every ship enters and leaves the port of Boston in full view of the windows of the house, and it may well be believed that a sharp lookout was kept up in the direction of the light-house. The first naval spectacle discerned from that post of observation, however, was a memorable and an auspicious one. It was the entrance of the Constitution into the harbor, on the 29th of August, 1812, after the capture of the Guerrière. I will copy the account of this event, and what immediately followed it, from the privately printed Memoir of my mother, by my eldest sister, of which I have already spoken.

"At Quincy, the ships in the harbor, especially those apparently of a warlike character, were anxiously watched. Toward evening, on the 29th of August, 1812, a frigate (recognized as the Constitution, commanded by Captain Hull) came in under full sail, and dropped her anchor beside Rainsford Island, — then the Quarantine Ground. The next morning, a fleet of armed ships appeared off Point Alderton. As they rapidly approached, the Constitution was observed to raise her anchor and sails, and go boldly forth to meet the apparent enemy; but, as the frigate passed the leader of the fleet, a friendly recognition was exchanged, instead of the expected broadside. They joined company, and the Constitution led the way to Boston. It was the squadron of United States ships, then commanded by Commodore Rodgers, unexpectedly returning from a long cruise.

"A few days afterwards, Hull, who had just taken the Guerrière, came with Decatur to breakfast at Quincy. When this incident was mentioned, he said: 'I must acknowledge, I participated in the apprehensions of my friends on shore. Thinking myself safe in port, I told my officers to let the men wash their clothes, and get the ship in order to go up to Boston; and, being excessively fatigued, went to my stateroom. I was sound asleep when a lieutenant rushed down, exclaiming, "Captain, the British are upon us! — an armed fleet is entering the harbor!" No agreeable intelligence, certainly; for I was wholly unprepared to engage with a superior force. But, determined to sell our lives as dear as I could, I gave orders to clear the decks, weigh anchor, and get ready for immediate action. I confess I was greatly relieved when I saw the American flag, and recognized Rodgers.' In speaking of the conflict with the Guerrière, he said: 'I do not mind the day of battle; the excitement carries one through: but the day after is fearful; it is so dreadful to see my men wounded and suffering.'

"These naval officers formed a striking contrast. Hull was easy and prepossessing in his manners, but looked accustomed to face 'the battle and the breeze.' Decatur was uncommonly handsome, and remarkable for the delicacy and refinement of his appearance."

This breakfast is one of the earliest of my own recollections. I was a very little child, but I remember perfectly well sitting on Decatur's knee, playing with his dirk, and looking up at his handsome face, the beauty of which struck even my childish eyes, and which I still seem to see looking at me from out the far past. I have no recollection of Hull at that time, but I often saw him in later years, and knew him well, as a very young man knows a distinguished elder. His manners certainly were easy as my sister describes them, and prepossessing in the sense of being eminently suitable to the man and characteristic of him. They were plain, bluff, and hearty, as became "a rough and boisterous captain of the sea," and indicated a good heart and a good temper, though not incapable of being ruffled on a sufficient occasion. I remember his telling the story of the fight with the Guerrière one day at my father's table in Boston. Poor Dacres, according to him, did not relish being beaten any more than "our wayward sisters" in the late Rebellion. One would infer that he must have been of the old-world breed of sea-dogs to which Commodore Trunnion belonged, rather than of the more polished modern school of naval officers. After he had struck his flag and was coming on board the Constitution, Captain Hull stood ready to receive his prisoner with his best manners, and said to him, as he came up the side, with the proper salute, "Sir, I am happy to see you." "Ugh, d——n you,

I suppose you are!" was the surly reply of John Bull, who thought his captor meant to insult him! Another thing I remember the Commodore said, which I record in the interest of my colored friends. Speaking of the fighting qualities of his sailors, he said: "I never had any better fighters than the negroes," — (I am afraid he spelled the word "with two *g*'s," — an orthography, according to Mr. Seward, fatal to the prospects of any Presidential candidate,) — "they stripped to the waist, and fought like devils, sir, seeming to be utterly insensible to danger, and to be possessed with a determination to outfight the white sailors." This testimony has been rendered superfluous, indeed, by the gallant record our black countrymen made for themselves, both by land and sea, during the late Rebellion; but it shows how groundless as well as despicable was the subserviency to slavery which excluded brave men for years from the service of their country, because they wore

"The shadowed livery of the burnished sun."

It was during this summer that a meeting took place at Quincy between Ex-President Adams and his sometime Secretary of State, Colonel Timothy Pickering, for the first and only time after the former had summarily dismissed the latter from office in 1800. The differences which occasioned that dismissal are matter of history, and need not be recapitulated here. They were of a nature, however, to prevent any personal intercourse between these eminent men — "good haters" both, after Dr. Johnson's own heart! — for the rest of their lives, excepting on this one occasion. It fell out on this wise. My father had been for several years one of the twelve trustees of the Massachusetts Society for Promoting Agriculture, during which time Mr. Adams had been its President. It was the custom of this excellent Board — and I believe it is one still honored in the observance — to encourage the consumption of the kindly fruits of the earth, besides promoting their production, by a monthly dinner at the houses of the trustees in turn. In consequence of the unfriendly relations of Mr. Adams and Colonel Pickering, the trustees had been debarred the privilege of inviting the latter gentleman to assist at any of their monthly festivals, which they regretted the more because he was as zealous in agriculture as in politics. This year, however, Mr. Adams had resigned his Presidency, and retired from the Board, on the ground that his age rendered the due discharge of the official and convivial duties of his post inconvenient to him. My father, knowing how interesting an addition the Ex-President always made to any party, invited him as a neighbor to meet his old colleagues once more at his table; and he readily agreed to come. The day arrived, and the host and hostess awaited the coming of their guests with no foreboding of anything out of the common way. But when the company began to arrive, one of the first to make his appearance was Colonel Pickering, who, happening to be in Boston that day, readily accepted the invitation of Mr. John Lowell to accompany him to Quincy, well knowing how welcome he would be. The welcome he expected was as cordial as he could desire, but my mother felt obliged, while giving it, to tell him whom he would presently encounter, that he might decide for himself whether to stay or return to town.

"I did not think of meeting Mr. Adams," he replied, "when I agreed to accompany Mr. Lowell hither, as I knew he had left the Board, and if my being here will occasion any uneasiness to yourself or Mr. Quincy, I will go away immediately. But, personally, I have no objection to meeting Mr. Adams."

Scarcely had this preliminary been adjusted, when Mr. Adams drove up. My father presented himself at the coach door, and made substantially the same statement of the existing state of affairs that my mother had just despatched, which the Ex-President received in the same spirit that his former prime minister had manifested.

"As your friend, Mr. Quincy," said he, "I shall be most happy to see Colonel Pickering."

Accordingly, after paying his respects to his hostess, he turned to Colonel Pickering, and they met with all the external cordiality of old friends who had been long separated, but never divided. The possible awkwardness of this meeting might have been heightened to less experienced men of the world, by the fact that

Mr. Adams was accompanied by his son-in-law, Colonel William S. Smith, whom he had nominated for Inspector-General, at the recommendation of Washington, when the army of 1798 was forming, and who had been rejected by the Senate, through the secret influence, as the Adams family believed, of Colonel Pickering.* Fortunately, however, the house at Quincy was not the Palace of Truth of the Genius Phanor, and everything was on velvet throughout the day. They took wine together, according to the good old-fashioned custom of the time; they talked over old times and old friends, told old-world stories, and made themselves exceedingly agreeable and entertaining to the company, and, we will hope, to one another. When the party broke up, and Colonel Pickering took his leave, he and Mr. Adams shook hands together, and expressed the pleasure they had had in each other's society, and parted, never to meet again in this world. After Colonel Pickering was gone, my mother expressed to Mr. Adams her hope that this unexpected meeting had not been unpleasant to him; for it had been a most interesting one to herself and the rest of the party. "No, madam," said he; "I certainly hope to meet Colonel Pickering in Heaven, and, next to Heaven, I surely should be willing to meet him here in your house."

I have already mentioned the odd sort of intimacy which had sprung up between my father and John Randolph. It would be difficult to imagine two men more dissimilar in character and opinions than they were, and yet the regard that they entertained for each other was a very real one. It is said that my father was the only friend Randolph ever had with whom he did not quarrel, first or last. In a letter to my mother, my father characterizes him thus: —

"Randolph is an eccentric character, with great faults and some virtues, — a creature of whim and momentary impulse. He is just what the hour makes him, — a true friend where he professes friendship, a bitter enemy where he declares it. To serve the one or depress the other, he will go to the world's end. As a politician he keeps Vir-

* Life and Works of John Adams, Vol. I. p. 539.

ginia always in his eye. While Massachusetts claimed to be her only rival among the States, he wreaked the vengeance of his patriotism upon her and her satellites, as he called the other New England States. Now New York has taken the ascendant, I can plainly perceive that the current of his bile is concentrating about the Hudson. Upon the whole, he is a man who will always have more enemies than friends."

Randolph had all the prejudices of his section and his caste against New England. He once said to my father: "I never intend to set my foot on the farther bank of the Hudson. But if I ever should, your house shall be the first that I will enter." He never did visit this part of the country, though it will be seen, by some of his letters by and by, that he did at one time seriously contemplate such a journey. But, notwithstanding his antipathy to the land of the Puritans, when the question came up as to where his nephew and adopted son and heir, Theodoric Tudor Randolph, should be educated, he surmounted it so far as to choose the oldest University in the country as the place where the youth was to be taught his humanities. Young Randolph was the son of Richard Randolph, John Randolph's elder brother, who died in 1796. At Mr. Randolph's request, my father took charge of the young man on his last journey home, and placed him at Cambridge, in the house and under the immediate eye of President Kirkland. He is described as a tall, swarthy youth, with a good deal in his looks that seemed to justify his claim, of which his uncle was so proud, to a descent from Pocahontas and Powhatan. He was a lad of fine abilities, and sufficiently attentive to his studies to take rank among the foremost in his class. Unhappily, his health failed towards the end of his college life, and he died in England before the class graduated; but the Corporation, nevertheless, gave him his degree, and his name appears regularly in the Triennial Catalogue. My father had a general oversight of young Randolph, and the charge of his money matters, which gave occasion to a tolerably continuous correspondence with the uncle, of which I shall give the greater part, under the years to which they belong.

MR. RANDOLPH TO MR. QUINCY.

"GEORGETOWN, July 8, 1812.

"DEAR SIR: — Your considerate and obliging letter has just reached me. I do not regret the detention here which has caused me to receive it. 'T is a source of great comfort to me to know that my son is under your kind protection, and I am unspeakably pleased to find that I am not singular in my approbation of his character and deportment. He is a creature almost of my entire formation, and I sometimes feared that my partiality might cause me to exaggerate his good qualities, and to be blind to his defects.

"I employ my last sheet of paper to acknowledge your attention to him and to me. Thanks are too poor to be offered in such a case. Your own bosom will tell you what I must feel on the occasion.

"'T is said our sovereign lord the P—— is exceeding wroth at the address of certain heretics to their constituents; * that he has pronounced that (except the overt act) it is treason; that he could have borne anything else; but this is proof of division, etc., etc. . . . . Accept my best wishes for Mrs. Quincy and yourself.

. . . . .

"JOHN RANDOLPH OF ROANOKE.

"The excessive heat has deterred me from commencing my journey. Be so good as to give my best love to Tudor, and present me respectfully to Mr. Kirkland. I shall write to them both as soon as I can get over my present depression of strength and spirits."

THE SAME TO THE SAME.

"RICHMOND, July 24, 1812.

"DEAR SIR: — By severe indisposition I have been detained here since the 12th of the month. Every art has been played off by government to affect the public mind in the State generally, and especially in my district, but with very little success. In my opinion there is a great but silent change in the current of public sentiment, by no means favorable to the Administration; but our general-ticket system will prevent its being felt in the Presidential election.

"I have just read the Newburyport Address and the Boston Resolutions. You men of New England are considered here as irreclaimable heretics, and we meditate to rescue the Cradle (may it not prove the Sepulchre!) of American liberty from the political infidels.

* The address of the minority in Congress.

You will see some resolutions of the County of Charlotte. Had General Dearborn and his friends preoccupied the Exchange, and passed resolutions, they would have been as fair an expression of the public opinion of Boston as these are of Charlotte. . . . . Thank you for the pamphlet. My best wishes attend Mrs. Quincy, and believe me, dear Sir, with much regard, your obliged friend and servant,

"JOHN RANDOLPH OF ROANOKE.

"My compliments to Mr. Otis. When you see Mr. Reed, greet him in my name."

THE SAME TO THE SAME.

"ROANOKE, Va., Aug. 2, 1812.

"DEAR SIR: — On my arrival here I found your very obliging and friendly letter of the 12th, together with Mr. Blake's Oration, for both of which I ask your acceptance of my best thanks. I received at the same time two letters from my son, in both of which he speaks as becomes him of your kind and marked attentions to him. On this subject I will repress my inclination to dwell. Your own bosom will tell you what must be my feelings towards you. It is a source of proud gratification to me to find that my boy holds no mean place in your estimation. Sometimes I have been inclined to think that I was led away by a natural but weak partiality. At others (after making ample allowance on this score), I have felt confident that he would impress all who saw him long enough to know him, that he was no ordinary boy.

"To return to the topic which has been under discussion during the last eight months. I fear you will 'look (in vain) to Virginia for *any* exertion to shake off the Incubus.' For though a majority of the people (hereabouts for example) disapprove the war, there is a general sentiment prevailing that this disapprobation should be suppressed to avoid an ill effect abroad. Another cause also operates. The only war within the memory of man (a few superannuated excepted) is the war of our Revolution. And that being a *civil* war, every man not entering heartily into the cause was justly deemed an enemy, and often treated as such. A fear of similar consequences under the present circumstances renders the greater part of the people shy and reserved. In fact, men are afraid to speak their sentiments. This state of things has emboldened Mr. Eppes to come forward as my opponent. My friends are very confident there is nothing to be feared from his exertions. Through the press, Administration have complete command of the public opinion of Virginia. I know but of two Opposition papers in the State, and the principal one (at Richmond) is utterly worthless and inefficient. Its inanity has destroyed its circulation.

"My health has been so extremely bad that I have seen nobody since I came home. When I left Washington, it was with a wish that I might never see it again. I have every inducement to withdraw from public life; none to remain in it, except a sense of barren duty, where hope finds nothing to achieve. My disorder admonishes me to lay aside my pen.

"With very high respect and regard, I am, dear sir, your obliged humble servant,

"JOHN RANDOLPH OF ROANOKE."

THE SAME TO THE SAME.

"ROANOKE, August 16, 1812.

"DEAR SIR: — Your letter of the 15th of July has just reached me, and I despatch these hurried lines to assure you that I am not unmindful of your very kind attention to Tudor, and that I am as deeply impressed as yourself can be with the importance of the present crisis. I hate the word, but there is none other ready at hand. My last, if it have reached its place of destination, will have informed you of the state of public sentiment in this quarter, where we are as ignorant of the temper prevailing in the Eastern States as the people of New Holland can be. I feel the full force of all that you have urged on the subject of the prevailing discontents in the Northern and Eastern sections of the United States, but I doubt whether any efficient opposition can be organized against the present ruling party in our country.

"For my own re-election I have no fears; but, although four out of five of our people disapprove the war and its advisers, yet a spirit prevails to support it so long as the constituted authorities shall enjoin that duty upon the nation; and to consider it, like the Revolutionary contest, as a struggle in which every man who does not rally round the standard of the government ought to be adjudged as disaffected to the cause of the country. In a few days I shall write you more at large. You will perceive that I have anticipated your idea as to a mode of communication between us which may baffle the spies of the post-office; for although I have nothing to say that I would not utter in the market-place, and which I have not repeatedly pronounced in my place on the floor of Congress, yet I do not choose to subject my private correspondence to the revision of these State inquisitors. I wrote to you from Richmond, and again since I got home. From time to time you may expect to hear from me through this channel. I was at last Charlotte Court; my constituents were anxious that I should address them publicly. In deference to their expectations I did so, and very general satisfaction was the result. I told them that, 'under different circumstances, all that I would have asked at their hands would have been an honest dismission; and such, had I consulted either my interest or my ease, would have been the petition which I should have preferred before them. But that I could not reconcile it either to my sense of duty or to my feelings of inclination to abandon them in the hour of trial and in the day of danger, *provided* it was their unbiased wish that I should continue to represent them. That if I had any cause to think (or should see any) that their confidence in me was in any wise withdrawn, or that they were indifferent in that behalf, I would willingly resign my pretensions to some more capable, but, I must be suffered to say, not more faithful Representative.'

"I dare not trust my pen with the subject of the Baltimore *Septembriseurs*, who have found among us 'an asylum for oppressed humanity.' We have yet no distinct accounts of this horrible transaction.*

"In haste, but with every good wish for yourself and Mrs. Quincy, I am, dear sir, very truly yours,

"JOHN RANDOLPH OF ROANOKE."

* The Baltimore Democratic mob of June 26 and 27, 1812, organized for the destruction of the Federal Republican newspaper. General Lingan, a Revolutionary officer, was most barbarously murdered, and General Henry Lee, "Light-Horse Harry" of the Revolution, father of Robert E. Lee, the leader of the Rebel forces, crippled for life. Alexander Contee Hanson, the editor of the paper, was left for dead, and never recovered fully from the injuries he received.

CHAPTER XII.

1812-1813.

MR. QUINCY'S LAST SESSION. — SPEECH ON THE ENLISTMENT OF MINORS. — FIRE-EATING TACTICS. — SPEECH IN BEHALF OF THE MERCHANTS. — DEFINES HIS POSITION AGAIN. — SPEECH ON THE INVASION OF CANADA. — EXCITEMENT CAUSED BY IT. — MR. CLAY'S DIATRIBE. — LACONIC REJOINDER. — LATER RELATIONS WITH MR. CLAY. — SPEECHES ON CLASSIFYING THE MILITIA AND THE PROHIBITION OF FOREIGN SEAMEN. — FELIX GRUNDY AND HIS CONSTITUENTS. — MR. QUINCY'S RELATIONS WITH MR. RANDOLPH. — AND WITH HARMANUS BLEECKER OF ALBANY. — TAKES A FINAL LEAVE OF CONGRESS.

MR. QUINCY left Boston for Washington on the 11th of November, 1812, in company with Senator Lloyd, and arrived, travelling by stage-coach, in the astonishingly short space of a week; for he took his seat on the 18th. He had formed the resolution not to take an active part in the deliberations of the House, experience having satisfied him "that resistance to whatever a majority had determined to do was hopeless, and that the will of the Cabinet was the law of the land." But it was easier to make than to keep such a resolve, especially for one of his ardent and impulsive temperament. On the third day after taking his seat he was on his legs making a speech, perhaps the most exasperating to the Administration he had yet uttered. It was on a bill "concerning the pay of non-commissioned officers"; but the occasion of his indignant remonstrance and protest was a clause in it which authorized the enlistment of minors without the consent first had of parents, guardians, or masters, which he stigmatized as nothing less than atrocious. I will give a few extracts from it as specimens of its character.

"The nature of this provision is apparent, its tendency is not denied. It is to seduce minors of all descriptions, be they wards, apprentices, or children, from the service of their guardians, masters, and parents. On this principle I rest my objection to the bill. I meddle not with the nature of the war; nor is it because I am hostile to this war, both in its principle and its conduct, that I at present make any objection to the provisions of the bill. I say nothing against its waste of public money. If eight dollars a month for the private be not enough, take sixteen dollars; if that be not enough, take twenty. Economy is not my difficulty. Nor do I think much of that objection of which my honorable friend from Pennsylvania (Mr. Milnor) seemed to think a great deal, — the liberation of debtors from their obligations. So far as relates to the present argument, without any objection from me you may take what temptations you please, and apply them to the ordinary haunts for enlistment, — clear the jails, exhaust the brothel, make a desert of the tippling-shop, — lay what snares you please for overgrown vice, for lunacy which is of full age, and idiocy out of its time.

"But here stop. Touch not private right, — regard the sacred ties of guardian and master, — corrupt not our youth, — listen to the necessities of our mechanics and manufacturers, — have compassion for the tears of parents.

. . . . .

"Mr. Speaker, what a picture of felicity has the President of the United States drawn in describing the situation of the yeomanry of this country! *Their condition happy, — subsistence easy, — wages high, — full employ.* To such favored beings what would be the suggestions of love truly parental? Surely that so much happiness should not be put at hazard, — that innocence should not be tempted to scenes of guilt, — that the prospering ploughshare should not be exchanged for the sword. Such would be the lessons of parental love. And such will always be the lessons which a President of the United States will teach in such a state of things, whenever a father of his country is at the head of the nation. Alas! Mr. Speaker, how different is this Message! The burden of the thought is, how to decoy the happy yeoman from home, from peace and prosperity, to scenes of blood, — how to bait the man-trap, — what inducements shall be held forth to avarice, which neither virtue nor habit nor wise influences can resist. But this is not the whole. Our children are to be seduced from their parents; apprentices are invited to abandon their masters; a legislative sanction is offered to perfidy and treachery; bounty and wages to filial disobedience. Such are the moral means by which a war not of defence or of necessity, but of pride and ambition, should be prosecuted. Fit means to such end!

"The absurdity of this bill consists in this, — in supposing these provisions to be the remedy for the evil of which the President complains. The difficulty is that men cannot be enlisted. The remedy proposed is more money, and legislative liberty to corrupt our youth. And how is this proved to be a remedy? Why, it has been told us, on the other side of the House, *that this is just the thing they do in France*, — that the age between eighteen and twenty-one is the best age to make soldiers, — that it is the most favorite age in Bonaparte's conscription. Well, Sir, what then? Are we in France? Is Napoleon our King? or is he the President of the United States?

. . . . .

"Sir, the great mistake of this whole project lies in this, — that French maxims are applied to American States. Now, it ought never to be lost sight of by legislators in this country, that the people of it are not and never can be *Frenchmen*, — and, on the contrary, that they are, and can never be anything but *Freemen*.

"The true source of the absurdity of this bill is a mistake in the nature of the evil. The President of the United States tells us that the Administration have not sufficient men for their armies. The reason is, he adds, the want of *pecuniary motive*. In this lies the error. It is not *pecuniary motive* that is wanting to fill your armies. *It is moral motive* in which you are deficient. Sir, whatever difference of opinion may exist among the happy and wise yeomanry of New England in relation to the principle and necessity of this war, there is very little, or at least much less, diversity of sentiment concerning the invasion of Canada as a means of prosecuting it. They do not want Canada as an object of ambition. They do not want it as an object of plunder. They see no imaginable connection between the conquest of that province and the attainment of those commercial rights which were the pretended objects of the war. . . . . They have no desire to be the tools of the ambition of any man or any set of men. Schemes of conquest have no charms for them.

"Abandon your projects of invasion, throw your shield over the seaboard and the frontier, awe into silence the Indians in your territory, fortify your cities, take the shackles from your commerce, give us ships and seamen, and show the people of that country a wise object of warfare, and there will be no want of men, money, or spirit.

. . . . .

"Now, Sir, of all the distinctions which exist in these United States, that which results from the character of the labor in different parts of the country is the most obvious and critical. In the Southern States all the laborious industry of the country is conducted by slaves. In the Northern States it is conducted by the yeomanry, their apprentices or children. The truth is, that the only real property in the labor of others which exists in the Northern States is that which is possessed in that of minors, the very class of which, at its most valuable period, this law proposes to divest them. The planter of the South can look round upon his fifty, his hundred, or his thousand of human beings, and say, 'These are my property.' The farmer of the North has only one or two 'ewe lambs,' his children, of which he can say, and say with pride, like the Roman matron, 'These are my ornaments.' Yet these this bill proposes to take from him, or, what is the same thing, proposes to corrupt them, — to bribe them out of his service; and that, too, at the very age when the desire of freedom is the most active, and the splendor of false glory the most enticing. Yet your slaves are safe, — there is no project for their manumission in the bill. The husbandman of the North, the mechanic, the manufacturer, shall have the property he holds in the minors subject to him put to hazard. Your property in the labor of others is safe. Where is the justice, where the equality, of such a provision?

. . . . .

"I know it is said, that in our country minors are subjected to militia duty; and so they are. But this very service is a proof of the position which I maintain: their obligation to serve in the militia is always subject to the paramount authority of the master and the parent.

"The law says, it is true, that minors shall be subject to militia duty. But it also permits the father and the master to relieve them from that obligation at an established price. If either will pay the fine, he may retain the service of the minor free from the militia duty. What is the consequence of all this? Why, that the minor always trains, not free of the will, but subject to the will of his natural or legal guardians. The moral tie is sacred. It is never broken. It is a principle that, cases of misconduct out of the question, the minor shall never conceive himself capable of escaping from the wholesome and wise control of his master or father. The proposed law cuts athwart this wise principle. It preaches infidelity. It makes every recruiting officer in your country an apostle of perfidy. It says to every vain, thoughtless, discontented, or ambitious minor: 'Come hither; here is an asylum from your bonds; here are wages and bounty for disobedience. Only consent to go to Canada, — forget what you owe to nature and your protectors, — go to Canada, and you shall find freedom and glory.' Such is the morality of this law.

"Take a slave from his master on any general and novel principle, and there would be an earthquake from the Potomac to the St. Mary's. Bribe an apprentice from his master, — seduce a son worth all the slaves Africa ever produced from his father, — we are told it is only a common affair. It will be right when there is law for it. Such is now the law in France!"

This speech called down upon its author the bitterest personalities and the most furious rage from the Administration leaders that had yet been wreaked upon him. Mr. David R. Williams* of South Carolina, who introduced the bill, declared Mr. Quincy's qualification of the clause as "atrocious" to be "a libel upon himself, which he threw back upon him who uttered it as a foul, atrocious libel on the committee. . . . . He threw it back in the teeth of the assertor as an atrocious falsehood." Mr. Troup of Georgia, with a classical zeal not altogether according to knowledge, said, "If in the days of Rome's greatness, if in the proud days of Grecian glory, a man could have been found base and hardy enough to withhold the young men from the public service, to turn them from the path of honor, or restrain them from the field of fame, he would have been hurled from the Tarpeian Rock, or consigned to the Cave of Trophonius!" And so on. It was a part of the political tactics of the Southern members to affect to consider denunciations of the measures they supported as personal insults to themselves. Mr. Quincy did not reply at this time; but took occasion afterwards, as will be seen, to expose the folly and fallacy of this assumption. The bill passed the House, but the objectionable clause was struck out in the Senate; only four voting for it, in consequence, as Mr. Quincy affirmed, of the opposition made to it, by himself chiefly, in the House of Representatives.

On the 14th of the next month he was again provoked to break silence by the following scheme, devised by Mr. Gallatin, the Secretary of the Treasury, to extract ten millions from the pockets of the merchants, under this pretence. By the terms of the Non-Importation Act the prohibited articles were to be for-

* David R. Williams, Member of Congress, 1805 to 1809 and 1811 to 1813 Governor of South Carolina, 1814 to 1816.

feited, of course, if imported. Just about the time of our declaration of war, England revoked her Orders in Council, in consequence of Bonaparte's revocation of his Decrees which had occasioned them. The news of the declaration of war had not yet reached England, and the American merchants there, taking it for granted that the Non-Importation Act would be repealed at once, if it did not expire by its terms on the revocation of the Orders, loaded their ships with the prohibited articles, openly and in entire good faith, and despatched them to the United States. But the act had not expired; war had been declared; the merchandise was forfeited, and, in strictness, three times its value besides. The penalty, however, Mr. Gallatin did not propose exacting. He only suggested that the half of the forfeiture which would go to the United States, if it were enforced, should be exacted, the half which would go to the informer being remitted. He claimed the power to do this by virtue of his office; but preferred first obtaining the consent of Congress. The speech which Mr. Quincy made on this proposition is mainly a careful argument against the right thus claimed by the Secretary to remit forfeitures at his pleasure, on such terms as he might judge best. The imposition of terms, he maintained, was limited to cases of wilful negligence or fraud. Where there was no pretence of the existence of these conditions, as in the cases in question, all he had to do was to remit the forfeitures, without taking advantage of innocent error to extort money for the government. It is not necessary to recapitulate his arguments on this point; but I will subjoin a few characteristic passages from the concluding part of the speech.

"I shall touch this subject of the restrictive system with as much delicacy as possible. I wish not to offend any prejudices. I know that the zeal and ardent affection which some gentlemen show for this restrictive system very much resemble the loves of those who, according to ancient legends, had taken philters and love-powders. The ecstasy of desire is just in proportion to the deformity of the object. I shall not, however, meddle with that topic any further than it is connected with the subject before the House.

. . . .

"I know it will be said that it is not proposed to confiscate the whole, but only a part. In other words, you will take not all that you want, but all that you dare. To this I reply, you have no right *to a single dollar, — not to a cent.* The merchants are free from all legal taint; they are free from all statute guilt. There is in the case neither 'wilful negligence nor fraud.' The Secretary of the Treasury does not pretend either; but this is his situation, and this is the secret of his application to Congress for their sanction to his exercise of this great discretionary power. Confiscate the whole of this immense amount, ruin hundreds and thousands on account of a breach of the letter of a penal statute, he dare not. Mitigate upon any principle which would aid the treasury in its necessities, he could not. He therefore transfers the whole matter to the broad shoulders of the Legislature.

. . . . .

"I shall not be able to speak upon this subject, I fear, without offending the nice sensibilities of some gentlemen in the House. Of late an opinion seems to be gaining ground upon this floor, that a member cannot denominate a doctrine or principle to be base or wicked, without attributing those qualities to those who may have happened to advocate such doctrine or principle. And this, too, notwithstanding he expressly declares that he has no intention of applying attributes to such persons, nor even intimating that their view is the same with his own upon the subject. I protest, Sir, against such a restriction of the rights of debate, as totally inconsistent with the necessary freedom of public investigation. It is not only the right, but it is the duty, of every man to whose moral perception anything proposed or asserted seems base or wicked, to brand such proposition or assertion with its appropriate epithet. He owes this duty not only to the public, but to the individual who has been unfortunate or mistaken enough to advocate such an opinion or make such assertion. And provided he does this as the state of his own perception on the subject, and without attributing motives or similar perceptions of the thing to others, not only there is no reasonable ground of offence, but, on the contrary, such a course is the only one reconcilable with duty. How else shall the misguided or mistaken be roused from their moral lethargy, or blindness, to a sense of the real condition or nature of things? What mortal has an intellect so clear as not sometimes to have his view of things doubtful or obscure? Whose moral standard is so fixed and perfect that it never fails him at the moment of need? If, after these explanations, any person takes an exception at the statement of my perceptions on this subject, and any hot humor should fly out into vapor upon the occasion, it has its liberty. I shall regard it no more than 'the snapping of a chestnut in a farmer's fire.'

"I say then, Mr. Speaker, that to my view, — let it be understood, Sir, I do not assert that it is even the true view, much less that it is the view of any gentleman who advocates an opposite doctrine, — I say that to my view, and for my single self, *I would as soon be concerned in a highway robbery as in this treasury attempt.* Sir, I think a highway robbery a little higher in point of courage, and a little less in point of iniquity. In point of courage there is obviously no comparison. In point of the quality of the moral purpose, the robber who puts his pistol to your breast only uses his power to get your property. He attacks nothing but your person. But in this treasury attempt the reputation of the victim is to be attacked to make an apology for confiscating his property. Guilt is alleged, — guilt of which he is clear by the terms of the law, — for the purpose of making him, though innocent, compound for escaping the penalty. What is this but making calumny the basis of plunder?

. . . . .

"I have been told, Sir, that this state of opinion ought to be concealed, — that it was calculated to offend. I have been also told, that we on this side of the House ought not to take any part in this debate, — that a party current would be made to set upon the question, and this to the merchants was inevitable ruin. To all this I have but one answer. My sense of duty allows no compromise on this occasion, nor any concealment. I stand not on this floor as a commercial agent, huckstering for a bargain. As one of the Representatives of the people of Massachusetts, I maintain the rights of these men, not because they are merchants, but because they are citizens. The standard by which their rights are proposed to be measured may be made the common standard for us all. There will soon be no safety for any man, if fines, penalties, and forfeitures be once established as the ways and means of the treasury.

"If I could wish that evil might be done that good might result, I should hope that you would confiscate the property of these merchants. If such a disposition really prevails in the national Legislature towards this class of men, it is desirable that it should be known. Act out your whole character; show the temper which is in you. The sooner will the people of the commercial States understand what they owe to themselves and to their section of country, when there is no longer any veil over the purposes of the Cabinet and its supporters.

"But it will be asked, What will become in the mean time of the individuals whose whole fortunes are at stake? Trembling for the prospects of themselves and their families, they stand like thrice-knouted Russians before the treasury Czar and Autocrat. I say, Sir let them be true to themselves, and true to their class, and true to their country, and they have nothing to fear. Let them remember that it is under the pretexts of law that all tyranny makes its advances. It bribes the avarice of the many to permit it to oppress the few. It talks of necessity. Necessity, — the beggar's cloak, the tyrant's plea. Let the merchants refuse all compromise, whether in the shape of loans, or of equivalents, or of commutation for extra profits. Let them scorn, while innocent, to pay any part of a penalty which is due only in case of guilt, — fly to the States, and claim their constitutional interposition, — interest their humanity to afford a shield against so grievous a tyranny. Above all, let them throw themselves upon the moral sentiment of the community, which will never countenance, when once made to realize the nature of the oppression. And let this be their consolation, that, as in the natural, so it is often in the moral and political world, — the darkest hour of the night is that which precedes the first dawning of the day."

It will be seen that my father took this occasion to expose and denounce the stratagem the Southern Administration-men habitually employed, for purposes of intimidation, of treating severity of language applied to the measure they introduced as insulting to themselves individually. He "defined his position," to use a later political formula, very clearly, and showed as clearly that he was not intimidated by the frantic scurrility of the attacks made upon him a few days before for his speech on the Enlistment of Minors. If any doubt remained on this point, it was certainly dispersed by his speech on the Invasion of Canada, which soon followed.

This famous speech — for the effect it had on friends and foes, its wide circulation and permanent reputation, may entitle it to be so described — was delivered on the 5th of January, 1813. It was, as he himself says of it, "most direct, pointed, and searching as to the motives and conduct of our rulers. It exposed openly and without reserve or fear the iniquity of the proposed invasion of Canada. In reprobating the true tendency and object of this project, I was sparing of neither language nor illustration. I openly and directly exposed the intention of the Administration to create the office of Lieutenant-General, and to raise Monroe to it, in terms so explicit and severe, that it was seen to be impossible to carry it into effect. It had previously been known and avowed." The great length of this speech, and the compactness of its argument, make it impossible for me to give a just idea of its force and spirit by extracts without absorbing more space than I can spare. Its invective is keen, its sarcasm bitter, its denunciations heavy and severe; but the facts from which these derive their sting or their weight are clearly stated and sustained, and it keeps well within the prescribed limits of parliamentary proprieties, avoiding all personal reflections and allusions not demanded and justified by the necessity which called for them. Its author might well say, on reading it over in his old age, that "he shrunk not from the judgment of after times." He considers the subject of the invasion of Canada, — 1st, as a means of carrying on the war; 2d, as a means of obtaining an early and honorable peace; and, 3d, as a means of advancing the personal and local projects of ambition of the members of the American Cabinet. As a means of carrying on the war, he denounces the invasion of Canada as "cruel, wanton, senseless, and wicked," — an attempt to compel the mother country to our terms by laying waste an innocent province, which had never injured us, but which had long been connected with us by habits of good neighborhood and mutual good offices. As a means of procuring peace, he ridiculed the idea that a powerful and haughty nation was likely to be intimidated or propitiated by a proceeding which touched her national honor, and irritated her national pride in the tenderest point. He exonerated the Cabinet, indeed, from being under this delusion; but it was on the ground that the invasion was undertaken by them for the very purpose of preventing a pacific solution of the questions at issue; affirming "that the embarrassment of our relations with Great Britain, and the keeping alive, between this country and that, of a root of bitterness, has been, is, and will continue to be a main principle of the policy of this American Cabinet." This view he supports by a review of the whole course of the Democratic Administrations in relation to England and France, from the time of the accession of Jefferson. From this point he naturally advances to the consideration of his third proposition, — that the invasion of Canada was intended to promote the personal objects of the Cabinet. The Democratic party having attained power by fostering the old grudge against England, and having maintained itself in power by force of that antipathy, a consent to the declaration of war had been extorted from the reluctant Madison as the condition precedent of his nomination for a second term of office. The invasion of Canada was demanded by the Hotspurs of the South and West as a proof of the sincerity of the Cabinet in its war policy, and as the condition of their support of its measures and of the Virginia succession. And he winds up his speech by charging the Cabinet directly with intending to invest Mr. Monroe, one of their own number, the actual Secretary of State and acting Secretary of War, and the pre-ordained successor of Mr. Madison, with the chief command of the army and the rank of Lieutenant-General. This premised, I subjoin a few specimens of the temper and spirit of this speech, which produced a profound sensation in Congress and throughout the country, and had the effect of defeating the contemplated elevation of Mr. Monroe.

"The bill brings necessarily into deliberation the conquest of Canada, either as an object in itself desirable, or inferentially advantageous by its effect in producing an early and honorable peace.

"Before I enter upon the discussion of those topics which naturally arise from this statement of the subject, I will ask your indulgence for one moment, while I make a few remarks upon this intention of the American Cabinet thus unequivocally avowed. I am induced to this from the knowledge which I have that this design is not deemed to be serious by some men of both political parties, as well within this House as out of it. I know that some of the friends of the present Administration do consider the proposition as a mere feint, made for the purpose of putting a good face upon things, and of strengthening the hope of a successful negotiation, by exciting the apprehensions of the British Cabinet for the fate of their Colonies. I know, also, that some of those who are opposed in political sentiment to the men who are now at the head of affairs laugh at these schemes of invasion, and deem them hardly worth controversy, on account of their opinion of the imbecility of the American Cabinet, and the embarrassment of its resources.

"I am anxious that no doubt should exist upon this subject, either in the House or in the nation. Whoever considers the object of this bill to be any other than that which has been avowed is mistaken. Whoever believes this bill to be a means of peace, or anything else than an instrument of vigorous and long-protracted war, is grievously deceived. And whoever acts under such mistake or such deception will have to lament one of the grossest, and perhaps one of the most critical, errors of his political life. I warn, therefore, my political opponents — those honest men, of which I know there are some, who, paying only a general attention to the course of public affairs, submit the guidance of their opinions to the men who stand at the helm — not to vote for this bill under any belief that its object is to aid negotiation for peace. Let such gentlemen recur to their past experience on similar occasions. They will find that it has been always the case, whenever any obnoxious measure is about to be passed, that its passage is assisted by the aid of some such collateral suggestions.

. . . . .

"I warn also my political friends. These gentlemen are apt to place great reliance on their own intelligence and sagacity. Some of these will tell you that the invasion of Canada is impossible. They ask, Where are the men, where is the money to be obtained? And they talk very wisely concerning common sense and common prudence, and will show with much learning how this attempt is an offence against both the one and the other. But, Sir, it has been my lot to be an observer of the character and conduct of the men now in power for these eight years past. And I state without hesitation, that no scheme ever was or ever will be rejected by them merely on account of its running counter to the ordinary dictates of common sense and common prudence. On the contrary, on that very account I believe it more likely to be both suggested and adopted by them. And — what may appear a paradox — for that very reason the chance is rather increased that it will be successful.

"I could illustrate this position twenty ways. I shall content myself with remarking only upon two instances, and those recent, — the present war, and the late invasion of Canada. When war against Great Britain was proposed at the last session, there were thousands in these United States, and I confess to you I was myself among the number, who believed not one word of the matter. I put my trust in the old-fashioned notions of common sense and common prudence. That a people which had been more than twenty years at peace should enter upon hostilities against a people which had been twenty years at war, — that a nation whose army and navy were little more than nominal should engage in war with a nation possessing one of the best-appointed armies and the most powerful marine on the globe, — that a country to which neutrality had been a perpetual harvest should throw that great blessing away for a controversy in which nothing was to be gained, and everything valuable put in jeopardy, — from these and innumerable like considerations, the idea seemed so absurd, that I never once entertained it as possible. And now, after war has been declared, the whole affair seems so extraordinary and so utterly irreconcilable with any previous suggestions of wisdom and duty, that I know not what to make of it, or how to believe it. Even at this moment my mind is very much in the state of certain Pennsylvanian Germans, of whom I have heard it asserted that they are taught to believe by their political leaders, and do at this moment believe the allegation that war is at present existing between the United States and Great Britain to be a '*Federal falsehood*.'

"It was just so with respect to the invasion of Canada. I heard of it last June. I laughed at the idea, as did multitudes of others, as an attempt too absurd for serious examination. I was in this case again beset by common sense and common prudence. That the United States should precipitate itself upon the unoffending people of that neighboring colony, unmindful of all previously subsisting amities, because the parent state three thousand miles distant had violated some of our commercial rights, — that we should march inland to defend our ships and seamen, — that with raw troops, hastily collected, miserably appointed, and destitute of discipline, we should invade a country defended by veteran forces at least equal in point of numbers to the invading army, — that bounty should be offered and proclamations issued inviting the subjects of a foreign power to treason and rebellion, under the influences of a quarter of the country upon which a retort of the same nature was so obvious, so easy, and in its consequences so awful, — in every aspect the design seemed so fraught with danger and disgrace, that it appeared absolutely impossible that it should be seriously entertained. Those, however, who reasoned after this manner were, as the event proved, mistaken. The war was declared; Canada was invaded. We were in haste to plunge into these great difficulties; and we have now reason as well as leisure enough for regret and repentance.

"The great mistake of all those who reasoned concerning the war and the invasion of Canada, and concluded that it was impossible that either should be seriously intended, resulted from this, — that they never took into consideration the connection of both those events with the great election for the chief magistracy which was then pending. It never was sufficiently considered by them, that plunging into war with Great Britain was among the conditions on which support for the Presidency was made dependent. They did not understand that an invasion of Canada was to be in truth only a mode of carrying on an electioneering campaign. But since events have explained political purposes, there is no difficulty in seeing the connections between projects and interests. It is now apparent to the most mole-sighted how a nation may be disgraced, and yet a Cabinet attain its desired honors. All is clear: a country may be ruined in making an Administration happy.

. . . . .

"Concerning the invasion of Canada as a means of carrying on the existing war, it is my duty to speak plainly and decidedly, not only because I herein express my own opinions upon the subject, but, as I conscientiously believe, the sentiments also of a very great majority of that whole section of country in which I have the happiness to reside. *I say, then, Sir, that I consider the invasion of Canada, as a means of carrying on this war, as cruel, wanton, senseless, and wicked.*

"You will easily understand, Mr. Speaker, by this very statement of opinion, that I am not one of that class of politicians which has for so many years predominated in the world, on both sides of the Atlantic. You will readily believe that I am not one of those who worship in that temple where Condorcet is the high-priest and Machiavel the God. With such politicians the end always sanctifies the means, — the least possible good to themselves perfectly justifies, according to their creed. the inflicting of the greatest possible evil upon others. In the judgment of such men, if a corrupt ministry at three thousand miles' distance shall have done them an injury, it is an ample cause to visit with desolation a peaceable and unoffending race of men, their neighbors, who happen to be associated with that ministry by ties of mere political dependence. What though these colonies be so remote from the sphere of the questions in controversy, that their ruin or prosperity could have no possible influence upon the result? What though their cities offer no plunder? What though their conquest can yield no glory? In their ruin there is revenge. And revenge to such politicians is the sweetest of all morsels. With such men, neither I, nor the people of that section of country in which I reside, hold any communion. There is between us and them no one principle of sympathy, either in motive or action.

. . . . .

"As there is no direct advantage to be hoped from the conquest of Canada, so also there is none incidental. Plunder there is none, — at least none which will pay the cost of the conquest. Glory there is none. Can seven millions of people obtain glory by precipitating themselves upon half a million, and trampling them into the dust? A giant obtain glory by crushing a pygmy! That giant must have a pygmy's spirit, who could reap or hope glory from such an achievement.

. . . . .

"It is easy enough to make an excuse for any purpose. When a victim is destined to be immolated, every hedge presents sticks for the sacrifice. The lamb who stands at the mouth of the stream will always trouble the water, if you take the account of the wolf who stands at the source of it. But show a good to us bearing any proportion to the multiplied evils proposed to be visited upon them. There is none. Never was there an invasion of any country worse than this in point of moral principle, since the invasion of the West Indies by the Buccaneers, or that of these United States by Captain Kidd. Indeed, both Kidd and the Buccaneers had more apology for their deed than the American Cabinet. They had at least the hope of plunder. But in this case there is not even the poor refuge of cupidity. We have heard great lamentations about the disgrace of our arms on the frontier. Why, Sir, the disgrace of our arms on the frontier is terrestrial glory in comparison with the disgrace of the attempt. The whole atmosphere rings with the utterance, from the other side of the House, of this word, 'Glory, glory,' in connection with this invasion. What glory? Is it the glory of the tiger which lifts his jaws, all foul and bloody from the bowels of his victim, and roars for his companions of the wood to come and witness his prowess and his spoils? Such is the glory of Genghis Khan and of Bonaparte. Be such glory far, very far from my country. Never, never, may it be accursed with such fame.

'Fame is no plant that grows on mortal soil,
Nor in the glistering foil
Set off to the world, nor in broad rumor lies;
But lives and spreads aloft, by those pure eyes
And perfect witness of all-judging Jove,
As he pronounces lastly on each deed.'

. . . . .

"Mr. Speaker, when I contemplate the character and consequences of this invasion of Canada, — when I reflect upon its criminality, and its danger to the peace and liberty of this once happy country, I thank the great Author and Source of all virtue, that, through His grace, that section of country in which I have the happiness to reside is in so great a degree free from the iniquity of this trangression. I speak it with pride, — the people of that section have done what they could to vindicate themselves and their children from the burden of this sin. That whole section has risen almost as one man for the purpose of driving from power, by one great constitutional effort, the guilty authors of this war. If they have failed, it has been, not through the want of will or of exertion, but in consequence of the weakness of their political power. When in the usual course of Divine Providence, who punishes nations as well as individuals, His destroying angel shall on this account pass over this country, — and, sooner or later, pass it will, — I may be permitted to hope that over New England his hand will be stayed. Our souls are not steeped in the blood which has been shed in this war; the spirits of the unhappy men who have been sent to an untimely audit have borne to the bar of Divine justice no accusations against us.

"This opinion concerning the principle of this invasion of Canada is not peculiar to me. Multitudes who approve the war detest it. I believe this sentiment is entertained, without distinction of parties, by almost all the moral sense, and nine tenths of the intelligence, of the whole Northern section of the United States. I know that men from that quarter of the country will tell you differently. Stories of a very different kind are brought by all those who come trooping to Washington for place, appointments, and emoluments, — men who will say anything to please the ear, or do anything to please the eye, of Majesty, for the sake of those fat contracts and gifts which it scatters, — men whose fathers, brothers, and cousins are provided for by the departments, whose full-grown children are at suck at the money-distilling breasts of the treasury, — the little men who sigh after great offices, — those who have judgeships in hand, or judgeships in promise, — toads that live upon the vapor of the palace, — that stare and wonder at all the fine sights which they see there, and most of all wonder at themselves, — how they got there to see them. These men will tell you that New England applauds this invasion.

. . . . .

"I shall now proceed to the next view I proposed to take of this project of invading Canada, and consider it in the light of a means to *obtain an early and honorable peace.* It is said, and this is the whole argument in favor of this invasion, in this aspect, that the only way to negotiate successfully with Great Britain is to appeal to her fears, and raise her terrors for the fate of her Colonies. I shall here say nothing concerning the difficulties of executing this scheme, nor about the possibility of a deficiency both in men and money. I will not dwell on the disgust of all New England, nor on the influence of this disgust with respect to your efforts. I will admit, for the present, that an army may be raised, and that during the first years it may be supported by loans, and that afterwards it will support itself by bayonets. I will admit further, for the sake of argument, that success is possible, and that Great Britain realizes the possibility of it. Now, all this being admitted, I maintain that the surest of all possible ways to defeat any hope from negotiation is the threat of such an invasion and an active preparation to execute it. Those must be very young politicians, their pin-feathers not yet grown, — and however they may flutter on this floor, they are not yet fledged for any high or distant flight,— who think that threats and appealing to fear are the ways of producing a disposition to negotiate in Great Britain, or in any other nation which understands what it owes to its own safety and honor. No nation can yield to threats what it might yield to a sense of interest; because in that case it has no credit for what it grants, and, what is more, loses something in point of reputation from the imbecility which concessions made under such circumstances indicate. Of all nations in the world, Great Britain is the last to yield to considerations of fear and terror. The whole history of the British nation is one tissue of facts tending to show the spirit with which she meets all attempts to bully and browbeat her into measures inconsistent with her interests or her policy. No nation ever before made such sacrifices of the present to the future. No nation ever built her greatness more systematically on the principle of a haughty self-respect which yields nothing to suggestions of danger, and which never permits either her ability or inclination to maintain her rights to be suspected. In all negotiations, therefore, with that power, it may be taken as a certain truth, that your chance of failure is just in proportion to the publicity and obtrusiveness of threats and appeals to fear.

. . . . .

"Surely, if any nation had a claim for liberal treatment from another, it was the British nation from the American, after the discovery of the error of the American government in relation to the repeal of the Berlin and Milan Decrees, in November, 1810. In consequence of that error, the American Cabinet had ruined numbers of our own citizens who had been caught by the revival of the Non-Intercourse law. They had revived that law against Great Britain under circumstances which now appeared to have been fallacious; and they had declared war against her on the supposition that she had refused to repeal her Orders in Council after the French Decrees were in fact revoked; whereas it now appears that they were in fact not revoked. Surely the knowledge of this error was followed by an instant and anxious desire to redress the resulting injury. As the British Orders in Council were, in fact, revoked on the knowledge of the existence of the French Decree of repeal, surely the American Cabinet at once extended the hand of friendship, met the British government halfway, stopped all further irritation, and strove to place everything on a basis best suited to promote an amicable adjustment. No, Sir, nothing of all this occurred. On the contrary, the question of impressments is made the basis of continuing the war. On this subject a studied fairness of proposition is preserved, accompanied with systematic perseverance in measures of hostility. An armistice was proposed by them; it was refused by us. It was acceded to by the American general on the frontiers; it was rejected by the Cabinet. No consideration of the false allegation on which the war in fact was founded, no consideration of the critical and extremely material nature to both nations of the subject of impressment, no considerations of humanity, interposed their influence. They renewed hostilities. They rushed upon Canada. Nothing would satisfy them but blood. The language of their conduct is that of the giant in the legends of infancy:

> 'Fee, faw, fum,
> I smell the blood of an Englishman;
> Dead or alive, I will have some.'

"Can such men pretend that peace is their object? Whatever may result, the perfect conviction of my mind is that they have no such intention, and that, if it come, it is contrary both to their hope and expectation.

. . . . .

"I will now reply to those invitations to 'union,' which have been so obtrusively urged upon us. If by this call to union is meant a union in a project for the invasion of Canada, or for the invasion of East Florida, or for the conquest of any foreign country whatever, either as a means of carrying on this war or for any other purpose, I answer distinctly, I will unite with no man, nor any body of men, for any such purposes. I think such projects criminal in the highest degree, and ruinous to the prosperity of these States. But if by this invitation is meant union in preparation for defence, strictly so called, — union in fortifying our seaboard, — union in putting our cities into a state of safety, — union in raising such a military force as shall be sufficient with the local militia in the hands of the constitutional leaders, the executives of the States, to give a rational degree of security against any invasion, — sufficient to defend our frontiers, sufficient to awe into silence the Indian tribes within our territories, — union in creating such a maritime force as shall command the seas on the American coasts, and keep open the intercourse at least between the States; — if this is meant, I have no hesitation: union on such principles you shall have from me cordially, and faithfully. And this, too, Sir, without any reference to the state of my opinion in relation to the justice or the necessity of this war. Because I well understand such to be the condition of man, in a social compact, that he must partake of the fate of the society to which he belongs, and must submit to the privations and sacrifices its defence requires, notwithstanding these may be the result of the vices or crimes of its immediate rulers. But there is a great difference between supporting such rulers in plans of necessary self-defence, on which the safety of our altars and firesides essentially depends, and supporting them in projects of foreign invasion, and encouraging them in schemes of conquest and ambition, which are not only unjust in themselves, but dreadful in their consequences; inasmuch as, let the particular project result as it may, the general effect must be, according to human view, destructive to our own domestic liberties and Constitution. I speak as an individual, Sir. For my single self, did I support such projects as are avowed to be the object of this bill, I should deem myself a traitor to my country. Were I even to aid them by loan, or in any other way, I should consider myself a partaker in the guilt of the purpose. But when these projects of invasion shall be abandoned, — when men yield up schemes which not only openly contemplate the raising of a great military force, but also the concentrating them at one point and placing them in one hand, — schemes obviously ruinous to the fates of a free republic, as they comprehend the means by which such have ever heretofore been destroyed; — when, I say, such schemes shall be abandoned and the wishes of the Cabinet limited to mere defence and frontier and maritime protection, there will be no need of calls to union. For such objects there is, there can be, but one heart and soul in this people.

"I know, Mr. Speaker, that, while I utter these things, a thousand tongues and a thousand pens are preparing without doors to overwhelm me, if possible, by their pestiferous gall. Already I hear in the air, the sound of 'Traitor!'—'British agent!'—'British gold!'—and all those changes of vulgar calumny by which the imaginations of the mass of men are affected, and by which they are prevented from listening to what is true, and receiving what is reasonable.

"Mr. Speaker, it well becomes any man standing in the presence of such a nation as this to speak of himself seldom; and such a man as I am it becomes to speak of himself not at all, except, indeed, when the relations in which he stands to his country are little known, and when the assertion of those relations has some connection with and may have some influence on interests which it is peculiarly incumbent upon him to support.

"Under this sanction, I say, it is not for a man whose ancestors have been planted in this country now for almost two centuries,—it is not for a man who has a family, and friends, and character, and children, and a deep stake in the soil,—it is not for a man who is self-conscious of being rooted in that soil as deeply and as exclusively as the oak which shoots among its rocks,—it is not for such a man to hesitate or swerve a hair's breadth from his country's purpose and true interests, because of the yelpings, the howlings, and snarlings of that hungry pack which corrupt men keep directly or indirectly in pay, with the view of hunting down every man who dare develop their purposes,—a pack composed it is true of some native curs, but for the most part of hounds and spaniels of very recent importation, whose backs are seared by the lash, and whose necks are sore with the collars of their former masters. In fulfilling his duty, the lover of his country must often be obliged to breast the shock of calumny. If called to that service, he will meet the exigency with the same firmness as, should another occasion call, he would breast the shock of battle. No, Sir, I am not to be deterred by such apprehensions. May Heaven so deal with me and mine as I am true or faithless to the interests of this people! May it deal with me according to its just judgments, when I fail to bring men and measures to the bar of public opinion; and to expose projects and systems of policy which I realize to be ruinous to the peace, prosperity, and liberties of my country!

"This leads me, naturally, to the third and last point of view at which I proposed to consider this bill,—*as a means for the advancement of the objects of the personal or local ambition of the members of the American Cabinet.* With respect to the members of that Cabinet, I may almost literally say, I know nothing of them except as public men; against them I have no personal animosity; I know little of them in private life, — and that little never made me ambitious to know more. I look at them as public men wielding powers, and putting in operation means and instruments, materially affecting the interests and prospects of the United States.

"It is a curious fact, but no less true than curious, that for these twelve years past the whole affairs of this country have been managed, and its fortunes reversed, under the influence of a Cabinet, little less than despotic, composed, to all efficient purposes, of *two Virginians and a foreigner.* When I speak of these men as Virginians, I mean to cast no odium upon that State, as though it were not entitled to its full share of influence in the national councils; nor, when I refer to one of them as being a foreigner, do I intend thereby to suggest any connections of a nature unworthy or suspicious. I refer to these circumstances as general and undoubted facts which belong to the characters of the Cabinet, and which cannot fail to be taken into view in all estimates of plans and projects, so long as man is constituted as he is, and so long as the prejudices and principles of childhood never fail to influence in different degrees, in even the best men, the course of thinking and action of their riper years.

"I might have said, perhaps with more strict propriety, that it was a Cabinet composed of *three Virginians and a foreigner,** because once in the course of the twelve years there has been a change of one of the characters. But, Sir, that change was notoriously matter of form rather than substance. As it respects the Cabinet, the principles continued the same, the interests the same, the objects at which it aimed the same.

"I said that this Cabinet had been, during these twelve years, little less than despotic. This fact also is notorious. During this whole period the measures distinctly recommended have been adopted by the two Houses of Congress with as much uniformity, and with as little modification, too, as the measures of the British Ministry have been adopted during the same period by the British Parliament. The connection between Cabinet councils and Parliamentary acts is just as intimate in the one country as in the other.

"I said that these three men constituted, to all efficient purposes, the whole Cabinet. This also is notorious. It is true that during this period other individuals have been called into the Cabinet. But they were all of them, comparatively, minor men, — such as had no great

* Mr. Jefferson, Mr. Madison, Mr. Monroe, and Mr. Gallatin.

weight either of personal talents or of personal influence to support them. They were kept as instruments of the master-spirits; and when they failed to answer the purpose, or became restive, they were sacrificed or provided for. The shades were made to play upon the curtain; they entered; they bowed to the audience; they did what they were bidden; they said what was set down for them; when those who pulled the wires saw fit, they passed away. No man knew why they entered; no man knew why they departed; no man could tell whence they came; no man asked whither they were gone.

. . . . .

"It is natural to inquire what are the projects connected with a Cabinet thus composed, and to what ends it is advancing. To answer this question, it is necessary to look into the nature and relations of things. Here the true criterions of judgment are to be found. Professions are always plausible. Why, Sir, Bonaparte himself is the very milk of human kindness; he is the greatest lover of his species in the world; he would not hurt a sparrow, if you take his own account of the matter. What, then, do nature and the relations of things teach? They teach this, — that the great hazard in a government where the chief magistracy is elective is from *the local ambition of states and the personal ambition of individuals.* It is no reflection upon any state to say that it is ambitious. According to their opportunities and temptations all states are ambitious. This quality is as much predicable of states as of individuals. Indeed, state ambition has its root in the same passions of human nature, and derives its strength from the same nutriment, as personal ambition. All history shows that such passions always exist amongst states combined in confederacies. To deny it is to deceive ourselves. It has existed, it does exist, and always must exist. In our political relations, as in our personal, we then walk most safely when we walk with reference to the actual existence of things, — admit the weaknesses, and do not hide from ourselves the dangers, to which our nature is exposed. Whatever is true, let us confess. Nations, as well as individuals, are only safe in proportion as they attain *self-knowledge*, and regulate their conduct by it.

"What fact upon this point does our own experience present? It presents this striking one, — that, taking the years for which the Presidential chair has been filled into the account, *out of twenty-eight years since our Constitution was established, the single State of Virginia has furnished the President for twenty-four years.* And, further, it is now as distinctly known, and familiarly talked about in this city and vicinity, who is the destined successor of the present President after the expiration of his ensuing term, and known that he too is to be a Virginian, as it was known and familiarly talked about, during the Presidency of Mr. Jefferson, that the present President was to be his successor. And the former was, and the latter is, a subject of as much notoriety, and to human appearance of as much certainty, too, as who will be the successor to the British crown is a matter of notoriety in that country. To secure this succession, and keep it in the destined line, has been, is, and will continue to be the main object of the policy of these men. *This is the point on which the projects of the Cabinet for the three years past have been brought to bear,—that James the First should be made to continue four years longer. And this is the point on which the projects of the Cabinet will be brought to bear for the three years to come,—that James the Second shall be made to succeed, according to the fundamental rescripts of the Monticellian dynasty.*

. . . . .

"The army for the conquest of Canada will be raised,—to be commanded by whom? This is the critical question. The answer is in every man's mouth. *By a member of the American Cabinet,—by one of the three,—by one of that 'trio' who at this moment constitute in fact, and who in effect have always constituted, the whole Cabinet.* And the man who is thus intended for the command of the greatest army this New World ever contained,—an army nearly twice as great as was, at any time, the regular army of our Revolution,—I say, the man who is intended for this great trust is *the individual who is notoriously the selected candidate for the next Presidency!*

. . . . .

"Mr. Speaker, what an astonishing and alarming state of things is this! Three men who virtually have had the command of this nation for many years have so managed its concerns as to reduce it from an unexampled height of prosperity to a state of great depression, not to say ruin. They have annihilated its commerce and involved it in war. And now the result of the whole matter is, that they are about to raise an army of fifty-five thousand men, invest one of their own body with this most solemn command, and he the man who is the destined candidate for the President's chair! What a grasp at power is this! What is there in history equal to it? Can any man doubt what will be the result of this project? No man can believe that the conquest of Canada will be effected in one campaign. It cost the British six years to acquire it, when it was far weaker than at present. It cannot be hoped that we can acquire it under three or four years. And what then will be the situation of this army and our country? Why, then the army will be veteran, and the leader a candidate for the Presidency! And whoever is a candidate for the Presidency, with an army of thirty thousand veterans at his heels, will not be likely to be troubled with rivals, or to concern himself about votes. A President elected under such auspices may be nominally a President for years; but really, if he pleases, a President for life.

"I know that all this will seem wild and fantastical to very many, — perhaps to all who hear me. To my mind it is neither the one nor the other. History is full of events less probable, and effected by armies far inferior to that which is proposed to be raised. So far from deeming it mere fancy, I consider it absolutely certain, if this army be once raised, organized, and enter upon a successful career of conquest. The result of such a power as this, intrusted to a single individual in the present state of parties and passions in this country, no man can anticipate. There is no other means of absolute safety but denying it altogether.

"I cannot forget, Mr. Speaker, that the sphere in which this great army is destined to operate is in the neighborhood of that section of country where it is probable, in case the present destructive measures be continued in operation, the most unanimous opposition will exist to a perpetuation of power in the present hands, or to its transfer to its destined successor. I cannot forget that it has been distinctly avowed by a member on this floor, a gentleman from Virginia too, (Mr. M. Clay,) and one very likely to know the views of the Cabinet, that '*one object of this army was to put down opposition.*'

"Sir, the greatness of this project, and its consequences, overwhelm my mind. I know very well to what obloquy I expose myself by this development. I know that it is always an unpardonable sin to pull the veil from the party deities of the day; and that it is of a nature not to be forgiven either by them or their worshippers. I have not willingly, nor without long reflection, taken upon myself this responsibility. But it has been forced upon me by an imperious sense of duty. If the people of the Northern and Eastern States are destined to be hewers of wood and drawers of water to men who know nothing about their interests, and care nothing about them, I am clear of the great transgression. If, in common with their countrymen, my children are destined to be slaves, and to yoke in with negroes chained to the car of a Southern master, they at least shall have this sweet consciousness as the consolation of their condition, — they shall be able to say, 'OUR FATHER WAS GUILTLESS OF THESE CHAINS.'"

Of this speech, and of the replies it called forth, Mr. Quincy thus speaks: —

"The plainness and directness of this attack were of such a nature, that, although all the minor herd of debaters poured out their wrath upon my head, it was deemed important enough that the untamed ferocious tongue of Henry Clay should be detailed to the service of responding to and prostrating the assailant. Accordingly, the House was resolved into a Committee of the Whole, and Speaker Clay descended from the chair to the floor, for the purpose, as one of his friends informed me, *of reducing me to the alternative of a duel or disgrace.* He consequently on this occasion exceeded himself in his characteristic power of insolent vituperation of his opponent, and unlimited laudation of the Administration.

. . . . .

"I do not wonder at the rage of these men. The truth is, I thrust the spear directly between the joints of the harness. I made a reply of about ten sentences, which my friends say was the best I ever made. I suppose the charm lay in its brevity. The palace and all its retainers are in a most tremendous rage, and if they had a Baltimore mob at command, I have no doubt they would show their indignation in a way perfectly in unison with their characters. I laid the mysteries of their power open to public inspection, and when you throw light upon an owl's nest, there is nothing like the agitation of the whole family."

The Democratic speakers who followed Mr. Quincy for the two or three days after the delivery of his speech — Mr. Rhea* and Mr. Grundy † of Tennessee, Mr. Widgery ‡ of the District of Maine, and Mr. Archer § of Maryland — devoted the chief of their speeches to attacks upon him with as much abusive skill as they had at command. But their puny invectives were thrown into obscurity by the philippic which Mr. Clay descended from

* John Rhea, Member of Congress from Tennessee, 1803 to 1815, and 1817 to 1823.

† Felix Grundy, born, 1770; in public life all his days, either in Tennessee or at Washington; Member of Congress, 1811 to 1814; Senator, 1829 to 1838; appointed Attorney-General by President Van Buren in 1838; resigned in 1840, and re-elected Senator; died the same year.

‡ William Widgery, born in Philadelphia, 1753; was a privateersman during the Revolution, and afterwards settled in Maine; was often in the General Court; Member of Congress from 1811 to 1813; died, 1822.

§ Stephenson Archer, Member of Congress, 1811 to 1817, and 1819 to 1821.

the chair to deliver on the 8th of January. This celebrated speech occupied the chief of two days, and was not finished until the third. The following extracts are all for which I can make room; but they contain the cream of his diatribe. The speech as reported is obviously much curtailed, and they that heard it testified that, in its modified form, as prepared for the press, it is far less bitter and abusive than as it fell from the speaker's lips.

"Next to the notice which the Opposition has found itself called upon to bestow upon the French Emperor, a distinguished citizen of Virginia, formerly President of the United States, has never for a moment failed to receive their kindest and most respectful attention. An honorable gentleman from Massachusetts (Mr. Quincy), of whom, I am sorry to say, it becomes necessary for me in the course of my remarks to take some notice, has alluded to him in a remarkable manner. Neither his retirement from public office, his eminent services, nor his advanced age, can exempt this patriot from the coarse assaults of party malevolence. No, Sir. In 1801, he snatched from the rude hands of usurpation the violated Constitution of his country, and *that* is his crime. He preserved that instrument in form and substance and spirit, a precious inheritance for generations to come, and for *this* he can never be forgiven. How impotent is party rage directed against him! He is not more elevated by his lofty residence upon the summit of his own favorite mountain, than he is lifted by the serenity of his mind, and the consciousness of a well-spent life, above the malignant passions and the turmoils of the day. No; his own beloved Monticello is not less moved by the storms that beat against its sides, than he hears with composure (if he hears at all) the howlings of the whole British pack, set loose from the Essex kennel! When the gentleman to whom I have been compelled to allude shall have mingled his dust with that of his abused ancestors, — when he shall be consigned to oblivion, or, if he lives at all, shall live only in the treasonable annals of a certain junto, — the name of Jefferson will be hailed as the second founder of the liberties of this people, and the period of his Administration will be looked back to as one of the happiest and brightest epochs in American history. I beg the gentleman's pardon; he has secured to himself a more imperishable fame. I think it was about this time four years ago, that the gentleman submitted to the House of Representatives an initiative proposition for an impeachment of Mr. Jefferson. The House condescended to consider it. The gentleman debated it with his usual *temper*, *moderation*, and *urbanity*.

The House decided it in the most solemn manner; and, although the gentleman had somehow obtained a second, the final vote stood *one* for the proposition, one hundred and seventeen against it! The same historic page that transmitted to posterity the virtues and the glory of Henry the Great of France, for their admiration and example, has preserved the infamous name of the fanatic assassin of that excellent monarch. The same sacred pen that portrayed the sufferings and crucifixion of the Saviour of mankind has recorded, for universal execration, the name of him who was guilty, not of betraying his country, but (a kindred crime) of betraying his God!

. . . . .

"But, Sir, I will quit this unpleasant subject. I will turn from one whom no sense of decency or propriety could restrain from soiling the carpet on which he treads, to gentlemen who have not forgotten what is due to themselves, the place in which we are assembled, nor to those by whom they are opposed.

. . . . .

"I am sensible, Mr. Chairman, that some part of the debate to which this bill has given rise has been attended by circumstances much to be regretted, not usual in this House, and of which it is to be hoped there will be no repetition. The gentleman from Boston had so absolved himself from every rule of decorum and propriety, had so outraged all decency, that I have found it impossible to suppress the feelings excited on the occasion. His colleague, whom I had the honor to follow (Mr. Wheaton), whatever else he might not have proved in his very learned, ingenious, and original exposition of the powers of this government, — an exposition in which he has sought, where nobody before has looked, and nobody after him will examine, for a grant of our powers, the preamble to the Constitution, — has clearly shown, to the satisfaction of all who heard him, that the power is conferred of defensive war. I claim the benefit of a similar principle, in behalf of my political friends, against the gentleman from Boston. I demand only the exercise of the right of repulsion. No one is more anxious than I am to preserve the dignity and liberality of debate; no member more responsible for its abuse. And if, on this occasion, its just limits have been violated, let him who has been the unprovoked cause appropriate to himself exclusively the consequences."

As soon as Mr. Clay had taken his seat, Mr. Quincy rose and spoke as follows. These few words were all the notice he saw fit to bestow on the personal attacks of Mr. Clay or of the other

Democratic speakers who preceded and followed him in the debate on this bill.

"Mr. Chairman, I do not rise to reply to the honorable the Speaker, who, it seems, has descended from the Chair in order to do that which no other member of this House was either willing to undertake or was deemed competent to perform. I should blush for myself and for the good and wise, the only portion of this community of whose applause I am ambitious, could I deem a reply necessary. As a public man, I never expect, I never wish, any other or further influence than what results from distinct principles, and those principles emanating from known or proved facts. He who refutes those principles, or disproves those facts, has my honor. He who misrepresents or mistakes either the one or the other has my pity or my contempt, according to the proportion of imbecility of head or corruption of heart which enters into the cause of such mistake or misrepresentation. I cannot put myself on the level of retort. That, in my observations, I did not pass the fair limits of parliamentary discussion is obvious from this, — that the honorable the Speaker himself, then presiding in this House, neither stopped me himself, nor permitted others to do it when it was attempted. So far as respects any personal reflections which have fallen from the honorable the Speaker, or may fall from other members, they have their liberty of speech. Such as my reputation was before Billingsgate opened its flood-gates, such it will remain after the odious flood shall have passed by."

This brief and pithy summing up of the conclusion of the whole matter, as far as he was concerned, was looked upon by Mr. Quincy's friends at the time as having been done in the best taste and in the most effectual manner, and I have no fear that their judgment will be reversed by history or posterity. Of this contemporary opinion he received many gratifying assurances which would have confirmed his own judgment as to the fitness of his course had confirmation been necessary. On the subject of Mr. Clay's avowed purpose of reducing him to the alternative of a duel or disgrace, he wrote as follows to his wife, immediately after this passage at arms was over, for the purpose of relieving her from any anxiety on the subject: —

"As it respects the Southern and Western men, they shall learn from me, if from no one else, that they are not to set up standards of duty or decorum for my part of the country. While I have tongue or pen, the ignorant part of the nation shall not assume to itself with impunity to lord it over the intelligent, nor the vicious over the virtuous. As to my *personal safety*, that is the last thing I think of. I am secured by my place in some measure, — more by my perfect sense of performed duty. Bleecker called me up out of bed a fortnight ago to tell me he heard at Georgetown there was some intention of a personal attack on me by some of the friends of the palace. I laughed at him. The storm was mere wind, as the event proved. They know their interest too well to resort to such means, and should they do it, I should not regret it on a public account. If men are not personally safe in this city who come here to perform their duty, it ought to be known, and I am as willing to have the proof made on me as on any other. But the truth is, there has not been one moment of real cause of such apprehension, nor should I have recurred to it had you not touched on the subject."

On the 26th of January he wrote: —

"The storm has subsided, and a most perfect calm is preserved on the floor. On reading my speech, I suspect the palace gentry find nothing so very violent and exceptionable in point of allusion and expression as they thought on its delivery; and there are so many truths, that they are willing to let it alone. My friends seem entirely gratified. Elisha R. Potter of Rhode Island said that 'it was the very thing. But,' added he, 'Quincy, as the old woman said of Whitefield, *there is no printing the manner*.'"

It was one of the characteristics of my father's temperament, that, though most sensitive to everything that might affect his true honor and real reputation, he was absolutely insensible to assaults made upon him, either by the press or in Congress, which he knew were not deserved. They seemed hardly to arrest his attention at the time, and made no permanent impression upon his mind. All the shafts, shaped with skill and tipped with malice, which the Administration orators, with Mr. Clay at their head, poured upon him in such showers, glanced off from his impenetrable indifference like native arrows from the hide of the armed rhinoceros. No one was ever more scrupulously anxious to make sure that his words and actions, as a public man, were exactly what they should be, and none more unaffectedly indifferent as to what was thought or said about the one or the other by friend or foe. As to Mr. Clay's share in this vain attempt to put him down, there is reason for believing that he was not altogether proud of it, after the passions of the time had cooled, and the occasion for the violence had passed away. In the last year of President John Quincy Adams's administration, during the winter of 1828–29, my father made his only visit to Washington after leaving Congress. According to the etiquette of the place, he made calls of ceremony upon all the members of the Cabinet, and among them he left his card at Mr. Clay's door. His visits were duly returned by all the other ministers; but nothing was heard of the Secretary of State. My father took it for granted that it was the memory of the old grudge that made Mr. Clay indisposed to meet him, even after the lapse of sixteen years, and thought no more about the matter. It happened, however, that the visiting-card had gone awry, and had never been received, which made Mr. Clay entertain precisely the same opinion as to my father's feelings towards himself. After the adjournment of Congress, a common friend (I think it was Mr. Everett) waited upon my father with an explanatory message from Mr. Clay, such as made a personal acquaintance possible between them. As the message was a verbal one, I have no means of giving its terms; but its substance as well as its form was satisfactory, and thenceforward bygones were bygones between the old antagonists. A few years later, in the autumn of 1833, Mr. Clay made a visit to Boston, on which occasion my father called upon him, and received him at the President's house in Cambridge, and introduced him officially to the students, who were assembled in the library for the purpose. He was never, however, an admirer of the personal character of Mr. Clay, nor a follower of his school of political economy. Though he took no active part in politics during the years when the American System was in question, he did not believe in it, and held to the last to the old Federal doctrine of free trade as the basis of national prosperity.

During the remainder of the session Mr. Quincy took part in the debates on all questions of national importance; but he only spoke twice at much length, — on the bill for classifying the militia, and on that for prohibiting the employment of foreign seamen on public and private vessels. The report of the first of these speeches is very meagre. He opposed the bill mainly on the ground that it proposed to make the militia the basis of a standing army, by the introduction of a system analogous to the French conscription. It passed the House, but was defeated or dropped in the Senate. The other bill, he wrote to his wife, was a mere tub to the whale, to make the Northern people believe that there was an inclination towards peace on the part of the Administration, shown in this plan for removing the occasion for search and impressment, and thus diminish the effect on the spring elections of Northern hatred of the war. The Federalists were especially urged to support the measure on the ground of its consistency with the stand they had always taken as to this matter. Mr. Quincy showed that there was no pretence for this assertion, and affirmed that the provisions of the bill were such as "no man in the nation ever advocated, or ever conceived as a scheme of practical policy, until it burst upon the astonished vision of the gentleman from Tennessee (Mr. Grundy)." The charge of inconsistency he retorted on the Democrats, urging that this bill was a direct contradiction of the assumptions on which they had resisted the right of search and of impressment even to the drawing of the sword. On this point he said: —

"Sir, if I wished to press far into the discussion of this bill, which I do not, I would ask, What has become of that great doctrine of the right of expatriation, so obtrusively and clamorously maintained, from the first establishment of our national government down to the present day, by the patrons and authors of this bill, their friends and supporters? Are all those choice topics of declamation to be abandoned? Are they forgotten by gentlemen on the other side of the House? If they are, will they be forgotten by this people? This bill proceeds upon the principle that the right of expatriation does not exist in the subjects of foreign governments. For, if it does exist, then such foreign government has no right to reclaim them, and we have no right to drive them home. The bill abjures this right of expatriation, and, in doing this, cuts up by the roots, not only the claim to protection of the individuals whom it contemplates to force back to the service of their respective sovereigns, but also your whole right to protect, beyond the limits of your local jurisdiction, even your naturalized citizens. . . . . It is extraordinary that men who have been, all their lives long, perfect knights-errant in favor of distressed foreigners, — who have set their spears in rest, and gone tilting all over the world in defence of oppressed humanity, — who have been inviting it to our shores with both hands, — should all at once turn round and pretend to be about to send them all home again, and leave them to the mercy of ancient systems and of their former masters.

"But this is not all. This great right of expatriation, which the advocates of this bill and their political friends have been maintaining these twenty years, in favor of all the world, is now denied by the bill to exist, even in our own citizens. The reciprocity of the bill consists in this, — that these, our citizens, should be forced home, according to the obligations of their natural allegiance. For on this principle alone have we a right to claim their return. Thus strange and mysterious is both the character and parliamentary course of this bill. . . . . For my part, I consider the bill as no pacific measure. Its true purpose is to give a peace aspect to the time, — to clear the atmosphere for a moment, so that the money-gudgeons may bite sharp at the treasury hook. I view it as a scheme intended to deceive the people, — to buoy them up with false hopes of peace, when the real intention is to continue the war. Under this belief it shall have no support from me."

This was Mr. Quincy's last speech in Congress. Mr. Grundy replied to the speech with sufficient asperity, and afterwards held the following conversation with my father, as described in a letter to my mother of the 16th of February, 1813.

"Concerning Grundy's asperity, it seems I have not yet received the whole. He is a perfect political jockey, and as good-humored as he is cunning. He said to me yesterday, 'Quincy, I thought I had abused you enough, but I find it will not do.' — 'Why, what is the matter now? I do not mean to speak again.' — 'No matter; by heavens, I must give you another thrashing.' — 'Why so?' — 'Why, the truth is, a d——d fellow has set up against me in my district, — a perfect Jacobin, as much worse than I am as worse can be. Now, except Tim Pickering, there is not a man in the United States so perfectly hated by the people of my district as yourself. You must therefore excuse me. By G——, I must abuse you, or I shall never get re-elected. I will do it, however, genteelly. *I will not do it as that d——d fool of a Clay did it,— strike so hard as to hurt myself.* But abuse you I must. You understand. I mean to be friends notwithstanding. By G—— I mean to be in Congress again, and must use the means.'

"I give you this anecdote because it is characteristic, and because it is illustrative of men, manners, and motives."

My mother appears to have written to my father to know how it happened that Randolph, who had paid high compliments, in one of his speeches, to Mr. Bleecker and Mr. Emott of New York, both of them Federalists of the first water, had passed himself over in utter silence. To this inquiry he made this wise and characteristic reply:—

"Randolph and I are upon friendly and confidential terms, as far as it is possible to be so with a man so wayward and versatile in his friendships and enmities as he has shown himself. With such a man one cannot feel himself wholly at ease. As to his studied compliments to Bleecker and Emott, and his silence with regard to me,— of which [Isaac P.] Davis spoke,— I never troubled myself to inquire the reason, or noticed the fact, as I never deemed him either the dispenser of fame or the criterion of character. I am not in the habit of permitting envy or jealousy in myself, or suspecting it in others. If there be any disposition in him not to do justice to me, of which I see no evidence, it is quite as likely to be the result of local politics as of any other cause. The truth is, that next to Timothy Pickering my name is the most obnoxious in the Southern States, and it would not aid Randolph on the hustings to have it said or shown that he had been paying compliments to so obnoxious a character."

In another letter to my mother, he says, speaking of Randolph:—

"As you seem to think John Randolph not inclined to be just to me, I will tell you an anecdote which occurred yesterday. He was sitting by the fire in the Capitol, and I said to him, 'Randolph, have you any news from Virginia?' 'Yes,' said he, very significantly, and put a letter into my hands from a Mr. Leigh, a gentleman of distinction there, who, in acknowledging the receipt of my speech from him, had expressed himself upon it in a style very far too flattering for me to repeat. Randolph evidently seemed gratified, although he did not say a word, except, '*That man's opinion is worth something, Quincy.*'

"I mention this by way of justice to him. On this topic, Bleecker showed me a letter from Chief Justice Kent of New York, whose approbation of my speech was unequivocal, and who desired him to express his thanks to me for my boldness, truth, etc., etc. So there is a balance for the scurrility to which I have been subjected."

The name of Mr. Bleecker reminds me that I should do my father's life less than justice if I failed to speak of the friendship which sprang up between himself and that excellent gentleman during the Twelfth Congress. Harmanus Bleecker — best and most silent of men! — was of pure Dutch descent, and was one of the few of their race who could speak the language of the founders of New Netherland. His public life, I believe, was limited to this one Congress, with the exception of a brief diplomatic service of which I shall speak presently. He was a lawyer by profession, — wise, learned, sagacious, the friend as well as the counsellor of his clients. "He asked only how best to serve the poor," writes one of his numerous pupils, — among whom were numbered many of the most eminent men of New York, — "and it was a sight worth seeing to witness his consultations with the quaint old people of Albany, where family sorrows or fortune's smile or frown were all talked over in the good old language of the Netherlands." He made no pretensions to forensic eloquence; but he was listened to by courts and juries with the respectful attention due to his knowledge, experience, and high character. No man, I am safe to say, ever had more friends or fewer enemies. My father entertained for Mr. Bleecker a friendship as warm as it was sincere, and his regard was reciprocated with feelings of cordial affection and admiration. Mr. Bleecker made frequent visits to Boston, where he was always a welcome guest at many of the best houses, and at none more welcome than our own. In this way the old intimacy was kept alive, and made an exception to almost all my father's Washington friendships, which too generally had faded out through the influences of time and separation.

I have said that Mr. Bleecker was the most silent, as well as the best of men. But this description must be taken with many grains of allowance. In general society he was eminently "a good listener," such as Dr. Johnson might have loved, and he used to remind me of that Englishman some French writer of the last century tells of, who affirmed that speaking spoiled conversation, — "*que parler c'est gâter la conversation.*" But when drawn out, or impelled to speak, he expressed himself, deliberately indeed and compactly, but in exact and well-chosen language, and always wisely and to the point.

Mr. Bleecker was appointed, in 1839, Minister to Holland, by President Van Buren, whose personal friend he was, and who seems, in defiance of the precedents of our diplomacy, to have regarded his peculiar fitness for the post, and especially his speaking the language of the court to which he was accredited, as no insuperable objection to the nomination. He made and left a most favorable impression on the court and society of the Hague, and, it may well be believed, had a thorough enjoyment of his official residence in the land of his ancestors. When he was first presented at court, the king said to him, "Sir, you speak better Dutch than we do in Holland!" which was no mere compliment, but a fact due to his speaking the classical Dutch of literature, untainted by the conversational corruptions of later times. Mr. Bleecker had lived a bachelor up to the time of his mission to the Dutch Court. Before his return, however, he had reformed that one error of his life by marrying a young Dutch lady, the daughter of a gentleman of distinction at the Hague, holding an important official position there, whose society gave a new happiness to the remainder of his life. He died at Albany in 1849, at the age of seventy years.

On the 4th of March, 1813, my father quitted Washington never to return to it in a public character. To use his own language: —

"I left Washington with the feelings of a man quitting Tadmor in the Wilderness, 'where creeping things had possession of the palace, and foxes looked out of the windows,' and sought refuge in home, and in the bosom of my family; with children dear to me as my heart's blood, with a wife wise, faithful, and beloved, with whom it was my destiny, by the will of Heaven, to pass fifty-three years in a felicity attained by few, surpassed by none."

CHAPTER XIII.

1813.

MR. QUINCY'S RETIREMENT FROM CONGRESS. — ORATION BEFORE THE WASHINGTON BENEVOLENT SOCIETY. — IN THE STATE SENATE. — REMONSTRANCE AGAINST THE WAR. — LOUISIANA RESOLUTIONS. — THE LAWRENCE RESOLUTIONS. — SETH SPRAGUE. — DISCONTENTS IN NEW ENGLAND. — MATTHEW LYON. — LETTERS OF JOHN RANDOLPH.

MR. QUINCY was barely forty-one years old when he thus withdrew, of his own free choice, from parliamentary life, after eight years of most assiduous service. There is no doubt that he might have remained in Congress for a much longer time had such been his wish, so decided a majority did the Federal party command in Boston, and so well content were they, as a body, with his course as their representative. His reasons for refusing to remain in Congress I have already given in his own words. That his deliberate judgment, in view of all the public and private reasons which led him to withdraw at this time from the scene of national politics, remained substantially unchanged, is doubtless true. But there were times when, in private conversation, he would seem to be a little shaken as to the wisdom of his course in thus leaving the national Legislature in the very prime of his life. He had prepared himself most laboriously and conscientiously for his Congressional duties, and he had so performed them as to gain the approbation of his constituents and to make himself one of the most prominent public men of his time. It is true that he had not succeeded in defeating the worst measures of the dominant party, nor even in materially modifying them; but to such success he could hardly have looked forward when he entered on his public life. His time, however, was by no means wasted, nor his labor lost. The stern remonstrance, the sharp rebuke, the keen sarcasm, with which he encountered the measures of the Administration, and exposed the motives which inspired them, helped to keep alive and make intelligent the opposition which in some degree held it in check, and in some cases caused it to change its course. Moreover, he had very early, as we have seen, discerned the insidious nature of the element of slavery in our institutions, — its disastrous influence upon the prosperity of the North, and its inevitable tendency to grow and strengthen itself, unless speedily and effectually checked, — and it was this feeling that pervaded and gave unity to his Congressional action. Perhaps no man did more than he to impress upon the general mind of New England the real source of the calamity of her people, and to implant the germs of that moral, religious, and political hostility to slavery which afterwards grew to such prevailing strength. It was natural enough that he should have sometimes felt, in later years, that he might have remained in Congress, through the years that the war with England lasted, advantageously to his country, and honorably to himself. And it would have been no unworthy ending of his Congressional career, could it have been rounded by a share in the glorious, though ineffectual struggle to stay the tide of slavery at the frontier of Missouri in 1820. But he judged otherwise at the time; and it would have made no practical difference in the result. He could not have changed or delayed the course of events, the direction of which he had so clearly foreseen and so distinctly predicted.

Almost immediately upon his return home, after taking his final leave of Congress, he had an opportunity of giving emphatic utterance to his sense of these growing dangers. The Washington Benevolent Society of Boston, the chief of an affiliation of organizations of that name extending through the State, partly charitable but mainly political, invited him to deliver an oration before them on the anniversary of Washington's first inauguration as President, the 30th of April, 1789. This association celebrated its feast-day with all the pomp and circumstance it could command, — a military escort, a procession, banners with appropriate devices, an oration, and appropriate exercises in the Old South Church. One especial feature of this procession was a company of school-boy Federalists, to the number of two hundred and fifty, dressed uniformly in blue and white, with Washington's Farewell Address, in red morocco, hanging round their necks, and with his gorget, which he had worn in the Old French War, attached to their banner. This gorget, the same which may be seen depicted in the portrait of Washington prefixed to the first volume of Sparks's Life, had been given to Mr. Quincy for this society by Mrs. Peter of Georgetown, D. C., a granddaughter of Mrs. Washington. It bears the arms of the Colony of Virginia, and has attached to it the very ribbon by which it hung round his neck on the day of Braddock's defeat. At the time of the dissolution of the society, soon after the peace of 1815, this interesting relic was presented by them to Mr. Quincy, and is still in the possession of the family.

Mr. Quincy's oration was a clear and able, if not exactly a dispassionate, exposition of the bearings of the slave ratio of representation upon the relative proportions of the political power of the different sections of the country. He showed by statistics the anomalous results which had flowed from this concession to slavery, multiplied and hastened by the annexation of foreign territory, to be erected into States as fast as they were needed to confirm the dominion of the slave-holders. "The new States govern the old, the unsettled the settled; the influences of emigrants prevail over those of the ancient natives; a black population overbalances the white; from woods and lakes and desert wildernesses legislators issue, controlling the destinies of a seaboard people, paralyzing all their interests and darkening all their prospects." He warned the people of Massachusetts that the cause of their commercial distresses lay deeper than embargo or war, and that the mere return of free trade and of peace would not cure the evils under which they suffered. These would be renewed in fresh forms as long as the control of the government was permitted to remain in the hands of the old Slave States and those to be carved out of the new territory acquired for this political purpose in flagrant violation of the Constitution. Undoubtedly passages in this oration, as well as in his famous Speech on the Admission of Louisiana, might be quoted by the advocates of the late Rebellion, in this country and in England, who have claimed for him the distinction of having been the original Secessionist, in confirmation of their assertion. But I think the dispassionate reader of the one, as well as of the other, will note a wide difference between the ground taken by him and that occupied by the oracles of the Rebellion, as I have already attempted to point out. It was the right of revolution that he vindicated, and the prerogative of the citizens to judge, at their own peril, when the injuries they endured justified a resort to that ultimate and supreme right. He really stood upon the ground of the Declaration of Independence, which was sophistically claimed as their own by the promoters of the slave-holding rebellion, and by its defenders on both sides of the Atlantic. If this were treason, he was a traitor to the end of his days, as I have said before, for he lived and died in this political faith. But I have no apprehensions as to the judgment which posterity will pass upon him as a statesman and a patriot, after reading his words in the light of the events which provoked, and of those which have justified them. I have room only for brief extracts from this oration; but I have conscientiously endeavored to select what its mislikers at the time would have considered its worst passages.

"Whenever the rulers of a nation become the mere heads of a party, the last and least consideration with them is the good of the people. How to secure their power, — how to manage the elections, — who is the fittest tool, — who will run the fastest, go the farthest, and hold out the longest for the least wages of corruption, — are the only inquiries. To give muscle and durability to their influence is the single end of their political system. For this, British antipathies are stimulated; for this, British injuries are magnified; for this, French affections are cultivated, and French insults and injuries palliated or concealed; for this, we had restriction; for this, embargo; for this, we have war; for this, war shall be continued; and, if peace come, for this, peace shall be concluded. For unprincipled ambition in power effects not even public good, except from corrupt motives.

. . . . .

"In treating of our condition, I shall not waste the hour in idle regrets or vain criminations. The hand of ruin is upon us and upon our cities. The deep and ancient root of the prosperity of Massachusetts is withering. Our commerce, navigation, and fisheries are gone. A whirlwind from the West is passing over those massy pillars of our greatness, and they are already prostrate. Lamentation and despair suit not the condition of freemen, — least of all, of the freemen of Massachusetts. To them it belongs to be mindful of the character of their ancestors, — men keen to discern and resolute to perform their duties, — generous spirits, whom power could not tempt, nor fraud ensnare, nor force subdue. The descendants of such men ought to blush at being satisfied with shuffling along from one mode of oppression to another, and from one stage of corruption to another; each individual happy, if his head escapes the bolt intended for the general ruin; content with life and precarious enjoyment to-day and to-morrow, careless of the long extent of time which is to come afterward. The grave will soon close upon us and our vain joys and vainer anticipations. You are fathers. What political inheritance do you leave to your children? Where lie the sources of the evils which we suffer? What are the remedies? What are our duties?

. . . . .

"The sources of our sufferings lie deeper than embargo or war, great as are both these evils. Washington foresaw and foretold that these men 'would be satisfied with nothing short of a change in our political system.'* But Washington himself did not foresee, nor could any human eye have foreseen, the change which in so short a space of time has been made in the internal relations of this country; much less could he have foreseen the change which artful construction and interested usurpation have made in the principles of our Constitution.

. . . . .

"It is a notorious fact, that, partly by the operation of the slave ratio in the Constitution, and partly by the unexampled emigrations into the West, the proportions of political power among the States of this country have changed since the adoption of the Federal Constitution in a degree as unanticipated as the result is eventful and ominous. On the proportion of its political power, in an association like ours, does the safety of every State which is a member of it depend. And reason teaches, and safety requires, that this proportion should have some reference to the nature and greatness of its interests.

. . . . .

"A free people have a right, and it is their duty, to inquire into the securities they possess for their liberties and properties; and to see

* Marshall's Life of Washington, Vol. V. p. 84 of the notes.

whether they be such as ought to give content to wise and virtuous minds. There is nothing mysterious in the fabric of our freedom. There is no divine right of Kings, or Presidents, or Congresses, in the whole compound. By the Constitution of the Commonwealth of Massachusetts it is made our duty frequently to resort to first principles. We have not only the right to examine the top and the shaft of the column of our liberties, but if it appear out of plumb, or out of level, it is made our duty to look at the corner-stones and see if they are not falling away. I know that, when these topics are touched, all the craftsmen — those who make profit by the shrines and are growing fat on the offal of the sacrifices — are in an uproar, and run about, crying, 'The Constitution is in danger. These things lead to a dissolution of the Union. Great is Diana of the Ephesians!' What? Are we not freemen? If to any individual the result of our political institutions appear incompatible with general or particular safety, shall he not speak? How, then, can the evils which we feel, or fear, be remedied or prevented? How else can we bring our existing Constitution to that test of experience which Washington has told us is 'the surest standard of its real tendency'? In my judgment, concealment in such case is not so much an error as a crime. For a crime it is for a citizen, in a free country, to see, or believe that he sees, distinct dangers surrounding the commonwealth and be silent concerning them, either through fear of personal responsibility, or in subserviency to the apathy or the prejudices of the times.

. . . . .

"The degree in which the proportions of political power among the States of this Union have been changed, by time and usurpation, since the adoption of the Constitution, admits of a very varied and extensive illustration. I shall confine myself to the statement of one or two facts, rather by way of indicating the state of things than describing it. This cannot be done, in all its relations, within the limits of the present occasion.

. . . . .

"The States of Virginia and Georgia together possess a white population but a little exceeding that of Massachusetts. Yet, through the effect of the slave ratio and the principles of the Constitution, while Massachusetts possesses in the Senate and the House of Representatives twenty-two votes, they possess thirty-three! All these States which I have named — Virginia, Georgia, Kentucky, Tennessee, and Ohio — have paid into the treasury of the United States, in customs, scarcely more than fifteen millions of dollars since the adoption of the

Constitution. The single State of Massachusetts has paid more than forty-two millions net revenue. Yet, upon every question touching the life-blood of our commerce, while Massachusetts, in both branches of the Legislature, has but twenty-two votes, those States have sixty-one! I state one other fact. The power attained in the House of Representatives by the effect of the slave ratio is twenty votes. The State of Massachusetts has but twenty. So that this great and ancient and once proud, but now, constitutionally speaking, humbled Commonwealth, has absolutely no more weight in the national scale than a species of beings in fact as destitute of political rights as the brute creation. Upon theoretical principles, can anything be more shameful? The practical effect is worse than the theory.

"Perhaps, however, it may be said that this evil is temporary, and that the causes which have produced this inequality are ceasing to operate. The fact is directly the reverse. The causes are permanent, progressive, and unlimited. All the policy of the government is shaped to strengthen them. The Constitution itself has been violated in order to augment the oppressive preponderancy of that quarter of the country.

. . . . .

"E[illegible]n this state of things, humiliating as it is, might be endured. No[illegible]tanding it presents little comfort for the present and less con[illegible]n for the future; notwithstanding it indicates this strange conditi[illegible] as the result of our political association, — that the new States govern the old, the unsettled the settled, — that the influences of emigrants prevail over those of the ancient natives, and that a black population outbalances the white, — that from woods and lakes and desert wildernesses legislators issue, controlling the destinies of a seaboard people, paralyzing all their interests and darkening all their prospects; — all this notwithstanding, still the condition might be endured, upon the principle that it was the fair result of the compact. We had agreed that all the people within the ancient limits of the United States should be placed on the same footing, and had granted an undoubted right to Congress to admit States at will *within the ancient limits.* We had done more: we had submitted to throw our rights and liberties and those of our children into common stock with the Southern men and their slaves, and had agreed to be content with what remained after they and their negroes were served.

. . . .

"But what shall we say to what is called the admission of Louisiana into the Union? What shall we say to the annexation of a territory greater than the whole of the old United States? — what to the asserted power — indeed already in one instance exercised — of making States beyond the Mississippi as unlimited in point of number as of extent? The indifference with which that usurpation has been viewed in this part of the country is an event as astonishing as it is ominous. . . . . Louisiana is spoken of as being an integral part of this nation, with as much indifference as though it had been admitted by an unquestionable authority. We hear of the intention of cutting it up into new States, with as much unconcern as though we had no interest in the matter. Yet every additional State augments that depressing inequality of political influence which already grinds our interests in the dust, rivets our chains, and makes more certain and hopeless the condition of our political servitude.

. . . . .

"This, then, is the undeniable condition of the people of the Commonwealth of Massachusetts. That proportion of political power which they possessed at the time of the adoption of the Constitution is gone, and the proportion which remains has not one characteristic of equality or justice, — whether we take age, or intelligence, or enterprise, or wealth, or physical strength, or population, as the measure of what is just and equal. This proportion, thus diminished, i[illegible]ry day diminishing still further, in a geometrical ratio, by the o[illegible]n of changes, partly the effects of the fair principles of our as[illegible]on and partly of usurpation. Such is the result of that 'expe[illegible] to which Washington refers us as the 'test of every constituti[illegible] Is this a state of things which ought to give content to wise and virtuous minds?

. . . . .

"As it is with the people of every State, so it is with the people of this Commonwealth, — the individuals composing this State owe to the people of the Commonwealth of Massachusetts an allegiance original, inherent, native, and perpetual. True it is that the people of this Commonwealth have transferred a certain specified portion of allegiance, originally due to them from the individuals composing their State, to a certain extrinsic association called the United States. This transferred portion of allegiance is not only limited in its nature, but it is also conditional. The condition is, that the principles of the Constitution should be preserved inviolate. Whether any such violation have occurred, or whether it be such as essentially affects the securities of their rights and liberties, are questions which the people of each of the associated States are competent not only to discuss, but to decide. And we in this Commonwealth have reason to thank the great Giver of every good gift that he has bestowed upon this people not only the right to make, but the power to support, any decision to which they may be called by a manifest violation of their liberties. If the people of the Commonwealth of Massachusetts shall ever become slaves, it will be from choice, and not from nature, — it will be, not because they have not the power to maintain their freedom, but because they are unworthy of it.

. . . . .

This war, the measures which preceded it, and the mode of carrying it on, are all undeniably Southern and Western policy, and not the policy of the commercial States. Now it is, in my apprehension, of little importance, if the vital interests of the Commonwealth of Massachusetts are destroyed, whether the blow be given through ignorance, indifference, or design. *Under these influences they are destroyed.* And if the apathy of the commercial States continue, and the present spirit of party render them blind to their natural interests, the policy which has wrought this destruction will be perpetuated. This policy perpetuated, we may call ourselves what we please, — in the eye of reason and common sense we are slaves; and I add, — for I know the natures of the predominating influences of those States, — slaves to no very desirable masters.

. . . . .

" This, then, is the undeniable condition of the United States. A sectional cabal governing them, not according to the true interests of any part, but solely according to the interests of their own ambition; deceiving and misleading the inland influences, corrupting and depressing the commercial. The basis of their power not temporary, but permanent, because it rests upon changes which time and usurpation have made in the relative proportion of the powers of the Constitution. What are the remedies? The spirit of Washington answers: 'Submit to no change by usurpation. If the distribution or modification of the constitutional power be wrong, let it be corrected in a constitutional way.'

" But how is this to be effected, weak, divided, and oppressed as are the commercial States? I answer, Let them be ashamed of the past. Be wise for the future. Put away these divisions. Let common interests cement your affections. Out from your councils, and out from your confidence, be every man who will not maintain the old foundations of New England prosperity. Follow no longer after the doctrines and commandments of men from the mountains. Contend earnestly for the commercial faith delivered by your fathers. And let him who will not stand up for it be to you worse than an infidel.

"Let ancient divisions cease, and the poor triumphs of party be forgotten in the contemplation of the interests of Massachusetts. The venerable name of government, the respect due to authority, the obtrusive pretensions of impostors in power, have misled many. Thank Heaven! the scales are fast falling from the eyes. The snare of the fowler is broken, and New England is escaping.

"But remember. It is not relief from commercial restrictions, nor yet the attainment of peace, nor yet the change of your rulers, that is to be the object of your struggles. Doubtless the jugglers will shift the hand when they see the old game is discovered. They understand well that the commercial influences are not to be crushed in a moment. Although the leviathan is hooked, he cannot be drawn at once and speared to the land. He must be played backward and forward at the end of the line, — now a little given, and then taken away, until, exhausted by idle efforts, the strength and adhesion of his parts gone, his fat shall be transferred to the mountains, and he shall remain, the skeleton of his former greatness, the scorn and the sport of his spoilers.

"People of Massachusetts! People of the commercial States! Look into the foundations of your security. Strive to bring back the principles and proportions of the Constitution to the standard of Washington. Nay, more, — by a great consentaneous and constitutional effort, strive to bring it back to the principles of wise and honorable safety. Look at the fact, that, by the operation of the slave ratio in the Constitution and by the unlimited power of making new States, partly the result of the provisions of the Constitution, partly of usurpation, the proportion of political power bears no relation to the proportion of your real interests. Recollect that this state of things is daily growing worse. Remember that the very blacks of the Southern States are equal in weight, in the political scale, to the whole State of Massachusetts. Is this a condition of things patiently to be borne by freemen, at least without one constitutional effort? If it be, we deserve what we endure. We deserve to be what we are, — of no more weight than slaves."

This oration was received by the Federalists in all parts of the country with the warmest applause. His old Congressional friends and other prominent members of the party sent him letters full of cordial agreement with its sentiments, and of high approval of its method. Mr. David B. Ogden, perhaps the head of the bar of New York at that time, wrote to him as follows, May 13th:—

"I have long been of the opinion that the course of public affairs in this country was such as naturally, and I believe intentionally, to destroy the weight and influence of the Northern commercial States, and I cannot but think the country under great obligation to you for placing the subject before the people in the strong and able manner in which it is done by this oration. The time has arrived when the truth must be spoken, and spoken plainly, or we are lost."

The following letter from Mr. Gouverneur Morris shows how strong party spirit must have been when it could suffer the idea of resisting the imposition of taxes for the purpose of providing for the payment of the interest of a public debt, legally contracted, to enter the mind of so eminent a disciple of the school of Washington and Hamilton.

"MORRISANIA, May 15, 1813.

"DEAR SIR:—Accept, I pray, my thanks for the oration you had the kindness to send. I have read it twice with renewed pleasure,—not merely as a composition, though in that respect excellent, but for the profound sense and just views which it displays. The subject you have broached must be pursued, and our national compact brought to the test of reason, matured by experience. That most important question must be thoroughly examined,—Can a commercial people harmonize with the masters of slaves? In the mean time, it is essential that taxes be opposed on the broad principle that it is impious alike to shed the blood of man in unjust war, and to support those who commit that impiety. Should it be objected, as it probably will, to favor lenders and their associates, that public faith is pledged, it may be replied that a pledge wickedly given is not to be redeemed; moreover, the pledge was not given, for acts of Congress violating the Constitution are void. The issue of paper money receivable in taxes was unconstitutional, because it was a violation of faith, previously pledged, that the produce of those taxes should be applied in payment of our old debt; and in like manner the second appropriation of the same taxes to a new loan was a violation of the first contract. The subscribers to that loan, therefore, will have no right to complain, for it was their duty to examine the validity of the act before they subscribed. Moreover, the refusal to lay taxes which could honestly be appropriated was in itself a sufficient warning. Let then the [illegible in the original] patriots who trusted after this warning apply for payment to the gentlemen who violated public faith in the very act by which they pretended to pledge it. Those who say they are the friends of peace will give themselves the lie, if, directly or indirectly, they furnish the means of war. And they must not pretend to be actuated by patriotic sentiment; for not only is the war unnecessary and unjust, but its professed object, if attainable, is inconsistent with our interest and our rights. Moreover, a satisfactory arrangement on the subject of impressment is in our power at any moment; for to obtain it requires neither the force of armies, the skill of generals, nor the dexterity of ministers. Let the first article of a treaty be proposed by us, and let it be the acknowledgment of a belligerent's right to take his subjects from neutral merchant-ships, as an unquestionable principle of public law. Let us then call on the British negotiator for a second article, containing such regulations of the practice of that right as they think convenient. We need not hesitate about submitting to conditions which they will submit to in their turn; for, as it is a sound maxim of legal prudence that no man need be wiser than the law, so it is a safe maxim of political prudence, that no nation need be prouder than the British.

"But essential as it is to peace that supplies be withheld, it is not less essential to the recovery of those rights which the commercial States have lost by their compact with slave-holders, and the subsequent abuse of that compact. I stop; for why should I give you the trouble to read what you have long since thought? This letter already so much exceeds all reasonable bound, that I must pray your pardon for what it contains, and extend it no further than to assure you of the esteem and respect with which I am yours,

"GOUVERNEUR MORRIS."

Colonel Pickering wrote to him from Washington, May 28th: —

"At Philadelphia, inquiry was made for your oration before the Washington Benevolent Society, and since my arrival here I have been requested to obtain a copy or two, from which an edition may be published in that city. I brought with me the copy you presented to me, and will transmit that to Philadelphia as soon as I receive it from some members of Congress who wish to read it. I suppose you have a parcel for distribution among your friends. At any rate, I pray you to send me some, if but two or three copies. . . . . We have not yet had a single document from the Executive. The majority are silent, probably canvassing to know the members who will support the plans of the Executive, whatever they may be."

His friend Mr. Elisha R. Potter, member of the House from Rhode Island, after paying his tribute of praise to the oration, goes on to give an account of a false alarm at the Capitol of the near approach of the British, which did but anticipate the true alarm which overtook it about a twelvemonth afterwards. The letter bears date July 19th.

"We have had nothing very interesting at this place until a few days past. Since the night before last all has been alarm and confusion. An express then arrived, informing that the British fleet were on their way up the Potomac with a fair whole-sail [*sic*] breeze, and that their object was this place. We soon afterwards heard that part of them were in the Potomac, and the remainder had gone to Annapolis, and were landing their forces at that place. We had many long faces among the war gentry yesterday morning. Secretary Armstrong, with the Regulars, City Volunteers, and Militia, left this city and went over the Eastern Branch, and went to Fort Warburton, and has not returned. The alarm has this morning a little subsided. We had a secret session yesterday for two or three hours, which gave an opportunity of hearing some patriotic speeches; but with those I was not much disturbed, as you know I am not much for war and fighting. If this place should be attacked, I shall neither run nor fight. My pride will not permit me to run, and I detest this war too much to fight."

Mr. Bleecker wrote from Albany, May 14th, speaking of this oration: —

"Its tone and spirit are approved by every one I have heard speak of it. I regret that there are not more copies in pamphlet form for distribution in this part of the country. It is particularly important that the facts and opinions you have so impressively stated should be extensively diffused in this State. Our people are yet blind."

The letter from Mr. Artemas Ward, — Mr. Quincy's successor for the First District, the son of the first Major-General commissioned in the Revolutionary war, and himself afterwards Chief Justice of the Common Pleas for many years, — from which the following extracts are made, contains some boarding-house gossip doubtless interesting to his correspondent, and some statements as to the distribution of taxation, and the exercise of the appointing power during the recess of the Senate, not uninteresting to any of us at this time. It is dated June 9th, 1813.

"I am at Captain Coyle's, and occupy the front upper chamber. I had my choice of what was left when I arrived. A total change has taken place in C.'s family. Not one has been there this session who were boarders in your days. How this happened I cannot tell, as I neither inquire into nor disclose family secrets. . . . . The present boarders are Mr. Stockton, Mr. Schureman, and Mr. Coxe, Representatives from New Jersey, Mr. Daggett, the successor of Mr. Goodrich, Mr. Webster, and myself. Mr. Stockton is a celebrated lawyer, — the first in his State. He has been before, some years ago, a member of the Senate and the House; but, like all other new members, does not feel that all the fight is his own. Mr. Schureman is a very sound, judicious, sensible man. Has heretofore been a member of the Senate and the House. Mr. Coxe is a gentleman farmer, sensible and scientific in his way, well educated, etc. Mr. Daggett is a lawyer of great celebrity, and a companionable, pleasant man. Mr. Webster you know. When I arrived at Washington I found the Jersey gentlemen in possession. Mr. Daggett came with an order from Mr. Goodrich for his birthright. Mr. Webster and myself took what was left. . . . . My accommodations are good, but I left much better at home, to which I cast many a longing look. . . . . The Chancellor of the Exchequer has not yet opened his budget. It is reported that it will soon be done. Mr. Pitkin says the Committee of Ways and Means have agreed upon a report, excepting as to the time when the bills are to go into operation, which they are about to report, imposing taxes. Mr. Eppes is for making the day far distant. He speaks of this session of Congress as being unnecessary, etc., and does not march up to the taxes with so bold a front as some of his brethren. There is, in my mind, good ground for believing that the leaders of the Administration party are much embarrassed. All agree that taxes are necessary; but when they put forth their hands and touch the bone and flesh of their several sections, each wishes to save his own, and, eventually, it is very possible they will not agree. . . . . The Executive business before the Senate undergoes much hard discussion. The late nomination of Gallatin has been the subject of very free remarks in that body, and the right of the President in the recess of the Senate to appoint him, questioned. It is denied that a vacancy had happened in the office to which he was appointed," etc.

The Mr. Webster mentioned in this letter was the celebrated orator, who began his long public life at this time as a Representative from New Hampshire. The nomination of Gallatin, of which Mr. Ward speaks, was to be one of the two special commissioners appointed to join Mr. Adams at St. Petersburg for the purpose of procuring the mediation of the Emperor Alexander between England and the United States. The appointment of Mr. Gallatin was resisted on the grounds mentioned by Mr. Ward, but especially because he still retained the office of Secretary of the Treasury, the duties of which were performed by the Secretary of the Navy. The nomination was finally rejected at this time, though it was confirmed on its renewal many months later. The other commissioner was James A. Bayard of Delaware, who had most ably represented his State in the House and the Senate since 1797. He had always been a consistent Federalist, and was one of those whom Mr. Jefferson honored by a posthumous attack, although he owed his first election to Mr. Bayard's preferring him to Burr as the least of two evils. His consenting to accept office at the hands of Mr. Madison was naturally an occasion of some suspicion and displeasure to his old political comrades. It was in reply to a letter from Mr. Quincy containing some intimation of this nature that Colonel Pickering wrote the following answer: —

Colonel Pickering to Mr. Quincy.

"Washington, June 17, 1813.

"Dear Sir: — I have this evening received your letter of the 10th, and will take due care of that enclosed.

"Although Mr. Bayard's conduct was not, on all occasions, just what I wished, yet in the main it was correct, according to *our views;* and he certainly possesses eminent talents. On my way hither I fell in with a gentleman of considerable distinction for intelligence and learning, — a native, though not a resident in Delaware. Speaking of Bayard he said: 'He is a man of supreme ambition. He is at the same time wealthy. Having abilities, wealth, and ambition, what can he want? Honors, — such honors *now* as may lead to the highest *hereafter*.'

"From the information of different gentlemen who conversed with

Bayard, I am satisfied that he expected the mission would effect a peace. He particularly said that his instructions were broad enough to render peace practicable.

"A discussion took place to-day on Mr. Webster's resolutions.* Mr. Grosvenor † spoke ably, and his colleague Oakley ‡ (who comes in Emott's place) displayed very great ingenuity. Grundy and Calhoun will probably exhibit to-morrow; and Webster, with Mr. Gaston § of North Carolina (a very eloquent man), I hope will close the debate. As much as many of the Executive party wish to prevent the inquiry, I am inclined to think the resolution will be substantially adopted; while I am aware that the most influential members of the ruling party are insensible to shame, and will therefore strain every nerve to crush the inquiry. Cheves and Lowndes have been silent. Taliaferro again contests Hungerford's election,‖ and attempted to set the whole election aside as irregular and illegal. Speaker Clay and Calhoun exerted themselves for the purpose; and the former especially, I am assured, is greatly mortified at his defeat; a majority of four declared the election valid, so far as that Hungerford should keep his seat, subject to a scrutiny of the polls.

"With great esteem and respect, I am yours,

"T. PICKERING."

Although no longer in Congress, Mr. Quincy had by no means retired from public life. At the spring election of 1813 he was chosen one of the Senators from Boston in the State Legislature; and his course there soon made him quite as prominent before the country, and as well abused by the Democratic orators and newspapers, as he had ever been in Washington. He easily took the lead in the Senate, and, in conjunction with his friends Lloyd

* Resolutions calling for information as to how and when the government obtained information concerning Bonaparte's Decree of April 28, 1811.

† Thomas P. Grosvenor of New York, member from 1813 to 1818; one of the best debaters in the House.

‡ Thomas J. Oakley was an eminent lawyer of New York; born, 1783; graduated at Yale College, 1801; Justice and Chief Justice of the Superior Court; died, 1857.

§ William Gaston was one of the most distinguished citizens of North Carolina, and a firm Federalist throughout; Member of Congress, 1813 to 1817. He was a graduate of Princeton College, and was a very cultivated and accomplished man. He died in 1844.

‖ John Taliaferro, who was many years in the House at different times, did not succeed in unseating John P. Hungerford now. Hungerford was a Revolutionary officer. He sat from 1813 to 1817.

and Otis in the House, — the former of whom had resigned his seat in the Senate of the United States, — presented a front of opposition, not to say resistance, to the war policy of the Administration scarcely less alarming to its fears than the successes of the enemy in those early days of the war. A remonstrance was agreed upon reprobating the war as impolitic and unjust after the repeal of the Orders in Council, — as having the color at least of being waged in alliance with France against England, — as having no just occasion in the vexed question of impressment, because that issue had never been presented to England as one of peace or war, and because the resources of negotiation had not been yet exhausted upon it. It went on to state that the Northern people, who had no need of Southern aid for their defence, had consented to the slave representation for the purpose of obtaining national protection for their commerce; but their commerce, far from receiving that protection, had been for years the object of a systematic course of hostilities from the general government, ending in its destruction by this war.

Another report was accepted at the same time, denouncing the purchase of Louisiana, on the grounds with which my readers are by this time sufficiently familiar, and proposing a joint resolution instructing the Senators and requesting the Representatives of the State to endeavor to obtain a repeal of the act of Congress admitting Louisiana into the Union. The report was accepted, and the joint resolution passed both Houses. This report was transmitted at once to Colonel Pickering, at Washington, by Mr. Quincy, from whom the following answer was received, with all despatch. His prophecy as to the secession of the Western States, as the consequence of that extension of territory, shows how inscrutable is the future of nations to the vision even of the most experienced and sagacious statesmen.

Colonel Pickering to Mr. Quincy.

"City of Washington, June 19, 1813.

"Dear Sir: — I this day received under your cover the Report of the Joint Committee concerning the admission of Louisiana as a State into the Union. That Massachusetts should express its opinion in the nature of a protest might be expedient; but, under my present view of the subject, I regret the proposed resolution instructing the delegates from Massachusetts to endeavor to obtain a repeal of the act of Congress for admitting Louisiana into the Union. You know the attempt must be fruitless. I presume that some who opposed the admission would not now vote to repeal. It seems to be one of those acts to which the saying applies, *Quod non fieri debet, factum valet.*

"I consider the thing as utterly hopeless. More States will be created, rather than the first disfranchised. The first and only remedy will be when the Southern Atlantic States shall open their eyes, and see their true interest in a close and firm connection with the Northern half of the Union. Then Congress will *equalize the public burdens;* and then the Western States with Louisiana will fly off. They will detach themselves, take to their own use all the Western lands, and leave the whole national debt on the shoulders of the Atlantic States.

"I am, dear sir, sincerely yours,

"T. Pickering."

The action of Mr. Quincy, however, which drew down the most violent denunciations of the war party upon his head was the report and resolution annexed, written and offered by him on the occasion of a vote of thanks to Captain Lawrence for the capture of the Peacock coming up from the House for the concurrence of the Senate. The report did ample justice to the naval skill and military and civil virtues of Captain Lawrence; but recommended — on the ground that previous votes of the same kind, in honor of other victorious officers, had been regarded by many conscientious persons as an encouragement to an unjust, unnecessary, and iniquitous war — that the following resolution be adopted in its stead, which was accordingly done: —

"*Resolved,* That in a war like the present, waged without justifiable cause, and prosecuted in a manner indicating that conquest and ambition are its real motives, it is not becoming a moral and religious people to express any approbation of military and naval exploits not immediately connected with the defence of our sea-coast and soil."

Whether this refusal to acknowledge the services of a gallant and meritorious officer, rendered in the course of his duty, was justifiable on the part of the Legislature, I shall not stop to consider. My readers are competent to decide that question for themselves. But it showed, in the most emphatic manner, the strength of political feeling and of party spirit at that time, made more intense and bitter by the general distress which the war brought upon all ranks of society. It was denounced at Washington as "moral treason," and the phrase "unbecoming a moral and religious people" became almost as much a popular by-word as "peaceably if they can, forcibly if they must," itself. In January, 1824, when the Democrats had obtained the control of the State, this resolution was ordered, by a strict party vote, to be erased from the journal of the Senate. This was done on the motion of Mr. Seth Sprague of Duxbury, an active Democratic politician ever since Democracy was, who expiated the services which he had thus ignorantly rendered to slavery during his prime of manhood, by the active, intelligent, and unwearied anti-slavery labors of his old age. This venerable man, who died in 1847 in his eighty-eighth year, often said to me that he wished he could be elected to the Senate once more, only that he might endeavor to undo what he had then done, — to expunge the expunging, and restore the record to the condition in which it stood before he touched it. Mr. Sprague was the father of Mr. Peleg Sprague, formerly a Senator from Maine in Congress, and latterly Judge of the United States District Court for Massachusetts, for many years.

The legislative action I have related was but a faint expression of the sense of injury felt by the majority of the people of Massachusetts, and indeed of New England. The hardships which the course of the Administration had brought to the door of almost every man in the Northern region, and especially in that portion of it which lies along the sea-coast, had set the face of New England as a flint against the war and its promoters. The feeling of disaffection to the general government outside the walls of the State-House was much deeper and more embittered than that which found utterance within them. In private circles and through the press the doctrine that the injuries inflicted upon the rights and interests of New England would justify the strongest measures for the vindication of the one and the maintenance of the other, was eagerly and passionately affirmed and argued. The intense excitement of those days extended itself over many months. That it did not break out into actual resistance was due to the settled habits of order and obedience to law in which the institutions of New England had bred and confirmed her people. And that this feeling was not confined to that region is shown by the following letter from Gouverneur Morris, a retired statesman and diplomatist, a man of fortune and elegant tastes, — one who had everything to lose, and nothing to gain, by a political convulsion.

MR. MORRIS TO MR. QUINCY.

"MORRISANIA, August 18, 1813.

"DEAR SIR: — Accept my thanks for your favor of the 10th. In the present state of public affairs our greatest danger is, I think, in the timidity of those who see and feel the present evils, but are distracted by the apprehension 'of what *may* happen' should the state of things be changed. The change, if it take place, must be effected by the very men whose moral condition produces that timidity. In ordinary cases, ambitious demagogues effect revolutions by stirring up the dregs of mankind to revolt against established order and the wholesome restraints of law. If that class of the community be now called into action, the country will be plunged in a still greater depth of distress, and have no hope of relief but from despotism, which, indeed, must soon take place if the present state of things continue unchecked. But those who fear for the future may console themselves by the reflection, that a change by mob power cannot be made. If, therefore, they will do their duty, the whole authority will be in their hands, and can be so modified and deposited as to secure *permanent*, *good*, *free* government. To develop this proposition would require a treatise instead of a letter, and is moreover unnecessary, for *you* must be convinced of it; and *they* are not convinced only because they look at what they *may* lose by action, and shut their eyes on what they *must* lose by inaction. I am ready to acknowledge the value of property, but I pray these gentlemen to consider that we are now on the down-hill road to that condition in which there is no property, — no, not in life itself, — because there is no security.

"I will not presume to say what steps should be taken, but I hold myself ready to follow any honest lead.

"Believe me, truly yours,

"GOUVERNEUR MORRIS."

One of the oddest conjunctions into which the changes and chances of political life brought my father was the one which made him the correspondent of Matthew Lyon, first of Vermont and afterwards of Kentucky, for several years a most notorious political actor on the Congressional scene. He was a native of Ireland, and came to this country as a redemptioner, or an emigrant whose services were sold for a term of years by the importer to pay for his passage and other expenses. He was bought by a citizen of Vermont, where in due time he grew into a conspicuous member of the Anti-Washington party. In 1797 he went to Congress, where he inaugurated, in January, 1798, the series of acts of personal insult and violence which have disgraced Congress from time to time from that day to this, by spitting in the face of Mr. Griswold of Connecticut on some occasion of offence he took at him. The House refusing to expel him, by a strict party vote, Mr. Griswold took justice into his own hands, and caned him in his seat a few days afterwards, for which irregular process of redress he too went scot-free, also by a party vote, neither the Administration nor the Opposition commanding the two thirds requisite for the expulsion of a member. Lyon acted with the Anti-Adams and Jeffersonian party for the chief of his Congressional career, carrying his professions of republican purism beyond even the canons set up by the most advanced section of the Democratic party, — as when he asked to be specially excused from accompanying the House to present the Address to President Adams in response to his Message, which was then the custom, on the ground that it was an anti-republican and slavish mimicry of monarchical customs. Later in the same year he was tried, convicted, fined, and imprisoned for libel under the Alien and Sedition laws, his party still refusing to expel him, on his return to his seat in the House, after the expiration of his sentence. At the end of his term he did not return to Vermont, but emigrated to Kentucky, from which State he obtained an election to the House in 1803. My father once asked him how he managed this matter. "By establishing myself at a cross-roads by which everybody in the district passed from time to time, and abusing the sitting member!" was his simple and satisfactory explanation of the phenomenon. During his membership for Kentucky he acted with the Federalists in opposition to the Embargo and the other restrictive acts of the Administration, which was probably the cause of his illustrating one of my father's favorite sayings, — "that politics, like misery, brings a man acquainted with strange bedfellows." His letters bear marks of an imperfect education, not unseldom of what Lord Chesterfield calls "auricular orthography"; but they indicate strength and energy of character and sound common-sense. Indeed, these qualities could not be wanting in one who carried his first election to Congress by means of a newspaper of which he was not merely the editor, but for which he cast the types, and made the paper out of bass-wood himself. I will give some brief specimens of his letters.

"I may tell you that I am very well pleased with the part Massachusetts has acted in the political drama before us. Her Governor has won my heart. Her Assembly have acted like men who sincerely loved their country. But the New England States are beaten in the political race for President. The mobbish Democratic spirit has carried the nation far on towards ruin. But I cannot, will not, despair for this nation, at the foundations of which I have labored with as much zeal as a devotee ever labored for Heaven or his God. You must not despair. Massachusetts must not despair. Let me see no disposition in her toward disunion. She must save the nation she created. She has the greatest power and influence to do so. She is now regenerated on the ancient principles of the Revolution. Let her move majestical toward the main object, the salvation of the nation, and all will be well."

"I acknowledge the long-suffering of your part of the nation is great, and your forbearance wonderful. But I hope New England will, in this very critical day, act like politicians and patriots. They must see that (as God would have it) those who caused the war are suffering most, or the constituents of those, while the Eastern people have the satisfaction to see the navy, which they have ever fostered, gaining laurels and making reprisals. The Western people are miserably disappointed in all their projects. Their friends are butchered and their efforts despised by their enemy, bringing home shame and disgrace to the doors of those bullying politicians in whom they placed too much confidence."

My father used to tell this characteristic story of Matthew

Lyon's method of managing his constituents. In those days of few newspapers and tedious postal communication, it was the custom of the members from the remoter and more thinly settled sections of the country to write political letters to their constituents, giving an account of what is now called "the situation," which were printed and distributed under their frank. One day my father asked Lyon how he avoided offending those of his constituents to whom he neglected to send his political missives, as it was quite impossible that he should remember them all. "I manage it in this way," he replied. "When I am canvassing my district, and I come across a man who looks distantly and coldly at me, I go up cordially to him and say, 'My dear friend, you got my printed letter last session, of course?' 'No, sir,' replies the man with offended dignity, 'I got no such thing.' 'No!' I cry out in a passion. 'No!! *Damn that post-office!*' Then I make a memorandum of the man's name and address, and when I get back to Washington I write him an autograph letter, and all is put to rights."

I will end this chapter with the letters of John Randolph belonging to the year 1813, — another of the strange bedfellows with whom politics had brought my father acquainted, though certainly as different a one from Matthew Lyon as nature, circumstances, and education could make two men.

Mr. Randolph to Mr. Quincy.

"Farmville (Va.), April 19, 1813

"Dear Sir:—I thank you very sincerely for your remembrance of me. Your letter, the Report on Impressment, and the newspaper containing the Celebration of the Russian successes in the town of Boston, have all been received. This festival does honor to those who planned and presided over it, and, as *primus inter pares*, I beg that you will present my best respects to Mr. Otis. In return for all these civilities, I have to tell you that my election is lost. The emissaries of government have been silently and secretly at work since last autumn, and while my friends indulged in a fatal security they have been undermined. My opponent has descended to the lowest and most disgraceful means, — riding from house to house, and attending day and night meetings in the cabins and hovels of the lowest of the people. He was present at fourteen of these preachings (seven of them held at night) the week before the election. . . . . . At the election for this county (Prince Edward) yesterday, Mr. E. said I had charged the Administration with being under French influence. In reply I told the freeholders that I would prove it, and did to their satisfaction. A notorious villain named Tom Logwood, from Buckingham, who was committed to the Penitentiary some years ago for forging bank-notes of the United States (I was on his jury), undertook to speak impertinently to me when on the bench. He had been seen laughing, talking, and drinking with E. at Buckingham. (N. B. Mr. Jefferson released him by a pardon.) I never saw such indignation. The scoundrel was obliged to take to his heels and make his escape home, or he would have been beaten to a jelly.

"Ignorant people were made to believe that the British fleet had come into the Chesapeake to aid my election; and the Russian mediation has also been played off with great effect on the uninformed. Gray will lose his election also. Sheffy is safe, and Breckenridge likewise. . . . .

"With every good wish, I am, dear sir, most truly yours,

"John Randolph of Roanoke.

"Pray give my love to Tudor."

The Same to the Same.

"Roanoke, May 23, 1813.

"Dear Sir:—You lay me under obligations which I know not how to requite, and yet I cannot help requesting a continuance of them. I have been highly gratified to-day by the receipt of your letter of the 5th, and the accompanying pamphlet. I have read them both with deep attention, and with a melancholy pleasure which I should find it difficult to describe. You are under some misapprehension respecting my opinions in regard to certain men and measures, — the true sources of our present calamities. They are not materially, if at all, variant from your own. It is time indeed to speak out; but if, as I fear, the canine race in New York have returned to their vomit, the voice of truth and of patriotism will be as the voice of one crying in the wilderness. I feel most sensibly the difficulties of our situation, but the question is as to the remedy.

"I had taken the same views (in one respect) of the election in this district that you have done. But, paradoxical as it may appear, I am convinced that the war and its authors are less popular in Virginia than ever, and that the result of the election here was owing to a fortuitous concurrence of events, some of them merely local and personal. The Russian mediation, however, was the great gull-trap. Legion could not believe that the government which accepted it would have any other object in view but peace; and the glory of the Russian victories, which should have called a crimson blush to the cheeks of the tools of Bonaparte, has thrown a false splendor around them, and given them a temporary reprieve from the sentence of public reprobation which impended over them. The incapacity and imbecility of the British Ministry has also contributed to give a false popularity to our own Administration. At the same time I would not have you expect relief from the *sympathy* of the Southern country, the people of which are prepossessed by the demons of faction and discord with no very favorable opinion of you. And, indeed, if our own privations and sufferings fail to open our eyes, you cannot take it unkind that we should continue insensible to the grievances of others seven hundred miles off. The history of the government of this country, if faithfully written, would sound like romance in the ears of succeeding generations, and be utterly discredited by them. But for this consideration I have sometimes thought that I would undertake the task. The oppression of Lord North's administration was lenity and compassion to the *régime* of the last six years. Mankind have ever been the dupes of professions, and imposed upon by names. We fondly thought that we were about to become an exception to the general laws of political philosophy, and our disgrace and punishment is like to be proportionate to our vanity and presumption.

"I find that our friend, Mr. Lloyd, has resigned his seat in the Senate, and for his sake I rejoice at his release from a state of bondage, not quite as abject, indeed, as that to which we were sometime subject, but irksome and odious to every high-minded man. . . . . .

"You have so often and so pressingly invited me to Boston, that I am at a loss how to reply, except by telling you that, if I can come, *come I will.* Be assured that I want no additional inducement to execute a plan that I have had long much at heart, and, if domestic matters will permit, I shall be Northward some time between midsummer and November. Hitherto I have not been able to add a single link to my chain.

. . . . .

"Be so good as to present me respectfully to Mr. Lloyd, and believe me, dear sir, with real regard, yours,

"JOHN RANDOLPH OF ROANOKE.

"My best respects to Mr. Otis."

THE SAME TO THE SAME.

"ROANOKE, June 20, 1813.

"DEAR SIR: — One of my New York papers received to-day contains the answers of the two branches of your Legislature to Governor Strong's excellent Address. In these state papers I think I recognize the pen of an old acquaintance, to whom I have been frequently obliged for the most sound and constitutional expositions of the principles of our heteroclite government. I think, too, that in the same print I can discern some traces of the less familiar style of *another* gentleman, to whom I beg to be mentioned in terms of the most cordial respect. My nature has become so degenerate and grovelling, during a double apprenticeship to the *art*, *mystery*, or *craft* of politics, that for the life of me I cannot envy, whilst I admire and esteem, the services which you are both rendering to your country. Neither can I, by the help of newspaper puffs, patriotic toasts, or Congressional rhetoric, work myself up into any serious regret that I am no longer under the abject dominion of Mr. H. Clay & Co. Not that I would be guilty of a contempt, or even insinuate anything in derogation, of Kentuckian suavity or courtesy, but, for the soul of me, I cannot be *bona-fidely* sorry, as one of their great orators would say, that I am here at home, where, like the Centurion, I say to one, Go, and he goeth, to another, Do this, and he doeth it, rather than under the discipline and *order* of the Calhouns, Grundys, and Seavers.

"You are likely to find in me at once a troublesome and unprofitable correspondent. Far removed from our provincial capital, I can procure nothing, even if it afforded anything of interest, to send you. And as all eyes are upon you at this time I must request you to furnish me with such publications as Boston affords, begging you to hold in remembrance that we have here a little school of intelligent freeholders upon whom such things are not thrown away. I have no doubt that hundreds, who, under the influence of artifice and temporary excitement, voted against me last April, now deplore it, and I must not fail to apprise you that the greater part of those who gave their suffrage to my competitor did it under the idea that it was the only chance to bring about *peace*. It was said that the government wanted peace, and the Russian mission was adduced in proof of it; but that such as you and I opposed them in *everything*, and the enemy would never grant us peace until we were more united. . . . . .

"Believe me, with best wishes for you and yours, and with the truest esteem, dear sir, your friend and servant,

"JOHN RANDOLPH OF ROANOKE."

THE SAME TO THE SAME.

"ROANOKE, June 28, 1813.

"DEAR SIR:—This day's mail brought me the report of your Legislature on the subject of the defence of Boston. The act of Congress of the 23d of April, 1808, for arming the militia, was, as you know, a bantling of my own nursing. I knew that the brat was hateful to the sight of the stepmothers of the Constitution, and foresaw that they would try to overlay it. I asked for an annual million, and they gave us a beggarly appointment of two hundred thousand dollars, the greater part of which they have contrived to embezzle, and the proceeds of the remainder they have distributed amongst their favorites. The terms of the act are imperative; they admit of no discretion; and if anything in the shape of political effrontery could have surprised me, I should have been astonished at the impudence with which this malfeasance and malversation has been, not merely palliated, but justified on the floor of Congress. Rely upon it, that, with all the unpromising appearances of the prospect in this quarter, there is a revulsion in the public sentiment. I have washed my hands of politics, but I cannot be insensible of the change which the matchless folly of our rulers is effecting in Virginia, and even in Kentucky, where the men of light and leading are gradually opening their eyes to the sins and fooleries of Administration. I beg you to present me most respectfully and cordially to Mr. Lloyd, ... and accept for yourself, dear sir, the assurance of my most sincere regard and attachment.

"JOHN RANDOLPH OF ROANOKE.

"I hope Tudor is not deficient in his duty to yourself and Mrs. Q. Pray offer to her my best wishes."

THE SAME TO THE SAME.

"ROANOKE, July 4, 1813.

"MY DEAR SIR:—Your welcome letter of the 18th of June has just now arrived. The papers to which you refer have not come to hand, but I confidently expect them by the next post. I have seen the *report*, however, in the New York Herald [Evening Post], and gave it a cursory reading. I thought I could recognize the hand that drew it.

"We are all here in a state of great alarm and distress. The Governor has called for more than one fourth of our effective men from every county far and wide. From those nearer the theatre of war a yet greater proportion has been demanded. The distress and alarm occasioned by this requisition do not arise from *fear* of the prowess of the *enemy*, but of the effects of the *climate* and *water* of the lower country, especially *at this season*, and the danger from *an internal foe*, augmented by the removal of so large a portion of our force. Of the result you can form no conception. 'I have seen more crying,' said an old neighboring freeholder to me this morning, 'since Friday (the 2d), than I have seen in all my life before.' If the cold-blooded insect whom God, for wise purposes, has inflicted upon us, (Pharaoh was plagued with some of the same species,) could have heard the shrieks of agonizing wives that yet ring in my ears, ... I am persuaded, some compunctious visitings of his reptile nature would have knocked at his heart. Perhaps you do not know that the climate and water of the lower country are *poisonous* to *our* constitutions, and that a stranger who would go to Norfolk at this *season* would be reckoned a *mad*, and certainly a *dead* man. To turn men who have been basking in the shade for two months, and never exposed to the sun, — to turn such men, at a *minute's warning*, into *soldiers*, and require them to march with a musket on their shoulders and a knapsack and four days' provisions at their backs, beneath this torrid sky, is to sign their death-warrant. Rely upon it, that the working of this campaign is against the faction which has plunged us all unprepared into this disastrous contest. The express who brought up our executive orders had not as much money as would pay for the hire of a horse. Twelve shillings lawful money would have been enough; instead of which he was furnished with a *power to impress*, and actually took the only horse of a *very* poor man in this neighborhood. Things are drawing to a head.

"I am much concerned at what you tell me respecting our friend Mr. Lloyd. I am truly sorry to hear of his attack, which the delicacy of his frame renders more alarming. Pray present me in terms of the most unaffected regard and respect to him and his lady. I regret the want of that sort of personal acquaintance with Mrs. Quincy that would entitle me to speak of her and to her in such language as my inclination prompts. She has my every good wish. . . . .

"Let me hope that you will cease to resemble Horace's old usurer, even in one particular, and give yourself to that society which has so many and such great demands upon you.

"In the hope of seeing you in the course of the summer or autumn, I am, dear sir, with the highest esteem, yours,

"John Randolph of Roanoke."

THE SAME TO THE SAME.

"ROANOKE, August 30, 1813.

"DEAR SIR: — A long time has elapsed since a letter passed between us. Without stopping to inquire who wrote last, I must indulge myself in congratulating you on the late glorious success of the Spanish arms in Biscay, and on the probable expulsion of the French from the Peninsula. This event is pregnant with the most important consequences. It would be impertinent in me to dilate on them to a person of your political knowledge and sagacity, but I cannot forbear naming *one* which touches ourselves more immediately. It may dispose our wretched Ministry to a serious endeavor at peace; for it will certainly shake in some degree their blind faith in the fortunes of Bonaparte. From such men little good can be expected, under any circumstances; but should they restore the blessings of peace to the country, it may be the means of averting incalculable mischief. Did you read Mr. Monroe's Report on Webster's motion, and compare it with the documents? How admirably the letter to Barton of July 14, 1812, tallies with the character given of it in page 8 of the Report! and how well the reasoning in page 9 *et seq.* is supported by the British 'Declaration,' and by Russell's letter of May 25, 1812! The incongruity between *Mr. Monroe's affirmation* (in page 8) and the *fact* (letter of July 14) seems not to have struck the attention of our editors. It is a most barefaced thing. Such is the degraded state of our country, that derision only is excited where indignation was wont to be roused.

"I suppose you are apprised of the deadly feud between M. and Armstrong. The partisans of the former keep no terms in speaking of the latter. There is no measure to their obloquy, if a great deal of truth mixed with some falsehood may pass by that name. It is, however, plain that the Cabinet *dare* not displace Armstrong. He is now gone on to 'organize victory' in Canada. What an admirable opportunity for some Villiers to bring another Bayes on the stage! 'Thunder and Lightning, by *General* D. R. W.' *

"The transactions of the last Congress have certainly weakened in a great degree the confidence of many well-meaning people in the Administration. I have observed with great pleasure the altered *tone* of the majority. The Hector is entirely laid aside, and they are forced patiently to submit to hear many galling sarcasms and yet more gall-

* David R. Williams, of South Carolina. See, *ante*, pp. 178, 276. He had been appointed a Brigadier-General, — one of the "political generals" of that time.

ing truths from the minority, who have asserted with a manly spirit their parliamentary rights. The war is so detested hereabouts that the under-spurleathers of the ministry are obliged to encourage their followers with the hope of a speedy peace. Our men in Norfolk are treated most barbarously. The commissariat and medical staff are upon the worst possible footing; and the *French* and Jews, of whom the trading population is composed, practise the vilest extortion upon their defenders, who, poor fellows! are compelled to sell their pay at forty per cent discount to obtain necessaries. The whole country watered by the rivers which fall into the Chesapeake is in a state of *paralysis*. We in this quarter are sending our wheat to *Fayetteville, on Cape Fear River*, to exchange it for *salt*, for which we have to pay at home fifteen shillings a bushel, lawful money. In short, the distress is general and heavy, and I do not see how the people can pay their taxes to both governments. When that operation commences, the discontent which has been so long smothered by a large portion of the people will break forth to the consternation of their rulers, whom they will lay upon the shelf with very little ceremony. It is only by obtaining entire control over the press south and west of Virginia (as well as in that State), and persuading the country that you and I and some others were the cause of all their difficulties, by encouraging the British, that they have been able to support themselves. But this delusion, like every other, must have an end. They will, however, find less difficulty in getting up some new imposture, than in devising *ways* and *means*.

"You consider yourself in retirement within an hour's ride of the metropolis of New England, whilst I am three days' tedious journey, over miserable roads, to the only spot in the State that deserves the name of a town, and that epithet will hardly apply to its present stagnant and deserted condition. I am, indeed, *hors du monde*, as well as *hors du combat*. It is to be hoped that a very few weeks will restore you to the society of your friends in Boston, whilst I have before me a long and dreary winter, interrupted only by the sordid cares of a planter. The variety and vexatious character of these interruptions can only be conceived by him who has been subjected to them. They remind me of Cromwell, when he turned farmer at St. Ives; for without vanity I may compare myself to what Oliver was *then*, and may with truth declare, that my 'mind, superior to the low occupations to which I am condemned, preys upon itself.' Sometimes I have thought of a certain *memoire pour servir*, etc.; sometimes of a 'letter.' Meanwhile week slips by after week, and month follows month, and nothing is done.

"One of the blessings of this war is, that I can procure none but French paper to write upon, and am even glad to get that, wretched as it is. I had a letter from Tudor about a week ago, with which I was much pleased. Be assured that his mother and myself are fully sensible of the claims which both yourself and Mrs. Quincy have upon his gratitude, and consequently upon ours.

"I would be glad to know how *you* like your new occupation of farmer; what quantity of land you cultivate, and with what success.

"I am, with the utmost sincerity, yours,

"JOHN RANDOLPH OF ROANOKE."

THE SAME TO THE SAME.

"ROANOKE, October 18, 1813

"DEAR SIR:— The delay in your reply to my light letter is amply compensated by the interesting views which you have given me of a subject, in comparison with which all others of a *public* nature dwindle into insignificance. As far as I can see, I perceive no variance in our opinions. I am not a man to put reliance on paper bulwarks when attacked by cannon and the bayonet. The parchment in the Rolls office I presume has undergone no erasures nor interpolations, (to ante-date or post-date *it* was unnecessary,) but the *Constitution* is changed. It can never get back to what it was. Old age can as soon resume the freshness and agility of youth. Not, however, that it was ever in my eyes that model of perfection which so many have pronounced it to be. You know I was an Anti-Federalist when hardly breeched. I did not then comprehend why I disliked the new system, but now I know that no such system can be *good*. Governments made after that fashion must have faults of their own, independent of such as are incidental to the nature of the institution, and perhaps inseparable from it.* To fit us, they must grow with our growth, and whilst they stubbornly protect the liberty of the subject against every attack, whether from the *one* or the many, must possess the capacity to adapt themselves, *at a minute's warning*, to the unforeseen emergencies of the state. I see nothing of this in our system. I perceive only a bundle of theories (bottomed on a Utopian idea of human excellence) and in practice a corruption the most sordid and revolting. We are the first people that ever acquired provinces, either by conquest or purchase (Mr. Blackstone says they are the same), not for us to govern, but that they might *govern us*,— that we might be ruled to our ruin by

* Daniel Lambert measured, when christened, for his wedding suit.

people bound to us by no common tie of interest or sentiment. But such, whatever may be the incredulity of posterity, is the fact. Match it, if you can, in the savage laws of Lycurgus, or the brutal *castes* of Hindostan.

"I *will* congratulate you on the accession of Austria to the cause of the Allies, although I confess my hopes are not high. Yet I look to the plains of Silesia and the Bohemian mountains for my deliverance from the incubus that has been weighing down my heart for many a long year.

"In answer to your most kind and flattering questions, I must tell you that *it is so*, because a Southern proprietor is a poor devil, and his overseer a prince. I had to discard one the other day for malversation and peculation in office, — a small affair compared with what we wot of in the 'great vulgar and the small' in the city of O.* and its dependencies. I wish you could have heard two worthy neighbors cautioning me against a contest at law with *an overseer* as a 'tremendous business, where, whatever may be the merits of the case, the employer is sure to be cast.' I knew, too, that they were right. Does not this fact throw great light on the state of society and manners? If a sagacious historian could stumble on it ten thousand years hence, it would give him a juster notion of what we are than a hundred volumes of 'Notes on Virginia.' *Hoc opus*, — the disease is not cutaneous, it is in the *bones* and the *marrow*, and there is nothing in our system to regenerate itself. We must pass from anarchy and corruption to military despotism. There is not a *third* alternative, as much as we have dabbled in political trigonometry, — no 'middle and most safe path.' There are no redoubts and fortifications within and behind which the citizen can find protection, — nothing to qualify or check in the remotest degree the power of the chief, whoever he may be, or whatsoever title please his ear. The country is *tabula rasa.* When once the liberty of the citizen is broken, like an army routed on the plains of Poland, we have no shelter, no refuge, but in the clemency of the victor. The pendulum vibrates from anarchy to despotism.

"The manner in which you speak of my son warms my heart towards you. I want to know your children, that I may love them. His intention of leaving college springs from the noblest motive My brother was not an economist, and he emancipated his slaves. Mrs. R., Tudor's mother, sustained this spring a heavy loss by fire;

* *Sic* in the original. Referring, doubtless, to some forgotten nickname for *Washington.*

and he knows that, whilst scoundrels have been holding me up to the nation as a British pensioner, they chuckle at the thoughts of the difficulties into which they *know* the times and my remote position from my property have involved me. Could I look on slaves as mere property, the means of extrication were obvious and easy; but I have indulged in a hope that they should never know another taskmaster. To visit your country lies very near my heart. That the prejudice which once existed there against me should be obliterated or succeeded by opposite (perhaps not more just) sentiments, is a subject of real gratification to me. I shall be proud, if, on an acquaintance which I am resolved to make with them, I shall be able to maintain my place in the good opinion of your countrymen. A few days since, I had a most severe affliction in the shape of rheumatism, which deprived me for a time entirely of the use of my limbs. I can now hobble about my solitary cabin. I forgot to add that I shall not indulge Tudor in his amiable desire to leave College before he graduates.

"I fear I am too late for the post. Believe me, dear sir, most truly, and with great regard, yours,

"John Randolph of Roanoke.

"I have a brother at Norfolk. In the regiment to which he is attached three hundred and twenty-four are sick. The hospital holds, by cramming, sixty. The poor creatures are dying like sheep, — ragged and without a blanket."

The Same to the Same.

"Richmond, December 11, 1813.

"Dear Sir: — Your valued letter was forwarded to me, a few days ago, at this place, where I have been just a month. But the night before it arrived, talking over the state of affairs with an old friend, we fell into the same train of thinking with yourself on the consequences of the present war. Without the same minute knowledge which you possess on the subject of New England, we both inferred that the war would eventually become less unpopular there, from its operating as an enormous bounty upon your agriculture and manufactures; and my friend undertook to predict that, by the time *we* sickened of the contest, *you* would support it.

"It is rather more just than generous in you to triumph over us; for be assured our sufferings are extreme. No State in the Confederacy has paid so dearly for the *war whistle* as the Ancient Dominion. Perhaps you will say, none deserved to pay more severely; but remember that our daughter, Kentucky, has been selling her whiskey and meat and meal and horses, and enjoying the chase of her favorite *red game*, whilst our only source of supply has been a little stale patriotism; and even in that staple commodity we are almost driven out of the market by her and her sister States. 'T is true we drive a little trade in tobacco, which pays for about the hundredth part of the dry goods which we import land-wise from the North. The balance is made up in specie; so that our banks, once the richest in the Union in that important article, are nearly drained of their last dollar, and, so far from being able to lend the State the amount of its quota of the direct tax, they are importuning payment of former advances to the sum of nearly four hundred thousand dollars, when our treasury has not an unappropriated cent. Do you wonder at this, when I state it as a fact, that the *straw* of a crop of wheat, near market, is worth more than the *grain!* and that flour, so far from being reckoned a *luxury*, as with you, is purchased by some planters as a cheaper food for their horses and oxen than oats or Indian corn! these last bearing a good price for the consumption of our towns. This relief, however, extends only a few miles around Richmond, Norfolk, and Petersburg.

"It appears to me that if England can (as she must, if the war continues) succeed in driving the American navigation off the ocean, and destroying the nursery of our seamen (the fishery and coasting-trade), it will not be a bad exchange for Canada, — supposing her to lose it. We have been, from the breaking out of the war of the French Revolution to the date of the Embargo (December, 1807), her most formidable commercial rival. Your ships, which once 'vexed every sea,' under-freighting even the penurious Hollander, are, I believe, not (like their hardy navigators) *long-lived*. Seven years, I think, are threescore and ten to them. The seamen who have left their European masters for our service will sail under the Russian or some other neutral flag. In short, I can see no motive in an able English Administration for making peace with us. My only trust is in their folly, — for, thank God, their Castlereaghs and Princes Regent are at least as low in the scale of intellectual beings as our Monroes and Presidents.

"I concur with you most cordially on the subject of this most detestable and unnatural war, — not to be matched except by the war of Lord North's government against our liberties; and even that was waged on motives less base than those which prompted the present accursed contest. *That* was a question concerning which honest men might differ. Not so *this*. Mark me, I speak of persons having access to *correct information*. On this subject I am glad to find one righteous man on our side. I mean Frank Key, who says: 'The people of Montreal will enjoy their firesides for this, and I trust for many a winter. This I suppose is treason, but, as your Patrick Henry said, "If it be treason, I glory in the name of traitor." I have never thought of those poor creatures without being reconciled to any disgrace or defeat of our arms.'

"As to the war in Europe, I have sad forebodings, notwithstanding some of my friends, men of much better information than myself, and especially on European affairs, are quite sanguine. Well may the tyrant rely upon his fortune. The ball that destroyed Moreau did him better service than his whole train of artillery besides. I consider that a victory would have been dearly purchased by the Allies at the price of his loss. I seem already to feel 'the wind of that blow which is to prostrate Europe at the feet of the modern Zingis.'

"By this time you are quietly fixed in your town residence, and I have no doubt return to the *opes et fumum strepitumque Romæ* with as much pleasure as you bade them adieu in the spring for your paternal shades. You are not now *procul negotiis*, but you have every other requisite which the poet deems indispensable to happiness; and even *that* is always within your reach. A ride of eight miles buries you in the solitudes of Quincy, whilst I have a weary journey of more than three days before I can reach my desolate habitation; and when there, I am shut out from all intercourse with the rest of the world, except through the tedious process of letter-writing.

"I dare hardly trust my pen on the subject nearest my heart, — my son. I am wrapt up in that boy, and it gives me pleasure to reflect that he is near enough to you to avail himself more frequently of the goodness of yourself and Mrs. Quincy towards him. Your kindness to this child will never be forgotten by us all. Your name and that of Mrs. Quincy is never mentioned by his mother or his brother without gratitude and respect for your generous protection extended to Tudor. May he live to make you the only suitable return, by fulfilling your flattering expectations of his future character.

"Bleecker is indeed all that you say of him, and *more*. He did write to me, and a most welcome letter it was.

. . . . .

"I had like to have forgotten to tell you that your University is decried in this quarter. The charge of Socinianism we once discussed together; but a heavier one is now advanced against you, — at least according to the maxims of this calculating age. 'T is said that your Principal and Professors take a pride in the extravagance of the students, and encourage it, whilst Yale zealously inculcates the sublime truths of 'Poor Richard's Almanac.' Be this as it may, some of our Southern youths have left a great deal of cash at Cambridge, and brought away nothing valuable in return for it. We are so much poorer in this quarter than you wealthy Bostonians, that we smart under an expense which you would scarcely feel. Whilst the students are treated as gentlemen, everything like profusion should be discountenanced by the Provost and his associates. I deemed it proper to apprise you of the fact that such reports are circulated, and with some industry. They have been the means of sending some of our young men to Yale instead of Harvard College.

"This letter is already too long to admit a word on the subject of the Speech from the Throne, even if it were worthy of a thought. I think it completes the anti-climax of the last five years. To mention in such a communication such names as Johnson, &c.! Except that it is liberal of praise to others, and somewhat scanty to himself, it might have been written by Don Iago. It is in his style. 'The imperious obligations of duty forbidding him to rout the enemy' in the *field*, he proceeds Hudibrastically to beat them in detail upon *paper! Ubi lapsi! Quid fecimus!*

"My best wishes attend you and all that are dear to you. How many children have you? Tell me their ages and names. I want to know all about you, for I am in truth, with the most affectionate respect, yours,

"JOHN RANDOLPH OF ROANOKE."

Whether there were any substantial grounds for these complaints of extravagant expenditures at Cambridge, I cannot say. That the President and Professors took a pride in them, if they existed, was of course a weak invention of the enemies of the College. Mr. Randolph, however, had some personal reasons for feeling sore on the subject. Young Randolph, though entirely free from vice and dissipation, according to the testimony of all the men of his time, was lavish in his expenditures, and, in particular, he inherited or shared his uncle's love for fine horses. Mr. Randolph did not forbid the indulgence of this taste in the young man, — indeed, he was probably rather proud of the figure he made by it, — but the expense was a source of serious inconvenience to him, his money income being very disproportionate to his nominal fortune. This letter was doubtless written under some irritation of mind from this cause.

John Randolph had a very great abhorrence of debt, and a very just sense of its degrading effect on the character. On one occasion in Congress, he suddenly interrupted himself in a speech on some other subject, and exclaimed: "Mr. Speaker, I have discovered the philosopher's stone. It is this, Sir, — PAY AS YOU GO! PAY AS YOU GO!!" His opinion on this subject is thus expressed in a letter to my father, which has been destroyed as containing matters too private for the public eye: —

"The muck-worm, whose mind 'knows no other work than money-keeping or money-getting,' is an object of pity and contempt. But I hold it essential to purity, dignity, and pride of character, that every man's expenses should bear a due relation to his means and prospects in life, and conceive few habits to be more destructive of all that is noble and manly about us, than a habit of profusion exceeding beyond all bounds those prospects."

CHAPTER XIV.

1814 – 1815.

REMOVAL FROM PEARL STREET. — WAR ALARMS AT QUINCY. — THE HUSSARS. — LETTERS OF RANDOLPH. — CONTINUED DISCONTENTS. — THE HARTFORD CONVENTION. — PEACE OF 1815. — REJOICINGS IN BOSTON. — POLITICAL CHANGES CONSEQUENT ON THE PEACE. — DEATH OF TUDOR RANDOLPH. — LAST LETTER OF THE RANDOLPH CORRESPONDENCE.

IN the year 1805 my father left the cheerful house in Pearl Street where he had passed so many happy years. On the northern frontier of the estate, facing on Oliver Street, he had built two houses, into one of which he removed his family. The situation was then a commanding one. The harbor was in full view in one direction, and in the other the prospect extended over the southern part of the town to the Brookline hills. The house itself was not as large or commodious as the one she had left; but my mother readily acquiesced in the change, the rather that she declined mingling in general society almost entirely during the winters my father was away. She made herself amends, however, by shortening the winters and lengthening the summers as best she might, and giving as many months as possible to her beloved country home at Quincy. Speculation and improvement, as it is called, which had already begun to lay waste the pleasant places in which Boston then abounded, in due time laid a ruthless hand on the slope of that one of the three hills on which sat the graceful town where my father's estate lay. The prospect from the Oliver Street house was first of all shut out by brick walls. Afterwards the terraces which climbed the hillside were levelled, the old elms felled, the blue-jays and golden robins driven from their ancient haunts, and a brick court called Quincy Place reigned in their stead. That part of the town, then and for many years later a creditable region to live in, inhabited by citizens of eminence and wealth, was for a long time given over to the very poorest of the population, and at the time I am writing it is in the very act of being removed and cast into the sea, in obedience to the demands of trade. The house in Pearl Street remained standing until 1845, when it gave place to the granite warehouses known as "Quincy Block," of which I have already spoken.

The happy summers at Quincy, however, were somewhat disturbed, during the years that the war lasted, by alarms, or apprehensions of them, of the enemy. There was a current belief that the British, should they propose making an attack on Boston, would land on my father's estate or thereabouts, and so take the town in flank. There were probably no good grounds for this opinion, as it is not likely that the British would attempt, with any force they could command on this side the Atlantic, when they had their hands so full on the other, to march through a thickly settled hostile country, intersected by streams, and with points all along their route capable of defence. The opinion was sufficiently prevalent with the authorities, however, to induce them to station a body of militia on the left bank of the river Neponset, separating Quincy from Dorchester, which was selected as the first point of defence should such an invasion be attempted. This circumstance materially increased the uneasiness inseparable from the exposed situation of the family at Quincy. As I have already related, every ship that enters or leaves the harbor can be seen from the windows of the house. And as the triumphant entry of Hull in the Constitution, after her victory over the Guerrière, had been discerned from that post of observation, so was the departure of Lawrence in the Chesapeake on his fatal quest of the Shannon, — doomed to "give up the ship," but only with his life; and with the telescope "the meteor-flag of England" could be seen from time to time flying at the masthead of men-of-war that prowled about the mouth of the harbor; so that it was no idle fear which suggested the probability of a midnight visit from a party of foragers or pillagers to that solitary shore.

One Sunday there was an alarm that the enemy had landed at Scituate, a dozen miles away. The news was announced in the meeting-house during Divine service. The congregation was dismissed at once, and the village was all astir with excitement. The bell rang, the drums beat to arms, and the volunteer companies marched to meet the enemy. It is unnecessary to say that they did not find him. The improbability of a military force landing nearly twenty miles from the intended object of attack, and marching towards it through a populous enemy's country, was overlooked under the excitement of sudden danger. The old people who remembered the days of the Revolution added to the fever in men's minds, and yet more in women's and children's, by stories of British ravages and outrages in that old time. This panic, however, soon passed away, though the feeling of possible danger was always present, and a state of preparation kept up. I suppose it was on the Sunday following this false alarm, that the militia companies, in uniform, attended service to return thanks for their escape from the assaults of their enemies; though it may have been after some more real and nearer danger. But the circumstance made a deep impression on my young mind by the delightful variety it gave to the usual monotony of Sunday.

My father, too, opposed as he was to the war, yielded to no one in determination to defend the soil of Massachusetts should it be invaded by an enemy. He assisted in the formation of a fine troop of volunteer cavalry, called the Boston Hussars, consisting chiefly, if not entirely, of Federal gentlemen, of which he was elected captain. They wore a splendid uniform, made after the pattern of one of the French regiments of the Imperial Guard, their dislike to Bonaparte and all his works not including his taste as to military costume; and, being well mounted, they formed the finest troop ever seen in New England before or since. Captain Quincy was afterwards promoted to the command of a squadron of horse, consisting of the Hussars and the Dragoons, with the rank of Major. He used to be concerned lest the enemy might land between Quincy and Boston, and thus cut him off from his command! Happily no such calamity occurred, and all his campaigns were confined to Boston Common and to an occasional escort of honor. On one occasion, when he was to perform this service for Governor Gerry, one of the Democratic newspapers announced that "Captain Quincy is going with his Hussars to bring Governor Gerry to town, *peaceably if he can, forcibly if he must!*" The older inhabitants of Boston yet speak of him mounted on his fine charger, Bayard, a beautiful animal, white as snow, his great personal advantages of face and figure set off by his superb uniform, as the finest sight of man and horse they remember to have seen. When all prospect of actual service was ended by the Peace of 1815, the Hussars were disbanded, the expense of keeping up the company being very great, and Major Quincy's military career came to an end. His horse Bayard was sold, and subsequently arrived at promotion which is worth the telling. One day my father came home in high good-humor, and asked my mother what she supposed had become of Bayard. "I have not an idea on the subject," said she. "Guess!" said he. "I can't guess," said she; "perhaps the king of Hayti has got him,"—that potentate being at the time much "bruited in men's minds." "But you have heard!" said he. "Never a word." "Well, you have guessed right. He now belongs to the king of Hayti." The purchaser exported the horse to Cape Haytien on speculation, where he was bought for the black King Christophe, and is said to have been the favorite charger of his sable Majesty.

I will insert in this place the letters my father received from Mr. Randolph during the year 1814.

Mr. Randolph to Mr. Quincy.

"Richmond, Jan. 7, 1814, Friday.

"Dear Sir:—On the subject of the war, I believe there is not a man in the United States who agrees more entirely with you than myself. As the mathematicians say, our opinions *coincide*. The late news from Leipsic has put the despondent Federalists here on the house-top; and in another week (perhaps) they will be in the cellar again. For my part I every day see less and less cause to hope for a restoration of the blessings we once enjoyed; and this opinion is founded at least as much upon the character of the party in opposition as upon that of those who administer, and their adherents who support or *suffer*, the government. The dictatorship (*as by law estab-*

lished) has not created half the sensation here as did the fall of sugar from thirty-five to twenty dollars per hundred-weight; or the rumor that Mr. King was nominated Minister to the Court of London. All heads here are agog for peace, and if Messrs. M. and M. give it to us, we shall '*ask no questions*' on the subject of the treasure, *blood*, and *honor* lost in this unnatural and hellish contest.

"My dear sir, with all our sins it must be allowed that we superabound in the first of Christian and of moral virtues, — charity. We are so full of the ass's milk of human kindness, that we shall soon learn to speak of Judas Iscariot as an *unfortunate* man. Such is the language which our *candor* prompts us to apply to Bidwell, Wilkinson, etc., etc.; and Federalists, ay, good Federalists too, do not hesitate to say of our precious rulers that Mr. M. is *now* seriously disposed for *peace* with England! Yet, if perforce they are driven to a cessation of active operations, they will have an armed *truce*, — a peace of restrictive measures, — 'a peace like a war.'

"The Continental System is to supply the place of *arms*, as *passion*, according to the crown lawyers, sometimes does in case of treason. But I must have done. Present my best wishes to Mrs. Quincy, and be assured that you will do me great injustice should you doubt the sincerity of the regard and esteem with which I am, dear sir, yours,

"JOHN RANDOLPH OF ROANOKE."

THE SAME TO THE SAME.

"RICHMOND, Jan. 29, 1814.

"DEAR SIR: — I should have acknowledged your letter of the 15th several days ago, but I received at the same time the communication which you had taught me to expect from Mr. Lowell. This had been so long on the way (having been addressed to Roanoke) that I found it necessary to write a hasty reply, lest I should incur the imputation of insensibility to Mr. Lowell's very polite and obliging attention. I therefore resolved to write 'to-morrow.' You know the rest. . . . . After my last to you was despatched, I was not without apprehension that I had been too hasty in that 'reproof' to which you so politely submit. The fact is, that you touched upon my leading infirmity, — my fond attachment to my nephew. This leads me sometimes to suspect that I play the fool on this subject, and seriously to fear that the praise which has been showered on the lad may be of lasting disservice to him through life. I have seen the effects of *puffing* on some young men who otherwise would have been respectable, but who were thereby converted into the most disgusting coxcombs imaginable. I had rather see Tudor a dull man without pretensions, than one of these over-educated and over-travelled youths, — such as the apostle of Democracy in Philadelphia, for instance, whose *skin* a member from New Jersey lately stripped over his head. It was a cruel punishment for being an ass. But I will not insult my son with the comparison.

"I have seen Mr. Otis's motion, and I assure you that no occurrence since the war has made so deep an impression upon me. It has had the like effect upon all seriously thinking people with whom I have conversed. What a game of round-about has been played since I was initiated into the mysteries of politics! I recollect the time when with Mr. Otis *State rights* were as nothing in comparison with the proud prerogative of the Federal government. *Then* Virginia was building an armory to enable her to resist *Federal usurpation.* You will not infer that I attach the least blame to Mr. Otis; far from it. I rejoice, on the contrary, to see him enlisted on the side of the *liberty of the subject and the rights of the States.* Pray give me some light on the subject of your proceedings. It was always my opinion that Union was the *means* of securing the safety, liberty, and welfare of the confederacy, and not in itself an *end* to which these should be sacrificed. But the question of resistance to any established government is always a question of expediency; and the resort ought never to be had to this last appeal, except in cases where there is reasonable prospect of success, and where the grievance does not admit of palliative or temporizing remedies. The one is a case to be decided by argument, the other by feeling. Verily, Mr. M.'s little finger is thicker than the loins of Lord North.

"I wish you would occasionally enclose me the Weekly Messenger, when it contains such pieces, for instance, as 'The Feasts of the Poets.' With best wishes to Mrs. Q. and your children, I am, dear sir, most sincerely yours,

"John Randolph of Roanoke."

The Same to the Same.

"Richmond, Feb. 8, 1814.

"Dear Sir: — Certain reports here, to which you cannot be a stranger, have caused much speculation and some uneasiness here. Pray give me a little light respecting the *serious* intentions of the Opposition in Massachusetts. Rash counsels are not always, *if ever*, wise. I trust we shall hold together, and live to reap the fruits of the late glorious events in Europe, on which I cordially congratulate you.

"I would like my nephew to see my reply to Mr. Lowell's letter on the subject of the University. Excuse this scrawl. I am, dear sir, sincerely and most faithfully yours,

"JOHN RANDOLPH OF ROANOKE."

THE SAME TO THE SAME.

"RICHMOND, March 1, 1814.

"Many thanks to you, my dear sir, for your information. It is highly interesting. I shall make no comment upon it, except to express a hope that Opposition with you will furnish its enemies with no handle against them. They will be delighted with some tub for the popular whale against the next election. I am informed that government have no other hope of pecuniary supply except from Boston; and that they confidently rely upon twenty per cent discount countervailing the patriotism of your moneyed men.

"I have just learned that Carlisle College is broken up by a conscription of Messrs. Binns, Duane, and Snyder. I believe this is the triumvirate by which Pennsylvania is governed. What intelligence for a parent, who fondly believes that his son is prosecuting his studies under some reverend divine, to hear that he is on the frontiers of Canada, a common soldier, 'a mere machine of murder,' destitute perhaps of the necessaries of life. Thank Heaven *my son* is under the protection of *Governor Strong* and the Legislature of *Old Massachusetts Bay*.* Why did you leave out that word *Bay* in your style and title? I like it. It was there in 1775. . . . .

"Tobacco has sold here as high as $13.10 per hundred-weight. This gives some relief to the planter; but on the whole we are vexed and oppressed in every shape that the *two* governments can devise.

"I am, dear sir, with great esteem and regard, yours,

"JOHN RANDOLPH OF ROANOKE."

THE SAME TO THE SAME.

"RICHMOND, March 22, 1814.

"DEAR SIR: — Let me return you my sincere and hearty thanks for your letter (of the 13th). It has afforded me great pleasure, as well on private as public account, — to use the fashion of speaking in this calculating age. You have judged rightly, in my poor opinion. Like you, I feel a veneration for the place of my residence, because it never belonged to any but the aboriginal proprietors and my ancestors, from whom it has descended to me in the direct line. The curse of

* Mr. Randolph always directed his letters to my father, "Boston, Massachusetts Bay."

slavery, however, — an evil daily magnifying, great as it already is, — embitters many a moment of the Virginian landholder who is not duller than the clod beneath his feet.

"I made a little excursion last week to the seat of my ancestors in the maternal line, at the confluence of James and Appomattox Rivers. The sight of the noble sheet of water in front of the house seemed to revive me. I was tossed in a boat for three miles, and sprinkled with the spray that broke over her.

"The scenes of my early youth were renewed. I do not wonder at the attachment of you New England men for your rocky shores and inlets and creeks, — that you cleave to them heedless of the siren song that calls you to the Western wilderness. The sight of the broad bay formed by the junction of the two rivers gave a new impulse to my being; but when the boat struck the beach, all was sad and desolate. The fires of ancient hospitality were long since extinguished, and the hearthstone cold. Here was my mother given in marriage, and here was I born, — once the seat of plenty and cheerfulness, associated with my earliest and tenderest recollections, now mute and deserted. One old gray-headed domestic seemed to render the solitude more sensible.

"The tombstone of the first Bolling who came to this country, about the period of the Restoration (1660), and who died (after marrying a granddaughter of Pocahontas) in 1709, is yet in very tolerable preservation; the stone is cracked, but the armorial bearings and epitaph quite fresh. Nothing, however, can be more melancholy than the aspect of the whole country on tide-water, — dismantled country-seats, ruinous churches, fields forsaken and grown up with mournful evergreens, — cedar and pine. But I am prosing.

"I said you had chosen wisely, — I mean for yourself and your children. But in your country the state of society is not changed, the whole fabric uprooted, as with us. Here the rich vulgar are everybody and everything. You can almost smell the 'rum and cheese, and loaf, lump, and muscovado sugar,' out of which their mushroom fortunes have sprung, — much more offensive to my nostrils than 'muck or merinos.' These fellows will 'never get rid of Blackfriars'; and they make up in ostentation for their other deficiencies, of which they are always conscious, and sometimes ashamed.

"I am under great uneasiness for Tudor. There is no field for him in his native country. Would you have him return here, attend a court every week, ride more miles than a post-boy, sleep *two*, perhaps *three*, in a bed, and barely make a support for himself and his horse? Such is the life of our country lawyers, who eke out their scanty gains by some paltry speculation at the sheriff's sales. Here a young man is shut out from the bar, and, indeed, the practice even to Wickham and his associates is far from being easy or lucrative. The afternoon, and the Sabbath are often broken in upon by the importunate client. New York, I suppose, affords the best field for a young man who will not lay aside civilization, and herd with the Grundys and Clays. Country life with us has few charms. One must give up society, and in a degree literature also. For after you have read your old books (if you have them to read) you can get no new ones.

"I have renewed my acquaintance (it was a slight one) with Horace this winter. Much as I admire him, I am yet better pleased with some of his imitators (not 'a servile herd'), among whom I reckon Warren Hastings, Pope, and the Horatii of Piccadilly. But I am so little of a pedagogue, — I ought to say a *scholar*, — that I prefer Lord Byron to all the poets from Virgil to Bavius. I have just finished his 'Bride of Abydos,' which some wiseacre of a printer advertised as the '*Bridge* of Abydos,' and led me to inquire of Tudor after it under that title, — a whimsical mistake; the 'Turkish Tale' appended to the title forbade all thought of the bridge of Xerxes, or of Leander's *substitute*. Lord Byron is a man of great powers, but they are not under his own control: they govern him. The dedication to Lord Holland brought to my mind most forcibly some passages in the 'English Bards and Scotch Reviewers.' His Lordship (Holland) must have much of the spirit of forgiveness. I doubt *her Ladyship*.

"What may be done in Europe I know not, but the 'Southern States' can take no share in the loan. Our banks were never so much pressed, and another year like the last will produce the most distressing embarrassments to them. Some of our people, particularly in my quarter of the country, are rich; but they were burnt a little with the first loan, and prefer to give one hundred and twelve for our new bank stock, after all the exactions of our Legislature, made more in the spirit of a Turkish Pacha than a free government.

"I see that Mr. *Ambi Dexter* * has not been adroit enough to take in you Yankees. The Chief Justice returned a few days since from Washington. He brings, however, nothing, except that Beau Dawson is on his last legs,— all the powers of nature, the *vis vitæ*, gone. Another of the war-makers is about to follow old Smilie to his dread account.

"Adieu, dear sir. My best wishes and regards attend you and

* The celebrated Samuel Dexter, who had separated himself from the Federalists during the war of 1812, and thus incurred the suspicion and censure of the opponents of the measure.

yours. If I were 'my own man,' as Jerry Sneak says, I might perhaps surprise you in your rural shades of Quincy; but if the war has affected *your* income, what must it have done with mine, whose estate (never under good management) depended for its revenue on open and direct export abroad, and chiefly to England?

"I am, with the most sincere respect and regard, dear sir, yours,

"JOHN RANDOLPH OF ROANOKE.

"At Washington they (you know who *they* are) are very sanguine respecting Plumer's election.* But if am to believe the papers, which I find some difficulty in doing on such subjects, Mr. Gilman is rechosen. I wish you would tell me what are the prospects of Mr. Dexter and his new friends in Massachusetts.

"Your quotation from Horace reminds me of a *jeu d'esprit* of our barrister Wirt on Mr. Wickham's offering to their brother Hay either horn of a dilemma.

'Wickham one day tossed Hay in court
On a dilemma's horn in sport;
Jock,† rich in wit and Latin too,
Cries, "Fenum habet in cornu."'"

THE SAME TO THE SAME.

"ROANOKE, Virginia, July 1, 1814.

"DEAR SIR: — It would require an essay to answer your inquiries; however, I will try what can be done within the compass of a letter. Before the Revolution the lower country of Virginia, pierced for more than a hundred miles from the seaboard by numerous bold and navigable rivers, was inhabited by a race of planters, of English descent, who dwelt on their principal estates on the borders of those noble streams. The proprietors were generally well educated, — some of them at the best schools of the mother country, the rest at William and Mary, then a seminary of *learning*, under able classical masters Their habitations and establishments, for the most part spacious and costly, in some instances displayed taste and elegance. They were the seats of hospitality. The possessors were gentlemen, — better-bred men were not to be found in the British dominions. As yet party spirit was not. This fruitful source of mischief had not then poisoned society. Every door was open to those who maintained the

* As Governor of New Hampshire. William Plumer, a seceding Federalist, was defeated by John Taylor Gilman. He had been elected in 1812, and was again in 1816.

† Old John Warden, a Scotch schoolmaster.

appearance of gentlemen. Each planter might be said, almost without exaggeration, to have a harbor at his door. Here he shipped his *crop* (tobacco), mostly on his own account, to London, Bristol, or Glasgow, and from those ports received every article of luxury or necessity (not raised by himself) which his household and even his distant *quarters* required. For these a regular order was made out twice a year. You may *guess* at the state of things when a bill of exchange on London for half a crown was sometimes drawn to pay for a dinner at *the ordinary*. Did a lady want a jewel new-set, or a gentleman his watch cleaned, the trinket was sent *home*. Even now the old folks talk of 'going home to England.'

"Free living, the war, docking entails (by one sweeping act of Assembly), but chiefly the statute of distributions, undermined these old establishments. Bad agriculture, too, contributed its share. The soil of the country in question, except on the margin of the rivers, where it *was* excellent, is (originally) a light, generous loam upon a sand; once exhausted, it is *dead*. Rice never constituted an object of culture with us. The tide swamps — a mine of wealth in South Carolina — here produce only miasma. You will find some good thoughts on this head, and on the decay of our agriculture generally, in our friend J. T.'s [John Taylor of Caroline] whimsical but sensible work 'Arator.'

"Unlike you, we had a *church* to pull down, and its destruction contributed to swell the general ruin. The temples of the living God were abandoned, the *glebe* sold, the University pillaged. The old mansions, where they have been spared by fire (the consequence of the poverty and carelessness of their present tenants), are fast falling to decay; the families, with a few exceptions, dispersed from St. Mary's to St. Louis; such as remain here sunk into obscurity. They whose fathers rode in coaches and drank the choicest wines now ride on saddle-bags, and drink grog, when they can get it. What enterprise or capital there was in the country retired westward; and in casting your eyes over the map of Virginia, you must look between the *North Mountain* and a line drawn through Petersburg, Richmond, and Alexandria for the population and wealth of the State. The western district is almost a wilderness. The eastern tract, from the falls of the great rivers to the shore of the Chesapeake, — the region above all others in United America the best adapted for commerce, — becomes yearly more deserted. Deer and wild turkeys are nowhere so plentiful in Kentucky as near Williamsburg. I say 'the shore of the Chesapeake,' because our *Eastern Shore* [the two counties that lie beyond that bay] must be excluded from this description. There the old Virginian character is yet (I am told) to be found in its greatest purity, although before the Revolution it was a poor, despised region. Here are the descendants of those men who gave an asylum to Sir W. Berkeley during Bacon's rebellion. The land, although thin, bears a good price, and is inhabited by a hospitable, unmixed people. On *this*, the western shore, land within two hours' sail of Norfolk may be bought for one half the money which the same quality would command one hundred and fifty miles from tide-water. The present just, necessary, and glorious war has not, as you may suppose, served to enhance its price. Perhaps, after all, you may say that I reassert a fact when asked for the cause. The country is certainly unhealthy, — more so than formerly; but this is only one of the causes of its depopulation. Bears and panthers have within a few years made their appearance in the neighborhood of the Dragon and Dismal Swamps.

"You are once more enjoying the 'uda mobilibus pomaria rivis' of Quincy. When you count over the *olentis uxores mariti* (if the dignity of a merino will brook such an epithet), and reckon your lambs before yeaning, you are not likely to be interrupted by any unpleasant Transatlantic recollections. Do you know that you have written a letter of three pages without a syllable on the subject of 'Foreign Relations'? This bespeaks the quiet of the heart within. You and I, whom the delators of the post-office are ready to swear they have detected in carrying on a treasonable correspondence, to be writing about 'old times' that 'are changed,' — 'old manners gone,' — tobacco and wool! . . . . The smaller critics would perhaps remind me that Horace's flock were of the hairy, or no-wool breed, and that they must have been goats. But that is by no means a necessary consequence. Did not Mr. Jefferson import sheep without wool (sent him, I presume, by some brother *savant* of the Academy of Lagado), and does Captain Lemuel Gulliver give us any reason to doubt that in point of antiquity that illustrious people flourished long before the age of Augustus? This valuable breed of sheep, although destitute of wool, had a double allowance of horns, — there being four to each head, two of them projecting like the fabled unicorn's. With these the ram actually tore out the entrails of a poor child in Washington, and killed it. (See Malthus on Population.) There is an apparent levity in this letter which is foreign to my real temper, at this moment especially. I do but mock myself. 'It may deceive all hearts save that within.' If you see Tudor, tell him his brother is better, much better.

"I am, dear sir, with great regard and truth, yours,

"John Randolph of Roanoke.

"We are to have peace forthwith. The hostages are *withdrawn.* The pacification of Europe settles the question of impressment. 'It has vanished into thin air.'

"July 4, 1814.

"P. S. Since writing the above I have been ruined by an inundation of the river on whose banks my lands lie. It rises beyond the Blue Ridge, indeed in the Alleghany Mountains; passes through the counties of Montgomery and Botetourt under its right name; issues from the mountains *incog.* under the appellation of Staunton; here receives the Little Roanoke; and on its junction with the Dan, about twenty miles below, resumes its true name, which it retains during the remainder of its course to the Sound.

"There have been heavy rains in the mountains, for we have not had more than enough. For twenty years there has not occurred such a calamity to the low grounds of this river. I have lost upwards of three hundred and fifty thousand tobacco *hills*, and a great deal of Indian corn, wheat, and oats."

The years of the war passed slowly and heavily over New England. Gloom and discontent pervaded all classes of people, always excepting the office-holders and contractors. As an absolute stop was put to commercial pursuits, then the chief occupation of the inhabitants of the seaboard towns, agriculture and the mechanic arts necessarily suffered from the paralysis of the great industry on which they mainly depended for profitable employment. There can be no doubt that a very wide-spread disaffection towards the general government prevailed among the most substantial and virtuous of the citizens of the New England States. They regarded the pretexts on which the war had been declared with contemptuous incredulity, believing them to be but the thin disguise of its real object. That object they believed to be the gratification of the malignant hatred the slave-holding States bore towards communities of free and intelligent labor, by the destruction of their wealth and prosperity. To this end the majority of the people of New England believed that the Constitution had been violated and perverted from its original purpose. Undoubtedly there were many among them who deemed that they were thus released from the moral and legal obligations imposed upon them by the sanction they had given to the national compact, and that it was their right, and might become their duty, to consider how much longer they should suffer themselves to be oppressed and ruined by a government which had forfeited its lawful claim to their obedience. It is no part of my business to censure or defend these opinions, but only to record the fact of their existence and of their extensive influence over men's minds. But these extreme opinions and violent passions, suggested and exasperated by positive suffering and actual distress, were not shared by the leading men of the Federal party, as a general thing, notwithstanding the railing accusations which have been brought against them. Their policy was to restrain the popular feeling of indignation against the national government, and to keep it within bounds, in the hope that time would bring a peaceful remedy of grievances and wrongs. But they knew that the public voice which demanded of the Legislatures of the New England States some concerted and effectual action for the vindication of those wrongs and the redress of those grievances, was as earnest as it was emphatic, and that there was danger of open resistance if it were not listened to; and hence came the famous Hartford Convention.

It has been the ill-fortune of that much abused assembly to be accused of designing an organized resistance to the general government, and a separation of the New England States from the Union, when in fact its purpose was to delay, at any rate, and if possible to defeat, such a catastrophe. Nothing could be more gratuitous than the obloquy, under which the eminent and excellent men who went up to Hartford on that errand lived and died, of having planned the dissolution of the Union. Their purpose was to prevent its being dissolved, if they could. And for this reason the Legislatures, when they came to elect delegates to the Convention, were very careful to choose men of known moderation of views and tried discretion of conduct. It was for this reason, my father believed and said, that he was passed by on that occasion. The prudent Federalists, when called upon to face this emergency, were afraid of his impetuous temperament and fiery earnestness. They dreaded lest he might express too well the spirit of those whose urgency extorted the

Convention. One useful piece of service, however, he rendered to the Convention, by making an accurate analysis of the effect which the slave ratio of representation had had upon the Presidential elections and upon all the most important doings of Congress since the close of Washington's Administration. This is contained in a long letter to Mr. George Cabot, afterwards the President of the Convention, dated December 9, 1814, written just before it met, at the request of that eminent gentleman. It undoubtedly helped to guide the action of the Convention in regard to that important matter. He always spoke of the Hartford Convention as a tub to the whale, as a dilatory measure to amuse the malcontents, and keep them quiet under inaction, until events might make action unnecessary. One day, while public attention was absorbed by speculations as to what the Convention, then sitting with closed doors, would do or propose, a friend met my father in the street, and said anxiously to him, "What *do* you suppose will be the result of this Convention?" "I can tell you exactly," was his reply. "Can you, indeed?" exclaimed the other. "Pray tell me what it will be." "A GREAT PAMPHLET!" he responded. And it was even so. Whether the calm and temperate address of the Convention to its constituent Legislatures, deprecating resistance even to unconstitutional and unlawful national action excepting in the last extremity, and the measures it suggested, of which the most material was to urge an amendment of the Constitution abolishing the slave representation, by making the number of voters the basis of representation, would have been sufficient to satisfy and restrain the people of New England had the war and all the mischiefs it brought with it lasted much longer, it were now only curious to inquire; for the peace which followed close upon the adjournment of the Convention effectually allayed the apprehensions to which its meeting had given rise, together with the irritations which had called for it.

The fall of Bonaparte, although it occasioned as genuine joy to New England as to the mother country herself, did not bring with it absolutely unalloyed satisfaction. There was reason to apprehend that the English Administration, triumphant over its gigantic foe, its army and navy released from the incessant service of so many years, might concentrate the whole force of the empire upon the power which it regarded as a volunteer ally of its mighty enemy, and administer an exemplary chastisement. No doubt many Englishmen felt, with Walter Scott, that "it was their business to give them [the Americans] a fearful memento that the babe unborn should have remembered," and there is as little question that infinite damage might have been done to our cities and sea-coast, and to the banks of our great rivers, had Great Britain employed her entire naval and military forces for that purpose. But, happily, the English people had had their fill of fighting for the time, and wisely refrained from an expenditure of blood and gold which could have no permanent result, and would only serve to exasperate passions and prolong animosities which it were far wiser to permit to subside and to die out. And, indeed, it is not unlikely that the attention of the English people had been so absorbed by the mighty conflict going on at their very doors, that they had not had much to spare for the distant and comparatively obscure fields across the Atlantic. The American war was but a slight episode in the great epic of the age. At any rate, the English ministry were content to treat with the American Commissioners at Ghent, and to make a peace which left untouched the pretended occasion of the war. The question of impressment, the only pretext for the war, was passed over in expressive silence, and peace was concluded, leaving "Sailors' Rights," the great watchword of the war party, substantially as they stood before hostilities began, excepting that our fishermen were deprived of the valuable privilege they then enjoyed of catching and curing fish on the shores of the Gulf of St. Lawrence. A conclusion, indeed, in which nothing was concluded! It was no unpoetical justice that Mr. Clay, who had been so forward in forcing the Madison Administration into the war, should have been one of the Commissioners who virtually confessed its failure to accomplish its ostensible purpose by signing this treaty of peace, — "a peace," as Sheridan said of that of Amiens, "which every one must be glad of, but no one could be proud of!"

However, there was small disposition to criticise the terms of the peace when the glad tidings first reached our shores. Both political parties were equally rejoiced to hear that the war was at an end, though for very different reasons; and the joy was the greater because the news was entirely unexpected. Only the night before, a very experienced and sagacious gentleman had declared, at my father's house, that the war would probably last for years to come. On Monday, the 13th of February, 1815, an express arrived at the office of the Columbian Centinel, in the incredibly short space of thirty-two hours, from New York, bearing a letter from Mr. Jonathan Goodhue, an eminent merchant of that city, telling of the arrival of the British sloop-of-war Favourite, under a flag of truce, bringing an English and an American messenger, charged with the custody of the treaty already ratified by his Britannic Majesty. The bells were at once set a-ringing as the readiest way of spreading the joyful news. I remember that a next-door neighbor, Eliza Cabot, afterwards well known by her writings, and for her marriage with Charles Follen, a faithful servant of liberty in the Old World and in the New, came breathless with haste into our house, and asked my mother if she knew why the bells were ringing. "For fire, I suppose, of course." "For peace! peace! peace!" exclaimed the messenger of glad tidings of great joy, in an ecstasy of that enthusiasm which made her presence so magnetic and her society so charming, in her old age as in her youth. It was a day given up to rejoicing which came from the heart; for there was no one, unless it were here and there a contractor, who was not sincerely and cordially glad that the war was over. Salutes were fired, the bells rang out their merriest peals, the volunteer companies and their bands filled the streets with such martial show and sound as they could furnish, the school-boys had a holiday, the whole population was in the streets, and even party spirit slept for that day, and Federalist and Democrat clasped each other's hands like ancient friends. The wharves, so long deserted, were again thronged, and the melancholy ships that rotted along them were once more bright with flags, and gay with streamers. Parties of sailors on sleds drawn by fifteen horses each, and with PEACE in large letters on the hat of the foremost man, made the town ring with their huzzas. And before night had fallen, crews were engaged, and preparations for voyages in forwardness. Commerce plumed her white wings afresh, so long clipped and crippled, and prepared to take her flight to all quarters of the globe. These rejoicings extended all along the seaboard, and stretched far into the inland, making glad all hearts, and none more glad than those of the promoters of the war in high places and in low.

Mr. Quincy, at the opening of the session of the Senate on that auspicious morning, moved the resolutions of thanksgiving proper to so glad an occasion, and was made Chairman of the Committee of Arrangements for the celebration of the event on the appropriate anniversary of Washington's birthday. That too was a day of universal joy, more regulated in its expression, perhaps, and tempered by religious services of thanksgiving, but flowing as genuinely from the heart as on that first memorable day of unlooked-for gladness. A procession under military escort, of which a main feature was a representation of the various trades, the men working at them as they went through the streets upon platforms drawn by horses, conducted the authorities of the State and the town to the Stone Chapel, where fitting religious and musical services were had. A dinner at the Exchange Coffee-house, at which Mr. Harrison Gray Otis presided, succeeded in the due order of the festivities, and the night was brilliant with fireworks and a universal illumination.

And so the war of 1812 ended, amid a general joy, — not for what it had brought to pass, but because it was at an end, and the industry of the Free States freed from its restraints and its burdens. The necessary provision for the payment of the interest of the national debt the war had created, and for its gradual extinguishment, soon renewed the old party divisions, though conducted with somewhat less of acrimony. The questions on which the politics of the period immediately following the war turned were almost purely financial. The Democratic party, still controlled by the Southern influences which compelled the war, sought successfully to make Northern commerce pay for the war which had crippled and all but crushed it, through the custom-house. The Federalists, led by Mr. Webster, opposed the imposition of further burdens upon the reviving trade of the North, and urged the continuance of a proportion, at least, of the direct taxes which the war had called for. Mr. Calhoun, however, prevailed, and the tariff of 1816 was adopted, which called into existence the great manufacturing industry of the North, the success of which, and the prosperity attending it, soon changed the political economy of its inventor, and called for the remedy of Nullification, to be followed in due time by Secession and Rebellion. In these discussions, however, Mr. Quincy took no very prominent part, although he shared in the doubts entertained by the Federalists generally as to the wisdom of a protective policy. He feared that its effect would be to change the character of the population of New England, and assimilate it to that of the great manufacturing centres of Europe. The experience of half a century has shown these fears to have been without substantial foundation. The Federalists, consisting to a great extent of educated and reflecting men, were too apt to draw from the experience of the Old World inferences as to the operation of political institutions and policies in the New, without making sufficient allowance for the infinite difference in the circumstances under which the experiments were tried. Holding to the opinion that "History repeats herself" (which she never does), they dreaded the renewal of the scenes which she describes in her tale of the ancient and modern republics, without sufficiently considering how much wider was the stage on which the American drama was enacted, and how much broader the influences which had formed the actors in it. It was their little faith in ideas that caused their disappearance from the world of American politics, and it was his unbounded faith in ideas that gave to Thomas Jefferson, in spite of all his faults of character and his inconsistencies and errors of public conduct, that controlling power over the minds of men which did not die with him, but is giving direction and shape to the history, not only of his own country, but of all Christendom.

On the 18th day of August, 1815, young Randolph died in

England, at Cheltenham, whither he had gone in search of the health he had lost. His death was a severe blow to his uncle, who looked upon him as the last representative of his line of the Randolphs, and who had every reason to believe that he would do credit to the name. The following letter closes the correspondence with my father, which was mainly owing to the residence of the young man at Cambridge. One or two letters of a later date will appear in their proper place.

MR. RANDOLPH TO MR. QUINCY.

"RICHMOND, Dec. 7, 1815.

"MY DEAR SIR:—Your letter, postmarked November 9, was forwarded to me from home, and received last night too late to answer it. I learned with the most unfeigned regret that you have been visited, and that not lightly, by one of the heaviest calamities that flesh is heir to.* But you have remaining offspring to hand down your name, and to exercise your affections, while I am left desolate and forlorn. You will readily conceive that my sympathy in your loss is not diminished by the circumstance of meeting on my arrival here the faithful servant who attended my child to Europe. He arrived about a fortnight ago from Liverpool, with the effects of his late young master, who died at Cheltenham on the 18th of August. This man's father was body-servant to mine, and accompanied his master to Quebec, by the way of Niagara and Montreal, soon after the annexation of Canada to the British Empire, when Albany was a frontier post. When my father mortgaged his whole estate, real and personal, to secure a debt of his brother to a London house, Syphax alone was excepted,—an honor of which he yet boasts. His wife was a favorite and confidential servant of my mother, born on my grandfather's estate. She died a few weeks after her mistress, in 1788. Stephen, her youngest child, was then at the breast, and a nursling with my youngest sister. They were of the same age. His fidelity and attention to Tudor was beyond example, and is attested by many Virginia gentlemen, several of whom were at Cheltenham and have lately returned home. You may judge of my attachment to him from these circumstances.

"In the summer a letter to my friend, Mr. Dandridge, Cashier of the Bank of Virginia, addressed to Charlotte Court House, was sent

* Referring to the death of two infant sons of my father, which took place in the course of 1815.

to Charlottesville (near Monticello), whither my letters are not unfrequently sent, as letters for that place are to Charlotte C. H., even with the treasury frank upon them. Charlottesville is, by mail route, one hundred and ninety miles from me, but in practice as far as Liverpool or London. When I did get the letter (which was mere accident) I was occupied by thoughts exclusive of business. Soon after I left home for this place, where I could best attend to such affairs. . . . .

"Mr. Eppes does not dispute my election. He has long ago abandoned the contest, declaring 'that his friends had deceived him.' On examination, my majority was more than doubled. It is expected that he will succeed Mr. Giles in the Senate.

"*December* 8. — As was expected, Mr. E. was elected by a great majority to fill the vacant seat of Mr. Giles. Men of all political parties agree that he is indebted to me for his seat; so that, if I am not *great* myself, I am the cause of greatness in others.

"My best regards to Mr. Lloyd. Of your kindness to my poor boy I shall ever entertain the most grateful remembrance. I know that, whilst he could feel, he felt upon this subject as he ought. When I reach the city of W. I hope to hear from you. Meanwhile, believe me, with great esteem and regard, dear sir, yours,

"JOHN RANDOLPH OF ROANOKE.

"In memory of Theodorick Tudor Randolph, Esquire, younger son of the late Richard Randolph, of Bizarre, Virginia, who departed this life at this place, on the 18th day of August, 1815, in the twentieth year of his age, this stone is placed by his afflicted uncle, John Randolph of Roanoke. This amiable and interesting young man fell a victim to the consequences of severe study, which compelled him to leave College about twelve months before his decease, and try the effect of relaxation and change of climate. In testimony of his merit as a scholar, the Corporation of Harvard University, Cambridge, North America, conferred upon him, at their annual Commencement, held on the 30th day of August, 1815, the degree of Bachelor of Arts, ignorant that he was then removed beyond the sphere of human applause or human censure.

"Pray suggest any alteration that seems proper."

CHAPTER XV.

1813 – 1823.

TEN YEARS OF LEISURE. — EXPERIMENTAL FARMING. — LETTER FROM JUDGE PETERS. — THE SUMMERS AT QUINCY. — EX-PRESIDENT ADAMS. — TRUMBULL'S PICTURE. — PRESIDENT MONROE'S VISIT. — SEPARATION OF MAINE FROM MASSACHUSETTS. — MR. QUINCY DROPPED FOR THE STATE SENATE. — SPEECH IN FANEUIL HALL. — RETURNED AS REPRESENTATIVE. — CONVENTION OF 1820. — THE MISSOURI COMPROMISE. — MR. DOWSE OF DEDHAM. — LETTER FROM JOHN RANDOLPH. — MR. DOWSE IN CONGRESS. — HIS LETTERS. — MR. QUINCY SPEAKER. — JUDGE OF MUNICIPAL COURT. — HIS LAW OF LIBEL IN THE MAFFITT CASE.

THE ten years of Mr. Quincy's life from 1813 to 1823 were years of comparative leisure. Though he was a member of the General Court for the chief of the time, his duties in that capacity were confined to a few months of the year, and were not of a very engrossing nature. In 1815, after the declaration of peace, he removed from Oliver Street, and took a lease of a house in Summer Street, one of the handsomest and most commodious in Boston, with ample stable-room and every convenience that was then thought essential to a gentleman's town residence. Here the winters were spent. The summers, which were always lengthened out at both ends as much as possible, were passed at Quincy. After leaving Congress, he took the management of the farm into his own hands. He was an enthusiast in whatever he undertook, and he entered into farming with all the zeal of his ardent temperament. His agricultural experience, like that of most gentleman farmers, was rather profitable to others than to himself. He was full of experiments, which, though not eminently successful as to the lucre of gain, were of great value to the farming interests of his neighborhood and of the State. He brought improved implements to the notice of the unbelieving farmers round about. He set an example in the matter of root culture, and of the succession of crops, which redounded to the general benefit, if not to his own personal advantage. And latterly he introduced the custom of soiling or stall-feeding of milch cows, and argued its merits in the agricultural papers of the day. These essays he collected and republished in his old age, as his last contribution to agriculture. One of his favorite schemes was the substitution of hawthorn hedges for the old-fashioned rail-fence of New England. They kept themselves in repair, he would say, and so saved the expense of renewing the fences of dead wood, which was a material item in the cost of farming. At one time his whole farm was fenced only with this verdurous wall, and the system worked exceeding well as long as the cattle were kept in the stalls. But when, in 1823, he was obliged to give up the supervision of his paternal acres for that of the city of Boston, and the tenant to whom he let them insisted on pasturing his cows, the hedges were found not to be equal to the occasion. A hedge might be sufficient to restrain the wanderings of the civilized cattle of England, which had been accustomed to be led into fat pastures for generations; but it was otherwise with the hardy kine of New Hampshire and Vermont, whence the herds of the lowland country were chiefly recruited, which, brought up to browse in the woods and on the mountains, made little account of any obstacle that offered itself in the shape of green leaves and twigs. The thorns they seemed to regard as an appetizing condiment, — a kind of *sauce piquante*, — thrown in to increase the pleasure of the meal. So, in the end, rail fences had to be provided to protect the hedges from the beasts. However, his experiment settled the hedge question as far as New England was concerned.

The following lively letter from Judge Richard Peters of Philadelphia was occasioned by my father's experimenting with the different kinds of hedges. Judge Peters was a man of great humor, and many of his *facetiæ* were current in conversation fifty years since; and it is likely some of them may still survive, as is the fate of such airy trifles, affiliated upon succeeding wits.

JUDGE PETERS TO MR. QUINCY.

"BELMONT, PENN., January 24, 1813.

"DEAR SIR: — I recently received very favorable accounts of the Newcastle thorn, and take the liberty of repeating my recommendation of it. I allow all you say about the species you have being *good enough;* but there are so many things worse than *bad* enough, that I do not see why we may not, *now and then,* indulge ourselves in the best we can get. Your career will be soon run out, and there is time enough to order McMahon to put you up in March a few for experiment.

"I thought you would have died a peaceful political death, but I see it is not in your nature. So much the better; for death-bed sayings are the most noticed and remembered. I once thought that *Parce puer stimulis et fortius utere loris* should be the minority motto, but I have long believed myself mistaken. It is not to your opponents that your protests are useful, but to those whose returning reason and patriotism will, one day, profit by them. You have anticipated the month of March by coming in like a lion; but it is not likely that you will go out like a lamb. I think that time will mend us (if chaos does not come too soon); but our progress will be slow. *When* our regeneration will be completed I do not undertake to prophesy.

"I was much pleased (as the scriveners say, *inter alia*) with your philippic against the delectable clause intended as a substitute for young conscripts. The trouble I have in hearing controversies about recruits would, indeed, have been lessened. I am annoyed more than the enemy has hitherto been by our pin-feather army. I had *gravely* to determine, against a learned argument of Mr. Dallas, that a widowed mother was a *parent* (the surest sometimes of the two), and had a legal as well as a natural relationship to her son.

"You eluded on your way to Washington all my inquiries, but I bear you no malice. I see plainly that you are not *hedging* there, whatever you do at home. I read many of the Congressional speeches, but not regularly. Dead votes, against reason and patriotism, give me the *hyp.* But I turn myself round, and recover as soon as I can. Many of you, I perceive, are uncalculating sticklers for *truth,* and expect to find it where *reasonable* men would not look for it. *You,* indeed, sometimes rouse the men of the woods, and may say, '*Non canimus surdis; respondent omnia silvæ.*' But there it ends.

. . . . .

"I began this letter with no other view than to remind you of the hedge thorn. Judging from your speeches, I avoid political discussion, lest you should think me a milk-and-water politician. So be it, for I live on meagre diet. The less I think on the politics of the day, the more happy I am. I do not fear to look at *truth* in your *concave mirror*, but as my glass has discharged the greatest portion of its sand, I seek the sunny sides of prospects, when the too-frequent clouds will permit. I nevertheless enjoy the dusky scenes of a Salvator Rosa, but most prefer the brilliant skies and illuminated landscapes of a Claude. You may pity me for this light propensity, but happy is he, in evil times, who can look on fraud, rebellion, guilt, and Cæsar 'in the calm lights of mild philosophy.' One is, however, like Garagantua in Rabelais, obliged sometimes to tickle one's self to produce a smile. I often feel bitterly our follies and disgrace. If I fly to bagatelles for amusement, I do not sympathize the less with those who have *only* reason and patriotism to oppose to superior and impenetrable numbers.

"I have sufficiently puzzled you how to decide, whether the garrulous or scribulous *senectus* merits most the *hunc tu Romane caveto*. It is high time then to conclude, with very sincere assurances of the esteem with which I am

"Your obedient servant,

"RICHARD PETERS.

"Before sealing my letter, a friend, who has lately visited New England, called on me. He describes your establishment at Quincy so as to interest me. He says you deserve, not a crown of thorns, but a chaplet of hawthorn-blossoms, for daring to enclose your grounds with anything but the dreary stone fences which disgust a Pennsylvanian. Your whole demesnes were eulogized so as to make us little stars hide our diminished heads. I hope the thorn will be the most prominent in my *mischianza*, and that you will, in your oblivion of the light and evanescent parts, not forget the Newcastle thorn. 'T is strange that I, who have not an enclosure other than of dead timber, should be anxious about your live fences. Perhaps self-reproach for not in early life beginning and continuing such essential improvements, which posterity would have thanked me for, has something to do with my desire to promote improvements in which you have engaged with commendable spirit. It seems, however, that we crow over you in some respects, for your *buildings* are composed of frail material, and your fences are indestructible. We have taken the opposite course. But had our enclosures been made as durable as are our buildings, our triumph would have been more profitably complete. It is well we have something to boast of."

So it fell out with my father's farming as it is apt to do with that of gentlemen who are not able or willing to give themselves entirely to the minute economies of the business, and are obliged to leave to others the small details, on a strict attention to which the prosperity of farming, as of every other calling, depends. It gave him much amusement, but cost him much money, — more than it was at all convenient to him to lose. The only profitable manufacture connected with his farm was one of salt, for which he established works along the length of his property on the sea-shore, and which made remunerative returns as long as the duty on salt was retained. His salt was always in particular request with the Cape Ann fishermen for curing their fish. But it was a pleasant life that he and his family led during those summers. The house was always filled with company. He delighted in exercising hospitality, and there was scarcely a Saturday in the year, in town or country, that was not solemnized by a regular dinner-party. Every afternoon in summer a succession of visitors thronged the house. In those days the universal summer dispersion of the well-to-do inhabitants of the town had not set in. Very few of the Boston gentlemen had country-seats, and the custom of exchanging their roomy and comfortable town houses for the narrow hospitalities of Saratoga and Ballston, then almost the only places of summer resort, was far from general. Sea-bathing was an undiscovered luxury, and the mountains had not yet been invented. Tours were slow, tedious, and expensive, and a visit to Niagara was more of an event in life then than one to the second cataract of the Nile is now. People stayed at home in their pleasant garden-houses, and gave summer parties to each other and to the visitors from the South and from Europe, who were always established in greater or less force in Boston during the hot months. The excursions which filled up the long afternoons left on their hands by the early dinner-hour of fifty years since often took the direction of Quincy. The neighborhood of Ex-President John Adams undoubtedly increased the number of these pleasant visitors, as no stranger of condition ever came to Boston without seeking an introduction to so celebrated a public man, and very few returned to town without taking my father's house by the way. His own personal celebrity, however, and the pleasantness of his home and domestic circle, were attractive enough in themselves, without that additional inducement, to secure a continual round of company. He had his books mainly at Quincy, and the exigencies of a growing family made it necessary to provide a small building apart from the main house, where he kept his library, and where he spent the chief of his time when at home, and not engaged in looking after his laborers or in the society of his visitors. His library was large for that day, and considerable even for this, and contained a very competent collection of the classics, and of the English and French authors. His journal, which he kept with tolerable regularity during portions of these years, bears testimony to the regularity of his literary industry and the variety of his reading. Law, ethics, Cicero, Lord Bacon, Madame de Staël, Colonial history, especially the part relating to the religious establishment, and the old English divines, made up a portion of his multifarious reading, often digested, analyzed, and commented upon. He also set down such anecdotes and bits of historical information as came to him in the course of each day, and particularly such as were communicated by Mr. Adams. Some of these may be worth recording, written down, as they were, fresh from the lips of the octogenarian statesman, although they may have already found their way into print; and I shall insert them occasionally in their order.

"*December* 4, 1818.—Rode to Quincy with W. S. Shaw and Colonel Trumbull, and dined with President Adams. Trumbull, a gentleman of the old school, greatly delighted at the patronage given by the national Legislature to the series of his paintings commemorating four great national events. The conversation turned on the character of Dr. Franklin. Adams said, that the suggestion made against Dr. Franklin, as not being hearty in his support of the Declaration of Independence, was a calumny. To his knowledge, he supported that measure at its earliest period, with energy and perfect devotion. Adams said, that he was present at the sittings of the Royal Academy of France, when Voltaire and Franklin both attended. As each appeared, the hall rang with acclamations. They approached each other. The cry was, 'Let them embrace, let them embrace!' They accordingly began to hug and kiss. The room rang with, 'Behold, Sophocles and Solon are embracing each other!'"

"*December* 5.—President Adams came to town to view the 'Declaration of Independence,' by Colonel Trumbull, now exhibiting at Faneuil Hall. President Adams, Trumbull, Prof. Farrar, Wm. S. Shaw,* dined with me. Colonel Trumbull said, that every portrait in his picture was taken from a real sitting of the individual, or from some existing picture of him, except that of Benjamin Harrison, which was only from general description, received from his son, the recently distinguished General Harrison. Adams said, that the portrait bore a general resemblance, but was not sufficiently corpulent. He well remembered, that, when engaged in signing the Declaration of Independence, a side conversation took place between Harrison, who was remarkably corpulent, and Elbridge Gerry, who was remarkably the reverse. 'Ah, Gerry,' said Harrison, 'I shall have an advantage over you in this act.' 'How so?' said Gerry. 'Why,' replied Harrison, 'when we come to be hung for this treason, I am so heavy, I shall plump down upon the rope and be dead in an instant; but you are so light, that you will be dangling and kicking about for an hour in the air.'"

I well remember being one of the party which accompanied Mr. Adams to see Trumbull's picture. Faneuil Hall was full of spectators when we arrived, and what impressed the scene upon my boyish memory was the respectful manner in which all the men took off their hats when Mr. Adams entered leaning on my mother's arm, and remained uncovered while he stayed. Room was made for him by common consent, so that he could see the picture to the best advantage. He seemed carried back to his prime of manhood, and to the most famous scene of his life, and he gave his warm approval to the picture as a correct representation of the Convention. "There is the door," said he, "through which Washington escaped when I nominated him as Commander-in-Chief of the Continental Army!" This picture

* William Smith Shaw, Harvard University, 1798, was the nephew of Mrs. John Adams. He was the Private Secretary of Mr. Adams during his Presidency, and afterwards Clerk of the District Court of Massachusetts. He was known chiefly by the sobriquet of "Athenæum Shaw," from the zeal and assiduity with which he labored in founding and building up the Boston Athenæum, which may almost be said to owe its existence to him. He died in 1826, æt. 48.

must be always interesting as an authentic collection of portraits, and an accurate representation of the Hall of Independence; and it pretends to be nothing more. At one time a shade of ridicule attached to this painting, because of John Randolph's splenetic description of it as "*a great shin-piece!*" — a most groundless sarcasm, as any one may see who will be at the trouble of counting first the *heads* and then the *shins* it portrays. That part of the subject is certainly as well managed as possible, if the venerable signers are to be allowed any legs at all.

"*January* 9, 1819. — In conversation with William Sullivan. He dined yesterday in company with General Coffin * of the British army. Coffin said, that he had the command of the first boat (being then Lieutenant of a transport ship) which landed the advance of the first regiment of British grenadiers at the attack of Bunker's Hill. As the boat touched the shore, a *three-pound shot from the American lines* passed lengthways over the boat, touched not a man, and beat out her stern. Further service with his boat being thus rendered impracticable, Coffin took a musket, joined the assailants, and was in the midst of the battle. He said that he had been since that time in many engagements, but never knew one, for the time it lasted, so hot and destructive. The anecdote proves what has been denied, — that artillery was used on the American side in the battle of Bunker's Hill."

In the summer after his accession to the Presidency, Mr. Monroe made a tour through the Northern States. He was received everywhere with the respect due to the head of the nation, and Federalists united with Democrats in doing him honor. Party spirit, in those old shapes, seemed almost extinct, and "the era of good feeling" to be indeed inaugurated. On the 7th of July, 1817, he dined with Mr. Adams, and after dinner, accompanied by his host, his suite, and the rest of the dinner-party, he paid Mr. Quincy an afternoon's visit. Bygones were bygones. Mr. Monroe did not seem to remember that Mr. Quincy had balked him of the Lieutenant-Generalship and the command of the army, and Mr. Quincy had forgotten that he had suspected the little gentleman of mild exterior before him of designing to

* General John Coffin was brother of Admiral Sir Isaac Coffin, Bart. They were natives of Boston, and took service with the Crown at the time of the Revolution.

use that power to destroy the liberties of his country. It was a lovely summer's day. The roses were still in bloom, and the hay-making was going on. I believe, however, that it must be confessed that my father had ordered a few loads of hay, which had been already housed, to be spread again at appropriate points of view, partly for the picturesque effect, but chiefly to afford the farm laborers an opportunity of seeing their President as he walked over the estate. After an animated and cheerful visit, the President returned to town, taking a last leave of his venerable predecessor, not without signs of strong sensibility on both sides.

The most important event in the history of the Commonwealth, during Mr. Quincy's service in the State Senate, was the separation of the District of Maine from Massachusetts, and its erection into a sovereign State. Thirty years before, previously to the adoption of the Federal Constitution, this action had been contemplated; but the time was not yet come when that dependency could well dispense with the fostering care of the parent State. Another generation found matters in a different condition, and Maine now conceived herself to have arrived at years of discretion, and to be fully competent to set up for herself. A coincidence of the interests of the two political parties favored the accomplishment of the measure at that time. The Democrats were in a small majority in the District, and the leading men among them hungered after the governorships and judgeships and senatorships, and all the other prizes of local ambition of which they were deprived by the predominance of the Federalists in the entire State. The Federalists of Massachusetts proper, on the other hand, feared lest the Democratic majority in the District might so increase, or be so managed, as to overthrow their supremacy in the State. But though the leaders of the two parties were thus ready for the separation, it took some time to prevail upon the people even of Maine to co-operate cordially with them. The Federalists of Maine considered it as hard treatment that they should be left naked to their enemies by the withdrawal of the sheltering hand of the mother State, and they made a resolute stand against the measure. It was first proposed in 1816, and most vigorously opposed by Mr. Quincy in the Senate. On one occasion his "Nay" was recorded alone against the otherwise unanimous voice of the Senators. He did not see how a State was strengthened by severing herself in twain, and held that such a loss of weight in the nation should not be incurred, excepting under the most imperative and unavoidable necessity. That such an absolute necessity then existed, was hardly pretended on either side. By this act Massachusetts would reduce herself from a State of the first rank in the Union to one of the second, and yield to New York the headship of the opposition to the Southern predominance, led by Virginia, which she had hitherto held. As to the arguments urged in private by the Federal leaders, drawn from the benefit that would accrue to the party in the State from the separation, — that it would, in the words of one of the chief of them, "give us a snug little Federal State for the rest of our lives," — Mr. Quincy refused to consider them, when treating of a question of general and permanent importance, which should be settled on fixed principles, and not by partisan expediency. But he warned his party friends that they would find themselves mistaken in their calculations, and that the effect of the separation would be exactly the opposite of what they anticipated. And so it proved, as we shall presently see.

An act was passed authorizing the holding of a Convention, and the taking of the sense of the people of the District on the subject. The Federalists of Maine complained of unfairness in the method of doing this, the management being in the hands of the favorers of the partition. But notwithstanding this, allowing that these complaints were well founded, the majority in favor of the separation was but about fifteen hundred in a comparatively light vote. The scheme went over for that time; but was a continued occasion of agitation in Maine, and of discussion in Massachusetts, until it was finally carried. The people of the District having, after two or three more trials, pronounced decisively in favor of separation, the question came up for final decision in 1819. Mr. Quincy again resisted the passage of the act, with all the energy of his character. He moved, first, that the act should not go into effect without having been first submitted to the people of Massachusetts; and, secondly, this resolution having been negatived, that the votes of two thirds of the people of the District should be given in its favor before it should take effect. He then recapitulated his arguments against the measure in a speech of two hours' length, but all in vain. The bill passed the Senate on the 15th of June, 1819, by a vote of twenty-six to eleven, and afterwards received the sanction of the House by one of a hundred and ninety-three to twenty-seven. Mr. Quincy, to the end of his life, regarded the stand he had taken as to this matter with much satisfaction, and he was especially proud of his having stood alone against the project in 1816. Talking once with Mr. John Quincy Adams on this subject, and referring to the circumstance of his single vote, Mr. Adams said, with a smile, "And that was not the only time, Mr. Quincy, that you played the part of Abdiel."

Mr. Quincy's daring to differ from the leaders of his party on this point probably was the occasion of their dropping him from their list of Senatorial candidates for Suffolk County at the spring election of 1820. His independence of action and outspoken energy in debate had made his Federal compeers look upon him as one whose political zeal might outrun his discretion, and who could not be depended upon in every partisan emergency. And it is not unlikely that the opinion they held of him, as one neither to hold nor to bind, stood in the way of his elevation to the Senate of the United States, — a distinction to which his faithful services in the House of Representatives, at a most critical period of our history, might not unreasonably have entitled him. I have in my possession a letter from Mr. Harrison Gray Otis, written in 1818, when Mr. Eli P. Ashmun contemplated resigning his seat in the Senate, to their common friend, Mr. John Phillips, strongly urging the claims of Mr. Quincy as Mr. Ashmun's successor, on the ground of his being the only man of the party who had subjected himself to a thorough and special training for public life. After speaking of the probability of Mr. Ashmun's resignation of his place in the Senate, Mr. Otis goes on: —

"Would not Quincy come? And if he would, why should he not be supported? He is the only man among us who had intended *ab initio* to pursue politics as a profession, and who has qualified himself by hard study for that department. He is proverbially industrious, and though an occasional expression or two have served as catchwords to injure his popularity, I have no doubt that in this Senate he would soon efface any petty prejudice existing against him, and be a very useful member. If you are of this opinion, you may easily ascertain his chance of success by touching a few persons lightly with *the tractors.** But do not quote me, unless you mean to ruin the plan, — though I am perfectly willing my good opinion of him should be known, whenever it may be thought *auxiliary* to others. Pray mind this distinction."

So that it is hardly possible that his name should not have been one of those taken into consideration on the several occasions of vacancies after his resignation of his seat in the House, and it is not unlikely that the choice of his party might have fallen upon him had he been of a more yielding and plastic clay. But, however this may have been, there is no doubt that it was a belief on the part of the Federal managers that his uncompromising and fearless course in public life, and especially in the matter of the separation of Maine, had damaged his popularity in Boston, that led them to omit his name when they came next to make up their list of candidates for the State Senate. Now, at that imperfect stage of our political development, the grand cardinal doctrine of modern politics, that of rotation in office, had not yet been discovered. It was fondly believed that the longer a competent man was retained in a public station, the better he was likely to be capable of performing its duties. The modern

* Referring to the metallic tractors of Perkins, a long-exploded quackery, which proposed to cure all diseases by the galvanic virtues of these instruments. In almost all old-fashioned libraries, especially of Federal families, will be found a volume of Hudibrastic verse, entitled "Terrible Tractoration," by Doctor Caustic, in which the system was held up to ridicule. By its side will be found another volume, in the same short metre, called "Democracy Unveiled," long since forgotten, like its companion, though famous and of many editions in its day. The author was Thomas Green Fessenden, afterwards an agricultural writer and editor. He graduated at Dartmouth in 1796, and died in Boston in 1837. He will be remembered rather by a kindly obituary article about him by Hawthorne, published in the American Monthly the same year.

improvements in our State institutions, and in the manner of administering them, which apparently have for their object to secure to the Commonwealth the largest possible amount of inexperience and incompetency for the management of its affairs, were not yet thought of. This treatment of Mr. Quincy was regarded by his personal friends, therefore, as unjust and ungrateful on the part of the wire-pullers of the party, in view of his long devotion and faithful services to it, and he was by no means insensible to their conduct himself. But he kept his temper and his counsel, and, without letting any one know his intentions excepting his wife, he went to the caucus in Faneuil Hall on the next Sunday evening, and took his place in the front row of the side gallery. As soon as the meeting was organized, he rose and addressed the moderator. His appearance there, which was evidently a general surprise, excited as general a curiosity to know what he was going to say and what course to take, — a curiosity probably not unmixed with anxiety on the part of those who had engineered the dropping of his name from the list of candidates. The hall was crowded to overflowing, and all were on tiptoe with expectation when he began his speech. First, he expressed his satisfaction at finding himself addressing a caucus in Faneuil Hall for the first time in near twenty years, he having been always a candidate for office of some kind, and it not being then the custom for candidates to address public meetings called to promote their own election. Then he proceeded to treat of the way in which he had been thrown overboard with such a mixture of pleasantry and good sense, and to urge the claims of the ticket, and especially of the gentleman substituted for himself, on the support of the people, in such a strain of humor, wit, and *bonhommie*, that the old walls shook with laughter and cheers, and he went out of the hall the most popular man in the town. Old citizens yet recall this speech as one of the most brilliant and telling they had ever listened to, and laugh at the recollection of it after the lapse of near half a century. The immediate effect of this sensible and judicious conduct was the unanimous demand of the party that he should represent the town in the Lower House, since he was shut out of the Upper, in obedience to which he was put at the head of the ticket for Representatives, and triumphantly elected.

In those days the State government was organized on the last Wednesday of May, according to the ancient custom of the Province from the earliest days of the emigration. The Governor and the General Court were qualified, and a short session held, during which business was arranged and committees appointed to sit during the recess. The change which not long afterwards was adopted, altering the time of the inauguration of the government to the first Wednesday in January, chiefly on the grounds of economy of time and money, resulted in small saving of either, while it destroyed an immemorial holiday, at the most beautiful season of the year, for a community that had too few holidays already. In January the long session was held, shortened by the work done to its hands by the committees in the recess, so that there was probably an actual saving of time under the old system. I well remember my father's buoyant satisfaction at finding himself for the first time a member of the popular branch of the Legislature of his native State. He said it was like being on the floor of Congress again. And, indeed, the Massachusetts House of Representatives at that time was by much the more numerous body of the two. At this first session provision was made for holding a convention of the people for the revision of the Constitution, such a measure being thought advisable in consequence of the erection of the District of Maine into a sovereign State. The preliminary motion was made by Mr. Quincy, who was made chairman of the committee charged with the consideration of the subject. An act was accordingly reported directing the people to give their ballots for or against the measure, and, if the majority should pronounce in the affirmative, the Convention was to be summoned by the Governor to meet in Boston on the third Wednesday of November. The people approved of the proposition, and Mr. Quincy was elected one of the delegates from Boston. In his journal of the time when this revision was in contemplation, he records the following conversation with Mr. Adams, who drafted the existing Constitution. The part Mr. Adams had in that fundamental act of legislation is recorded in his life, and is a part of history; but this lively assertion of his claim as a legislator is too characteristic to be omitted: —

"*May* 31. — In the course of the past month I had one or two conversations with the Hon. John Adams concerning the expediency of a revision of our State Constitution. Among other things, I asked him who drafted the Constitution of Massachusetts. The old man answered, 'This right hand!' holding it up. 'There was a great committee appointed to sit during the recess of the Convention, which accordingly adjourned for some time. This committee appointed James Bowdoin, Samuel Adams, and myself a sub-committee. These gentlemen insisted that I should take the paper to Braintree, where I then resided, and make the draft. This I accordingly did; and I completed the whole, except the article relative to religion. This I found I could not sketch, consistent with my own sentiments of perfect religious freedom, with any hope of its being adopted by the Convention, so I left it to be battled out in the whole body. This was the case. The other parts were adopted as I had drafted them, with some alterations.'

"In relation to the state of religious sentiment at that period, the veteran said, 'that there was in 1780 more open, avowed infidelity, three to one, than at the present day, and that thirty years before the case was worse.'"

Mr. Adams was elected, unanimously, a delegate from Quincy, and upon the assembling of the Convention on the 15th of November, he was almost unanimously elected its President. This honor he had to decline on account of his great age, and Chief Justice Parker was chosen in his stead. A seat, however, was assigned to him on the right hand of the President, which he occupied during the sessions that he attended. I was in the gallery the next morning, and saw his reception by the Convention, the whole body rising, taking off their hats, and remaining uncovered when he was introduced by the committee charged with that complimentary service, and conducted to the place of honor appointed for him. In those days the good old parliamentary custom of the members of the popular branch wearing their hats during the sessions of the House, the Speaker in the chair and the speaker on the floor only being uncovered, had not yet been reached by modern degeneracy. The great number of the members of the Massachusetts House then, ex ceeding that of the House of Commons now, made the head, as my father used to say, the most convenient peg possible for the hat. But the custom had come down from times when the hat had a symbolic signification which it has long since lost.

Mr. Quincy took an active part in all the debates and doings of the Convention, and had his full share in determining its action. It was a body whose character and discussions were very honorable to the State. It was made up of the men of the greatest weight and distinction in both the political parties. All the professions were represented by their most learned and eminent members, and the yeomanry and mechanics sent up substantial and intelligent men of their callings to help reform the State. Few polities, of whatever name or extent, could furnish an assembly of equal numbers more distinguished for talent, learning, good sense, and fitness for the task of revising the fundamental and vitalizing law of a great commonwealth.

The following extracts from my father's journal belong to about this period: —

"*June* 2. — In the evening at F. C. Gray's. Gray stated that he had, as he apprehended, satisfactorily ascertained that Jonathan Sewall was not the writer of Massachusettensis. That Judge Chipman, now in Boston, from Nova Scotia, as one of the commissioners under the treaty with Great Britain, had stated to him that he was a student of law with Sewall, in 1774, and copied at that time his political speeches for the press; that Sewall wrote *Philanthropos*, which he (Chipman) copied, and used to carry out to Milton to Governor Hutchinson, who revised and gave them their last corrections. That in 1774 Daniel Leonard moved from Taunton, having been appointed to an office in the customs, and that he (Chipman) was recommended to Leonard by Sewall as an assistant in his office, and that he was employed by Leonard in copying Massachusettensis and sending them to the printer. As Chipman may have mistaken the essays he thus copied, and as Leonard is now living, Gray stated to the club that he had sent a copy of the late publication of Massachusettensis and Novanglus, containing President Adams's Preface, to Leonard, for the purpose of ascertaining the fact."

"*June* 4. — In the evening visited President Adams, — told him of

Gray's story relative to Massachusettensis. He said that he knew all the time that Leonard was suspected to be the author; but he never believed it, because he never thought Leonard able to write it. That it exhibited, indeed, more labor than Sewall was accustomed to expend on his compositions, and such interior marks of Sewall"s mind, that, if Leonard did write it, he was quite sure he was indebted to Sewall, either for the general turn of thought, or for subsequent corrections."

It was probably this conversation that led Mr. Adams to change his long-settled opinion that Jonathan Sewall was the author of those celebrated papers. The next year he expressed this change of opinion in a letter quoted in a note to the Preface to Novanglus, in his grandson's edition of his works.*

"*July* 10. — In the evening visited Hon. John Adams. He related to me the following anecdote of my father and himself. During the time of the operation of the Boston Port Bill, when the loss of trade and the general stagnation of business in consequence of that measure threatened the town with utter destruction, and the poor with the greatest misery and distress, 'your father,' said he, addressing me, 'made a famous speech, in his usual nervous and eloquent style, on the duty of a general co-operation in measures which should exhibit the unanimity of all classes of the town, and their determination to endure every privation, and concluded with some resolutions proposing, during the continuance of that measure, general tables to be provided for all the citizens at the common expense. The proposition excited great noise and uproar; some shouted, some hissed. For my part,' said he, 'I was for supporting the proposition of your father. And, after some previous remarks, I said, that the manner in which the suggestions of my friend Mr. Quincy had been received reminded me of one of the sonnets of John Milton: —

'"I did but prompt the age to quit their clogs
By the known rules of ancient liberty,
When straight a barbarous noise environs me
Of owls and cuckoos, asses, apes, and dogs."'

. . . . .

* Vol. IV. p. 10. Jonathan Sewall was an eminent lawyer, successively Solicitor and Attorney-General under the Crown, to which he adhered in 1775. He married Esther, daughter of Edmund Quincy, brother to Colonel Josiah Quincy, and sister of the wife of Governor Hancock. He was the father of Chief Justice Jonathan Sewall of Quebec, and of Mr. Stephen Sewall, K. C., of Montreal.

"President Adams said of Joseph Hawley, that he was 'an Israelite indeed, in whom there was no guile,' — of considerable eloquence, and unquestionable talent, but that he had always a vein of melancholy, which finally terminated in something like distraction. He said also of Timothy Ruggles, the leader of the Tory party in the House of Representatives, that he was a man of great wit, and, although not fluent, one of the most majestic persons he ever heard. In the early part of his life he had been a lawyer, but left the profession and took a colonel's commission in the year 1755. He served during the whole war until the Peace of 1763. He took refuge in Boston, and went with the British to New Brunswick, in which Province he died (1795), at a very advanced age."

"*July* 30. — Passed evening with President Adams. Conversation turned on Botta's History of the United States, which he had just seen. He agreed with Jefferson that it was the best extant; he thought, however, that it was written with the intention of giving an impression to the world of the great influence of France in effecting the independence of the United States. He considered him as being inclined to give an undue credit to the Southern States in producing that event. 'One thing,' said Adams, 'I confess touched my vanity. Botta has adopted the ancient plan of putting speeches into the mouths of the actors in his history; and the debate relative to the Declaration of Independence is carried on in this volume between John Dickinson and Richard Henry Lee. Now the truth is, that Lee said very little on that subject on that occasion. The debate was in fact between John Dickinson and John Adams.'

"Speaking of the indications of discontent in France, he said, monarchy must come down in the Old World, which, sooner or later, must submit to the representative system. Indeed, that it was now nothing to what it was formerly, and, as light and knowledge increased, it must be ameliorated. He considered the French Revolution as having tended greatly to impede the improvement in the condition of mankind. Before that event the old governments were everywhere gradually growing better. The severity of the ancient *régime* was softening; torture and the Inquisition were abolished except in Spain, and there existed but as the shadow of what they once were. But that tempest fell upon Europe, and produced such terror everywhere that the natural progress of the principles of liberty was checked. Those terrors were, however, now dissipating, and the ancient prejudices and influences must yield to the effect of learning and the general diffusion of knowledge in the world."

During the winter of 1820 the public mind of the whole country was agitated by the discussion of the question whether or not Missouri should be admitted into the Union with a constitution making slavery one of its organic institutions. This is not the place, even had I the time and space, to enter into the philosophy or the facts of that momentous transaction. The people of the North were brought into unwonted unanimity by the imminence of this threatening peril. Democrats, as well as Federalists, were of one mind, with scarcely an exception, as to the fatal nature of the concession demanded by the Slave States. Had all the Senators and Representatives of the Northern States truly represented the opinions of their constituents, an effectual stand might have been then made against the encroaching arrogance of the slave power. While this mighty question hung in the balance, public meetings were held all over New England to throw the weight of public opinion into the Northern scale, and Boston was not behindhand in speaking her sense of what the crisis demanded. A great meeting was held in Faneuil Hall, at which it may well be believed Mr. Quincy assisted. He was one of a large committee, taken from both political parties, to report an address on the subject, which was written by Daniel Webster chiefly if not entirely. It was small satisfaction to Mr. Quincy to see his prophecies as to the consequences of Jefferson's *coup d'état* of 1803 so soon begin to be fulfilled, — a beginning only of their accomplishment which reached over the next forty years.

The following letter from John Randolph was in reply to one introducing to his acquaintance Mr. Edward Dowse of Dedham, who served during the first session of that famous Congress as the Representative of his District. Mr. Dowse had married Mr. Quincy's maternal aunt, Hannah Phillips. They left Boston at the time of the yellow-fever in 1797, and, going to Dedham for a few weeks, they remained there for the rest of their lives. Mrs. Dowse's sister, Mrs. Sarah Shaw, widow of Major Samuel Shaw of the Revolutionary army, lived with them. These ladies were twins, and so closely resembled each other as to be undistinguishable the one from the other by their nearest friends, excepting by a slight difference of dress. The country-people round about were accustomed to speak of the three as "Mr. Dowse and his two wives"! Yet they never spoke of them but with love and gratitude, for their bounty was only limited by their means, and their charity neither began nor stayed at home. Any life of my father would be imperfect without a tribute of affectionate remembrance to these beloved relatives, and especially any written by me, who am daily reminded of them by the roof that shelters me, by the trees they planted, and by the river that they loved. They were childless, and he was the only son of their only sister, and consequently his relation to them was all but filial, and they well supplied to his children the grandparents these had never known. They and he were perhaps drawn yet nearer to each other by some sense of a common injustice. His grandfather and their father, William Phillips, of whom I have spoken in my earlier chapters, influenced by the desire of keeping together the large fortune he had accumulated, bequeathed it almost entire to his only son, leaving to my father, the only representative of one of his daughters, absolutely nothing, and but a very moderate provision to Mrs. Dowse and Mrs. Shaw. His son, William Phillips, for many years Lieutenant-Governor, and noted for his large munificence, public and private, in some degree made amends to his sisters for this distinction in his favor, and yet more liberally from time to time during his lifetime and by his will to his nephew, who always rendered to him the duty and service of an affectionate son. Mrs. Dowse and Mrs. Shaw did not change to the end of their long lives the fashion of the dress of their prime, and they remained until long into this century in look and manners examples of the gentlewomen of the pre-Revolutionary period. Mr. Dowse had been much about the world, and was one of the first Americans who engaged in the trade with China, after it was opened to us by the Peace of 1783. For many years, however, he lived in retirement at Dedham, exercising the most abundant hospitality to his friends, and relieving all the poverty and suffering he could find out. No one who ever knew him could forget the eager cordiality of his manners, and the almost passionate demonstrativeness of his temperament. When I was a lad, and fresh from the first of many readings of Fielding's epic novel, I used to liken him to Mr. Allworthy; and yet there was an enthusiasm and simplicity of character about him — though he had known cities and the manners of many men, though he had seen Garrick and Foote, and heard Burke and Sheridan — which savored rather of Parson Adams, that still more exquisite creation of "the prose Homer of human nature." But it is time to return to John Randolph's letter, from which the revered and beloved images it casually conjured up have lured me away.

Mr. Randolph to Mr. Quincy.

"Washington, December 18, 1819.

"Sir: — I am under a threefold obligation to you for the pleasure of your letter, of Mr. Dowse's acquaintance, and the perusal of your lively and interesting address. I take them in the order of succession; and this obligation would have been earlier acknowledged but for my having been obliged to go the next day to Baltimore, whence I have just returned. The morning after its receipt I devoted to the reading of your address to the Massachusetts Agricultural Society, by which I was at once instructed and entertained, and had my hand on the goose-quill to express my thanks to the writer, when one of the harpies that flit about these regions, and which neither Virgil nor I need describe to you, 'soused down' upon me and made my time his prey. I say *his*, for this vampyre bat — neither bird nor beast in political zoölogy — was of the masculine gender.

"If I knew anything, I would communicate it to you, but I find myself as raw as if I had been just catched in the backwoods and caged for a legislator.

"Yesterday I had the pleasure to hear of you through our mutual friend, Mr. Bleecker.

. . . . .

"I am, sir, your obliged and most obedient friend and servant,

"John Randolph of Roanoke.

"P. S. My sight has so failed me that I can hardly read or write. I do not distinctly see a single character traced by my pen.

"Qu. Address p. 9, pyramidically or pyramidally?"

[N. B. Either spelling is correct.]

The excellent Mr. Dowse, however, had one defect in his almost perfect character; —

"Yet one fault he had, but that was a *thumper!*"

He was *a Democrat*, — a Democrat of the Democrats! Considering that he and my father held such diametrically opposite opinions on points which they both regarded as vital to the best interests of their country, and this with all the earnestness of temperaments of extraordinary ardor, it is honorable to them both that this divergence of politics never divided them from one another personally, or abated the warmth of their mutual friendship. Mr. Dowse held very different opinions of Mr. Jefferson from those Mr. Quincy entertained. They had known each other personally, — I believe, abroad, — and it is probable that Mr. Dowse was not unaffected by the personal influence of which Mr. Jefferson had so large a gift. At any rate, he was a personal and political admirer of that renowned leader, and they had interchanged friendly offices with one another. I have in my possession a mighty punch-bowl bearing Mr. Jefferson's cipher and his famous motto, "REBELLION TO TYRANTS IS OBEDIENCE TO GOD," which was part of a dinner-set which Mr. Dowse had had made for him, at his request, in Canton, when he was Secretary of State. Mr. Dowse having been unduly delayed in China, Mr. Jefferson had been obliged to provide himself with another service. Mr. Dowse refused to allow his friend to take the superfluous set off his hands, which he was entirely willing to do, and found a purchaser for it in a gentleman of Boston, whom the cipher suited, and who did not object to the motto. The punch-bowl and a pair of pitchers he retained *in rei memoriam*. To his consistent adherence to the Democratic party in the midst of social surroundings of a strongly Federal tendency, Mr. Dowse undoubtedly owed his nomination to Congress, and his winter in Washington that memorable year, to which he always recurred as the most delightful he had ever spent, for personally and socially he was a great favorite there. He was deeply impressed with the vital importance of the business which absorbed the thoughts of Congress and the nation. "I shall never regret having come to Washington," he wrote to his wife, "because it has given me an opportunity to exert my best efforts, however feeble, to prevent the extension of slavery in our country." I will indulge myself with inserting a few extracts from this domestic correspondence, as alike honorable to his clearness of insight and his consistent love of liberty, and curious as contemporary records of an actor in a passage of history so full of fate.

"*December* 20, 1819. — I spent an hour at the President's house last evening, in pleasant conversation, Mrs. Monroe becoming, as it were, at once, an old acquaintance. She is a New York lady, — a very handsome woman, elegant, easy, and affable in her manners. The President invited me to dine with him next Friday, and mentioned he intended to invite the foreign ministers."

Mr. Monroe was a former acquaintance of Mr. Dowse, and had spent the night before entering Boston, in July, 1817, at his house in Dedham.

"*January* 8, 1820. — I am on one of the committees, and have no leisure left, unless I forego the debates in the House, where are displayed such powers, such eloquence, as at least rivals the British Parliament. I confess (and it shows the power of prejudice to beguile the understanding) that I have never properly appreciated our friend Quincy. He is here spoken of with admiration, and his last letter to me on the Missouri question delights all his friends. In political wisdom on this question he is inferior to no one. Such men as he ought to be in public life.

"There is here a great assemblage of talent on the floor of Congress, — some who might emulate the Athenian orator, whose 'resistless eloquence wielded at will that fierce democratie.' To-morrow comes on the great question of the Missouri Territory, the people of which are sufficiently numerous to become a State, and claim to be admitted as such; and they also claim the right of holding slaves. The question will be productive of much zeal, not to say animosity, on both sides.

"I wish you could be present sometimes, and hear John Randolph's wit. It is the most delicate, and, at the same time, the keenest.

. . . . .

"If Quincy was here he would be of great service to us on the great question of the Missouri Territory. To be an able statesman in such a government as ours, a man should commence his career early in life. The Southern people have a great preponderancy of talent against us.

. . . .

"*January* 26. — Yesterday began a sort of skirmishing on the Missouri business. This preparatory manœuvring will to-day probably lead on the shock of battle. The question is undoubtedly of immense importance. On one side, the passions, as well as the present and apparent interests, of the Southern people, are deeply engaged; and, to my sorrow, I perceive that they have drawn over some of our Yankees. The cause of humanity, religion, and sound policy is the motive, I firmly believe, which influences the other.

. . . .

February 5. — Missouri, Missouri, engages all attention. Scarcely ever was so great a question agitated before a human tribunal. A host of talents is brought into the field. In the Senate, things have gone against us deplorably, owing to the defection of our Yankees. For slaves, twenty-seven; against slavery in Missouri, sixteen. I am rejoiced that Otis is on our side. The leading members of the Senate are now spectators in our House, where they find themselves surpassed, I suspect, not only in numbers, but in eloquence. I wish Quincy was here to stem the torrent.

. . . .

"I have thought that the oratorical and parliamentary talents were possessed almost exclusively by the slave-holding States. But to my great joy I find it is not so. There are good men of great minds and acquirements on our side, and it fills me with delightful reflections, a kind of awe at the real grandeur of the human character, to find it capable of such expansion.

. . . . .

"If sound policy, if reason, if religion, if virtue, can ever successfully combat against the love of money, — the sole root of all this evil, — then shall we come off victorious in this great Missouri question.

"Randolph finished his speech yesterday, not much, I suspect, to his own satisfaction. He said his nerves were unstrung, and his bodily and mental powers in a state of prostration; and so they appeared to be. Not all *his* talents are adequate to sustain the cause he has embarked in.

. . . . .

"As to putting Maine and Missouri together, in my opinion it was a jockeying trick, just worthy of ostlers in a livery-stable; and I suspect Clay and Holmes were at the bottom of it.

. . . . .

"*March* 3, 1820. — Slavery is allowed of as far as thirty-six and a half degrees of latitude. Some people think the Missourians themselves will interdict slavery from their new State. It would be their present glory, and permanent happiness, if they should do so. I feel most wofully mortified and cast down at the result of our Missouri Bill. For slavery, ninety; against it, eighty-seven. Four of our side stayed out at the final taking of the question; and four more went over and joined the slaveholders, which operated as equivalent to eight against us. The whole counted as twelve against us, who ought to have been for us. Whether this proceeded from weakness or treachery, I will not pretend to say. People talk pretty much as if this had been brought about by sly, underhand Executive influence. I do not pretend to judge, or to form any opinion about it; but if there were strong reasons to think so, Monroe ought to be turned out of the next Presidency. I consider our nation now as disgraced in the eyes of the civilized nations of the earth. We had it in our power to stop the progress of slavery, and *we chose to let it go on*." *

At the second session of the General Court, January, 1821, the Speaker of the House, Mr. Elijah H. Mills of Northampton, was elected United States Senator, and Mr. Quincy was chosen Speaker in his stead. For this office he was eminently fitted by his long parliamentary experience, and by his peculiar talent for the despatch of business. The next May he was re-elected to the Speakership, but resigned it before his term of office expired to take the post of Judge of the Municipal Court of Boston. This was a jury court for the trial of all offences not capital committed in the town of Boston. Its jurisdiction was exclusively criminal. During the short time he remained on the bench, he manifested, not only great discrimination and humanity in the administration of criminal justice, but a facility in mastering and applying the principles of law to the facts in evidence somewhat remarkable in one who had been so long withdrawn from professional life. The most important case that came before him was that of Joseph T. Buckingham, editor of the Galaxy, a weekly paper conducted with great spirit and much ability, for a libel on John N. Maffitt, a notorious Methodist minister of that day, and father of the notorious Rebel corsair of

* Mr. Dowse resigned his seat in Congress at the end of the long session, and spent the rest of his life at Dedham, where he died in 1828, in his seventy-third year.

the same name. This case excited a very general interest, especially among the religious public, whose displeasure Mr. Buckingham had incurred by very great plainness of speech as to some prominent members of it. Mr. Quincy ruled, that a defendant under indictment for libel might be allowed to prove that his allegations were true, and that they were published with good motives and for justifiable ends. He argued that the common-law doctrine, that the truth could not be admitted in evidence under an indictment for libel, — or, as usually put, that "the greater the truth, the greater the libel," — was overruled by the express provision of the Constitution of the State, which made a specific reservation for its citizens of the liberty of the press, — a liberty unknown, as such, to the common law, — and declared that all parts of that law repugnant to that liberty are not to be considered law under the Constitution. Under this ruling evidence was admitted to prove the truth of the charges against Maffitt, and Mr. Buckingham was acquitted. This was the first time that such a ruling had been made in the case of an ordinary indictment for a libel on a private individual, and it excited much discussion and no little censure at the time. But Mr. Quincy's law of libel has prevailed, and is now the established rule in this country and in England.

In the year 1820 my father left the house in Summer Street for the one on the corner of Hamilton Place and Tremont Street, which was given to him by his uncle, Lieutenant-Governor Phillips, where he lived until he removed to Cambridge in 1829. The house was not, in itself, so large or so good as that he left, but its situation on the Common, commanding a view of the distant country and the western sky, made it a much more agreeable one to live in. It was a change in every respect satisfactory to himself and his family, and nine very happy winters were spent under that roof.

CHAPTER XVI.

1823 – 1828.

Mr. Quincy's Views and Acts as to Poverty and Crime. — Nomination for First Mayor of Boston. — Party Complications. — Elected the Second Year. — The House of Industry. — Of Correction. — Of Reformation for Juvenile Offenders. — Improvement in the Police. — The Fire Department. — Schools. — The High School for Girls. — Faneuil Hall Market-House. — Visits of Lafayette. — Life of Josiah Quincy, Junior. — Visitors. — Fourth of July Oration. — Death of John Adams. — Correspondence. — Randolph's last Letter. — Mr. Quincy as a Municipal Magistrate. — Loses his Election. — His Address on leaving the Office.

THE great social problems which have not yet ceased to vex political philosophers — how best to provide for the poor and to treat the vicious and the criminal members of society — had long and deeply engaged Mr. Quincy's thoughtful consideration. The growth of population demanded some change in the old almshouse system, which had come down from the Colonial times, and which answered sufficiently well for the early days when paupers were few. The town of Boston, though its population amounted to but little more than forty thousand souls, was closely built, and the almshouse in its heart ceased to be suitable or sufficient for the growing necessities of the place. Soon after entering the General Court in 1820, Mr. Quincy moved for an inquiry into the subject of pauperism, and was made chairman of the committee raised for the purpose. Returns were called for from all the towns in the State, giving their methods and experience in the matter of providing for the poor. From such returns he made a report, submitted the next January, which condensed the experience of England and Massachusetts as to the various methods of dealing with pauperism. This report was printed and circulated, by order of the Legislature, throughout the State, and I believe the improved system of treating the dependent poor, — especially the institution of town farms, — which has replaced the old ways, was greatly advanced by the distribution of that report, if it did not absolutely date therefrom. The next May Mr. Quincy was appointed by the town chairman of a committee on the same subject, and, in pursuance of the recommendations of the report he made to the town, the committee was authorized to provide a House of Industry, where the able-bodied poor could support themselves in part, and where the impotent from age or infirmity could be comfortably lodged and cared for. A tract of land was purchased in South Boston, then a thinly inhabited district, and a suitable building erected. Like all changes, even for the better, this one met with its share of opposition. The Overseers of the Poor, a body elected by the town, strenuously resisted this change in the disposition of the paupers in their charge, and it was not fully completed for several years, in consequence of their persistent opposition. Popular prejudice was aroused against this innovation on the ancient usages. It was pronounced cruel to compel the poor to leave the town in which they had lived all their lives, and the paupers themselves were almost ready to rise in rebellion against their oppressors. And so kind and gentle was the spirit in which those unfortunates were treated in those days, that none were colonized to South Boston excepting with their own consent, while the town government lasted. Some of these sturdy beggars, with a spirit worthy of a better cause, resolutely refused to change their quarters, declaring "that they had not gone into the almshouse to work"!

Mr. Quincy's experience as a criminal judge had made him consider the bearings of poverty upon the welfare of society yet more deeply, as well as those of vice and crime with which he was called upon more immediately to deal. In March, 1822, in his charge to the grand jury, he treated at large of these three topics, and showed their relations to one another in a very lucid manner, and indicated those reforms in the treatment of the criminal classes, such as classification and separation in penitentiaries, and the substitution of private for public executions, which have since been almost universally adopted in the Northern States.

The intelligent zeal he had shown in the matter of these much-needed reforms, together with his well-tried integrity and activity, suggested him to those inhabitants of the town who were the most conversant with its municipal affairs as the fittest person to organize the new form of government, after it had been determined to exchange the old popular rule by town meetings for one by a civic corporation. This change Mr. Quincy resisted by speech and pen as long as there was any chance of defeating it. He believed the pure democracy of the town meeting more suited to the character of the people of New England, and less liable to corruption and abuse, than a more compact government. But his opposition was vain; the city charter was granted by the Legislature, and accepted by the people, and he presided on the 28th of March, 1822, as moderator of the last town meeting ever held in Faneuil Hall. A body of the most substantial citizens, and the most experienced in conducting the town affairs, invited him to stand as candidate for the office of Mayor, on no party grounds whatever, but solely on account of his eminent fitness for the work of organizing the new government. He accepted their invitation, never dreaming of the office being made one of the prizes of party. The Federal leaders, however, did not take this view of the matter, and they had arranged it that Mr. Harrison Gray Otis, who just then resigned his seat in the United States Senate, should be the first Mayor of Boston, as the stepping-stone, it was believed, to the Governorship of the State. They accordingly nominated him, and Mr. Quincy was placed in a most delicate position, between what he owed to his friends whose nomination he had accepted, and his obligations to his party, which had set up a candidate of its own. This proceeding of the Federal managers did not please the citizens who had made Mr. Quincy their first choice, and they would not release him from his promise; and although his most valued personal friends and his most honored relatives urged him to withdraw, and so prevent a breach in the Federal party, he felt himself bound to stand by the men who stood by him. At the election he would have been chosen, beyond a doubt, had not the Democrats, the night before, set up Mr. Thomas L. Winthrop, without the knowledge of that gentleman, and to his great displeasure, which drew off votes enough to defeat the election.

Mr. Quincy had much the largest vote, and lacked only about a hundred of an absolute majority. He gladly seized the opportunity of withdrawing his name, and, Mr. Otis's friends doing the same thing by him, Mr. John Phillips was elected at the next choice. Mr. Phillips retiring at the end of his year, Mr. Quincy was elected his successor without material opposition.

On the 1st of May, 1823, he was inaugurated as the second Mayor of Boston, in Faneuil Hall, and entered at once upon the discharge of his new duties with characteristic activity and zeal. During the mayoralty of his predecessor, the administration of the affairs of the city had not differed materially from that of the town it had superseded. Mr. Phillips was a man of excellent abilities, sound judgment, and sterling integrity. He retained his seat in the State Senate and his place as its President, and performed the duties of his civic office in the spirit and after the fashion of a faithful chairman of the Selectmen under the town government. Mr. Phillips was strictly my father's contemporary, and perhaps his most intimate and valued friend from boyhood. His death, which occurred very suddenly in June, 1823, was severely felt and deeply deplored by my father, as the heaviest loss he had met with since that of his mother. Mr. Phillips had been in the public service of Massachusetts, in one station or another, for almost the whole of his mature life, and the State had no more trusted and respected citizen. He will be known, however, to the present generation, and hereafter, chiefly as the father of his celebrated son, Mr. Wendell Phillips.

Mr. Quincy's first step towards the establishment of a more vigorous administration of affairs was to claim the privilege of doing the chief of the work himself. He made himself chairman of all the committees of the Board of Aldermen, and took the laboring oar into his own hand. The opposition of the Overseers of the Poor to the removal of the paupers from the almshouse in Boston, the condition of which had grown to be absolutely disgraceful to the city, prevented the completion of that favorite measure of his until 1825, when it was finally effected. The evils attendant on the promiscuous mingling of the honest poor with rogues and vagabonds were mitigated by the establishment of the first House of Correction, properly so called, in Boston, during the first year of his mayoralty. A building in the jail-yard was used at first for this purpose, but the establishment was afterwards removed to South Boston, near the House of Industry. The separation, more important yet, of the young convicts from the old in places of penal restraint, led to the establishment of a House of Reformation for Juvenile Offenders, the results of which, both direct, in the large proportion of young persons who were saved to society by its means, and indirect, by the encouragement which its successful experiment has given to the system elsewhere, have been of the happiest nature. These institutions were long regarded as models in their several kinds, and Mr. Quincy always looked upon them with peculiar satisfaction as being largely creations of his own. The House of Reformation for Juvenile Offenders excited the particular admiration of Messrs. Beaumont and De Tocqueville, when they visited Boston in the course of the inquiries with which they were charged by the French government. They expressed an earnest wish that such an institution could be established in France; "but," M. de Tocqueville added, "it would be essential to its success that Boston should lend to it the first superintendent and organizer of her own institution," — the Rev. Eleazar M. P. Wells, D.D., whose life has been one long service of the unfortunate and suffering classes.

The internal police of the city was another matter which called for the anxious attention of the new Mayor. The maintenance of order, the abatement of nuisances, the protection of the public health, the suppression of impudent vice, and the swift and sure overtaking of crime, devolved upon him, and with no sufficient force to fulfil these demands of his office. The policing of cities was very imperfectly understood in this country, or in England, until the reform initiated by Sir Robert Peel. Mr. Quincy had to work with such instruments as law and custom afforded him, and he used them to the best advantage. The entire police force then consisted of a constabulary twenty-four strong, and a body of eighty night-watchmen, of whom not more than eighteen were on duty at the same time! It seems hardly credible that a city of between fifty and sixty thousand inhabitants could have been kept in peace and safety by so small a force, and I apprehend that it was without a parallel in this country or in Europe. But the population of Boston at that time was singularly homogeneous. The great Irish and German emigrations had not then set in. The city was eminently English in its character and appearance, and probably no town of its size in England had a population of such unmixed English descent as the Boston of forty years ago. It was *Anglis ipsis Anglior,* — more English than the English themselves. The inhabitants of New England at that time were descended, with scarcely any admixture of foreign blood, from the Puritan emigration of the seventeenth century. They kept the peace and maintained order themselves, without the need of guardians to take care of them. The number of constables and watchmen was not increased during Mr. Quincy's mayoralty, and all he could contribute towards their efficiency was care in the selection of the men, and the appointment of a competent head, under the style of the City Marshal.

Still, quiet and well-ordered as Boston was, in general, there was one disgraceful district which had set at defiance for years the attempts of the town authorities to reduce it to order. Infamous houses were openly maintained, the resort of the worst part of the population. Murders had notoriously been committed there, and it was believed that by no means all had been brought to light. The head of the old town police told Mr. Quincy that this nuisance could not be abated without a military force. No man's life would be safe that should attempt it. Mr. Quincy asked him if vice and villany were too strong for the police; to which he replied: "I think so. At least, it has long been so." "There shall be at least an attempt to execute the laws," said the Mayor; and he proceeded to make it. On examining the terms of the City Charter, he found that he had not the powers under it necessary for a summary suppression of this nest of vice and villany, so he was obliged to act only in his capacity of a Justice of the Peace throughout the Commonwealth. His first step was to issue a warrant for the arrest of the fiddlers who inspired the orgies of the dance-houses, under an old Provincial statute never repealed, aimed at those troublers of the night-watches; and his next, to take away the licenses of all the tippling-shops and bar-rooms in the region round about. Deprived at once of music and of drink, the enemy succumbed to the authority of law without resistance. The nuisance was thoroughly abated, and, though vice might not have lost half its mischief, it was stripped of much of its grossness, and public decency was no more insulted by its flaunting insolence. That part of the town is now covered with the houses of respectable and wealthy citizens, many of whom probably do not know to whose heritage they have succeeded. On another occasion a riot was proceeding in another part of the town, for the purpose of destroying some houses of ill-fame. The constabulary were entirely insufficient for the work to be done, and Mr. Quincy, casting about for a proper force, bethought him of the draymen, or truckmen as they were then denominated. I believe the long narrow vehicle on two wheels, for the conveyance of heavy burdens, called "a truck," is now extinct, but it was then the chief one in use; and the truckmen, generally owning their horses and trucks, were a very substantial and respectable, as well as a burly and resolute set of men. A word to one or two of the leaders among them brought the brotherhood to the aid of the Mayor, who, placing himself at their head, and making the proper strategic dispositions, swept the rioters out of the street by mere force of muscle, and sent them about their business.

Another department of urgent importance to the city, which it was Mr. Quincy's good fortune to put upon a better footing than ever before, was the Fire Department. This existed in a very primitive form when he came into office. Engines were provided by the town, manned by voluntary companies, and officered by fire-wards elected by the people. The engines were of small power, and at a fire depended entirely for their supply of water upon fire-buckets passed along lines of volunteer spectators reaching to the nearest pump. It was the theoretical right of the fire-wards to compel all and singular they met to fall into the line, and tradition said they had been known in times past to knock recusants down with the pole which was the ensign of their office. But persuasion was the only influence used within the memory of man, and the scene at a fire was one of the least en couraging manifestations possible of the democratic principle reduced to practice. It was assumed to be the duty of every citizen to rush to the scene of action at the first stroke of the fire-bell, carrying with him his buckets, and perhaps a bag for the rescue of valuables from the flames. And, as a general rule, the confusion was great in proportion to the number who came with the best dispositions to be of service, but who too generally were only in the way. The single mind of a commander-in-chief, as necessary at a fire as in a battle, was wanting, and consequently even the imperfect means at hand were not turned to the best account. New York and Philadelphia were both of them in advance of Boston in this particular, and Mr. Quincy, as the magistrate charged with the safety of the city, was greatly desirous of adopting the latest improvements for putting out fires. But he had most determined opposition to encounter. The old ways had been good enough for their fathers, and why not for them? The introduction of hose for the supply of the engines was ridiculed, and denounced as absurd, and almost wicked. The purchase of engines in New York and Philadelphia was an affront to the mechanics of Boston. The cisterns or reservoirs which were provided at convenient points to make sure of a sufficiency of water were "the inverted monuments of Quincy's extravagance." It was not without difficulty that the necessary powers for a reorganization of the department were obtained from the Legislature, and, when obtained, the inhabitants, whose consent was to be first had, sanctioned the change by a majority of only about a hundred. The system thus introduced, though far enough from the admirable one which now exists, soon commended itself to the entire community by the greater sense of security which it inspired, of which the fact that the insurance companies at once, of their own accord, reduced their rates by twenty per cent, was a satisfactory proof.

The circumstance of the greatest local interest in Mr. Quincy's municipal administration was the building of the Faneuil Hall

Market-house. The conveniences for the provisioning of the city were at that time of a very limited description, and one of the first considerations which occurred to him after entering on his office was, how these could be enlarged and improved without great expense to the city. From first to last he encountered opposition in every shape, — of the selfish interests of the property-holders whom it was necessary to buy out, of the parties whose vested interests in the old state of things were endangered, of demagogues who were ready to lay hold of any occasion of persuading the people that they were in danger of ruin, and of cautious citizens who dreaded the creation of an unmanageable city debt. I have not the space, nor would it be generally interesting at this day, to trace the whole progress of this remarkable transaction; and I cannot state the result better or more compactly than he has done it himself in his Municipal History of Boston.* "A granite market-house, two stories high, five hundred and thirty-five feet long, fifty feet wide, covering twenty-seven thousand feet of land, was erected at the cost of one hundred and fifty thousand dollars. Six new streets were opened, and a seventh greatly enlarged, including one hundred and sixty-seven thousand square feet of land; and flats, docks, and wharf-rights obtained of the extent of one hundred and forty-two thousand square feet. All this was accomplished in the centre of a populous city, not only without any tax, debt, or burden upon its pecuniary resources, but with large permanent additions to its real and productive property." The land made by filling up the dock on a part of which the Market-house stands sold for enough to pay the whole expense of the operation, while the taxable property of the city was increased by the value of the warehouses built upon it. It was thought not inappropriate by many citizens of that day, that the building should bear the name of the magistrate whose pains and skill had virtually made a free gift of it to the city. But this suggestion was overruled, and his name given only to the large hall over the centre of the Market-house. But I believe that the people to this day know

* A Municipal History of the Town and City of Boston during two Centuries, from September 17, 1630, to September 17, 1830, p. 74.

and speak of it only as "The Quincy Market," a derivation of the title which its contriver regarded as much more honorable to himself, as proceeding directly from the sovereign fountain of honor, than if it had been formally conferred.

It is hardly necessary to say that Mr. Quincy gave great attention to the condition and improvement of the public schools, and I believe they had never been in a better state than they were during his official term. The only innovation which was attempted in his time upon the old customs of the town was an experimental High School for girls, which had a brief trial of a year or two, and was then abandoned. The suggestion of the establishment of a school for carrying the education of girls to as advanced a point as that of boys in the Latin and High Schools, was one which naturally commended itself to the general public, and the experiment was fairly tried under the mastership of Mr. Ebenezer Bailey, a teacher of great experience and skill. In one sense it only succeeded too well. The number of candidates fit for admission was entirely beyond the capacity of the school-house at the start, with the prospect of growing still larger every year. And in one important respect the plan was found not to work as its projectors had expected it would. The majority of the girls who could pass the preliminary examination were found to come from the wealthier classes, who could purchase for them special instruction, or were competent to afford it themselves. More than half the candidates came from private schools. Without going into the details of the question, the practical objections to the scheme seemed insuperable, and it was abandoned. This conclusion of the whole matter gave rise to great discontent, and brought much obloquy upon Mr. Quincy, who was known to regard the plan as impracticable, although the city government, as a body, consented to the final action. He submitted patiently to be the object of this popular injustice, being fully persuaded in his own mind that the course the matter took was right and necessary. And his judgment on this point was confirmed by the fact that the scheme was not revived until after many years, when it took the form of the present admirable Normal School, of which Boston has just reason to be proud.

The visit of General Lafayette to the United States occurred during Mr. Quincy's mayoralty, and it was his good fortune to invite and welcome him to the hospitalities of Boston. It was a season of general joy, unbroken by a whisper of dissent, in which both political parties, and every religious sect, and all conditions of men, united in expressing their gratitude to the early friend of their country. As soon as it was known that General Lafayette proposed coming to America, the City Council of Boston directed the Mayor to invite him to land in their city, from which he had sailed when he took his departure from the country more than forty years before. The following correspondence accordingly took place between them:—

Mr. Quincy to General Lafayette.

"United States of America, Boston, March 20, 1824.

"Sir:—Your intention to visit the United States has been made known to its citizens by the proceedings of their national Legislature. The city of Boston shares in the universal pleasure which the expectation of so interesting an event has diffused; but it has causes of satisfaction peculiarly its own. Many of its inhabitants recollect, and all have heard, of your former residence in this metropolis,—of the delight with which you were greeted on your second visit to this country,—and of the acclamations of a grateful multitude which attended you, when sailing from this harbor, on your last departure from the United States,—and also of that act of munificence by which in later times you extended the hand of relief in their distress. These circumstances have impressed upon the inhabitants of this city a vivid recollection of your person, and a peculiar interest in your character, endearing you to their remembrance by sentiments of personal gratitude, as well as by that sense of national obligation with which the citizens of the United States are universally penetrated. With feelings of this kind the City Council of Boston, in accordance with the general wish of their constituents, have directed me to address this letter to you, and to express the hope, that, should it comport with your convenience, you would do them the honor, on your ensuing visit to the United States, to disembark in this city, and to communicate the assurance that no event could possibly be more grateful to its inhabitants,—that nowhere could you meet with a more cordial welcome,—that you could find nowhere hearts more capable of appreciating your early zeal and sacrifices in the cause of American freedom, or more ready to acknowledge and honor that characteristic uniformity of virtue with which, through a long life, and in scenes of unexampled difficulty and danger, you have steadfastly maintained the cause of an enlightened civil liberty, in both hemispheres.

"Very respectfully, I am your obedient servant,

"JOSIAH QUINCY."

GENERAL LAFAYETTE TO MR. QUINCY.

"PARIS, May 26, 1824.

"SIR: — Amidst the new and high marks of benevolence the people of the United States and their representatives have lately deigned to confer upon me, I am proud and happy to recognize those particular sentiments of the citizens of Boston which have blessed and delighted the first years of my public career, and the grateful sense of which has ever since been my reward and support.

"I joyfully anticipate the day, not very remote, thank God, when I may revisit the glorious cradle of American, and in future, I hope, of universal liberty. Your so honorable and gratifying invitation would have been directly complied with, in the case to which you please to allude. But while I profoundly feel the honor intended by the offer of a national ship, I hope I shall incur no blame by the determination I have taken to embark as soon as it is in my power on board a private vessel. Whatever port I shall first attain, I shall with the same eagerness hasten to Boston, and present its beloved, revered inhabitants, as I have the honor to offer it to you, sir, with the homage of my affectionate gratitude and devoted respect.

"LAFAYETTE."

Lafayette arrived in New York on the 16th of August, 1824, and four days afterwards left that city for Boston, and entered upon the triumphal progress in which he passed through the land. He arrived at the house of his old companion in arms, Governor Eustis, on the evening of the 23d, where he passed the night. The next morning he was escorted by a cavalcade of citizens to the city, at the boundary of which he was met by Mr. Quincy, who received him with the following address: —

"GENERAL LAFAYETTE: — The citizens of Boston welcome you on your return to the United States, — mindful of your early zeal in the cause of American Independence, grateful for your distinguished share in the perils and glories of its achievement. When, urged by a generous sympathy, you first landed on these shores, you found a people engaged in an arduous and eventful struggle for liberty, with apparently inadequate means, and amidst dubious omens.

"After the lapse of nearly half a century, you find the same people prosperous beyond all hope or precedent, — their liberty secure, sitting in its strength, without fear and without reproach.

"In your youth you joined the standard of three millions of people, raised in an unequal and uncertain conflict. In your advanced age you return and are met by ten millions of people, their descendants, whose hearts throng hither to greet your approach and to rejoice in it."

Here Mr. Quincy was interrupted by the shouts of the multitude around, and, after pausing until the tumult had in some degree subsided, he thus continued: —

"This is not the movement of a turbulent populace, excited by the fresh laurels of some recent conqueror. It is a grave, moral, intellectual impulse. A whole people in the enjoyment of freedom as perfect as the condition of our nature permits recur, with gratitude increasing with the daily increasing sense of their blessings, to the memory of those who, by their labors and in their blood, laid the foundation of our liberties.

"Your name, sir, — the name of Lafayette, — is associated with the most perilous and most glorious periods of our Revolution, — with the imperishable name of Washington, and of that numerous host of heroes which adorn the proudest archives of American history, and are engraven in indelible traces on the hearts of the whole American people.

"Accept, then, sir, in the sincere spirit in which it is offered, this simple tribute to your virtues. Again, sir, the citizens of Boston bid you welcome to the cradle of American Independence, and to scenes consecrated with the blood shed by the earliest martyrs in its cause."

General Lafayette then made the following reply: —

"The emotions of gratitude and love which I have been accustomed to feel on my entering this city have ever been mingled with a sense of religious reverence for the cradle of American, and, let us hope it will be hereafter said, of universal liberty. What must be, sir, my feelings, at the blessed moment when, after so long an absence, I find myself again surrounded by the good citizens of Boston — when I am so affectionately, so honorably welcomed, not only by my old friends, but by several successive generations, — when I can witness the prosperity, the immense improvements, that have been the just reward of a noble struggle, virtuous morals, and truly republican institutions!

"I beg of you all, beloved citizens of Boston, to accept the respectful and warm thanks of a heart which has, for nearly half a century, been particularly devoted to your illustrious city."

The procession wound slowly through the shouting streets, every window, every balcony, and every roof being alive with eager spectators. "But where is the *mob?*" demanded the General of Mr. Quincy, who had left his own carriage, and taken his place by the side of Lafayette in his barouche, after the formalities of reception were finished. "This is all we have to show you, sir, in the way of mob." Lafayette declared afterwards, that the crowd which greeted him in the streets of Boston appeared to him "like a picked population out of the whole human race." It was a delicious day, — clear, cool, and calm, — in perfect accordance with the joyful and brilliant scene. Lafayette passed through the principal streets, and between rows of the school-children on the Common, to the State-House, where he was officially received by Governor Eustis, and thence to the house making the corner of Park and Beacon Streets, facing on Beacon Street. It was then a club-house, and it was offered to the city by the club for the purposes of this great hospitality. The city had the house completely furnished and provided with a proper staff of servants, and put their guest into his own house; and within those walls he was the host, and they the guests.

In the evening, after a great civic dinner at the Exchange Coffee-house, he visited Mr. and Mrs. Quincy at their town house in Hamilton Place, where a party of friends were invited to meet him. Mrs. Quincy received him with the grace and sweetness which marked her manners; and a young friend of the family, a gentleman of great refinement and sensibility, declared, thirty years afterwards, that he accounted it one of the felicities of his life that he was present at this introduction, and heard the fitness and elegance of her few words of welcome. This, however, was the second visit he had paid that evening. The first, as was fit, was given to the widow of Governor Hancock, his hostess on his former visits to Boston. As he was passing through the streets that morning, in the midst of all the tumult of welcome, he remembered his old friend, and said to my father, "Pray tell me, is the widow of John Hancock yet alive?" "O yes," was the answer, "and I have no doubt that we shall see her at one of the windows as we pass by." "If you see her, have the goodness to let me know it," replied Lafayette. As they were passing along what is now Tremont Street, fronting the Common, my father espied the venerable dame seated in an honorable post of observation on a balcony overlooking the scene. "There is Hancock's widow, General," said he. "Tell the coachman," said the General, "to draw up opposite the place." This being done, Lafayette rose and saluted her with a profound bow, which she returned by as profound a courtesy, the crowd cheering the pair with great enthusiasm. And hers was the first private house which he entered in Boston.

His reception at Cambridge the next two days — Commencement and the annual celebration of the Phi Beta Kappa Society — was but a continuation of the same warm-hearted welcome. No one who was present on Thursday, when Mr. Everett delivered the Oration before the Society, concluding it with a peroration of welcome to Lafayette, can ever forget the scene. The audience was largely made up of studious and professional men, not usually demonstrative in their ways; but the eloquent words of the orator, and the more eloquent presence of the nation's guest, roused it to the highest pitch of enthusiastic excitement. Tears from eyes unused to weep rolled down furrowed cheeks, and old men, as well as young men and maidens, were fairly taken off their feet by the very tempest and whirlwind of the passion of that glorious hour. On these two days Lafayette had an opportunity of showing that remarkable readiness of mind of his, which, if it were not talent, since it is the fashion to deny this to him, was at least an excellent substitute for it. As a general rule, on occasions of formal receptions, the speeches are written beforehand, and copies exchanged, so that the spontaneousness may be properly prepared. As my father was conducting Lafayette to Cambridge on Commencement morning, they were stopped in Cambridgeport by a deputation of the inhabitants, headed by Judge

Samuel P. P. Fay, on horseback, who made a suitable address of welcome in the name of the citizens of Cambridge. It was an entire surprise, but Lafayette replied with perfect fluency and appropriateness, making all the proper complimentary allusions to the Revolutionary history of the town, in as finished a manner as if he had had a week to write it in. At the dinner of the Phi Beta Kappa Society on Thursday, called up by the drinking of his health with all the honors, he concluded a felicitous speech with a classical compliment to Mr. Everett, as happy — if a trifle hyperbolical — as perhaps was ever made. From the circumstances of the case, all of which I do not now remember, my father was satisfied that it was literally an impromptu. It was to this effect, — "The young American Cicero of to-day, 'Quæ est in hominibus tanta perversitas, ut, inventis frugibus, glande vescantur!'" *

Lafayette always spoke of himself as an American, when referring to the days of the Revolution. One evening at a party my mother said to him, "The American cockade was black and white, was it not, General?" "Yes, madam," he replied, "it was black at first; but when the French came and joined *us*, we added the white in compliment to them!" On the day of his arrival, an old soldier would press through the crowd in the State-House, and cried out, "You don't remember me, General; but I was close to you when we stormed our redoubt at Yorktown." (It will be remembered there were two redoubts to be carried, essential to the success of the movement, one of which was assigned to Lafayette and his American division, and the other to the French troops.) "I was just behind Captain Smith. You remember Captain Smith? He was shot through the head just as he mounted the redoubt." "Ah, yes, yes! I remember," returned Lafayette. "Poor Captain Smith! *But we beat the French! We beat the French!!*"

On Sunday he dined with Mr. Adams at Quincy, and afterwards visited my father's family at his country-seat. "That was not the John Adams I remember!" said he, sadly, — a sentiment which was reciprocated by Mr. Adams, who said, the next time

* Cicero, Orator. Cap. 9.

some one of the family saw him, "That was not the Lafayette that I remember!" It would have been strange if it had been, considering that more than forty years (and such years!) had passed over their heads since they last parted.

Shortly after Lafayette's departure from Boston he introduced two distinguished and interesting persons to my father by letter. The first was Colonel Huger of South Carolina, whose attempt to rescue him from his imprisonment at Olmutz made him doubly interesting just at that time. The letter of introduction is as follows: —

GENERAL LAFAYETTE TO MR. QUINCY.

"NEW YORK, September 20, 1824.

"MY DEAR SIR: — I have been so happy in our intimacy, and so sensible of your kindness to me, that I consider this letter of introduction as an act of gratitude to Colonel Huger, towards whom you know my Olmutz obligation. Be pleased to welcome and present him to my Bostonian friends; both of which I am sure you will do very heartily. Happy I would be to accompany him to Boston, and to find myself again in that dear city; but I am proceeding to the South, and must defer to the next spring the gratification to tell you in person how gratefully and affectionately I am your most sincere friend,

"LAFAYETTE.

"My son and M. Levasseur beg their respects to be presented to you and your family, to whom I request you to offer the affectionate and grateful sentiments which bind me to you, your lady, and children."

I copy from my sister's unpublished memoir of my mother her account of Colonel Huger's visit.

"After Lafayette returned to New York, he wrote to Mr. Quincy, on the 20th of September, to introduce Colonel Huger; in speaking of whom, during his visit, he had said, 'I never saw Huger but for ten minutes; but for ten years his countenance was never absent from my mind.' On the 2d of October a party consisting chiefly of members of the Common Council of Boston dined with Mr. Quincy; and at the name of Colonel Huger, associated with that of Lafayette, every countenance expressed animated interest. Mrs. Quincy, on receiving him, said, 'We all are under obligations to you, Colonel Huger, for your attempt to rescue Lafayette from Olmutz.' 'I only did my duty, madam,' was his reply. 'I considered myself the representative of the young men of America, and acted accordingly. If I have deserved their approbation, it is a full reward.'

"Colonel Huger, in 1824, was about fifty-one years of age, — manly and polished in his personal appearance and address, his countenance and manner indicative of self-command. His conversation marked him as a man of honor and integrity, extensive information, and knowledge of the world; evincing singular modesty respecting his own claims and opinions, and great deference for those of others. In contradicting a statement in the newspapers, that he was in early life acquainted with Lafayette in America, he said: 'When Lafayette first arrived on the coast of Carolina, accompanied by the Baron de Kalb and several officers, they were pursued by British cruisers, and were very anxious to land. My father then resided on North Island; and two of his negroes, being out in a boat late in the evening, were boarded by another boat containing Lafayette and the Baron de Kalb, and were induced to pilot them to my father's house. As the depredations of British vessels caused great alarm, doors and windows were barred against these officers; but when they succeeded in making themselves known, they were hospitably received, and the next day attended to Charleston, on their way to join the American army. I was at that time a child of three years old, and have no recollection of these circumstances, except from hearing them often mentioned by my family.'"

The next day, Sunday, Colonel Huger spent at Quincy with our family, and after dinner he gave us a detailed account of his Olmutz attempt. I well remember the breathless interest with which it was listened to, and could record most of the particulars. But this has been already done in an authentic shape. It is a curious illustration of the slight circumstances on which important matters turn, that had Huger spoken to Lafayette in French instead of English, and said, "Allez à Hoff," and not "Go to Hoff," the escape would have been effected. The necessary arrangements had been made at Hoff for expediting the flight of the prisoner; but Lafayette understood the direction to be "*Go off*," and, taking his way at random, was soon overtaken and carried back to captivity. Colonel Huger, I remember, amused us with an account of the singular privilege he had enjoyed just before, in New York, of seeing himself represented on the stage. It was in a drama, got up to order, entitled "The Castle of Olmutz," in which he was made to be in love with the governor's daughter, who assisted in the evasion.

The other letter of introduction was as follows:—

GENERAL LAFAYETTE TO MR. QUINCY.

"BOSTON, September 4.

"MY DEAR SIR:—Count Vidua, a distinguished Piedmontese, after having travelled over a great part of the Old World, as it is called, is now on a tour through the United States. He has been introduced to me in very high terms by my friends Humboldt and Ségur. Permit me to recommend him to your kind notice. Present my affectionate regard to your family, and believe me forever your sincere and grateful friend,

"LAFAYETTE."

Count Vidua was the son of a prime minister of the king of Sardinia, and a man of high intelligence, infinite curiosity, and vast information. Mr. Adams said that he put questions to him concerning the American Revolution which no other foreigner had ever asked. And I have before me a letter from him to my father, describing the collection he had made of works relating to the early history of the country, and asking for assistance in procuring others, and also information as to "the political, beneficent, municipal, literary, commercial, and manufacturing institutions and establishments" of the country, and especially everything in relation to the public schools; which shows the extent of his knowledge, and his thirst for more. He says that he had consulted with Mr. Webster about printed works on general politics and the Federal Constitution, and "observed with pleasure that he had already collected all, or almost all, the remarkable writings on this topic." I well remember the Count. He was the ugliest and most ungainly of mortal men. The Great President would have shone a marvel of grace and beauty by his side. But he had withal an air of distinction and high breeding which qualified his personal disadvantages, and his conversation was full of curious interest and intelligent observation. President John Quincy Adams said of Count Vidua, whose thirst for universal knowledge so strongly resembled his own, that, "after talking awhile with him, he would forget his looks, and think him absolutely a handsome man!" The following extract from my father's journal I insert here, although it relates to a second visit which Count Vidua paid to Boston: —

"Count Charles Vidua, son of the late prime minister of the king of Sardinia, with M. Niederstetter, Prussian Chargé d'Affaires, passed the evening with my family at Quincy. Two Englishmen also, recently graduated at Cambridge, England, Mr. St. Aubyn and Mr. Hallam, were of my company.

"Vidua has travelled through the greater part of Europe, Russian Asia, Palestine, to the Upper Cataracts of the Nile, and through Lapland, — is now on a visit to the United States. Scrutinizing, inquisitive, intelligent, — a collector of everything connected with the history of this country. He considered the Unitarianism of this part of the country as little else than *pure Deism;* and, though denied, yet to be such in fact. It is true, Unitarians spoke of Christ as 'our Saviour,' — Christ, 'our Redeemer'; but it was very plain that the notion they affixed to it was that of quality and not of power, and the terms were used as matter of honor, as when we call a man 'Your Excellency,' — but all feeling of reverence, as being a peculiar emanation from the Divine nature, was lost, or not felt. This he thought a great mischief. Speaking on politics, he observed that nothing had so much shaken him as to the future destinies of the United States as the near success of Jackson to the Presidency, since the fact indicated the strong hold military prowess had on the affections of the people of the United States. Vidua is uncommonly intent in researches upon the history and present state of this country. Niederstetter is gentlemanly and well-informed. The two Englishmen also were travelling for purposes of improvement, and seemed well-informed and interesting young men."

Baron von Niederstetter was the Prussian Minister at Washington, and as handsome as the Piedmontese nobleman was ugly. Messrs. St. Aubyn and Hallam were modest, cultivated, and high-bred English gentlemen, of which class we did not see many examples in this country in those days. The former I presume to be the Cornish gentleman who has lately (1866) received a baronetcy from Lord Derby, Sir Edward St. Aubyn, of St. Michael's Mount, whence

"The great Vision of the guarded Mount
Looks towards Namancos and Bayona's hold!"

During the year 1824, my father gave much of his leisure to the preparation of the memoir of my grandfather, which was published in the spring of 1825, just fifty years after the death of its subject. In this pious work he was greatly assisted by my eldest sister, Eliza Susan Quincy. Its progress was a source of constant interest to the family; but the secret of its intended publication was so well kept, that no hint of it got wind, and the first intimation that any person beyond the family circle and the printing-office had that such a book was thought of, was the advertisement on the morning it appeared. It was very handsomely got up, and so carefully corrected that it was absolutely without a misprint. Its value as illustrating the times immediately preceding the Revolution is, I believe, allowed by all students of that passage of our history. The following testimony of Mr. Webster on this point has been preserved by my sister in her memoir of my mother. In his great discourse on the laying of the corner-stone of Bunker Hill Monument, June 17th, 1825, he had introduced this quotation from my grandfather as illustrative of the spirit of the Revolutionary fathers. "The sentiment of Quincy," said Mr. Webster, "was full in their hearts. 'Blandishments,' said that distinguished son of genius and patriotism, 'will not fascinate us, nor will the threats of a halter intimidate; for, under God, we are determined that wheresoever, whensoever, or howsoever we shall be called to make our exit, we will die freemen.'" On the evening of that immortal day Mr. and Mrs. Webster gave a great party to General Lafayette in the house in Summer Street where they then lived. A door had been opened between Mr. Webster's house and that of Mr. Israel Thorndike, thus throwing the two into one, and it was a very brilliant assembly, from the number of eminent persons collected there, — many foreigners and distinguished Americans from all parts of the country having resorted to Boston on that memorable occasion. At this party, my mother having thanked Mr. Webster for his compliment to Josiah Quincy, Jr., the following conversation ensued: —

"'There is no need of my help in that cause,' was his reply. 'The memoir Mr. Quincy has published will be an enduring monument. It is one of the most interesting books I ever read, and brings me nearer than any other to the spirit which caused the American Revolution. Josiah Quincy, Jr. was a noble character. I love him because he loved the law. How zealous he was in seeking out the celebrated lawyers, in copying their reports, in studying the laws of the different Colonies! There are no such men now-a-days. Who keeps such journals?' Mrs. Quincy replied, 'I hope you do, Mr. Webster.' 'No, I do not. The times are far different. The members of Congress do not write such letters now.' Referring to the scene of the morning, he then said: 'I never desire to see again such an awful sight as so many thousand human faces all turned toward me. It was, indeed, a sea of faces I beheld at that moment.' Doctor Warren informed Mrs. Quincy that he had put the Memoir of Josiah Quincy, Jr. under the corner-stone of the Bunker Hill Monument, among the memorials of the Revolution."

The visit of Lafayette at this time was very brief, and he was the guest of Mr. Lloyd, then Senator from Massachusetts. On the evening before the 17th, he attended a reception given by my mother in Hamilton Place, and on the 18th he paid his farewell visit to Mr. Adams at Quincy, accompanied by my father. Mr. Adams was then ninety years of age, and the parting, never to meet again on earth, of these two men of the Revolution was a touching and impressive scene. In the evening Lafayette attended the Boston Theatre, where an overwhelming multitude assembled to take their last leave of their fathers' friend and their own. The following letter from Lafayette was the last my father received from him on this side the Atlantic, just before this Bunker Hill visit. It is written in just about the pretty kind of broken English which he spoke.

"Albany, June 12, 1825.

"My dear Sir: — Thus far have I come to redeem my sacred and most cordial pledge. We shall reach Boston on the 15th. I will tell you, between us, that I have been informed the Legislature intend to receive my personal respects; in which case it becomes proper for me to be arrived two days before the Bunker Hill ceremony. As to what I am to do, I cannot do better than to refer myself to your friendly advice, and shall hastily offer you and family my most affectionate, grateful respects,

"Lafayette.

"I would have been very happy to celebrate with you the Fourth of July, but am obliged to set out on the 20th to visit the States of Maine, New Hampshire, Vermont, and will proceed down the North River to New York, then to Philadelphia, Baltimore, Washington, and the seats of the Virginia Ex-Presidents, so as to embark on the 15th of August."

During the years that Mr. Quincy was Mayor of Boston his wife and family spent the summers at Quincy, as before. He himself remained in town to be ready for any unexpected emergency, paying frequent visits to his country-house, but seldom spending the night there. The farm he let, retaining only the grounds appertaining to the house. He maintained his custom of giving a dinner-party almost every Saturday, and in the summer these entertainments were always had at Quincy. He had somewhat enlarged the material of his dinner-company since his mayoralty, in consequence of his determination to break up the ancient custom of the town authorities, of feasting at the public expense. To these convivial customs he put a peremptory end; but, by way of consolation to the afflicted officials, he made it a rule to invite all the city government, in convenient detachments, to dine with him, at least once a year, either in town or at Quincy. Almost all strangers of condition, either from Europe or other parts of the United States, brought letters of introduction, or were visited *ex officio*, and were generally entertained at his table. Among these I recall the Duke Bernhard de Saxe Weimar, the second son of the friend of Goethe. His Highness expected to find Indians in the streets of Boston, and expressed great surprise that ladies should venture so far into the wilderness as the Falls of Niagara; and he had provided good store of books, clothes, arms, and other necessaries, supposing that such articles were not obtainable in the strange land to which he was bound. He was a man of fine presence, and of good intelligence on matters with which he was more familiar than the internal condition of the United States. He arrived in the Dutch sloop-of-war Pallas, commanded by Captain Ryk, afterwards Admiral, a lively, homely little man, covered with orders and decorations. One of the officers of the Pallas was M. Van

Tromp, a descendant of the famous Admiral who

"With his broom swept the chops of the Channel."

When this young gentleman was introduced to Mr. Adams, the Ex-President waved his hand over his head, and called out, "Hurrah for Van Tromp!" The officers of the Pallas gave a dance on board ship in return for the civilities they had received. Then there was Colonel Wilson, the son of the famous Sir Robert, who was himself *aide de camp* to Bolivar, and had seen battles in the cause of South American independence. He was a very young man then, and afterwards rose to distinction in the diplomatic line, and died not long since Sir Belford Wilson, K. C. B. Then there was the Baron Wallenstein, connected with some one of the Continental legations at Washington, small, plain, polished, full of knowledge, speaking and writing English as few Englishmen can do, an animated talker, and a most agreeable companion. I think I have heard that his later career was not prosperous, and his end unhappy. But the procession of these images of past days might well fill up more space than I have left myself, should I let it go on. They come like shadows, and like shadows let them depart, with those of the honored, the revered, the beloved, with which they are inextricably mingled in the memory of those long-gone days. I will not withhold, however, my father's account of a visit from General Morgan Lewis of New York, who, after serving in the army of the Revolution, and filling the offices of Chief Justice and Governor of his native State, finished his public career as one of the Major-Generals of the army of 1812. It is copied from one of his occasional fragmentary journals.

"*September* 24. — P. M. At Quincy on a visit to family. Morgan Lewis, his daughter, Mrs. (Maturin) Livingston, and two daughters, also Mr. Schley and lady, passed the evening with my family. Visited old President Adams, accompanied by Lewis and Schley. Found the old man in body weak and helpless, bearing all the marks of extreme old age. His mind vigorous and active, though slow in its operations. The conversation turned upon the mission which he, Doctor Franklin, and Edward Rutledge executed by the order of Congress in 1777, when they met Lord Howe, at his request, on Staten Island.

'Lord Howe,' said Mr. Adams, 'spoke with great feeling of the monument which Massachusetts had raised to his brother* in Westminster Abbey; and said that nothing would give him so great pain as to witness the fall of a State to which his family owed so great a distinction. Doctor Franklin replied, "Your Lordship may be assured that we shall do our best endeavors that your Lordship may be spared so great suffering." Lord Howe told us,' said Mr. Adams, 'that his orders were such that he could not receive us in the character of envoys or commissioners from Congress; that his instructions were, to open negotiations and hear proposals from any British subjects. I replied,' said Adams, 'that the only character in which I could not meet his Lordship was that of a British subject.'

"I told Mr Adams that news had just arrived that his son, the present President of the United States, had set out on a visit to him. It was unexpected. 'Well,' said he, 'I shall then see him once more. I had thought I had taken leave of him forever. God be thanked!'

"In the evening conversed with Lewis on various events of our Revolution. He is now seventy-one years of age; had entered early into the war of the Revolution, and continued in the army until the end. He said that the capture of General Lee was, in his opinion, the most fortunate event of the war; that if it had not happened, he thought there would have been great danger that Washington would have been superseded. He said that Samuel Adams was the head of the party in Congress opposed to Washington, and that Gates of New York and Mifflin of Pennsylvania were both concerned in it. Both Gates and Mifflin had personal causes of discontent. They each had respectively requested commands of Washington, which, from his sense of public service, he was compelled to deny. After the battle of Brandywine, Gates and his adherents could not conceal their satisfaction at the event, as they thought it would effect a riddance of him from the command of the army. . . . .

"Mr. Schley had been personally acquainted with the late William Pinkney at the bar of Maryland. He considered him one of the most able men our country had ever produced, — a man of constant and infinite labor, — yet possessed with the foolish vanity of desiring that his labored effusions should appear the effect of genius and of sudden inspiration. He concealed, therefore, as much as possible his studies, and was in the habit of resorting to a thousand poor tricks and contrivances, that his arguments might appear spontaneous. His love for

* The Lord Howe who was killed July 6, 1758, in the unsuccessful expedition against Ticonderoga, in the Old French War.

the profession of the law was extreme, which he took every possible occasion to avow and to evidence."

The following scrap of history from the same journal is worth preserving: —

"*September* 23. — In evening, with Lieutenant-Governor Phillips. He told me this anecdote of the late Samuel Adams. At the time of the Convention in Massachusetts for the adoption of the Federal Constitution, Adams and Hancock were known originally to be opposed to it. Those in favor of it had used various means to excite the people, and among others a meeting of the mechanics and others was held at the Green Dragon. To the opinion of those who met there, Adams was peculiarly alive. It happened that one day in the later period of the session Adams dined with Mr. Phillips. During dinner it was announced that a meeting had just been held at the Green Dragon, at which it was voted that '*we will have* the Federal Constitution.' 'Well,' said Adams, 'if *they will* have it, they *must* have it'; — and from that time he voted in favor of it."

The election of Mr. John Quincy Adams to the Presidency of the United States, in February, 1825, gave a new and peculiar interest to the intercourse of our family with the great statesman whom it was his singular felicity to follow in the highest office in the nation. At the visit which he paid to his father in September, 1825, we had frequently the curious satisfaction, never probably to be had again, of seeing two Presidents of the United States together, the one the son of the other. It is a happiness to be permitted to remember the glow of delight which lighted up the countenance and kindled anew the eyes of the father as he looked proudly on his son and successor, — a happiness enhanced by the remembrance of the great parliamentary career of John Quincy Adams, which has placed him apart from the vulgar herd of Presidents, and made his name only less illustrious than those of Washington and of Lincoln. The last time that John Adams was in my father's house, where he had been the welcome and honored guest of three generations, was on the 30th of September, 1825, when he entered and left it leaning on the arm of his son, the President. He frequently afterwards drove to the door and held audiences at the carriage-window, but his infirmities hindered him from getting out. In the winter of 1826 my elder brother paid a visit to Washington, and proposed extending his journey into Virginia; which, however, he was prevented from doing. Mr. Adams gave him this characteristic letter of introduction to Mr. Jefferson. It was the last he ever addressed to his famous successor, and is one of the last he ever wrote. At least, there are none of later date, excepting a couple of answers to invitations to public meetings, in his grandson's edition of his Works.

TO THOMAS JEFFERSON, EX-PRESIDENT OF THE UNITED STATES, MONTICELLO.

"QUINCY, January 14, 1826.

"MY DEAR SIR:—Permit me to introduce to your acquaintance a young lawyer by the name of Josiah Quincy, with the title of Colonel, being aid to our Governor. The name of Colonel Quincy, I believe, has never been extinct for nearly two hundred years. He is a son of our excellent Mayor of the city of Boston, and possesses a character unstained and irreproachable. I applaud his ambition to visit Monticello and its great inhabitant; and, while I have my hand in, I cannot cease without giving you some account of the state of my mind. I am certainly very near the end of my life. I am very far from trifling with the idea of death, which is a great and solemn event; but I contemplate it without terror or dismay,—*aut transit, aut finit.* If *finit,* which I cannot believe and do not believe, there is then an end of all: but I shall never know it; and why should I dread it?—which I do not. If *transit,* I shall ever be under the same constitution and administration of government in the universe; and I am not afraid to trust and confide in it. I am, as ever, your friend,

"JOHN ADAMS.

On the 4th of July, 1826, the Jubilee of American Independence was celebrated throughout the United States. The Reverend Henry Ware, Junior, had accepted the invitation of the city authorities of Boston to deliver the Oration on that day. Unfortunately, he was taken ill about a week before the anniversary, and was prevented from fulfilling his engagement. The city government then made a unanimous request to Mr. Quincy to perform the duty in his stead. Though the shortness of the time might have well excused his refusal, he would not permit his natural fear of doing himself less than justice on an occasion that demanded the best powers of the best man to stand in the way of the due performance of the ceremonies of the day. This Oration was probably none the worse for the rapidity with which it was written, as the topics were not far to seek, and their treatment required rather spirit and life than meditation and research. It was certainly very well done, and sets forth the changes in political condition which the Revolution had caused, and the material development which the nation had undergone because of those changes, during half a century, in a clear, impressive, and eloquent manner. In enumerating the great Bostonians whose names are indissolubly connected with the Revolution, he thus spoke of Mr. Adams:—

"Especially shall he not be forgotten, now or ever, — that ancient citizen of Boston, that patriarch of American Independence, of all New England's worthies on this day the sole survivor. He, indeed, oppressed by years, sinking under the burdens of decaying nature, hears not our public song or voice of praise, or ascending prayer. But the sounds of a nation's joy, rushing from our cities, ringing from our valleys, echoing from our hills, shall break the silence of his aged ear; the rising blessings of grateful millions shall visit with a glad light his fading vision, and flush the last shades of his evening sky with the reflected splendors of his meridian brightness."

At the moment these words were uttered Mr. Adams was still alive; but before the rejoicings of the day were over, the news came that he had died on that immortal anniversary. He had failed rapidly for the last two or three days, but he retained his faculties almost to the latest moment. The very last time he left his house was on the 1st of July, when he was lifted into his carriage to return a visit which my mother had paid him the day before. Having told her of this intention, he could not be dissuaded from fulfilling it, and drove to the house, and held his last audience with the family at the carriage-window. The news of his death was not believed at first, the coincidence being almost too extraordinary for credence. But five days later yet greater astonishment fell upon the people, when it was announced that

Thomas Jefferson had also died on that day of jubilee. A solemn amazement filled the land as the strange intelligence spread, that these two long and eventful lives had been closed by deaths so fortunate on the fiftieth anniversary of the most illustrious event in their history and in that of their country. Due observances were had everywhere in honor of their lives and in memory of their deaths, but none more striking or enduring than that held in Faneuil Hall, by the city of Boston, when Daniel Webster delivered his great discourse in the presence of John Quincy Adams, President of the United States, and of an audience in numbers and character worthy of the extraordinary occasion.

I will here insert a few letters belonging to the year 1826. The correspondence with Bishop Cheverus expresses on my father's side the cordial respect and affection with which that admirable prelate was regarded by men of all religious persuasions in the city where he long resided, and tells on the part of the Bishop how cordially that love and esteem was reciprocated by him. M. de Cheverus, an emigrant of the French Revolution, was the first Catholic Bishop of Boston. Shortly before the death of Louis XVIII. he was summoned to France to become Bishop of Montauban. It was with reluctance that he obeyed the royal command, and left the humble charge he had so long held in the very seat of "the Protestantism of the Protestant religion." He was subsequently translated from Montauban to fill the seat once occupied by Bossuet at Meaux, and afterwards to the Archiepiscopate of Bordeaux. In 1838 he received a Cardinal's hat from Pope Gregory XVI. Just before the fall of Charles X., Cardinal Cheverus was made a Count, and a member of the Chamber of Peers, but this dignity he lost by the Three Days of July.

Mr. Quincy to Bishop Cheverus.

"Boston, January 2, 1826.

"Reverend and dear Sir:—I cannot permit your excellent friend, the Rev. Mr. Taylor, to depart, with an intention to proceed directly to Montauban, without bearing with him some evidence of my remembrance, and of those deep traces of respect which your long residence in this city, and the uniform course of your conduct as a man and a Christian minister, have impressed upon the hearts of all who had the happiness of knowing or observing you.

"Be assured, sir, as there is none who feels more strongly this sentiment than myself, so there is no one who is happier to seize every suitable occasion to express it to yourself and others. Your memory is very precious and dear among us. Though absent, you are not forgotten, nor will be, so long as the generation which was contemporaneous with your residence in this city survives.

"The Rev. Mr. Taylor well supplied your place in the congregation over which you once presided, and in the city. Having learned of you the nature and character of our inhabitants, his course was shaped in a manner at once faithful to his flock and acceptable to those whose religious faith was not coincident with his. We part with him in friendship, with respect, and with regret. . . . .

"I remain, with great respect, most truly yours,

"JOSIAH QUINCY."

BISHOP CHEVERUS TO MR. QUINCY.

"MONTAUBAN, April 8, 1826.

"DEAR AND HONORED SIR:—The Rev. Mr. Taylor has just forwarded to me your kind and welcome letter of January 2d. It has not been for want of strong and repeated recommendations from me that the general wish in Boston has not been complied with at Rome.* But the one who is now appointed is a worthy prelate, and was highly respected in New York and in Charleston, South Carolina. I have known him long since, and I have no doubt that he is already popular among my dear fellow-citizens of Boston.

"I know that he will have your kind support, which has been so useful and so acceptable to myself.

"If, as you have the goodness to assure me, I am not forgotten in Boston, I can say, with truth, I do not forget Boston. So dear and familiar is the name of the beloved city, that even in conversation I say Boston instead of Montauban, and this often; and I am then told, 'You love Boston better than Montauban, but we defy the Bostonians to love you more than we do.' I must acknowledge that here, as well as in America, love and respect are given me much beyond my deserts. A new Mayor of this city (the King appoints him) was installed two months since. I was present, and thought much of the Mayor of Boston. In the inaugural speech the Viscount de Gironde, the new

* Doubtless that the Rev. Father Taylor should be appointed Bishop of Boston, in the place of Bishop Cheverus.

magistrate, paid me a very handsome compliment. He went so far as to say, that it was his most ardent wish to follow my steps, and to take my paternal administration, which had made this city a city of brothers, for the model of his, and by so doing to entitle himself to my kindness, and deserve my esteem.

"I must confess I felt gratified, but I am not less so by the very kind and handsome testimony which your letter bears to my conduct while in Boston. The approbation of the noble-minded Mayor of Boston is indeed a valuable meed, and his friendship and esteem are treasures. Will he have the goodness to assure my fellow-citizens and friends in Boston, that my adopted country, and its kind and so dear inhabitants, will always be objects of my affectionate gratitude.

"With affectionate respect, dear and honored sir, I remain your most obedient humble servant,

"† John, Bishop of Montauban."

The following letter from John Randolph was in reply to one introducing my brother to his acquaintance, on the occasion of the same visit to Washington which procured the letter from Mr. Adams to Mr. Jefferson which I have already given. It is the last letter my father ever received from him, and its liveliness, wit, and pathos make it a fit conclusion of their correspondence.

Mr. Randolph to Mr. Quincy.

"Washington, February 20, 1826.

"Dear Sir: — Your letter was 'right welcome unto me,' as my favorite old English writers sing or say, but much more welcome was the bearer of it. Son of yours, even with far less claims from his own merit than this gentleman obviously possesses, shall never be shown my 'cauld shoulther.' I hope that you'll pardon my using the Waverley tongue, which I must fear bodes no good to the good old English aforesaid, and which I shall therefore leave to them that like it, — which I do not, out of its place, — and not always there. In short, I have not catched the literary 'Scotch fiddle,' and, in despite of Dr. Blair, do continue to believe that Swift and Addison understood their own mother tongue as well as any Sawney 'benorth tha' Tweed.' Nay, further, not having the fear of the Edinburgh Reviewers before my eyes, I do not esteem Sir Walter to be a poet, or the Rev. Dr. Chalmers a pulpit orator. But, as I do not admire Mr. Kean, I fear that my reputation for taste is, like my earthly tabernacle, in a hopeless state.

"The fuss made about that mountebank, who is the very fellow — although not 'periwig-pated' — that Shakespeare describes, has, I confess, disgusted me not a little. What are we made of, to take sides in the factions of the circus (green or blue), and to doat upon the professions of 'feeling' and 'sentiment' and 'broken-heartedness' from the lips or pen of a fellow whose vocation it is to deal in those commodities, — who has a stock of them in his travelling pack, like an Irish fortune-hunter on a visit to a 'young ladies' seminary' of learning anything but good? For my part, like Burchell in the Vicar of Wakefield, I say nothing, but cry, 'Fudge!'

"By the common law, stage-players come under the description and penalties of vagrants and sturdy beggars. To be sure, Shakespeare was on the stage, and Garrick and Siddons and Kemble were stage-players; but, you know, *exceptio probat regulam.*

"I did not (when I began) intend to have turned the page, but must do it to say, that the stage comes emphatically under Lord Byron's sweeping ban and anathema against the world, as

'One wide den of thieves, or — what you will.'

"My right hand has forgot its cunning. With great respect and every good wish to you and yours, I am, dear sir, your obedient servant,

"JOHN RANDOLPH OF ROANOKE."

"P. S. — I often think on 'Auld Lang Syne' [more Scotch]. Though 'seas between us broad have rolled' since those days, I have a perfect recollection of most of them. I can see you now just as you were when a certain great man that now is was beginning to be, — but why revive what is better forgot? One thing, however, I will revive (what I shall never forget), your kindness to my poor boy, — 'the last of the family,' — for I am nothing; it will soon be utterly extinct. He lies in Cheltenham churchyard. I bought the ground. I need not say that it was my first pilgrimage in England. As you go from the Town to the Spring, he lies on the right hand* of the pathway through the churchyard, leaving the church on your left."

The following note from Mr. Randolph to my brother is too characteristic to be omitted: —

* "Close to the wall there is an iron railing and a stone, put up, like all other things done by agency of distant people, very badly. They thought that I would never see it; charged a high price; and I was indebted to one of poor Tudor's schoolfellows for its repair, not very long before I saw it. I think I sent you a copy of the epitaph."

MR. RANDOLPH TO MR. J. QUINCY, JUNIOR.

"CAPITOL HILL, Dawson's, No. 2, Thursday.

"If Mr. Josiah Quincy, Junior, will waive ceremony, and accept this return for his card from an old and very infirm man, Mr. Randolph will be very glad to see his father's son (not Mr. R.'s, but Mr. Q.'s father's) at any time before half past ten or eleven in the morning, or between the adjournment of the Senate and eight o'clock, which is Mr. R.'s bedtime. Mr. R. is much obliged to Mr. Q. for the letter which he was so good as to leave here yesterday. It gave him great pleasure once more to hear from one with whom he had passed through some trying political scenes; and for whom he then entertained, and hopes always to cherish, sentiments of great esteem and regard."

These letters from Lafayette need no preface or explanation.

GENERAL LAFAYETTE TO MR. QUINCY.

"LA GRANGE, July 20, 1826.

"MY DEAR SIR: — Former letters of acknowledgment have expressed my grateful feelings for the precious volume you have sent me before my sailing for Europe. It has interested me in the highest degree, not only on account of its literary merit, and my warm affection for the author, but still more so from a sense of lively concern in the first times of the Revolution, and of admiration for the great and devoted patriot whose memoirs have been published in a manner worthy of him. Nor will I omit to observe that, in the beauty of the material execution, I find daily occasion to satisfy European visitors with the state of book-printing and book-binding in the city of Boston.

"A book has been printed in Boston by E. G. House, 1824, containing an account of my happy visit to the United States, from August 15th to October 19th. I wish you may have the kindness to trace it up to the author, and express the pleasure and gratitude with which I have read it. Should he have completed the series of gratifying records, I beg you to send me the following parts.

"I am at a great distance from you, dear friends, but my heart is constantly with you; and among the numerous objects, presents, keepsakes, by which I am surrounded, as a sort of continuation of my delightful American thirteen months, you need not I hope being told that the two beautiful drawings of my young friend hold a conspicuous and peculiarly cherished place.

"Since we are returning to those times of which I shall ever think with inexpressible delight, permit me to ask whether the measure we have recommended to the possessor of the first gun that was fired in the Revolution has been attended to, — to have a plate and inscription affixed to it, so that this precious relic of this first signal for the emancipation of the world be never mislaid.

"It is needless to say I am deeply interested in reading the intelligence which through letters and newspapers come to me, three times a month, from the United States. It is to me a language better understood than European style. The city of Boston had a large share of oratory honors in the last session of Congress. To the papers of this side the Atlantic, I refer you for British and Continental information. The discrepancy which to the credit of most European nations exists between governed and governors, is particularly remarkable with respect to the affairs of Greece. The situation of that interesting, spirited people, given up as they have been by every one of the pretended Christian powers, is far from being desperate. Assistance is much wanted, but would be effectually applied.

"With the most affectionate respects and good wishes to you, to Mrs. Quincy, to the whole family, daughters and sons, I am forever your devoted, grateful friend,

"LAFAYETTE.

"George and Levasseur beg to be respectfully remembered. Remember me also to our dear friends in the beloved city of Boston."

THE SAME TO THE SAME.

"LA GRANGE, November 13, 1827.

". . . . You will hear of the great event at *Navarino*. How far the governments of France and England will have been pleased to hear that the joke has been carried so far by their naval representatives I don't pretend to determine, but they must join in our joy and our praises. The fact is, that the two gallant admirals, along with that of Russia, indignant at the breach of faith, and the horrors committed in the Morea by Ibrahim Pacha, and at the murder of the officers bearing the flag of truce, have utterly destroyed the fleets of Turkey and Egypt, and the vessels — sixty they say — which the Austrian government had lent as transports to assist in the destruction of their fellow-Christians of Greece. Now the diplomatists will be busy in patching up the business, preventing wars, and stifling freedom in the best way they can; but heroic Greece is saved from imminent danger, and I have much confidence in the patriotism, talents, and dexterity of their worthy President, Capo D'Istria. . . . .

"CHAMBRE DES DEPUTÉS.

"The dissolution of the Chamber of Deputies by the French Ministry can only be explained on account of their fears of a progressing public spirit, which might render their chance less advantageous in one or two years. That measure has been so calculated as to give the liberal electors no time to have previous meetings, to think of their candidates, nor in many instances to return to their places of election, while everything had been previously underhand arranged to serve the views of government. I think, however, in the state of the public mind, that a good number of *Deputés* will be patriots, and a still greater number anti-ministerialists. It is, I believe, out of the power of the French government to prevent my being re-elected by the same district where I have been lately nominated, — the less so, as a part of those they had iniquitously excluded have since been able to recover their rights.

"Remember me most respectfully and affectionately to Mrs. Quincy, to all the family, and to our particular friends in the beloved city of Boston, and believe me forever your affectionate, grateful friend,

"LAFAYETTE."

At the time my father was engaged in his inquiries into the cause and cure of poverty, vice, and crime, he had had an occasional communication and exchange of publications with Mr. Roscoe, the historian of the Medici, who, it is well known, was greatly interested in those questions. When Mr. Quincy published the life of his father in 1825, he sent a presentation copy of the work to that excellent writer and benevolent man, as a mark of his respect and esteem. In return he received the following answer, which, besides the gratifying testimony it bears to the merits of the memoir, is interesting for the enlightened humanity it breathes, that had already done so much towards mitigating the bloody code of English penal law

MR. ROSCOE TO MR. QUINCY.

"TOXTETH PARK, NEAR LIVERPOOL, July 10, 1826.

"SIR: — From the time I received your obliging letter of the 28th April last, and perused the very interesting volume which accompanied it, of the life of your excellent father, it has been my constant intention to express to you my sincerest thanks, as well for the pleasure and information you have afforded me, as for the honor you have done me.

"It is with real satisfaction I perceive that the lives of those distinguished individuals who signalized themselves as the founders of the liberties of your country have of late been brought forward in a manner worthy of their character; and amongst these your memorial of your father will ever hold a distinguished rank. This is a monument which a son may indeed be proud to raise to a father, and which, instead of being confined to some solitary spot, extends his fame wherever there are heads to think and hearts to feel. I have lent your volume to the small circle of my family and particular friends, and have been gratified in hearing it uniformly spoken of by them with the same sentiments of admiration and affection which I have so truly felt myself.

"I have also to thank you for the two Tracts which you have had the goodness to transmit to me, and in which I am happy to perceive a striking coincidence of opinion with some of those which I have myself ventured to avow, in my observations on penal jurisprudence.

"Disappointed, as I confess myself to have been, in the effect of my publications, I find no disposition to relax in the slightest degree from the sentiments I have endeavored to establish, and which are in fact intended to demonstrate that criminal law, like every other human institution, ought to have its foundation in benevolence, and not in resentment, cruelty, and revenge; that, at all events, it is easy to restrain the wicked from crimes by imprisonment, and to make them provide for themselves by labor; and that, whilst this is the case, there can be no pretext for the severities, punishments, and judicial murders which have hitherto been considered as essential to the safety of society and the repression of crime.

"With the sincerest wishes for your health and happiness, and the most grateful acknowledgments for your kind communication, believe me most respectfully, dear sir, your very faithful and obedient servant,

"W. Roscoe."

In this chapter I have endeavored to relate, in as brief a manner as possible, the facts of Mr. Quincy's mayoralty, dwelling the longest on those which are likely to be most interesting to the general reader at this late day. The changes which he introduced were of great and permanent benefit to the city, and it is not too much to say that the citizens at this time, after the lapse of near forty years, are daily the better for his administration. It may be safely affirmed that he was a model municipal magistrate. He gave his entire time and attention to the duties of his office, and he left the city beautified, the police improved, the fire department reformed, and all things connected with the comfort and safety of the citizens in better condition than they had ever been before. He utterly refused to favor any of his personal friends in the matter of public improvements or contracts, and shunned so carefully even the appearance of self-seeking on his own account, that it was popularly said, "He stood so straight as to lean backward." His administration had been too upright and straightforward not to create many enemies, as well as many friends. He said from the beginning that no man could do his duty in such an office without being turned out of it. His own experience fulfilled his prediction. After being five times re-elected without much opposition, — once, at least, without any at all, — his official life came to an end at the election of 1828. In reforming the fire department he had created a very powerful political body, as well as a very useful practical one. To this body he gave offence by refusing to appoint a person chief engineer, whom he did not regard as suitable for the place. An excited opposition was rallied against him by the partisans of the rejected candidate, which all the elements of hostility his conduct in office had excited helped to swell. After two trials, at each of which he had a large plurality, but lacked rather less than a hundred votes of an absolute majority, he withdrew his name, and peremptorily refused to allow it to be used again in the canvass, and Mr. Harrison Gray Otis was elected his successor. Though he had foreseen that such must be the ending of his official career, he was far from insensible to the treatment he had received from his fellow-citizens in return for his indefatigable and disinterested services, the rather that the contest had been conducted in a spirit of personal bitterness and malignity which he had deserved only by his resolute devotion to the interests of the city. Accordingly, he summoned a meeting of both branches of the city government on the last day of his official service, and delivered an address, in which he recapitulated the doings of his term of service, showing the falsity of the various charges that had been urged against him, by the unanswerable arguments of facts and figures, as well as of logic. From its temporary and local character it will not be much known or read hereafter, but it is full of the eloquence of truth, reason, and an honorable sensibility. Its peroration will make a fitting conclusion of this chapter.

"And now, gentlemen, standing as I do in this relation for the last time in your presence and that of my fellow-citizens, about to surrender forever a station full of difficulty, of labor and temptation, in which I have been called to very arduous duties, affecting the rights, property, and at times the liberty of others; concerning which the perfect line of rectitude — though desired — was not always to be clearly discerned; in which great interests have been placed within my control, under circumstances in which it would have been easy to advance private ends and sinister projects; — under these circumstances, I inquire, as I have a right to inquire, — for in the recent contest insinuations have been cast against my integrity, — in this long management of your affairs, whatever errors have been committed, — and doubtless there have been many, — have you found in me any thing selfish, any thing personal, any thing mercenary? In the simple language of an ancient seer, I say: 'Behold, here I am; witness against me. Whom have I defrauded? Whom have I oppressed? At whose hands have I received any bribe?'

"Six years ago, when I had the honor first to address the City Council, in anticipation of the event which has now occurred, the following expressions were used: 'In administering the police, in executing the laws, in protecting the rights and promoting the prosperity of the city, its first officer will be necessarily beset and assailed by individual interests, by rival projects, by personal influences, by party passions. The more firm and inflexible he is in maintaining the rights and in pursuing the interests of the city, the greater is the probability of his becoming obnoxious to the censure of all whom he causes to be prosecuted or punished, of all whose passions he thwarts, of all whose interests he opposes.'

"The day and the event have come. I retire — as in that first address I told my fellow-citizens, 'If, in conformity with the experience of other republics, faithful exertions should be followed by loss of favor and confidence,' I should retire — 'rejoicing, not, indeed, with a public and patriotic, but with a private and individual joy'; for I shall retire with a consciousness weighed against which all *human suffrages* are but as the light dust of the balance."

CHAPTER XVII.

1828-1833.

MR. QUINCY ELECTED PRESIDENT OF HARVARD UNIVERSITY. — THE PRESIDENT'S HOUSE. — REMOVAL TO CAMBRIDGE. — INAUGURATION. — LETTERS OF JUDGE STORY, MR. ADAMS, MR. WEBSTER, GENERAL LAFAYETTE, AND ARCHBISHOP CHEVERUS. — CAMBRIDGE SOCIETY. — CHANGES IN DISCIPLINE AND INSTRUCTION. — OFFICIAL AND PRIVATE INTERCOURSE WITH THE STUDENTS. — PHILOSOPHY OF PREVENTION. — THE COMMONS HALL. — NEW TEST OF COLLEGE RANK. — THE VOLUNTARY SYSTEM. — THE LAW SCHOOL. — LETTER FROM CHIEF JUSTICE MARSHALL. — CENTENNIAL CELEBRATION IN BOSTON. — PRESIDENT QUINCY'S ADDRESS. — LETTER TO LAFAYETTE. — DESCRIPTION OF LAGRANGE. — DEATH OF LAFAYETTE. — LETTER TO HIS SON. — GENERAL JACKSON'S DOCTORATE.

AT the time Mr. Quincy ceased to be Mayor of Boston, the Presidency of Harvard College was vacant by the resignation of the Reverend Dr. John Thornton Kirkland. The claims of many eminent gentlemen to that important position were the matter of general discussion in society, and of grave consideration on the part of the academic functionaries on whom the responsibility of selection rested. Mr. Quincy had never been regarded as a candidate for the office. The nature of the occupations of his past public life did not suggest his elevation to the headship of the oldest University in America, and, until just before the election of December, 1828, his hold upon the mayoralty was regarded as sure and steadfast for as many years as he might choose to retain it. Immediately, however, after his refusal to be again a candidate for that office, his name began to be talked of in connection with the Presidency of the College. The best friends of the institution, and especially the Fellows, constituting the Corporation, from whom the nomination was originally to proceed, very soon were of one mind as to his peculiar fitness for the place at that particular time. The Corporation then consisted of the Reverend Dr. Eliphalet Porter; Mr.

Justice Charles Jackson, late of the Supreme Court of the State; Mr. Justice Joseph Story, of the Supreme Court of the United States; Nathaniel Bowditch, LL. D. and F. R. S., the author of the Navigator, and the translator of Laplace; Mr. Francis Calley Gray; and Mr. Ebenezer Francis, the Treasurer. On the 15th of January, 1829, the Corporation nominated Mr. Quincy unanimously as President of the University. He felt the honor deeply which the confidence of such men in his fitness for so novel and difficult a situation implied; but he was unaffectedly doubtful on the point himself. On mature consideration, however, he thought he saw it to be his duty to accept the office, should the nomination be confirmed by the Board of Overseers. The confirmation was not as unanimous as the nomination had been. The clergy had been accustomed to regard the Presidency of the College as belonging, in a manner, to their body, from which, indeed, it had always been filled since its establishment, excepting in the case of President Leverett, more than a century before. This feeling, and also a little leaven of old partisan prejudice, prevented his receiving a unanimous vote in the Overseers. But the majority in his favor was a decided one, and on the 29th of January, 1829, his election was completed.

The general community approved of the choice with great unanimity, though there were some apprehensions that he might not be able readily to adapt himself to duties so different from those of his former life. But it was generally understood that the finances of the College had been in a state of great disorder. Dr. Kirkland, the model of a dignified clergyman, an accomplished scholar, a polished gentleman, bland and courteous in his intercourse with the students, by whom he was greatly beloved, and universally popular in society for his genial graces, was not a man of business, and had no natural or acquired talent for the management of money. Judge John Davis, of the United States District Court, who was Treasurer of the College during the whole of Dr. Kirkland's Presidency, unfortunately was not fitted to make good his deficiencies in this particular. A learned lawyer, and a man of great general erudition, he had rather the tastes and habits of a retired scholar, than those of a man of affairs. Between them both, without the slightest impeachment of their personal integrity, the College finances had fallen into almost inextricable confusion. Though the financial experience and skill of the Corporation, and especially of Dr. Bowditch and Mr. Francis, had already placed the funds on a safe basis, it was thought important that a man of the world, accustomed to business, should be placed at the head of the University. Mr. Quincy was very generally allowed to be the man to satisfy this necessity.

The chief sacrifice which this change in the order of his life called upon my father and his family to make was that of the summers at Quincy. The duties of his office requiring his residence for the whole year at Cambridge, my mother did not think it worth her while to be encumbered with two establishments for the sake of the few weeks of vacation she could give to Quincy. For seventeen summers, therefore, that beloved abode — occupied indeed by other members of the family — was no longer the home of my father's immediate household. The sacrifice, however, was cheerfully made, in view of the circumstances which demanded it. The President's house, which could claim the great American antiquity of more than a hundred years, and had been the abode of eight of his predecessors, was fitted up for its new occupant. The ceilings were low, as was the custom when it was built, but the rooms were large, and their arrangement not incommodious, and, when suitably furnished, had a very comfortable, old-fashioned look, and for more than sixteen years were the scene of unbroken domestic happiness and of an abounding hospitality. To this new home the family removed towards the end of May, 1829, and on the 2d of June the inauguration took place.

It was an event in which the neighboring city and the State generally felt a warm interest. In those days the connection between the city and the College was much closer than it is now. The growth of the one and the other seems rather to have separated them than to have drawn them nearer together. The various College festivals were objects of interest and conversation in Boston as they occurred, to a degree now utterly unknown. Commencement was a legal holiday (it still is one at the banks and the

Custom-House), and its heroes and its deeds were at least one day's wonder. Rich and poor resorted to Cambridge on that day; the roads between the towns were crowded with carriages, horsemen, and foot-passengers, and the streets of Cambridge all alive with strangers who had come up to the anniversary. The inauguration of a President, being a ceremony of rarer occurrence, caused a yet greater excitement, and brought larger numbers together. It was nearly twenty years since the last one had taken place, and this circumstance, together with Mr. Quincy's prominence in Boston as a public man for so many years, made his inauguration an unusually attractive occasion. It was a very fine day, — the crowds without were great, and the attendance within the good old parish church — very ill replaced, as a scene for academic ceremonies by the newer one — was numerous and brilliant. It was the last inauguration, I believe, at which the addresses of the Governor and the President to each other and to the public, incident to the induction into office of the one by the other, were made in Latin, according to immemorial academic usage. At the inauguration of President Everett, and I think also at that of President Sparks, worthy Mr. Briggs was Governor, who did not possess among his many good qualities and gifts a knowledge of the Latin tongue. It must have been a cross to so excellent a scholar as Mr. Everett to miss this just opportunity of airing his Latinity, and to one so wisely regardful of good usages to be thus obliged to deviate from the ancient paths at his very entrance upon his office. And thus the custom fell into desuetude, and will probably never be revived. At Mr. Quincy's initiation, however, Governor Lincoln was fully competent to discharge properly his part in these introductory ceremonies, and they went off with great success. When the newly made President, wearing his academic robes of office, seated himself in the ancient chair from which the degrees have been given from time immemorial, and assumed the square cap, he was saluted by the cheers of the undergraduates and the applause of the whole audience. His Inaugural Address in English concluded the formal ceremonies of the day. A dinner followed, in the Commons Hall, given to all Masters of Arts, and also to all the students, — which academic hospitality has been impracticable on later occasions by reason of the great multiplication of the undergraduates. A reception was held by Mrs. Quincy in the evening, which was attended by all that was best in the society of Boston and Cambridge, and also by many strangers, graduates, and others, who had come up to grace this occasion. An illumination of the College buildings by the students made a brilliant conclusion to the welcome of the new President to his new home and his new duties.

The following letters, touching his leaving the mayoralty and entering upon the presidency, belong to this place.

Judge Story to Mr. Quincy.

"Washington, January 14, 1829.

"Dear Sir: — An hour ago I had the pleasure of receiving your farewell address. I have read it through carefully and deliberately. I sit down to thank you for it with my heart full of gratitude for your services. It is a most triumphant answer to all the calumnies against you, and is absolutely irresistible in its statements. I admire it for its masculine strength, its severe truths, its forcible — because plain — eloquence, and its moral dignity. The *mens sibi conscia recti* is visible everywhere.

"No man could regret more than myself your non-election. No man felt more confidence in your singleness of purpose, and firmness and public virtue. I cannot but lament what you so mildly denominate a mere exercise of the power and right to change. If such noble experiments so begin and so end, where and what is our security for the future in the course of our free governments? But I forbear. I ask you still to remember me as one who honored you in office, but who now feels that your title to his admiration and respect was but feebly understood, because it was never dependent upon office, and strengthens by the departure of its forms and its trappings.

"I am, dear sir, with the truest regards, and I trust you will allow me the privilege of so subscribing myself, your most obliged friend,

"Joseph Story."

Mr. Adams to Mr. Quincy.

"City of Washington, January 15, 1829.

"My dear Sir: — I have received the copy which you had the goodness to send me of your address on taking leave of the office of

Mayor. I have read it with deep interest, and take it not for flattery, if I say admiration. No event which has occurred for years had given me more sincere concern than the failure of your re-election.

"Too long absent, and too far distant, to be conversant with the details of your administration, I was not competent to form a judgment concerning them; but the impress of your mind and heart upon the condition of our beloved city was too deeply stamped for me to be insensible to it, and I regarded your removal from her service as a public calamity. Your address has proved that the parts are all congenial to the whole, and that your improvements of the city are not only striking to the superficial eye, but in the interior solid, compact, and durable.

"It must afford you constant gratification during the remainder of life, that the good you have done is permanent; that you have elevated to a higher standard the character of the city itself. This praise is your own, and cannot be taken from you. If it is not understood now, it will be felt hereafter.

"With my most fervent prayers for the prosperity of the city, I can wish her no better fortune than that your successors may have equal claims to the title of her benefactors with yourself.

"Accept the assurance of my unaltered and unalterable friendship.

"JOHN QUINCY ADAMS."

MR. WEBSTER TO MR. QUINCY.

"WASHINGTON, January 25, 1829.

"MY DEAR SIR: — I have just closed the perusal of your address, and am not willing to lose a moment in expressing the pleasure, and, allow me to say, *the pride* with which I have read it. In my opinion it is in the highest degree just, manly, sensible, — full of proof of independence, conscious integrity, and proper self-respect. While you have done yourself no more than justice, you have made an exhibition of the measures of the city administration and of their effects which cannot fail to gratify your friends and all good citizens. Heaven punishes folly by granting it its desires; and this penalty I imagine they who were mainly active in producing this change will feel hereafter, if they do not feel it now. Although I deeply regret that change, on public accounts, I yet think it clear that the events which produced it, the feeling which those events have excited, and the use which you have made already, and *which I trust you will still further make*, of the occasion, will enable you to retire from the government of the city with more solid and brilliant reputation than almost any other state of things which could be reasonably anticipated would have conferred.

"I pray you to make my most friendly regards acceptable to Mrs. Quincy and your family, and to believe me, dear sir, with constant esteem, your obedient servant,

"DANIEL WEBSTER."

GENERAL LAFAYETTE TO MR. QUINCY.

"PARIS, January 27, 1829.

"MY DEAR SIR: — The session of the Chambers has opened to-day, and while I regret my country life, I find here a pleasing compensation in the enjoyment of an American society.

"There has been lately in France not a presidential, but a ministerial question, which has occasioned some excitement. M. de Polignac, the French Ambassador to England, having been called to Paris, by special order of the King, to occupy the department of foreign affairs, public opinion has repelled this representative of the counter-revolutionary party. So that it has been supposed M. de La Ferronnays was better than everybody knows him to be, and matters have been patched up with temporary substitutes. The King's speech of this morning confirms the opinion that the French troops will not long be continued in Greece, and that the boundaries will not extend much farther than the Morea. A narrow system, in my opinion, which is to be attributed not to the more liberal dispositions of the French government, but to the jealousy of England in everything that concerns a question of trade, or of liberty, out of their own island.

"I hear the monument is going on finely. A drawing of Washington's statue in the State-House has greatly pleased me. May the beloved city of Boston continue in every sort of prosperity and happiness.

"Present my most affectionate regards to Mrs. Quincy, to your daughters and sons. Remember me to our friends.

"Most truly and affectionately yours,

"LAFAYETTE."

THE SAME TO THE SAME.

"PARIS, February 26, 1829.

"MY DEAR SIR: — We have just now received the account of your being elected President of the University, for which, as one of its oldest members,* and your affectionate friend, I find a double cause

* Lafayette was made a Doctor of Laws at Cambridge in 1784.

to rejoice. I have been highly gratified to welcome our Boston friends and the letters from you of which they were the bearers. We are this winter happy in the society of a good number of American ladies and gentlemen, among whom I find a consolation for the otherwise very unpleasant obligation to be five or six months absent from La Grange. After having, forty years ago, contributed in France to a constitutional system where the rights of man had been fairly acknowledged, and where many principles of the American school had received their execution, I have seen the result of our labors in a great measure overturned by the convulsions of anarchy, the combinations of imperial despotism, and the prejudices of a restoration, so that now, with the aid of public, peaceful opinion, and an honest but timid majority in the Chamber of Deputies, we must by very slow steps recover some inadequate mites of what had been established on a broad basis, with almost universal assent. Yet some progress is made and will continue to increase; but quick-step, although old men have no time to wait, is not the march of the day.

"I hope, my dear friend, you will have sent me the publication relative to your mayoral magistracy. Be pleased to remember me very affectionately to Mrs. Quincy, to your daughters and sons, to Mr. Webster, and other friends in Boston and Cambridge. My son begs to be respectfully, cordially mentioned, and I am with all my heart your friend,

"LAFAYETTE."

ARCHBISHOP CHEVERUS TO MR. QUINCY.

"BORDEAUX, April 25, 1830.

"DEAR AND HONORED SIR: — I have received with pleasure and gratitude your kind favor and your address on leaving the Mayor's office, but I have not had the happiness of seeing as yet the esteemed bearer of them, Dr. Kirkland.

"The sentiments you express towards me in your letter I deeply feel and duly appreciate. It is no small honor and gratification to me to be remembered and esteemed by such a man as the Honorable Josiah Quincy. I have not forgotten his eloquence in Congress, his zeal and services as Mayor, and I see from afar his new and successful exertions as the chief of the University. I know him equal to any situation. There is none ever so high and arduous that he would not render both more beneficial to his country and more honorable.

"I was delighted with your address. Along with the delightful consciousness of having well and nobly done, you have commanded the respect, the admiration, and the gratitude even of those who had not voted for you.

"May Harvard long flourish under your direction and auspices! May every blessing attend you here and hereafter!

"The bearer of this, my beloved friend and pupil, the Rev. Mr. Byrne, may give you all the details of my present situation. It is attended with many difficulties and anxieties. I often regret my peaceable abode and ministry in dear Boston, and miss more than I can express the many esteemed friends I had there.

"With high and affectionate respect, I remain, dear sir, your most obedient, humble servant,

"† JOHN, ARCHBISHOP OF BORDEAUX."

The new President and his family were welcomed to Cambridge with the most cordial kindness by the families of the Professors, and of the principal inhabitants of the town. The society of Cambridge was then, as it has always been, distinguished for its refinement and high cultivation. It was upon a simple and inexpensive footing, which made the showing of hospitality general and easy, and this was extended to the new-comers on every hand. Almost every evening of that pleasant summer was filled up with parties in their honor. Among others, Mrs. Craigie, whose house had been the scene of the brief wooing of my father and mother more than thirty years before, appeared again in society, after a long seclusion, and filled her beautiful rooms with a brilliant assembly to meet her old friends and new neighbors.

President Quincy, in the mean time, applied himself with his constitutional industry to the duties of his new office. With all due deliberation he made his observations on the state of things in the College, and considered how it could be best improved, and gradually introduced such changes in its discipline and instruction as his experience and knowledge of the world suggested. The doubts which some of the friends of the College had entertained, that he would lack the power of adapting himself to the government of young men, and their fears that he would be too severely strict in his dealings with them, were soon dissipated by the development of his plan of administration. It soon appeared that his fitness for his place was not limited by his experience in business matters, which had first suggested him as a fit man to fill it. This part of his duties, indeed, he discharged with eminent success. With the assistance of the other able men associated with him in the Corporation, he placed the finances of the College on a footing of perfect safety, and their condition when he left office was more flourishing than it had ever been before. But his heart's desire was to make the College a nursery of high-minded, high-principled, well-taught, well-conducted, well-bred gentlemen, fit to take their share, gracefully and honorably, in public and private life. His knowledge of the world, and long and close intercourse with men, had taught him how to approach and influence the sons, as well as the fathers. The pervading principle of his treatment of the undergraduates was to make them a law unto themselves, by the development of a sense of honor and self-respect, which should make severity of discipline unnecessary. He happily illustrated this philosophy of his in an after-dinner speech at the inauguration, or the first Commencement, of his successor, Mr. Everett, by a quotation from Prior's "English Padlock." "I have always been guided, in my treatment of the undergraduates," said he, "by the rule laid down by 'famed Matt Prior' for that of the ladies: —

'Be to their faults a little blind;
Be to their virtues very kind;
And clap your padlock on the mind!'"

In his intercourse with them he always took it for granted that they were gentlemen and men of honor. He never questioned the truth of any story any of them told him, when in academic difficulties, however improbable it might be. That statement was accepted as the truth until it was overthrown by implacable facts and inexorable evidence. Then, beyond doubt, the unhappy youth was made to know the value of a good character by the inconvenience attending the loss of it. Still, even in such cases, every kindly encouragement was extended to the offender to rehabilitate himself in his own self-respect and the good opinion of his superiors. President Quincy took a truly fatherly interest in the young men, kept himself singularly well informed as to their characters and conduct, and introduced an unprecedented freedom of personal intercourse with them, without in the slightest degree compromising his personal dignity, or weakening their respect for him. He had a strong sense of the importance to young men, at the forming period of life, of mingling in the society of ladies, and of their elders and superiors, as a part of education. In these views his wife fully concurred, and cheerfully lent her aid. For several winters after the removal to Cambridge, she opened her house every Thursday evening to the little world of Cambridge society, to which the larger world of Boston often contributed its contingent; and to these receptions, or *levees*, as they were termed, the students were freely invited, and freely came. After a few years these *soirées* were held only once a fortnight, instead of weekly; and when at last they were discontinued, I believe there was but one feeling of regret on the part of all who frequented them, and they are still recalled, by those whose recollections run back so far, as among the pleasantest memories of their lives. And there can be no doubt as to the beneficial influence of these receptions, while they lasted, on the manners and morals of the young men.

One of President Quincy's maxims of government was that discontents are much more easily prevented than cured, and his practice was in accordance with it. I will give two instances. At the time of his accession to office the ancient institution of the Commons Hall still existed. Though all the students were not required to sit at the board spread by the College, still a great proportion of them did so from mingled motives of convenience and economy. The table was provided by a contractor, who, though not the worst of his class, thought naturally more of his own profit than of the contentment of the hungry lads whose meat he was to provide in due season. In all time, since the memory of man, the Commons were the fertile source of discontent and disturbance. Almost every rebellion against the constituted authorities had begun in the Commons Hall, and, it must be owned, if all tales be true, not always without palliation, or even justification. This occasion of offence the new President removed merely by requiring the tables to be properly served, simply, but plentifully and neatly, — a device which seems never to have occurred to his predecessors. As the table service of the contractor was not such as the spirit of the age and the habits of the students when at home demanded, the President took this matter into his own hands, and ordered a set of china from Liverpool, with the College buildings, or some of them, on each piece, and replaced the dubious metal which did the duty of silver with genuine articles, each authenticated with the College arms. These changes removed all complaints, and I believe no breach of discipline began in the dining-hall after they were effected.

This is one of the stories he used to tell on this point. One day the contractor came to him, and complained that the students would persist in toasting their bread at the stove, to the manifest detriment of the forks employed in that chemical experiment. He said it had always been a matter of complaint, but that no Faculty had yet been found equal to the emergency. "What did they do when you complained?" inquired the President. "Why, they would admonish the offender, and, in case of a repetition of the practice, they would suspend or dismiss him." "But that seems rather hard measure," expostulated the President. "Pray, do not you have your own bread toasted for breakfast in winter?" "Certainly I do," returned the contractor to this *argumentum ad hominem;* "but I cannot afford to toast the bread of all the College on my present terms." "Very good," the President replied; "*toast the bread*, and charge the additional expense in your bill!" And so the great toast question was settled forever.

Another cause of dissatisfaction among the students was the way in which their academic rank was determined, and the College honors distributed. There was no exact rule for the settlement of this matter, and rank and honors were given upon a kind of general average of merit, on which point there was often a difference of opinion between the Faculty and the students. Sometimes it was thought the former were influenced in their decisions by the personal qualities of a candidate, which would enable him to make a creditable appearance on a public day, to the injury of a painstaking fellow-student whose merits were not set off by equal advantages of manner or appearance. Whether or not there were any grounds for these suspicions of partiality, — exercised not so much in favor of the person as of the College, as was generally admitted, — they did exist, and gave rise to that sense of injustice which is so hard for any of us, but especially for the young, to bear. Mr. Quincy set himself to devise a remedy for this wrong, real or imaginary, and invented the system which has removed all possibility of complaint on this head, as far as complaint can be made impossible among human beings, ever since. By this plan the merit of every College exercise is valued according to a scale of numbers, — say from one to eight, — by the professor or tutor, at the time of its performance. The sum of the whole, after deducting the amount of certain other numbers for small delinquencies, such as absences from lectures, or from chapel at daily prayers or on Sunday, make up the rank of each individual, — being the sum of his merits less that of his demerits. Mr. Quincy labored over this scheme most industriously at its inception, and, I think, actually kept the account himself until he had reduced it to a matter of mathematical certainty. Upon this plan there can be no injustice done, excepting by the officer making the original record at the time of the performance of each exercise, which is a thing not to be supposed possible. So entirely has this matter of the relative rank of the students been made mathematically exact, that the highest position has once or twice been decided by a difference of one or two out of scores of thousands, and in one case, at least, there were two friendly rivals whose sums of merit were exactly equal. The question has lately been mooted as to the expediency of changing the existing system of instruction for one allowing a wider range of individual choice in studies, and substituting for the ascertaining of proficiency by the present plan of accurate detail a more general one by rigid examinations. That some alteration of this kind will be made in our academical arrangements is not improbable, considering that the average age at which students now enter college is more mature by several years than the average of forty years ago. But until this revolution is accomplished, the system of "marks" introduced by

Mr. Quincy more than thirty-five years ago will probably hold its own as the best possible under the existing arrangements.

It is but just to President Quincy to say, that he endeavored to introduce a system of elective studies, by which the student's time could be more largely given to those departments of knowledge towards which he had a particular bent, or to which his parents or guardians wished his attention to be more particularly directed, than could be done on the old plan. No man could be more fixed in the faith that a competent knowledge of the ancient languages was the only sufficient foundation for a liberal education, in its proper signification, than President Quincy; but he was not so bigoted in this belief as to insist upon it that all men, of all capacities and tastes, should be rigidly confined to one unchangeable *curriculum* of studies. He was strongly in favor of the adoption of the voluntary system, as far as it was compatible with the condition of the College, and the means of instruction it could command. And, in effect, the elective experiment was tried more thoroughly, and on a broader scale, in his time, than it has ever been since. In the words of his third successor, President Walker, in an admirable memoir of my father, prepared for the Collections of the Historical Society, "If it should still be objected that he did not do as much as was expected for academic reform, the answer is found in the fact, that he did more than the College has been able to retain. At the present moment, though a reaction is understood to be now going on in favor of the elective or proper university system, that principle is not carried out and applied to anything like the same extent as under President Quincy's administration."

About the time Mr. Quincy entered upon the Presidency, Nathan Dane, illustrious for having drawn up the Northwestern Ordinance, by which slavery was forever excluded from the regions northwest of the river Ohio, founded the professorship of law which bears his name, and Judge Story was appointed the first Professor. That eminent jurist accordingly removed to Cambridge; and the feeling of mutual respect and regard which before existed between him and Mr. Quincy ripened into a warm and intimate friendship. The reorganization of that important branch of the University was therefore strictly contemporaneous with Mr. Quincy's entrance upon office, and he was actively efficient in promoting its progress and interests. The next year Mr. Dane advanced a sum of money sufficient to authorize the Corporation to provide the building known as the Dane Law College. On the dedication of this building, in October, 1831, to the purposes of the School, Mr. Quincy delivered an address, which was published and widely distributed. The following letter from Chief Justice Marshall contains his testimony to the value of such a school as one of the departments of a university.

"RICHMOND, December 10, 1832.

"DEAR SIR: — I am much indebted to you for the renewed proof of your recollection given by sending me a copy of your address at the dedication of Dane Law College. You have added to my respect for that estimable gentleman, who has bestowed a large portion of the acquisition of a valuable life on an institution which promises to be so advantageous to the profession he had adopted. I had not supposed that law was so negligently studied in your country, whatever it may be in the South, as you represented. But, however this may be, you satisfy me entirely that it may be read with greatly increased benefit in an institution connected with your University. I can very readily believe that 'to disincorporate this particular science from general knowledge is one great impediment to its advancement.' The vast influence which the members of the profession exercise in all popular governments, especially in ours, is perceived by all; and whatever tends to their improvement benefits the nation.

"I am, with great respect and esteem, your servant,

"J. MARSHALL."

Having thus briefly related the changes introduced by President Quincy into the instruction and general discipline of the undergraduates during his term of office, I will now return to the facts of his personal biography. The year after his removal from Boston to Cambridge, the second century from the first settlement of Boston was completed. It was thought proper by the city authorities, in compliance with the general wish of the citizens, to celebrate so interesting an anniversary by the usual commemorative services. President Quincy was selected as one eminently suitable to deliver the Address, in view of his descent from one of the founders of the city, and of his long official connection with it. He performed this duty with great care, and his discourse is perhaps the most finished, in point of style, of all his smaller productions. The celebration was held on the 17th day of September, 1830, which was given up to the holiday pleasures of the occasion. The formal services took place in the Old South Church, and the Address was received with great approbation. It traced the republican institutions of New England, as they now are, to their small beginnings, and showed the jealousy with which the founders of our secular and ecclesiastical polity guarded against the smallest infringement of civil and religious liberty. It affirmed that the idea of absolute independence of the mother country was almost, if not quite, contemporaneous with the emigration, and that the Revolution was but the complement of the scheme of the first generation of the Pilgrims. It explained the necessity, and asserted the wisdom, of the ecclesiastical policy of the early settlers, and defended them against the railing accusations of inconsistent bigotry which yet form so large a part of the stock in trade of shallow and malignant enemies of New England. It showed that their course was one of plain self-defence and simple common-sense, and that to their successful assertion of it we owe that perfect toleration of all sects, and absolute freedom in matters of religious faith and practice, which we now enjoy. These positions, political as well as ecclesiastical, were not permitted to pass unchallenged, and they were attacked both in this country and in England; but President Quincy was content to leave his statements and arguments to their own weight, and declined any controversy on the subject. As this Address has been long out of print, I will give a few passages of its peroration as specimens of its character, tone, and style. After a rapid but clear account of the political, moral, and religious condition of New England, he thus goes on: —

"If, after this general survey of the surface of New England, we cast our eyes on its cities and great towns, with what wonder should we behold, did not familiarity render the phenomenon almost unnoticed, men, combined in great multitudes, possessing freedom and the consciousness of strength, — the comparative physical power of the ruler less than that of a cobweb across a lion's path, — yet orderly, obedient, and respectful to authority; a people, but no populace; every class in reality existing which the general law of society acknowledges, except one, — and this exception characterizing the whole country. The soil of New England is trodden by no slave. In our streets, in our assemblies, in the halls of election and legislation, men of every rank and condition meet, and unite or divide on other principles, and are actuated by other motives, than those growing out of such distinctions. The fears and jealousies which in other countries separate classes of men, and make them hostile to each other, have here no influence, or a very limited one. Each individual, of whatever condition, has the consciousness of living under known laws, which secure equal rights, and guarantee to each whatever portion of the goods of life, be it great or small, chance or talent or industry may have bestowed. All perceive that the honors and rewards of society are open equally to the fair competition of all, — that the distinctions of wealth, or of power, are not fixed in families, — that whatever of this nature exists to-day may be changed to-morrow, or, in a coming generation, be absolutely reversed. Common principles, interests, hopes, and affections are the result of universal education. Such are the consequences of the equality of rights, and of the provisions for the general diffusion of knowledge, and the distribution of intestate estates, established by the laws framed by the earliest emigrants to New England.

"If from our cities we turn to survey the wide expanse of the interior, how do the effects of the institutions and example of our early ancestors appear, in all the local comfort and accommodation which mark the general condition of the whole country! — unobtrusive indeed, but substantial; in nothing splendid, but in everything sufficient and satisfactory. Indications of active talent and practical energy exist everywhere. With a soil comparatively little luxuriant, and in great proportion either rock, or hill, or sand, the skill and industry of man are seen triumphing over the obstacles of nature; making the rock the guardian of the field; moulding the granite, as though it were clay; leading cultivation to the hill-top, and spreading over the arid plain hitherto unknown and unanticipated harvests. The lofty mansion of the prosperous adjoins the lowly dwelling of the husbandman; their respective inmates are in the daily interchange of civility, sympathy, and respect. Enterprise and skill, which once held chief affinity with the ocean or the sea-board, now begin to delight the interior, haunting our rivers, where the music of the waterfall, with powers more attractive than those of the fabled harp of Orpheus, collects around it intellectual man and material nature. Towns and cities, civilized and happy communities, rise, like exhalations, on rocks and in forests, till the deep and far-sounding voice of the neighboring torrent is itself lost and unheard, amid the predominating noise of successful and rejoicing labor.

"What lessons has New England, in every period of her history, given to the world! What lessons do her condition and example still give! How unprecedented, yet how practical! How simple, yet how powerful! She has proved that all the variety of Christian sects may live together in harmony, under a government which allows equal privileges to all, exclusive pre-eminence to none. She has proved that ignorance among the multitude is not necessary to order, but that the surest basis of perfect order is the information of the people. She has proved the old maxim, that 'no government, except a despotism with a standing army, can subsist where the people have arms,' to be false. Ever since the first settlement of the country, arms have been required to be in the hands of the whole multitude of New England; yet the use of them in a private quarrel, if it have ever happened, is so rare, that a late writer of great intelligence, who had passed his whole life in New England, and possessed extensive means of information, declares, 'I know not a single instance of it.'* She has proved that a people of a character essentially military may subsist without duelling. New England has at all times been distinguished, both on the land and on the ocean, for a daring, fearless, and enterprising spirit; yet the same writer† asserts that, during the whole period of her existence, her soil has been disgraced but by *five* duels, and that only *two* of these were fought by her native inhabitants! Perhaps this assertion is not minutely correct. There can, however, be no question that it is sufficiently near the truth to justify the position for which it is here adduced, and which the history of New England, as well as the experience of her inhabitants, abundantly confirms, — that, in the present and in every past age, the spirit of our institutions has, to every important practical purpose, annihilated the spirit of duelling.

"Such are the true glories of the institutions of our fathers! Such the natural fruits of that patience in toil, that frugality of disposition,

* See "Travels in New England and New York, by Timothy Dwight, S.T.D. LL. D., late President of Yale College," Vol. IV. p. 334.

† Ibid., p. 336.

that temperance of habit, that general diffusion of knowledge, and that sense of religious responsibility, inculcated by the precepts, and exhibited in the example, of every generation of our ancestors!

"And now, standing at this hour on the dividing line which separates the ages that are past from those which are to come, how solemn is the thought, that not one of this vast assembly — not one of that great multitude who now throng our streets, rejoice in our fields, and make our hills echo with their gratulations — shall live to witness the next return of the era we this day celebrate! The dark veil of futurity conceals from human sight the fate of cities and nations, as well as of individuals. Man passes away; generations are but shadows; — there is nothing stable but truth; principles only are immortal.

"What, then, in conclusion of this great topic, are the elements of the liberty, prosperity, and safety which the inhabitants of New England at this day enjoy? In what language, and concerning what comprehensive truths, does the wisdom of former times address the inexperience of the future?

"Those elements are simple, obvious, and familiar.

"Every civil and religious blessing of New England — all that here gives happiness to human life, or security to human virtue — is alone to be perpetuated in the forms and under the auspices of a free commonwealth.

"The commonwealth itself has no other strength or hope than the intelligence and virtue of the individuals that compose it.

"For the intelligence and virtue of individuals there is no other human assurance than laws providing for the education of the whole people.

"These laws themselves have no strength, or efficient sanction, except in the moral and accountable nature of man disclosed in the records of the Christian's faith; the right to read, to construe, and to judge concerning which belongs to no class or caste of men, but exclusively to the individual, who must stand or fall by his own acts and his own faith, and not by those of another.

"The great comprehensive truths, written in letters of living light on every page of our history, — the language addressed by every past age of New England to all future ages, is this: *Human happiness has no perfect security but freedom; freedom, none but virtue; virtue, none but knowledge; and neither freedom, nor virtue, nor knowledge has any vigor, or immortal hope, except in the principles of the Christian faith, and in the sanctions of the Christian religion.*

"Men of Massachusetts! citizens of Boston! descendants of the early emigrants! consider your blessings; consider your duties. You have an inheritance acquired by the labors and sufferings of six successive generations of ancestors. They founded the fabric of your prosperity in a severe and masculine morality, having intelligence for its cement, and religion for its groundwork. Continue to build on the same foundation, and by the same principles; let the extending temple of your country's freedom rise, in the spirit of ancient times, in proportions of intellectual and moral architecture, — just, simple, and sublime. As from the first to this day, let New England continue to be an example to the world of the blessings of a free government, and of the means and capacity of man to maintain it. And in all times to come, as in all times past, may Boston be among the foremost and the boldest to exemplify and uphold whatever constitutes the prosperity, the happiness, and the glory of New England."

The correspondence between my father and Lafayette was kept up as long as the latter lived, one letter a year at least being exchanged by them. The winter after the Revolution of July, 1830, my father addressed the following letter to Lafayette, which contains its own excuse for the delay of his congratulations on the successful issue of the Three Days.

Mr. Quincy to General Lafayette.

"Cambridge, January 30, 1831.

"Dear Sir: — Permit me to join the voice of my country, as of the truly great and good of every land, and express my congratulations for the unexampled success of the events which have recently distinguished France, and my admiration of the part you have acted in them. I should have done so earlier, but I knew the multitude of communications of this kind with which you must be oppressed, and I was willing to postpone my gratification, out of respect to your convenience and the better rights of others. I need not tell you of the intense anxiety which has been felt by your friends on this side the Atlantic, when they perceived you were putting to risk the fame you had acquired through the sacrifice and suffering of a long life, and placing your great name again in the front ranks of a revolution as critical, perhaps, as any the world has ever witnessed. The recollection of the scenes which succeeded the events of 1789 added strength to their fears. It was not realized that the lapse and lessons of forty years had materially changed the character of the French people.

Like convulsions — a reign of anarchy, succeeded by a reign of despotism — were anticipated. How wonderfully, how joyfully, have their anticipations been proved groundless! With what pride do your friends perceive the prudence as well as the predominance of your genius. A revolution in the great capital of France, effected without other bloodshed than that which flowed in the first and inevitable combat. A new dynasty established, united by its relations with the ancient prejudices of the people, yet severed, by the character of the immediate sovereign and his family, from all that excited fears in the friends of a well-regulated freedom. That this revolution has been as yet bloodless, except in battle, is attributed here to the mild influences of your character. May your designs and desires relative to this eventful topic be accomplished. May those influences of your virtues which are seen and acknowledged in whatever there has been of hope and honor in this revolution be continued. May you forever attach to your memory what your sacrifices and labors so well deserve, — the name of father of two nations, and the hero of both worlds. You well know, sir, this is not the language of compliment, nor yet of an individual. It is that of the whole American people. It is, or will soon be, that of all France, of Europe, and the world. In the elevated and yet critical situation in which you stand, your American friends see nothing but new opportunities for putting to proof and for giving occasion of success to those virtues and influences which have already been instrumental of good to America, and to France. They are yet solicitous to be assured that the mild and humane principles which have so uniformly characterized your life continue to sway those around you, and that the throne of Louis Philippe shall have its foundations laid sure on the principles of mercy. Pardon, sir, these expressions of respect and honor, which the personal affections my acquaintance with you implanted in my bosom have compelled.

"You did me the honor in your last letter to me to request that I would transmit to you a small publication of mine, on declining the re-election to the Mayor's office of Boston. With this request I complied, and accompanied the pamphlet with a letter by Dr. Kirkland. I mention this fact lest I should seem insensible of the honor conferred on me by your request, as I have reason to apprehend that the pamphlet and letter never reached your hand. Encouraged by your former expressions of interest, I now transmit an address delivered by me at the request of the city authorities of Boston, in September last, on the second centennial anniversary of the settlement of that city. Should you find a few moments for its perusal, I think you will perceive the character of our ancestors in New England placed in a truer light than that in which it had been accustomed to be viewed, and those features of their character usually deemed most objectionable softened, if not vindicated.

"I am, sir, with great respect, your friend and obedient servant,

"JOSIAH QUINCY."

In the autumn of 1833, the year before the death of Lafayette, my sister Margaret visited Europe with her husband, the late Mr. B. D. Greene, and when in France paid a visit to La Grange, of which she wrote a description to my father. I am sure my readers will pardon me for varying the monotony of my narrative by the insertion of this charming episode.

LA GRANGE.

Extract from a letter addressed to President Quincy by his daughter Mrs. B. D. Greene.

"We intended to defer presenting your letter of introduction to General Lafayette until our return from Italy. The General, hearing through a friend that your daughter was in Paris, came in person to see us, accompanied by his son George Washington and two ladies of his family. At his urgent request, we passed the first night at 'La Grange,' on our way to Italy, quitting Paris on the 8th of December, 1833.

"We arrived at four o'clock, and, having sent François forward to announce us, found the gates open, and servants ready to receive us. The hall of entrance is ornamented by flags, and the stone staircase lined by jars of flowers. Upon the landing-place we were most cordially welcomed by Madame Lasteyrie, the daughter of Lafayette, and one of his granddaughters. They conducted us through a large apartment to the *salon*, where a bright wood-fire presented a most cheerful aspect in the dark autumnal evening. Lafayette now entered, received us in the kindest manner, and presented us to the ladies as 'representatives of very dear friends.' He then accompanied Mr. Greene to his apartment, while the young lady attended me to mine; in both were fires burning and servants in waiting. At six returned to the *salon*, where the family then at the chateau were presented to us by Lafayette. They considered their number reduced almost to solitude; but twelve persons sat down at dinner, besides ourselves. I was conducted by Lafayette to the fine old *salle à manger* (a stone hall with groined roof), placed at his right hand, and was the recipient of all kind attentions. The dinner passed very agreeably, and, on adjourning to the *salon*, we found assembled the great-grand-children of Lafayette then at the chateau, pretty specimens of French children, of various ages.

"Upon the centre-table were the water-colored drawings of the Adams and Hancock Houses, painted by Susan. Lafayette read aloud the inscriptions, spoke of her kindness in presenting them to him, and the value they possessed.

"The ladies expressed their interest in the drawings, and had much to say concerning the General's visit to Boston and Quincy. Coffee was served at ten, tea at half past eleven, and, after an animated and agreeable evening, the company retired.

"At ten the next morning we joined the ladies and some of the gentlemen in the *salon*, and at eleven Lafayette, preceded by his beautiful little dog, entered; all the company rising at his entrance,— a mark of respect paid whenever he entered or left the apartment. He gave Mr. Greene several letters of introduction to various dignitaries in Italy, and, after speaking in high terms of the Princess Charlotte Napoleon,* presented me with a letter addressed to her in Florence, requesting me particularly to make her acquaintance, as he was certain it would prove a mutual pleasure. Then, taking my hand and saying, 'Come, dear friend,' he led me down stairs to breakfast, *à la fourchette*,—beginning with soup and ending with coffee. In the room adjoining the *salon* are portraits of the Presidents of the United States; the books presented by you to Lafayette were upon a table, round which the family were accustomed to assemble to read the letters and newspapers, giving accounts of Lafayette's reception and progress in America.

"The American flag draped one side of this apartment. Flags possessing different histories adorn many of the walls of the chateau. Among them that of the 'Brandywine,'—the frigate placed by the government of the United States at the disposal of Lafayette, upon his return to France. Upon his arrival this flag was presented, at his request, as a souvenir of the voyage, and of his friendship with the officers.

"We were then invited to visit the library, Lafayette's bedroom, dressing-room, and other apartments. In these are collections of various presents of every description and value, given to Lafayette during his last visit to the United States. The dressing-room is hung

* The daughter of Joseph Bonaparte.

with portraits, prints, and pictures; — among these are the drawings by Susan which were shown to us last evening.

"The library is a charming room. Lafayette requested me to observe his desk, which was placed at a window commanding a view of the farm, etc.

"We were shown a variety of gifts and relics, each possessing some interesting story, told by Lafayette in his endearing manner. A short walk round the grounds followed. The chateau has been in Madame Lafayette's family for six hundred years. Fisher's pictures of it are excellent.

"At four our carriage was announced, and the ladies, with Lafayette, accompanied us to the door of the hall, offering good wishes and affectionate farewells. Lafayette tenderly embraced me, thanked us for visiting him at so late a season, and, waving his hand, exclaimed, 'Adieu, dear friends,' as we were driven away. We consider it a great privilege to have seen him at La Grange, surrounded by his family. He seemed in good health, but was constantly attended by a servant, who assisted him in rising. A favorite dog, — a *chien-loup*, — white as snow, never quitted him, and received from him a lump of sugar at meals.

"The unceasing affection and respect shown to Lafayette by all around him was very striking to an American.

"The visit in all its details will remain a most interesting and unique episode in my experience."

During the absence of my sister and her husband in Europe, Lafayette died, in 1834. After their return home my father addressed the following letter to M. George Washington Lafayette, which will fitly conclude that interesting passage of his life.

To G. W. Lafayette.

"Cambridge, January 24, 1835.

"Dear Sir: — The return of my son-in-law and daughter (Mr. and Mrs. Greene) from Europe, and their interesting recollections of their visit to La Grange, call upon me to express, both in their behalf and my own, the gratitude we have felt for all the kindness thus experienced from your lamented father and the ladies of his family.

"How pleasing would it have been to us had we been permitted to have made this expression of our feelings to that father! A father, — so loved, so honored, and now so mourned, — beyond the lot of any other being of our race! For where in all history is there a name concentrating on itself such a universal and overflowing honor and affection as Lafayette?

"It was not, however, my purpose to touch a theme on which the eloquence of the New World, as well as that of the Old, has been already employed and exhausted. My object in this letter was wholly of an individual and personal character. The gratification my whole family received by the kind reception given to those two beloved members by your father and his family claimed from me a distinct expression of gratitude.

"To you, sir, as his son and representative, I cannot deny myself this privilege of uttering feelings which I am not permitted to express to him. Be assured, sir, that the hours passed at La Grange by those highly favored children of mine were to them the happiest and most cherished in recollection of all those spent in their tour in Europe,— although in every other respect most happy.

"Accept, sir, these expressions of our feelings, and with them the best wishes for your happiness, and for that of all that may be dear to you, from your obliged friend and servant,

"JOSIAH QUINCY."

In the summer of 1833 General Jackson, then just entering on his second administration, made his tour through the Northern States. He was everywhere received with the respect due to the head of the nation. And his recent dealings with South Carolina and Nullification had in some measure qualified, even in Massachusetts, the feelings of dislike and distrust which his election and his earlier administration had created at the North, and especially in New England. No President, not even Washington himself, had a more splendid welcome to Boston than General Jackson. At the time of the visit of President Monroe in 1817, it had been thought due to his high station that the University should confer upon him her highest degree. In the light of this precedent my father considered it the duty of the authorities of the University to do the same honor to President Jackson. The Corporation were of the same opinion, as were such of the Overseers as could be got together at an informal meeting. President Jackson was evidently much gratified at the compliment, and expressed his sense of the proffered honor in suitable terms. A special academic session was had in the chapel of the University on the 26th of June. The chapel was entirely filled with the members of the Corporation and Overseers, the Faculty, the students, and the general public. When the procession entered, the whole audience rose and remained standing until the two Presidents had taken their seats on the platform in front of the pulpit. The General submitted graciously to the Latin, bowed generally in the proper places, and received his parchment in eloquent silence, which was broken by general applause. After his reception among the sons of Harvard, he held a levee at the President's house, which was attended largely by the members of the University and the inhabitants of the town. Nothing could be more soldierly and gentlemanlike than the bearing and manners of General Jackson, when he was upon his good behavior; and much of the prejudice which had raged against him, and which soon revived with the war he declared against the United States Bank, disappeared before the charm of his personal presence. This academic action was made the occasion of much ridicule and of many virulent attacks upon my father. Party spirit, which had slept for a moment, soon awoke again, and the same outside influences which the next year fostered the intestine disturbances of the College seized on this occasion to cast odium upon him. At the next regular meeting of the Overseers, whose consent was necessary to confirm the degree, but which could not be had in proper form for want of time at the moment, there was an attempt to invalidate the transaction, or at least to censure it. But precedent, common sense, and the custom of learned bodies in the Old World overbore the attempt, and General Jackson lived and died a Doctor of Laws, entitled to all the privileges and pre-eminences thereunto appertaining.

CHAPTER XVIII.

1833 – 1845.

Sir Augustus Foster. — Correspondence with President Quincy. — College Disturbances in 1834. — Celebration of 1836. — Dangerous Situation of the Library. — Gore Hall built. — Growth of the Observatory. — Built and equipped mainly by President Quincy's Efforts. — Profitable Purchases of Lands. — History of Harvard College. — Letter from Chancellor Kent. — From James Grahame, the Historian. — Correspondence and Friendship with him. — Memoir of Grahame. — Republication of his History of the United States. — Dealings with Mr. Bancroft. — President Quincy resigns his Office. — Reasons for his Resignation. — Results of his Administration. — Testimony of President Walker. — His Last Commencement. — Takes Leave of Cambridge. — Returns to Boston.

DURING my father's life at Washington he had made the acquaintance of Mr. Augustus John Foster, who was there first as Attaché and Secretary of the British Legation, and afterwards as Minister. After serving his time as Secretary of Legation in this country, he was promoted to be Chargé d'Affaires at the Court of Stockholm, whence he was transferred, after the removal of Mr. Jackson, to Washington, in 1811. He was an agreeable and accomplished young man, and a friendly intercourse existed between himself and my father during their common residence at Washington, and he paid one or two visits to Quincy when they were both off duty at the capital. Naturally enough, their common detestation of Bonaparte, and dread of the universal empire of the French, drew Mr. Foster and the Federal members of Congress together, of whom, as will be seen presently, he always retained a kindly remembrance. He was a gentleman of good descent, being the son of Mr. John Thomas Foster of Dunleer, County Louth, and Lady Elizabeth Hervey, daughter of the eccentric fourth Earl of Bristol and Bishop of Derry, and granddaughter of Pope's "Lord Fanny" and Molly Lepel. After the death of Mr. Foster, Lady Elizabeth married, in 1809, the fifth Duke of Devonshire, thus succeeding the celebrated Duchess Georgiana, famous in the last century for her beauty and Whig zeal, and historical for the part she took in behalf of Mr. Fox in the great Westminster election of 1784. Mr. Foster was British Minister at Washington at the time the war of 1812 was declared, and did all in his power to prevent it. Receiving the news of the repeal of the Orders in Council at Halifax, on his way home, he prevailed on the Admiral in command on the North American Station to suspend proceedings against captured American vessels, in the hope that the removal of that one great pretext for hostilities might lead to a pacification. In the same spirit he induced Sir George Prevost, who commanded the land forces, to propose to General Dearborn an armistice until the action of the American government in this new state of things could be known. General Dearborn agreed to this proposition; but the things that made for peace found no favor in the eyes of the war party at Washington. The Cabinet refused to ratify the armistice, or to consent to a mutual suspension of proceedings in the prize courts, and the war went forward on the one issue of impressment, with what success we have already seen. Mr. Foster subsequently was Minister to Denmark and to Sardinia, was made a Privy Councillor, a Knight Grand Cross of the Hanoverian Guelphic Order, and, in 1831, a Baronet.

After more than twenty years' separation Sir Augustus Foster renewed his acquaintance with my father by the following cordial letter, which led to an occasional correspondence.

SIR AUGUSTUS FOSTER TO PRESIDENT QUINCY.

"TURIN, September 30, 1833.

"MY DEAR SIR: — I should hardly venture to recall myself to your recollection, if I had not learnt from Dr. Bigelow, whom I accidentally met on board the steamboat of the Rhone, that you were very well, and comfortably estatablished in your native State, and at the head, if I mistook not, of the University. I am sorry that neither you, nor any other of my Washington friends, ever give any letter for me to your countrymen who come to travel in Europe. I should at all times be happy to see them, if their hurry to go South would allow them to stop a day or two at Turin. I was in hopes Dr. Bigelow would have made us a visit on his return from Naples; but I conclude he did not pass this way. I am busily engaged in putting my notes together which I collected during my double residence in the United States, with a view to getting them in order for printing some years hence, and, as I have set down naught in malice, but, on the contrary, found much to praise, I trust you will not be dissatisfied with the book.

"You have had enough of nonsense from Mrs. Trollope and other silly people, who saw nothing but the dark side, and who did not deserve such kind treatment as they met with, being merely land-jobbers or book-jobbers, instead of travellers for information.

"You would much oblige me if you could get me any short account of the mode in which schools are conducted, and tutors educated for the purpose, in Connecticut or Massachusetts, where the system seemed to be excellent, and also if you could procure for me the memoirs of your uncle,* the immediate successor of Washington, which I remember appeared piecemeal in a Boston paper, but which I was never able to get in an entire state.

"I scarcely venture, after such a separation, to inquire after your family. . . . . I have been married since the year 1815,† and have three boys, the eldest of whom, now seventeen years old, I sent this year to Edinburgh to be prepared for the University of Cambridge. The second is destined for the Church, and the third for the law. If any of yours ever travel this way, don't fail to recommend them to call on me.

"I was in correspondence with poor Randolph not many months before he died. Did you not smile at his punctiliousness about pronunciation in his dying moments, when the doctor would so obstinately say *omnipo'tent?*

. . . . . .

"I suppose there are but few in Congress now of our old New England friends, whom we remember in the wide waste of the Federal city. I should like to know if Pitkin is still flourishing? And Hunter of Rhode Island? But I am come to the end of my paper. Begging you to receive my best wishes for the continued prosperity of yourself and family. I am, my dear sir, very truly yours,

"AUG. J. FOSTER."

* It is unnecessary to say that Sir Augustus was mistaken as to this relationship. The middle name of President John Quincy Adams has often led strangers to infer a nearer blood relationship than actually exists between the two families.

† Sir Augustus Foster married Lady Albinia Jane Hobart, sister of the fifth Earl of Buckinghamshire, and a descendant of John Hampden. Lady Albinia Foster, I believe, still survives.

PRESIDENT QUINCY TO SIR AUGUSTUS FOSTER.

"CAMBRIDGE, Massachusetts, March 7, 1834.

"MY DEAR SIR: — I have had the great pleasure of receiving your letter of the 30th of September, and should have replied earlier had not public and official duties prevented my reciprocating your kind expressions of recollection. Availing myself of your permission, I have transmitted a letter of introduction to you to my son-in-law, B. D. Greene, Esq., who, with my daughter, is now in Italy. He is a man of science, and chiefly devoted to the pursuits of natural history. On the death of his father, whose widow is a sister of Lord Lyndhurst, he has entered a second time on a tour of Europe.

"Your proposed work on the United States I doubt not will be characterized by candor and correctness, and be a valuable addition to the mass of knowledge concerning a period of American history not without its interest and its lesson. I say nothing concerning the already perished travels of the Trollopes, the Fiddlers, the Halls, and the Hamiltons, since you entertain so just an opinion of them. These birds of passage have skimmed over this country like vultures over the surface of the Carolinas, pouncing upon whatever is corrupt, and passing by whatever is sound or healthful, as adapted neither to their taste nor scent.

"The American Almanac for 1831, which I send, contains a concentrated account of the schools in the United States. Satisfactory information on the same topic can be found in Rich's View of the United States, published in London, 1833. I know of no memoir of the late President John Adams; the publication to which you allude, and which appeared in the form of a pamphlet, is now out of print. I also send you Dwight's History of the Hartford Convention.

"There must be at Turin resources of which you perhaps are not aware, relative to this country, in the extensive and valuable collections of books and pamphlets made by Count Vidua, son of a prime minister of the King of Sardinia, which I understood were transmitted to Italy some ten years ago. At the time I was Mayor of Boston he brought letters of special introduction to me, and I aided him in his researches. He was possessed with an insatiable thirst for visiting foreign countries, and died somewhere in the East Indies.

"It gives me great pleasure to hear of the happy prospects of your family, and, in reply to your kind inquiries after mine, I have the happiness to state that my wife is still preserved to me. We have two sons and five daughters, and are descending into the vale of life with as many causes of gratitude as belong to human lot.

"At the solicitation of the Corporation of Harvard University I accepted some years since the presidency of that seminary, and now reside at Cambridge. It is an office of superintendence, and not of instruction. My social relations are extremely pleasant, — not the less so by their having withdrawn me from any direct connection with the politics of the country. As I advance in life, the selfishness and virulence which distinguish them have become disgusting to me.

"Death has indeed made sad havoc among the ranks of those who enjoyed your acquaintance at Washington. Pitkin still lives, and occupies himself with the statistics and history of his country; Dana, Hillhouse, and Pickering are gathered to their fathers. Poor Randolph! America could well have spared a better man. In a highly civilized state of society, and possessing a cultivated intellect, he had the temper and spirit of his savage ancestress, Pocahontas. His tomahawk was continually in his hand, and his scalping-knife ever hung at his side. His warfare was never of the regular, but always of the partisan character. Enemies he could not destroy he never failed to cripple. Those he could not conquer, he was apt to leave skinned alive. Before his death his eccentricities had become so great that he was thought by many to be deranged. But peace to his ashes. Hunter is, I am told, alive, but forgotten.

"Five-and-twenty years have produced an almost total change in the relations of society. Those whom you knew in active life are either gone or grown old. A race of politicians have succeeded, formed in a school more consonant to the changeful humor of the times than that in which their predecessors had been educated. They steer the ship of state by the winds of popular favor, before which they run, which they never seek to stem, which they dare not resist. So long as the tempestuous sea of liberty has sea-room for such sailing, the navigators who hold the helm will be such as they now are. To my eye, however, she is in the midst of breakers, which if she escape it will be by good luck and not by seamanship. The relations of this country are vast and unparalleled, and results are constantly occurring which seem to set at defiance both sound reason and experience. Your own country also seems to me well inclined to enter on the career of revolution, for I cannot see anything less in the (measures*) of reform which seem to be contemplated. All I can say is,

'Tu, nisi ventis
Debes ludibrium, cave!'

* Word illegible in the press-copy.

"It will always give me pleasure to hear from you. Whatever local publication you may wish to obtain, you may always command by giving me notice of it. . . . .

"With every wish for your happiness and for that of your family, I am, my dear sir, very truly yours,

"JOSIAH QUINCY."

SIR AUGUSTUS FOSTER TO PRESIDENT QUINCY.

"TURIN, July 12, 1834.

"MY DEAR SIR:—I have been in hopes to see your daughter and son-in-law for some weeks. The weather being so hot, I made sure of their coming northward, but I now begin to despair of it, and have written to our Minister at Florence to inquire after them, having heard from Mr. Temple Bowdoin, whom I accidentally met in the street, that they were there.

"I am much obliged to you for your friendly reply, and for the books which you were so good as to send me, particularly the History of the Hartford Convention. That is, of course, very interesting to me.

"The Italian gentleman (M. Vidua) whom you knew at Boston died, I am sorry to say, three or four years ago, in one of the Dutch or Philippine Islands, of the effects of an injury he received from slipping his leg into some hot sulphur while examining a *solfatara*. He was a great traveller, and two of his countrymen are putting his notes in order; but I am sorry to say, that those relating to the United States are believed to have been burnt, as he had deposited them with the Sardinian Consul at Bordeaux, who executed literally some order which he gave him years previously, to burn his papers in case of his death occurring without his having claimed them. This order was supposed to have been given from a fear of their not being arranged in a manner to do honor to his memory; but his old father and his old friends here are in despair at it. Luckily, every person with whom he left papers did not think it necessary to act up to his order for burning; but, unfortunately, those on the United States had been deposited at Bordeaux.

"I cannot say when any notes of mine will see the day, as diplomates must be more cautious than other people. But it amuses me to put my recollections together; and I feel a spur in looking at the stupid assertions and reflections of so many book-makers who have visited your country full of prejudice and vulgarity, and who describe the fungous populations of Irish or Germans, or Atlantic settlers at the West, as if they were natives, and very often in total forgetfulness of the old line, '*Cœlum, non animum mutant.*' Captain Hall was here last winter and amused me with his criticisms, which smacked rather of editorial jealousy, on Rush's book, which seems to me a very good-humored, harmless account of England, far different from our own Bulwer's, and I dare say popular enough in the United States, where people must find much information on the every-day sort of matter introduced into it.

"I have now got a leave of absence, and we shall be first joined by my three boys, and then travel homewards and go to a country-place I have hired for the season in Norfolk, to be near *our* Cambridge, where I shall put my eldest in October. I sadly fear, therefore, we shall not have the pleasure of seeing Mr. and Mrs. Greene, but I expect to hear about them from Mr. Seymour,* and I should be sorry not to be able to do the honors of this place to them; for there are several clever and scientific people here, and, though not given so much to the arts as the rest of Italy, yet is Turin highly respectable as a capital, and much the most national people are here of any in the peninsula. They were indeed esteemed by Bonaparte above all the others, and much employed by him. And I am particularly acquainted with Plana, the Professor of Astronomy, and with Boucheron, Professor of Latin Eloquence.

"I will now conclude, with many congratulations on your prosperous situation every way, and beg you will give my best remembrances to Mrs. Quincy.

"Yours most truly,

"A. J. FOSTER.

"I beg you to employ me, if I can be of use to you at any time."

The following is the last letter my father received from Sir Augustus Foster, which I will insert in this place, although it belongs chronologically to a somewhat later page. My brother and sister, Mr. and Mrs. Greene, visiting Europe a second time in 1838-39, my father again gave them letters to his old friend, of which, unfortunately, they were again prevented from availing themselves.

* Then British Minister at Florence; now Sir George Hamilton Seymour, G. C. B. He was Minister at St. Petersburg at the breaking out of the war with Russia, as will be remembered by all familiar with that passage of recent history.

SIR AUGUSTUS FOSTER TO PRESIDENT QUINCY.

"TURIN, July 18, 1839.

"MY DEAR SIR:—I was very much pleased to get another letter from you, though sorry to see written on the back of it that the bearer, your son-in-law, could not deliver it in person, by which I know not when I shall have the pleasure of making Mr. Greene's acquaintance. Turin would not have furnished, I fear, much nourishment for his favorite tastes, though the indigenous flowers are thought so well of, that I once sent a collection of them to the Horticultural Society, at their particular desire; and the owners of landed property are beginning to take an interest in planting. Milan, however, is far beyond them in botanical knowledge, and at Monza is a first-rate garden.

"I was happy to see you were in good spirits at the time of your writing, and could joke upon my Notes, although you say so much of Death and Fate, and your being destined perhaps to read them in Kingdom-come. And why? Are you so very old? I own I thought you still a good bit under sixty. But I remember you used to have a fling every now and then, in the olden time, at the fate of us mortals being to vegetate and rot, though this consideration never seemed to oppress your spirits. For my part, as it was once my chance to cross Hyde Park with M. Delille, *valet de chambre* of Louis XV., when he was one hundred and seven years old, and who, although he had had to hide . . . . in Robespierre's time . . . .* was still a spruce fellow, and walked as straight as an arrow, I never can bring myself to believe but what I am still a youngster. However, I have my three sons just now all with me, who now and then waken me up from so agreeable a dream; and, as in your country such youngsters may already be provided with other youngsters almost able to shove them also off the stage, I conclude your mementos are more stringent than mine, and therefore make you feel more near the edge of the great precipice.

"Now, with respect to my Notes, you must observe that I am still in office; and, though they are nearly ready for printing, yet they must not come forth till I am free,—though I doubt if they will be thought much of when they do come forth. This, however, I will tell you,—that I have a foible for your division of the country of Transatlantidis, that is, for New England, which I look upon as nearly as much superior to the districts south of the Susquehanna as Old England is to Hungary or Sicily. J. Randolph once told me that slaves were neces-

* The details of the hiding of this veteran are really too unsavory for the eye of this squeamish generation.

sary to form a gentleman; but J. Randolph knew little of Connecticut and Massachusetts, and would have made an excellent Russian nobleman. Did you ever hear of his having presented his letters of credence to the Emperor at St. Petersburg on his knees? It is a positive fact.

"I shall be much flattered by receiving a copy of your History of the American Cambridge University, and it will be a pleasure to trace with you its origin up to where it branched off from the parent stream, and then to the common source from whence the united channels, English and New English, were derived.

"Knowledge has, I fear, become almost unfashionable, from the weight of books and stupendous volumes which absolutely encumber the earth on every possible subject, and frighten the votaries of ease; and few are the heads now-a-days which can expect to equal, in concentration at least of acquirement, those of the fifteenth or sixteenth centuries, while books of reference under everybody's hand make us independent almost of studying. It is a great pity, but it cannot be helped; and even reading the classics over again, or quoting them, is become far less common than it used to be.

"When my eldest son, who has been attached to my mission for about two years, shall get into the diplomatic saddle, which I hope will happen in a year or two, I shall hope to get leave to retire to enjoy '*Otium cum dignitate*,' shouting out, '*Inveni portum: Spes et Fortuna valete!*' And why may I not entertain some hopes of seeing you in England? You will come over some day or other, and I trust I shall have a visit from you if you do.

"I observe by the date of your letter, December 10, 1838, that your work must be out; and, if so, may I request you to send me the copy you are so good as to promise me to my address, 'Foreign Office, Downing Street.'

"I beg to repeat my best wishes for you and your family, and believe me very truly and sincerely yours,

"A. J. FOSTER."

I believe the work on America which Sir Augustus Foster contemplated never saw the light. He retired from diplomatic life the year after the above letter was written, 1840, and returned to England. His life of various and useful public service came unhappily to a tragical conclusion. His health gave way under a complication of disorders which finally resulted in insanity, in an access of which he committed suicide, by cutting his throat, at his seat of Branksea Castle, Dorsetshire, on the 1st of August, 1848. He is represented at present by his second son, Sir Cavendish Hervey Foster, who is in Holy Orders, his eldest son and successor having died in 1857.

In the year 1834 President Quincy established a new rule of action in relation to the undergraduates, in the face of violent opposition outside the walls of the College as well as within them. That this should have been the case may seem a little surprising to simple citizens who have never enjoyed the advantages of a collegiate education. The new principle was this, — that, where flagrant outrages were committed against persons or property by members of the University, within its limits, they should be proceeded against, in the last resort, like any other citizens, before the courts of the Commonwealth. Non-academical persons found it hard to understand why young gentlemen in the possession of privileges of education superior to those they had themselves enjoyed should therefore be exempted from the penalties of the violated laws of the land, which would be inexorably visited on themselves or their sons in like case. Still, the application of this simple principle produced a prodigious ferment among the students, which was stimulated and encouraged by parties in Boston, and even by a portion of the press. It is not impossible that a wish may have existed in some quarters that President Quincy should be driven to resign his office, which, undoubtedly, would not have remained vacant for lack of candidates for the succession. But all parties, young and old, in College and out, reckoned most egregiously without their host, if they thought he was to be driven from a post of duty by any outcries that boys or men could uplift. He had not fought with the wild beasts of the Congressional Ephesus for eight years, to be frightened from his propriety by any such uproar. I do not recollect all the particulars of this disturbance, nor is it worth while to rake them up at this distance of time. Suffice it to say, that, although the students of that day were extremely well-conducted and gentlemanlike in their deportment as a general rule, yet it was a rule not without the exceptions necessary to prove it. In so large a flock it was nothing strange that a few black sheep should be found. Wanton injury of a disgraceful kind was done to some part of the College buildings. An inquiry was instituted by the officers of the College, and every possible effort made to get at the root of the matter by a purely academical investigation. All attempts were in vain, through the evasions or refusals to testify of the parties examined, under the duress of that *esprit du corps* which obtains generally in such collections of young men. After every effort to sift the matter academically, and to deal with it only as a College offence, had been made and failed, the President gave notice, on behalf of the Faculty, that the case would be laid before the Grand Jury, and the power of the law invoked to extort the testimony necessary to the discovery of the offender. This announcement gave rise to the fermentation among the students of which I have spoken, and which also extended to the general community. The students saw one of their immemorial privileges — that of exemption from public prosecution for offences committed within the College walls — in peril, and they were almost, if not altogether, of one mind as to the atrocity of the innovation. Parties outside, from various motives, took the part of the young men, and protested against this departure from the principles of "paternal government," to which only the ingenuous youth of Harvard should be subjected. As if the duty as well as the right of the tenderest of fathers was not perfect to call in the protection of the laws against the violence of his own sons! It would hardly be credited if I should describe the vehemence with which this question was discussed, or the virulence with which the Faculty, but especially the President, was assailed by certain prints.

All this commotion, however, disturbed not his purpose or his peace in the slightest degree. He was resolved that the precincts of the University should not be made the sanctuary of ruffianism while he was at the head of it, and that the property intrusted to his care should not suffer from wanton mischief, if the laws of the State were sufficient to protect it. And he was sustained in his course, not only by the Corporation and the Faculty, but by the most weighty and considerable citizens, and by all who saw the matter in the light of common-sense. His opinions and feelings on this subject are better expressed than I can do it in a letter to Judge Daniel Appleton White of Salem, — who was, to use his own words, "one of the earliest, dearest, most truly valued and beloved of all his friends," and who had written to him to express his cordial approbation of what he was doing, — of which the following is an extract: —

> "As to the opinion that the tribunals of the State are never to be resorted to on occasions of this kind, I am prepared to show that it is most corrupting to our youth, — the greatest source of the temptations to outrage, to falsehood, and combinations, which, in every period of the history of our College, have been its trouble and disgrace.
>
> "The subject is of vast interest. So far from *never resorting to tribunals of justice*, the true principle is, that outrages of this kind, which are the effect of combination, should never be allowed to be passed over without an investigation *competent to develop and detect*, and that a College Faculty, after having used all the means of the parental and domestic character to ascertain the offender without success, should be placed under a *positive obligation never to fail to apply to the tribunals*. There is no reason why youth in our colleges should feel or believe that they are under less liabilities than youth of the same age in the community; or that, because they are gentlemen's sons, and have the highest motives and noblest inducements to good conduct, the same act shall be deemed sport in them, which, if done by the son of a laborer or mechanic, he must take his place in the *jail* or State's prison."

Influenced by these views of his duty, President Quincy went forward and discharged it fearlessly and fully. Had he been vulnerable to "paper bullets of the brain," volleys enough were showered upon him to deter him from its performance. Every day newspapers were sent to him, with the trenchant passages carefully marked, so that the shaft might not miss of its aim. The perusal of these diatribes was usually reserved for the tea-table, when they were read aloud for the diversion of the family; and they were carefully preserved, for the benefit of posterity, by one of my sisters, in a scrap-book, which is destined to be deposited, by the request of one of my father's honored successors, in the archives of the College, *in perpetuam rei memoriam*. All his popularity with the students vanished. An eminent gentleman lately told me, that he used to look upon my father at that time as "the wickedest old man that ever lived," and that this was the general opinion of the College. But he established his point, and that so effectually, that I believe there has been no occasion to resort to the State courts since then, or, if so, it has been accepted as an inevitable necessity. The Board of Overseers at their next meeting appointed a committee, on the motion of Mr. John Quincy Adams, of which he was the chairman, to report upon this matter. Mr. Adams made a detailed report, sustaining the course of the President and Faculty in every particular, which the Board accepted unanimously by yeas and nays. Before quitting this subject, I may as well say here, that, on the day of the last Commencement at which he presided, the members of the class which had been the one mainly implicated in these troubles waited upon him in a body, and made him an address expressive of the change of opinion which ten years had worked in them all as to his official conduct and his moral character.

On the 17th of September, 1836, the completion of the second century since the foundation of the College was duly celebrated. It was an anniversary of singular interest, and its celebration was most brilliant and successful. Sons of Harvard came from every quarter of the country to do honor to their common mother on her two-hundredth birthday. The weather was perfect, and the scene eminently beautiful and touching. Fifteen hundred graduates, and a great number of friends of the College besides, assembled in honor of the occasion. President Quincy delivered the Address to the Alumni in the church, where appropriate exercises were had, in which he gave a succinct account of the origin and growth of the College. This afterwards grew into the "History of Harvard College," in two volumes, which was published five years afterwards, of which I shall speak again. As no hall belonging to the College was sufficient for the company assembled, a pavilion was erected in the grounds adequate to receive them all for the festivities which crowned the day. Mr. Harrison Gray Otis, as one of the oldest and most eminent of the graduates, had been invited to preside at the dinner; but the sudden death of Mrs. Otis preventing his attendance, his place was most admirably and appropriately filled by Mr. Everett, then Governor of the State. It need not be said that he performed his festive duty with infinite grace and felicity. In the evening the Colleges were illuminated, and a reception was held at the President's house, which was attended by great numbers of distinguished strangers who had been called together by the anniversary, and of the principal inhabitants of Boston, in addition to the society of Cambridge itself. It was a day never to be forgotten by those who had the good fortune to see it.

The two principal permanent additions which were made to the College in its literary and scientific departments in President Quincy's time, and largely through his personal influence and exertions, were the new library building, Gore Hall, and the Astronomical Observatory. The library had long since outgrown the limits of Harvard Hall, where it had been deposited for more than seventy years, and demanded more room in which to extend itself, as well as a place of greater security from fire. The library was unavoidably exposed to accident by fire, or to injury from wanton mischief, in consequence of the College bell being hung in the belfry on Harvard Hall. This circumstance made it necessary to leave the outer door unlocked, during the night, for the early admission of the bell-ringer. In the course of some repairs upon the building, after Mr. Quincy's accession, a loaded shell was found concealed in it, stolen from the United States arsenal in the neighborhood, the fuse of which had happily gone out before reaching the charge. It was believed that this crime had been committed by a student who had been expelled shortly before my father's inauguration, I believe for stealing books from the library. This circumstance naturally increased greatly the President's anxiety for the safety of this most precious possession, for which he felt himself responsible; and, also, it was one main reason for his determination to establish the precedent that students guilty of crimes of violence against persons or property should enjoy no immunity, because of their academic status, from the penalties of the laws of the land. He wrote a pamphlet, setting forth the urgency of the case, and petitioned the General Court to make an appropriation for a new library building, (the professors of the theological seminaries at Andover and at Newton joining in the prayer,) but failed to convince the collective wisdom of the State that it was any affair of theirs.

But he was determined to accomplish this object, which was essential to the growth of the library, as well as to its safety; for obviously it was vain to expect liberal donations to a collection which already had not room where to bestow its present possessions, and which was exposed to the same calamity which had destroyed the original library in 1764, to the irreparable loss of the College and the public.

Fortunately the Corporation had at their disposal the munificent legacy of Governor Christopher Gore, which had wisely been left at their disposal without conditions. As almost every department of instruction needed reinforcement, it was matter of grave and mature deliberation, extending over several years, whether so large a sum should be invested in stone and mortar, instead of in the enlargement of the opportunities and advantages for the imparting of knowledge. The urgent necessity of the case, however, decided the Corporation to apply Governor Gore's legacy to the erection of a fire-proof building, capable of receiving the existing library and the large additions which it was reasonable to believe would be made to it as soon as room was provided for them. The corner-stone was accordingly laid on the 25th of April, 1838, and the library removed to its new depository in August, 1841. The building is one of the few connected with the College which make any pretensions to architectural beauty, and is creditable to the taste, as well as the forecast, of the authorities by whom it was constructed. The faith in which Gore Hall was built, that the furnishing of a proper and safe receptacle for the library would be the means of attracting donations to it, has become already sight. In proof of which, I will state that, almost immediately after the library had been removed to Gore Hall, President Quincy obtained, by subscription, almost for the asking, more than twenty-one thousand dollars for the purchase of books. This he was induced to do, in part, as an answer to the disapprobation expressed by many persons — among them some of the best friends of the College — at this disposition of Governor Gore's money. When the appropriation was made, it was in the belief that the contemplated building would be sufficient to accommodate all the accumulations the library would be likely to receive during the present century. In about twenty-five years since its occupation its space has been entirely filled, and more than filled, and an enlargement of its walls is already imperatively called for by the necessities of its growth. Mr. Quincy had endeavored, many years before, to inspire the graduates and the general public with a due sense of the importance of providing for the enlargement and safety of the library, but without success. It was therefore doubly gratifying to him to have his views thus liberally carried into effect, and that under his own immediate influence and direction as the head of the University.

The most enlightened friends of the College, and all everywhere especially interested in the advancement of science in this country, had long felt the importance of having an Astronomical Observatory attached to this, the oldest of American colleges, because of the obvious convenience of such a connection, and of the advantage and credit which each institution would derive from the other. Mr. John Quincy Adams, when Secretary of State, and afterwards when President, had strenuously urged upon the Corporation the importance of establishing an Observatory at Cambridge as near the Colleges as possible, and proved his sincerity by offering to give one thousand dollars (a much larger sum forty years ago than now) towards this object, if the necessary funds could be raised within a specified time. Mr. Quincy had entered into this proposition with his usual zeal at that time; but nothing came of it then. But after his establishment at Cambridge he began to feel his way more definitely towards the accomplishment of this object, and never lost sight of it till it was done. In all his proceedings in this direction it may be well believed that he had the earnest encouragement and help of his illustrious colleague in the Corporation, Dr. Nathaniel Bowditch, though that great man did not survive to witness the success of the undertaking. The first step towards the completion of the design was the purchase of a house on a slight elevation in the neighborhood of the Colleges, sufficiently convenient for the purpose, where the infant institution first began its life. In 1839 a new impulse was given to the movement by the opportunity of securing as Observer Mr. William Cranch Bond, of Boston, who was at that time employed by the United States government in a series of scientific observations in connection with the Exploring Expedition in the South Seas, and who was provided with a proper apparatus for that purpose. The consent of the government at Washington being first obtained for the removal of the apparatus and the observations to Cambridge, Mr. Bond was appointed Observer, and the necessary funds obtained for the alterations in the house and the additions requisite to fit it for its new uses, chiefly by the influence and exertions of the President. The instruments — other than those already owned by the College and those brought with him by Mr. Bond — which were wanting for the purposes of the small beginnings of the Observatory were furnished by the liberality of the American Academy of Arts and Sciences.

The experience of a few years, however, showed that a building constructed expressly for the purpose, and instruments of a more perfect description, were indispensable to the performance of the proper office of an Observatory. Just at this time the magnificent apparition of the comet of 1843 had turned the thoughts of all sorts of men to the wonders of the heavens. President Quincy seized the opportunity, and, by his personal representations mainly, obtained the funds necessary for building the present Observatory and equipping it with its necessary apparatus, especially with the great equatorial telescope, second only, at the time it was procured, to that at Pulkowa. The large sums necessary for these purposes President Quincy obtained, with small urgency, from the enlightened munificence of the capitalists and merchants of Massachusetts, chiefly of Boston, who entered into the plan with a zeal highly honorable to their intelligence and liberality. This was the crowning glory of his administration, and fitly rounded it by a service of enduring value to the University and to the world. His interest in the Observatory did not cease with his official life, but continued to the end of his days. It was through his influence that his relative and former ward, Edward Bromfield Phillips, of the Class of 1845, a young man of large fortune, bequeathed the sum of one hundred thousand dollars to the general purposes of the Observatory, and which was received only too soon through his untimely death. Mr. Quincy was a member of the Visiting Committee of the Observatory until his death, and in 1855, wishing to pay the legacy his father had left to the College in the event of his own death under age, he gave the sum of ten thousand dollars as a fund to defray the expenses of its publications.

During Mr. Quincy's Presidency his familiarity with affairs and his experience in the management of property enabled him to do the University good service in the matter of the purchase of lands — important then to its purposes, and of greatly increased value now — on reasonable terms. He conducted a negotiation of some intricacy with the First Parish in Cambridge, by which he succeeded in obtaining for the College the site formerly occupied by the old meeting-house, which had seen the Commencements of many years; where the pew in which Washington had sat during the siege of Boston could be pointed out; and where the Convention had been held in 1779 which framed the Constitution of Massachusetts of 1780, — that model of a government for a free commonwealth, almost every departure from which has been a blunder and a misfortune. By the same operation he obtained the parsonage house, which stood near the corner of what is now Quincy Street. These two purchases helped to round the College grounds, with which same object President Quincy completed other purchases, amounting in all to about nine acres, the possession of which is of inestimable value to the University. He also obtained at a fair bargain the land on which the Observatory stands, and that appertaining to it, the worth of which has been very greatly enhanced since then by the rise in the price of real estate in Cambridge.

In 1840 Mr. Quincy's "History of Harvard College," in two volumes, appeared, his Address at the Centennial Celebration having grown under his industrious hands to that size. It is safe to say that he has exhausted that interesting portion of the history of New England, which will never need to be written again. It was done with the most conscientious care, all his statements being made after a strict verification by contemporary records and authorities, and the narrative is condensed, clear, and concise. He found himself obliged to speak of some of the favorite characters of Massachusetts history in a different tone from that used regarding them by previous writers. Particularly, he felt obliged to paint the Mathers in darker colors than those in which they are usually portrayed. His account of the behavior of Governor John Hancock towards the College, in his capacity as Treasurer, placed the character of that celebrated person in a new light, not altogether so flattering as that in which it is usually displayed. The work was received, however, by the friends of the College with much favor, as a general thing, and he was held to have judged in the main righteous judgment in the cases as to which he had felt himself obliged to differ from the traditional opinions as to the characters of famous men.

Chancellor Kent to President Quincy.

"New York, March 8, 1841.

"My dear Sir:—I have just finished the perusal of the two volumes of your 'History of Harvard University,' and I cannot refrain from returning you my grateful thanks for the deep interest your talents, accuracy, principles, and taste, and the beautiful sketches of your daughter, have enabled me to take in the work. It is, in point of mechanical execution, a work worthy of the dignity of the subject. It is the history of all the illustrious men in church and state who have adorned the annals of Massachusetts for the last two centuries, and you have vindicated and illustrated their fame with equal candor, liberality, force, and elegance. . . . . I admire and revere the uniform wisdom and fairness, learning and accomplishments, of the authorities of the University, and the fortitude and perseverance with which they sustained the interests of the institution, and its pure and catholic character, amidst all difficulties and opposition.

"I hope I have not been too intrusive; and I beg leave to add my best respects to Mrs. Quincy and your family, and to assure you of the great respect and esteem of your obliged servant,

"JAMES KENT."

In the year 1836 Mr. James Grahame, the author of a History of the United States which has not yet obtained the general reputation in this country to which its profound research, judicial impartiality, clear method, and transparent style justly entitle it, and which it cannot fail ultimately to secure, transmitted for safe-keeping in the library at Cambridge a small manuscript, containing a list of the authorities he had used in the preparation of his great work. In the year 1839 the University bestowed upon Mr. Grahame the honorary degree of Doctor of Laws, in testimony of the sense the governing authorities entertained of the obligations under which he had laid the American department of the republic of letters. The formal communications incident to these transactions grew into a cordial and friendly correspondence between President Quincy and Mr. Grahame, which was kept up until terminated by the death of that excellent and accomplished man. The following letter sets forth in mild and candid terms the objections which were expressed by other eminent gentlemen, through the religious press, as to the treatment of the character of the Mathers. Mr. Quincy's answer to Mr. Grahame is the one he would have made to his Cisatlantic critics, had he not thought it best to let his narrative, supported by the authorities he cites, be its own defence.

MR. GRAHAME TO MR. QUINCY.

"5 PLACE DE LAUNAY À NANTES, July 4, 1841.

"MY DEAR SIR: — I write while I am scarce able to manage a pen. Let me begin by felicitating you on this anniversary, and joining with you in the gratitude which it claims from us to Almighty God. The 4th of July is a glorious date for North America, and, I trust, the dawn of a long and happy day for her and for all the world.

"A week ago I received a copy of your History of Harvard University. . . . . The enfeebled state of my health has obliged me to decline for a long time all study or mental exertion; but I have not been able to refrain from looking into your History, of which, however, I have read little more than one hundred pages. All that I have read commands my respect and admiration, but the beginning engages my love. Nothing can be more interesting, or more nobly worthy the noble subject, than your exordium. I shall express my opinion more distinctly and freely than would become a letter to you in the next edition of my own historical work.

"As you advance, you wound some of my prejudices. The Mathers are very dear to me, and you attack them with a severity the more painful to me that I am unable to demur to its justice. I would fain think that you do not make sufficient allowance for the spirit of their times. My heart and judgment are with them in point of doctrine. From their views of discipline my judgment utterly revolts. Yet in a deep corner of my heart, quite unassailable by reason, there lies intertwined with my being a tender love for the primitive Puritans and the old charter of New England. I do not despair of your indulgence. I regard the primitive Puritans much as I do the Scottish Covenanters, — regretfully disapproving and completely dissenting from many of their views and opinions, especially their favorite scheme of the intertexture of church and state, which appears to me not merely unchristian but antichristian. But I candidly embrace all that is purely *doctrinal* in their system, and regard their persons with a proud, jealous love that makes me indulgent even to their errors. Carrying their heavenly treasures in earthly vessels, they could not fail to err. But theirs were the errors of noble minds. How different from the cunning of knaves, fools, and lukewarm professors! I forget what poet it is who says,

'Some failings are of nobler kind
Than virtues of a narrow mind.'

"Farewell, my dear sir. Believe me, with highest respect and esteem, your faithful friend,

"J. GRAHAME."

MR. QUINCY TO MR. GRAHAME.

"CAMBRIDGE, September 20, 1841.

"MY DEAR SIR: — I am grieved to find by your favor of July last that your health has been assailed and is yet precarious, and unite my prayers to those of your friends and relatives, that a life so deservedly dear to them, and in which so much has been done for truth and literature, should long be spared to their affections and hopes.

"The kind thoughts you express concerning my History are justly valued. I am not insensible to the pleasure of being *laudatus a laudato viro*, nor do I object to any criticism proceeding from a sound judgment and a kind spirit.

"I was aware of the favorable tendencies of your mind towards the Puritans. Those of my own mind are not less strong and decided. The subject of my History was not selected by me. It was forced upon me by accident. It was undertaken and pursued as an official duty, with a determination on the one hand to derive no profit from its sale should it result in pecuniary gain, and a like determination to indemnify the institution should it result as I anticipated, and as will be the case, in pecuniary loss. I early found that my researches would compel me to exhibit certain favorites of parties in church and state in lights very different from those in which they appear in popular histories, and even in which they had stood among my own prejudices. I adopted, therefore, the principle of placing in my Appendix every new document from which such different views resulted, at length. Affording every reader opportunities to judge for himself concerning the correctness of those I presented, taking the law of history as laid down by the Roman orator as an undeviating rule of conduct, — *ne quid falsi.* I am not conscious of having deviated from this law in any case.

"The difference to which I allude is most remarkable in respect to the Mathers among the divines, and to Hancock among the politicians. It was impossible to write the history of the College without bringing their conduct under animadversion. I am perfectly willing to leave the truth and justice of my history in relation to them to the decision of future times. The work is too local and individual to excite a general interest in it. My determination to raise in it a monument to every benefactor of the College, be he small or great, humble or high, renders it unavoidably a collection of details in themselves of very limited attraction. But my object was usefulness to the College, and I thought I should in no way be more serviceable to it than by making its history a medium of expressing its gratitude. Although the path of fame may thus have been neglected, that of duty has been followed.

"I enclose official acknowledgments to you and your brother for the books presented to our library. They are highly valued, not only for their intrinsic worth or curiosity, but from the evidence they convey of your interest in our institution.

"Hoping this correspondence will be neither infrequent nor soon interrupted, I am, most respectfully, your obedient servant,

"JOSIAH QUINCY."

This admirable person died in just a year, wanting a day, from the date of his last letter, on the 3d of July, 1842, the eve of that great American festival in which he felt all an American's interest and pride. At the request of the Massachusetts Historical Society, my father prepared a brief memoir of the life of Grahame, which was afterwards prefixed, at the request of the historian's family, to the American edition in four volumes of his History, corrected and enlarged by himself, published in Boston in 1845. My father took an active interest in this publication, and corrected the press himself. The friendship which had existed between my father and Mr. Grahame yet continues between their respective families, and is maintained by a cordial correspondence.

The Memoir of Grahame which my father prepared for the Massachusetts Historical Society was the occasion of involving him in an unpleasant controversy with Mr. George Bancroft, who followed Mr. Grahame in the field of American history. Grahame, in treating of the course pursued by John Clarke, the agent of Rhode Island and the Providence Plantations, to procure from Charles II. the charter under which that commonwealth flourished for nearly two centuries, said that "Clarke conducted his negotiation with a baseness that rendered the success of it dearly bought." In a note to the passage of his own History relating to that period, Mr. Bancroft, after eulogizing the general character of John Clarke, said, "*The charge of 'baseness' in Grahame*, I. 315, *edition of* 1836, IS GRAHAME'S OWN INVENTION!"—an imputation against an historian of most solicitous accuracy and a gentleman of unblemished honor as gross and offensive as language could well convey. Mr. Grahame felt the affront as any man of sensibility and self-respect must have done, and his sense of it was conveyed to the American public by his friend Mr. Robert Walsh, formerly editor of the National Gazette of Philadelphia, then residing at Paris, in a letter to the New York American. But though the pain he had given to Mr. Grahame by this aspersion had been thus brought to the notice of Mr. Bancroft, years passed away with no proper offer of reparation. Accordingly, when preparing the revised edition of his History, to be published after his death, Mr. Grahame appended the following severely temperate note to the passage which had called forth the insult:—

"Mr. Bancroft has, with a strange lack of courtesy and correctness, reproached me with having *invented* the charge I have made against Clarke. I am incapable of such dishonesty; and sincerely hope that Mr. Bancroft's reproach is, and will continue, on his part, a solitary deviation from candor and rectitude."

My father well knew that the publication of this note would inevitably provoke Mr. Bancroft to an angry reply, but his sense of duty as an editor would not permit him to suppress it. Having no disposition, however, to have an altercation with Mr. Bancroft, he did not mention the matter in the Memoir, and made no use of the evidence as to the full particulars of Mr. Bancroft's conduct towards Mr. Grahame, which had been forwarded by that historian's family, together with the revised copy of the history. On the 4th of March, 1846, Mr. Bancroft addressed a letter to Mr. Joseph T. Buckingham, editor of the Boston Courier, complaining of "a groundless attack" upon himself, and "a grievous wrong" to the memory of Clarke, contained in the recently republished History of Grahame. The letter charged Mr. Quincy with giving publicity to his (Grahame's) personal criminations of himself (Mr. Bancroft); with lending his aid to the promulgation of Grahame's "renewed detraction" of Clarke; and with stepping forward to "defend the new version of the *calumny*, accompanied by an impeachment of his [Mr. Bancroft's] 'candor,' 'correctness,' and 'rectitude.'" The "new version of the calumny" refers to a change of phrase adopted by Mr. Grahame, because of the displeasure which his strictures on Clarke had excited "in some of the *literati* of Rhode Island," in which he substituted for the word "*baseness*" the periphrasis "*suppleness of adroit servility*," — one of the few cases in which it must be confessed strength does not suffer from dilution. The letter to the Courier ended with these words: "*Mr. Quincy owes it to me, and owes it to the memory of the dead whom he has wronged, to correct the statements he has put forth; and, as he published Grahame's work by subscription, he should send a copy of the correction to every one of his subscribers.*"

On this hint Mr. Quincy spoke. He began by thanking Mr. Bancroft for the last suggestion, and promised that every subscriber to the History should have a copy of his reply, and that it should have, if possible, as extensive a circulation as the History of Mr. Grahame or that of Mr. Bancroft. I have not room for any detailed account of this trenchant pamphlet. Its title conveys its substance in little. It runs thus: "The Memory of the late James Grahame, Historian, etc., vindicated from the Charges of 'Detraction' and 'Calumny' preferred against him by Mr. George Bancroft, and the Conduct of Mr. Bancroft towards that Historian stated and exposed." I think all impartial readers of the pamphlet will admit that, in this case at least, the campaign came up to the proclamation. Mr. Quincy cites anew the authorities which led to Grahame's severe condemnation of Clarke, and shows that his expression of opinion was supported by the statements of Chalmers and Hazard, writers of unquestioned accuracy and fidelity; and he shows the entire insufficiency of Mr. Bancroft's attempt to justify his imputation to Mr. Grahame of falsification of history, even if the facts he alleged in his own defence should be admitted to be true. This main matter despatched, he gives in full the particulars, previously withheld, of the conduct of Mr. Bancroft towards Mr. Grahame from the beginning, with which the Grahame family had furnished him, which presents a melancholy or an amusing picture, according to the mood of the reader, of the littlenesses into which personal rivalship and literary jealousy can betray even men of unquestionable talent and extensive experience of the world.

The following letter from Sir John F. W. Herschel, the astronomer, the intimate friend and a near connection by marriage of Mr. Grahame, will fitly conclude this interesting passage of my father's life.

SIR JOHN F. W. HERSCHEL, BART., TO PRESIDENT QUINCY.

"COLLINGWOOD, HAWKHURST, KENT, October 29, 1845.

". . . . Allow me to congratulate you on your having brought your labors in this matter [the Memoir of Mr. Grahame] to a close, in a manner calculated to give the highest satisfaction to the friends of your historian, and to enhance his reputation in America. Independent of other considerations, you have produced in this Memoir a remarkably pleasing, *uninflated*, and able work, which will not be without its influence on your own literary fame so far as its style is concerned, and which, from the motives which have prompted you in its production, must win for you the hearty approbation of all good men, be their political or national views what they may.

"Believe me, dear sir, your faithful and obedient servant,

"J. F. W. Herschel."

The superintendence of Grahame's History was the last business which occupied my father's time and thoughts at Cambridge. The Preface bears date the 9th of September, 1845, which was after his resignation had taken effect, and about a week before his removal to Boston. When he accepted the Presidency, it was on the express understanding with the Corporation that he should not be asked to stay after the expiration of four years, if he should wish then to end his relations with the University. He had voluntarily stayed four times the stipulated term. He had more than passed the appointed age of man, yet was not his eye dim nor his strength abated. There was no apparent reason why he might not continue fit for the office for ten years longer. But he was resolved that he would leave his post when the wish was yet general that he should remain at it, and before there could be the faintest suspicion that his powers were beginning to fail him. Besides, Mr. Edward Everett was just returned from his residence at the English court. The general voice of the graduates and of the public named him as the proper person to succeed to the Presidency, whenever my father should vacate it. Mr. Everett was also my father's first and last choice. After Dr. Kirkland's resignation, and before he himself had been thought of for the office, Mr. Everett was his favorite candidate; and it was only the consciousness that it was not to be expected that so young and so able a man would be content to settle himself permanently in an academic retirement that prevented him from pressing the nomination at that time. But now that Mr. Everett had run the career of public honors, — after ten years in Congress, four in the Governor's chair, and as many in the most brilliant diplomatic position in Europe, — it seemed as if the fitting time had come when he could bring his honors, his long experience, his consummate scholarship, and his rare gift of speech, and lay them cheerfully at the feet of his *Alma Mater*. My father resolved not to stand in the way of one whom he esteemed the man of men for the office he held. He took his measures accordingly, no one knowing his intention, excepting his family at Cambridge, until the moment of action. He called a meeting of the Corporation in Boston, and took Judge Story along with him in his carriage, who had not a suspicion of the purpose for which the meeting was called. At the meeting he gave in his resignation of his office to the Board, to take effect after the next Commencement. The Fellows were entirely taken by surprise, and at first utterly refused to entertain the proposition. At least, they would not accept his resignation until he had had some further time to reflect upon it. But he had anticipated this action, and taken his measures accordingly. That morning he had given, in confidence, a copy of his letter of resignation to Mr. Hale, of the Daily Advertiser, with directions to have it appear the next morning. The letter was already in type. It was too late to recall it. Expostulation would be only a waste of breath. So his resignation was perforce accepted according to its terms.

It was very fortunately timed. All the conditions which he had wished should accompany it were satisfied. There could be no question as to his perfect physical and mental competency to perform the duties of the office. All connected with the University, its general and immediate governments, the graduates, and the undergraduates, were unanimous in their regrets at his leaving, and in their wish that he should remain. He had done all that he intended to do when he took office. Under his administration the finances of the University had been reduced to order, and its funds largely increased. The instruction had been enlarged and improved in every direction. He had connected his name permanently with its history by three most important additions to its usefulness. The Law School, though in existence when he became President, had but a name to live. Under him it had grown into proportions worthy of its great office, — the formation of sound lawyers, learned judges, and able statesmen. Gore Hall had been built and dedicated to the uses of the library, — a fit receptacle for that function which is to a university what the brain is to a man. And he might claim as his especial work the establishment and equipment of the Observatory. He might with truth affirm that he left the institution in every particular in the most flourishing condition, both as to prosperity and usefulness, that it had ever been in from its foundation. And on this point I can cite the authentic testimony of President Walker, my father's third successor, who thus spoke of him at the dinner of the Alumni, July 19, 1866: "I have been led to review with some care his administration of the College, and the effect of it has been greatly to increase my sense of the obligations the College is under to him. Sixteen years of more devoted, unremitting, unwearied work in the service of a public institution were never spent by mortal man. And when we call to mind the state of things at the time of his appointment, it seems to me that he will be forever remembered as THE GREAT ORGANIZER OF THE UNIVERSITY."

On Commencement Day, then, the 27th of August, 1845, he took leave of his office and retired to private life. The fact of its being his last appearance in his official capacity caused a larger attendance than usual of the Alumni, especially of those who had received their education under his auspices. It was a day of great and general interest. My father was now in his seventy-fourth year, but time had touched him with a gentle hand, and he hardly seemed older than he did at his inauguration. His figure was still erect, his step firm and elastic, his voice clear and resonant, his presence and manner, in making the Latin addresses and giving the degrees, as full of grace and dignity as at his first Commencement. He was eminently qualified for all occasions of public representation by his noble head and gracious countenance, his fine person, and the ease and grace of his movements. After he had conferred the degrees for the last time, the Governor, Mr. Briggs, rose and read the resolutions written and offered by John Quincy Adams, and passed unanimously that morning by the Overseers upon his resignation being officially communicated to them. He was taken entirely by surprise, but replied in a few feeling and fitting sentences, which left nothing to be desired. The reception at the President's house was very numerously attended, and all sorts of people seemed desirous of manifesting their respect for his character and their sense of his services. His relations with the officers of instruction and government had always been of the most cordial and confidential description. Having no charge whatever of teaching connected with his functions, he kept himself advised of the manner in which each professor and tutor did his work, and frequently made visits of inspection and examination, so that his superintending eye should be ever felt by all parties to be upon them. In the arrangement and direction of studies he took an intelligent and active share, endeavoring to make the labors of the teachers as easy and agreeable as was consistent with their duty to the taught. These gentlemen took a proper occasion to express their feelings of respect, gratitude, and affection in an address couched in fit and touching words.

With the undergraduates also, the President, as a general thing, was very popular, although I have had occasion to speak of a signal exception to the general rule. But though, on other occasions than that one, he was not unfrequently called on to administer discipline which exposed him to temporary dissatisfactions and dislikes, I believe there were none, even of the sufferers, who did not ultimately acknowledge the justice and clemency of his academical administration. The undergraduates paid him the parting and graceful compliment of requesting him to sit for his bust, to be placed in the library of the University. This work was admirably performed by that eminent artist, Thomas Crawford. As a portrait-bust, and as a work of art, it is of the highest merit, and does equal justice to the subject and the sculptor. Of what was then regarded by the young men as the heaviest to be borne of all their afflictions, the President showed his readiness to share the burden. Morning prayers were then held at a very early hour, — at six in summer, as I remember, and at the earliest moment at which it was possible to read in winter. During the sixteen years of his administration he never missed a single morning prayer from illness, and only three in all, — and this occasioned by his attendance on court at Concord as a witness on business of the College. He was always in his seat in the chapel, facing the students, before they or the officiating officer arrived. During this long term of service, moreover, he had been absent from the religious services in the chapel on Sundays but one half-day, when he was called away by the last illness of a near relative. During his term of office, also, he never attended the theatre nor permitted card-playing in the President's house, though both before and after he had no objection to a play, nor to a solemn game of whist. I will not affirm that his example in these respects had the effect of producing absolute conformity to it on the part of the undergraduates; but he was resolved that he should not be known to indulge in amusements which were forbidden to them by the laws of the College, and for their indulging in which he might have to administer its discipline.

A residence of sixteen years in Cambridge could not be broken up by my father's family without emotion at the remembrance of the many happy hours they had spent there, and the many friends they would leave behind them. They were years of unbroken prosperity and happiness. Neither death nor sickness had entered their doors, with the single exception of that of my mother's mother, whose *euthanasia* at ninety-three was rather like translation than death. It was a life of continual variety. Boston was so near, that the family were not separated from the society of that city, while they had in addition the polished and cultivated circle which had gathered around the College. Many valuable and permanent friendships grew out of that Cambridge sojourn, which were not left behind at the return to Boston. Every stranger from abroad, or from other parts of this country, found his way to Cambridge, and to the President's house, and many interesting and valuable additions, foreigners as well as natives, were made to the acquaintanceships, and sometimes to the friendships, of my father and his family. And there was, after all, no real separation from the Cambridge circle. For years, Saturday was "Cambridge day" at my father's house, when his friends from Cambridge were sure of finding him and the ladies of his household at home, and sure, too, of a cordial welcome to his fireside and to his table. On the 16th of September, 1845, the removal was completed, and my father entered upon the last stage of his long journey through life.

CHAPTER XIX.

1845-1855.

HOUSE ON BEACON HILL. — PREPARATIONS TO MEET OLD AGE. — DIARY. — MEMOIR OF MAJOR SHAW. — CLASSICAL RECREATIONS. — HIS BOOKS. — TASTE IN ENGLISH LITERATURE. — HIS FARMING. — EXTRACTS FROM DIARY. — CONVERSATIONS WITH JOHN QUINCY ADAMS. — GENERAL ST. CLAIR. — DEATH OF MR. ADAMS. — FRENCH REVOLUTION OF 1848. — CORRESPONDENCE WITH MR. BROOME. — MR. HEYWOOD, M. P. — THE "PLEA FOR HARVARD." — DEATH OF HIS WIFE. — HIS CHARACTER OF HER. — HISTORY OF THE BOSTON ATHENÆUM. — MUNICIPAL HISTORY OF BOSTON. — THE KOSSUTH BANQUET. — PURCHASE OF THE CITY WHARF. — VISIT OF DR. KANE. — OPPOSES THE UNION OF BOSTON WITH CHARLESTOWN. — HIS OPINION OF LARGE CITIES. — MR. ADAMS'S DIARY, AND THE COLLEGE TROUBLES OF 1834.

TWO or three years before resigning the Presidency, my father bought the house in Beacon Hill Place, at the corner of Bowdoin Street, in anticipation of this event. It stands on the precise spot where Beacon Hill once stood, — the highest and the fairest of the three hills which gave to Boston its original name of Trimountain. Its site is yet the highest point of the peninsula. Here he and his family spent the next ten or twelve winters. The house was near those of his son and of one of his married daughters, and sufficiently central in its position for convenience; but otherwise neither the situation nor the house itself was entirely satisfactory to the family, and it was gladly exchanged, in 1857, for the one on Park Street, facing the Common and the sunset, which he occupied during the rest of his life, and where his daughters yet live. He and his books, however, were sufficiently well accommodated; and here he enjoyed the first sweets of absolute leisure. He was not entirely without outside occupation, however, as he held extensive trusts, and managed all his own private affairs without asking the assistance even of his own sons. But these filled but a small portion of his time, the greatest part of which was at his own disposal, free from the importunate demands of public duty. His health being unbroken, and all his faculties in the highest condition they had ever been in, he might reasonably reckon on eight or ten years more of life. He could hardly have anticipated that his life would last nineteen years longer. But he set himself as resolutely to work to meet these novel conditions of repose as he ever had done to encounter the various activities of his former life. Three days before his seventy-fourth birthday, February 1st, 1846, he began a diary as a part of his scheme for keeping off the inroads of old age. He says: —

"I am soon about to enter my seventy-fifth year. Indolence and indifference to labor are the dangers of old men. *Manent ingenia senibus modo permaneat studium et industria*, says Cicero in his *De Senectute*. As one mode of putting to proof this doctrine I undertake this diary, an attempt I have often made, and, through engagements of an active life, as often have failed to execute. I have at length the felicity of being my own master, — relieved from the servitude of place and office, and have entire liberty to devote my time according to my duty to myself and Heaven.

"*Deus nobis hæc otia fecit*, — and may my mind never fail to think of, and refer to Him with gratitude and love, all the blessings which through his bounty I enjoy."

This diary he continued, with occasional interruptions and omissions, up to the end of 1863, six months before his death, when he had all but completed his ninety-second year. It fills three thick closely written small octavo volumes, and contains perhaps as intimate and candid self-communings as diary ever did. I shall make frequent extracts from it as I tell the story of his old age, as the best possible statement of his thoughts, opinions and feelings. I only regret that the inexorable limits of this volume will compel me to give so few of them. On his birthday, three days later, he says: —

"*February* 4, 1846. — My birthday, on which I enter my seventy-fifth year. What an expanse of past time appears in the retrospect, crowded with figures once material, now shadowy, yet dear to the memory as light to the eyes, with whom I too must soon unite, and be forgotten, or be remembered only as it were by mental twilight!

"Chiefest and dearest among these is *my mother*, — the truest, the faithfulest, and the most self-sacrificing. No one ever surpassed, few ever equalled, her maternal affection.

> 'O name forever blessed, forever dear,
> Still breathed in sighs, still uttered with a tear.'"

He accepted the philosophy of Cicero as to the efficacy of constant activity in keeping the mental powers in repair during old age, and certainly proved its truth by his own example. And he used to re-enforce the authority of the great Roman by a more homely apophthegm of John Adams's, which he was fond of repeating. When Mr. Adams was in the very last stages of life, my father asked him one day how he had managed himself so as to keep his faculties entire up to ninety years. To which he replied, "By constantly employing them. The mind of an old man is like an old horse, — if you would get any work out of it, you must work it all the time!" Acting on this principle, my father set himself solid tasks of work, requiring painstaking and research, and his lighter recreations of literature were of a kind that most men would put down in the category of hard study. He began early in 1846 his Municipal History of Boston, and, contemporaneously with it, the preparation of the Journals of his uncle, the husband of his mother's sister, Major Samuel Shaw of the Revolutionary army, kept during his voyages to Canton, he having been the first American to open the trade with China, after peace and independence made it practicable, and the first American Consul at that port. My father performed this labor of love at the request of the late Robert Gould Shaw, Major Shaw's nephew, prefixing to the Journals a Memoir of the writer, to whose memory he pays this affectionate tribute.

"It was my happiness in my early youth to enjoy the privilege of his acquaintance and correspondence; and now, after the lapse of more than fifty years, I can truly say, that, in the course of a long life, I have never known an individual of a character more elevated and chivalric, acting according to a purer standard of morals, imbued with a higher sense of honor, and uniting more intimately the qualities of the gentleman, the soldier, the scholar, and the Christian."

This work appeared in 1847, and is a curious and interesting contribution to the materials for American history. The Memoir is largely compiled from Major Shaw's letters to his family, and gives the story of the war, through the whole of which he served, from the point of view of a subaltern officer. The Journals contain a lively description of his adventures in China and the East Indies generally, of the great commerce between which regions and the United States he may be said to have been the pioneer.

My father's favorite recreation, in the intervals of these serious occupations, was reading the ancient classics. He was an excellent Latin scholar, and had always kept up his familiarity with the Roman authors, especially Cicero and Horace, with quotations from whom his Diary absolutely bristles. On journeys he always took a little Horace with him, made expressly for the pocket, — the gift of his friend and mine, the late Henry Russell Cleveland, an elegant scholar and most amiable man, too early lost to his friends and to society, — and there were few days in which he did not hold some converse with the Sabine bard. Many of the Odes he knew by heart, and I imagine that there were few that he had not so known at one time or another of his life. He wrote Latin easily and correctly, and his academic addresses are very creditable specimens of modern Latinity. He was a moderately good Greek scholar, as goodness is reckoned in this age and country, and he never entirely neglected the Greek exemplars, though he did not turn them over with daily and nightly hand, as he might be said to do those of Rome. I sometimes found him busy over Thucydides or Demosthenes, but oftener with Xenophon or Homer. His successor in office, President Walker, — certainly a competent authority in the case, — came to the conclusion, after looking into the matter for a specific purpose, that he was the best classical scholar of all the Presidents of Harvard up to his time. One day when he was President he attended an examination of undergraduates in some Greek author. One of the young men gave a certain rendering of a particular passage, which the presiding professor criticised and corrected. After the examination was done and the lecture-room cleared, the President remained behind, and, carefully closing the door, came up to the professor and told him that his version of the passage was wrong, as well as that of the student, and gave him what he himself held to be the true one,—which the learned professor, upon fuller consideration and examination, candidly admitted to be the fact. His collection of the Latin and Greek classics was almost complete, though the editions were mostly old-fashioned, and some of them obsolete,—good, sturdy, old-world friends, clad in vellum or old calf. He had the Olivet edition of Cicero, which Gibbon says "may adorn the shelves of the rich," in six large quartos, ed. 1742, elegantly bound in the style of a hundred years ago, and that of Ernesti, which, according to the same supreme authority, "should lie on the tables of the learned"; but his favorite copy for use was the beautiful duodecimo edition of the Foulis brothers, of Glasgow, in twenty volumes, A. D. 1748, also from the text of Olivet, excellently printed by those Scotch Elzevirs. He knew that this text had lost the high repute it enjoyed in the last century, but it was good enough for him. The volumes bear the marks of thorough and frequent reading; and the one that contains the treatises *De Officiis*, *De Senectute*, and *De Amicitia*, has had to be new backed to save its life. His Lucretius was also from the Foulis press, and was the presentation copy from the printers to Doctor Franklin. His fine Plutarch in twelve volumes was once the property of Talleyrand. But he was no bibliomaniac, and the few books he had interesting in the eyes of that frantic generation came to him rather by accident than by pains. His lexicographical apparatus was good;—in Latin, besides the large Ainsworth in two quarto volumes, the yet larger and more perfect Forcellinus in two folios;—in Greek, besides Schrevelius and Hedericus, Suidas, Scapula, and Stephanus. He subscribed, more than thirty years before his death, for the splendid Paris edition of this last-named greatest of lexicons, and he watched for the later *fasciculi* with eager interest, as if he had a long life of Greek before him. The last *fasciculus* rejoiced his eyes a very short time before he died.

His taste in English reading was formed according to the canons of the last century. Shakespeare and Milton—the latter as prose-writer as well as poet—were his constant companions in age as in youth. Lord Bacon was often in his hand and on his lips, as were the older divines. And—I almost fear to state the fact in the ears of this generation — he regarded Pope as a great poet, and could draw upon the youthful stores of his memory for great numbers of those smooth verses. Indeed, he was very much what Margaret Fuller (Madame d'Ossoli) described her father to have been, — "a Queen Anne's man,"— and he had not much relish for the lighter literature of the last thirty or forty years. Childe Harold, even, he had never read until he was seventy-five years old. His judgment upon it, as recorded in his journal, February, 1846, is that which will probably be the final sentence of posterity.

"Childe Harold is evidently a poetic embodiment of the poet's own discontent with life and the world; yet it is apparent there is more of affectation than reality in this constantly obtruded disgust.

. . . . .

"His descriptions are splendid, his command of language despotic; but the poem is evidently the work of a diseased mind, and as little indicative of a genius to be envied or desired, as the hectic flush of fever is of the ruddy bloom of youthful health."

Historical and biographical works of the day he read with avidity, and recorded his opinions of them in his Diary, some of which I may extract from time to time.

The removal from Cambridge restored my father and his family to their country home at Quincy. They returned thither in the summer of 1846, for the first time since 1828, and every summer has been passed there since then. My father took the management of his farm into his own hands again, with as much enjoyment as at the time of his first experience, and I believe with less loss. He retained this oversight and direction for the next ten years, and then relinquished it to his eldest son, who also has a country-house on the estate. This occupation gave him much wholesome amusement, and no doubt contributed to his length of life. During these first years his serious task was the preparation of his Municipal History of Boston; but he found time to write, besides, the History of the Boston Athenæum. He had been one of the earliest promoters of that excellent institution, — for fourteen years one of its Trustees, and for nine its President. When the corner-stone of the present library-building was laid, in April, 1847, he delivered an address, reciting briefly its early history. This, at the request of the Trustees at the time, he enlarged to the extent of a volume of some three hundred and fifty pages, including short notices of the lives of its projectors and founders. This work was published at the beginning of 1851.

"*November* 8. — Rose at four o'clock. In the morning visited J. Q. Adams. I found him apparently unconscious that he had been visited by a paralytic affection, yet deeming his case critical; but self-possessed and resigned. One part of his conversation was at once curious and gratifying to me. 'I have never said to you, Mr. Quincy, how much I approved your resigning your Presidency of Harvard College under the circumstances in which you were, — in full health and success, and with every indication of the power of protracted usefulness, — out of regard to your advanced period of life, and solely from a wish to have what remained to you of it at your own command, unembarrassed by official obligations. I consider that act as the crowning glory of your life, and characteristic of great wisdom.'

"I expressed to him my sense of obligation for the manner in which, in 1834 – 35, when assailed by an internal rebellion, encouraged systematically by external discontent, he had come forward in an unqualified spirit in my defence. I told him I had never ceased to be grateful for the aid he afforded me on that occasion. He said he was conscious of the service he had rendered me, and had always considered the opportunity then afforded him of doing me justice as one of the happiest of his life."

"*December* 1. — Visited J. Q. Adams, who is slowly convalescing, — his mind active and self-collected. He spoke of the Observatory at Cambridge; said he had come to Boston prepared to write his report on that subject, as chairman of the Committee of the Overseers, and on this account regretted this attack of illness, which would preclude his fulfilling that duty; expressed his great pleasure at the prosperity of the Observatory under the joint care of Professor Peirce and Mr. Bond and his son; considered them all highly qualified, and possessing the right zeal.

"He spoke of the Observatory at Washington as being erected in a mean way, and under false colors, no appropriation having ever been made for it by Congress; and in one of their acts of appropriation for the navy, they inserted a clause that no part of it should be applied to an Astronomical Observatory. He regarded the course of Congress on this subject as guided by a spirit of malevolence and ill-will toward himself. When President of the United States, he had expressly recommended the establishment of a National Observatory. His interest in it had been frequently manifested, yet everything had been done to exclude him from any influence in it; and it had been at last established in a way which he denominated mean, from personal hostility toward himself.

"*December* 4.—Visited President J. Q. Adams. He said he did not understand some of the grounds taken by Webster at the Philadelphia dinner. What was it to Whigs, if Polk did not pursue the policy of Jackson? By condemning Polk is it his intention to laud Jackson? The wisdom or the principles of Jackson was poor ground for Whigs to stand on. I stated to him the retort of the Boston Post to Webster's assertion, in Faneuil Hall, that 'Polk had made the war upon Mexico, and ought to be impeached for it,'—'which,' says the Post, 'comes very poorly from the mouths of Whigs,—every one of whom, except sixteen, voted deliberately that the war was the act of Mexico.' 'Yes,' replied Adams, 'by that vote the Whigs have taken the ground from under themselves. They have nothing to stand upon. They have voted the war unavoidable, and have committed themselves to support it.'"

"*March* 21.—Resumed reading Cicero's Tusculan Disputations, and abstracted his most important remarks."

"*May* 26.—Read, in the 'Memoirs of the Academy of Inscriptions,' an explanation of passages in Homer, Horace, Juvenal, and Josephus.

"To indicate that the only path to honor was virtue, the Romans built a temple to each, and so joined them together that there was no access to the former but through the latter."

"*June* 6.—In the evening my drawing-room was crowded with my children and grandchildren, it being the fiftieth anniversary of Mrs. Quincy's and my marriage. A meeting full of the most joyous feelings, without sorrow of any kind, and the heart oppressed with gratitude to Heaven which language has no adequate power to express. Received from each of my children some token of affection, grateful and appropriate."

"*September* 24.—George W. Turner, of Wheatland, near Charlestown, Jefferson County, Virginia, called and introduced himself to me, visited my farm, and conversed on agriculture. He breakfasted with me, and accompanied me in my carriage to Boston to the Mechanics' Fair; and I gave him letters to Cambridge. I was much pleased with him. Educated at West Point, after passing six years in the army and visiting Europe he has settled as a planter. Intelligent, well-informed, modest, and gentlemanly." *

"*October* 17. — Passed the evening with President J. Q. Adams. The conversation turned on Governor Bowdoin's 'All-Surrounding Orb.' He said he had read this paper lately, and thought it had not received the justice it merited from the public; that, considering the state of astronomical science of the period, it was quite as respectable as Buffon's theory of the formation of the world, and as the modern theory of a central sun. It must be remembered, that, when Bowdoin wrote, Herschel had not made his discovery of the new planet, which gave new light and impulse to the human mind, — that Bowdoin supported his theory by many plausible, and some strong arguments."

"*November* 21. — Visited by Elisha Whittlesey of Ohio, formerly Member of Congress from that State. Intelligent and well-informed, of practical talents and sound judgment. The conversation once turned on General St. Clair, the unfortunate commander against the Indians in 1794, and who had been equally unfortunate in the army of the Revolution. On both occasions no blemish was cast on his courage or capacity. 'In 1815,' said Whittlesey, 'I saw St. Clair on the top of one of the western spurs of the Alleghany Mountains, living in a log hut, and keeping a tavern for a livelihood. He had lost his documents of his expenditures when in command of the army by accidents incident to Indian warfare, and, although he repeatedly solicited Congress for remuneration, his claims were neglected. He had letters in his possession, which I have seen, entirely approbatory of his conduct, from General Washington. I found him a man of commanding aspect, six feet in height, reading in his log hut. He received me as a soldier and a gentleman of the old school, supporting his mortifications and his poverty with great dignity.'"

"*February* 25, 1848. — I have to record the loss of the friend of my youth, of my manhood, and of my old age, — John Quincy Adams, — who died at the Capitol, in Washington, on the 23d instant, on the spot where his eloquence had often triumphed, and where his worth and powers were shown, and are now acknowledged. Death, which shuts the gate of envy and opens that of fame, has at length introduced him to the rewards of a life of purity, labor, and usefulness spent in the service of his country. The language of sorrow and lamentation is universal. His memory is embalmed in the hearts of his countrymen. No tongue but speaks his praise, — well deserved, but hardly earned

* This unfortunate gentleman was killed at Harper's Ferry by a shot from the engine-house, at the time of John Brown's invasion of Virginia.

by a life of unceasing labor and untiring industry. Friend of my life, farewell! I owe you for many marks of favor and kindness. Many instances of your affection and interest for me are recorded in my memory, which death alone can obliterate.

'Multis ille bonis flebilis occidit,
Nulli flebilior quam mihi.'"

"*March* 10. — Attended the reception of the remains of John Quincy Adams at Faneuil Hall, by my son, J. Quincy, Jr., as Mayor of the city, from the Committee of Congress, consisting of a delegate from every State in the Union, who had attended them from Washington. In the evening met the committee at my son's house. Mr. Tallmadge was particularly interesting to me as the son of one of my Congressional friends most dear to my heart. Gave and received many reminiscences of his father."

"*March* 11. — Attended the solemn and very interesting ceremonies at the funeral of my friend, John Quincy Adams, in the presence of the delegates of twenty-six States, appointed by the House of Representatives of the United States to attend his remains to their last resting-place, at Quincy.

"*March* 27. — This evening the news of the Revolution in Paris, and the flight of Louis Philippe, is confirmed; and also the adoption of a republic as the government of France.

"The attempt to establish a republic in France will end like all her other attempts: first, in the despotism of the many; next, in that of the few; and, lastly, in that of an individual. France has not one element of a republic. She has voted, indeed, that death shall not be the penalty for political crimes, — may it prove true! — but the passions and the interest of parties are not to be restrained by votes. The experience of the sufferings of the Revolution of 1790 may limit the tendency to bloodshed; but men acting in masses are never made the wiser by the experience of others, or by their own."

Early in 1848 my father had the following letter from his old Congressional comrade James M. Broome, formerly Senator from Delaware. His answer, while glowing with the pleasure of a revived friendship, yet breathes the authentic forebodings of his too prophetic soul in its sadder ending.

MR. BROOME TO MR. QUINCY.

"PHILADELPHIA, March 20, 1848.

"MY DEAR SIR: — Every political movement which has tended to swallow up the old United States, and to transfer the seat of empire beyond its limits, has brought to my memory and heart your prophetic speech in opposition to the admission of new States beyond our national boundaries.

"For a long time I hoped that the moral, political, and pecuniary influence of the 'Old United' would cure the evils under which they labored at their union, and that, by becoming more alike, we should be better able and more willing to resist invasion in future.

"This hope is now gone, and I fear that we shall be ruled by people aliens to our race, and antipodes to everything which may be wise, virtuous, and good in our laws and institutions. I know of nothing to stop the acquisitions, until we shall fill up the outlines of Doctor Thornton's visionary scheme of uniting *all* America under one government, to be composed of thirteen confederations like the United States, the thirteen Presidents of which shall meet in grand council on the Isthmus of Darien, and regulate the general concerns as the United States do to the States, &c., and then, to use the Doctor's pleasant conceit, the Eagle of Freedom shall stand on the Isthmus, with her right wing over the Northern hemisphere, her left wing over the Southern, and her *tail* over the West India Islands, picking the eels out of the Pacific Ocean, — unless, indeed, this ill-constructed empire shall previously break by its own weight.

"I did not intend to say more to you now than to ask you if you can procure for me a pamphlet copy of your speech, and to assure you and Mrs. Quincy of my unabated regard for both; for I have so much to say to you that I cannot trust myself to say anything by letter.

"The truth is, that Providence, who surrounds us with forgetfulness of recent things to make us let go our hold on life by degrees, brightens our recollections of the long past when life was full of hope, and suffers us to call them up at pleasure, and even to bring before us our friends from the grave.

"With great regard, yours,

"JAMES M. BROOME."

MR. QUINCY TO MR. BROOME.

"BOSTON, March 27, 1848.

"MY DEAR SIR: — I will not attempt to express the pleasure I derived when, on opening your favor of the 20th instant, I recognized the steady hand and the steadfast mind of one who, more than forty years since, impressed himself on my memory and heart by common views, common feelings, and a conformity of principles, with a depth which time has not obliterated, nor separation nor want of intercourse materially diminished. He lives, then; he breathes this vital air; he still enjoys the light of the sun and the sight of this goodly universe; but how, and where? Does he sit solitary in his advanced years, or is he gladdened by the cheerful voices of children and descendants? Had you said more about yourself, your letter would have been thrice welcome. The multitude of my departed friends draws those which survive with a triple cord nearer the heart.

"That I owe this evidence of recollection to the desire of obtaining a copy of a speech which I had thought buried in oblivion, 'in the family vault of all the Capulets,' was a circumstance not the less flattering to my pride, nor the less indicative of your friendship; but when, in the kindly warmth of ancient sympathy, you apply to it the epithet 'prophetic,' and declare that the events of the passing period have brought it 'to your memory and heart,' I feel something of the excited exaltation of the Latin poet: —

'Sublimi feriam sidera vertice.'

Such are the transitory dreams of a flattered vanity, destined immediately to awaken into the consciousness of the utter disregard and forgetfulness to which it is destined.

"I have found a copy of that effort, and transmit it, as you request, in company with this letter. I have read it *to-day for the first time* since it was published, in 1811; and I rejoice that I see so little to regret either in its temper or language, and nothing at all to be ashamed of in the argument. Had my view of our constitutional duty been then maintained as it ought to have been, and the States been called upon individually to sanction the admission of new States beyond the ancient limits of the original thirteen, the precedent would have been conclusive, and at this day we should not have heard of Texas or Mexico as adjuncts to our Union. Congress would not in such case have dared to assume, as they have done, the power of voting into the Union new States beyond the ancient limits, by its own exclusive authority, and thus turned their limited powers into a practical despotism. The consequences of these assumptions I could represent, — inevitable and not distant; but there is a recklessness in the political influences of the period which sets at defiance all the warnings of history and experience, spurns all evidence and all argument, and paralyzes endeavors by making success hopeless. Let them be powerful as they may, passion and party spirit will make them

'Ora, Dei jussu non unquam credita.'

"For myself, I hear the hollow voice of the rushing waters, foretelling the coming storm, — for come it will, — though probably, thank God! neither in your day nor mine. Even now I feel the upheaving of the advancing tempest, I see the broken columns of our Union, and realize the grinding of their massive materials as they dash against each other — *not without blood.*

"Pardon the effervescence of an old man's feelings and fears, and let me know how time passes with you, and assure yourself always of the remembrance and the regard of yours,

"JOSIAH QUINCY."

The gentleman named in the next passage from the diary was Mr. James Heywood, F. R. S., member for North Lancashire in the third and fourth Parliaments of the present reign, and still active in all liberal movements in England.

"Visited by James Heywood, an Englishman, an Oxonian, and a member of Parliament; also by M. Kœppen, a learned Dane, for several years Professor in the University at Athens, Greece. Heywood is every inch an Englishman, — in look, manner, and bearing, — highly educated, but reserved in society. A reformer in principle, but apparently wise and practical in his views. He took a high rank at Oxford, but having been educated by Dr. Carpenter, and being liberal in his views on the subject of religion, he refused to sign the Thirty-nine Articles, and was of consequence refused a degree. He said Puseyism was all-prevalent at Oxford, and that, in appointing to professorships, it was made a criterion of qualification, to the exclusion of men more highly adapted to the offices than those appointed. This had gone so far as to create a disposition towards reaction; and measures were in train to induce the crown to interfere by the exertion of its prerogative.

"Heywood sent for my acceptance the 'History of the English Universities' by Huber, in three volumes, translated from the German at his instance and expense, he being the proprietor of the work. It is very useful and curious."

"*November* 1. — Sent a copy of my 'History of Harvard University' to him. He accompanied me to Cambridge, and visited the Colleges, the Observatory, President Everett, and Professor Agassiz."

In January, 1849, my father wrote a pamphlet entitled "A Plea for Harvard," to counteract what he conceived to be the beginnings of an attempt to change the name of the University from "Harvard College," its ancient corporate name, or "Harvard University," a style which the Constitution of Massachusetts permitted it to assume, to "The University at Cambridge in New England," — the Triennial Catalogue of 1848 and the smaller semiannual Catalogues for that year and the two previous years appearing with that name upon their title-pages, and the one for 1848-49 having a note appended to it justifying the change. And President Everett, holding the just opinion that the institution had fairly outgrown the proportions of a college, and assumed those of a university, and thinking that the time had come for bestowing upon it its due title, was in the habit of so styling it in his official writings and speeches. In this opinion his predecessor did not share, and, fearing that the innovation might grow into a custom and a precedent, he made this reclamation against it, which was well received by the graduates and the public; and the ancient landmark was restored, and has remained unremoved unto this day.

Thus the first years of my father's green old age passed on, filled up with the tranquil and happy occupations of which these extracts from his Diary afford examples. The months from May to November were always spent at Quincy, and those from November to May in town. Until the spring of 1850 my mother had her average of health, and enjoyed these alternations, and the varied pleasures attending them, with all the keenness of her impressible and sympathetic nature. She held that the main elements of happiness in life were personal independence, a love of literature, and a love of the country. These elements, finely mixed in her own nature, she encouraged her children to develop in themselves by her precept and example. She had an exquisite perception of the beauties of nature and of books, and the keenest relish of them, while her manners, at once dignified and engaging, and her great gifts of conversation, fitted her to derive the highest enjoyment from general society, to which she ever lent grace and animation. The sensibility of her organization, mental and physical, would have been almost too acute for happiness, had it not been qualified by the soundest judgment and the most infallible good sense. She had been most emphatically the helpmate of her husband in all the various activities of his life, and she had the happiness to witness and to share the honor and reverence which accompanied his old age for five years after he had entered into its rest. But in the winter and spring of 1850 the shadows of approaching calamity began to gather over the household that had seemed for so many years to be exempt from bereavement and sorrow. Her health rapidly failed, and it was plain that the healing art could do no more for her than to make easier her descent to the grave. She was removed to Quincy, and there, in the scenes she loved best, she gradually passed away, with every mitigation that assiduous affection could afford her. The sweet influences of nature, and the blessed magic of books, helped to charm away the hours of pain and weariness. Not long before her death she asked one of my sisters to read aloud to her one of Jane Austen's novels, adding, with an excusing smile,

> "For so to interpose a little ease,
> Let my frail thoughts dally with false surmise!"

In the perfect possession of her mental powers, and knowing exactly her condition, she awaited patiently and calmly the hour of death. She died on the first day of September, 1850, having all but completed her seventy-seventh year. Three days afterwards the funeral services were performed by the Reverend William Parsons Lunt, the minister of the parish, in the presence only of her family, excepting Mr. Charles Francis Adams, who claimed the privilege of an hereditary friendship, and his wife. My father, attended by my brother and myself, proceeded through a driving storm of wind and rain to Mount Auburn, where he buried her in his own new tomb, wherein was never man yet laid. The next record in his diary is nearly two months later.

"*October* 30. — During the period intervening since the last entry in my diary, my heart has been too full, my loss too great, to yield me any pleasure in the retrospect. After an illness commencing in March last, on the 1st of September my wife, the companion of my life, one who had been for more than fifty-three years its solace, its support, its joy, its reliance, was taken from me. It is the will of Heaven. I submit, but nature cannot be stayed in vindicating its affections. Life is not, it cannot be to me hereafter, what it once was. . . . Though afflicted, I have no reason to use any language but that of gratitude, confidence, and trust. But the heart turns involuntarily to all it has lost, — the truth of her affections, the faithfulness with which she performed her duty under every aspect of life and fortune, the devotedness of her mind to all the objects embraced within the female sphere, the pure and elevated tone of her intellect, and the exquisite taste, sensibility, and delicacy which gave to her a charm and a power which extended far beyond the domestic circle, and was recognized by all who had the privilege of her companionship. Happy and beloved in life, in her illness resigned, acquiescent, anxious only to assuage the grief of those around her, her thoughts seemed concentrated upon one purpose,— that of preserving her self-possession. Not a word of complaint or anxiety escaped her. In the last week of her life she was engaged in reading works of taste and literature, with the same delight and the same critical acumen for which she was distinguished; and she would not allow a word of sorrow or regret to be uttered on her account. Once, indeed, she heard, as I stood by her bedside, an involuntary sigh escape me. Turning toward me with a look of inexpressible tenderness, she exclaimed, 'O, don't sigh! there is nothing to sigh about!' In this tone her spirit maintained itself to the last, departing apparently with no more anxiety about the future than if she was about, at the proper season, to quit her residence in the country for that in the city. It is impossible for any death to be in manner more dignified, or in mode more desirable."

My father soon sought the relief from the presence of this great grief which study and occupation could afford. He busied himself with finishing his History of the Boston Athenæum, which had been delayed, as he says himself, by circumstances for which he was not responsible, adding: —

"I am well repaid for all the difficulties and trouble attending it by the satisfaction I feel at having been instrumental in preserving the memory and services of some of my early friends, and by having done justice, though feebly, to their merits."

This work was very well received by the proprietors of the Athenæum and the general public; and, besides recording the services and characters of several excellent and accomplished men whose memories were fading out of the minds of this generation, it brought the importance of maintaining such an institution distinctly to the attention of the community. Two or three years later he came to the rescue of the Athenæum from a proposition to make it the nucleus of a public library for the use of the citizens at large. My father thought this would be an unwarrantable deviation from the original design of the institution, and inexpedient, besides, in many other points of view. His pamphlets had the effect of defeating the plan, and it were not, perhaps, too much to claim for him that they and his History materially helped to revive the public interest in the Athenæum, and to promote the movement which soon afterwards placed it on its present enlarged and permanent foundation.

"*November* 14, 1850. — In the evening read Thucydides. His declaration that his work was intended to be *κτῆμα ἐς ἀεί, an everlasting possession*, for mankind, indicates that he possessed the spirit which rendered his work what it is, — immortal."

"*December* 28. — From half past eight o'clock till eleven engaged in writing a report on the Observatory, then rode to Quincy. Returned at two in the afternoon on business. Read four Odes of Horace, one of Burns; then on business of the farm till eight o'clock; visited Jonathan Phillips till nine; the rest of the evening at my son's house.

'Multa petentibus
Desunt multa; bene est, cui Deus obtulit
Parca, quod satis est, manu.'"

"*December* 29. — A violent snow-storm prevented my going to church. Continued the report on the Observatory; also, read one of the odes of Burns. The state of the weather gave effect to one of his happy effusions: —

'O Nature! all thy shows and forms
To feeling, pensive hearts have charms;
Whether the summer kindly warms
With life and light,
Or winter howls, in gusty storms,
The long, dark night.'"

In 1852 he published his "Municipal History of the Town and City of Boston from its Foundation to the Year 1830," being the first two centuries of its existence. It is chiefly devoted to the later history of Boston, after it became a city, under his own administration and that of Mr. Phillips; but it tells all that there is to tell of the previous story of the town, with curious illustrations of the state of society and the customs of the place in its early days, drawn from its records and other original sources. It is compactly and tersely written, and must always hold a high rank among the local histories which have multiplied so much of late years. This work finished, and before it was through the press, he began upon his Memoir of John Quincy Adams, on the ground that he found regular occupation necessary to his happiness. He had been appointed in the year 1848, by the Massachusetts Historical Society, to write a sketch of the life of Mr. Adams, to be published with their Transactions. He proposed to himself at first to do no more than this; but the subject grew upon him and gave him occupation and amusement for the next six years, and at last took upon itself the dimensions of a volume.

DIARY. "*May* 1.—Being invited to the legislative banquet given to Kossuth at Faneuil Hall, I deemed it my duty to attend. I had the gratification to find that, though long separated from such scenes, my presence was not disregarded. As I took my seat I was greeted by the whole assembly. My address to Kossuth, though spontaneous, was well received by him and by the audience. Such tributes it is no shame to any man to acknowledge to be gratifying, particularly when accompanied by a consciousness that they have been the result neither of subserviency to the many, nor abandonment of the interests of the few."

All who were present on that most interesting occasion must remember the graceful meeting of the old American statesman and the young Hungarian hero, the fitness of their words, and the enthusiasm of the company.

In the autumn of 1852 a transaction occurred, my father's part in which is too characteristic to be omitted in any account of his life. When he was carrying out the operations which resulted in the building of the market-house, he had made a wharf, called the City Wharf, opposite its eastern end. This wharf he considered to be of particular importance to the rest of the wharf property on the harbor, and he held that the city should always keep the control of it. The lease of this wharf expired in September, 1852, and the city government proposed selling it by auction to the highest bidder. As soon as my father saw the advertisement of the sale, he wrote a letter to the Mayor remonstrating against this action, and giving his reasons why it should not be taken. Not satisfied with this, he immediately followed up his letter by a personal interview with that magistrate, in which he urged his objections with fresh earnestness. The Mayor seemed impressed with his arguments, and submitted his letter to the committee having the matter in charge. The sale, however, went forward, and on the day appointed my father went to Faneuil Hall to witness it as a spectator. When the bidding ceased at the point of four hundred thousand dollars, he was moved to take a part in the competition, "irresistibly impelled," as he says in his Diary, "by an influence of the origin of which I was wholly unconscious." It is not impossible, however, that the origin of this irresistible influence was the knowledge he had, above all other men present, of the value of the property. It was finally knocked down to him at four hundred and eleven thousand dollars; and the announcement was received by the numerous company of competitors and spectators with loud cheers. He stated to them that he had not acted as a speculator, but merely for the purpose of giving the city government an opportunity to reconsider their action in the premises. Should they refuse to do so, he was very willing to take the risk of the purchase. This announcement was received with renewed cheering. Accordingly he wrote to the Mayor offering to relinquish his purchase if the city government would bind itself and its successors not to part with the property for the space of twenty years. This offer being refused, he kept the estate, and its improvement and management gave him occupation for the rest of his life.

DIARY. "*February* 15, 1853. — Visited Cambridge with Dr. Kane, a surgeon in the navy, of great enterprise and apparently indomitable will. As surgeon he attended the American expedition to the North Pole in search of Sir John Franklin, and is now appointed to command a second expedition to the Arctic Circle. He is confident that there is an open sea under the Pole, in which he is of opinion Franklin may be imprisoned, and is determined, if possible, to make the fact certain. From character, spirit, practical skill, and scientific attainment, he seems well adapted to the enterprise."

"*February* 7, 1854. — Read Webster's reply to Hayne, and Parkman's History of Pontiac's Conspiracy, a work of great merit, written with much apparent labor and research, and graphic descriptions of absorbing interest. The characteristic traits of Indian life, motives, and feelings are sketched with a hand that well deserves to be called masterly. I have seldom read a work with more entire approbation."

"*March* 29. — Some friend has sent me a sermon on old age by Theodore Parker. It has the vivacity and generalization of his style. Instead of a sermon, it consists of a series of fancy sketches, pencillings by the way. Some things are represented according to nature, some are imaginary, others mistaken. So far as my experience goes at the age of eighty-two, I cannot agree that it is the characteristic of old age to lose the love of new things and new persons, and think the old to be better. On the contrary, almost everything at the present time seems to me to be better; and I do not limit this feeling and opinion to physical improvements and accommodations, but extend it to morals and religion. It is true, that with increasing population crime has increased, but with it a counteracting spirit is in action aiming to repress these consequences, accompanying which is an enlarged sense of public duty, willing to make sacrifices of time, labor, and money for the general improvement and comfort of our race. And as to persons, although love of the lost gradually fades away with time, and exists more in memory than feeling, yet the love of the friends who remain to us is increased in intensity by the bereavements to which, in the course of nature, age is compelled to submit."

"*March* 30. — What Parker says of pains and infirmities I do not realize. This may be the effect of original constitution, having always been favored with health, and somewhat to what he calls 'the religion of the flesh,' which is unquestionably a means of preventing its infirmities. . . . . I can truly respond to his anecdote of Dr. Priestley, who, in his eightieth year, preached that 'old age was the happiest time of life.' I would only modify this language by the acknowledgment that all my life has been as happy, and more happy than I have deserved, and the experience of the present is in unison with the past."

In the autumn of 1854 an attempt was made to effect a union of the cities of Boston and Charlestown. This proposition my father resisted to the best of his ability. He wrote a strong pamphlet on the subject, of which he distributed a large edition at his own expense. Whatever effect it had was on the citizens of Charlestown, for a large majority of those of Boston who voted on the question — only about a third of the legal voters — went for the union. The vote of Charlestown defeated the scheme. His principal reasons for his opposition are thus written down in his Diary, and perhaps it may not be amiss to put them on record here. What he deprecates most is

"A change in the wise policy of our ancestors, founded upon the division of our population into small municipalities, and introducing gigantic cities, which, by removing the interests of the community from the inspection of the inhabitants, introduces among them an indifference to public affairs, and opens temptations to the selfish, the unprincipled, and intriguing to get the management of city affairs, resulting in making all the concerns of a city the objects of the plunder of wretched adventurers without patriotism, guided by no other motives than private gain or political advancement."

Nearly a year later he thus speaks of the revelations of Mr. J. Q. Adams's Diary, which Mr. Charles F. Adams had lent to him for consultation when writing Mr. Adams's life, as to a matter of personal interest to himself.

"*November* 3, 1855. — The morning chiefly employed in copying from J. Q. Adams's Diary a graphic detail of the proceedings of the Board of Overseers of Harvard College, and of the committee appointed by them on my report, as President of that institution, on the disturbances in that College in 1834. The whole detail is very curious and interesting, exhibiting the base passions which endeavored to implicate me, and the spirited defence made by Mr. Adams in my behalf. A number of political rivals thought they had me at disadvantage, and would probably have given me great trouble had not Adams had the courage and the friendship to interpose in my behalf. I have always appreciated his conduct on that occasion, and cherished for him a grateful heart. But until I had the reading of this diary, I never understood the malignity with which I was assailed, nor the laborious zeal with which I was defended by Mr. Adams. I always knew that those troubles were fanned from without, if not enkindled there. A newspaper of the city was devoted to the discontented youth, and I always believed that a political rival who had applied to be appointed President of the seminary before I was chosen, as was well known, was the most active in encouraging these malcontents. The diary of Mr. Adams explains the motions and motives of this vermicular enemy.

. . . .

"I was gratified to find the course of the College was maintained by such men as Benjamin Pickman, John Wells, Richard Sullivan, Lemuel Shaw, James Savage, Dr. Lowell, and Dr. Francis.

"The particulars of that debate, through the lapse of time, have been obliterated from my memory, which this report of Mr. Adams has revived in my mind, bringing with it a renewed sense of my obligation for the spirit and laborious zeal with which he defended me and the government of the College."

Josiah Quincy

Æt LXXXIX

CHAPTER XX.

1854 – 1863.

His Interest in Politics. — Abhorrence of the Fugitive Slave Law. — Letter from Washington Irving. — The Assault on Mr. Sumner. — Letter to Mr. Hoar. — Address at Quincy. — Letters from Professor Silliman and Mr. Sumner. — Letter to Mrs. Waterston. — Fremont Campaign. — Writes "Whig Policy Analyzed." — Reception of Mr. Sumner. — Election of Mr. Burlingame. — Defeat of Fremont. — Removal to Park Street. — Visit from Richard Cobden. — Letter from Mr. Motley. — From Lord Lyndhurst. — Election of Lincoln. — Breaking out of the Rebellion. — His Faith in the Result. — Letter to Captain Quincy. — Meets with a disabling Accident. — His Personal Habits. — Bereavements. — Religious Opinions. — Address to the Union Club. — Death of Colonel Shaw. — Letter to President Lincoln. — Correspondence with Professor Cairnes. — Conclusion of his Diary.

IT must not be supposed that Mr. Quincy was unobservant of the portentous events which made up the history of the years since he resigned the Presidency of the University, or indifferent to them. In the annexation of Texas, the war with Mexico, and the incorporation of the territory wrested from that republic with our own, he saw the literal fulfilment of his prophecies of near half a century before. The compromises of 1850, and especially the Fugitive Slave Bill, he regarded as inevitable consequences of the dominion which the Slave Power had obtained over the policy and destinies of the country. All these calamities, and the yet greater ones of which they might be the precursors, he considered the logical results of the *coup d'état* of 1803, by which Mr. Jefferson established the precedent that foreign territory might be made an integral portion of the domain of the United States by the mere act of Congress, without first obtaining the consent of the people in their sovereign capacity. During the years of his headship of the University he had abstained, as a matter of academical decorum, from taking any active part in the politics of the day. And now, although they had assumed a much more menacing aspect than ever before, he still felt a strong reluctance to mingling again with them, natural enough in view of his age and long retirement from the political arena. Still he could not see the battle raging without an instinctive desire to be in the midst of it again. The recollection of the *certaminis gaudia*, — "the rapture of the strife," — which he had felt so keenly in the old time, might well invite him to engage in a contest which was but the continuation of the fierce struggles of his prime. The enforcement in Boston of the Fugitive Slave Law in 1851, and yet more in 1854, stirred his spirit deeply. It appears from his Diary that he intended attacking that infamous enactment through the press in 1851, and that he had bestowed much pains in preparation for it; but, for some reason which does not appear, it did not see the light. On the occasion of the rendition of Anthony Burns, on the 2d of June, 1854, the blackest day that Boston had seen since her history began, he fled from the spectacle of that great disgrace. He says in his Diary: —

"*June* 2. — Left Boston as early as possible to avoid the painful scene of a human creature restored to bondage by the arm of the law. The public sentiment so averse to the measure, that a body of troops, and cannon loaded, were deemed requisite to carry the law into execution. Such was the opposition manifested. Events indicative of discontents, which are at no distant period, if not removed, to be the source of irretrievable discords and dangers to the continuance of our Union."

In the winter of 1854, indeed, he attended the public meeting held in Faneuil Hall on the occasion of the Repeal of the Missouri Compromise, to join in the general protest against that infamy. Though he had declined acting as one of the Vice-Presidents of the meeting, he was spied out by the crowd, who demanded him so loudly and earnestly that he had to comply, and, to use his own words, "addressed them briefly, though wholly unprepared. It resulted in my own conviction that my mind was yet at my command, and not without satisfaction to others, judging from the fact that it has exposed me to that '*pessimum genus inimicorum, laudentes.*'"

The next August he was invited to attend the Whig State Convention, and went accordingly, though he had never accounted himself as belonging to the Whig party. Being called upon to speak, he took the opportunity to express his opinions very distinctly as to the recent horror enacted in Boston, of which he gave a briefly energetic recital.

"The obligation," he said, "incumbent upon the Free States to deliver up fugitive slaves, must be obliterated from the Constitution at every hazard. . . . . . We have seen our Court-House in chains, two battalions of dragoons, eight companies of artillery, twelve companies of infantry, the whole constabulary force of the city police, the entire disposable marines of the United States, with artillery loaded for action, all marching in support of a Prætorian band, consisting of one hundred and twenty select friends and associates of the United States Marshal, with loaded pistols and drawn swords, — and all this military preparation and array, for what purpose? To escort and conduct a poor, trembling slave from a Boston Court-House to the fetters and lash of his master!

"This display of military force the Mayor of this city officially declared to be necessary on the occasion. Nay, more, at a public festival he openly took to himself the glory of this display, declaring that by it life and liberty had been saved, and the honor of Boston vindicated!

. . . . .

"This scene, thus awful, thus detestable, every inhabitant of this metropolis, nay, more, every inhabitant of this Commonwealth, may be compelled again to witness, at any and every day of the year, at the will or the whim of the meanest and basest slaveholder of the South."

He significantly added, that the obliteration of the obligation to return fugitive slaves was as much for the benefit of the slaveholders as of the people of the Free States. On their own ground, of course, that slavery was an institution that should be preserved. And the result has proved the truth of his assertion. Nothing, perhaps, prepared the way to the sudden destruction of the slave system more effectually than the Fugitive Slave Law. It helped to educate the Northern mind thoroughly up to that point.

His speech was well received by the body of the Convention,

the greater part of whom, doubtless, soon made part of the new Republican party, though I apprehend it was not altogether well pleasing in the ears of the leaders of the moribund Whig organization, who yet hoped against hope for slaveholding help in their extremity.

As time passed on, and the resolute purpose of the slaveholders to make slavery coextensive with the Union, by overriding the common law, declared and enforced in many of the Free States by statute, making every slave a freeman who was brought within their frontiers through the act of the master, and by the forcible intrusion of slavery into reluctant Territories by the national arm, became more and more apparent, the resistance of the true patriots of the Free States to these aggressions on their own rights, as well as on those of the negroes, became more and more pronounced. In these feelings, and in every disposition to defeat designs so fatal to liberty, Mr. Quincy shared, and soon made himself prominent in the first great struggle between slavery and freedom for ascendancy in the country, in which John C. Fremont was selected as the champion of the North. The outrages in Kansas, and the cowardly attempt upon the life of Senator Sumner in his place by one slaveholder with a bludgeon, supported by another with a revolver, aroused his indignation, in common with that of all honest men, and led him to unite with them in an attempt to limit, if it could not be destroyed, the system thus fruitful of treachery, cruelty, and crime.

But before entering upon this passage of his life I must find room for the following cordial letter from Washington Irving, and for a few extracts from his Diary.

Mr. Irving to Mr. Quincy.

"Sunnyside, March 17, 1856.

"My dear Sir: — I must apologize to you for delaying so long to answer your very kind letter, and to acknowledge with many thanks the receipt of the copy of the Life of Major Shaw. I feel much interested by the account you gave of the late Colonel Tallmadge, and of your intimacy with him when you were in Congress together. Those were gallant days when you and he served together in Congress. It was a great intellectual treat to attend in the galleries. There were noble champions in both parties, and a wonderful array of talent. I had the pleasure of hearing you speak repeatedly, and I recollect being struck at one time with the noble scorn with which you spoke of the miserable party hacks, 'the earth-spirited animals' trudging along in the traces, in the hope of receiving their allotted portion of provender. I am recalling vaguely a noble invective which you may have forgotten. Of the high-spirited, high-minded orators of that day I believe you are almost the only one left. But I feel it an honor to address one of the *élite* of those intellectual combatants. Believe me, with the highest respect, &c., yours very truly,

"WASHINGTON IRVING."

"*June* 23.—This morning I accompanied on board the Cambria my sons-in-law and my daughters, Mr. and Mrs. Greene, and Mr. and Mrs. Waterston, and their daughter, Helen Waterston. They sailed for Liverpool, intending to spend a year in Europe. Heaven grant them a safe voyage, a happy excursion, and a return in health, whether I am permitted to be here to receive them or not! Very precious are they to my heart, by the ties of nature and society, but much more so by a uniformity of affectionate intercourse. I can most truly, in the language of the poet, address the Cambria,

'Reddas incolumem precor,
Et serves animæ dimidium meæ.'"

In the interval between this entry and the next extract the assault on Mr. Sumner was perpetrated. The letter my father speaks of was one addressed to Mr. E. Rockwood Hoar, now one of the Justices of the Supreme Court of Massachusetts, in reply to one inviting him to attend the annual Unitarian festival. This invitation he declined for the following reason.

"My mind is in no state to receive pleasure from social scenes and friendly intercourse. I can think or speak of nothing but of the outrages of slaveholders in Kansas, and the outrages of slaveholders at Washington,—outrages which if not met in the spirit of our fathers of the Revolution (and I see no sign that they will be), our liberties are but a name, and our Union will prove a curse."

After recounting the more recent villanies,—the Fugitive Slave Law, the repeal of the Missouri Compromise, the invasion of Kansas, and the help given it by the government, and, finally, the cowardly assault on Mr. Sumner,—he thus proceeds:—

"In my opinion, it is time to speak on the house-top what every man who is worthy of the name of freeman utters in his chamber and feels in his heart. By a series of corruption, intrigue, and cunning, bribing the high by appointments of state, the low by the hope of emoluments, — playing between the parties of the Free States, and counteracting one by the other, — by flattering the vain, paying the mean, and rewarding the subservient, — the slaveholders have, in the course of fifty years, usurped the whole constitutional powers of the Union, have possessed themselves of the executive chair, of the halls of Congress, of the national courts of justice, and of the military arm, leaving nothing of hope to the spirit of freedom in the Free States but public speech in the Legislature and the ballot-box. The one, a slaveholder's mob is crushing in Kansas; the other, a deputation from the slaveholders of the House of Representatives have attempted to crush in the Senate by a slaveholder's bludgeon.

"My heart is too full. If I should pour forth all that is in it, both paper and time would fail me. Truly, I am yours,

"JOSIAH QUINCY.

"QUINCY, May 27, 1856."

"*May* 28. — My letter to Hoar published by him, and well received by the public, and large editions called for. My thoughts are so absorbed by the events of the day that I can attend to nothing else."

This letter to Mr. Hoar was followed almost immediately by an address delivered in Quincy, at the request of its inhabitants, on "The Nature and Power of the Slave States, and the Duties of the Free States." In this address he showed, with great clearness and energy, the effect of slavery upon the character of the slaveholders, the origin and growth of the supremacy of slavery in the councils of the nation, and the duties of the North in that hour of danger. He said, on this point: —

"The Free States are then, undeniably, at this day, in that very state of things in which the warning voice of Washington declared 'RESISTANCE TO BE THEIR DUTY.' During more than forty years, the spirit of a continued series of encroachments has established over them *the worst of all possible despotisms*, — THAT OF SLAVEHOLDERS."

And he thus concludes the whole matter : —

"At the coming election, I cannot doubt that the Free States, in which the greatest proportion of practical wisdom, active talent, and efficient virtue exists, will take possession of this government; restore to the Constitution the proportions of power established by Washington; reinstate, in full force, that barrier against the extension of slavery called 'the Missouri Compromise'; make Kansas a Free State; and put an end forever to the addition of any more Slave States to this Union; — duties to be fulfilled *at every hazard*, even of the dissolution of the Union itself. If this Union is destined to break to pieces, it cannot fall in a more glorious struggle than in the endeavor to limit the farther extension of slavery, — that disgrace of our nation, and curse of our race."

This address was very widely circulated, and doubtless, together with his previous letter to Mr. Hoar, had an appreciable effect in the arousing and directing the spirit of the Northern States in the great Presidential campaign then about to open. He received many letters of grateful acknowledgment of this timely service from different sections of the country. One or two of these will not be out of place here. That of Professor Silliman of New Haven, one whom all men delighted to honor, shows that there was at least one other octogenarian in whom the call of the crisis renewed the spirit and energies of youth.

Professor Silliman to Mr. Quincy.

"New Haven., Conn., August 6, 1856.

"Dear Sir: — Be pleased to accept my best thanks for your powerful, searching, and truthful address delivered at Quincy. Years sit so lightly on your head, that even your handwriting retains the characteristic roundness and fulness of bygone days, and the clearness and vigor of thought and glow of patriotism have suffered no eclipse, and now shine as they shone half a century ago.

"Mere compliment I avoid from taste, and abjure from principle, but both taste and principle unite in the approbation this effort elicits from me.

"The development which you, sir, have made in giving the history of the rise and progress of the slave oligarchy is confirmed by my own distinct recollections; for although never engaged in political life, I have ever been a diligent student and observer of our public affairs, and I well remember the Louisiana purchase, and the fearful anticipations with which it was contemplated at the time by our wisest and best men.

"You remember, no doubt, our brilliant Senator, Uriah Tracy, whose wit, often sparkling and brilliant, was suppressed under the influence of his anxious forebodings, when, in conversation with myself, he predicted some of the results which you have so powerfully portrayed.

"I could wish that your address were stereotyped and thrown out broadcast, by thousands, over the breadth and length of the land,—the South not excepted,—were it indeed possible that it should find admission in those regions, where truth on the subject of slavery is excluded with Neapolitan rigor.

"Without claiming a response to this voluntary expression of feeling, I remain, with the greatest respect, your obliged friend,

"B. SILLIMAN."

These letters from Mr. Sumner, the first written when he was seeking health among the mountains of Pennsylvania, after the murderous attempt upon his life, and the second from Philadelphia, need no introduction. They breathe the reverence and love which he always showed towards my father, who returned his regard with all but paternal affection.

MR. SUMNER TO MR. QUINCY.

"CRESSON, ALLEGHANY MOUNTAINS, PENN., August 12, 1856.

"MY DEAR SIR:—I have throbbed with gratitude as from time to time I read your words,—first the letter, and now your address. The letter gave a just tone to public sentiment, and now the address touches to the quick the character of slaveholding civilization, and also the extent to which it has usurped the government,—the very theme which I have intended to discuss from my seat at this session, were I permitted to reach it.

"Among all your productions, marked always by rare vigor and eloquence, and elevated by noble sentiment, I think this last may proudly take its place as inferior to none. They speak of old age as second childhood. In you it is second youth. *Macte nova virtute*, &c. Believe me, my dear and ancient friend, with much regard, sincerely yours,

"CHARLES SUMNER.

"P. S.—My health is slowly re-establishing itself in this mountain air, but it is still uncertain when I shall be able to make any intellectual effort."

THE SAME TO THE SAME.

"PHILADELPHIA, September 7, 1856.

"MY DEAR SIR: — I am grateful for your letter and all its sympathy; but I am more grateful still for what you are doing to sway the public mind. You, indeed, are our good *Cid Campeador*, and I hope that you will not sheathe for a moment the brightness of your falchion. Another such blow as that on Mr. Choate will complete the work in Massachusetts.

"The tyranny of this Administration is maddening. As I read to-day the instructions with regard to Kansas, I felt that all old wrongs are made decent by the shameless atrocity of these proceedings.

"I have left the mountain and reached this place. I am now quite comfortable, but I am disheartened by finding how little I can bear. I walked a mile slowly yesterday, and then, as a penalty and token of my feebleness, was doomed to lie awake all night, hearing every clock strike till daybreak. This is hard; for it seems to postpone the period when I can take part in our contest. But why should I repine? You are in the field, to supply all our omissions.

"Ever sincerely yours,

"CHARLES SUMNER."

In the interval between these letters of Mr. Sumner, Mr. Quincy wrote a letter occasioned by one addressed by Mr. Rufus Choate to the Whig State Committee of Maine, in which that florid orator endeavored to frighten the Maine Whigs from their propriety, by setting forth the horrors sure to ensue upon the election of Colonel Fremont. These terrors Mr. Quincy treated in the strain of lively ridicule, which was the best antidote for them. It was one of his happiest effusions, and no one would suspect, from its wit or its logic, that it proceeded from an octogenarian. It had an immense circulation, especially in Maine, and was believed to have had a prevailing influence in carrying that State for Fremont. To this fact I have had very recently the authentic testimony of ex-Governor Israel Washburn, of Maine, whose services to the country in the early days of the Rebellion are freshly and gratefully remembered by us all, who voluntarily assured me, in the strongest terms, of the immense support which the Republican party in Maine at that time derived from the weight of my father's name, character, and words.

The domestic letter which follows will vary the political seriousness which characterizes the mass of my father's utterances at this period.

TO MR. AND MRS. R. C. WATERSTON.

"QUINCY, MASS., August 3, 1856

"MY DEAR DAUGHTER AND SON-IN-LAW: — My letter must be a joint concern, for I have neither time nor head to make two of it. Confidentially, I have been these several weeks past so absorbed by thoughts relative to the state of this country, that I can neither think. speak, nor dream of anything else. The truth is, when a man gets to that age when 'the grasshopper is a burden,' whatever gets under the legs and wings of the insect is embarrassed, and acts only in one direction, and confines itself to one subject, as the limbs of that animal permit. I hope soon to throw off that burden, and chirp again in my old age, as the grasshopper aforesaid does in the spring. In the mean time I shall send you, in company with this letter, an evidence that my brain has not been wholly rendered *effete* under the influence of that animal, but that it has some activity yet, and that there is a reasonable hope that intellectual vitality may for a time, at least, be granted to me. As to things abroad, your sisters and nephews and brothers and brothers' wives must keep you up to the times; my life has been chiefly in my study. I know only that it has been a most glorious season for haying, both as it respects quantity and time for harvesting. My farmer assures me he has put in nearly one hundred tons of English hay, and more to be got in yet. My corn is flourishing, my barley excellent, rye abundant, and my general products so great, that for aught I know I must pull down my barns and build greater. This, however, I will not do, lest I should be tempted, like the man in the Scripture, to say things which might lead to consequences I would avoid; so I have determined to stack all my surplus out, and escape the speechifying temptation, and so also escape the penalty.

"I know not if I ought to enter on more grave and serious topics, but I will, however, gratify your thoughtful propensities by telling you confidentially that Tiger is as grave as a judge, Fritz has taken up his old lodgings with Joe and Sam, at the other house, and Bruno catches rats in the morning, and comes in every evening to be fondled and sleep, until he goes to take up his night's lodging with Tiger.

"As to the domestic state, it is pretty much as you left it. . . . . And all the daughters are as good as good can be, — and, sometimes I think, a little better. As to the other house, my son and his lady, Mary, and the two young men, are all as happy as possible in this world of care and uncertainty. Mary sings like an Italian nightingale, — so that I can hear her high notes here in my dwelling-place, — not much to my edification, but very much to my astonishment. . . . . .

"Now if this is not a good letter, I know not what is. It wants to be perfect only the assurance that I am ever your affectionate father and father-in-law,

"JOSIAH QUINCY."

As the time of the election approached, Mr. Quincy shared in the animated excitement and intense anxiety which went before it. There were no apprehensions as to the Presidential vote of Massachusetts. That Fremont would carry the State by a majority of many thousands was an absolute certainty. The chief interest of the election in Massachusetts, and which was largely shared everywhere, North and South, lay in the contest between Mr. Anson Burlingame and Mr. William Appleton for the representation in Congress of one of the Boston Districts. The former had just made himself conspicuous in Congress by a speech, which Mr. Quincy characterized, in a pamphlet of which I shall speak presently, as "timely, just, appropriate, and honorable; and which if the people of Massachusetts fail to support, they will thus far, in my judgment, be disgraced in all time, present and future." Mr. Appleton was the candidate of the Whig party, which, in the same pamphlet, Mr. Quincy characterizes as the embodiment of the cotton-growing and cotton-spinning interests, the identity of which he had demonstrated, and under the influence of which "Massachusetts had been led into a course of policy which has made her the reproach and ridicule of slaveholders, while she has been a pander to their power and contributed to their success." It was in particular contemplation of this election that he wrote this pamphlet, entitled, "Whig Policy Analyzed and Illustrated," in which he traced the decline and fall of that once powerful party to its subserviency to the slaveholders, and its futile endeavors to obtain their aid for the elevation of Mr. Webster to the Presidency and the adoption of the policy of protection to manufactures. He maintained that it was to their unqualified support of the later course of Mr. Webster, and especially of his Speech of the Seventh of March, 1850, that the Whigs owed that loss of power and popularity which they acknowledged and deplored. After sketching the course of the Whig party as to the Nebraska and Kansas questions and the repeal of the Missouri Compromise, — "verbal demonstrations soon succeeded by acquiescence," — he showed that the necessary effect and natural purpose of their nomination of Mr. Fillmore were to defeat Colonel Fremont and secure the election of Mr. Buchanan. From all these premises he affirms that the majority of the citizens of Massachusetts had been driven to the conclusion, "that the present remnants of the Whig party are no longer true supporters of constitutional liberty, but in truth representatives of the united interests of cotton-growers and cotton-spinners, and as being nothing else in this Union but the Northern wing of the Slave Power." This pamphlet was very extensively circulated, and was one of the great forces of that critical election, as well in other parts of the country as in Boston and Massachusetts. Mr. Burlingame was elected by a very small majority, after a struggle in which no means were spared to defeat him. It was enough, however, to give the *coup de grace* to the Whig party in Boston, its last retreat. It then perished from off the earth, and all endeavors to resuscitate it under other forms and names have signally failed of success.

The day before the election, November 3d, was given up to a public reception of Mr. Sumner, on his first return to his native city after the attempt of slavery upon his life. Mr. Quincy was invited to make the welcoming address at the boundary of the city, which he most cheerfully did, and did well. This is the record of these days in his Diary: —

"*November* 3. — Mr. Sumner was received at the Boston line by a cavalcade of at least a thousand horsemen, collected in Boston and the vicinity. He was there addressed by me, and afterwards in front of the State-House by the Governor of the Commonwealth, and afterwards escorted to his own house. The proceedings of the occasion were highly honorable to the State."

That Mr. Buchanan prevailed over Colonel Fremont only

through the frauds of the Pennsylvania election, I need not tell. Mr. Quincy felt the disappointment at the time keenly, in common with all the enemies of the Slave Power; but he bated no jot of heart or hope, and still believed that the Right was sure to prevail in the end.

The years succeeding the great struggle of 1856 between slavery and freedom for the possession of the nation, were passed by my father in the usual occupations and recreations which filled up the leisure of his old age. He kept up a constant interest in public affairs, and was never backward in expressing his opinions concerning them as occasion offered, but he took no active part in them. His serious occupation during the next two years was his "Memoir of John Quincy Adams," which was published in the autumn of 1858. It contains a clear and succinct narrative of Mr. Adams's life,—chiefly of his public life, —perhaps as complete a one as could be compiled from the materials at his command, chiefly such as were open to all the world. The passages in the following most interesting letter from Mr. Motley, the historian, relating to this work, contain a gratifying testimony to its merits, and an admirable characterization of its subject.

MR. MOTLEY TO MR. QUINCY.

"WALTON ON THAMES (ENGLAND), NOV. 23, 1859.

"MY DEAR SIR:—Very long after the date,—29 January, 1859, —which you were so kind as to write, together with your honored name, in the blank leaf of the copy of your admirable life of John Quincy Adams, did the volume reach me. It has been in my possession, indeed, but a very few weeks; but I have already read it through carefully once, besides studying many passages of it many times.

"I thank you most sincerely for your goodness in presenting me with the book. To have known and venerated its *author* from my earliest youth, I shall always consider one of the great privileges of my life. I esteem myself still more fortunate in being able to find sympathy with my own political views, and with my own convictions as to the tendency and aspects of the American commonwealth, in one of so large and elevated a mind, and so wide an experience, as yourself. This is an epoch in which, both in Europe and America, the despotic principle seems to be uppermost, in spite of all the struggles of the oppressed to free themselves. . . . .

"At home, the battle between the Slave Power in alliance with the Mob Power, and the party which believes in the possibility of a free republic, governed by the laws of reason, and pursuing a path of progress and civilization, is soon I hope to be fought out, without any compromise. The party of despotism is, I trust, at the next Presidential election, to be fairly matched against the party of freedom, and one or the other must go down in the conflict.

"I ought to apologize for making this digression from the topic of my letter; but knowing your sentiments on the great subject of liberty, it was impossible for me to say less; nor was it easy, in thinking of John Quincy Adams, the very breath of whose existence was the love of freedom, not to speak of the great object of his pure and illustrious career. I was much struck with a brief analysis which you give, on pages 374, 375, of his view of our government. 'The Constitution neither of the United States nor of Massachusetts can, without a gross and fraudulent perversion of language, be termed a Democracy. They form a mixed government, compounded not only of the three elements of democracy, aristocracy, and monarchy, but with a fourth added element, confederacy. The Democrats are now the most devoted and most obsequious champions of executive power, — the very life-guard of the commander of the armies and navies of this Union. The name of Democracy was assumed because it was discovered to be very *taking* among the multitude; yet, after all, it is but the investment of the multitude with absolute power.' . . . .

"It seems to me that human liberty, and its result, human civilization, have not been in so great danger as now for many years. Men have grown so familiar with the ugly face of despotism, both in Europe and America, that they really begin to love it. It is for this reason that — especially at this epoch — your life of Mr. Adams is most welcome. I wish it could be made a text-book in every public school and college in the Free States of America. It is a statue of gold raised by most worthy hands to him who most deserved such an honor.

"Allow me to say, that, from a literary point of view, your work seems to me remarkably artistic and satisfactory. The portraiture of the just man, with his solid, unshaken mind, tenacious of his noble purpose in the midst of the '*civium prava jubentium*,' is a very finished one.

"I never had the honor of his personal acquaintance, but I have always felt — without being thoroughly aware of my reasons — that he was among the small band of intellectual, accomplished, virtuous, and patriotic statesmen, not only of our country, but of all countries.

"There are always plenty of politicians in the world, but few statesmen; and there are sometimes eloquent patriots who are sadly deficient in culture, and others still more lamentably wanting in still more important endowments. But here was a scholar, — a ripe and rare one; a statesman trained in the school of Washington; a man familiar with foreign courts and laws and tongues; a life-long student, ever feasting on the nectared sweets of divine philosophy, and yet a busy, practical, and most sagacious administrator of political affairs; a ready debater; an impetuous and irresistible orator; and a man so perfect in his integrity that it was as impossible for him to be intimidated, as to be cajoled or bribed. The wonder is, not that such a man should have lost his re-election to the Presidency, but that he ever should by any combination have arrived at it at all.

"But this is not a pleasant reflection. Would that he were to be the candidate of the Republicans in 1860. It would almost be a triumph to be defeated under such an indomitable chief.

'Et cuncta terrarum subacta
Præter atrocem animum Catonis.'

"I must once more thank you most warmly for the noble portrait you have given us of the patriot, philosopher, and statesman; and for yourself pray accept my sincerest wishes for your health and happiness.

"Believe me, my dear sir, most respectfully and truly yours,

"J. Lothrop Motley."

In 1859 my father renewed his acquaintanceship with his celebrated contemporary and townsman, Lord Lyndhurst. He had known his lordship when in America, about the year 1794, as young Mr. Copley. Lord Lyndhurst was about four months my father's junior, and the tradition runs that the same nurse went from Mrs. Quincy to Mrs. Copley. At any rate, it is certain, I believe, that they were both introduced into the world by no less celebrated a person than Doctor Joseph Warren, afterwards the General who fell on Bunker Hill. In the year 1827 my father set on foot a plan, first suggested by President John Adams, of purchasing by subscription Copley's picture of Charles I. demanding the Five Members, and he had actually nearly raised the money, when for some reason I do not recollect it came to nothing. In 1859 he revived the plan, and finding the survivors of the first subscription, and the sons of those deceased, ready to come into it, he entered into correspondence with Lord Lyndhurst, and obtained the picture for fifteen hundred guineas, the price at which it had always been held. It was given by the subscribers to the city, and is now in the City Library. It is valuable as a fine specimen of the master, and as a collection of historical portraits. From this circumstance began an occasional exchange of slight gifts and letters, two of which I will here insert.

LORD LYNDHURST TO MR. QUINCY.

"GEORGE STREET, April 20, (1859.)

"DEAR MR. QUINCY:—The date of this letter is as above (April), the temperature is that of January. Everything seems like the weather,—disagreeable and unsettled. Among other evils, you have sent us over an American pugilist, to strive with our so-called champion. The scene has been most disgraceful,—a scandal to civilization. The particulars you will see in that universal instructor, the Times.

"The Buchanan question rests upon a nice distinction; and as to the St. Juan affair, it does not, I regret to say, promise an easy settlement. Here in Europe the clouds are heavy and dark. It is impossible to read the mysterious governor of France. The characters are unintelligible. All confidence in him is at an end. No one ventures to foretell what is to come next. His avowed policy is, one thing at a time, and for this he quotes Napoleon the first. But the Italian affair is not yet finished, so there will be some respite.

"The greatest of calamities would be a war with our American descendants. I hope both countries will ever strive to avoid such a fearful event.

"With great regard and respect, yours,

"LYNDHURST."

THE SAME TO THE SAME.

"GEORGE ST., LONDON, February 3, 1860.

"DEAR MR. QUINCY:—I have to thank you for the present of your Memoir of the late Mr. Quincy. The book was sent to me by Mr. Winthrop, who is somewhere on the Continent. I have read the memoir with great interest, as a most valuable addition to the catalogue of our American worthies. The volume contains, I find, among much valuable matter, the report of a speech of Lord Chatham's upon a proposal for reconciliation with America. We have so few accounts, or, I should say, reported specimens of his eloquence, that every addition will be welcomed with eagerness. Mr. Quincy appears to have caught his style of eloquence with admirable skill.

"We are here in Europe in a very uncomfortable and anxious state. Everything seems unsettled; and we watch with anxiety the intentions and movements of our ALLY, the Emperor of the French. We heard yesterday of Mr. Amory * at Nice; his health has improved by his journey.

"I sincerely hope that this letter will find you in good health and vigor.

"I remain very faithfully yours,

"LYNDHURST."

During the Presidential campaign of 1860, my father felt the warmest interest in its whole progress, from the nomination to the election of Mr. Lincoln. He did not join personally in the canvass, as he had done four years before. There was no especial call upon him then to exchange his retirement for the tumult of politics. During the dreadful winter of 1860–61, when the audacity of the Rebels seemed to be equalled only by the pusillanimous vacillation of the Executive, he shared in the anxiety which agitated every loyal mind in view of the uncertainties of the situation. But when the reverberation of the cannonade of Fort Sumter startled the whole North into a consciousness of its condition and its duties, there was no younger heart that beat higher in that exultant uprising of a great people than his. He confessed that he learned to know his countrymen better, through the light of that glorious hour, than he had ever done before. He said to me, in one of those days, "Now *I know* we are going to be a great nation! I never felt sure of it before." And his clear intuition discerned that the abolition of slavery must follow the Rebellion as a moral and political necessity. In the first days of doubt and apprehension as to this matter, when the Secretary of State was assuring foreign nations that emancipation was no part of the purpose of the government in putting down the Rebellion, when generals were endeavoring to conciliate the Rebels by threatening to crush slave insurrections with an iron hand where there were no slaves to rise, and when officers were returning loyal fugitives to Rebel masters, my father

* Mr. James S. Amory of Boston, who married a niece of Lord Lyndhurst.

had no doubt or fear as to the issue. As slavery had drawn the sword, he saw that it must perish by the sword. He had a clear perception of the immense difficulties with which Mr. Lincoln had to contend, and made allowance for the early delays and uncertainties of his conduct accordingly. He always believed in the President's honesty of purpose and practical sagacity, and would join in none of the censures which sincere men were too ready to launch at his head in the first year and a half of the war. When I was going to Washington in the spring of 1862, I asked my father whether he had any word to send to the President, if I should be fortunate enough to see him. "Tell him," he replied, "that I have watched his course carefully from the first, and that I have not yet seen the first mistake that he has made." I had the happiness of a short interview with that illustrious person, and, finding that he knew all about my father's earlier and later history, I gave him the message, and I well remember the smile of pleasure which lighted up his worn and weary face as he answered, "To have such an expression of approbation from Josiah Quincy is indeed a gratification and an encouragement!"

His faith and hope never wavered in all the vicissitudes of the war. He was certain of success in the midst of defeat, and saw light shining from behind the darkest cloud; and this although he felt his full share of the inconveniences arising from the derangement of affairs by the war. At the breaking out of the Rebellion, his grandson, Samuel Miller Quincy, the second son of his eldest son, raised a company for the Second Massachusetts Regiment, — a band of brave men led by gallant young gentlemen of the best blood of New England, nearly all of whom, with four fifths of the rank and file, died that their country might live. The following letter, and the extracts from my father's Diary of a later date, but referring to the military service of his grandson, are too honorable to both parties to be omitted.

MR. QUINCY TO CAPTAIN QUINCY.

"QUINCY, July 20, 1861.

"MY DEAR GRANDSON: — All that I hear of you and of the regiment to which you belong is in a high degree gratifying. Heaven grant that all future reports from you and from it may, for a long time, if not forever, be alike grateful. I have no shrinking in my feelings as I realize your approach to the field of battle, and to the other dangers incident to the life you have chosen.

"You will recollect, that when you first told me of your intention, or rather inclination, to join the army, and asked my opinion and advice, that I refused *both*, and abstained from any look or expression indicative of the state of my mind on the subject, stating to you that the whole responsibility of such a step must rest upon yourself, free from any influence of mine, or any indication of my wishes or opinions. When, self-moved, self-sustained, and self-directed, you cast your lot into the army, and took your station in the regiment, I did not refrain from expressing my entire approbation and gratification at your course, knowing, as I did, from your statement and my knowledge of your character, that you were impelled into the service from no vain, unworthy motive, or necessity, but solely from a sense of duty to your country, excited by your personal situation and position in life, and impelled, as you yourself stated to me, 'by a feeling that your great-grandfather, at such a time, and on such a call, and in your circumstances, would not have failed to respond in like manner to the voice of his country. I approved the motive, I honored the spirit, and was deeply touched by the feelings your explanation developed. Yes, my grandson, going to the field with such motives, and under such impulses, no event is to be feared, none deprecated. The laurels you win, should you be permitted to gather any, will be bright with a glory more than human; for they will not have sprung from the ground, but from a sense of duty, well considered and well performed, impelled by the purest and highest motives which can influence the human heart, and called for by your country, under circumstances as imperious and blameless as ever excited a nation.

"But if such happiness is not destined to be yours, and that Almighty hand which distributes his lot to every human being shall decide that yours is to be that of a victim to the cause to which you have devoted yourself, neither you nor your friends will have any cause of regret at your course, or complaint. The Great Disposer of events may, according to his infinite wisdom, have shortened a life which you and they had hoped to be long and prosperous. But with what certainty? His means of disappointing the hopes of man are not confined to the field of battle. He may have foreseen that protracted life would not have been to you a benefit or a blessing, and that in kindness, as well as wisdom, he has bestowed on you the privilege and glory of a martyr to the cause of freedom and of virtue, in defence of your country's safety, and of the liberty, the rights, and the most precious moral and social prospects of the human race. Is any human lot more glorious, or desirable ?

" Pardon, my dear child, this outflowing of an old man's heart, which, among the many objects of its affections, the events of the day unavoidably concentrate upon you. In whatever they may result, be assured of the approbation, the love, and the never-ceasing prayer for you of your grandfather,

"JOSIAH QUINCY."

" *March* 2, 1863. — My grandson, Samuel Miller Quincy, took leave of me to return to the army, which he entered at the commencement of the civil war, as Captain in the Second Massachusetts Regiment. At the battle of Cedar Mountain he received two wounds, one in the side, the other through the left foot, was made prisoner, and lay eight weeks in the Rebel hospital. He returns to his regiment as its Colonel. On taking leave he said, 'Be assured I know that I am your grandson, and that I will do nothing unworthy your name.'

" I replied, 'You have already shown that you are an honor to it.' May God bless and keep him in health and safety ! "

Colonel Quincy took command of his regiment and led it at Chancellorsville, but he found that he had returned to active service too soon. He resigned his Colonelcy of the Second Regiment, but, after a further season of rest, became Colonel of the Eighty-First Colored Regiment at Port Hudson, and afterwards in New Orleans, of which city he was at one time Military Mayor, and where he was afterwards detailed as President of the Commission of Claims. While there he received the brevet of Brigadier-General.

But this is in advance of my story. In December, 1861, my father met with an accident, from the effects of which he never fully recovered. It was merely slipping from a chair by his bedside upon the floor, but he received an injury in the hip, which prevented him from walking without assistance for the rest of his life. For three or four months he kept his bed, but afterwards was able to go down stairs to his books for the day, and to drive out regularly. As he suffered no pain in consequence of this accident, it may possibly have saved him from worse injury, as it did certainly contribute to his personal comfort. For it effectually prevented his venturing into the public streets, where, from his age and deafness, he was exposed to constant danger, and where indeed he had been seriously injured a year or two before. And, besides, it reconciled him to having a body-servant in constant attendance upon him, which his independent personal habits would have otherwise made intolerable to him. His general health stood the confinement perfectly well, and was never broken by any distemper but the most incurable of all, — old age. His freedom from disease, after the maladies of childhood were over, was absolute, and he had met with very few accidents. He had, however, one very narrow escape in the year 1828, the last year of his Mayoralty. He was walking in Broad Street, when a ladder, seventy feet long, fell upon him. His head passed between the rounds in the precise middle of the ladder, the weight of which struck him to the ground senseless, but with no greater injury than fracturing the *scapulæ* of both shoulders, from which he recovered in a few days. Had not the accident been attended by all these conditions, he must have been killed on the spot. Dr. John C. Warren pronounced it the most remarkable escape he had ever known in the course of his practice, and the Rev. Dr. Channing said to him, in view of it, "Mr. Quincy, there must be some very important work for you yet to do in this world!"

In the year 1857, he visited his old school-boy haunts at Andover in company with my brother. He went over the house where he had spent eight years under the charge of the good Parson French and his wife, revisited the grounds where he used to play, and sat again on the stone where seventy years before he buckled on his skates upon the borders of Pomp's Pond, a beautiful little wooded lake, so called from Pompey Jackson, a negro who lived in a hut on its banks, formerly a slave of Mr. Jonathan Jackson,* who emancipated him by deed, for con-

* This excellent man (H. C. 1762) was the father of the late Judge Charles Jackson, Dr. James Jackson, and Mr. Patrick T. Jackson. He was the son of Edward Jackson (H. C. 1726) and Dorothy Quincy, daughter of Judge Edmund Quincy (*ante*, p. 3). He had been a member of the Continental Congress, and was Treasurer of the College at the time of his death in 1810.

science' sake, before the Bill of Rights abolished slavery in Massachusetts in 1780. Pompey, I think, served in the Revolutionary war, and he lived down to my own school days, and died at somewhere about a hundred years old. My father spent the night at the tavern, and was to visit the Academy the next morning and address the boys. At breakfast, however, he had a sudden seizure of some kind, which he verily believed would carry him off. The doctor was sent for, and he was soon out of danger, but quite incapable of keeping his engagement. While my brother was away keeping it for him, the doctor kept watch by his side, and, remarking on the signs of a good constitution, well kept, which he observed, he said, "I should judge, sir, that you have been exempt from acute attacks of fevers and the like during your life." "You are wrong there," replied my father; "I came near dying of a fever once, and, what is a little odd, it was in this very town." "Indeed," responded the doctor, "I had never heard of it. It must have been before I came to the town. Pray, when was it?" "In the year *seventeen hundred and eighty!*" — he having been carried through a bad scarlet-fever in that year by good Mrs. French.

My father had inherited a fair average constitution from his ancestors, but not one of those iron frames which neither neglect, nor excesses, nor hardly time itself can subdue. His father died young, and his mother in middle life. His grandfather, who died at seventy-four, reached the greatest age of any of his paternal ancestors. His own longevity and perfect health he attributed, and I believe with truth, to the rational and philosophical care he took of himself, — to his fidelity to what Theodore Parker calls "the Religion of the Flesh." That he was strictly temperate, I need hardly say. I have already told how he was saved from all excess in wine, when such excess was not uncommon, and even from the most moderate indulgence, by a headache, which invariably chastised the one, as well as the other, for the greater part of his life. Though, during his dinner-giving days, he always kept a good cellar of wine, — importing and laying down a pipe of Madeira every year, as was the genial custom of gentlemen in those days, now unhappily fallen into decay, — it was for his friends and not for himself that he maintained it. At morning and night, for many years, he limited himself strictly to very moderate, plain meals of a fixed amount, which he never exceeded. At dinner, he ate with a hearty and healthy appetite whatever was set before him, holding that one plentiful meal was demanded by nature, and no more. He had, too, he himself hardly knew how, many years ago arrived at the knowledge that the skin was an important part of the animal economy, and one within the control of man. He accordingly paid great and regular attention to that function, long before the gospel of baptism was so widely preached and so generally received as now. And he attached especial importance to the air bath, and to careful grooming with the flesh-brush and hair-gloves, which last he held to be as good for Christians as for cattle. For more than thirty years, since his accession to the Presidency of the University, his habits had been entirely sedentary. He never walked or rode for exercise merely at any period of his life. To answer the necessity for muscular exercise, he invented for himself a system of what would now be called "Light Gymnastics," which he practised morning and night in his bed-room or dressing-room, up to the time of his disabling accident. This custom, he believed, greatly contributed to preserve him from the ills which so often assail the sedentary man.

I have related, in telling my father's doings as President, how he never failed to set the sleepy students an example of rigid punctuality at morning chapel. He deserves the less credit for this example, however, in that he had contracted, long years before, the habit of rising every morning, winter and summer, at four o'clock, so that he had been long astir before the prayer-bell rung out its unwelcome summons. This excess in early hours, however, like every other excess, brought its penalty along with it. Nature would not be cheated of her dues, and, if they were not paid in season, she would exact them out of season. Accordingly, my father was sure to drop asleep, wherever he might be, when his mind was not actively occupied; sometimes even in company, if the conversation were not especially animated, and always as soon as he took his seat in his gig, or "sulky," in which he used to drive himself to town. It was good luck, and the good instinct of his horses, that carried him safe through for so many years. Morse — as well known to successive generations of students, first as stage-coachman and afterwards as omnibus-driver, as old Hobson the carrier was to those of the English Cambridge in Milton's time — begged my father's coachman to take some order about the President's somnambulic expeditions, as he (Morse) had more than once nearly upset the omnibus in getting out of his way. One day, Mr. John Quincy Adams, who was addicted to the same vice of intemperate early rising, with much the same consequences, was visiting my father, who invited him to go into Judge Story's lecture-room, and hear his lecture to his law class. Now Judge Story did not accept the philosophy of his two friends in this particular, and would insist that it was a more excellent way to take out one's allowance of sleep in bed, and be wide awake when out of it, — which he himself most assuredly always was. The Judge received the two Presidents gladly, and placed them in the seat of honor on the dais by his side, fronting the class, and proceeded with his lecture. It was not long before, glancing his eye aside to see how his guests were impressed by his doctrine, he saw that they were both of them sound asleep, and he saw that the class saw it too. Pausing a moment in his swift career of speech, he pointed to the two sleeping figures, and uttered these words of warning: "Gentlemen, you see before you a melancholy example of the evil effects of early rising!" The shout of laughter with which this judicial *obiter dictum* was received effectually aroused the sleepers, and it is to be hoped that they heard and profited by the remainder of the discourse.

My father's occupations were not materially affected by his hurt after he was permitted to quit his bedroom and return to his library. He received his friends as before, and was visited by almost every stranger of eminence from abroad or from other sections of this country. One of the latest and the most honored of these welcome guests was Richard Cobden, who visited him in the summer of 1862, at Quincy. It did not seem probable, as they sat and talked together in the light of that summer's day, that the English statesman, then in the prime of his life and his greatness, would survive by less than a year the American Nestor, who had already seen three generations of breathing men. Yet so it was ordered. My father was able even to attend several of the public days at Cambridge, where he was always received with the most cordial enthusiasm, the whole audience usually rising, and giving him cheer upon cheer, while every allusion to him was greeted with rounds of applause. The eye that saw him blest him, and the ear that heard him bore witness to him. He attended the inauguration of his fifth successor, the Reverend Dr. Thomas Hill, on the 4th of March, 1863, and the meeting of the Alumni on the day after Commencement in the same year, less than a year before his death, on both which occasions he made admirable speeches, needing no allowance to be made for him because of his burden of more than ninety years. His birthdays were always remembered by the general public, as well as by his personal acquaintances, and his house was always visited by troops of friends upon those anniversaries with genuine congratulations and good wishes. Thus his life declined with slow and almost unperceived decay, the most revered and honored man of the city in which he lived.

But while his latter days thus went down blest with all that should accompany old age, he was not exempted from the bereavements and sorrows which are also its inevitable attendants. The doom of man was not reversed for him. Though Death had entered that happy home but once in so many years, he had cast his shadow across its threshold, and darkened its light. In the midsummer of 1858 his granddaughter, Helen Ruthven Waterston, the only surviving child of his daughter Anna, died at Naples, in her seventeenth year. I need not describe the grief which the untimely blighting of this fair blossom brought to him, as to us all. Of this dear child the poet Bryant thus speaks in his "Letters from Spain": "I confess I felt a degree of pride in so magnificent a specimen of my countrywomen as this young lady presented, — uncommonly beautiful in person, with a dignity of presence and manner much beyond her years, and a sweetness no less remarkable than the dignity." And the poet

Whittier has made her the motive of one of the most exquisite of his recent lesser poems. It is that entitled, "Naples. — 1860. Inscribed to Robert C. Waterston." In November, 1860, my father lost by death a beloved daughter-in-law in the prime of matronly goodness and beauty, who had always shown him the duty and love of a daughter, and whom he did not distinguish in his affection from the children of his blood. Two years after, in 1862, his son-in-law, Benjamin D. Greene, died, — respected by men of science on both sides the Atlantic as a botanist of eminence, and honored and beloved, for the elements of strength and sweetness finely mingled in his character, by all to whom the retiring modesty of his nature permitted him to be intimately known.

Under these bereavements, and in the prospect of his own approaching death, he was sustained by a full persuasion of another life, and by the continual sense of the superintending presence of a beneficent Deity. He seldom spoke of his religious opinions or devotional feelings, and it is to the revelations of his Diary that those who knew him best owe the knowledge of their character and extent. During the period which preceded the schism in the Congregational churches of New England, and at the time it took place, he always sympathized and sided with the liberal party. From the time of the settlement of his schoolfellow and friend, Dr. Kirkland, over the New South Church, until that divine was translated to Cambridge, he attended on his ministrations. From that time until he himself succeeded his friend in the Presidency of the University, he sat under the preaching of William Ellery Channing, in the church in Federal Street, and had a keen enjoyment of the genius and eloquence of that great man. But he never called himself a Unitarian, nor took any part in denominational discussions. Indeed, in a speech he delivered before the Board of Overseers of Harvard University, February 6, 1845, in vindication of that institution against sundry charges contained in a minority report presented by Mr. George Bancroft, he expressly disclaims the name. "I never did, and never will, call myself a Unitarian; because the name has the aspect, and is loaded by the world with the imputation, of sectarianism." That he accepted the distinctive doctrine of that denomination of Christians appears by the following extract from his Diary.

"*August* 20, 1854. — I lay aside, for myself, all further thought or argument concerning the Divine unities. Let any man cast off the prejudices and prepossessions of childhood, and read the fifth chapter of Milton's Treatise concerning the Scripture Christian Doctrine, and it seems to me impossible for any mind thus freed from the trammels of preconceived opinion not to be brought to the same conclusions with this great divine and greatest of poets."

But he regarded doctrinal differences as of slight importance, especially as to matters beyond the grasp of the human intellect. His catholicity of spirit fraternized with "all who profess and call themselves Christians," and who prove their title to the name by their lives. His opinion as to religious disputes he sometimes expressed in the words of his favorite poet, —

"For modes of faith let graceless zealots fight;
He can't be wrong whose life is in the right."

And in his Diary for 1854, a few days before the entry I have just given, he records this confession of his faith, containing what seemed to him the conclusion of the whole matter.

"*July* 23 (*Sunday*). — From the doctrines with which metaphysical divines have chosen to obscure the word of God, — such as predestination, election, reprobation, &c., — I turn with loathing to the refreshing assurance which, to my mind, contains the substance of revealed religion, — 'In every nation, he who feareth God, and worketh righteousness, is accepted of Him.'"

Though my father died before the end of the war, he lived long enough to see the approaching victory of the nation. On the 1st of January, 1863, a new and acceptable year of freedom dawned upon the people, as well the free as the slaves. He had foreseen that emancipation must be the issue of an appeal to arms of slaveholders in behalf of slavery; but he none the less rejoiced that his eyes were permitted to see the great day of deliverance. On that immortal day he received from President Lincoln an imperial photograph portrait of himself, accompanied by the following note from Mrs. Lincoln. It will ever hold, as may be readily conceived, an honored place among the household treasures of the family.

MRS. LINCOLN TO MR. QUINCY.

"EXECUTIVE MANSION, December 30, 1862.

"Mrs. Lincoln presents her most respectful compliments to the Honorable Mr. Quincy, and begs leave to present to him what their friends consider an excellent photograph of the President, who desires to be particularly remembered to him, desiring that it may reach him on the first day of the New Year, and trusting his health may be good and his valuable life long."

Upon the formation of the Union Club in Boston, for the purpose of sustaining the President in his public course, my father was one of the earliest members, and, though he declined the presidency of it, which was given to Mr. Everett, he made an address to the Club, on the 27th of February, which was afterwards printed and widely dispersed. He began by saying that he could not excuse himself, on the ground of his age, from joining this association, because he regarded the existing war "as involving a crisis in the condition of the whole human race, from which no human being has a right to shrink." He set forth briefly the object of the Confederacy, chiefly in the words of its Vice-President, Stephens, — to put an end to the agitating question concerning African slavery, by establishing it as the normal condition of the African, and founding the new government "upon this great physical, philosophical, and moral truth, — the first in the history of the world based upon it." Mr. Quincy then proceeded thus: —

"There is now no possible doubt concerning the object and nature of the Constitution of this Confederacy, — that it is to establish among the whole human race a new form of civilization. In conformity with its principles, the founders of it give public notice to the nations of the earth, that the old form of civilization has been by them abrogated, leaving no loop-hole or pretence for any nation or individual to escape from the dilemma, or from the duty, of either abandoning the old or resisting the new form of civilization. The enslaving of Africans is, on the principle of this Confederacy, no longer a mere power to be exercised when an individual could be bought, inherited, or stolen, but is founded on an immutable principle of assumption, that the African race have been constituted by God and nature unequal to the Caucasian; including, not the duty of the latter to aid them in rising in the scale of civilization, but the right of reducing them to a state of forced servitude, and of depriving them of all social and moral rights, — of liberty, property, and even life; having no property in themselves, their wives, nor their offspring, — all being holden at the will, and subject to the control, of the Caucasian master. To this condition, the Constitution of this Confederacy reduces the whole African race; and, while declaring these to be its principles, their founders claim the privilege of being admitted into the society of the nations of the earth! Principles worthy only of being conceived and promulgated by the inmates of the infernal regions, and a fit constitution for a confederacy in Pandemonium!

"Now, as soon as the nature of this Constitution is truly explained and understood, is it possible that the nations of the earth can admit such a Confederacy into their society? Can any nation, calling itself civilized, associate, with any sense of self-respect, with a nation avowing and practising such principles? Will not every civilized nation, when the nature of this Confederacy is understood, come to the side of the United States, and refuse all association with them, as, in truth, they are, *hostes humani generis?* For the African is as much entitled to be protected in the rights of humanity as any other portion of the human race.

"As to Great Britain, her course is, in the nature of things, already fixed and immutable. She must, sooner or later, join the United States in this war, or be disgraced throughout all future time; for the principle of that civilization which this Confederacy repudiates was by her — *to her great glory and with unparalleled sacrifices — introduced into the code of civilization;* and she will prove herself recreant if she fails to maintain it."

During this year he recorded almost daily in his Diary his occupations, his readings, and his visitors. I can make room for but very few of them.

"*March* 3. — Visited by Mr. F. Bassett. In familiar conversation on men and historical events, he told me that Mr. Webster once said to him, that 'the speeches of Mr. Quincy in Congress were the best and ablest ever delivered in that body on the influence of slavery.' All this may be extravagant, but I look back upon the exertions I made in my Congressional life, and see in my speeches but little to regret in point of language and manner,—nothing in point of principle."

"*March* 20.—I have read during the last month four of Shakespeare's plays,—King John, Richard II., and Henry IV. in both Parts."

The summer of 1863 was made memorable in the history of the war by the enlistment of colored regiments at the North. The first regiment which went thence to the field was the 54th Massachusetts, under the command of Robert Gould Shaw, the grandson of my father's life-long friend of the same name, whom I have already had occasion to mention. I need not repeat the story of that regiment, nor tell again the tale of Fort Wagner. There is no brighter and no sadder page in American history than the one that records it. For its record proves that the black race, to whom the first privilege the American people had accorded was that of fighting and dying in their behalf, had shown the deliberate courage, the capacity for discipline, the coolness in danger, the dash or patience as need demanded, and the subordination to authority, which make the best veteran troops. They proved their right to liberty and to citizenship, by seeking them in the face of greater and more terrible dangers than any their white fellow-soldiers had to fear. But the same record tells how the gallant and generous youth that led them fell at their head. Possessed of every advantage of fortune and social condition, blest with every virtue that can grace pure and ingenuous youth, adorned by every accomplishment of education and every charm of person and manner, bound by every tie of affection that can hold a human heart closest to earth, he left it all and cast in his lot with the lowliest and most despised of his countrymen, in life and in death, that he might deliver them and his country. Many brave men have been as faithful to duty and died as nobly as he, and have been as deeply mourned; but it was his fortune to connect his name with the era in the history of the nation when the black race was called to its help and its deliverance. This great epoch in our annals Colonel Shaw baptized with his heart's blood, and with it his name will be inseparably and forever united.

On receiving the news of the attack upon Fort Wagner and the death of Colonel Shaw, Mr. Quincy addressed this letter to his father, Mr. Francis George Shaw, of Staten Island, N. Y.: —

MR. QUINCY TO MR. SHAW.

"QUINCY, August 17, 1863.

"Although I am aware how delicate is the endeavor, and how difficult the fit moment, of mingling sympathy with suffering, yet I cannot refrain from uttering the deep grief of my heart, and communicating to you and your lady my sad coincidence of feeling with you on your bereavement. It is not for me to speak to you of that faith and trust in the wisdom and goodness of the All-disposer, who distributes to us mortals happiness and sorrow as seems best for us to His infinite will. Your own minds have already sought and been consoled by the assurance that 'whatever He gives, He gives the best.' But I may be permitted to recall the many causes of gratitude and consolation which are united with your loss, rendering it at once conspicuous by virtue and permanently useful as an example. Your son gave his life in defence of the integrity and laws of his country. He yielded it in association with an oppressed race contending for freedom and the rights of human beings. He fell in a conflict selected, and on the spot assigned, by the authorities of his country, — in a service for which only the highest bravery is selected, and which none but the bravest spirits would accept. He fell with brave men, contending for liberty and their rights, and was buried with them in a grave which will be hallowed and celebrated in all future time, whenever and so long as the rights of human beings shall have an advocate, martyrdom in their defence shall have a eulogist, and the spirit of chivalry, ennobled by union with virtue and religion, shall be honored and reverenced.

"My friend, let these truths assuage griefs which they cannot prevent. Could long life, if permitted to your son, do more, — or have given to him a more prosperous or immortal career? In sympathy for your sorrows, I am truly your friend,

"JOSIAH QUINCY."

The next month he was moved by the admirable letter of President Lincoln to the Convention of Illinois, maintaining the justice and necessity of his course, especially in the matter of the Emancipation Proclamation, to address to him the following letter. It was not originally intended for the press, but, having found its way thither, I give it here entire, together with the President's reply, as concluding not unfitly or ungracefully my father's communications with the public.

Mr. Quincy to President Lincoln.

"Quincy, Massachusetts, September 7 1863.

"Sir: — Old age has its privileges, which I hope this letter will not exceed. But I cannot refrain from expressing to you my gratification and my gratitude for your letter to the Illinois Convention, — happy, timely, conclusive, and effective. What you say concerning emancipation, your proclamation, and your course of proceeding in relation to it, was due to truth and your own character, — shamefully assailed as it has been. The development is an imperishable monument of wisdom and virtue.

"Negro slavery and the possibility of emancipation have been subjects of my thought for more than seventy years; being first introduced to it by the debates in the Convention of Massachusetts for adopting the Constitution, in 1788, which I attended. I had subsequently opportunities of knowing the views on that subject, not only of such men as Hamilton, King, Jay, and Pickering, but also of distinguished slaveholders, — of both the Pinckneys, of William Smith of South Carolina, and of many others. With the first of these I had personal intercourse and acquaintance. I can only say that I never knew the individual, slaveholder or non-slaveholder, who did not express a detestation of it, and the desire and disposition to get rid of it. The only difficulty, in case of emancipation, was, what shall we do for the master, and what shall we do with the slave? A satisfactory answer to both these questions has been, until now, beyond the reach and grasp of human wisdom and power.

"Through the direct influence of a good and gracious God, the people of the United States have been invested with the power of answering satisfactorily both these questions, and also of providing for the difficulties incident to both, of which if they fail to avail themselves, thoroughly and conclusively, they will entail shame on themselves, and sorrow and misery on many generations.

"It is impossible for me to regard the power thus granted to this people otherwise than as proceeding from the direct influence of a superintending Providence, who ever makes *those mad whom He intends to destroy.* The only possible way in which slavery, after it had grown to such height, could have been abolished, is that which Heaven has adopted.

"Your instrumentality in the work is to you a subject of special glory, favor, and felicity. The madness of Secession and its inevitable consequence, civil war, will, in their result, give the right and the power of universal emancipation sooner or later. If the United States do not understand and fully appreciate the boon thus bestowed on them, and fail to improve it to the utmost extent of the power granted, they will prove recreant to themselves and to posterity.

"I write under the impression that the victory of the United States in this war is inevitable.

"Compromise is impossible. Peace on any other basis would be the establishment of two nations, each hating the other, both military, both necessarily hostile, their territories interlocked, with a tendency to never-ceasing hostility. Can we leave to posterity a more cruel inheritance, or one more hopeless of happiness and prosperity?

"Pardon the liberty I have taken in this letter, and do not feel obliged in any way to take notice of it; and believe me ever your grateful and obliged servant,

"JOSIAH QUINCY."

PRESIDENT LINCOLN TO MR. QUINCY.

"EXECUTIVE MANSION, WASHINGTON, September 12, 1863.

"DEAR AND HONORED SIR: — Allow me to express the personal gratification I feel at the receipt of your very kind letter of the 7th of September, and to thank you most cordially for its wise and earnest words of counsel.

"Believe me, my dear sir, to be very respectfully and sincerely your friend and servant,

"A. LINCOLN."

On the 28th of October my father removed from Quincy to Boston for the last time, as he himself seems to have foreboded.

"*October* 28. — The monsoon gale of existence has continued to fill the sails of my life ever since August last. To-day I take leave of my summer residence at Quincy, possibly — probably — for the last time. Life, at all times uncertain, is at ninety-two the last running of the sands of its glass. I have but little of its grains remaining; but I neither wish to multiply nor reduce them."

"*November* 2. — Began to read J. E. Cairnes's work 'On the Slave Power and the Causes and Issues of the American Contest,' — a work of great merit, evidencing a very thorough knowledge of the subject."

"*November* 3. — Continued reading Cairnes's 'Slave Power.' Went to the polls and threw my vote for the Republican ticket."

He was so much pleased with Professor Cairnes's admirable work, that he wrote to him a very long letter about it, — altogether too long for insertion, — one of the last and one of the best he ever wrote. The answer of Professor Cairnes did not arrive until four days before my father's death, but I insert it here as its most convenient place.

Mr. Cairnes to Mr. Quincy.

"74 Lower Mount St., Dublin, June 4, 1864.

"Dear Sir: — I trust it is not yet quite too late to thank you for the very great gratification you have afforded me by your interesting and much prized letter, which reached me, I am ashamed to say, so long as some six months ago.

"It is indeed reassuring, and gives me a confidence in the soundness of my view of the American civil struggle which few other testimonies could give, that my book should have received the sanction of your knowledge, experience, and sagacity, — a sanction, too, which has been conveyed in terms of such liberal commendation as have afforded me, I assure you, very lively satisfaction. . . . .

"I read your views on American politics with much interest, and I am entirely disposed to follow you in your opinion that the universal diffusion of sound popular education, together with the just distribution of the land of the country among its people, are *the* two poles on which turn the destinies of American democracy, — conditions which, as you justly remark, have been realized in the United States, and more emphatically in New England, for the first time in the history of the world.

"I think you will have observed, notwithstanding some disappointing side-eddies, that, on the whole, the movement of opinion in this country has been satisfactory since you wrote. The old cant about the non-slavery character of the contest has been effectually silenced by the course of events. I think, too, that people here are beginning to understand better, and to regard with more sympathy and respect, the 'Union' feeling. The unparalleled tenacity, moreover, with which the North sticks to its purpose, combined with the courage and endurance exhibited in the campaigns of the last two years, — in a word, the accumulating manifestations of high national character in the

American people, are producing silently, but I think steadily, a healthy effect, which, I have no doubt, will show itself in our future intercourse. At present we are watching with extreme anxiety the tremendous struggle in Virginia.

"Believe me, dear sir, most respectfully and truly yours,

"J. E. CAIRNES."

"*November* 26. — Thanksgiving, a day of joy, gratitude, and thankfulness. Had eighteen at my table, consisting of sons, daughters, sons-in-law, daughters-in-law, grandchildren, and great-grandchildren, — all happy, united, good, and prosperous. In the evening many visitors; among others, Charles Sumner, Mr. Bowen of Tennessee, and Mr. Hoffman, the Recorder of New York."

"*November* 27. — At Cambridge. Attended the meeting of the Committee on the Observatory. Mr. Bond read his report. Present, Mr. Mitchell, R. C. Winthrop, Ingersoll Bowditch, President Sparks, R. T. Paine, and others. Went through all the rooms, — that of the great telescope, the library, and the other instruments."

Thus the ninety-second year of my father's life wore away in the performance of duties, in the enjoyments of society, and in the recreations of literature. There was no symptom of even diminished activity and sprightliness of mind. He was as alive to the events of the day and to the pleasures of conversation as ever he had been. By his wise philosophy of life he had made maturity reach far into the years usually the domain of old age. Towards the end of 1863, however, he evidently foreboded that the days of darkness approached. Though there were no outward and visible signs of failing nature more than had long existed, he probably had secret intimations that the end could not be deferred much longer. It was under the influence of this presentiment that he ended his Diary, on the evening of the last day of the year, 1863, with this fit and beautiful conclusion: —

"*December* 31. — With the close of the year comes the conviction that the time has come to close this Diary forever. The light of the sun is withdrawing; but, blessed be Heaven, the light of the evening star reveals the hope of a coming immortality."

CHAPTER XXI.

1864.

LAST SCENE OF ALL. — HIS NINETY-SECOND BIRTHDAY. — ILLNESS. — LETTER TO MR. DABNEY. — REMOVAL TO QUINCY. — INTEREST IN PUBLIC AFFAIRS. — DEATH. — FUNERAL. — TRIBUTES TO HIS MEMORY. — LETTERS FROM MR. CHARLES F. ADAMS AND MR. J. L. MOTLEY. — HIS PERSONAL APPEARANCE. — STORY'S STATUE. — BUSTS AND PORTRAITS. — HIS DELIBERATION OF SPEECH. — HIS LIFE IN THE PASSING DAY. — HIS PART IN THE ANTI-SLAVERY REVOLUTION. — CONCLUSION.

THERE is not much more to tell. My father's ninety-second birthday was welcomed by his many friends with all their usual demonstrations of affectionate interest and respect. Not long after that day, however, he was attacked by an epidemic influenza, from the effects of which he never recovered. But he rallied sufficiently in a few weeks to take the long drives which were his latest recreation. His mental faculties were not weakened, but they grew more and more sluggish. When aroused, they were as clear and sound as ever, as I think will be shown by the following letter, the last he ever wrote, to his valued friend of many years, Mr. Charles W. Dabney, the American Consul at Fayal.

"MY DEAR MR. DABNEY: — I have this moment received your favor of the 17th February, and cannot refrain from immediately acknowledging the gratification your kind, respectful, affectionate reminiscence confers, lest old age should put a *veto* upon my powers, which I find precarious and changeful. Your 'regard' will be found written on my heart, where all your many kind remembrances are inscribed with a permanency which death only can obliterate.

"You had occasion for the interest you express for my state of health. About the 1st of February I was assailed with what is called *influenza*, in a style more appropriate for a younger man. At the age of *ninety-three*, nature does not recuperate after the fashion of an earlier period of life. Accordingly I have been ever since prostrated in my bed, and am yet little more than a child, dependent for getting up, and for all locomotion, on an assistant. This is almost the first letter I have written for these six weeks; but my respect and interest in you and yours have made me unmindful of old age and sickness. Your letter was a *panacea* for all trouble.

"I shall probably never write to you again. But no matter. We shall soon (greet *) each other in another world, and renew the intimacy we have had in this. Until which time, adieu. God be with you. In life or death, forever yours,

"JOSIAH QUINCY."

Happily, during these last few months he suffered no pain. But the charm of living was gone. Weariness of life and longing for death came over him. He slept for the most of the time, by day as well as by night, but he longed for "the sleep that knows no waking." One day he said to me, "Remember, when I am in my grave, I shall be where I wish to be!" It was not the impatience of discontent, but the longing of a tired child for its bed. It was the instinct with which kind Nature has provided her children, to make the inevitable hour welcome and grateful when it comes in her due course. When the time of the annual flitting to the country came, and his daughter suggested it to him, he said: "I am willing to go with you to Quincy. Do just as you please about it. But remember, I wish my funeral to take place from Boston. In Boston I was born, in Boston I have lived, and from Boston I choose to be buried. Promise me this."

On the 3d of June, accompanied by two of his daughters, he was removed to Quincy, passing for the last time through the streets of the city he loved so well. He was able to be dressed and down stairs as a general thing, and to take carriage exercise almost every day. The last time I saw him was the day but one before he died. I had driven my daughter over, and we arrived just before he returned from his last drive. He was lifted from the carriage by two men, and was the very image of extreme old age. He looked kindly at us, and said a few words, but was too much fatigued to talk much. I had no notion, however, that it was the last time I should see him in life. There was no apparent reason why he should not continue at least through the

* Word illegible in MS.

summer. He still took an intelligent interest in the news of the day. His daughters read the newspapers to him every morning, and he kept himself advised of the events of the war as they occurred. The last event which excited his particular attention and admiration was the great engineering feat of Colonel Bailey, — pronounced by Admiral Porter in his despatch, "without doubt, the best ever performed," — by which he saved the flotilla of gunboats on the Red River, and probably shortened the war by one or two years. This great action roused my father to fresh life. He had the report read twice over to him, and then, as if he had seen of the travail of his soul and was satisfied, he exclaimed, "THAT IS TRUE GLORY! I will hear no more."

Though there was no especial reason for expecting the end just when it came, he was himself evidently daily looking and hoping for it. "He repeatedly took leave of his daughters," my eldest sister writes, to whom I am indebted for the particulars of those of his last days when I was not able to be with him, "thanking them for their affectionate attentions, and saying, 'I am sorry to leave you, but I wish to go; I have had a remarkably long, prosperous, and happy life, blessed in my children, grandchildren, and great-grandchildren. It is time that I should go. Weep not, mourn not, for me!'" Even on the morning of the last day of his life, there was no especial reason for supposing that it had indeed come. So little, that my brother, who lives on the estate, after visiting him in the morning, went to keep an engagement to address an Agricultural Society at Framingham, and so missed the closing scene. There was no time to send for me, and thus neither of his sons was present when he died. But our absence was fitly supplied by the presence of his three daughters, the friends, companions, and guardians of his old age, whose cheerful society, unremitting watchfulness, and assiduous affection had given grace, comfort, and happiness to his latter days. My sister thus describes the end. "On Thursday, the 30th of June, he was evidently losing strength, and did not leave his chamber; but it was not until noon on the 1st of July that it was perceived that a great change had occurred. No one was with him but his attendant and his three daughters during the last peaceful hours, until, as quietly as an infant sinks to slumber, he ceased to breathe, and the spirit returned to God who gave it!"

As soon as his death was known, Mr. Frederick W. Lincoln, the Mayor of Boston, came in person to learn the wishes of the family as to the funeral, with the necessary arrangements for which in the city he charged himself in his official capacity. The funeral took place on Tuesday, July 6th, from the Church in Arlington Street. The services were impressively performed by the Reverend Ezra Stiles Gannett, D. D., assisted by the Reverend John D. Wells, the minister of Quincy. Notwithstanding that it was the time of the summer dispersion of the citizens, the church was entirely filled. The lines of Sir Henry Wotton, prime favorites with the dead, —

> "How happy is he born or taught
> Who serveth not another's will," —

were sung by the choir, and were surely never more fitly applied. The members of the City Government, the President, Fellows, and Faculty of the University, the Judges of the Supreme Court, many members of the bar, and clergymen of the different religious denominations, and many citizens who had known him in his various public functions or in private life, made up the attendance. Mr. Everett, Mr. Robert C. Winthrop, Colonel Thomas Aspinwall, Dr. Oliver Wendell Holmes, and four ex-Mayors of Boston, were the pall-bearers. As the procession moved, all the bells of the city were tolled, and the flags on the State-House and the other public buildings were hung at half-mast. The funeral was accompanied by the civic authorities and other functionaries as far as the line of the city at Cambridge Bridge, whence it proceeded, attended only by the family and their immediate friends, to the cemetery at Mount Auburn. At the chapel of the cemetery a short service was held by the Reverend President Hill, after which, laying him by the side of his wife, we left him to the rest he had so yearned for.

His death called forth tributes to his character and public services from the press in all parts of the United States. The two Boards of the City Government of Boston, the Overseers and Faculty of the University, the various learned societies of which he was a member, and the political associations to which he belonged, or with which he was in sympathy, paid homage, always sincere and touching and sometimes eloquent, to his memory. Of the many private letters which the family received on the occasion of my father's death, I shall gratify my own feelings, as well as my sense of what is due to him, by inserting the two following, addressed to myself by his friends and my own, Mr. Charles Francis Adams, now Minister at the Court of St. James's, and Mr. John Lothrop Motley, then holding the same diplomatic position at the Court of Vienna, but who is more widely known, and will be always remembered, as the historian of the Dutch Republic. They express the feelings with which the generation that grew up to manhood when he was past the middle term of life regarded him, in a manner honorable to all parties.

Mr. Adams to Mr. E. Quincy.

"London, 29 July, 1864.

"My dear Edmund: — I thank you for thinking of me so far as to send me a copy of your notice of your father's life in the Tribune, at the same time with your letter announcing his demise. When, on the day before my departure from Boston, I took leave of him, I admit that I thought it unlikely that I should see him again. But as time wore on, and my term of service here appeared to be drawing to a close, the prospect of returning to find him still among us grew by no means so unreasonable. I began to think him a fair candidate for the small list of centenarians in the catalogue of graduates of Harvard University. My vision was at last rather suddenly dispelled, and he is no more. With him disappears, I think, the very last of the men whom I associate with my earliest impressions of life in America. It is but a few days short of forty-seven years ago that I first saw him at his own mansion in Quincy, — since which period his name and person have been continuously connected in my mind with every friendly office towards three generations of my family. I need not say to you how rarely this happens to any one in America. It is not common anywhere in the midst of the vicissitudes of this world. I shall cherish the recollection for the remainder of my days, as of an event which, at least in my experience, cannot occur again.

"It is rare that an individual leaves so unspotted a record behind him as your father has done. Born in the lap of fortune, this neither emasculated his vigor nor impaired his integrity. He never refused to assume a responsible trust, and never failed to acquit himself in it with honor. Glory enough for any man!

"This peaceful termination of a long and well-spent life is not a matter to justify any language of condolence with his family. They could not have wished for him anything else, as he could not have hoped for more.

"I pray you to believe, yourself, and to assure the other members of your father's family, that no more ardent admirer of his character can be found than your affectionate friend,

"C. F. Adams."

Mr. Motley to the Same.

"Vienna, 7 August, 1864.

"My dear Quincy: — I thank you very sincerely for your letter of July 15th, which reached me a few days ago. I thank you also for the Tribune, containing the biographical sketch. As I take the Daily Tribune, I had already received the paper in due course, but I was very glad to have a second copy, although I trust erelong to possess it in a more enduring shape. You were quite right, of course, to publish it first in a journal enjoying justly so very wide a circulation.

"I wish most earnestly that I could talk to you by the hour together about your father. To write is so unsatisfactory, — I mean to write a letter, — because, if one enters on such a subject at all, one never knows where to stop. A letter is not a volume, and less than a volume would hardly suffice to say all that ought to be said about Josiah Quincy.

"The graceful and heartfelt eulogies which have already sprung up like flowers from his new-made grave, have been sufficient to prove to you, and to all who have the honor of belonging to him, how firmly established he was in the affections and the esteem of the best part of the American people. But upon that point you could hardly have had a doubt. I feel, however, in attempting to speak of him, as if it were impossible to avoid saying what has just been said all around you, by so many, and so much more eloquently than I could say it. Let me thank you, however, for assuring me that he honored me with his personal regard, — that he was kind enough to look with indulgence on my poor labors in literature. I had the happiness of hearing this from himself, and I was always very proud of his approbation. From the time when I first came into his presence as a very young Junior soon after his inauguration at Cambridge, down to that delightful dinner at Quincy, — do you remember it? — in the summer of '61, just before my departure for this post, he was always most kind, genial, and friendly to me, and I have always appreciated his kindness to the full. I shall say no more of that. But really I am afraid to trust myself to speak of him as I really think. I don't like the language of exaggeration and weak enthusiasm, and yet I have always had a very great admiration of his character and of his intellect.

"The only thing I have always regretted is, that he retired so soon from public life, — I mean from national public life. He lost but little, but we lost much, — more, perhaps, than can now be measured. The influence from first to last of such high probity and such clear vision on the course of affairs, had it been directly exerted by him during the long period in which he preferred retirement from the national service, could not but have been most wholesome for us all. Boston and the University gained the best of municipal magistrates and of presidents, but the senate and the council-board at Washington lost more than was thus gained. What I especially admired about your father was that he was so purely an American. I hate the word aristocracy, as applied to the Transatlantic world, for it is philosophically and practically a misnomer and a vulgarism. If an aristocracy *can* exist with us, — that is to say, a privileged class, founded on birth and territorial possessions, — then is our whole system a sham and a lie, and the sooner Jeff. and his slave-dealing oligarchy take possession of the whole country the better. Therefore I certainly shall not make use of the term in regard to him, but I shall borrow the expression of our friend Wendell Holmes, and speak of him as the type and the head of the Brahmins of America. A scholar, a gentleman, descended of scholars and gentlemen, a patriot and the son of a patriot, well known to all who know America, — an upright magistrate, an eloquent senator, a fearless champion of the Right, a man of the world, a man of letters and a sage, with a noble presence from youth onwards, which even in extreme old age did not lose its majesty, and which gave a living and startling contradiction to the great poet's terrible picture of man's 'seventh age,' — what better type could those of us who are proud of America, and who believe in America, possibly imagine? More than all, what I especially honor and admire him for is that he most fully believed in America, and most respected his country exactly in the midst of this war and *because* of the war.

"If there is anything that inspires my inexpressible loathing, my infinite contempt, it is the senseless gabble with which the hack-politicians of Europe entertain each other about our 'wicked war,' our 'miserable war,' our 'causeless war,' our 'hopeless war.' Had there been no war, we should indeed have been wicked, miserable, hopeless.

"I can stand anything but the crocodile regrets which our enemies express for the 'fratricidal conflict.' When the commonwealth was sliding smoothly down into the infinite abyss, during the last forty years, we were the 'Great Republic.' Now that we are struggling upwards and onwards, into the daylight, through sacrifices of blood and treasure, and with an almost superhuman energy such as the history of no country in the whole world can show, we are the objects of compassion, or of contempt, for the little folks looking on from across the water, whose souls are not large enough to comprehend a portion of the grandeur of this greatest encounter of passions, principles, and intellectual powers ever waged upon the earth.

"And in this, our conflict with the Devil, the same little spectators think that the Devil has already gained the victory, merely because they wish well to him. They call upon us to give it up and worship him, that the whole world may be happy together, — especially the cotton-brokers. Don't they wish we would?

"You may suppose, therefore, how I echo the passage in the last part of your memoir: — 'Far from being cast down by the disturbance of public and private affairs consequent upon the civil war, he looked upon that war as the most hopeful sign that he had seen during his long life of the future of his country. He used to say, after the war had begun, that he now believed that we were going to be a great nation, of which he never felt sure before.'

"I think I had better not say any more. You know how much I honored and admired your father, and you have yourself given so truthful and noble a portraiture of him, that it would be almost an impertinence in me to do more than express my sympathy with what you have written, and with what you feel.

"Let me say, however, that your memoir (which I called a sketch merely, for want of any other word) strikes me as admirably written. I have read it twice, with the deepest interest. Don't you intend to enlarge it to a volume, and publish it as such? Your father set you the example in his admirable biography of his father, which you ought to follow at once.

"It will always be a pleasant remembrance to me that I knew so well those twin Nestors of England and America, your father and Lord Lyndhurst. I saw much of Lord Lyndhurst during the latter years of his life, and I had more than once the pleasure of being the bearer of friendly greetings and remembrances from the one to the other. Lord Lyndhurst, too, had preserved his intellectual faculties undimmed, and I heard him deliver a speech in the House of Lords on his eighty-eighth birthday, — a vivid, interesting, logical argument, on a constitutional question. In private he was kind, genial, playful, — never senile, — to the last. He was deeply interested in our affairs, and had a sincere affection for the land of his birth. He too was a handsome old man; but his physiognomy was disfigured by a brown wig, and he had almost entirely lost the use of his legs.

"The attractive and commanding personal appearance of your father is as familiar to me as if he stood before me now. It was so remarkable that I can never cease to regret that the statue which was ordered from William Story was never completed, — I believe for want of funds. I do wish that something could be done now; and I should like to join in any plan. I saw the model in Rome, which was admirable.

"I have been talking on, without saying anything very new. I have not expressed deep regret at your father's departure. Lasting sorrow for such a euthanasia would be ill-timed. There is always a fear, too, that the body *may* outlive the mind, — and so calm and peaceful an ending before that fear could find a place is in itself a relief. Still, I know well that these considerations must come later, and the personal grief for his passing away must claim its place.

"I beg you to accept for yourself, and for the other members of your family, my sincerest and heartfelt sympathy, and believe me ever, my dear Quincy, very faithfully yours,

"J. L. MOTLEY.

"My wife desires her kind remembrances."

The statue of which Mr. Motley speaks is still in the studio of the sculptor. The artist put his heart, as well as his genius, into this work, for he loved and revered its subject as the friend of his own youth and of his father's prime. Competent judges have assured me that it is surpassed by no modern portrait statue, if it may not be pronounced absolutely the best of all. My father was an eminently handsome man, even down to extreme old age. His fine set of teeth, which he kept entire till his death, doubtless contributed to preserve the majestic proportions of his countenance. A bust taken of him about 1826 by Horatio Greenough might well pass for the head of an Apollo or a Jupiter. I have already spoken of the fine bust by Crawford in the College Library, which is a most accurate likeness, as well as an admirable work of art. Four portraits of him remain. The first by Stuart, taken in 1806, when he was in "the prime of manhood where youth ends," in the earlier and highly finished style of that master; the second, also by Stuart, taken twenty years afterwards, in his later and freer manner, which has been engraved for this work; the third by Page, in 1842, in his robes as President of the University, taken when he was just entering upon his green old age; and the fourth by Wight, painted some ten years later, at the request of the class of 1829, which is deposited with the collections of the Massachusetts Historical Society.

He was not a fluent speaker in his later years, nor yet a rapid talker, seeming to choose his words and sentences with almost too deliberate care; but what he said at last, in public speech or private conversation, was always full of ripened thought, fitly uttered, and richly illustrated from the stores of his reading and experience. And yet I have been told by ear-witnesses that his speech was swift enough in the fiery conflicts of his Congressional days. He was, too, always extremely happy in impromptu speeches, ready repartees, epigrammatic toasts, and quips of fancy, which made him an incomparable presiding officer at public dinners. He was never a *laudator temporis acti*, nor ever affirmed that the former days were better than these. Quite otherwise. He was always ready with examples from his own memory to prove the exact contrary. He did not live in the past, as many old men do. Perhaps one reason of his retaining his mental vigor so long and so well was owing to the intenseness with which he lived in the day that was passing over his head. Thus he kept at least abreast of his time to the last, and saw in the great events of his old age the logical consequences of those of his prime, which were hastening to a conclusion he had foreseen, and labored to bring to pass, but had not hoped to see with his mortal eyes.

From the first moment of his entering public life, even before going to Washington, he had discerned and resisted the power fatal to liberty given by the Constitution to slavery. And I think I am safe in saying that no public man saw more clearly, and resisted more persistently, the growing predominance of the Slave Power than he. Resistance to that Power was indeed the inspiration of his whole Congressional life. Whatever specific shape the measures might take which he opposed and protested against, it was the Slave Power behind them that he attacked. And it may not be too much to say, that his voice crying in that wilderness prepared the way for the great deliverance, the advent of which he lived to see. And when, in the conflict of 1856, he took down his old sword, and threw himself into the ranks of a new generation, it was because it was the same battle for freedom, bequeathed to the sons, in which he had led the sires. His stainless private life, his sterling public spirit, his perfect disinterestedness, free from all by-ends and self-seeking, his laborious fidelity in honorable posts of duty, were acknowledged by the men among whom he lived, and rewarded by their gratitude, affection, and reverence. But it is to the part he bore in the great revolution which was going forward all his life, and is not ended yet, that he will owe — should such be awarded to him — a place in the permanent history of his country.

INDEX.

THE END.

Cambridge: Stereotyped and Printed by Welch, Bigelow, & Co.

www.ingramcontent.com/pod-product-compliance
Lightning Source LLC
LaVergne TN
LVHW021229110826
845150LV00002B/283

* 9 7 8 1 4 2 5 5 6 2 9 1 5 *